"Here will love its last attentions pay,
And place memorials on these beds of clay;
Large level stones lie flat upon the grave,
And half a century's sun and tempest brave.
But many an honest tear and heartfelt sigh
Have followed those who now unnoticed lie;
Of these what numbers rest on every side,
Without one token left by grief or pride!
Their graves soon levelled to the earth, and then
Will other hillocks rise to other men.
Daily the dead on the decayed are thrust,
And generations follow—dust to dust."

CRABBE.

"The long flat stones,
With nettles skirted and with moss o'ergrown,
That tell in homely phrase who lie below."

BLAIR'S "GRAVE."

SIR WALTER SCOTT'S MONUMENT,
EDINBURGH.

MONUMENTS

AND

MONUMENTAL INSCRIPTIONS

IN

SCOTLAND.

BY THE

Rev. CHARLES ROGERS, LL.D., F.S.A. Scot.,
HISTORIOGRAPHER TO THE HISTORICAL SOCIETY OF GREAT BRITAIN.

VOL. I.

A HERITAGE CLASSIC

LONDON:
PUBLISHED FOR THE GRAMPIAN CLUB.

1871.

A Facsimile Reprint
Published 1997 by

HERITAGE BOOKS, INC.
1540E Pointer Ridge Place
Bowie, Maryland 20716
1-800-398-7709

ISBN 0-7884-0684-1

A Complete Catalog Listing Hundreds of Titles
On History, Genealogy, and Americana
Available Free Upon Request

THE GRAMPIAN CLUB.

Patron.

HIS ROYAL HIGHNESS THE PRINCE OF WALES.

HIS GRACE THE DUKE OF ARGYLL, K.T., *President*.
ABERDEEN, UNIVERSITY OF.
ADAMSON, EDWARD, ESQ., M.D.
AITKEN, J., ESQ., M.D.
ALEXANDER, LIEUTENANT-COLONEL, W.R.E.
ALEXANDER, LOUIS CHARLES, ESQ., LL.D.
ANDERSON, JOHN, ESQ.
ANDERSON, GEORGE, ESQ.
ANDERSON, JAMES, ESQ., Q.C.
ARNAUD, JOHN MACAULAY, ESQ.

THE MOST HON. THE MARQUIS OF BUTE, *Vice-President*.
THE RIGHT HON. LORD BORTHWICK, F.S.A. SCOT., *Vice-President*.
BADENOCH, REV. G. R.
BAILLIE, JAMES WILLIAM, ESQ., of Culterallers.
BAIN, JOSEPH, ESQ. F.S.A. SCOT.
BATTEN, EDMUND CHISHOLM, ESQ., of Aigas, M.A., F.R.S.E.
BEATTIE, ALEXANDER, ESQ., J.P.
BEATTIE, JOSEPH, ESQ.
BENNET, RICHARD, ESQ.
BERRY, WALTER, ESQ., F.S.A. SCOT.
BISHOP, F., ESQ.
BOYD, MARK, ESQ., of Merton Hall.

BRAIKENRIDGE, REV. GEORGE WEARE, F.S.A. SCOT.
BRASH, RICHARD ROLT, ESQ., M.R.I.A.
BROWNE, LIEUTENANT-GENERAL WALTER JOHN, C.B.
BUCHAN, PATRICK, ESQ., PH.D.
BLACKIE, JOHN, ESQ.

CAMPBELL, JAMES, ESQ.
CAMPBELL, DAVID, ESQ.
CAMPBELL, MAJOR PEMBERTON.
CABBELL, BENJAMIN BOND, ESQ., F.R.S., F.S.A., F.G.S.
CABBELL, BENJAMIN BOND, ESQ., JUN.
CHALMERS, J. A., ESQ., F.S.A. SCOT.
CHRISTIE, JONATHAN HENRY, ESQ.
CIBRARIO, COUNT, *Honorary.*
CLARK, GEORGE T., ESQ.
COULTHART, JOHN ROSS, ESQ., F.S.A. SCOT.
CRAIG, SKENE, ESQ.
CROLL, A. ANGUS, ESQ.
CRUIKSHANK, GEORGE, *Honorary.*

THE RIGHT HON. THE EARL OF DALHOUSIE, K.T., *Vice-President.*
DROUYN DE LHUYS, HIS EXCELLENCY EDOUARD, MEMBER OF THE INSTITUTE, AND PRESIDENT OF THE AGRICULTURAL SOCIETY OF FRANCE, *Honorary.*
DALLAS, A. G., ESQ., of Dunain.
DALZIEL, JOHN, ESQ.
DALTON, JAMES CARTER, ESQ.
DAVIDSON, DUNCAN, ESQ., of Tulloch.
DAVIDSON, JAMES W., ESQ.
DAVIDSON, J. E., ESQ.
DAVIDSON, JAMES, ESQ., of Ruchill.
DE CHAUMONT, F., ESQ., M.D.
DENNY, PETER, ESQ.
DOUGLAS, EDWARD OCTAVIUS, ESQ., of Killichassie.
DRUMMOND, GEORGE STIRLING HOME DRUMMOND, ESQ., of Blair Drummond.
DRYSDALE, HECTOR, ESQ.
DUNCAN, ALEXANDER, ESQ.

Elphinstone, The Right Hon. Lord.
Edgar, Andrew, Esq., LL.D.
Euing, William, Esq., F.R.S.E., F.S.A. Scot.

Farquharson, Robert O., Esq., of Haughton, F.S.A. Scot.
Ferguson, Robert, Esq.
Finnie, John, Esq.
Fleming, J. W., Esq., F.R.C.S.
Fowler, John, Esq., of Braemore.
Francis, Edward James, Esq.
Fraser, William Nathaniel, Esq., of Tornaveen.
Fraser, Francis Garden, Esq., of Findrack.

The Right Hon. the Earl of Glasgow, *Vice-President.*
Garland, E. W., Esq.
Gibbon, Alexander, Esq.
Gliddon, Alfred, Esq., City Bank, 159, 160, Tottenham Court Road, London, *Treasurer.*
Gooden, J. Christopher, Esq.
Gordon, Samuel, Esq.
Gordon, Alexander, Esq.
Gordon, John, Esq.
Graeme, Captain Alexander, R.N.
Graham, Peter, Esq.
Gray, John Edward, Esq., LL.D., F.R.S., F.L.S.
Greenshields, John B., Esq., F.S.A. Scot, of Kersc.
Grieve, John, Esq.
Guthrie, James, Esq.

The Right Hon. Lord Houghton, F.S.A., *Vice-President.*
Home, Major John Ferguson, of Bassendean.
Hepburn, William Crichton, Esq.
Hunter, David, Esq., of Blackness.

Innes, Rev. J. Brodie, of Milton Brodie.

Jessett, Claude, Esq.

KING, COLONEL W. ROSS, of Tertowie, F.R.G.S., F.S.A. SCOT.

KINLOCH, GEORGE R., ESQ.
KEITH, REV. WILLIAM, M.A.
KIELL, GEORGE MIDDLETON, ESQ.

LAGOS, HIS EXCELLENCY BARON DE A., *Honorary.*
LAING, ALEXANDER, ESQ., F.S.A. SCOT.
LAMB, JAMES J., ESQ.
LARKING, J. W., ESQ.
LEGGE, REV. JAMES, D.D., LL.D.

THE RIGHT HON. THE EARL OF MAR, *Vice-President.*
MACDONALD, JOHN D., ESQ., M.D., F.R.S.
MACFARLANE, REV. W. O., M.A.
MACFARLANE, W. H., ESQ.
MACGREGOR, P. COMYN, ESQ., of Brediland.
MACINTOSH, ALEXANDER, ESQ.
MACINTOSH, CHARLES FRASER, ESQ., of Drummond, F.S.A. SCOT.
MACKAY, JOHN, ESQ.
MACKENZIE, JOHN WHITEFORD, ESQ., W.S., F.S.A. SCOT.
MACKENZIE, CAPTAIN ALEXANDER, of Springfield.
MACKENZIE, KEITH STEWART, ESQ., of Seaforth.
MACKENZIE, SIR KENNETH, BART.
MACKINNON, WILLIAM ALEXANDER, ESQ., C.B.
MACLEOD, R. B. E., ESQ., of Codboll.
MACINNES, DONALD, ESQ.
MARTIN, SIR J. RANALD, C.B.
MAXWELL, SIR WILLIAM, BART., of Monreith.
MCBURNEY, ISAAC, ESQ., LL.D., F.E.I.S., F.S.A. SCOT.
MENELAUS, WILLIAM, ESQ.
MCCOSH, WILLIAM, ESQ.
MENZIES, SIR ROBERT, BART.
MONTGOMERIE, HUGH EDMONDSTON, ESQ., F.S.A., F.A.S., F.R.C.S.
MOORE, GEORGE, ESQ., M.D.

MURCHISON, SIR RODERICK IMPEY, BART., K.C.B., F.R.S., F.R.S.E., D C.L., LL.D., Member of the Institute of France, *Vice-President.*
MURDOCH, PETER, ESQ.
MUSCHET, JOHN S., ESQ., M.D., of Birkhill.

ORDE, SIR JOHN POWLETT, BART., of Morpeth.
OLIPHANT, T. L. KINGTON, ESQ., of Gask.
OSCAR, H.R.H. PRINCE, *Honorary.*

THE RIGHT HON. THE EARL OF ROSSLYN, *Vice-President.*
RAMSAY, ROBERT HAMILTON, ESQ., M.D.
RAMSAY, ANDREW CROMBIE, ESQ., LL.D., F.R.S., V.P.G.S.
RAE, JOHN, ESQ., LL.D., F.S.A.
REED, EDWARD J., ESQ., C.B.
RIDER, WILLIAM, ESQ.
ROGERS, REV. CHARLES, LL.D., F.S.A. SCOT., Snowdoun Villa, Lewisham, S.E., *Hon. Secretary.*
ROSS, GEORGE, W. H., ESQ., of Cromarty.

THE RIGHT HON. THE EARL OF STRATHMORE, *Vice-President.*
SAGASTA, HIS EXCELLENCY M. P., *Honorary.*
SCOTT, THOMAS D., ESQ.
SEMPLE, DAVID, ESQ., F.S.A. SCOT.
SHAIRP, PRINCIPAL JOHN C.
SION COLLEGE, LONDON.
SMITH, ALEXANDER, ESQ.
SHAW, CHARLES, ESQ.
STEWART, BALFOUR, ESQ., LL.D.
STEWART, CAPTAIN ROBERT WESTWOOD, F.G.S., F.R.A.S.
STEWART, CHARLES A., ESQ., of Achnacone.
STEWART, CHARLES, ESQ., R.A., F.S.A. SCOT.
STEWART, C. J., ESQ.
STRATTON, THOMAS, ESQ., M.D., R.N.
STUART, THE RIGHT HON. SIR JOHN, F.S.A. SCOT.
SWINTON, A. CAMPBELL, ESQ., of Kimmerghame, F.S.A. SCOT.
SWITHINBANK, GEORGE EDWIN, ESQ., LL.D., F.S.A. SCOT.
SYKES, COLONEL WILLIAM HENRY, F.R.S., F.G.S., F.R.A.S., M.P.

TREVELYAN, SIR WALTER CALVERLEY, BART., F.S.A., F.G.S., F.S.A. SCOT.
TAYLOR, W. J., ESQ.
TENNANT, ROBERT, ESQ.
TENNENT, GILBERT RAINEY, ESQ.
TOD, ALEXANDER, ESQ.
TURNER, THOMAS AUBREY, ESQ.
WEIR, ARCHIBALD, ESQ., M.D.
WILLIAMS, MAJOR W. E., F.S.A. SCOT.
WILSON, GEORGE FERGUSON, ESQ., F.R.S.
WILSON, WILLIAM THORBURN, ESQ., of Burnside, F.S.A. SCOT.
WIZSNIEWSKI, PRINCE ADAM, *Honorary.*
WRIGHT, REV. J. G., LL.D.

YULE, MAJOR-GENERAL P., F.S.A. SCOT.

PREFACE.

MONUMENTS are as milestones in the pathway of civilization. In early times memorial stones were not reared. When tribes became communities, unhewn stones were set up to perpetuate their heroes. As nations arose, cairns were heaped in celebration of national triumphs, or to denote the graves of princes. When the Israelites crossed Jordan, they placed twelve stones in memorial of the event; on their establishment as a nation they erected tombs in honour of their prophets. Decorated mummy tombs were common in ancient Egypt; the pyramids, which are clearly monumental, were built about two thousand years before Christ. The Assyrians constructed imposing edifices in celebration of their kings. The Greeks adorned their tombs with elegant sculptures; these at length assumed magnificent proportions, such as the celebrated Mausoleum at Halicarnassus. In Italy the Romans substituted the adorned sepulchral chambers of Etruria by spacious structures, which while honouring the dead suited the convenience of the living. Alike among eastern and western nations the *barrow*, or sepulchral mound, was superseded by the *cromlech*, which in its turn was exchanged for the Runic cross and other sculptured forms.

The memorial stones which form the subject of this work belong to a class usually termed modern. They began to be reared in the thirteenth century, but were then reserved for kings and warriors and churchmen. At the Reformation churches and abbeys were found studded with the cenotaphs of ecclesiastics; these, with the statues of saints and martyrs, were held as idolatrous, and thrown down. For two centuries afterwards, monumental tablets were disallowed in churches; while even in churchyards ornamental monuments were discommended. In respect of such memorials a more cultivated taste arose some sixty years ago. To encourage that taste, and to aid in preserving existing monuments, this work was originated. But the publication may be found useful to some who take no concern in monumental affairs; to the student of Family History it will yield convenient assistance—while to those interested in the memorials of National History it will convey information otherwise inaccessible.

An absolutely complete work was scarcely to be attained. For his performance the author claims only such an approach to completeness as might be accomplished by unwearied diligence. His inquiries were commenced in 1861. In August of that year he addressed a circular letter, accompanied with a schedule, to the whole of the parochial clergy. A schedule was afterwards despatched to the parish schoolmasters. In the principal Scottish journals information has been repeatedly solicited. Local antiquaries have been addressed. A tour was prosecuted throughout the principal counties, including nearly every portion of the Lowlands.

If the author has had frequently to regret that parochial functionaries have been unable to spare an hour or two in procuring information for a national work, and on a subject associated with the memory of their predecessors, he has on the other hand had occasion to rejoice in many intelligent and obliging coadjutors. For materials used in the present volume he has been under especial obligations to the Very Reverend Dean Ramsay, David Laing, Esq., LL.D., and John

Alexander Smith, Esq., M.D., Edinburgh; William Euing, Esq., Glasgow; David Semple, Esq., Paisley; William McDowall, Esq., Dumfries; A. Campbell Swinton, Esq., of Kimmerghame; the Rev. John Struthers, Prestonpans; and Mr. Andrew Currie, sculptor, Darnick. Every work bearing on the history of Scottish tombstones, and the various local and provincial histories have been examined; while the inscriptions and epitaphs contained in the collections of Monteith and others have been carefully utilized. Of modern publications none has proved more useful than Dr. Hew Scott's "Fasti Ecclesiæ Scoticanæ," a work which in minute and accurate details of ecclesiastical biography is altogether unrivalled. For greater convenience of reference an index is appended to each volume.

SNOWDOUN VILLA,
    LEWISHAM, S.E.,
        September, 1871.

CONTENTS.

	PAGE
EDINBURGHSHIRE	1
ST. GILES'S	15
GREYFRIARS	19
ST. CUTHBERT'S	57
ST. JOHN'S	72
LADY YESTER'S	80
LADY GLENORCHY'S	81
BUCCLEUCH	81
CANONGATE	85
OLD CALTON	91
NEW CALTON	96
HOLYROOD ABBEY	99
RESTALRIG	116
SOUTH LEITH	118
NORTH LEITH	121
ROSEBANK	124
WARRISTON	125
DEAN	130
DALRY	144
GRANGE	146
NEWINGTON	154
BORTHWICK	156
COLINTON	156
CORSTORPHINE	157
CRICHTON	159
DALKEITH	159
DUDDINGSTON	161
GLENCROSS	163
INVERESK	165

	PAGE
KIRKLISTON	168
KIRKNEWTON	169
LASSWADE	171
LIBERTON	175
NEWBATTLE	177
PENICUIK	177
LINLITHGOWSHIRE.	
ABERCORN	179
BATHGATE	180
CARRIDEN	181
DALMENY	181
ECCLESMACHAN	182
LINLITHGOW	182
QUEENSFERRY	183
TORPHICHEN	183
UPHALL	184
HADDINGTONSHIRE.	
HADDINGTON	186
ABERLADY	199
ATHELSTANEFORD	200
DUNBAR	201
GLADSMUIR	206
NORTH BERWICK	207
ORMISTON	209
PRESTONKIRK	211
PRESTONPANS	212
SALTON	217

CONTENTS.

	PAGE		PAGE
Spott	218	St. Boswell's	260
Tranent	219	Wilton	261

BERWICKSHIRE.

	PAGE
Ayton	221
Bunkle	221
Chirnside	222
Coldingham	222
Coldstream	223
Dunse	224
Earlston	225
Eccles	226
Edrom	227
Foulden	228
Hutton	228
Lauder	229
Longformacus	229
Merton	230
Mordington	234
Polwarth	235
Swinton	235
Westruther	236
Whitsome	237

ROXBURGHSHIRE.

	PAGE
Ancrum	238
Bowden	239
Castleton	239
Cavers	240
Eckford	241
Ednam	242
Hawick	243
Jedburgh	245
Kelso	248
Lilliesleaf	248
Linton	249
Melrose	250
Roxburgh	258
Smailholme	260

PEEBLESSHIRE.

	PAGE
Broughton	262
Eddleston	262
Kirkurd	263
West Linton	263
Lyne	265
Manor	265
Newlands	266
Peebles	267
Skirling	271
Traquair	271
Tweedsmuir	272

SELKIRKSHIRE.

	PAGE
Selkirk	274
Yarrow	275
Ettrick	280

DUMFRIESSHIRE.

	PAGE
Dumfries	283
Annan	295
Caerlaverock	297
Canonbie	299
Closeburn	299
Dornock	300
Dryfesdale	301
Dunscore	301
Durisdeer	302
Eskdalemuir	304
Glencairn	305
Gretna	306
Hoddam	308
Holywood	309
Johnstone	309
Keir	310
Kirkconnel	310
Kirkmahoe	311

CONTENTS.

	PAGE
KIRKMICHAEL	312
KIRKPATRICK-JUXTA	313
LANGHOLM	313
LOCHMABEN	314
MIDDLEBIE	314
MOFFAT	315
PENPONT	316
RUTHWELL	316
SANQUHAR	318
TINWALD	319
TORTHORWALD	321
TUNDERGARTH	322
TYNRON	322
WAMPHRAY	323
WESTERKIRK	324

KIRKCUDBRIGHTSHIRE.

ANWORTH	326
BALMACLELLAN	327
BALMAGHIE	328
BORGUE	329
CARSPHAIRN	329
CROSSMICHAEL	330
DALRY	330
GIRTHON	331
KELLS	332
KELTON	335
KIRKCUDBRIGHT	336
KIRKMABRECK	338
KIRKPATRICK-IRONGRAY	339
MINNIGAFF	340
NEW ABBEY	342
RERRICK	343
TERREGLES	344
TONGLAND	345
URR	345

WIGTONSHIRE.

GLASSERTON	347
LESWALT	347
OLD LUCE	347
PENNINGHAM	348
STRANRAER	348
WHITHORN	348
WIGTON	349

AYRSHIRE.

AUCHINLECK	358
AYR	360
BEITH	364
COLMONELL	365
CUMNOCK	365
CRAIGIE	366
DAILLY	368
DUNDONALD	368
DUNLOP	370
FENWICK	372
GALSTON	375
IRVINE	377
KILBIRNIE	379
WEST KILBRIDE	382
KILMARNOCK	384
KILMAURS	388
KILWINNING	388
KIRKMICHAEL	389
LARGS	389
LOUDOUN	393
MAUCHLINE	396
MAYBOLE	396
MONKTON	397
MUIRKIRK	398
STEVENSTON	399
STEWARTON	400
STRAITON	401
TARBOLTON	401

RENFREWSHIRE.

CATHCART	403
EAGLESHAM	405
EASTWOOD	407

	PAGE		PAGE
GREENOCK	409	DALZIEL	446
HOUSTON	415	DOUGLAS	447
INCHINNAN	415	GARTSHERRIE	450
INNERKIP	416	GLASFORD	451
KILMALCOLM	416	GLASGOW	452
LOCHWINNOCH	416	THE CATHEDRAL	457
PAISLEY	417	THE COLLEGE	465
RENFREW	433	TRON CHURCH	469
		RAMSHORN	469
LANARKSHIRE.		THE NECROPOLIS	470
AIRDRIE	435	SOUTHERN NECROPOLIS	491
AVONDALE	436	SIGHTHILL CEMETERY	494
BIGGAR	437	JANEFIELD CEMETERY	499
BLANTYRE	438	WOODSIDE CEMETERY, AN-	
BOTHWELL	439	DERSTON	501
CAMBUSNETHAN	439	GOVAN	501
CARLUKE	443	HAMILTON	502
CARMICHAEL	444	LANARK	504
CARNWATH	444	LESMAHAGOW	505
CRAWFORDJOHN	445	WANDELL	506
DALSERF	446	WALSTON	506

MONUMENTS

AND

MONUMENTAL INSCRIPTIONS IN SCOTLAND.

EDINBURGHSHIRE.

EDINBURGH is a city of monuments. Sovereigns, statesmen, warriors, poets, and philosophers are all commemorated with befitting honours. The monuments are of every class, from the lofty Gothic spire down to the simple tablet.

The monument to Sir Walter Scott, in Princes Street, claims a first notice. It is the *chef-d'œuvre* of Scottish memorial art; in elegance of construction it has never been excelled. Sir Walter Scott died on the 21st September, 1832. On the 24th day of the same month a circular letter was issued convening a meeting at the rooms of the Royal Society of Edinburgh, to consider the best means of suitably commemorating the illustrious departed. At this meeting a committee was appointed to arrange a general meeting of the citizens for more maturely considering the course of action. This general meeting was held on the 5th October, under the presidency of the Lord Provost, and a resolution in favour of a national monument to Sir Walter was moved by the Duke of Buccleuch, and seconded by the Earl of Rosebery. Sir John Forbes, Bart., then announced that he was instructed by the Bank of Scotland, and other banks in Edinburgh, creditors of the deceased baronet, to subscribe £500 "in token of their appreciation of the honourable feelings which induced him, after his embarrassments in 1826, to dedicate his talents during the remainder of his life in insuring the full payments of his debts."

Differences arose as to the character of the monument. An auxiliary committee formed in London devoted their subscriptions of £10,000 to liquidate the debt on the library and museum at Abbotsford; and committees formed at Glasgow, Selkirk, and Perth resolved to appropriate their funds in rearing memorial statues of Sir Walter in their several localities.

In November, 1833, the original Edinburgh committee had collected £5,534, a sum sufficient to insure the construction of a substantial monument. It was now resolved to deliberate about the site. Among the sites suggested were the following:—The space in the Lawn Market, bounded on the east by St. Giles' Church; the west end of Princes Street, opposite to St. John's Church; the foot of St. David Street, near Queen Street Gardens; the open space at Picardy Place, head of Leith Walk; the rocky angle at the north-east corner of the Calton Hill; Charlotte Square, at the west end of George Street; the centre of Moray Place; and Randolph Crescent.

The committee, suspending their decision on the question of a site, advertised in thirty-two newspapers, requesting that designs might be sent to the secretary before the first day of September, 1836. Fifty-five designs were offered. For the best three the committee adjudged prizes of fifty guineas. One of the prize designs bore the signature "John Morvo," the name of a famous master mason, commemorated by an inscription in Melrose Abbey. It was assumed by George Meikle Kemp, author of the drawing, then a working joiner. Kemp had studied the peculiarities of Gothic architecture in different parts of the kingdom, and latterly added to his scanty emoluments by making architectural drawings. The committee, dissatisfied with all the designs received, including those to which they had assigned prizes as the best, advertised a second time. Among those who joined in the new competition were Sir William Allan, David Roberts, R.A., and William H. Playfair, the well-known architect. Kemp lodged an improved drawing of his original design. It represented an elaborately decorated Gothic tower, and was adopted by a majority of twenty-one to ten at a meeting of the general committee, held at Edinburgh on the 6th April, 1838. At the same time Mr. John Steell, the distinguished sculptor, was commissioned to prepare a marble statue of Sir Walter Scott, to be placed under the lofty canopy of the basement arch. The site was ultimately fixed in Princes Street, at the foot of South St. David Street. The architect had designed the monument to reach the height of 180 feet, but the funds at the disposal of the committee did not justify their proceeding with it on so large a scale. The reduction of the design was opposed, and in May, 1840, an auxiliary committee undertook that the plan should be fully carried out.

An Act of Parliament securing the site having been obtained, the foundation stone of the monument was on the 15th August, 1840, laid by the Right Honourable Sir James Forrest, of Comiston, Bart., Lord Provost of the city, and Grand Master Mason. A metallic plate deposited in the foundation stone bore the following inscription, composed by Lord Jeffrey:—

"This graven plate, deposited in the base of a votive building on the 15th day of August, 1840, and never likely to see the light again till all the surrounding structures are crumbled to dust by the decay of time, or by human or elemental violence, may then testify to a distant posterity that his countrymen began on that day to raise an effigy and architectural monument to the memory of Sir Walter Scott, Bart., whose admirable writings were then allowed to have given more delight, and suggested better feelings to a larger class of readers in every rank of society than those of any other author, with the exception of Shakspeare alone, and which were therefore thought likely to be remembered long after this act of gratitude on the part of the first generation of his admirers should be forgotten. He was born at Edinburgh, 15th August, 1771, and died at Abbotsford, 21st September, 1832."

The monument was, at the cost of upwards of £1,500, founded on the solid rock, fifty-two feet below the level of Princes Street. The structure, which presents the form of an open crucial Gothic spire, may be thus described:—From each corner of a raised platform of masonry rise elegantly clustered columns, from which spring four grand Early English arches, that converge into a vaulted roof, crossing each other by ribbed groinings with beautifully carved bosses, and terminating in a richly ornamented pendant or drop centre. The arches are successively supported by projecting buttresses, also arched upon clustered columns, and which after ascending to the first gallery spring into the open air to the height of ninety-eight feet, and terminate in pinnacles beautifully carved with crockets, and crowned with richly ornamented finials. The connecting buttresses are decorated as they rise with large niches, adorned with brackets and canopies; and each of the abutment towers, at the height of the first gallery, has two chaste and tastefully wrought gargoyles in the form of grotesque griffins. The pilasters which separate the different clustered pillars that support the vaulted roof of the Gothic temple are crowned with finely ornamented capitals, containing likenesses of sixteen Scottish poets. The lateral towers are connected with the centre one by means of flying buttresses, and with spandrils and crockets. The four principal arches and buttresses sustain an open trellis, which extends round the building in front of the first gallery; and level with this gallery is an apartment used as a Waverley Museum. From the gallery rises the principal tower. On each side is an arched window. A flying staircase leads to the third gallery. Around are towers, buttresses, pinnacles, arches, crockets, corbels, and finials, in all the rich profusion of Gothic architecture. On reaching the fourth gallery the view is grand in the extreme. At each successive stage are elegantly sculptured niches, intended for statues illustrative of the Poet's works. The height of the monument (increased beyond the original design) is 200 feet 6 inches above the level of Princes Street; it is ascended by 289 steps.

The monumental statue of Sir Walter represents him in a sitting attitude, with the ample folds of a Scottish plaid hanging loosely about him, and his favourite hound Maida at his feet. The artist has seized the moment when the great novelist has just recorded some of his imperishable thoughts in the volume which is in his hand, and he has successfully communicated to the features a look of complete abstraction; while the dog, as if startled by the closing of the book, is in the act of lifting up its head to catch the expression of its master's countenance. The statue was inaugurated in 1846. The block of white Carrara marble from which it was chiselled contained 200 cubic feet, and weighed upwards of twenty-five tons. The monument is constructed of sandstone from Binny quarry. The funds raised by the original and auxiliary committees amounted to £17,243 4s. The sum of £1,871 12s. 8d. was expended in procuring subscriptions. For the statue Mr. Steell received £2,000; eight small statues cost £179 5s. 10d.; a sum of £460 3s. 5d. was lost by a contractor, and a railing was erected at the expense of £147 13s. 6d. The balance, amounting to £12,584 8s. 6d., was expended in the monumental fabric.*

Notwithstanding the most persevering exertions, the auxiliary committee were obliged to discontinue their labours without obtaining sufficient funds to provide statues for all the niches. Of these thirty are still unoccupied, but a vigorous effort is now being made by Mr. James Ballantine, the ingenious poet, to complete the work. The sum of £2,000, Mr. Ballantine conceives, will suffice to provide the remaining statues. The museum-room is being fitted up under the direction of Mr. Cousin, the city architect. It is hoped that, in carrying out these improvements, some method may be discovered to conceal the iron balustrade which, appearing in the staircase above the arched windows, impairs the beauty of the fabric as seen from St. David Street.

In point of magnitude, and the grandeur of its site, the Nelson monument on the Calton Hill next claims attention. This structure consists of a circular tower on an octagonal basement,

---

* In preparing an account of Sir Walter Scott's monument I have been mainly indebted to a MS. work entitled "History of the Subscriptions for Erecting the Monument to the Memory of Sir Walter Scott at Edinburgh, compiled from the Minute Books and Vouchers of the Original and Auxiliary Committees, by John Castle, Secretary to the joint committees," 1852. 4to. This MS. volume was bequeathed by Mr. Castle to the Faculty of Advocates. Mr. Castle died a few years ago, and his volume is preserved in the Advocates' Library.

which together are upwards of one hundred feet in height. It was erected in 1815; in front is the following inscription :—

"To the memory of Vice-Admiral Horatio Lord Viscount Nelson, and of the great victory of Trafalgar, too dearly purchased with his blood, the grateful citizens of Edinburgh have erected this monument, not to express their unavailing sorrow for his death, nor yet to celebrate the matchless glories of his life; but by his noble example to teach their sons to emulate what they admire, and like him, when duty requires, to die for their country. MDCCCV."

On the flagstaff of the Nelson monument a huge ball is rigged, which, moved by mechanism adjusted at the Observatory, drops daily at one o'clock.

Twelve massive columns, with an entablature, situated on the most elevated portion of the Calton Hill, originally intended as a portico to a larger structure, constitute what is termed the *National Monument*. The proposal to rear a great cenotaph in commemoration of the heroes who fell in the land and sea battles of Napoleon's reign was suggested in 1816, at a meeting of the Highland Society. The Parthenon at Athens was adopted as a model, and the erection was to consist of a great church with a cemetery. The sum of £6,000 was subscribed at once, and in 1822 the subscribers were incorporated by Act of Parliament, and empowered to raise the sum of £50,000, in shares of £25 each. When George IV. was at Holyrood Palace, in August, 1822, the foundation stone was laid with splendid ceremonial by Royal Commissioners, under the presidency of the Duke of Hamilton, Grand Master Mason. But success did not attend the subsequent efforts of the projectors. The sum of £13,500 was raised from first to last, and the amount, deducting expenses, appropriated in constructing the portico.

A proposal has been instituted to place on the Calton Hill a monument to King Robert the Bruce, from a spirited design, prepared by Mr. George Cruikshank. A model of the proposed monument was lately exhibited to the Queen at Windsor Castle. It consists of a statue of the patriot king, to be cast in bronze, and resting on an upright block of unhewn granite. King Robert, arrayed in the hauberk of the period, covered with the royal surcoat, is in the act of sheathing his sword, and the expression of his countenance, full of benignity, gives token that victory has been achieved. The pedestal shares the simplicity of the figure by which it is surmounted. On the reverse is a figure of Britannia joining the two shields of Scotland and England. Opposite are represented boughs of laurel and weeping willows intertwined, and beneath are two hands, male and female, interclasped, surrounded by a wreath of flowers. This elegantly devised memorial will certainly be erected either at Edinburgh or at Bannockburn.

A monument on the Calton Hill of elegant Greek architecture, resembling "The Lantern of Demosthenes" at Athens, and executed by W. H. Playfair, commemorates the celebrated Professor Dugald Stewart. At the south-east corner of the hill a rectangular monument celebrates the genius and worth of Professor John Playfair, the eminent mathematician.

On the Calton Hill is an elegant monument to Robert Burns, reared in 1830 at the cost of £3,000, after a design by Thomas Hamilton. Of this elegant memorial, the cupola is a copy of the monument of Lysistratus, at Athens. The interior is tastefully fitted up as a museum; it contains, among other interesting memorials, the Poet's bust, by Brodie, a sword-cane which he carried as an officer of excise, the stool on which he sat while correcting proofs in Creech's printing office; a painting of "Tam o' Shanter," by James Drummond, R.S.A.; and letters written by the poet, his sons, the Colonels Burns, and his father and paternal uncle, Robert Burns.

In front of the Register House stands a fine equestrian statue of the Duke of Wellington, on a pedestal of Peterhead cyenite, thirteen feet in height. The duke's horse is in the act of rearing, the forepart being elevated, with the head raised and drawn back. The weight of horse and rider is thrown upon the hind legs and flowing tail, which the position of the animal causes to touch the ground. The horse is a magnificent charger, full of strength and action. The figure of the duke is excellent, with an accurate likeness. Calm and self-possessed, he guides his horse with his left hand, while with his right he points forward, in the act of directing the field. From his shoulders a military cloak falls in graceful folds. The statue is of bronze. It was modelled and cast by Mr. Steell at the cost of £10,000. It is fourteen feet in height, and weighs twelve tons. The statue was publicly unveiled on the 18th June, 1852. On the occasion a masonic procession marched to the spot, headed by the Duke of Athole, Grand Master Mason; an address was delivered by the Duke of Buccleuch.

On the top of the Royal Institution, fronting Princes Street, rests a colossal statue of her Majesty Queen Victoria. It was reared in 1844, by public subscription. Her Majesty honoured the sculptor, Mr. Steell, with several sittings; she is represented seated on her throne, with a diadem on her brow. In her right hand she holds the sceptre, and her left hand leans on an orb, emblematic of her extended sway. The statue is four times the size of life.

Within Princes Street gardens, and on the right and left front of the Royal Institution, are elegant monumental statues of Allan Ramsay, author of "The Gentle Shepherd," and of Professor John Wilson. The monument to Allan Ramsay was executed by Mr. Steell, on the commission of the late Lord Murray. The statue, cut in Carrara marble, is ten feet eight inches in height, and in the sculptor's studio weighed eighteen tons. The poet, in the quaint costume of his period, stands in an easy attitude, and is in the act of composing. In his left hand he holds a book, the back of which he presses to his breast. The right arm is close to his side, the fore-arm being slightly elevated; in his hand is a pencil, held in readiness to inscribe the thought with which he is busy. The right foot is advanced, and the body leans back slightly on the left, imparting an air of ease and dignity. The statue rests on a pedestal of Binny stone, decorated on the sides with medallion portraits of Lord Murray the founder, Mrs. Ramsay, wife of the poet's son Allan, General Ramsay, a grandson of the poet, and Lady Campbell and Mrs. Malcolm, the poet's granddaughters. The monument was erected in March, 1865.

Professor Wilson's monument occupies the corner of Princes Street gardens, at the left front of the Royal Institution. The statue, one of Mr. Steell's happiest impersonations, is eleven feet eight inches in height. The careless ease of the professor's ordinary dress is adopted, a plaid which he was in the habit of wearing supplies the required drapery, and the trunk of a palm tree gives a rest to the figure, while it symbolizes his principal poem. The lion-like head and face thrown slightly upward express impulsive genius evolving itself in fruitful thought, —the glow of fancy animating every feature. In his right hand the professor grasps a pen, and clutches the plaid which hangs across his breast. His left hand rests negligently in the leaves of a half-open MS. The limbs loosely planted, yet firm and vigorous, correspond with the grandly elevated expression of the countenance. The pedestal is simple and appropriate.

In the centre of St. Andrew's Square a tall fluted column, in the style of Trajan's pillar, commemorates Henry Dundas, first Viscount Melville. It was reared in 1821 at the cost of £6,000, chiefly defrayed by gentlemen connected with the navy. The height is 136 feet, and the diameter at base 12 feet. A circular pedestal on the top supports a statue of Lord Melville, 14 feet in height.

On the east side of St. Andrew's Square, in the recess in front of the Royal Bank, a bronze statue, in Roman costume, leaning on a charger, represents Lieutenant-General Sir John Hope, afterwards fourth Earl of Hopetoun. This distinguished military commander was born on the 17th August, 1766. He entered the army in his sixteenth year, and in 1793 became Lieutenant-Colonel in the 25th Foot. He was present at the battle of Alexandria in 1801, and negotiated the convention for the surrender of Cairo in the same year. In the Peninsular War he served with distinction. He commanded the left wing of the British army at Corunna, and on the death of Sir John Moore took the chief command. In 1813 he commanded the left wing at the battle of Nivelle. He afterwards distinguished himself in the campaign of the Pyrenees. Lord Hopetoun died at Paris on the 27th August, 1823. This monument (one of four raised to his memory) was erected in 1835, after a model by Campbell.

A colossal bronze statue of George IV., by Chantrey, at the junction of George Street and Hanover Street, commemorates his Majesty's royal visit to Scotland in 1822. It was erected in 1831.

A bronze statue of William Pitt, also by Chantrey, and which, like the former, rests on a granite pedestal, stands at the crossing of Frederick Street and George Street; it was reared in 1803.

A monumental statue of Dr. Thomas Chalmers, now preparing in the studio of Mr. Steell, will be placed at the crossing of George and Castle Streets. The proposal to commemorate Dr. Chalmers by a monument at Edinburgh was originated by Dean Ramsay in 1847, and was revived at a meeting held in November, 1869, under the presidency of the Earl of Dalhousie. Upwards of £3,000 have been subscribed.

At Melville Crescent a monumental statue of Robert, second Viscount Melville, commemorates the regard and esteem in which he was held by his friends and fellow-countrymen. The statue, which was executed by Mr. Steell, is of bronze, and in height measures nearly twelve feet. His lordship is represented leaning with his right arm on a square truncated pillar, which being set angularly admits of an easy and graceful *pose*. The right leg is slightly advanced, and stands quite clear; and the left, which sustains the greater part of the weight, is at the lower part also clear of the cloak, which, falling loosely from the shoulders and over the right arm, supplies the requisite drapery. The head is bent forward with an expression of attention. Robert Dundas, second Viscount Melville, was born on the 14th March, 1771, and studied at the High School of Edinburgh and in Emanuel College, Cambridge. In 1802 he became M.P. for Mid-Lothian. In 1807 he was President of the Board of Control. On the death of his father, the first Lord Melville, in 1811, he obtained a place in the House of Peers, and was appointed Keeper of the Privy Seal of Scotland. In 1812 he became First Lord of the Admiralty, and in 1814 was elected Chancellor of St. Andrews University. He was a member of several administrations, and held office in two royal commissions for visiting the universities of Scotland. Lord Melville died at Melville Castle, Mid-Lothian, on the 10th June, 1851, in his eightieth year.

At the junction of St. Colme Street with North Charlotte Street has (in questionable taste) been placed the richly carved Eleanor cross, reared by grateful citizens to commemorate the philanthropy and Christian work of the late Miss Catherine Sinclair. This admirable gentlewoman was sixth daughter of the celebrated Sir John Sinclair, Bart., of Ulbster, and was born on the 17th April, 1800. She was for many years resident in Edinburgh, where she took an active part in promoting the interests of the industrial classes, and in every charitable undertaking. In the literary world she is known as the author of many interesting works. She died at Edinburgh on the 6th August, 1864. Her monument was designed by Mr. David Bryce, R.S.A. On a broad platform of stone two and a half feet in height rests the base proper of the cross, consisting of three massive steps, each two feet in height. The monument is hexagonal, with buttresses at the angles, and the total height is sixty feet. Above the base the structure is divided into three stages, in the two lower of which the sides are finished with arched recesses surmounted by pediments, and otherwise ornamented. The upper stage consists of a crocketed pyramidal spire.

Two monuments adorn the esplanade of the castle. That situated nearer the castle is a bronze statue by Campbell of Frederick, Duke of York and Albany, K.G., second son of George III., and commander-in-chief; it was reared in 1839. The other presents the form of a Runic cross, and is thus inscribed:—

" Sacred to the memory of the officers, non-commissioned officers, and private soldiers of the 78th Highland Regiment, who fell in the suppression of the mutiny of the native army of India in the years 1857 and 1858. This memorial is erected as a tribute of respect by their surviving brother officers and comrades, and by many officers who formerly belonged to the regiment, A.D. 1861."

In Parliament Close, occupying the narrow space between St. Giles' Church and the Parliament House, stands the equestrian statue of Charles II. During the rejoicings which in the city attended the event of the Restoration, the Corporation resolved to rear a statue in honour of the restored king, and an artist at Rotterdam was commissioned to execute the work. The statue was reared in 1685, when the artist was recompensed with a payment of £2,580 Scots, or £215 sterling.* The site selected is not very creditable to the taste of Edinburgh citizens, for while the statue is dwarfed by the high buildings which surround it, it occupies the spot where were entombed the remains of John Knox, the illustrious reformer.† After the conflagration of 1700, which destroyed the range of buildings in Parliament Close, the statue was temporarily deposited in the Calton jail; it was afterwards placed on a new and handsome pedestal, in which were inserted two marble tablets. These tablets present the following inscription:—

" Augustisimo magnificentissimo
CAROLO SECUNDO,
Britanniarum Galliarum & Hibernie
Monarchae
Invictissimo
Cujus Natalitijs providentia arrisit Divina Asterisca Meridiano eodem momenti conspicua qui postquam adolescentiam in acie sub patre, exegisset illo demum, obtruncato, jus finim, per biennium strenue quidem sed improspere vendicavit Rebellioni namq; sæpius

* Maitland's " History of Edinburgh," Edinb., 1753, fol. p. 105.
† A square stone inscribed with the initials " J. K., 1572," a few feet to the west of the statue, denotes the spot where it is supposed the reformer was buried, but Dr. Daniel Wilson is inclined to believe that the monument stands directly over the Reformer's grave. The locality formerly constituted a portion of the churchyard of St. Giles. See Dr. Daniel Wilson's " Memorials of Edinburgh," vol. i., p. 84.

victrici impar, solum prope per decennium vertere coactiis ess in exteris autem Regionibus divinis excubijs. Pactis dolis minis armis Incubatoris non obstantibus Munitus, & custoditus, instar solis tandem, clarioris e nubibus, in regna sua sine cæde expostliminio reversus Ecclesiam politiam Civilem pacem Commercium erexit, auxit, firmavit et stabilivit. Bello dein Batanico insignis, stative devenit inter bellantes vicinos belli pacisque Arbiter Rebellione denique pristina nuper repullulante Palladis non Martis ministerio Basiliscum in ipso ovo compressit contudit et conculcavit huic ergo miraculorum principi summa in pace et gloria."

Of this inscription the following translation is presented in the Appendix of "The Life, Prophecies, and Times of Alexander Peden" (Edinburgh, 1849) :—

"To the Most August, Most Magnificent, and Most Unconquered Charles II., Monarch of Great Britain, France, and Ireland, at the moment of whose birth Divine Providence smiled auspiciously, by causing a bright star to shine forth at noonday; who, after having spent his youth in arms under his father (and the latter being beheaded), strenuously, but without success, contended for nearly two years for his rights. But, unequal to cope with rebellion, too often victorious, he was compelled for about ten years to retire into foreign countries. Yet, guarded and defended by divine protection, in spite of the proffered guiles, threats, and arms of the usurper, at length, after the Restoration, he arose brighter, just as the sun when he emerges from the obscuring clouds, and returned, without bloodshed, to his kingdom and to his rights. He erected, augmented, remodelled, and strengthened the Church, the civil polity, the peace, and the commerce of his kingdoms. After this he shone forth illustriously in the Dutch war, waged between neighbouring belligerents, and became the arbiter both of peace and war. Finally, when the old rebellion sprung up anew, he struck it down—trampled it in the dust, more by the assistance of Pallas, the goddess of wisdom, than by Mars, the god of war; and thus crushed the basilisk (or cockatrice) in its eggs. To this prince of miracles, therefore, be the highest glory now that he is in the enjoyment of peace!"

Within the Parliament House are marble statues of several distinguished lawyers. Duncan Forbes of Culloden, Lord President of the Court of Session, who died in 1747, is commemorated by the French sculptor, Roubiliac. The statue of Lord President Blair, (son of the author of "The Grave,") who died in 1811, was executed by Chantrey. Robert Dundas of Arniston, Lord Chief Baron of Exchequer, who died in 1819, is represented in marble at the cost of the county of Edinburgh. There is a colossal statue of Henry, first Viscount Melville, by Chantrey; a statue of Lord Cockburn by Brodie; and admirable representations of Lord Jeffrey and Lord President Boyle, both from the chisel of Mr. Steell. A statue of Sir Walter Scott in freestone is preserved in the Advocates' Library.

Among the mural monuments in the vestibule of St. Giles' Church, several possess special interest. Dr. Carson, Rector of the High School of Edinburgh, is on a handsome tablet thus commemorated:—

Memoriæ Sacrum
Aglionbii Ross Carson, A.M., LL.D., S.R.E.S.,
Scholæ Regiæ Edinensis
Per Viginti Quinque Annos
Rectoris

Multo ingenii acumine præditus, Linguarum tam Recentium quam veterum Literarumque Humaniorum scientia præ ceteris spectabilis, Quadraginta fere annos juventuti hujus urbis formandæ operam dedit; His et artibus clarum sibi nomen conquisivit.

Pius, plurimis ornatus virtutibus, Honesta decora, laudanda fideliter excolendo, civium suorum gratiam conciliavit.

Benevolus, pacificus, verecundus, simplex, vixit amicis carus; Discipulis, familiaribus, Liberis, summum sui desiderium sublatus reliquit.

Natus A.D.   Obiit A.D.
MDCCLXXIX.   MDCCCL.

A handsome cenotaph commemorates Major-General Sir Robert Henry Dick, K.C.B. K.C.H., of Tullymet, who was killed at Sobraon on the banks of the Sutlej on the 16th February, 1846, while gallantly leading his division within the enemy's trenches. Sir Robert was Lieutenant-Colonel of the 42nd Regiment, and this handsome tribute to his valour was reared by his brother officers.

Marble tablets erected by their brother officers celebrate the heroism of Captain James Ranald Burt, of the 6th Bengal Light Cavalry, who died at Ferozepore on the 8th May, 1846, aged thirty-five; of Lieutenant George Hill Sprott, of the 2nd Bengal

European Regiment, who fell at the battle of Goojerat on the 21st February, 1849; and of John Marriott Aytoun, of the 94th Regiment, who was killed in action in the Punjaub on the 4th May, 1860.

There are elegant marble cenotaphs in honour of the officers, non-commissioned officers, and privates of the 72nd and 93rd Regiments, who fell in action or died from wounds and disease during the suppression of the mutiny in India in 1857-8.

A tablet supported by a massive bracket celebrates the philanthropy and Christian devotedness of George Lorimer, Dean of Guild, who lost his life while seeking to save the lives of others during the destruction by fire of the Theatre Royal, 13th January, 1865. A marble tablet, reared at the expense of friends "in token of their esteem and affection," commemorates Patrick Robertson, one of the Senators of the College of Justice. This learned judge and most agreeable companion was son of James Robertson, Writer to the Signet, and was born at Edinburgh on the 17th February, 1794. He passed advocate in 1815, and speedily attained high reputation as a pleader. His strength lay chiefly in his sarcastic humour, which has rarely been equalled. In 1842 he was elected Dean of Faculty, and in the year following was promoted to the Bench. In 1848 the students of Marischal College, Aberdeen, elected him as Lord Rector of that university. He died suddenly from a stroke of apoplexy on the 10th January, 1855. Lord Robertson published several volumes of poems, but his poetical merits were not equal to his forensic and conversational talents. His *bon-mots* and brilliant sallies of wit are pleasantly remembered by the citizens of Edinburgh, among whom his name is "familiar as a household word."

In the interior of St. Giles' Church is the recently restored monument of the Regent Murray.* The remains of Lord James Stewart, Earl of Murray, were interred in the south aisle of

---

* This monument is situated partly below the west end of the present centre lobby of the Old Church, and partly below the west side of the pulpit leading from the outer lobby to the body of the church, when entering from Parliament Square.

this church on Sunday, the 14th February, 1569-70, after a sermon preached on the occasion by Knox. Above the vault in which the body was entombed an altar-tomb was constructed, to which was attached a brass plate, inscribed with a Latin inscription, composed by Buchanan. The south aisle of the church remained an open thoroughfare for nearly two centuries; and when it was converted during the last century into a parish church the Regent's monument was defaced, and the brass plate torn off. Chiefly through the exertions of Mr. David Laing, with the co-operation of the Scottish Society of Antiquaries, the late John, twelfth Earl of Moray, was in 1865 induced to restore the monument of his progenitor. The restoration was effected under the superintendence of Mr. David Cousin, city architect, who has succeeded in reproducing the original aspects. The brass plate which had been secured by the family on the dilapidation of the fabric, is re-attached, and two inscriptions added, with the dates of the erection and the repair. In the "Proceedings of the Society of Antiquaries of Scotland" Mr. Laing has presented an interesting narrative of the negotiations attendant on the restoration of this national memorial, with "The Compte" of the original cost found in the family archives. He has enhanced the interest of his narrative by engravings of the monument in its restored form, and of the plate containing the inscription.*

In the quadrangle of the College opposite the entrance archway, is a marble statue by Brodie, of Sir David Brewster, who at the time of his decease held the offices of Principal and Vice-Chancellor of the university. Immediately in front of the School of Arts in Adam Square, James Watt is commemorated in a statue by Slater. The great inventor is seated, and in the act of applying a pair of compasses to a drawing which rests upon his knee. This monumental statue was erected in 1853.

In October, 1869, Mr. William Chambers, of Glenormiston, then Lord Provost of Edinburgh, made the judicious proposal

* "Proceedings of the Society of Antiquaries of Scotland," vol. i., pp. 181—196; and vol. vi., pp. 49—55.

that buildings and localities in the city associated with historical personages or interesting events should be denoted by suitable inscriptions. We subjoin a list of some of the localities which Mr. Chambers suggested as entitled to commemoration, and the inscriptions proposed.

On the tenement at the north-west corner of Drummond Street, opposite the College, at present containing Drummond Street Hall, Mr. Chambers proposed to inscribe—" On this spot, at Kirk of Field, stood the house in which Henry Stuart, Lord Darnley, was blown up by gunpowder, in the morning of February 10, 1567."

On the tenement at the corner of High Street, and entrance to Hunter Square, the lower part of which comprehends a draper's shop—" Here stood the old building known as the 'Black Turnpike,' occupied by Sir Simon Preston, Lord Provost of Edinburgh, and in which Mary Queen of Scots was lodged on her surrender at Carbery Hill, 15th June, 1567."

On the tenement in Riddle's Court, Lawn Market, over the doorway of the stair in which is the warehouse of Mr. Glass—" The house of Bailie Macmoran, in which took place two memorable banquets given by the city of Edinburgh to King James VI., with his Queen, Anne of Denmark, and her brother, the Duke of Holstein, 24th April and 2nd May, 1578."

On the front of the Merchants' Hall, Hunter Square—" George Buchanan, the eminent Scottish historian and reformer, closed his mortal career in a house in Kennedy's Close, near this spot, 28th September, 1582."

On the old timber-fronted tenement, High Street, opposite Niddry Street—" Here Allan Ramsay, the eminent Scottish poet, carried on business as author and bookseller at the sign of the 'Mercury,' 1721; and here were first published his 'Gentle Shepherd' and other works."

On the front of the building, head of St. John Street, Canongate, first floor, entering on west of arch—" Here resided Tobias Smollett on his visit to Edinburgh, 1766—the visit which occasioned his 'Humphrey Clinker.'"

On the building to be erected near the head of College Wynd, on the spot (now a wood yard)—" Near this spot stood the house in which Sir Walter Scott was born, August 15, 1771."

On the tenement erected in St. Mary Street, at corner of Boyd's Entry, belonging to the Catholic Institute—" This edifice occupies the site of Boyd's Inn, at which Dr. Samuel Johnson alighted on his celebrated tour to the Hebrides, August 17, 1773."

Shortly after the lamented death of H.R.H. the Prince Consort it was resolved by the citizens of Edinburgh to commemorate his virtues by a monument. After various competitions a design by Mr. John Steell was adopted, and he was authorized to proceed with its execution. The selected design may be thus described :—A great pedestal of Peterhead granite, enriched with bas-reliefs and subsidiary groups of statuary, supports an equestrian statue of the Prince. The structure, oblong in ground-plan, is formed in three stages. The first, which presents faces of plain masonry about four feet in height, has at each angle a square projection supporting a group of figures. Over this rises the second stage, which has its sides covered with quotations from Prince Albert's published speeches. The third stage, or pedestal proper, is richly moulded, and exhibits on each side a bas-relief in bronze illustrative of the Prince's tastes, or of leading events in his life. One represents the auspicious marriage by which his Royal Highness became connected with the British Crown. In another he appears in the act of opening the International Exhibition of 1851. These occupy the two sides of the oblong, while at the ends there are representations of the Prince in the act of distributing rewards of merit, and a subject showing his Royal Highness in his domestic relations. Under the centre of each bas-relief a group of emblematic objects, suggestive of the Prince's honours and pursuits, rests on the ledge formed by the projection of the second stage beyond the base of the third. The groups of statuary on the first stage represent people of all classes in the act of approaching the Prince with gestures of affectionate reverence. The site of the monument has not been definitely fixed, but a majority of the subscribers have indicated a preference for the centre of the east side of Charlotte Square Gardens. On that site, unquestionably the first in the city, it is hoped the monument will be reared.

After the Reformation, vigorous efforts were made by the Town Council of the city, and also by the General Assembly, for the discontinuance of interments in the Collegiate Church of St. Giles and its adjacent churchyard. In answer to a memorial of the Town Council, Queen Mary, on the 17th August, 1562, granted the "zaird," or grounds of the Greyfriars Monastery, as a burial-place to the citizens. It is sufficiently interesting to remark that the last notable person interred in St. Giles' Churchyard was John Knox, in November, 1572, while his great contemporary, George Buchanan, is the first noted individual known to have been buried in the grounds of the Greyfriars.* Buchanan died on Friday, the 28th September, 1582, and his funeral took place on the following day. Neither he nor Knox has been honoured with a memorial stone. The dust of Knox is surmounted by the effigy of a profligate king. A flat or *through*-stone which covered the grave of Buchanan has long since disappeared; it had sunken in 1701, when the City Chamberlain was instructed to have it raised, and the inscription cleared—a work which he did not perform. Latterly the stone was discovered and placed on the grave of a sexton. Some years ago a humble blacksmith erected at Buchanan's grave a small memorial stone, to compensate for the neglect of an ungrateful country. Buchanan's skull, torn from his grave, got into the hands of Mr. John Adamson, who in 1623 became Principal of Edinburgh University. It is now preserved in the College Library; it is thin and transparent.

One of the earliest monuments in Greyfriars Churchyard is that of George Heriot, father of the celebrated founder of the hospital.† Built

---

* Introduction, by Mr. David Laing, to "Epitaphs and Monumental Inscriptions in Greyfriars Churchyard," Edinburgh, 1867. 12mo.

† The magistrates and council, on the 30th November, 1610, empowered George Heriot, the "founder of the hospital," and David Heriot, sons of the deceased George Heriot, elder, goldsmith, to erect a tomb to the said deceased George Heriot in the Greyfriars Kirkyard. — *Town Council Records.*

in the east wall of the church, it bears the following inscription :—

> "Viator, qui sapis, unde sis, quid sis, quidque
> futurus sis, hinc nosce.
> Vita mihe mortis, Mors vitæ janua facta est ;
> Solaque mors mortis vivere posse dedit.
> Ergo quisquis adhuc mortali vesceris aura,
> Dum licet, ut possis vivere, disce mori.
> G. H., 1610."

By Mr. Robert Monteith, author of "The Theater of Mortality," is presented the following metrical translation :—

> "Passenger, who art wise, hence know whence you are, what you are, and what you are to be,
> Life, gate of death ; Death, gate of life to me,
> Sole death of death gives life eternallie.
> Therefore, whoever breath draws from the air,
> While live thou may'st, thyself for death prepare."

A small stone marked "J. E. M." denotes the burial-place of James Douglas, fourth Earl of Morton, Regent of Scotland. He was second son of John George Douglas of Pittendriech, younger brother of the sixth Earl of Angus. By his marriage with Lady Elizabeth Douglas, only child of James, third Earl of Morton, he obtained on her father's death his title and estates. In 1563 he became Lord High Chancellor. Having joined Darnley in effecting the death of Rizzio he was obliged, with his accomplices, to escape to England. He subscribed the bond to protect Bothwell against the charge of being concerned in the murder of Darnley. At the battle of Langside he was one of the principal commanders, and continued warmly to support the Protestant side against the adherents of the Queen. He was appointed Regent on the death of the Earl of Mar in 1572, but his avariciousness rendered him unpopular. In September, 1577, he resigned office and retired to Lochleven. Subsequently gaining possession of Stirling Castle and the King's person, he proceeded to wreak vengeance on his adversaries. These combined for his destruction, and accusing him of being accessory to the murder of Darnley, subjected him to trial for the offence. By the court he was declared "art and part" guilty, and was condemned. On the day following his sentence, being the 2nd of June, 1581, he was beheaded at Edinburgh. The instrument used in his decapitation was called *the Maiden:* he had himself brought it into Scotland from Halifax, in Yorkshire. His head was placed on the tolbooth, and his body, wrapped in a coarse cloth, was consigned to the burial-place of criminals. By the authority of James VI. his head was taken down from the tolbooth on the 9th December, 1582, and buried at this spot. Whatever were his offences as Regent, Morton was innocent of participation in the crime for which he suffered. The instrument of his death is preserved in the Antiquarian Museum.

John Nasmyth, chief physician to James VI., is commemorated thus:—

Hic situs est Joannes Nasmithius, e Posso familio non obscura in Twedia, civis Edinburgensis, Serenissimæ Regiæ Majestatis, et Galliarum Regis prætoriæ e Scotia cohortis, protochirurgus; omnibus piæ vitæ officiis egregie functus; qui Londini, dum apud regem munia sua obit utriusque gentis luctu, fatis concedens, corporis exuvias huc translatas (qui ejus in patriam fuit animus) cœmiterio hoc condi voluit: regi, patriæ et amicis, quæ habuit et debuit, ad extremum usque persolvens. Obiit ætatis suæ anno 57, ad 16 cal. Octobris, ciciccxiii., Reverti, unde veneris, quid grave est?

Ars mihi, vim contra Fortunæ; Tartara contra,
Est data, divino munere, firma fides.
Grata fuit regi cœlorum hæc, illa Monarchæ
Supremo, in terris; plura ego nec volui.

Here lyes a flow'r that, with the too much haste
Of fates cut down, did in her blossom waste;
In whose untimely fall fond man may see
Youth, vigour, strength, what mortal things they be.
What graver eye, contemplating thy dust,
O happy Nasmyth, after thee will trust
The smiles of nature? or presume to say
This well-set morn foresigns a hopeful day?
O may thy grave, untainted like thy years,
Grow, ever green, bedewed with sister-tears;
Who envies not thy good, but grieves to be,
By ling'ring life, so long disjoyn'd from thee.
"O death, where is thy sting? O grave, where is thy victory?"

John Nasmyth died at London on the 16th September, 1613, at the age of fifty-seven.

A handsome monument with the following Latin inscription celebrates John Layng, Keeper of the Signet, who died in 1614:—

" Quam natura dedit mortali corpore clauso,
Dum spes exilii sustinet una moras,
Vita fuit ; nec vita fuit : mors, nescia mortis,
Posse dedit vita jam meliore frui."

Monteith thus translates :—

" The life me nature gave, while pent in clay,
Hopes of escape supporting the delay,
It was not life : death, ignorant of death,
To me a life far better did bequeath."

A plain monument indicates the family burial-place of Sir Thomas Hope, the celebrated lawyer, and founder of the noble House of Hopetoun. Son of an eminent merchant, he distinguished himself at the trial of the six ministers who, in 1606, were arraigned at Linlithgow on a charge of high treason, because they had, in ecclesiastical matters, resisted regal authority. In 1626 he was appointed Lord Advocate to Charles I.; he was created a baronet in 1628. In 1638 he took part in framing the National Covenant; he supported the legality of the famous General Assembly of that year. By Charles I. he was appointed Lord High Commissioner to the General Assembly of 1643. He died in 1646; he saw two of his sons appointed Judges of the Supreme Court. Sir Thomas Hope's family monument is thus inscribed :—

Sir Thomas Hope of Craighall, Bart., 1628.
" At spes non fracta."

The family burying-ground in which are interred several of the descendants of Sir Thomas Hope, Bart., of Craighall, advocate to King Charles I. Also, Dame Elizabeth McDowall, the wife of Sir Archibald Hope, Bart., of Craighall, and daughter of William McDowall, Esq., of Castle-Semple, born April, 1742, died October, 1778. Here lies the body of Isabella Hope, relict of Colonel William Cullen of Parkhead, and eldest daughter of Sir Archibald Hope, Bart., and the above Dame Elizabeth McDowall, born 26th April, 1760, died 23rd May, 1842. Of Christian humility and fortitude, she was one of the few who survived the eventful shipwreck of the Winterton, East Indiaman, off Madagascar, in August, 1792.

'Blessed are the pure in heart.'—Matt. v. 8.

"In memory of William Cullen, M.D., physician in Edinburgh, second son of Colonel Cullen, born 27th April, 1798, died 28th May, 1828; and Archibald Hope Cullen, eldest son of Colonel Cullen, born 11th March, 1792, died 14th May, 1850."

On the handsome mausoleum of Thomas Bannatyne are these inscriptions:—

> Hodie mihi; cras tibi.
> Vita quid est hominis? flos, umbra et fumus, arista,
> Illa malis longa est; illa bonis brevis est.

> "If thou list, that passest by,
> Know who in this tombe doth ly;
> Thomas Bannatyn, abroad
> And at home who served God.
> Though no children he possest,
> Yet the Lord with meanes him blist.
> He of them did well dispose,
> Long ere death his eyes did close.
> For the poore his helping hand,
> And his friends his kyndness fand;
> And on his deare bed-fellow,
> Jennet Macmath, he did bestow,
> Out of his lovelie affection,
> A fit and goodlie portion.
> Thankfull she herself to prove,
> For a sign of mutuall love,
> Did nor paines nor charges spair
> To sit up this fabrick fair;
> As Artemise, that noble frame,
> To her deare Mausolus' name.

He died 16th July, 1635, of his age 65.

"O that men were wise to { Know the multitude of those that are to be damned; the paucity of those that are to be saved; and the vanity of transitory things. Understand evil committed, good things omitted, and the loss of time. Foresee the danger of death, the last judgment, and eternal punishment.

Sir Thomas Henryson of Chester is on his monument commemorated thus:—

"Sanctæ et individuæ Trinitati solæ, honor et gloria in æternum. Amen.
"D. Thomas Henryson a Chesters eques.
"Mors unius vita omnium. Beati qui moriuntur in domino. Christus in vita et morte lucrum.
"Jugum jugo valide excussum.
"Felicissimæ memoriæ clarissimorum virorum, ingenuorum adolescentium, innoxiorum, infantium, lectissimarum, fœminarum sanctissimarum matronarum, hic sparsim recubantium, gloriosum servatoris Domini nostri Jesu Christi adventum expectantium, et generalem universæ carnis resurrectionem in Domino opperientium, Dominus Thomas Henrysonus, Eques, senator, vi. Calend Octobres posuit mœstissimus: anno Christi CICICCXXXVI."

On the same monument are commemorated by Latin inscriptions Dr. Edward Henryson, Doctor of the Civil and Canon Law, and Alexander Henryson, Judge of the Consistory Court at Edinburgh, together with several other members of the Henryson family.

The celebrated Alexander Henderson is commemorated by a monumental obelisk erected by his nephew. There are the following inscriptions:—

"Memoriæ Sacrum D. Alexandri Hendersonii, regi à sacris, Edinburgensis ecclesiæ pastoris, ibidem academiæ rectoris, academiæ Andreanæ alumni, amplificatoris, patroni; qui, contra grassantes per fraudem et tyrannidem prælatos, libertatis et disciplinæ ecclesiasticæ propugnator fuit acerrimus; superstitionis, juxta et succrescentium sectarum, malleus; religionis cultusque divini purioris vindex et assertor constantissimus: in quæ cum omni cura et cogitatione incumbens, assiduos, cum in patria, tum in vicino Angliæ regno, labores ecclesiæ utiles, sibi gloriosos exantlavit, extremum spiritum effudit, die 19 Augusti, 1646, ætatis 63.

      "Reader, bedew thine eyes,
      Not for the dust here lyes;
      It quicken shall again,
      And ay in joy remain;
      But for thyself, the Church and States,
      Whose woes this dust prognosticates.

"Hanc quisquis urnam transiens spectaveris,
Ne negligenter aspice,
Hic busta magni cernis Hendersoni,
Pietatis hic bustum vides.

"No negligent spectator may
Look on this tomb at all;
This tomb of greatest Henderson,
And duty we may call.

"Vir fuit divinus, ac plane eximius, et omni virtutis genere, tum pietate imprimis, eruditione, prudentia, illustris; regi serenissimo, et utriusque regni ordinibus, juxta charus; cui hoc monumentum, pietatis ergo, erigendum curavit Georgius Hendersonus ex fratro nepos; ipse sibi eternum, in animis bonorum reliquit."

Alexander Henderson was born in 1583, and studied at the University of St. Andrews. He was, hrough the influence of Archbishop Gladstanes, presented to the church living of Leuchars, Fifeshire, and was in 1615 inducted forcibly into the charge. He was then a supporter of episcopacy; he subsequently changed his views and became a zealous upholder of Presbyterianism. He opposed the adoption of the five Articles of Perth in 1618, and resisted the use of the Service Book in 1637. He preached in the Greyfriars church on the 28th February, 1638, when the National Covenant was renewed, and presided as Moderator of the memorable General Assembly held at Glasgow in the following November. On two subsequent occasions he was chosen Moderator of Assembly. He was Rector of Edinburgh University, and instituted a Professorship of Oriental Languages in that seat of learning. With a view to conciliate the Presbyterians, Charles I. appointed him his chaplain on his visit to Scotland in 1641. Henderson was entrusted with various important missions; he was one of the commissioners who represented the Scottish Church at the Assembly of Divines at Westminster, and he was honoured with several interviews by Charles I., when he endeavoured, though unsuccessfully, to bring the king over to Presbyterianism. He died in 1646. At the Restoration the inscriptions on his tombstone were obliterated; they were restored at the Revolution.

James Murray of Deuchar, who died on the 30th April, 1649, is thus celebrated:—

S.D., J.M., L.H.G.

"Monumentum Jacobi Moravii, de Deuchar, 1649.

"Jacobus Moravius, ex antiqua Morav. a Philiphaugh familia ortus, civitate Edinburgena, donatus, in ea mercaturam feliciter exercuit, et magistratus honorem sæpius meruit; Gulielmi Mauli, civis præclari, filiam Bethiam uxorem duxit, ex qua plures liberos suscepit, et ex ijs tres filios superstites reliquit, cum filia una. Jacobo Eliseo civi honorifico, nupta. Opum, non tam custos, quam œconomus honestissimus; in literatos, munificus; in egenos, insigni charitate beneficus. Sic piam vitam placida secuta est mors, prid. Kal. Maij. anno æræ Christianæ MDCXLIX. ætatis suæ, quarto sexti, supra decimum, lustri. Optimo Charissimoque patri plorantes filij, Jacobus Eques, Rob. et. Pat. Moravii Parentarunt."

The inscription is thus rendered by Monteith:—

"Stay, passenger, and shed a tear,
For good James Murray lyeth here;
He was of Philiphaugh descended,
And for his merchandise commended.
He was a man of a good life,
Marry'd Bethia Maul to 's wife;
He may thank God that e'er he gat her—
She bare him three sons and one daughter.
The first he was a man of might,
For which the king made him a knight;
The second was both wise and wyllie,
For which the town made him a baillie;
The third a factor of renown,
Both in Camphier and in this town
His daughter was both grave and wise,
And she was married to James Elies."

Archibald Tod, who was Provost of the city from 1651 to 1654, is commemorated thus:—

D. O. M.

"Quod caducum habuit, hic deponi jussit, Archibaldus Tod, urbis Edinburgenæ a mortalibus civis; vir procul omni fuco, & sine fastu probus; quater matrimonia junctus; at, ex prima tantum conjuge Helena; filia Joannis Jackson, civis præclari, unicam natam superstitem reliquit Katharinam, uxorem Davidis Wilkie, civis honorifici, & hoc anno 1656, ædilis. Ipse vero, seu pace juvante, seu bello adversante, pro patria & urbe semper, idem magistratus honorem æque meruit, ter prætor, bis ædilis, septies urbis præfectus, & per sex lustra βελευτης. Obiit multum desideratus 5to Idus Februarii, anno 1656, ætatis LXXI.

> " Here worthy Provost Tod doth ly,
> Who dy'd and yet who did not die.
> His golden name in fame's fair roll,
> Claims the liferent tack of a soul.
> Edinburgh, in this man alone,
> Lost both a father and a son ;
> For twice three lusters that he sat
> In council, for her publique state ;
> For two years care of late, which more
> Avail'd than fifty twice before ;
> For the great pains he then did take,
> T' avert the cry, Kill, burn, and sack ;
> Sure he deserves a tomb of jeat,
> Or one of purest porphyrite.
> And ev'ry house should bring a stone,
> To build him a mausoleon.
> But outward pomp he still did flye,
> And thus, in singale dust would lye."

John Milne, Master Mason to the King, and member of Parliament for the city of Edinburgh, is commemorated by a handsome monument. The inscriptions run thus :—

"Bina quater ac trina post repetita lustra peracta, vitæ hujus lubricæ, hic dormienti molliter, Joanni Milne, Regio de Milneorum stirpe sexto protofabro Murario, artis architectonicæ, eximie perito, artificum Edinorum saepius Archidecano, Publicis in Regni comitiis metropolis non semel delegato, considerato, fido ; viro animi dotibus supra sortem exculto, corporis forma spectabili, probo, cordato, pio, omnibus colendo ; monumentum hoc qualecunque Robertus, ex fratro Nepos, Patruo virtutum et officii æmulus successor, gratitudinis ergo posuit. Obiit 24 Decembris anno 1667, ætatis suæ 56.

> " Great artisan, grave senator, John Milne !
> Renowned for learning, prudence, parts, and skill,
> Who in his life Vitruvius' art had shown,
> Adorning others' monuments ; his own
> Can have no other beauty than his name,
> His memory and everlasting fame.

> Rare man he was, who could unite in one
> Highest and lowest occupation;
> To sit with statesmen, councillor to kings,
> To work with tradesmen, in mechanick things;
> Majestick man, for person, witt, and grace,
> This generation cannot fill his place."

His descendant, namesake, and successor is thus celebrated:—

> "Reader, John Milne, who maketh the fourth John,
> And, by descent, from father unto son,
> Sixth master mason to a royal race
> Of seven successive kings, sleeps in this place."

These epitaphs celebrate Alexander Bethune of Longhirdmonston, Writer to the Signet:—

"Hic jacent exuviæ Alexandri Bethune de Longhirdmonston, Signeto Regio Scribæ; ex prisca & præclara familia de Balfour ortum habentis. Vir erat prudentia, pietate, & industria, haud leviter imbutus. Ex uxore sua Marjorana Kennedie, cum qua triginta annos conjunctissime vixit, numerosam sobolem suscepit: ex quibus, septem mares, cum una filia, & dobus nepotibus, hic una tumulantur. Obiit 9 Novembris 1672, ætatis suæ 57.

> "Amidst two nephews and sev'n sones heir lyes
> One of good birth, was prudent in his wayes;
> And tho' God blist him in his law profession,
> To conquest riches, and a large possession,
> Himselfe he never valu'd by these things,
> But by the grace that Christ's salvation brings.
> So he, by Christian prudence, did acquire
> More than the world's gaine or the heart's desire:
> Of godly, sober, just, the blessed name,
> And left unto posteritie his fame.
> Just doing, speaking, writing, was his glorie,
> Above all elogies of worldlie storie."

A massive tomb commemorates Sir George Mackenzie of Rosehaugh, the celebrated lawyer. This distinguished individual was nephew of the Earl of Seaforth. He was admitted advocate in 1659, and soon earned a high reputation as a pleader. In 1661 he was one of the council at the trial of the Marquis of Argyle for high treason. After the Restoration he was appointed a judge in the criminal court, and was soon afterwards knighted.

In 1669 he became parliamentary representative of the county of Ross. He was appointed King's Advocate in 1677, and thereafter became a keen adversary of the Presbyterians. The State prosecutions which he conducted against the adherents of the Covenant brought him the designation of "the bloody Mackenzie." When in 1686 James VII. abrogated the penal laws against the Papists, he retired from his office as King's Advocate, but it was afterwards restored to him. In 1689 he founded the Advocates Library, and in the following year retired to Oxford to dedicate his remaining years to classical studies. He died at London on the 8th May, 1691. Sir George Mackenzie published works on law, history, and antiquities, which in 1722 were collected by Ruddiman and printed in two folio volumes. Long after his death the humbler citizens of Edinburgh regarded his monument with aversion.* It formerly bore the following inscription:—

"Reliquiæ sacræ D. Georgii Mackenzie a valle Rosarum, equitis aurati, Simonis filii, Coleni comit. de Seafort nepot. Natus æræ Christi anno 1636. Per annos XXXI. foro in Supremo causarum patronus. Ab anno 1677, regius advocatus; regibus Carolo II. et Jacobo VII. a secretioribus conciliis. Patriæ decus, religionis vindex, justitiæ propagator, juris regii assertor strenuus et indefessus; collegii juridici, sive prudentiam summam sive eloquentiam eximiam, sive instruenda jurisconsultorum bibliotheca curam, et locupletanda munificentiam spectes, ornamentum imprimis illustre; comitatis exemplar; eruditorum Mæcenas eruditissimus; omnibus carus si perduellium colluviem excipias. A quorum violentia, patriam, patriæque patrem, cum ore, cum calamo, accerrime vindicavit; virulentiam jure et justitia temperavit; ferociam rationis viribus repulit, ac tantum non domuit. Monarchiæ genius tutillaris, fama, eloquio, morum integritate, factis et scriptis clarus vixit, Ecclesiæ, reipublicæ, liberis et amicis. Maii die octavo anno 1691, in Domino obiit desideratissimus."

Within Sir George Mackenzie's tomb were interred the remains of Sir George Lockhart, Lord President of the Court of Session, who was murdered by John Chiesley of Dalry in returning from church

---

* Children were wont to call in at the keyhole,—
"Bluidy Mackinyie, come oot if ye daur,
Lift the sneck and draw the bar!"

on the 31st of March, 1689. Sir George was second son of Sir James Lockhart of Lee, a judge in the Court of Session. He endured some persecution under the government of Charles II. In 1685 he was returned to the Scottish Parliament for the county of Lanark, and was about the same time appointed Lord President. John Chiesley, to whose violence he fell a victim, was father of the noted Lady Grange; he sought to avenge himself for a decision of the President compelling him to maintain his wife and children. According to Monteith the following lines were formerly inscribed on the President's tomb :—

> "So falls our glory with one fatal blow,
> Gone is that head which did us justice show;
> That tongue from which such well-tuned words did come,
> And charmed us all, is now for ever dumb,
> Which with such evenness justice did dispense,
> As universal judge of wit and sense.
> His pointed wit did in us hope create
> To see our Church healed, and our tott'ring State.
> This stroke doth make them vanish into air,
> Leaves us behind to languish in despair.
> So when a boist'rous wave doth overwhelm
> The skilful pilot that should guide the helm,
> And yet the enragèd ocean still doth roar,
> The passengers must doubt to reach the shore.
> O heavens! by such a horrid murder must
> So brave a man's be mixed with common dust?
> Monster, what tiger would thy length have gone?
> Ravilac, Clement, Gerard, are outdone;
> Fatal it seems in pleading to excel,
> Just so Rome's pride and glory, Tully fell."

Lord Roystoun, Lord of Session, cousin and son-in-law of Sir George Mackenzie, who died in 1744, is also interred within his tomb.

The Martyrs' Monument ‡ was reared in 1706 by James Currie,

---

‡ Within the southern compartment of the churchyard, which is still enclosed with the original iron gate, were placed upwards of 400 prisoners captured at the battle of Bothwell Bridge, in 1679. They were treated with great cruelty, being allowed only four ounces of bread daily as food, and during five months of winter were compelled to sleep in the open air, almost without covering. Many died from exposure, and the remainder, consisting of 257 persons, were thrust on board ship at Leith with the view of being transported to Barbadoes; but the vessel being wrecked, only forty of the number were saved.

merchant, Pentland, and others; it was renewed in 1771. The inscriptions follow:—

> " Halt, passenger, take heed what you do see—
> This tomb doth shew for what some men did die:
> Here lies interr'd the dust of those who stood
> 'Gainst perjury, resisting unto blood;
> Adhering to the covenants and laws;
> Establishing the same: which was the cause
> Their lives were sacrific'd unto the lust
> Of prelatists abjur'd: though here their dust
> Lies mixt with murderers and other crew,
> Whom justice justly did to death pursue.
> But as for them, no cause was to be found
> Worthy of death; but only they were found
> Constant and stedfast, zealous, witnessing
> For the prerogatives of Christ their King;
> Which truths were seal'd by famous Guthrie's head,
> And all along to Mr. Renwick's blood;
> They did endure the wrath of enemies,
> Reproaches, torments, deaths, and injuries.
> But yet they're those who from such troubles came,
> And now triumph in glory with the Lamb.

"From May 27, 1661, that the most noble Marquis of Argyle was beheaded, to the 17th February, 1688, that Mr. James Renwick suffered, were one way or other murdered and destroyed for the same cause about eighteen thousand, of whom were executed at Edinburgh about an hundred of noblemen, gentlemen, ministers, and others, noble martyrs for Jesus Christ. The most of them lie here.

"Rev. vi. 9.—And when he had opened the fifth seal, I saw under the altar the souls of them that were slain for the word of God, and for the testimony which they held:

"10.—And they cried with a loud voice, saying, How long, O Lord, holy and true, dost Thou not judge and avenge our blood on them that dwell on the earth?

"11.—And white robes were given to every one of them; and it was said unto them that they should rest yet for a little season, until their fellow-servants also and their brethren, that should be killed as they were, should be fulfilled.

"Chap. vii. 14.—These are they which have come out of great tribulation, and have washed their robes, and made them white in the blood of the Lamb.

"Chap. ii. 10.—Be thou faithful unto death, and I will give thee a crown of life."

The following inscriptions have been added at a later date:—

> "Yes, though the sceptic's tongue deride
> Those martyrs who for conscience died—
> Though modern history blight their fame,
> And sneering courtiers hoot the name
> Of men who dared above be free,
> Amidst a nation's slavery;—
> Yet long for them the poet's lyre
> Shall wake its notes of heavenly fire;
> Their names shall nerve the patriot's hand
> Upraised to save a sinking land;
> And piety shall learn to burn
> With holier transports o'er their urn." *
>
> (JAMES GRAHAME.)

> "Peace to their mem'ry! let no impious breath
> Sell their fair fame, or triumph o'er their death.
> Let Scotia's grateful sons their teardrops shed,
> Where low they lie in honour's gory bed;
> Rich with the spoil their glorious deeds had won,
> And purchas'd freedom to a land undone—
> A land which owes its glory and its worth
> To those whom tyrants banished from the earth."

"For the accomplishment of this revolution, the three kingdoms lie under no small debt of gratitude to the Covenanters. They suffered and bled both in fields and on scaffolds for the cause of civil and religious liberty; and shall we reap the fruit of their sufferings, their prayers, and their blood, and yet treat their memory either with indifference or scorn? No; whatever minor faults may be laid to their charge, whatever trivial accusations may be brought against them, it cannot but be acknowledged that they were the men who, 'singly and alone,' stood forward in defence of Scotland's dearest rights, and to whom we at the present day owe everything that is valuable to us as men or as Christians."†

Marjorie Brodie, spouse to James Brown, feltmaker, is thus commemorated:—

---

* "History of the Covenanters," vol. i., p. 349.   † *Ibid*, vol. ii., p. 364.

"Here lyes inter'd her corps in hopes to rise,
Whose soul's above, with Christ, in Paradise;
When both unite, a matron grave and just,
Faithful and careful in her husband's trust;
Not gaudie kept her shop, went not abroad,
Virt'ous and charitable, serving God;
Prudent, obliging, in her ways discreet,
At home, abroad, did for her husband's credit;
He, mindful of her worth, moved this intent
For badge of love t'erect this monument."

In the burial vault of Trotter of Morton Hall, John Trotter, who died in 1641, is celebrated in a Latin epitaph:—

"Mors patet, hora latet, anno 1641.
John Trotter and Janet Macmath.

Octoginta ultra Trotterus vixerat annos;
Progenie felix, ambitione carens.
Publica privatus curavit; semper egenis
Aut opere, aut opibus, contulit almus opem."

Monteith supplies the following metrical translation:—

"Death is most sure;
Unseen its hour; 1641.
'Bove eighty years John Trotter liv'd,
And saw his issue fair;
He from ambition all was free,
A property most rare.
Tho privat, publick was his mind;
He guardian to the poor;
Whom to assist, by pow'r or wealth
He labour'd ev'ry hour."

The following acrostic constitutes the elegy of Thomas Fisher, Treasurer of Heriot's Hospital, who died on the 26th March, 1711 :—

"T he debt which man by birth contracts, he must
 By death repay, adjoining to the dust;
H ad goodness, grace, or truest candour been
 Exeem'd from fate, he death had never seen.
O h! the contagion of our father's fall,
 To certain death has doom'd his offspring all.
M ausoleum he merits well to have,
 And not the common cell of homely grave;

A s being, by Heaven's tender care, set o'er
 The good town's treasure and George Heriot's store.
S ince his first breath did thro' his nostrils pass,
 Of virtues all the mirrour bright he was;
F urnishing mortals with examples fair
 Of ev'ry action, honest, great, and rare;
I njured Ed'nburgh to his wings did fly,
 For sudden help from hardest je'pardy,
S cotland from him in epitome, did draw,
 A matchless map of truest Burgal law.
H eroick actions ever did attend
 Him all his life unto his blessed end,
E ndearing goodness did him so exalt,
 'Bove burgers all, below the enamled vault
R eward of virtue, glory; and the pen
 Of learned ones him stile, FISHER OF MEN.

EPITAPH.

" Here lies the perfect and the upright man,
Of charity and righteousness the plan;
Scotland with joy as glad that he was born,
As now in tears his funeral doth mourn."

There is a handsome monument to Dr. Archibald Pitcairn, the celebrated physician and poet. Born at Edinburgh on the 25th December, 1652, he prosecuted his medical studies in Paris, and having obtained the degree of M.D. from the Medical Faculty at Rheims began to seek practice in his native city. In 1692 he became Professor of Physic in the University of Leyden, but after a short interval returned to Edinburgh. In 1691 he was admitted a Fellow of the College of Surgeons; he subsequently held the chair of Medicine at Edinburgh. He died in 1713. His library was after his decease purchased by Peter the Great of Russia, but many of his original MSS. were scattered and lost. His works were printed at Venice in 1733, and in 1781 Dr. Charles Webster published an account of his life and writings. Dr. Pitcairn's tomb is inscribed thus:—

"Here lyes Doctor Archibald Pitcairn, who died 26th day of October, 1713, aged 61. Also, Elizabeth Pitcairn, his daughter, who died the 18th day of March, 1718; Elizabeth Stevenson, his widow, died 5th October, 1734; Margaret Pitcairn, his daughter, died August, 1777; Janet Pitcairn, Countess of Kellie, his daughter, died 7th June, 1776; Lady Ann Erskine, his last surviving grandchild, one of the best of women, died 18th March, 1803.

"Ecce mathematicum, vatem, medicumque, sophumque,
Pitcairnum magnum hæc urnula parva tenet.
Ergo, vale, lux Scotigenum, princepsque medentium.
Musarum columen deliciæque, vale."

Dr. Pitcairn's monument was in 1800 restored by the Edinburgh Æsculapian Club.

A Latin epitaph commemorates the talents and worth of Professor Colin Maclaurin, the eminent mathematician. He was born at Kilmodan, Argyleshire, in February, 1698, and studied at the University of Glasgow. In his nineteenth year he was by competition elected to the chair of Mathematics in Marischal College, Aberdeen; and in 1725 was preferred to the Mathematical Professorship at Edinburgh. He died in 1746. The following is his elegy :—

"C. M., nat. MDCXCVIII.; ob. MDCCXLVI.

"Infra situs est Colin Maclaurin, matheseos olim in Acad. Edin., Prof. electus ipso Newtono suadente.

"H. L. P. F.

"Non ut nomini paterno consulat,
Nam tali auxilio nil eget,
Sed ut in hoc infelici campo,
Ubi luctus regnant et pavor,
Mortalibus prorsus non desit solatium;
Hujus enim scripta evolve,
Mentemque tantarum rerum capacem,
Corpori caduco superstitem crede.

"Non omnis moriar, ridebit munus inane carminis ac tumuli spiritus alta petens. Non fasces, non purpuram, non extructas in altum divitias, non ingenium artibus atque scientiis utcunque ornatum et imbutum, sed animum communi utilitati inservientem, dignitas sequitur."

These rhymes commemorate John Barnett, student of "Phisick," who was born in 1733, and died in 1755 :—

" Peace, gentlest Shade, this from a Brother's hand,
Who must not say what justice would demand ;
Yet this I must (not each proud marble can),
The dust beneath was truly once a man.
From virtue's pleasing paths he never rov'd,
Of man a lover, and by man belov'd;
For others' ills he griev'd, contemn'd his own,
To none severe save to himself alone.
To him fair Science oped her useful page,
Rich with experience and the spoils of age.
Too early lost, lamented here he lies,
Nipp'd like a rose-bud, ere it blows it dies;
Death, lest mankind he from the tomb should save,
Snatched him thus early to the peaceful grave."

Thomas Ruddiman, the eminent grammarian, has the following simple epitaph upon his tombstone :—

"Sacred to the memory of that celebrated scholar and worthy man, Thomas Ruddiman, A.M., keeper of the Advocates Library near fifty years. Born October, 1674, within three miles of the town of Banff; died at Edinburgh, 19th January, 1757, in his eighty-third year.

Post obitum benefacta manent æternaque virtus
Non metuit stygiis ne rapiatur aquis.

"This tablet is erected as a respectful tribute, by his relative William Ruddiman, M.D., 1801."

Ruddiman was in 1695 appointed parish schoolmaster of Laurencekirk. Through the influence of Dr. Archibald Pitcairn he obtained in 1700 a subordinate appointment in the Advocates Library; he added to his emoluments by transcribing Chartularies and practising as an auctioneer. In 1714 he published his "Rudiments of the Latin Tongue," and in the following year edited and published the works of Buchanan in two folio volumes. About the same time he joined his brother Walter in establishing a printing-house. He became proprietor and printer of the *Caledonian Mercury*. In 1730 he was appointed principal keeper of the Advocates Library, an office which he retained till 1752, when he tendered his resignation. He edited the works of Livy in four volumes duodecimo when nearly eighty. He died in 1757, at the age of eighty-three.

One of the principal celebrities whose remains rest in Greyfriars Churchyard is Allan Ramsay, the poet. His tombstone is thus inscribed :—

"In this cemetery was interred the mortal part of an immortal poet, Allan Ramsay, author of 'The Gentle Shepherd,' and other admirable poems in the Scottish dialect. He was born in 1686, and died in 1758.

> "No sculptur'd marble here, no pompous lay,
> No storied urn, no animated bust;
> This simple stone directs pale Scotia's way
> To pour her sorrows o'er her poet's dust.
>
> "Though here you're buried, worthy Allan,
> We'll ne'er forget you, canty callan;
> For while your soul lives in the sky,
> Your 'Gentle Shepherd' ne'er can die."

Allan Ramsay was remotely connected with the noble family of Ramsay of Dalhousie. He commenced life as apprentice to a wig-maker in Edinburgh; he afterwards became a hair-dresser on his own account. After a period he adopted the book trade, and at his own shop published his "Tea-table Miscellany" and the "Evergreen," two collections of Scottish songs and ballads. His "Gentle Shepherd" appeared in 1725. He established a circulating library, the first of the kind in Scotland. He built a house (Ramsay Lodge) at the head of the mound, where he resided during the last twelve years of his career. He died on the 7th January, 1758. His tombstone was erected about fifty years after his decease.

The Rev. James Hall, "Minister of the Gospel, Edinburgh," who died in 1781, aged fifty-five, is thus commemorated :—

> "Blameless in life, even from his early youth,
> Unknown to wander from the paths of truth,
> He lived; but did not live on bread alone,
> The word of Life his comfort, heaven his home.
> His constant aim the soul of Christ to win,
> A friend to sinners, yet abhorr'd their sin.

> Firm to the truth, by sacred influence mov'd,
> Mild yet severe; even in reproof belov'd.
> This to thine honour, more than this thy due,
> On earth the Christian's life was shown in you."

A handsome tombstone celebrates George Goldie, manager of the British Linen Company, who died on the 26th September, 1785, aged seventy-nine. The inscription, prepared by his wife and children, is as follows:—

> "God gave, and God resumes, be grief resigned
> To every mandate of the sovereign mind;
> Yet for a while must wounded Nature smart,
> And mourn her loss in bitterness of heart:
> Friend, father, husband, all that life endears,
> At once demands and vindicates our tears."

The following inscription celebrates Sir James Hunter Blair, chief magistrate of the city, and its representative in Parliament:—

"Sir James Hunter Blair, the son of Mr. John Hunter, merchant, Ayr, was born there in 1741. He was apprenticed to the Messrs. Coutts, bankers in Edinburgh, 1756, and Sir William Forbes and he became partners in the concern in 1763. He married Miss Blair of Dunskey, 1770, and in 1781 was chosen Member of Parliament for Edinburgh; three years after he became chief magistrate of the city. The erection of the South Bridge was arranged by his persevering exertions. Hunter Square and Blair Street derive their names from him. Sir James died in 1787."

On the same tombstone are commemorated Major-General Thomas Hunter Blair, C.B., sixth son of Sir James Hunter Blair, Bart., who was born 5th October, 1782, and died 31st August, 1849. Also Anne Hunter Blair, daughter of Sir James Hunter Blair, and wife of William Mure of Caldwell, who died in 1854.

A handsome monument, reared to the memory of the Rev. Adam Gib, one of the ministers of the Secession Church, and leader of the Antiburghers, proceeds thus:—

"Sacred to the memory of the Rev. Adam Gib, an able and faithful minister of Christ; endued with a large share of natural talent, improved by education, study, and use: in language concise, clear, nervous, and expressive; with freedom, acuteness, zeal, and assiduity, he long preached the pure doctrines of the Gospel, and contended to instruct, warn, and reprove a degenerate and declining age. Born 15th April, 1714, he died on the 14th of June, 1788, ætatis 74."

Mr. Gib joined the Associate Presbytery when he was a student in the College of Edinburgh. He was licensed in 1740, and in 1741 was settled as Minister of a new congregation in Nicolson Street, Edinburgh. He greatly distinguished himself by his loyalty and patriotism during the Rebellion of 1745, when the insurgents held possession of Edinburgh. In 1746 he took a leading part with the Antiburghers during the memorable schism of that year. He died in 1788.

These simple lines denote the grave of Isabel Muir, who died 1st May, 1790, aged 65 :—

"It is God's will that I most dye,
And this my burial place should be.
Reader, while you read, time is past;
As I am now, you must be at last;
Then haste, oh haste, make no delay;
Make peace with God for the long day."

In Greyfriars Churchyard repose the remains of Dr. William Robertson, the eminent historian. This distinguished individual was born in the manse of Borthwick, in 1721. Having studied at the University of Edinburgh he was licensed to preach in 1741, and two years afterwards was appointed to the church of Gladsmuir. An eloquent speaker in the General Assembly, he was recognised as leader of the Moderate party. In 1759 he was promoted to Lady Yester's Church, Edinburgh. His "History of Scotland during the reigns of Queen Mary and James VI." appeared in 1759, and at once established his literary reputation. He was appointed Chaplain of Stirling Castle, and one of the king's chaplains for Scotland. In 1761 he was preferred to the Principalship of the University of Edinburgh, and translated to Greyfriars Church. Soon afterwards he was constituted Royal Historiographer for Scotland, with a salary of £200 per annum. In 1769 he published his history of the Reign of Charles V. in three quarto volumes, receiving for the copyright £4,500. His History of America appeared in 1777. After a period of feeble health he died, on the 11th June, 1793, in his seventy-first year. His tombstone is inscribed thus:—

"In hoc conduntur sepulchro reliquiæ summi viri, ingenio, judicio, doctrina præstantis; suavissima indole, puris moribus, assidua benignitate, omnibusque privatis virtutibus; suis quam maxime cari; sacrosancti evangelii ministri fidelis, prædicatoris eloquentis; in Ecclesia Scotiæ administranda presbyteri mitis, prudentis, felicis; Academiæ Edinburgenæ præfecti meritissimi; historici gravis, diserti, candidi, sagacis; cujus memoriam non exigua hæc et ruitura monumenta, sed scripta ipsuis ære perenniora vetabunt mori, atque in omne ævum testabuntur tale sui seculi et patriæ, artibus ingenuis, et scientia frugifera, literisque elegantibus jam tum florentissimæ, decus et lumen extitisse Gulielmum Robertson, S.S.T.P., Natus est A.D. MDCCXXI., obiit A.D. MDCCXCIII."

On Dr. Robertson's tomb are tablets commemorating the Honourable William Robertson, Senator of the College of Justice, the Principal's eldest son, who died 20th November, 1835, aged eighty-two, and Lieut-Col. David Robertson M'Donald, youngest son of Principal Robertson, who was born 7th April, 1761, and died 7th September, 1815.

Dr. Hugh Blair is interred near the burial-place of Principal Robertson, and is commemorated by the following inscription carved on a stone in the south wall of New Greyfriars Church:—

"Infelici hoc in campo, ubi effunduntur suspiria et lacrymæ sepultus est Hugo Blair, S. S. Theol. Doctor; Ecclesiæ Scotiæ et Academiæ Edinburgenæ, per annos pene sexaginta, decus et tutamen; in cathedra Academica criticus eximius; in rostro templi orator perelegans; maritus amantissimus, amicus fidelis, vir bonus. Natus 7mo Aprilis, 1718, terram cum cœlo commutavit 27mo Decembris, 1800, anno ætatis 83tio. Tertio jam condito lustro post obitum viri venerabilis, hunc lapidem ponendum curabant alumni virtutis memoriæ studiosi."

Descended from the old family of Blair of Ayrshire, and great-great-grandson of the celebrated Robert Blair, Minister of St. Andrews, Hugh Blair was son of a merchant in Edinburgh, who subsequently held office in the Excise. Having studied at the University of Edinburgh, he was in October, 1741, licensed to preach. In the following year he was ordained Minister of Collessie, Fifeshire, but in less than a year thereafter he was elected second Minister of the Canongate. In 1754 he was translated to Lady Yester's, and in four years afterwards was promoted to the High Church. Having delivered lectures on literary composition in the college, he was, in 1762, appointed Professor of Rhetoric and *Belles Lettres.* His lectures on Rhetoric, subsequently published, have long been held as a standard work. Dr. Blair was a patron of Robert Burns, and also of James Macpherson when he first undertook to collect the traditional poetry of the Highlands. The first volume of his celebrated Sermons appeared in 1777. The fifth and last volume prepared by him for the press was published posthumously in 1801.

The Rev. John Erskine, D.D., minister of Old Greyfriars from 1758 to 1803, is commemorated by a window of stained glass in Old Greyfriars Church, and also by a tombstone. He was proprietor of Carnock, in Fifeshire, which he inherited from his ancestors. His father, John Erskine of Carnock, was a celebrated lawyer, and author of "The Principles of the Law of Scotland." He was born on the 2nd June, 1721, was licensed in 1743, and in 1744 was ordained Minister of Kirkintilloch. He was subsequently translated to Culross, and in 1758 to the New Greyfriars. In 1767 he was associated with Dr. William Robertson in the collegiate charge of Old Greyfriars parish. Dr. Erskine was leader of the Evangelical party in the General Assembly, and maintained an extensive correspondence with eminent divines both on the Continent and in the provinces of North America. He died suddenly on the 18th January, 1803. His character and mode of preaching are described in *Guy Mannering.*

A tombstone celebrates by a Latin inscription Andrew Dalzel, Professor of Greek in the University of Edinburgh. The inscription is as follows:—

"Memoriæ sacrum Andreæ Dalzel, multos per annos in Academia

Edinense Græcarum Literarum Professoris; viri in vita amati, in morte defleti, animo benigno, moribus cultis et urbanis, omni denique doctrina liberali et virtute ornatissimi; cujus ita erat comitate condita gravitas, ut animos discentium et sibi mirum in modum conciliaret, et amore literarum quo ipse flagrabat vehementer incenderet. Nat. Prid. non. Oct. MDCCXLII., ob. sext. Id. Dec. MDCCCVI."

Professor Dalzel, the son of humble parents, was born in the parish of Kirkliston, Linlithgowshire. Through the interest of the Earl of Lauderdale, in whose family he had been tutor, he was by the Town Council appointed to his Professorship. As an instructor of youth he was widely celebrated. In 1789 he was elected principal clerk to the General Assembly, being the first layman who ever held that office. Professor Dalzel died on the 8th December, 1806.

The following rhymes celebrate the virtuous qualities of Dame Darcy Brisbane, daughter of Thomas Brisbane, of Brisbane, and widow of Sir Walter Maxwell, of Pollok, who died at Edinburgh on the 2nd July, 1810 :—

> " Now she has dropt her cumbrous clay,
> And joyful soars the shining way;
> While kindred spirits spread their wings,
> And bear her to the King of kings.
> Long had she known the Saviour's love,
> And fixed her heart on things above.
> Long had she run, with even pace,
> A useful, not uncertain race.
> With various gifts and graces fraught,
> By the unerring Spirit taught,
> She warned, allured, with fervent zeal,
> Nor dared religion to conceal.
> And now she shines in endless light,
> In all her Father's glories bright.
> A spotless robe to her is given,
> And all the glorious joys of heaven,
> She sees with joy the Saviour's face,
> And sings the triumphs of His grace;
> Then casts her crown beneath His throne,
> And glory gives to God alone."

A monument, reared by " a few admirers of his genius," denotes the burial-place of Duncan Ban Macintyre, the celebrated Gaelic bard. The following verse, extracted from his poems, is engraved on the monument as his epitaph:—

"MARBH RANN AN UGHDAIR DHA FEIN.

"Fhir tha'd sheasamh air mo lic
Bha mise mar tha thu'n drast;
'S i mo leaba'n diugh an uaigh
Cha-n'eil smior no smuais 'am chnaimh;
Ged tha thusa laidir òg,
Cha mhair thu beò ged fhuair thu dail;
Gabh mo chomhairle 's bi glic
Cuimhnich tric gu-n tig am bàs."

This inscription has been thus translated:—

"You that stand upon my gravestone,
I have been as you are now.
To-day the grave is my bed,
And there is no marrow in my bones.
Though you get respite, you will not live.
Take my advice, and be wise.
Remember oft that death will come."

Macintyre was born at Glenorchy on the 20th March, 1724, and died at Edinburgh on the 14th May, 1812.

A long Latin inscription commemorates the learning and personal qualities of Alexander Fraser Tytler, Lord Woodhouselee. This distinguished judge, eldest son of William Tytler, author of the "Inquiry into the Evidence against Mary, Queen of Scots," was born at Edinburgh on the 15th October, 1747. In 1770 he passed advocate, and in 1780 was appointed Joint Professor of Civil History in the University of Edinburgh. In 1790 he obtained the office of Judge Advocate of Scotland, and in 1802 was appointed a Lord of Session. He died at Edinburgh on the 5th January, 1813. Of his numerous publications, his "Lectures on Universal History," and his "Essays on the Principles of Translation," retain popularity. On the same tombstone is commemorated Patrick Fraser Tytler, youngest son of Lord Woodhouselee, and author of the "History of Scotland" which bears his name. This estimable and learned person was born at Edinburgh on the 30th

August, 1701. In 1813 he was called to the Bar, but he did not seek practice as an advocate. He published in 1819 his "Life of the Admirable Crichton," which was followed by the Lives of Sir Thomas Craig of Riccarton, and of John Wycliffe. At the advice of Sir Walter Scott he undertook his "History of Scotland," and in order to obtain authentic information he proceeded to London, where he conducted extensive researches in the State Paper Office. The first volume of the "History" was issued in 1828, and the ninth and last in 1843. Mr. Tytler published subsequently in Mr. Murray's Family Library " Lives of Scottish Worthies," three vols., 12mo. In 1833 he edited and printed as a gift to the Bannatyne and Maitland Clubs, " Memoirs of the War carried on in Scotland and Ireland in 1689—1691, by Major-General Hugh Mackay." Mr. Tytler latterly suffered from broken health. He died at Great Malvern, on the 24th December, 1849, in his fifty-ninth year. His character is thus represented on his tomb :—

"Of his genius and his taste, his historical and biographical works are a sufficient memorial; of his pure converse and delightful manners, his serene temper and lovely disposition, recollections are garnered up where only they can be preserved—in the hearts of his friends; of his piety, his faith, his hope and love, the record survives in heaven.

"' Blessed are the pure in heart, for they shall see God.' "

A tombstone denotes the burial-place of William Creech, the eminent publisher. Son of the Rev. William Creech, Minister of Newbattle, he was born on the 21st April, 1745. By his father he was intended for the medical profession, but preferring the concerns of trade, he became apprenticed to Mr. Kincaid, bookseller in Edinburgh, with whom he subsequently entered into partnership. His shop was the resort of the *literati* of the capital. He conducted business for forty-four years with remarkable success, and held the office of Lord Provost of the city from 1811 to 1813. The first Edinburgh edition of Burns' poems was issued from his printing office. He died unmarried on the 14th January, 1815.

Helen Blake, wife of Peter Leslie, who died on the 14th November, 1818, is by her husband lamented in these lines :—

"She was!
But words are wanting to say what.
Think what a wife should be,
And she was that."

Henry Mackenzie, author of "The Man of Feeling" and other works, is thus comemorated on the family tombstone :—

"Here rest the mortal remains of Henry Mackenzie, who as an author, for no short time and no small part, supported the literary reputation of his country; whose writings, by beautiful and pathetic fancy, ingenuity and justice of thought, by elegance and delicacy of style, by refined moral sentiments and religious purity, have attained classical celebrity : not therefore to commemorate these writings, or to record his fame as an author, is this stone erected, but as a memorial of the love and affection of the widow and the children he left behind to lament his loss, who saw in all the relations of his life the practice of the virtues his writings inspire, and in his prospect of death the peace of Christian faith and hope. 1 Thess. iv. 13—18. Born in Edinburgh, August 6, 1745; died in the same place, January 14, 1831."

Henry Mackenzie was son of Joshua Mackenzie, physician in Edinburgh. He studied law and became attorney for the Crown. "The Man of Feeling," his first and most popular work, appeared in 1771; it was followed in 1773 by "The Man of the World," and in 1777 by "Julia de Roubigné." In 1779-80 he edited the *Mirror*, of which the papers were issued twice a week. The *Lounger*, a periodical of similar character, appeared weekly from 1785 to 1787 under his editorial care. He contributed to the Transactions of the Royal Society of Edinburgh, and of the Highland Society of Scotland. He attained the advanced age of eighty-six.

Within the family tomb of Henry Mackenzie rest the remains of Joshua Henry Mackenzie, his eldest son, a Senator of the College of Justice; he died on the 17th November, 1851, aged seventy-four.

On a family tombstone is recorded the name of James Wolfe Murray of Cringletie, a Senator of the College of Justice. Lord

Cringletie died in 1836 at the age of seventy-seven. His daughter, Alicia Stewart, who died young, is commemorated in these lines :—

> "Pluck'd from its stem the bud before the flower
> Had felt the blight of winter's chilling hour;
> Warned from a life with griefs and sorrows fraught,
> When Time its tale of tears had scarcely taught,
> Her fragile form here found that sacred rest
> Her soul had sought in mansions of the blest."

Dr. Thomas McCrie, the learned biographer of John Knox, is on his tombstone thus celebrated by the members of his flock :—

"In memory of Thomas McCrie, D.D., the biographer of John Knox, &c., &c., born 1772, died 1835. A Christian and a patriot, in him were united the softer virtues of private life with the high disinterested spirit of the times, which his writings have illustrated. Raised by his genius as an author to eminence in the world of letters, he rose still higher, in the estimation of his flock, by his affectionate fidelity as a minister of Jesus Christ, under the banner of the Original Secession; he contended with unfaltering firmness for the principles of the Reformation, the memory of whose champions he has vindicated and embalmed in the page of imperishable history.

"His congregation, among whom he laboured for nearly forty years, have erected this memorial of his worth and of their gratitude."

Dr. McCrie was born at Dunse; he studied at Edinburgh, and was some time employed in tuition. In 1795 he became a licentiate of the Associate Presbytery of Kelso, and soon after was called to minister to a congregation in Potterrow, Edinburgh. In 1806 he separated with three others from the General Associate Synod on the ground of their having departed from the principles of their founders in reference to the powers of the civil magistrate. He formed what was styled the Constitutional Associate Presbytery, which in 1827 was joined by another body of protesters who together assumed the designation of Original Seceders. In 1811 Dr. McCrie issued the first edition of his "Life of John Knox," which was afterwards enlarged. In the pages of the *Christian Instructor* in 1817 he vindicated the Covenanters from the unhappy attack of Sir Walter Scott in the "Tales of my

Landlord." His "Life of Andrew Melville" appeared in 1819, and was followed by his "Memoirs of William Veitch and George Bryson." He published subsequently "History of the Reformation in Italy," and "History of the Reformation in Spain." Dr. McCrie died at Edinburgh on the 5th August, 1835.

A handsome mausoleum forms the burial-place of the family of Adam of Blair Adam, Kinross-shire. It presents the following inscriptions :—

"The Right Honourable William Adam, Lord Chief Commissioner of the Jury Court, a Privy Councillor, and Lord Lieutenant of the county of Kinross, eldest son of John Adam of Blair-Adam, was born on the 2nd August, 1751, passed advocate 1773, elected to Parliament in 1774, called to the English bar in 1782. He took a prominent part in the proceedings of the House of Commons until he vacated his seat in 1795. Associated with Mr. Fox and the small number of eminent men who exerted their powerful talents to uphold the principles of the Constitution during the progress of the French Revolution, he was conspicuous in his endeavours, although in vain, to prevent the antiquated law of lease-making being illegally used against the liberty of the subject. He lived, however, to see his views adopted by the amendment of that law. He was made King's Counsel in 1796, and appointed Chancellor of the Duchy of Cornwall in 1806, in which year, on the formation of the Granville Administration, he was returned to Parliament for the counties of Kincardine and Kinross, and sat for the former until 1811. From an early period he had devoted his attention to the improvement of the administration of justice in Scotland, and when it was resolved in 1815 to establish trial by jury in civil causes, he was placed at the head of the court. The distinguished talent, the unwearied zeal, and patient attention by which he overcame the difficulties attending so great a change in the jurisprudence of Scotland, together with the admirable temper, the kindness of demeanour, and the urbanity he displayed in the execution of this arduous undertaking, have been publicly recorded by those over whom he presided. The energy of his character was no less exhibited in the district in which his estate is situated, where works of vast extent and great utility, suggested by his foresight and completed by his influence, are lasting marks of his unwearied exertions for the public benefit. He was distinguished by his extensive knowledge and enlightened conversation, his judgment in the conduct of affairs was remarkable, and his advice was sought by persons of all ranks. The useful assistance and liberal encouragement he afforded to the numerous objects of his solicitude and regard will long be remembered as striking proofs of his active benevolence and the kindness of his heart. He died in Edinburgh on the 17th February, 1839, in the enjoyment of the profound respect of the public, the admiration of his friends, and the affectionate love of his family.

"William George Adam, third son of the Lord Chief Commissioner, born in London, 6th December, 1781. He was entered at Lincoln's Inn in 1799, called to the Bar in 1806, and appointed King's Counsel in 1824. The accuracy of his knowledge and talents for business established him at an early period in full employment at the Bar; but his declining health obliged him ultimately to confine himself to the practice of Parliament. His career and success were preeminent, for to his professional acquirements he added independence of conduct and a high and honourable bearing which commanded the respect and confidence of those tribunals before which he practised. His strength, however, was unequal to the incessant labour, and his health was rapidly giving way, when by the friendship and spontaneous kindness of Lord Chancellor Brougham he was appointed, in 1831, Accountant-General of the Court of Chancery. But this comparative ease came too late; the seeds of disease had sunk too deep to be removed, and overpowered by a complication of maladies, he died at his cottage in Richmond Park, on 16th May, 1839, and was interred in the churchyard of Mortlake. His unbending integrity, his high sense of honour, his boundless generosity of spirit, had secured to him alike the regard and attachment of public and private friends, whilst the mildness of his disposition and his other endearing qualities rendered him the delight of those who witnessed the progress of his blameless course in the privacy of domestic life.

"John Adam, of Blair-Adam, in Kinross-shire, eldest son of William and Mary Adam. Firm in adversity, non-elated by prosperity, the serenity of his temper and the kindness of his nature were the source of happiness to his family, and a blessing to all within his influence. His taste and spirit of improvement were most distinguished. He died in June, 1792, aged 71. His remains are interred here.

"John, the second son of John Adam, of Blair-Adam, was educated at Eton School, where his amiable qualities and his distinction as a scholar gave great hope of future eminence. He died in London in 1769, aged 16. His remains are deposited in Grosvenor Chapel.

"Mary, the wife of William Adam, architect, a daughter of Robertson, of Gladney, in Fife, a woman of exemplary virtue and good sense. She died in 1761, aged 62. Her remains are interred here.

"Jean, the wife of John Adam, of Blair-Adam, daughter of John Ramsay, a son of Ramsay of Abbotshall, in Fife; a woman of great virtue and good sense. Died 1795, aged 74. Her remains are interred here.

"Francis, the fifth and youngest son of the Lord Chief Commissioner, was a merchant in London. Actuated by a high sense of honour, he undertook a voyage to Demerara for the arrangement of some arduous affairs. His brother (Rear-Admiral Adam) accompanied him—a signal instance of family affection. Francis was seized with the yellow fever on their voyage home, and on the 8th of June, 1820, aged 29, he expired in his brother's arms. His remains were committed to the ocean. Put up by his father in July, 1827.

"John Adam, eldest son of the Lord Chief Commissioner, was born 4th May, 1779. In June he sailed for Bengal, in the Civil Service of the East India Company. He passed through various offices of great trust and labour, and in 1819 was placed in the Supreme Council. The usual time of holding that station being completed, he was reappointed, and from January to August, 1823, he acted as Governor-General, a period which required decision, firmness, and energy. His character and services have been extolled by the public voice of India. His extensive knowledge, his elevated views, his indefatigable zeal, his exemplary integrity, and the wisdom of his measures, have been publicly recorded by the Supreme Council of Bengal, and by those who preside over the affairs of India in England. Ill-health—the effect of climate, fatigue, and anxiety—compelled him, in March, 1852, to embark for England. His surviving parent and family expected to have seen in ripened manhood what early youth had promised—to have beheld his benign countenance, to have enjoyed his enlightened discourse, to have been soothed by his warm affection, to have witnessed his active benevolence; but he died on the 4th of June, 1825, on his voyage home, and his remains were committed to the ocean. This stone is inscribed to his private virtue. His public services will be recorded in the history of British India. Put up by his father in July, 1827.

"Eleanora, the wife of the Right Hon. William Adam, Lord Chief Commissioner of the Jury Court, a daughter of Charles, the tenth Lord Elphinston, of exemplary goodness, unassuming manners, and superior understanding. She died in London, 4th February, 1800, aged 53. Her remains are deposited in Grosvenor Chapel. Put up by her husband in July, 1827.

"Erected in 1750 by John, the eldest son of William Adam, architect; repaired, and surrounding inscriptions put up, in 1827, by William, the son of John.

"The Right Hon. Sir John Leach, Knt., Master of the Rolls. He died in Edinburgh, the 14th day of September, 1834, aged seventy-four years. He was appointed Chancellor of the Duchy of Cornwall in 1816, Chief Justice of Chester in 1817, Vice-Chancellor of England and one of His Majesty's most honourable Privy Council, 1818, Master of the Rolls, 1827. His revered remains are deposited in this mausoleum by permission of the Lord Chief Commissioner, his early and most valued friend. This memorial was placed by his affectionate brother, Thomas Leach."

To the narrative inscribed on the mausoleum may be added that the Lord Chief Commissioner was nephew of Robert and James Adam, the celebrated architects. His grandfather, William Adam, born at Kirkcaldy in 1728, likewise possessed an eminent reputation as an architect. By a course of professional industry he purchased Blair Adam estate. Admiral Sir Charles Adam, eldest son of the Lord Chief Commissioner, was Governor of Greenwich Hospital, and one of the Lords of the Admiralty; his son, William Patrick Adam, of Blair Adam, now represents the county of Kinross.

A tombstone with a short Latin inscription commemorates Robert Blair of Avontoun, Lord President of the Court of Session. This eminent judge was fourth son of the Rev. Robert Blair, author of "The Grave;" he was born in 1741, and passed advocate in 1764. He was in 1789 appointed Solicitor-General, and in 1801 elected Dean of Faculty. In 1808 he was appointed to his office of Lord President. He died on the 18th May, 1811. On the same tombstone is commemorated Captain Robert Blair, of the 2nd Dragoon Guards, grandson of Lord President Blair, who died at Cawnpore on the 28th March, 1859.

A small tombstone denotes the burial-place of John Beugo, engraver of Nasmyth's portrait of Burns prefixed to the first Edinburgh edition of his poems. Beugo was born at Edinburgh on the 7th May, 1759, and died on the 13th December, 1841.

A tombstone celebrates the worth of Robert Cadell of Ratho. Mr. Cadell is entitled to remembrance as the spirited and successful publisher of the Waverley novels. He was born at Cockenzie, Haddingtonshire, on the 16th December, 1788, and became partner of Archibald Constable in 1809. He had as his first wife, Elizabeth Constable, his partner's daughter, who died on the 16th July, 1818, and whose name is inscribed upon his tombstone. In 1826, after the failure of Constable and Co., he became sole publisher of Sir Walter Scott's works. He acquired the joint copyright in 1827, and after Scott's death he paid £30,000 for the remaining share. After a prosperous career he died at Cockenzie on the 20th January, 1860.

A short inscription on a tombstone, engraven with several other names, denotes the resting-place of George Dunbar, Professor of Greek. This accomplished scholar was born at Coldingham, Berwickshire, in 1774. He was bred a gardener, but being injured by an accident he betook himself to study. His scholarly abilities recommended him as assistant to Professor Dalzel, of the Greek chair in the University of Edinburgh, and on his death in 1805 he was appointed successor. In his efforts to advance the study of Greek literature he was unwearied. He compiled an excellent Greek dictionary. Professor Dunbar died on the 6th December, 1851.

Dr. Carson, Rector of the High School, was interred in this churchyard. He was born at Holywood, Dumfriesshire, in 1780; studied at Wallacehall Academy and the University of Edinburgh, and in 1801 was elected Master of the Grammar School, Dumfries. In January, 1806, he was elected one of the Masters of the High School, Edinburgh, and in 1820 was on vacancy promoted to the rectorship. He resigned office in 1845, and died at Edinburgh on the 4th November, 1850. Dr. Carson was a profound classical scholar. A monument to his memory has been erected in the vestibule of St. Giles's Church.

The names of other prominent persons whose mortal remains have been consigned to Greyfriars Churchyard must be simply enumerated :—

William Cowper, Bishop of Galloway and Dean of the Chapel Royal, died 15th February, 1619, aged 53 ; Sir William Oliphant King's Advocate, died 13th April, 1628, aged 77 ; Sir James

Skene, Bart., of Curriehill, President of the College of Justice, died 15th October, 1633, aged 54; David Aikenhead, Lord Provost of the city, died 13th August, 1637, aged 71; George Jamesone, the eminent painter, born 1587, died 1644; Sir David Falconar of Newtoun, President of the Court of Session, died 15th December, 1685, aged 46; William Annand, Dean of Edinburgh, born 1633, died 13th June, 1689; Sir James Falconer of Phesdo, one of the Senators of the College of Justice, born 16th August, 1648, died 10th June, 1706; Sir Hugh Cunningham of Bonnington, Provost of Edinburgh and Founder of the Merchants' Maiden Hospital, died 16th December, 1710, aged 67; Sir John Medina, the eminent painter, died 5th October, 1710; James Watson, printer and editor of the Scottish Collection of Poems, which bears his name, died 1722; Sir Robert Whyte of Bennochy, Physician to the King and Professor of Medicine in the University of Edinburgh, died on the 15th April, 1766, aged 51; Patrick Grant of Elchies, Senator of the College of Justice, born 1691, died 1754; William Ged, inventor of the art of stereotyping, died 1749; Alexander Nisbet, author of the "System of Heraldry," born 1672, died 1725; Alexander Smellie, F.R.S.E., author of "The Philosophy of Natural History," died 24th June, 1795, aged 54; Joseph Black, M.D., Professor of Chemistry, died 26th November, 1799, aged 71; Sir John Home, Bart., of Blackadder, Vice-Admiral of the Blue, died 2nd May, 1803; Catherine Wilson, first wife of Francis Jeffrey, died 8th August, 1805, aged 28 years; Alexander Gibson Hunter of Blackness, died 9th March, 1812, aged 41; Henry Siddons, died 12th April, 1815, aged 40; William Brown, M.D., born 14th November, 1757, died 28th November, 1818; Alexander Christison, Professor of Humanity in the University of Edinburgh, died 25th June, 1820, aged 69; Sir John Peters, Consul-General for the Netherlands, died 19th June, 1826, aged 81; the Rev. John Campbell, D.D., one of the Ministers of the Tolbooth Church, Edinburgh, died 30th August, 1828, aged 70; Gilbert Innes of Stow, died 26th February, 1832, aged 81; William Trotter of Ballindean, born 10th November, 1772, died 16th August, 1833; the Rev. Andrew Brown, D.D., Minister of the Old Church, and Professor of Rhetoric in the University, died 19th February, 1834, aged 71; Lieut.-Colonel John Farquharson, late of the 42nd Regiment, and Lieut.-Governor of Carlisle, died 3rd November, 1835, aged 82; the Rev. Robert Anderson, D.D., one of the Ministers of Old Greyfriars, died 24th January, 1837, aged 69; General Sir James Hay, K.C.H., died 11th February, 1837, aged 72; William Wallace, LL.D., Professor of Mathematics in the University of Edinburgh, died 28th April, 1843, aged 74; Adam, Lord Gillies, Senator of the College of Justice, born at Brechin, 29th April, 1766, died at Leamington, 24th December, 1842; Alexander Monypenny, W.S., born 23rd March, 1778, died 15th June, 1844; Alexander Falconar of Falcon Hall, died 10th December, 1847; Sir Alexander Charles Maitland Gibson of Clifton Hall, Bart., born 21st November, 1755, died 7th February, 1848; John Jeffrey (brother of Francis Jeffrey), born 25th March, 1775, died 3rd July, 1848; Alexander Boswell, Writer to the Signet, died 30th August, 1850, aged 69; James L'Amy, Esq., of Dunkenny, Sheriff of Forfarshire, died 15th January, 1854, aged 81; David Simpson of Teviot Bank (father of General Sir James Simpson, who was appointed Commander-in-chief in the Crimea, June, 1855), died 1st January, 1806; Patrick Miller of Dalswinton, born 1731, died 9th December, 1815; John Kay, the eminent caricaturist, born April 1722, died 21st February, 1826; James Gillespie Graham of Orchill, the eminent architect, died 21st March, 1855, aged 78; John Learmouth of Dean, died 11th December, 1858, aged 69; Daniel Scrymgeour, Inspector of Schools, died 2nd March, 1859; the Rev. David Barclay Mellis, Minister of the Free Church, Tealing, died at Edinburgh the 27th May, 1861, aged 60; General Henry James Riddell, K.H., died 8th March, 1861; Robert Riddell, Advocate, born 29th May, 1797, died 18th April, 1862; John Porteous, Captain of the City Guard, who was executed by the mob on the 8th September, 1736, was on the following day interred in Greyfriars Churchyard.

An elegant memorial window in Old Greyfriars Church commemorates the celebrated George Buchanan; it was erected by the late Mr. James Buchanan of Moray Place. In the same church are memorial windows in honour of the Rev. Dr. James Finlayson, minister of the High Church and Professor of Logic in the University, who died on the 28th January, 1808; Principal Robertson, the historian; the Rev. Dr. John Inglis, minister of Greyfriars; the Rev. Robert Trail, minister of Greyfriars, who died in May, 1716, aged seventy-four; and of Dr. Robert Anderson, also a minister of the church, who died on the 24th January, 1837, aged sixty-nine.

Within Old Greyfriars Church an elegant medallion by Mr. John Hutchison, R.S.A., commemorates Dr. Robert Lee, minister of the church, who died on the 14th March, 1868.

On the north wall of New Greyfriars Church an inscription denotes a former burial-place of the family of Lauder of Lauder. Among those commemorated is Sir Andrew Dick Lauder of Grange, sixth Baronet, of Fountainhall, who died 16th December, 1820.*

From Monteith's "Theater of Mortality" we extract the following inscriptions:—

Tomb of Elizabeth Hay, spouse to George Drummond, bailie, died 1673 :—

"Let no dry eyes indifference confess,
When ev'n a stone doth so just grief express;
Here the best wife, mother, and friend doth ly,
In whom none but herself a fault could spy.
Here grief and love show in their noble strife,
Him, a kind husband, her a matchless wife;
She to her husband herself in life resigned,
And here he her to heaven hath consigned."

* In Mr. James Brown's valuable work, "The Epitaphs and Monumental Inscriptions in Greyfriars Churchyard," are presented lists of eminent persons interred in the churchyard. These lists include the names of the more noted citizens of Edinburgh during the last two centuries. Those who desire to obtain a more intimate acquaintance with the history and annals of the churchyard we have great pleasure in referring to Mr. Brown's work.

James Brown, who died in 1691, had bemoaned his wife who pre-deceased him in these lines :—

> "Here lyes interr'd her corps, in hopes to rise,
> Whose soul's above with Christ in paradise,
> When both unite; a matron grave and just,
> Faithful and careful in her husband's trust;
> Not gaudie, kept her shop, went not abroad,
> Vert'ous and charitable, serving God,
> Prudent, obliging, in her ways discreet,
> At home, abroad, did for her husband's credit;
> He mindful of her worth moved this intent,
> For badge of love, t'erect this monument."

A parent laments his children thus :—

> "Though marble, porphirie, and mourning touch
> May praise these spoils, yet can they not too much;
> For beauty lost and fame this stone doth close
> One earth's delight, heaven's care, a purest rose.
> And shouldst thou, reader, but vouchsafe a tear,
> Upon it other flowers shall soon appear,
> Sad violets and hyacinths, which grow
> With marks of grief, a publick loss to show."

The following is common to Scottish graveyards :—

> "A soul prepared needs no delays,
> The summons comes, the saint obeys;
> Swift was her flight and short the road,
> She closed her eyes and saw her God."

A female who died 12th November, 1675, aged forty-six, is celebrated in these lines :—

> "A nature sweet grace did enamel o'er,
> A modest mind a great wit did decore;
> Her comely features vertue did excel,
> Her dust here lyes, her soul with Christ doth dwell."

A child of seven years, daughter of Alexander Swinton of Mersingtoun, advocate, had these lines upon her tombstone :—

> "The sweetest children are but like fair flowers,
> Which please the fancy for some days and hours;
> They soon spring up, but ere they be well grown,
> They fade away, their place is no more known;

> Only their death, sure, leaveth such a smart,
> That grief's engraven on the parents' heart."

The following lines commemorated a youth who died in 1699:—

> "O death, O grave, why so severe?
> E'en youth must see thy look austere,
> This young man did by living die,
> By death he lives eternally."

Here is an epitaph alike pervaded by sentiment and poetry:—

> "You'll say, alas, he's dead! he cannot die;
> He's only changed to immortality.
> Weep not for him who has no cause of tears,
> Hush then your sighs and calm your needless fears;
> Run such a race as you again may meet,
> You'll find your conversation far more sweet,
> When purged from dross, you shall unmix'd possess
> The purest essence of eternal bliss."

The following is composed creditably:—

> "By Him whose conquests through the world are known,
> I to my first original am thrown,
> My earth lies here, my better part's above,
> And lives,—so I, not death, the conqu'ror prove.
> Yet lest the stingless terror boast
> Of what he's won, and what he thinks I lost,
> He that's almighty and for ever true,
> Engaged this dust should rise and conquer too!
> What I possess secures me what's to come,
> My clay shall be refined, then sent for home."

The Rev. James Hall, who died 8th December, 1781, is thus commemorated:—

> "Blameless in life, e'en in his early youth
> Unknown to wander from the paths of truth,
> He lived; but did not live on bread alone,
> The word of God his comfort, heaven his home.
> His constant aim the love of Christ to win,
> A friend to sinners, yet abhorred their sin;
> Firm to the truth by sacred influence moved,
> Mild yet severe, even in reproof beloved;
> This to thine honour, more than this thy due,
> On earth the Christian's life was shown in you."

The blessedness of the future life is thus happily portrayed on an existing tombstone :—

> "Now she has dropt her cumbrous clay,
> And joyful soars the shining way,
> While kindred spirits spread their wings,
> And bear her to the King of kings.
> Long had she known the Saviour's love,
> And fix'd her heart on things above.
> Long had she run with even pace
> A useful, not uncertain race,
> With various gifts and graces fraught,
> By the unerring Spirit taught,
> She warn'd, allured with fervent zeal,
> Nor dared religion to conceal.
> And now she shines in endless light,
> In all her Father's glories bright;
> A spotless robe to her is given,
> And all the glorious joys of heaven.
> She sees with joy her Father's face,
> And sings the triumphs of His grace,
> Then casts her crown beneath His throne,
> And glory gives to God alone."

ST. CUTHBERT'S CHURCHYARD.

In the vestibule of St. Cuthbert's Church a decorated marble tablet erected in 1842 commemorates by a Latin inscription the genius and learning of John Napier of Merchiston, inventor of the Logarithms. This remarkable man was born in Merchiston Castle, near Edinburgh, in 1550. He was eldest son of Sir Alexander Napier, Master of the Mint to James VI., by his first wife, daughter of Sir Francis Bothwell, a Lord of Session. He was educated at St. Salvator's College, St. Andrews; after travelling abroad, he devoted himself to mathematical studies. For many years he directed his inquiries to the discovery of a short method of calculation to facilitate the solution of trigonometrical problems. In 1614 he produced his book of Logarithms. His invention rendered his name celebrated over Europe. He died at Merchiston Castle in April, 1617, and was buried in St. Giles Church. His eldest son was the first Lord Napier.

A marble tablet in the vestibule of St. Cuthbert's Church is thus inscribed:—"Here lyes the corpse of the Honble. Sir James Rocheid of Inverleith, who died on the 1st of May, 1787, in the 71st year of his age." Sir James was second and last Baronet of the old family of Rocheid of Craigleith and Inverleith. His daughter and co-heir, Mary, married Sir Francis Kinloch, Bart., of Gilmerton; her third son on succeeding to the estates of his maternal grandfather assumed the name of Rocheid. The family is extinct.—Also in the vestibule of the church a marble tablet commemorates the Rev. William Paul, minister of the second charge of the parish, who died on the 27th October, 1802, in the forty-eighth year of his age and twenty-fourth of his ministry. Mr. Paul was translated from Newbattle in 1786; he was Chaplain in Ordinary to the King, and was held in high esteem for the fidelity and earnestness of his ministrations.

The Rev. Sir Henry Moncreiff Wellwood, Bart., minister of the first charge of St. Cuthbert's, is commemorated by a mural tablet. This distinguished divine was son of the Rev. Sir William Moncreiff, seventh Baronet of Tippermalloch and Minister of Blackford, Perthshire. Educated at the Universities of Glasgow and Edinburgh, he was licensed in 1771, and in the same year ordained successor to his father in the parish of Blackford. In October, 1775, he was translated to St. Cuthbert's parish. He became leader of the evangelical section of the church; in 1785 he was elected Moderator of the General Assembly. He died on the 9th August, 1827, in the seventy-eighth year of his age, and fifty-sixth of his ministry. For forty-three years he held the office of collector of the Ministers' Widows' Fund, and he was one of the original members of the Society for benefiting the sons of the clergy.

The oldest tombstone in the churchyard is a mural tablet in memory of Henry Nisbet of Dean, who died in 1692. Among the older mortuary enclosures is one containing the remains of the celebrated Mr. Robert Pont. This eminent clergyman and civil judge was born at Culross about the year 1524. He studied at the University of St. Andrews, and afterwards improved himself in law at the universities of the Continent. In 1559 he was sent by the kirk-session of St. Andrews as a Commissioner to the first General Assembly, and in 1563 was appointed by the Assembly their commissioner to visit the diocese of Moray. He was chosen moderator of Assembly in 1570, and was four times thereafter elected to that office. In 1571 he was appointed provost of Trinity College, and a senator of the College of Justice. In 1574 he became collegiate minister of St. Cuthbert's; he was translated to St. Andrews, Fifeshire, in 1582. In 1587 he was nominated by the king to the temporality of the Bishopric of Caithness, but the General Assembly declined to ratify the appointment. He died on the 8th May, 1606, in his eighty-second year, and the forty-fourth of his ministry. His tombstone became a subject of dispute, as appears by a minute of the Privy Council, dated 4th June, 1607: —" Having befoir his death ordered his grave stone with some epitaphs thereon, and Mary Smyth, his relict, on a vain curiositie having removit that stone and made another, the kirk session complaines thereof to the councill, who preferrs her stone to his, and discharges the session to trouble her anent the laying thereof on her husband's grave." Mr. Pont's tombstone is adorned with a Latin inscription.

In Mr. Pont's burial-place is interred the Hon. Patrick Robertson, a senator of the College of Justice (see *ante*).

A mural monument commemorates John Grant cf Kilgraston, assistant judge in the island of Jamaica. He was elder son of Peter Grant, the last of the lairds of Glenlochy, and held office as assistant judge in Jamaica from 1783 to 1790. He died on the 25th March, 1793.

A tombstone celebrates the virtues of Dr. James MacKnight, one of the ministers of the Old church, and author of " The Harmony of the Gospels." This learned divine was son of the Rev. William MacKnight, minister of Irvine, and was born on the 17th September, 1721. In May, 1753, he was ordained to the ministry at Maybole, Ayrshire. His "Harmony of the Gospels" appeared in 1756, and his "Truth of Gospel History" in 1763. In 1769 he was elected Moderator of the General Assembly, and in the same year was translated to Jedburgh. In 1772 he became minister of Lady Yester's church, Edinburgh; he was subsequently preferred to the Old church. He published in 1795 a translation of the Apostolical Epistles. He died on the 13th January, 1800.

A handsome mausoleum commemorates Alexander Murray, Lord Henderland, a senator of the College of Justice, who died on the 16th March, 1795. On this monument are inscribed the names of William Murray of Henderland, eldest son of the preceding, who died 3rd October, 1854, and of Sir John Archibald Murray, second son of Lord Henderland, who after holding the offices of Recorder of the Great Roll, and Lord Advocate, was raised to the Bench as Lord Murray in 1839. Lord Murray died on the 7th March, 1859. On this monument is also commemorated Mary, wife of Lord Murray and daughter of William Rigby, Esq., of Oldfield Hall, Cheshire, who died on the 2nd October, 1861. Lord and Lady Murray, it is recorded, evinced such unwearied zeal in doing good, that their departure was felt as a general loss.

John Mason, "Student of Physic," who died in 1763, at the age of twenty-seven, is commemorated in these lines:—

> "O Death, O Grave, why so severe,
> E'en youth must see
> Thy looks austere;
> This young man did by living die,
> By death he lives eternally."

These lines are inscribed on the tombstone of Jacobina Curtis, wife of Archibald Lumsdaine, who died in 1809 :—

> "Hark from the tomb a solemn sound!
> 'Prepare, prepare,' it cries,
> 'To drop your body in the dust—
> Your soul to mount the skies.'"

More ambitious verse is inscribed on the gravestone of Eliza Dunbar, wife of Captain Tod, who died in 1804 :—

> "Ah! whither fled, ye dear illusions, say?
> Lo! pale and silent lies the lovely clay.
> How are the roses on that cheek decayed,
> Which beauty's bloom to every eye displayed?
> Health on her form each sprightly grace bestowéd,
> With life and thought each speaking feature glowéd.
> Fair was the blossom, soft the vernal sky,
> Elate with hope, we deeméd no tempest nigh;
> When lo! a whirlwind's instantaneous gust
> Left all its beauties withering in the dust."

By a marble slab is commemorated John, fifteenth Earl of Glencairn, who died at Coats, near Edinburgh, on the 29th September, 1796, aged forty-six. At his death the earldom became dormant. His lordship's elder brother, who died in 1791, was a warm patron of the poet Burns.

A monument celebrates the ministerial faithfulness of the Rev. Neil McVicar, Minister of St. Cuthbert's, who died on the 29th January, 1747, in the seventy-fifth year of his age and forty-eighth of his ministry. From the office of military chaplain at Fort William, Mr. McVicar was transferred to St. Cuthbert's church in May, 1707; he was appointed almoner to the king in 1729. An anecdote of him is related in connection with Prince Charles Edward's triumphal entry into Edinburgh after the battle of Prestonpans. On the following Sunday he preached to a promiscuous audience, many of whom were opposed to the reigning family. During prayer he expressed the petition that "the young man recently come amongst us in search of an earthly crown may soon obtain what is far better, a heavenly one."

A tombstone marks the burial-place of Major-General Mark Napier, who died on the 10th June, 1809. He was son of Francis, fifth Lord Napier, by his wife Lady Henrietta Hope, third daughter of the first Earl of Hopetoun. His family are interred in the churchyard.

A monument denotes the burial-place of William Jobson of Lochore, who died on the 19th December, 1822, and of his wife, Mrs. Rachel Stuart, who died on the 15th August, 1863. Jane, only child of Mr. and Mrs. Jobson, married on the 3rd February, 1825, Lieutenant Walter Scott, eldest son and heir of Sir Walter Scott, Bart. She subsequently became Lady Scott of Abbotsford.

A tombstone celebrates the Rev. Thomas Fleming, D.D., minister of Lady Yester's, who died on the 19th July, 1824, in the seventieth year of his age and forty-sixth of his ministry. To Lady Yester's church he was translated from Kirkcaldy in October, 1806. He aided in revising the translation of the Scriptures into Gaelic, and was author of several useful publications.

The Rev. John Johnstone, minister of Roxburgh Place Chapel of Ease, is commemorated by a tombstone. He was a native of Edinburgh, and was licensed to preach by the Presbytery of the Relief Church on the 12th July, 1807. In July, 1808, he was ordained to the third congregation, then worshipping in Carrubber's Close, and afterwards in Roxburgh Place. In 1829 some of his members desired to introduce an organ, a proposal which, being keenly opposed, led to its use being prohibited by the Relief Synod. Mr. Johnstone consequently withdrew his connection with the Relief Church, and in 1833 obtained admission into the Church of Scotland. He died suddenly on the 3rd September, 1833.

A monument commemorates the Rev. George Paxton, D.D., who died on the 9th April, 1837. Dr. Paxton was born at Dalgowry, Haddingtonshire, in 1762; he ministered successively at Kilmaurs and Stewarton in connection with the Associate Synod. Subsequently he became pastor of the congregation of the Associate Church worshipping in Infirmary Street, Edinburgh, and was Professor of Divinity in the connexion. His "Illustrations of Scripture" is a well-known work.

The Rev. John Jamieson, D.D., the distinguished antiquary, and author of the Scottish Dictionary, rests in this churchyard. Dr. Jamieson was born at Glasgow in 1758. For many years he ministered as pastor of a congregation of Antiburghers at Forfar. In 1797 he undertook the pastorate of the Associate Congregation in Nicolson Street, Edinburgh. His Dictionary of the Scottish language appeared in 1809-10 in two quarto volumes. In 1811 he published his "History of the Culdees." His last publication, "Views of the Royal Palaces of Scotland," appeared in 1828. Dr. Jamieson was member of many of the learned societies. He latterly enjoyed a pension on the Civil List. His death took place at Edinburgh on the 12th July, 1828.

An elegant monument, erected by admiring and attached friends, commemorates Robert Jameson, advocate, son of the preceding. He died on the 31st December, 1834.

A tombstone denotes the grave of the Rev. David Dickson, minister of New North Church, Edinburgh. This reverend gentleman was proprietor of Persilands, Lanarkshire, and was successively minister of the parishes of Liberton and Bothkennar, and of the Canongate Chapel of Ease, Trinity College, and New North Church, Edinburgh. He died on the 3rd August, 1820, in the sixty-seventh year of his age, and forty-fourth of his ministry.

Attached parishioners have reared an elegant monument, adorned with appropriate sculptures, to the memory of the Rev. David Dickson, D.D., minister of St. Cuthbert's. Dr. Dickson was translated to St. Cuthbert's from the Chapel of Ease, Kilmarnock, on the 16th May, 1803. He was a zealous promoter of benevolent enterprises, and for many years held the secretaryship of the Scottish Missionary Society. He contributed to the "Edinburgh Encyclopædia," and the *Edinburgh Christian Instructor*. He died on the 28th July, 1842, in the sixty-third year of his age and forty-first of his ministry.

A small obelisk marks the burial-place of Adam McCheyne, Writer to the Signet, who died on the 24th February, 1854. On the same monument is commemorated his son, the Rev. Robert Murray McCheyne, minister of St. Peter's Church, Dundee. This popular and gifted clergyman was born at Edinburgh on the 21st May, 1813. He studied at the High School and University of the city, and was licensed to preach in 1835. After a period of ministerial employment in the united parishes of Larbert and Dunipace, he was, in November, 1836, ordained to the pastoral charge of St. Peter's Church, Dundee. In 1839 he accompanied a deputation from the Church of Scotland on a mission to Palestine. He died after a short illness on the 29th March, 1843. Mr. McCheyne was an earnest and most effective preacher.

In the new portion of the burial-ground rest the remains of Mrs. Anne Grant, commonly styled "of Laggan" the amiable and accomplished authoress. Daughter of Duncan M'Vicar, an officer in the British army, and, through her mother, descended from the ancient Argyleshire family of Stewart, of Invernahyle, she was born at Glasgow on the 21st February, 1775. Her infancy was spent in America, where her parents had settled for a time. Returning to Scotland in 1768, Mr. M'Vicar was appointed barrack-master of Fort Augustus. There his daughter became acquainted with the Rev. James Grant, chaplain to the Fort, to whom, on his becoming parish minister of Laggan, she was married in 1779. On the death of Mr. Grant, which took place in 1801, Mrs. Grant removed with her family of young children, first to Stirling, and afterwards to Edinburgh. During her married life she had evinced some poetical talent, but it was not until her widowhood that she ventured on a publication. Three thousand subscribers were procured for a volume of poems which she published in 1803. This was followed by her "Letters from the Mountains," a work which materially enhanced her literary reputation, and considerably stimulated a taste for Scottish scenery and traditions. Mrs. Grant was much cherished in the literary society of the capital. In 1825 she obtained a pension on the Civil List. She died on the 7th November, 1838, at the age of 84. Her "Memoir and Correspondence" appeared in 1844.

An elegant monument with a medallion denotes the resting-place of John Abercrombie, M.D., the eminent physician and philosophical writer. He was born at Aberdeen on the 12th October, 1780. Having become qualified as a physician at the University of Edinburgh, he commenced in his twenty-third year to practise in that city. He was appointed physician to Heriot's Hospital, and physician to the King for Scotland. In 1830 he published his work on the "Intellectual Powers," which gained him a wide reputation as a philosophic thinker. He was a zealous promoter of benevolent institutions, and enjoyed the highest reputation as a consulting physician. In 1835 he was elected Lord Rector of Marischal College, Aberdeen. He died suddenly on the 14th November, 1844; his remains were honoured with a public funeral.

A monument commemorates the Rev. David Welsh, D.D. This eminent divine was son of a farmer at Moffat; he was born in that parish on the 11th December, 1793. Educated at the University of Edinburgh, he was licensed to preach in 1816. In March, 1821, he was ordained to the pastoral charge of Crossmichael; he was subsequently translated to St. David's Church, Glasgow; and was, in 1831, appointed to the Professorship of Church History in the University of Edinburgh. In 1842 he was chosen Moderator of the General Assembly. At the opening of the Assembly the following year, he announced the determination of a large number of his brethren to leave the Establishment and constitute the Free Church. Dr. Welsh died suddenly on the 24th April, 1845. He several years held the secretaryship of the Scottish Bible Board. For a time he edited the *North British Review*.

A monument has been erected to Andrew Combe, M.D., and to the members of his family. Dr. Combe was born at Edinburgh, on the 27th October, 1797. Having prosecuted his medical studies at Edinburgh and on the Continent, he commenced practice as a physician in 1822. He was, in 1836, appointed physician to the King of the Belgians, but after a short period was compelled to resign the office from infirm health. He died at Gorgie Mill, near Edinburgh, on the 9th August, 1847. Dr. Combe obtained wide celebrity from his phrenological speculations. His works on physiology are held in estimation.

A small obelisk indicates the sepulchre of Robert Archibald Smith, the eminent composer of Scottish music. Mr. Smith was born at Reading, in Berkshire, on the 16th November, 1780. In his 20th year he settled at Paisley, where he formed the acquaintance of Robert Tannahill, whose best songs he set to music. In 1823 he became precentor in St. George's Church, Edinburgh. His numerous musical works are much valued. He died at Edinburgh on the 3rd January, 1829.

By a tombstone is commemorated Dr. Andrew Thomson, minister of St. George's. This eminent divine was born at Sanquhar, in the county of Dumfries, on the 11th July, 1779. His father, Dr. John Thomson, was in succession minister of Sanquhar and Markinch, and one of the ministers of Edinburgh. He was licensed in 1802, and in the same year was ordained minister of Sprouston, Roxburghshire. In 1808 he was translated to the East Church, Perth; and in 1810 was presented to New Greyfriars Church, Edinburgh. He now commenced the *Christian Instructor*—a periodical which under his editorial care obtained much favour in religious circles. He contributed valuable articles to the "Edinburgh Encyclopædia." In 1814, on the opening of St. George's Church, he was appointed its first pastor. Dr. Thomson took a prominent part in the Apocryphal controversy; he was keenly opposed to the Scriptures being printed along with the Apocrypha. In the General Assembly he was an eloquent debater, and leader of the Evangelical party. He died suddenly on the 9th February, 1831.

A monument denotes the grave of James Donaldson, founder of the great hospital which bears his name. Mr. Donaldson was a printer in the city. He died in October, 1830, bequeathing £200,000 for the erection and endowment of an hospital for the maintenance and education of 300 children. Donaldson's Hospital, a spacious quadrangular structure, built from a design by William H. Playfair, was completed in 1850; it is one of the most imposing erections in the city.

A tombstone celebrates the pious labours of the Rev. Henry Grey, D.D., minister of St. Mary's Church, Edinburgh. This eminent clergyman was successively minister of St. Cuthbert's Chapel, New North Church, and St. Mary's Church. To the last charge he was admitted in 1825. In the celebrated controversy in regard to the books of the Apocrypha being printed along with the authorized Scriptures, he supported the practice. In 1843 he joined the Free Church, and in the following year was elected Moderator of Assembly. On the celebration of his jubilee in 1851, several bursaries were endowed in the Free Church College in association with his name. He died on the 13th January, 1859, in the eighty-first year of his age and fifty-ninth of his ministry.

The Rev. William Innes, D.D., minister of Elder Street Church, is commemorated by an obelisk. This reverend gentleman was son of the Rev. James Innes, minister of Yester. He was licensed to preach in 1792, and in the following year was appointed minister of the second charge of Stirling. With Mr. Robert Haldane, of Airthrey, he associated in his religious enterprises. Having adopted sentiments of Independency, he tendered the resignation of his charge, but he was deposed from the ministry in October, 1799. He accepted an educational and ministerial appointment at Dundee; but a controversy having arisen on the subject of baptism, he adhered to those who preferred the adult mode, and removed to Edinburgh. In that city, beside ministering to a congregation in Elder Street, he conducted business as a bookseller. He died on the 3rd March, 1855, at the age of eighty-five. Dr. Innes was author of numerous publications, chiefly theological.

A tombstone denotes the burial-place of William Home Lizars, the eminent engraver, who died on the 30th March, 1859; and of his brother John Lizars, surgeon, who died on the 21st May, 1860.

A small monument commemorates Thomas de Quincy. This distinguished writer was born in Manchester, on the 15th August, 1786. He was educated at Oxford, and, being possessed of an independent fortune, he early established his residence at the Lakes of Cumberland. In 1819 he removed to Lasswade, near Edinburgh. He died at Edinburgh, on the 8th December, 1859. De Quincy was a brilliant magazine writer—his articles being pervaded by genial humour and curious speculation. His most celebrated work is "The Confessions of an Opium-eater." His habits were eccentric; he frittered away a fine fortune, and reduced himself to indigence.

A plain mural monument is inscribed with the name of James Alexander Haldane. This gentleman, the younger of two remarkable brothers, was born at Dundee, on the 14th July, 1768. His father, Captain James Haldane, of Airthrey, died a fortnight before his birth, and his early upbringing devolved on his mother, a woman of eminent piety. He was educated at the High School and University of Edinburgh; and in his seventeenth year entered the service of the East India Company as a midshipman on board the *Duke of Montrose*. At sea the religious impressions of his youth were some time forgotten, but afterwards returned with resistless efficacy. In his 25th year, when he became commander of the *Melville Castle*, he caused public worship to be celebrated on board, and Bibles and religious publications to be distributed among his men. He subsequently resigned his appointment; and, returning to Edinburgh, began to preach as an itinerant. During the summer of 1797, he made a missionary tour in the northern counties. He was afterwards ordained to the pastorate of Circus Chapel, Edinburgh. He latterly adopted Baptist views. Captain Haldane died on the 8th February, 1851, in his eighty-fourth year. He published several theological and other works.

A tombstone, with a sculptured medallion, commemorates George Meikle Kemp, architect of the Scott Monument. This ingenious person was born early in the century, on the southern slope of the Pentland Hills. The son of a shepherd, he received a very ordinary education, and while still young was apprenticed to a joiner. He early devoted himself to the study of Gothic architecture, and performed long journeys to examine remarkable specimens of the art. He spent some time on the Continent examining the more celebrated Gothic structures. Returning to Edinburgh in 1825, he occupied himself with architectural drawing, and in this line obtained considerable employment from the leading architects. In 1838, when premiums were offered for the best design for a monument to Sir Walter Scott, he became a competitor, and was ultimately successful. His design has been described (See *ante*). When the foundation stone of the monument was laid on the 15th August, 1840, Mr. Kemp was appointed superintendent of building operations. On the evening of Wednesday, the 6th March, 1844, while proceeding along the Union Canal to meet some boats laden with stones for the monument, he missed his footing in the darkness of the night and fell into the canal, where he perished. His remains were accompanied to St. Cuthbert's burying-ground by a large number of the citizens. On his tombstone these lines have been inscribed:—

> "Hope still cheers us while we mourn;
> Fame strews laurels o'er his urn;
> See yon structure cleave the sky;
> Dream not genius e'er can die."

There is a monument in this churchyard to John Lee, D.D., Principal of the University of Edinburgh. This distinguished divine was born of humble parents at Stow, Edinburghshire, in 1780. He studied medicine, passed as M.D., and became surgeon apothecary in a military hospital. He afterwards qualified himself for the ministry, and preached in London. In 1808 he was presented to the church of Peebles, and four years thereafter became Professor of Church History at St. Andrews. In 1820, he accepted the professorship of Moral Philosophy in King's College, Aberdeen, intending to lecture one-half of the session at Aberdeen, and the other at St. Andrews. His intention was changed by an overturn of the stage-coach, which nearly proved fatal to him. From St. Andrews he removed to Edinburgh to become collegiate minister of the Canongate. In 1824 he was chosen a University commissioner, and was appointed minister of Lady Yester's Church. In 1827 he was elected depute-clerk of the General Assembly; in 1828 he delivered lectures as substitute Professor of Theology in the University of Edinburgh. He was appointed, in 1830, one of the King's Chaplains. In 1835 he exchanged Lady Yester's for the Old Church, Edinburgh. In 1837 he became Principal of the United College, St. Andrews. In 1838 he was named secretary of the Bible Board. The Deanery of the Chapel Royal, and principalship of Edinburgh University, came in 1840. In 1843 the professorship of Divinity was added to the principalship. In 1844 he was both Moderator and Principal Clerk of the General Assembly. He died on the 2nd May, 1859, in his eightieth year, and the fifty-second of his ministry. His lectures on the "History of the Church of Scotland," published posthumously, are a valuable contribution to ecclesiastical history.

On a tombstone commemorative of his wife and two infant sons, Mr. William Penney, advocate (now Lord Kinloch), has inscribed these lines :—

> "Sacred to memory not alone,—
> Love hath a wider scope,
> Through mercy made by faith its own;
> Sacred not less to hope."

A tombstone celebrates George Lorimer, Dean of Guild, who died 13th January, 1865. Mr. Lorimer is also commemorated by a mural monument in the vestibule of St. Giles' Church (See *ante*).

A tombstone commemorates certain members of the family of Ferrier. James Ferrier, one of the principal clerks of Session, died on the 18th January, 1829. His son, John Ferrier, W.S., died on the 23rd November, 1852; his wife, Margaret Wilson, sister of Professor John Wilson, died on the 5th January, 1853. Their son, James Frederick Ferrier, Professor of Moral Philosophy at St. Andrews, whose name is also recorded on this tombstone, attained a first rank among Scottish metaphysicians. He was born at Edinburgh, in November, 1808, studied at the Universities of Edinburgh and Oxford, and in 1832 was called to the Scottish Bar. He did not seek legal practice, but dedicated himself sedulously to literature. He was elected to the chair of Universal History at Edinburgh, and some years afterwards was preferred to the professorship of Moral Philosophy at St. Andrews. His celebrated work, "The Institutes of Metaphysics," appeared in 1854. Professor Ferrier died at St. Andrews, on the 11th June, 1864. His remains were interred in the Cathedral churchyard of that city.

The other notable persons commemorated in St. Cuthbert's Churchyard, are the following:—

The Rev. Thomas Pitcairnes, minister of St. Cuthbert's from 1735 to 1751; he died on the 13th June, 1751, in the thirty-second year of his ministry. Mrs. Mary Megget, daughter of William, 5th Lord Cranstoun, by his wife Lady Jane Ker, eldest daughter of William, 2nd Marquis of Lothian; she died on the 10th April, 1768. Mrs. Jane Bruce, widow of Captain Andrew Bruce, who died on the 10th August, 1794. The Rev. James Robertson, Professor of Oriental Languages in the University of Edinburgh, who died the 26th November, 1795. James Erskine, of Alva, senator of the College of Justice, by the title of Lord Alva, who died on the 17th May, 1796. Sir John Ogilvy, 5th Baronet of Innerquharity, who died in March, 1802. The Rev. David Black, minister of Lady Yester's, who died on the 25th February, 1806, in his forty-fourth year and twenty-first of his ministry. Bain Whyte, writer to the Signet, who died in 1818. George Winton, architect, who died on the 30th November, 1822. Henry Dewar, of Lassodie, who died on the 19th January, 1823. David Steuart, Lord Provost of Edinburgh, who died 19th May, 1824. Lieutenant-Colonel George Hutchison, who died 24th July, 1828. Alexander Sutherland, author of "Tales of a Pilgrim," and editor of the *Edinburgh Observer*, who died on the 30th June, 1831. The Rev. Thomas Snell Jones, minister of Lady Glenorchy's Chapel, who died the 3rd March, 1837, in his eighty-third year and fifty-eighth of his ministry. Francis Georgiana Vans, daughter of Robert Vans Agnew, of Barnbarrow, Wigtonshire, who died the 18th February, 1840. Sir Richard Bemptde-Johnstone Honyman, Baronet, of Armadale, who died on the 24th February, 1842. The Rev. Archibald McLean, pastor of the Baptist Church, Edinburgh, who died December 21st, 1842. Sir William Drysdale, of Pitteuchar, who died on the 4th June, 1843. John Montgomerie Bell, Sheriff of Kincardineshire, who died 11th May, 1844. John Alexander, M.D., first physician to the Queen for Scotland, who died 14th November, 1844. Rear-Admiral James Haldane Tait, who died

7th August, 1845. George Murray, Captain 52nd Regiment, and 4th son of Sir Patrick Murray, of Ochtertyre, who died 24th February, 1866. Robert Louis, of Plean, who died 2nd September, 1856. George Ross, advocate, son of Admiral Sir John Lockhart Ross, Bart., of Balnagowan, who died on the 17th March, 1861.

A handsome mausoleum commemorates several members of the family of Gordon, of Cluny.

CHURCHYARD OF ST. JOHN'S EPISCOPAL CHURCH.

Among the eminent persons who have been commemorated in this churchyard, may be first named Sir Henry Raeburn. This distinguished painter was born at Stockbridge, Edinburgh, on the 4th March, 1756. His parents having died while he was still young, he was educated by his brother William, who apprenticed him to a goldsmith. He began to paint miniatures, which being in demand, he was encouraged to execute portraits in oil. With letters from Sir Joshua Reynolds he proceeded to Italy, where he prosecuted artistic studies for two years. Returning to Edinburgh in 1787, he established himself as an artist. He painted the portraits of most of his distinguished contemporaries. Many of his portraits have been engraved. He was elected member of the leading academies of Europe; and in 1822 received the honour of knighthood. He died on the 8th July, 1823.

A monument commemorates Neil, 3rd Earl of Rosebery, K.T., who died 25th March, 1814; also his Countess.

The Rev. Archibald Alison, author of "Essays on the Nature and Principles of Taste," rests in this churchyard. This eminent divine was born at Edinburgh, in 1757; he studied at the University of Glasgow, and became an Exhibitioner at Baliol College, Oxford. After holding some ecclesiastical preferments in

England, he was in 1800 elected minister of the Episcopal Chapel, Cowgate. The congregation having removed to St. Paul's Church, York Place, he continued to officiate there till 1831, when failing health compelled him to retire from ministerial duty. Mr. Alison died on the 17th May, 1839, in his eighty-second year.

Dr. William Pulteney Alison, M.D., LL.D., eldest son of the preceding, and Professor of the Practice of Physic in the University of Edinburgh, has also here found a resting-place. He died in 1855. Professor Alison was author of various works in medical science and was much distinguished for his efforts to mitigate the sorrows of the labouring poor.

To this place of sepulture were consigned the remains of Professor Sir William Hamilton, Bart. This distinguished philosopher was born at Glasgow, in March, 1788. He studied at Glasgow College; and, obtaining a Snell exhibition, proceeded to Baliol College, Oxford, where he obtained first-class honours. In 1813 he passed advocate. After much diligent research, he established his right to the baronetcy of Hamilton, of Preston, which had remained in abeyance since 1701. In 1821 he was elected to the chair of Universal History in the University of Edinburgh; and in 1836 was preferred to the chair of Logic. He died at Edinburgh, on the 6th May, 1856. Sir William Hamilton edited the works of Thomas Reid and Dugald Stewart. Since his death his lectures and memoir have been published.

A memorial stone denotes the grave of Macvey Napier, Professor of Conveyancing in the University of Edinburgh, and successor of Francis Jeffrey as editor of the *Edinburgh Review*. Mr. Napier was son of John Macvey, of Kirkintilloch, and was born in 1777. He adopted his mother's family name of Napier. He obtained his professorship in 1825, and in 1837 was appointed one of the principal clerks of Session. In 1824 he edited a supplement to the *Encyclopædia Britannica*, in six volumes quarto. In 1829 he became editor of the *Edinburgh Review*, which he conducted for seventeen years. He died at Edinburgh, on the 11th February, 1847, in the seventieth year of his age.

The remains of Miss Catherine Sinclair, whose public monument has been noticed (See *ante*), rest in this churchyard.

In St. John's Churchyard rest the remains of Professor George Moir, the eminent lawyer and essayist. A native of Aberdeen, he studied law at the University of Edinburgh, and was called to the Bar in 1825. As a writer he first attracted public notice by an article on Spanish Literature in the *Edinburgh Review*. He was then in his twenty-fifth year; till the period of his death he continued to furnish papers to the leading serials, especially *Blackwood's Magazine*. He was in 1838 elected Professor of Rhetoric in the University of Edinburgh, an office which he resigned in 1840, when he was appointed Sheriff of Ross-shire. He was in 1858 preferred to the Sheriffship of Stirling; and was in 1864 elected Professor of Scots Law in Edinburgh University. Professor Moir died on the 19th October, 1870, aged seventy-one.

To St. John's burying-ground were consigned the remains of James Syme, the late distinguished surgeon. Professor Syme was born in Kinross-shire, where his father inherited a small estate. Having studied surgery under Liston, he settled in Edinburgh, where he attained a high reputation as a practitioner and lecturer. In 1835 he was appointed Professor of Clinical Surgery in the University. He was elected to a similar chair in University College, London, in 1847, but he resigned this post after two years, and was re-installed in his former chair at Edinburgh. He held a high reputation as a skilful operator. Of his numerous publications his work "On the Excision of Diseased Joints" has obtained a first rank. Owing to his exertions a new Infirmary is about to be reared at Edinburgh. Professor Syme died on the 26th June, 1870. He was surgeon to the Queen for Scotland.

In the interior of St. John's Church a series of elegant monumental tablets bear the following inscriptions:—

"In testimony of affection and respect for the memory of the Right Rev. Father in God, James Walker, D.D., Cambridge, late Bishop of this Diocese and Primus, his clergy and some lay friends have dedicated this monumental tablet. Born January 24th, 1770; ordained Deacon 1793; ordained Priest 1805; consecrated Bishop March 7th, 1830. Died March 5th, 1841."

"Sacred to the memory of Major General Sir John Campbell, Baronet, C.B., who served throughout the first Burmese war, under his distinguished father, Lieutenant-General Sir Archibald Campbell, Baronet, G.C.B., K.C.T.S. He commanded the 38th Regiment for fourteen years, and as Brigadier General fought at Alma and at Inkerman. He fell while gallantly leading on at the assault of the Redan, 18th June, 1855. His remains were laid in the cemetery on Cathcart's Hill, near Sebastopol. His widow dedicates this tablet, near the remains of his revered parents, to the memory of a beloved husband.

A monument has also been erected in Winchester Cathedral by the 38th Regiment, in which he served for thirty-three years, as a testimony of respect, sincere affection, and esteem.

"'Them also that sleep in Jesus will God bring with him—2 Thess. iv. 14.'"

"Sacred to the memory of Captain James Robertson, 9th Regiment Madras Native Infantry, and assistant Commissary General, third son of the late Colonel David Robertson Macdonald, of Kinloch-Moidart. Born 22nd July, 1806. He died on board the *Bucephalus* on his passage to the Cape of Good Hope, lat 25° 9' south, long. 62° 31' east, February 15th, 1851."

"This tablet is erected by Jeannette Stanley in memory of her beloved husband, Edward Stanley, senr., captain of H.M. 57th Regiment of Foot, Knight of the Tower and Sword of Portugal. Born A.D. MDCCCXVI. He fell in the Crimea, November 5th, MDCCCLIV., while in command of his regiment, and on the following day his remains were committed to a soldier's grave on Cathcart's Hill.

"'Cast down but not destroyed.'—2 Cor. iv. 9."

"In memory of Douglas Charles Turing Beatson, Lieutenant 14th Bengal Native Infantry, who hardly recovered from a wound received at Ferozeshuhur on the 21st December, 1845, was again wounded 10th February, at Sobraon, and died at Ferozepore, 16th February, 1845, aged 24. The officers of the 14th Regiment place this monumental tablet as a record of their affection and esteem for a lamented fellow soldier and friend.

"'Thou therefore endure hardness as a good soldier of Jesus Christ.'—2 Tim. ii. 3."

"Sacred to the memory of Lieutenant-Colonel Thomas Graham, youngest son of General Alexander Graham Stirling, of Duchray and Authyle, and late of the First or "The Royal Regiment," who died at Haslar Hospital on his return from the Crimea, 2nd November, 1855, in the forty-sixth year of his age and thirtieth of his service. The mortal remains of Colonel Graham rest in the family burying-ground, Port of Monteith. But this tablet has been dedicated by his brother officers to record the unchanged love and honour with which during the entire period of his service his companions in arms regarded his character and conduct. "By grace ye are saved."

"Sacred to the memory of Lieutenant James Cruikshank, 36th Regiment Madras Native Infantry, and eldest son of the late Alexander Cruikshank, Esq., of Keithock, Forfarshire. He died at sea, 16th October, 1857, aged 32 years. This tablet has been erected by his brother officers as a mark of their esteem and regard."

"This Tablet, erected by Susan Jane Ballard, is sacred to the memory of her beloved uncle, Alexander Bruere Tod, late of H.E.I.C. Civil Service, Bengal, and during twenty-five years a member of this congregation. He died "looking unto Jesus," March 20th, MDCCCLIII., aged LXVIII.
"'As in Adam all die, even so in Christ shall all be made alive.' —1 Cor. xx. 22."

"In memory of Captain Archibald Sinclair, R.N., fourth son of the Right Honourable Sir John Sinclair, Baronet. Born 20th September, 1801; died 1st June, 1859. On three occasions Captain Sinclair saved the lives of others at the immediate hazard of his own. He leaped overboard and rescued from drowning in one instance a boy, in another a seaman, and in the third an officer of his own ship.
"'I know that my Redeemer liveth.'—Job xix. 25."

"Sacred to the memory of Alex. Lawrence Tweedie, Capt. 36th Royal Madras N.I., who died on his passage from India, 19th November, 1858, aged 38 years. This tablet is erected by his brother officers, to whom he was endeared by many amiable qualities, in token of their esteem and regard."

"This tablet records the deaths (within a space of two months) of a father and mother whose beloved memory seven orphan children cherish and revere. Rupert John Cochrane, Esq., of Halifax, N.S.,

ST. JOHN'S CHURCHYARD.

died in London, 28th June, 1851, aged 50 years; and was buried at Battersea. Isabella Maccomb Cochrane, of New York, United States, America, died in Edinburgh, 3rd September, 1851, aged 42 years; and was buried in the Dormitory attached to this chapel.

"'The Lord gave and the Lord hath taken away: blessed be the name of the Lord.'—Job i. 21."

"Sacred to the memory of Elizabeth Bannerman, Dowager Lady Ramsay, eldest daughter and co-heiress of the late Sir Alexander Bannerman, of Elsick, Bart., and widow of Sir Alexander Ramsay, of Balmain, Bart. Born April vii., MDCCLXVI.; died December xi., MDCCCXLIV.

"'She stretched out her hand to the poor.'—Prov. xxxi. 20."

"This tablet is erected by four surviving children to the loved and honoured memory of their parents, Captain William Hunter, H.E.I.C.S. Died instantaneously within this house of God, Sunday, April 30th, 1843. Mary Knox, his wife, died at Ryde, Isle of Wight, February 2nd, 1850.

"'Blessed are the pure in heart, for they shall see God.'—St. Matt. v. 8."

"To the honoured memory of Captain John Woodburn, 44th Bengal Native Infantry, and Commandant of the 5th Disciplined Hindostanee Regiment of Infantry, in the service of His Majesty the late Shah Soojah Ool Moolk, who nobly fell at the head of a small band of devoted followers in action with an overpowering number of Ghilzie insurgents, near Ghuznee, in Affghanistan, on the 4th of November, 1841. This cenotaph has been erected by the surviving British officers of that service, friends and companions in arms, who deeply lamented his untimely fate, knew and admired his great skill as a soldier, his sterling worth and honesty as a man."

"Sacred to the memory of Sir John Robison, R.N., late Secretary to the Royal Society of Edinburgh, who, inheriting from his father an ardent love of philosophy, was like him distinguished in the pursuit of physical science. Died vii. March, MDCCCXLIII. This tablet is erected by two surviving children to the beloved memory of a kind and affectionate father."

"In memory of Mary Ann, the beloved wife of Major General Mayne, C.B. Born 1st January, 1795; died 29th June, 1841. This monumental tablet is erected by her bereaved husband as a tribute of his love and affection."

By all who venerate wisdom, sanctity, and virtue, let this stone be held for ever sacred in memory of the Right Reverend Daniel Sandford, D.D. in the Scottish Episcopal Communion, Bishop of Edinburgh, to record the gratitude of a Church, which to his piety, prudence, and meekness, was mainly indebted for its union and prosperity, and of a congregation which for thirty-eight years he led by teaching and example in the ways of truth, peace and godliness. This monumental tablet was erected by the vestry of the chapel of St. John. Born July 1st, 1766; died January 14th, 1830.

The following brief sketch of Bishop Sandford has been kindly supplied by Dean Ramsay:—

"Daniel Sandford was second son of Rev. Dr. Sandford, Shropshire; he was born at Delville, near Dublin, the residence of Dean Delany, in 1766. His father held preferment in the Irish Church. He represented a very ancient family in Norfolk; he served long in the Irish Church, and died early in life. His widow was sister-in-law of Mrs. Chapone, of literary celebrity. An able woman, she took much pains in the education and upbringing of her family. The well-known Mrs. Harriet Bowdler was her intimate friend, and was the friend of Daniel, her son, for sixty years.

Daniel was educated at Southampton under the charge of a clergyman; and entered a commoner at Christ Church, Oxford, in 1789. Among his friends and associates were the late Earl of Liverpool and Lord Bexley. Distinguished as an accurate and accomplished scholar, he won the Christ Church prize for Latin composition. During vacation, at the Duchess of Portland's, he became a zealous student of botany; he was also a capital rower. Mr. Sandford in 1790 married Miss Douglas, a near connection of the Queensberry family; the same year he was admitted to holy orders. He came to Edinburgh in 1792: he was intimate with Blair, Robertson, Dugald Stewart, Playfair, and other eminent literary Scottish characters. Charlotte Chapel, in Rose Street, was opened for Divine service under his ministry in 1797. It was said that Mr. Sandford's preference for the Church lost him a bequest of £70,000 from an eccentric old relative. For some time he officiated out of the jurisdiction of Scottish Bishops. He joined the Episcopal Church of Scotland in 1803. He was himself consecrated a Bishop of the Church in 1806. In 1818 he became incumbent of the beautiful church of St. John's. His acceptance of the Scottish Episcopate, it is supposed, prevented his having English preferment. He had always very delicate health, and died 1st January, 1830, in full faith and hope. Bishop Sandford's character as a scholar, divine, and Christian is well portrayed in the work published by his son, Archdeacon Sandford. He was an acceptable and serious preacher. His deep and earnest study was the Greek New Testament, of which he was an accurate and judicious critic. He published during his lifetime sermons, and after his death his son, the Archdeacon, published extracts from his diary, which he kept with great care for many years, and which forms a very accurate picture of his mind and opinions. His son, Sir Daniel Sandford, Professor of Greek in Glasgow college, was one of the most distinguished scholars of his time."

In St. John's Church are many elegant memorial windows. Among these are windows commemorative of George, Earl of Morton, who died 31st March, 1858; Baron Clerk Rattray, of Craighall; W. W. Hay Newton, of Newton; and "Isabella, for twenty-nine years the beloved and faithful wife and friend of Edward B. Ramsay, Incumbent of St. John's." In the churchyard is commemorated Sir William Arbuthnot, Bart., Lord Provost of Edinburgh, who died in 1829. In the "Dormitory" of the church were deposited the remains of Mrs. Anne Scott, wife of Walter Scott, Writer to the Signet, and mother of Sir Walter Scott, Bart., the illustrious novelist. She died on the 24th December, 1819.

LADY YESTER'S CHURCHYARD.

Lady Yester's Church was founded by Margaret, Lady Yester, previous to her death, 15th March, 1647. According to Monteith, her ladyship was thus commemorated "on the north side of the vestiary":—

> " It's needless, to erect a marble tomb:
> The daily bread, that for the hungry womb,
> And bread of life thy bounty hath provided,
> For hungry souls, all times to be divided;
> World-lasting monuments shall reare,
> That shall endure, till Christ himself appear.
> Pos'd was thy life; prepar'd thy happy end;
> Nothing, in either, was without commend.
> Let it be the care of all who live hereafter,
> To live, and die, like Margaret Lady Yester:
> Who died 15th March, 1647. Her age 75."

Lady Yester was third daughter of William Kerr, 3rd Earl of Lothian, and wife of James, 7th Lord Yester.

In the churchyard, according to Monteith, a monument was thus inscribed:—

"Hic, aut alibi, forsan nullibi, condenda sunt ossa Joannis Mackenzie, et Margaretae Hay, sortis humanae sociorum, casta cura radamantium, fidei praemia, non morum, humili spe praestolantium. Hoc quippe quadrum, in ulnas quinque patens, ab urbico senatu, sibi suisque sepeliundis impetrarunt, anno solis justitiæ. MDCCII."

The inscription has been thus rendered:—

"Here, or elsewhere, perhaps nowhere, are to be laid up the bones of John Mackenzie and Margaret Hay, mutually loving with chaste care—rewards of their faith, not works in humble hope expecting. For this square place, extending to five elnes, from the town council, to bury them and their heirs they obtained in the year of the Sun of Righteousness 1702."

LADY GLENORCHY'S CHAPEL.

Above the pulpit a monumental tablet commemorates Willielma Maxwell, Viscountess Glenorchy, founder of the church. The inscription is as follows:—

"In memory of that most excellent lady, Willielma Maxwell, Viscountess Glenorchy. Few characters in the religious world were better known or more universally and justly respected. Her many amiable personal qualities and superior understanding, improved by education, genuine religion, reading and experience, greatly endeared her to her numerous acquaintance, her family and select friends. And this house, with several other places of worship in Scotland and England, founded by her, together with large sums she bequeathed to the Society for Promoting Christian Knowledge, will be a lasting monument how much she had at heart the glory of the Redeemer, and the best interests of mankind. She died July 13th, 1786, aged 43, and her remains are deposited in the centre of this church. This monument was erected as a tribute of respect by her executrix, Lady Maxwell."

Lady Glenorchy was daughter and co-heir of William Maxwell of Preston, and wife of John Lord Glenorchy, son of John, third Earl of Breadalbane. Zealously interested in religious concerns, she devoted herself, after the death of her husband in 1771, to the erection and endowment of places of worship in the localities in which she happened to reside. A memoir of her life, with extracts from her Diary and Correspondence, was published in 1822 by the Rev. Thomas Snell Jones, D.D., minister of her chapel at Edinburgh.

BUCCLEUCH CHURCHYARD.

In the burial-ground attached to Buccleuch Church (formerly St. Cuthbert's Chapel of Ease) are several interesting memorial stones. Among those associated with the names of prominent persons are the following:—

A mural tablet in memory of Dr. Thomas Blacklock, with the following Latin inscription, composed by Dr. Beattie:—

"Viro Reverendo Thomæ Blacklock, D.D., Probo, Pio, Benevolo, Omnigenâ Doctrinâ Erudito, Poetæ sublimi; ab incunabulis usque oculis capto, at hilari, faceto, amicisque semper carissimo; qui natus xxi. Novemb., MDCCXX., obiit vii. Julii, MDCCXCI: Hoc Monumentum Vidua ejus Sara Johnston, mœrens P."

Deprived of eyesight in his childhood, Dr. Blacklock compensated for his misfortune by composing verses and cherishing the society of his ingenious and learned contemporaries. One of the first to recognise the genius of Robert Burns, it was owing to his counsel that the great Scottish bard relinquished his intention of leaving his native country. Dr. Blacklock was ordained minister of Kirkcudbright in April, 1762, but owing to oppositions from his parishioners, he demitted the charge in October, 1765. He afterwards resided at Edinburgh, where he died on the 7th July, 1791, in his seventieth year. Dr. Blacklock was much esteemed for his conversational powers, and was beloved for his benignity.

At the north-east corner of the churchyard a tombstone is inscribed—

"To the memory of Mrs. Alison Rutherfurd,* widow of Patrick Cockburne, Esq., Advocate, who died 22 November, MDCCXCIV., and of her son Captain Adam Cockburne, who died 22 August, MDCCLXXX."

Mrs. Cockburn composed the song beginning,—

"I've seen the smiling of fortune beguiling."

Daughter of Robert Rutherfurd of Fernylee, Selkirkshire, she was born about 1710. In 1731 she married Patrick Cockburn, youngest son of Adam Cockburn of Ormiston, Lord Justice Clerk, who died 16th April, 1735, in his seventy-ninth year. Patrick was admitted advocate in January, 1728; he died at Musselburgh on the 29th April, 1755. Mrs. Cockburn survived her husband

* The Christian name of this gentlewoman has been a source of difficulty to her biographers. She is styled Alicia in the Index of Johnson's "Musical Museum," and Sir Walter Scott describes her as Mrs. Catherine Cockburn.

upwards of forty years. Personal recollections of her, communicated by Sir Walter Scott to Mr. Robert Chambers will be found in his "Scottish Songs" (Edinburgh, 1829).

A mural tablet commemorates David Herd, editor of the collection of "Scottish Songs" which bears his name. Herd was born at Balmakelly, parish of Marykirk, Kincardineshire, on the 23rd October, 1732.* Though descended on his mother's side from the old family of Low of Balmakelly, he was uninfluenced by ambition, and did not attain a position higher than that of clerk to an accountant. His tombstone is thus inscribed:—

"Near this stone are interred the remains of Mr. David Herd, writer; a man of probity, of a kind and friendly disposition, of mild, tolerant principles, and a taste in ancient Scottish literature. Not solicitous to shine nor anxious to become rich, he lost few friends and made few enemies. These qualities had their influence, for they averted many of the wants and evils of declining years. He died a bachelor, aged eighty-six, upon the 10th of June, 1810."

On the east wall a tablet is inscribed,—

"The burial-place of Flora, eldest daughter of Macleod of Rasay, wife of Colonel James Mure Campbell of Rowallan, county of Ayr. She died 8th September, 1780, a few hours after giving birth to her only child, Flora, who afterwards became Countess of Loudoun."

About the centre of the north wall rest the mortal remains of Dr. Alexander Adam, rector of the High School. A mural tablet is thus inscribed:—

"Memoriæ sacrum Alexandri Adam, florentissimæ scholæ regiæ Edinensis, per annos xl. et amplius rectoris indefessi, meritissimi; viro ingenio, doctrina, industria, literarum suavitate penitus imbuti insignis, quas ipse et præceptis, et exemplo, mira felicitate discipulis suis commendavit. Natus viii. cal. Julii, 1741, obiit xv. Januarii, 1810; eodem die quo filius ejus natu maximus efferebatur."

Dr. Adam was born of humble parents in the parish of Rafford, Elginshire. In his seventeenth year he proceeded to the University of Edinburgh. During the first portion of his attendance he endured

* We have ascertained the correct date of his birth from the register of his native parish. It has been misstated.

the utmost privation. In his nineteenth year he was elected head master of Watson's Hospital, and in 1768 was promoted to the Rectorship of the High School. His "Principles of Latin and English Grammar" appeared in 1772, and his "Roman Antiquities" in 1791. He died on the 18th December, 1809, in his sixty-eighth year. His remains were honoured with a public funeral. Dr. Adam introduced the study of Greek into the High School, and greatly extended the educational reputation of that seminary.

A tombstone commemorates Andrew Duncan, senior, M.D. This eminent physician was born at St. Andrews, on the 17th October, 1744. Having passed surgeon, and obtained his degree of M.D., he began in 1774 to deliver lectures at Edinburgh on the Theory of Medicine. In 1790 he was elected President of the College of Physicians. Soon afterwards he obtained the chair of the Institutions of Medicine in the university. In 1821 he was appointed first physician to the king for Scotland. He died on the 5th July, 1828. Besides providing valuable contributions to medical literature, Dr. Duncan founded a public dispensary and the Horticultural Society of Edinburgh. He also established the Royal Lunatic Asylum at Morningside.

A tombstone commemorates the Rev. Robert Hamilton, D.D., Professor of Divinity in the university. Dr. Hamilton was son of the Rev. William Hamilton, minister of Cramond, subsequently Professor of Divinity at Edinburgh. He was born on the 19th May, 1707. Educated at the High School and University of Edinburgh, he obtained licence in 1730, and in 1731 was ordained to the ministry at Cramond. In 1736 he was translated to Lady Yester's Church, Edinburgh. He was promoted to Old Greyfriars in 1750, and in 1754 was elected Professor of Divinity. He was chosen Moderator of the General Assembly in 1754, and was again elected to the chair in 1760. In 1766 he was appointed Dean of the Order of the Thistle. He died on the 3rd April, 1787, in the eightieth year of his age, and fifty-seventh of his ministry.

Tombstones commemorate the Rev. Janes Bain, of the family of Easter Livilands, Stirlingshire; James Stormouth, of Lednathy,

W.S., who died 20th October, 1817; and Thomas Riddell, yr., of Carrieston, who died 18th April, 1826.

Henry Francis Duncan, who died in 1805, in his fourteenth year, is thus commemorated:—

> "If rising virtues claim the poet's tear;
> If worth, if genius wake soft pity's sigh,
> Who will not weep o'er Henry's youthful bier?
> Who will not grieve that worth like his should die?
>
> "Sweet youth, farewell! yet long we'll mourn thy doom,
> Long kindle incense at affection's shrine;
> And oft we'll wander to thy early tomb,
> And oft in sorrow read this tender line.
>
> "Here Henry rests, a youth beloved by all,
> His parents' hope amid declining years;
> More could I say, but friendship's sacred call
> Demands this tribute of my bursting tears."

CANONGATE CHURCHYARD.

Canongate Churchyard contains much honoured dust. Here is the simple gravestone erected by Robert Burns over the remains of the poet, Robert Fergusson. The following inscription, composed by Burns, is engraved upon it:—

"Here lies Robert Fergusson, Poet, born September 5th, 1751, died October 16th, 1774.

> "No sculptured marble here, nor pompous lay,
> 'No storied urn, nor animated bust.'
> This simple stone directs Pale Scotia's way
> To pour her sorrows o'er her Poet's dust."

On the back are these words:—"By special grant of the Managers to Robert Burns, who erected this stone, this burial-place is ever to remain sacred to the memory of Robert Fergusson." Fergusson's reputation as a poet has considerably waned; his compositions are seldom read. He was intended for the Church, but he subsequently sought employment as a clerk. Before his twentieth year he contributed verses to Ruddiman's *Weekly Magazine*. Fond of society which his power of song enabled him to adorn, he fell into habits of dissipation and became insane. He died in a lunatic asylum at the age of twenty-four.

Alexander and John Runciman, brothers, eminent as historical painters, are commemorated in this churchyard. Alexander was born at Edinburgh in 1736. In 1750 he became apprentice to a firm of house-painters; after various experiences he established himself as an historical painter in the city. Through the patronage of Sir James Clerk, of Penicuik, he was afterwards sent to Italy. On his return in 1771 he was appointed Master of the Academy for Drawing lately established at Edinburgh. The paintings in the hall of Penicuik are his greatest work. He died suddenly on the 21st October, 1785. John Runciman died in his twenty-fourth year while on a professional visit to Naples in 1768. An elegant tablet with medallion busts of the brothers was placed in the west wall of Canongate Church in 1866 at the expense of the Royal Scottish Academy. The sculpture was executed by Mr. Brodie.

In Canongate Churchyard were deposited the remains of Dr. Adam Smith the distinguished Political Economist. He was born at Kirkcaldy on the 5th June, 1723. In his third year he was stolen by gipsies, but was soon recovered by a relative. Of a delicate constitution, he evinced an early aptitude for reading, with a singularly retentive memory. He studied at the University of Glasgow and at Baliol College, Oxford. Disappointed in obtaining suitable employment in England, he returned to Kirkcaldy in 1746. In 1751 he was elected Professor of Logic in Glasgow University; he was subsequently preferred to the chair of Moral Philosophy in the same college. He published his "Theory of Moral Sentiments" in 1759, which was followed by his treatise on the origin of languages. In 1763 he resigned his Professorship to accompany the young Duke of Buccleuch in Continental travel. He returned to Britain in 1766, and spent the next ten years in studious retirement. His "Inquiry into the Wealth of Nations" appeared in 1776, in two volumes, quarto. Appointed a Commissioner of Customs he established his residence in Edinburgh. He was in 1787 elected Rector of Glasgow University. He died in July, 1790.

Near the grave of Dr. Adam Smith a handsome mausoleum denotes the resting-place of Professor Dugald Stewart. This profound and amiable philosopher was born at Edinburgh on the 22nd of November, 1753. Having studied at the Universities of Edinburgh and Glasgow, he was appointed successor to his father as Professor of Mathematics in Edinburgh College. In 1785 he exchanged his chair for that of Moral Philosophy. The first volume of his "Philosophy of the Human Mind" appeared in 1792. In 1800 he added a course of lectures on Political Economy to the usual course of his chair. In 1806 he procured the sinecure office of gazette-writer, with a salary of £600 a year. He relinquished his professorship in 1810, retiring to Kinnoul House on the banks of the Forth, where he enjoyed the society of literary friends. He died at Edinburgh on the 11th June, 1828. Professor Stewart's Monument on the Calton Hill has been noticed.

An elegant monument commemorates Sir William Fettes, Bart., on two occasions' Lord Provost of Edinburgh, and founder of the institution which bears his name. Sir William died on the 27th May, 1836. His monument was reared "by the trustees of the Fettes endowment out of respect for his benevolence in making a provision for the children of his less fortunate fellow-countrymen."

A monument celebrates Walter, Lord Ogilvy, who died at Paris on the 21st March, 1824.

A tomb denotes the burial-ground of the family of Lord Macleod, now represented by the Countess of Cromartie. Within the enclosure are deposited the remains of Isabel, daughter of Sir John Gordon, Bart., of Invergordon, and relict of George, third Earl of Cromartie, who died 23rd April, 1769, and of John, Lord Macleod, son of the preceding, who died the 2nd April, 1789. Along with his father, Lord Macleod adhered to the fortunes of Prince Charles Edward. They were captured by a party of Lord Sutherland's militia at Dunrobin Castle in April, 1746, and were sent prisoners to London. Both were convicted of high treason, the Earl being sentenced to death and his estates forfeited. The capital sentence was remitted. Lord Macleod was pardoned. With the permission of the British Government he accepted military service in Sweden. He was appointed aide-de-camp to the king. Returning to Britain in 1777 he raised two battalions of Highlanders and became colonel of the 71st Foot, with which he served in India. In 1784 his estates were restored to him. Other members of the family are interred in the Canongate Churchyard.

A handsome monument perpetuates the worth and public spirit of George Drummond, Lord Provost of Edinburgh and founder of the Royal Infirmary. This benevolent and energetic individual was son of George Drummond of Newton, a cadet of the ancient house of Drummond of Stobhall. He was born on the 27th June, 1687. At the age of twenty he was appointed Accountant-General of the Excise. He gave early information of the rising under the Earl of Mar in 1715, and, joining the royal forces with a body of volunteers, fought at Sheriffmuir. In 1725 he was elected Lord Provost of Edinburgh, an office which he filled on five subsequent occasions. He established the Royal Infirmary in 1736. During the Rebellion of 1745 he again joined the army, and was present at the battle of Prestonpans. He laid the foundation-stone of the Royal Exchange in 1753, and of the North Bridge in 1763. Five professorships in the University were constituted by his enterprise. He died on the 4th December, 1766, in his eightieth year. His remains were honoured with a public funeral. A bust of Provost Drummond was placed in the hall of the Royal Infirmary.

A tombstone has been reared in honour of John Jardine, D.D., one of the ministers of the Tron Church, Edinburgh. This eminent clergyman was son of the Rev. Robert Jardine, successively minister at Glencairn and Lochmaben, Dumfriesshire. He was born at Lochmaben on the 3rd January, 1716. Licensed as a probationer in 1736, he was ordained minister of Liberton in 1741. In 1750 he was translated to Lady Yester's Church, Edinburgh, and in 1754 was preferred to the Tron Church. He became Chaplain in Ordinary to the King, one of the deans of the Chapel Royal, and Dean of the Order of the Thistle. He died suddenly while attending the General Assembly on the 30th May, 1766, in the fifty-first year of his age and twenty-first of his ministry. Dr. Jardine projected the first *Edinburgh Review*, which was published in July, 1755, but was discontinued in the following year. By his marriage with a daughter of Lord Provost Drummond he became father of Sir Henry Jardine, who is also commemorated by a tombstone in this churchyard.

Sir Henry Jardine was born at Edinburgh on the 30th January 1766. In 1790 he passed as a Writer to the Signet, and three years afterwards was appointed Solicitor for Taxes in Scotland. In 1820 he became King's Remembrancer, having for many years held the deputy office. He was knighted in 1825. He died on the 11th August, 1851. Sir Henry Jardine was an ingenious antiquary and elegant scholar.

A mortuary enclosure inscribed with the single word "Ramsay" denotes the burial-place of James Ramsay, Bishop of Ross. Son of Principal Ramsay of Glasgow College; he was successively minister of Kirkintulloch and Linlithgow. In 1670 he was appointed Dean of Glasgow; and in the following year Bishop of Dunblane. In 1673 he was translated to the Bishopric of Ross. He died at Edinburgh, 22nd October, 1696.

A tombstone commemorates Charles Alston, M.D., Professor of Botany. This eminent physician was born in 1683; he studied at the University of Glasgow and afterwards at Leyden. In 1738 he was appointed to the Chair of Botany and Materia Medica in the University of Edinburgh. By his numerous medical and other scientific works he laid the foundation of that fame which Edinburgh has since enjoyed as a school of medicine. He died on the 22nd November, 1760.

Dr. John Walker, Professor of Natural History at Edinburgh, is interred in the churchyard. Son of the Rector of the Canongate Grammar School, he studied at the University of Edinburgh, and was licensed by the Presbytery of Kirkcudbright in 1754. In 1758 he was ordained to the pastoral charge of Glencross, from which he was translated to Moffat in 1762. In 1779 he was appointed Regius Professor of Natural History and Keeper of the Museum in the University of Edinburgh. Along with his academical appointment he retained his clerical office. In 1783 he was translated to Colinton. He was elected Moderator of the General Assembly in 1790. Professor Walker died on the 31st December, 1803, at the age of seventy-three.

A tombstone is consecrated to the memory of Thomas Hardy, D.D., one of the ministers of Edinburgh and Professor of Church History in the University. He was son of the Rev. Henry Hardy, minister of Culross and proprietor of Navity, Fifeshire. Licensed as a probationer in 1772, he was in the following year ordained minister of Ballingry. He was translated to the High Church, Edinburgh, in 1784, and two years afterwards was preferred to the New North Church and to the Professorship of Church History. In 1793 he was elected Moderator of the General Assembly. He died on the 21st November, 1798, in his fifty-first year. Dr. Hardy was instrumental in forming the "Society for the Benefit of the Sons of the Clergy." He was author of several works and a leader in the General Assembly.

A monument denotes the resting-place of Henrietta, Viscountess Duncan, relict of Admiral Lord Viscount Duncan of Camperdown. She was second daughter of the Right Honourable Robert Dundas of Arniston, Lord President of the Court of Session. She died at Edinburgh in December, 1822.

A monumental enclosure contains a memorial tablet in memory of Robert Suttie, fourth son of Sir George Grant Suttie of Balgone, Haddingtonshire. He died in February, 1843.

A monument celebrates Sir Robert Crawfurd Pollok, Bart., of Pollok, who died on the 7th August, 1845.

A tombstone marks the grave of Robert Forsyth, author of "Beauties of Scotland," and other works. Mr. Forsyth was born at Biggar on the 18th January, 1766. In his twentieth year he obtained licence as a preacher, but having no prospect of a settlement, he studied law and became an advocate. At the Bar he attained considerable distinction; he published several valuable works. He died in 1845. His memoir has been published.

John Ballantyne, printer and bookseller, one of the attached friends of Sir Walter Scott, is interred and commemorated in this churchyard. He was born at Kelso in 1774. Originally engaged in merchandise in his native town, he proceeded to Edinburgh in 1805, where he was sometime employed as clerk in the printing office of his brother, James. Through the good offices of Sir Walter Scott, he was in 1808 established as a partner in the firm of Ballantyne and Co., Publishers, Hanover Street. The poem of the "Lady of the Lake" was issued by this firm. John Ballantyne subsequently added to his emoluments by practising as an auctioneer. After a period of feeble health, he died at Edinburgh on the 16th June, 1821, at the age of forty-seven. He was possessed of a kind and generous nature, combined with a strong sense of humour.

On the east wall of the churchyard a monumental slab is inscribed thus :—

"Here lye the mortal remains of John Frederic Lampe, whose harmonious compositions shall outlive monumental registers, and with melodious notes, through future ages perpetuate his fame, till time shall sink into eternity. His taste for moral harmony appeared through all his conduct. On the 23rd of July, 1751, in the forty-eighth year of his age, he was summoned to join that heavenly concert with the blessed choir above, where his virtuous soul now enjoys that harmony which was his chief delight upon earth.

"In vita felicitate dignos mors reddit felices."

OLD CALTON BURIAL-GROUND.

In this place of sepulture, a monument protects the remains of David Hume, philosopher and historian; he bequeathed money for its erection.

Hume was born at Edinburgh on the 26th April, 1711. His father, Joseph Home of Ninewells, Berwickshire, was remotely connected with the noble family of Home. The philosopher (who preferred to spell his name Hume) studied at Edinburgh University with a view to the legal profession. Conceiving an aversion to the law, he attempted merchandise at Bristol; he subsequently travelled abroad, improving himself in literature. He published in 1737 his "Treatise on Human Nature," and five years afterwards two volumes of essays. Subsequent to 1745 he became guardian to the young Marquis of Annandale. He was afterwards secretary to General St. Clair during his expedition to Canada and embassy at the courts of Vienna and Turin. In 1752 he published his "Political Discourses," which attracted immediate attention. In the same year he was appointed keeper of the Advocates Library, Edinburgh, with a small salary which he devoted to charitable purposes. In 1754 he issued the first portion of his "History of England," which he completed in 1762. He went to France in 1763 as secretary to Lord Hertford's embassy. At Paris he became acquainted with Rousseau, who repaid his substantial kindness with the basest ingratitude. In 1766 he became Under Secretary of State for the Home Department; in 1769 he returned to Edinburgh, with an annual revenue of £1,000. After a period of feeble health he died on the 25th of August, 1776.

An obelisk, eighty feet in height, commemorates the Political Martyrs of 1793; it is thus inscribed :—

"To the memory of James Muir, Thomas Tyshe Palmer, William Skirving, Maurice Margarot and Joseph Gerald. Erected by the friends of Parliamentary Reform in England and Scotland, 1844. 'I have devoted myself to the cause of the people; it is a good cause; it shall ultimately prevail. It shall finally triumph.' Speech of Thomas Muir in the Court of Justiciary, on the 30th of August, 1793. 'I know what has been done these two days will be re-judged.' Speech of William Skirving in the court of Justiciary on the 7th of January, 1794."

A tombstone commemorates the Rev. John Barclay, commonly

known as the Berean. He was son of a farmer at Muthill, Perthshire. At St. Andrews University he adopted the peculiar theological views of Professor Archibald Campbell, maintaining that faith in Christ, and the assurance of personal salvation, are inseparable; that a real Christian only can or ought to pray, and that it is absurd for a believer to pray for an interest in Christ, which he ought to feel assured he already has. The public avowal of these opinions rendered Barclay obnoxious to his clerical brethren, who though not depriving him of his status as a probationer, prevented his admission into the pastoral office. Compelled to secede from the Church of Scotland, he became founder of a sect called the Bereans. He died at Edinburgh on the 29th July, 1798, at the age of sixty-five.

A tombstone commemorates the poet, Richard Gall. This short-lived bard was born at Dunbar in 1776. He was employed in the *Edinburgh Courant* printing-office, and subsequently was engaged as travelling clerk to the proprietors. At an early age he composed verses: several of his songs continue to be popular. He enjoyed the intimacy of Hector Macneil and of Thomas Campbell, author of "The Pleasures of Hope." With the poet Burns he maintained a friendly correspondence. He died of a pulmonary complaint on the 10th May, 1801, in his twenty-fifth year.

Archibald Constable, the distinguished publisher, is interred and commemorated in this churchyard. He was born on the 24th February, 1773, at Kellie, parish of Carnbee, Fifeshire. He commenced business as bookseller in High Street, Edinburgh, in 1795, and his shop immediately became the resort of persons of learning. In 1800 he started the *Farmer's Magazine,* a quarterly publication, and in 1801 became proprietor of the *Scots Magazine.* In October, 1802, he issued the first number of the *Edinburgh Review,* which greatly extended his reputation as a publisher. From his premises "The Lay of the Last Minstrel" proceeded in 1805. With few exceptions the whole of Sir Walter Scott's subsequent poems and works of fiction were produced under his auspices. In 1812 he became proprietor of the *Encyclopædia Britannica,* of which he issued the fifth edition with a supplement. He suffered insolvency in 1826, his liabilities exceeding a quarter of a million. He died on the 21st July, 1827, in his fifty-third year. Mr. Constable was a munificent patron of literature, and a generous friend. His insolvency was consequent on a monetary panic; the event shattered his health, which was never re-established.

William Blackwood, another eminent bookseller, is interred in this burial-ground. He was born at Edinburgh on the 20th November, 1776. After a long apprenticeship to a bookseller, he commenced business in 1804 on his own account. For some time he dealt in old books only. In 1816 he disposed of his stock and became publisher. He issued the first number of *Blackwood's Magazine* in April, 1817; henceforth he became one of the foremost of Scottish publishers. He died at Edinburgh on the 16th September, 1834, at the age of fifty-eight. Mr. Blackwood held office as a magistrate, and took a deep interest in civic affairs.

A handsome obelisk reared by public subscription commemorates Charles Mackay, of the Theatre Royal. Mr. Mackay was a native of Glasgow. He obtained wide celebrity for his successful personification of *Bailie Nicol Jarvie* in the drama of "Rob Roy," and for his embodiment of other creations of the author of "Waverley." He died on the 2nd November, 1857.

David Roberts, R.A., has commemorated his parents by a tombstone which is thus inscribed:—

"Sacred to the memory of John Roberts, shoemaker of Stockbridge, who died 27th April, 1840, aged eighty-six years, and was here interred. As also his wife, Christian Ritchie, who died 11th July, 1845, aged eighty-six years. There are also interred near the same spot three of their children; Christian, aged two years, Alexander, aged seven years, and John, aged nine years. This stone is erected to their memory by their only surviving son, David Roberts, member of the Royal Academy of Arts, London, who gratefully attributes much of his happiness and success in life to their parental care and solicitude, combined with the virtuous example which in their own conduct they placed before him during his early years."

By an affectionate relative a Gothic spire has been erected to the memory of Dr. George Wilson, Professor of Technology in the University of Edinburgh and Director of the Industrial Museum of Scotland. This eminent philosopher was born at Edinburgh on the 21st February, 1818. Having studied at the University of Edinburgh, and University College, London, he became Surgeon in 1837, and M.D. in 1839. For many years he delivered chemical lectures at Edinburgh in the Extra Academical School. In 1855 he was appointed Professor. He died on the 22nd November, 1859, at the age of forty-one. Dr. George Wilson's more esteemed works are his "Text-book of Chemistry," "Researches on Colour Blindness," "The Five Gateways of Knowledge," and his memoirs of John Reid, M.D., and Edward Forbes.

Professor John Playfair, whose monument on the Calton Hill has already been noticed, was interred in this churchyard. This celebrated mathematician was born at Benvie, Forfarshire, on the 10th March, 1748. In his eighteenth year he became candidate for the Professorship of Mathematics in Marischal College, Aberdeen, and though unsuccessful, highly distinguished himself in a public competition. In 1773 he was ordained minister of Liff and Benvie in succession to his father. This charge he resigned in 1782 to become tutor in the family of Ferguson of Raith. In 1785 he was appointed joint Professor of Mathematics in the University of Edinburgh, a chair which he exchanged for that of Natural Philosophy in 1805. He died on the 19th July, 1819, in his seventy-second year. His principal works are "Elements of Geometry," "Outlines of Natural Philosophy," and "Illustrations of the Huttonian Theory of the Earth."

Among the other notable persons commemorated in Old Calton burial-ground are the following :—Thomas Hamilton, Architect of the High School, Edinburgh; the Rev Thomas Thomson, minister of the Relief congregation, James Place, Edinburgh, died 16th April, 1819; Major Archibald Argyle Campbell of the 42nd Regiment, died 27th January, 1809; John Carruthers of Holmains, died 20th October, 1809; Robert Spottiswood, a field officer in the service of the East India Company, died 31st August, 1828; John

Boyd of Maxpoffle, died 22nd July, 1861; and the Rev. John Dunlop Paxton, minister at Musselburgh, died 10th January, 1864. A mortuary enclosure protects the remains of several members of the family of the Rev. Dr. Robert S. Candlish, minister of Free St. George's Church, and Principal of the New College.

NEW CALTON BURIAL-GROUND.

New Calton Burial-ground is separated from "the old" by Regent's Road. A tombstone commemorates David Allan, the eminent historical painter. Born at Alloa on the 13th February, 1744, he early displayed artistic tastes, and by some opulent persons in Clackmannanshire was sent to Rome, where he remained sixteen years. He afterwards resided in London. In 1786 he was appointed successor to Alexander Runciman as Director of the Academy of Art, Edinburgh. His edition of "The Gentle Shepherd" with characteristic etchings appeared in 1783. He died at Edinburgh on the 6th August, 1796.

A monument celebrates the memory of the Rev. Dr. John Inglis, minister of Old Greyfriars. This distinguished divine was youngest son of the Rev. Harry Inglis, minister of Forteviot, and was born in 1763. Having studied at the University of Edinburgh he was licensed to preach in 1785. In 1786 he was ordained to the pastoral charge of Tibbermuir. To Old Greyfriars Church, Edinburgh, he was translated in 1799. In 1804 he was chosen Moderator of the General Assembly. He died at Edinburgh on the 2nd January, 1834. Dr. Inglis published an able work on the "Evidences of Christianity" and a "Vindication of Ecclesiastical Establishments." He originated the General Assembly's scheme of India Missions.

By a monument is commemorated Sir William Miller, of Barskimming, Bart., Lord Glenlee. Son of Sir Thomas Miller, Bart.,

NEW CALTON BURIAL-GROUND.

Lord President of the Court of Session, he was admitted Advocate in 1777, and raised to the bench in May, 1795. He retired from his public duties in 1840, and died in 1846. Lord Glenlee was a sound lawyer and an intelligent antiquary.

A handsome mausoleum records the worth and genius of Robert Stevenson, the eminent engineer. Mr. Stevenson was born at Glasgow on the 8th June, 1772. He was at first intended for the ministry, but afterwards devoted himself to engineering, in which he was encouraged by his step-father, whom he succeeded as Superintendent of Northern Lighthouses. He erected twenty-three lighthouses, that of the Bell Rock being his principal work. He proved the superiority of malleable iron rods for railways over those of cast iron formerly used. Mr. Stevenson died at Edinburgh on the 12th July, 1850.

An elegant monument by Patric Park commemorates Andrew Skene, the eminent lawyer. Son of Dr. George Skene, Professor of Natural History in Marischal College, he was born at Aberdeen on the 26th February, 1784. In 1806 he passed Advocate, and soon obtained a wide practice. In 1834 he was promoted as Solicitor General. He died on the 2nd April, 1835.

In New Calton Churchyard rest the remains of Dr. David Ritchie, minister of St. Andrew's Church, and Professor of Logic in the university. Dr. Ritchie was a native of Methven, Perthshire. He was licensed to preach in 1789. In 1798 he was ordained assistant and successor at Penicuik. In 1800 he was admitted minister of the first charge, Kilmarnock; he was translated to St. Andrew's Church, Edinburgh, in the following year. In 1807 he obtained his professorial chair. He presided as Moderator of the General Assembly in 1814. Dr. Ritchie died on the 10th January, 1844.

A monument celebrates the piety and learning of Dr. John Brown, minister of Broughton Place Church, Edinburgh. This eminent divine was grandson of the Rev. John Brown, author of the "Self-Interpreting Bible," and was born in the parish of Whitburn, Linlithgowshire, on the 12th July, 1784. Having studied for the Secession Church, he was ordained to the ministry at Biggar in February, 1806. He was translated to Rose Street Church, Edinburgh, in 1822, and afterwards became pastor of the church in Broughton Place. In 1834 he was elected Professor of Exegetical Theology. He took a leading concern in several important religious movements, much to the satisfaction of his people, who on the completion of the fiftieth year of his ministry presented him with a large donation; this he generously handed to the fund for the relief of aged ministers. Dr. Brown died at Newington, Edinburgh, on the 13th October, 1858, in his seventy-fourth year. He was honoured with a public funeral. Dr. Brown's expository works are much valued.

These lines are inscribed on a tombstone erected by Thomas Ord, equestrian, in memory of Clara Jane, his infant daughter, who died on the 2nd January, 1834:—

> "The rose that decked thy cheek is dead,
> The ruby from thy lips has fled,
>   Thy body's lost its breath;
> And the pure smile that used to play
> Upon thy brow has passed away
>   Before the touch of death.
> But oh! thou wert to mortal eyes,
> Like some pure spirit from the skies,
>   Awhile to bless us given;
> And sadly pining for the day
> To spread thy wings and flee away
>   Back to thy native heaven;
> Thou wast beloved by all before,
> But now a thing that we adore."

The mortal remains of the following notable persons rest in this burial-ground:—

James Haig, of Blairhill, died 8th October, 1833; Major-General William Turner, C.B., died 29th April, 1839; Admiral Alexander Fraser, died 29th December, 1829; David Pratt, of Seggie, died 31st December, 1841; Admiral John Graham, of Coldoch, died 3rd June, 1854; William Handyside, late of St. Petersburg, died 26th May, 1850; William Fraser, of Broughton

Place, died 29th August, 1862; George Boyd, publisher, Edinburgh, died 1st February, 1843; John Hume, of the General Register House, died 7th December, 1849; Robert Kinniburgh, teacher of the Deaf and Dumb Institution, Edinburgh, died 28th August, 1851; John R. Greig, Esq., of Lethangie, died 4th July, 1859; and Colonel John Simpson, who died 20th June, 1836.

HOLYROOD ABBEY CHURCHYARD.

The Abbey Church of Holyrood was founded by David I. early in the twelfth century. Within it were crowned several kings and queens. It was the scene of the marriage of James II. to Mary of Gueldres; and of the marriage of James III. to Margaret of Denmark. Here James IV. received from the Papal Legate the purple crown and richly decorated sword which Pope Julius II. sent as gifts to that monarch. Within the fabric Mary Stuart took in wedlock the hand of Darnley. The church was frequently dilapidated. By Edward II., in 1322, it was partially demolished. It was burnt by Richard II. in 1385; mutilated by the English invaders in 1547; and stripped during the angry tumult of the Reformation. The choir and transepts have disappeared. Of the north and south aisles which remain, a large portion is paved with incised slabs—a species of sepulchral memorials common in Continental countries in the fourteenth and fifteenth centuries. Of these old memorial stones the majority are illegible and broken. The oldest legible inscription is the following, which surrounds a floriated cross with a decorated base:—

"Hic jacet dns. Robertus Cheyne, xii. prior hujusce monasterij qui obiit xvii. die Sept. An. Dni. MCCCCLV."

In the south-east corner of the chapel is the royal vault, secured with a grated iron door. Here were deposited the remains of David II.; James II.; Prince Arthur, third son of James IV.;

James V., and his first queen, Magdalene of France; Arthur, Duke of Albany, second son of James V.; and Henry, Lord Darnley. According to Fordoun, David II. died in Edinburgh Castle in 1371, and was buried near the high altar—an elaborate Latin epitaph being inscribed upon his tomb. This long since disappeared. In the Advocates Library a MS., supposed to be in the handwriting of Sir Robert Sibbald, presents the narrative of a search made in the royal vault in 1683. We present it entire:—

"Upon ye xxiv of January, MDCLXXXIII, by procurement of ye Bischop of Dumblayne, I went into ane vault in ye south-east corner of ye Abbey Church of Halyrudehouse, and yr. were present ye Lord Strathnavar and E. Forfare, Mr. Robert Scott, minister of ye Abbey, ye Bishop of Dumblayn, and some utheris. Wee viewed ye body of King James ye Fyft of Scotland. It lyeth within ane wodden coffin, and is coveret wyth ane lead coffin. There seemed to be haire upon ye head still. The body was two lengths of my staf, with two inches more, that is twae inches and mare above twae Scots elne; for I measured the staf with ane elnwand afterward.

"The body was coloured black with ye balsam that preserved it, which was like melted pitch. The Earl of Forfare took the measure with his staf lykeways. There was plates of lead, in several long pieces, louse upon and about the coffin, which carried the following inscription, as I took it from before the bishop and nobleman in ye isle of ye church:—

"Illvstris Scotorvm Rex Jacobvs Ejvs Nominis v .Etatis
Sue Anno xxxi Regni vero xxx Mortem Obüt In
Palacio De Falkland 14 Decembris Anno Dni. MDXLII
Cvjvs Corpvs Hic Traditvm Est Sepvltvre.

"Next ye south wall, in a smaller arch, lay a shorter coffin, with ye teeth in ye skull. To the little coffin in the narrow arch seemeth to belong this inscription, made out of long pieces of lead in the Saxon character:—

"Magdelena Francisci Regis Franciæ
Primo-genita Regina Scotiæ, Sponsa Jacobi V.
Regis. A.D. MDXXXVII. Obüt.

"There was ane piece of a lead crown, upon the syde of whilk I saw two *floor de leuces* gilded; and upon ye north side of ye coffin lay two children, none of the coffins a full elne long, and one of them lying within ane wod, the other only the lead coffin.

"Upon ye south syde, next the King's body, lay ane gret coffin of lead, with the body in it. The muscles of the thigh seemed to be entire; the body not so long as King James the Fyth, and ye balsam stagnating in sum quantity at ye foote of ye coffin: there appeared no inscription upon ye coffin.

"And at ye east syde of ye vaults which was at ye feet of ye other coffins, lay a coffin with the skull sawen in two, and ane inscription in small letters, gilded upon a square of ye lead coffin, making it to be ye bodye of *Dame Jane Stewart, Countesse of Argyle*, MDLXXXV., or thereby, for I do not well remember ye yeare. The largest coffin I suld suppose to be that of Lord Darnley's, and the short coffin, Queene Magdalene's."

Jane, Countess of Argyle, mentioned in this narrative, was wife of Archibald, the fifth Earl, and natural daughter of James V. by Elizabeth, daughter of John, Lord Carmichael. She was at supper with Queen Mary when Rizzio was murdered in her presence on the 9th March, 1566. At the baptism of James VI. she stood sponsor for Queen Elizabeth. After her death her body was enclosed in a magnificent coffin with gilded compartments, and was deposited in the royal vault. That vault has latterly received the dust of Mary of Gueldres, queen of James II. This munificent princess was originally interred in Trinity College Church, which was erected by her bounty; but when that structure was taken down in 1848, her remains were removed and deposited in this place. The Duchess de Grammont, of the dynasty of the Bourbons, who died in exile on the 30th March, 1803, was interred in this royal sepulchre.

Near the royal vault is the burial-place of Jane, Countess of Roxburghe, governess to the children of James VI. She died on the 7th October, 1643.

In the southern aisle a tablet on one of the pillars commemorates Adam Bothwell, Bishop of Orkney, who officiated at the marriage of Queen Mary and the Earl of Bothwell. His father, Francis Bothwell, was a senator of the College of Justice; he was one of the four bishops who embraced the Reformed doctrines.

The following is his epitaph:—

"Hic reconditus jacet nobilissimus vir, Dominus Adamus Bothuelius, Episcopus Orcadum & Zethlandiæ; commendatarius Monasterii

Sanctæ Crucis, senator & consiliarius regius: qui obiit anno ætatis suæ 67. 23 die mensis Augusti, anno Domini 1593.

> Nate, senatoris magni; magne ipse senator;
> Magne senatoris, triplice laude, parens;
> Tempore cujus opem poscens ecclesia sensit;
> Amplexa est cujus cura forensis opem;
> Vixisti, ex animi voto: jam, plenus honorum,
> Plenus opum, senii jam quoque plenus, obis.
> Sic nihil urna tui, nis membra senilia, celat;
> Teque vetat virtus vir tua magne mori,
> I fælix, mortem requie superato suprema;
> Sic, patriæ & liberis, fama perennis erit.
>   Æternum vive, atque vale."

Monteith thus translates:—

"Here lies interred a most noble man, Lord Adam Bothwell, Bishop of Orkney and Zetland; Commendator of the Monastery of Holy Rood, Senator of the College of Justice, and one of the Lords of his Majesty's Privy Council; who died in the sixty-seventh year of his age, 23rd day of the month of August, in the year of our Lord 1593."

> "Thy praise is triple, sure; thyself, thy sire,
> Thy son, all senators, whom men admire.
> The stagg'ring state by thee was quickly stayed,
> The troubled Church from thee got present aid.
> Thou livedst at thy wish; thy good old age
> In wealth and honours took thee off the stage.
> Thine aged corpse interrèd here does lie,
> Thy virtues great forbid your name to die.
> Go, happy soul, and in thy last repose
> Vanquish thou death, and all its fatal blows;
> Thy fragrant frame shall thus eternal be
> Unto thy country and posterity."

On the south wall a monument commemorates, by a short Latin inscription, Alexander Hay, of the Park family, Clerk Register and Lord of Session, under the title of Lord Easter Kennet. He obtained various offices and honours. In 1589 he accompanied James VI. to Denmark as private secretary. He died on the 19th September, 1594. His younger son, Sir Alexander Hay, became a Judge in the Court of Session, under the title of Lord Newton.

HOLYROOD ABBEY CHURCHYARD.

A mural monument, thus inscribed, commemorates Jean, Countess of Eglinton, who died in 1596:—

"D. I. H.
"Here lyes ane Nobil and maist vertuous Ladie, Deame Jeane Hamilton, Countas of Eglingtoun, Dochtor to James Duke of Schattillarot, sometyme Governor of this Realme. She deceast in December MDXCVI."

A memorial tablet celebrates Lord James Douglas, otherwise styled Sir James Douglas, of Parkhead, nephew of the Regent Morton. His wife was only child of William, Master of Carlyle; who died in the lifetime of his father, Michael, fourth Lord Carlyle. In 1596 Sir James Douglas slew James Stewart, Earl of Arran, an unworthy favourite of James VI., to avenge the wrongs of his uncle the Regent. He was, in 1608, killed in the High Street of Edinburgh, by William Stewart, Arran's nephew. His tombstone is inscribed thus:—

"Heir lyes ye noble and potent Lord James Douglas, Lord of Cairlell, air and heretrix yarof; wha was slaine in Edinburghe ye xiii day of July in ye zeier of God 1608. Was slain in 48 ze."

On the north side of the church a monumental tablet is thus inscribed:—

"D. O. M.

"Here lyeth Dame Margaret Ross, daughter to James Lord Ross; and Dame Margaret Scott, daughter of Walter Lord Buccleugh, and sister to Walter Scott, Earl of Buccleugh. She was married to Sir George Sterline, of Keir, Knight and Chief of his name; and having lived a pattern and paragon for piety and debonairitie beyond her sex and age, when she had accomplished 17 years, she was called from this transitory life to that eternal 10 March, MDCXXXIII. She left behind her an only daughter, Margaret, who in her pure innocency soon followed her mother, the 11th day of May thereafter, when she had been twelve months shown to this world, and she lyeth near unto her, interred.

"D. Georgius Sterline de Keir, eques auratus, Familiæ Princeps Conjugi dulcissimæ, poni curavit MDCXXXIII.

Though *Marble, Porphirie,* and mourning *touch*
May praise these spoils, yet can they not so much;
For beauty lost, and fame this stone doth close
One, earth's delight, heav'n's care, a spotless *Rose;*
And shouldst thou, reader, but vouchsafe a tear
Upon it, other flowers will soon appear;
Sad violets and hyacinths which grow
With marks of grief a public loss to show."

In the north-west tower an altar-tomb, formed of Italian marble, commemorates Robert, Viscount Belhaven, Master of the Horse to Charles I. This royal favourite was son of Malcolm Douglas, of Mains, and was in youth Page of Honour to Prince Henry. He gradually rose in royal favour, obtaining a succession of offices at court. By Charles I. he was raised to the rank of Privy Councillor, and was in 1633 created Viscount Belhaven. His monument was reared by Sir Archibald and Sir Robert Douglas, his nephews and heirs. A recumbent figure of his lordship, in his robes of state, and wearing a coronet, is sculptured in Parian marble. Within an arched recess is presented the following inscription:—

"D. O. M.

"Quod reliquum apud nos est, hic conditur Roberti Vice-comitis de Belhaven, Baronis de Spot etc. Regi Carolo, a secretioribus consiliis, et inter familiares intimi quippe qui et prius.

Henrico Valliæ gratissim. ejusq. stabulis præfecterat. Illo vero fatis cedente, patri Carolo nunc rerum potito, in quæsturam domus, adscitus est, singulari favoris gradu accept., re et honoribus auctus. In juventute Nicolæ Moraviæ Abercarniæ comarcho natæ ad octodecim non amplius menses unicæ uxoris in puerperio simul cum fœtu extinctæ lectissimo consortio fruebatur. Ingravescente senectute ab aulico strepitu (ut morum illico et malorum temporum pertæsus) se subtrahens in patriam reversus est. Archibaldum et Robertum Duglassios Equites auratos, primævi fratris filios, terris et bonis, præter quæ testamento legavit æqua lance divisis hæredes scripsit, qui, memoriæ ejus, gratitudinis suæ pignus, hoc monumentum poni curarunt. Ingenium quod literis cultura non implevit sagacitate natura supplevit. Indolis bonitate et candore nulli cessit facile succendi at dum loquimur facilius defervescere ei in moribus quod æque ab omnibus vix acciperetur unicum erat Fide in Regem; Pietate in Patriam Officiis in amicos charitate in egenos nulli secundus cui in prosperis modus et comitas in adversis constantia et magnanimitas ad supremum usque diem invaluere obiit Edinburgi prid idus Januarii anno ab incarnatione Messiæ supra CIƆIƆCXXXIX° ætatis vero ultra clymactericum magnum, tertio."

Lord Belhaven's epitaph has been translated thus :—

"Here are interred the remains of Robert, Lord Viscount Belhaven, Baron of Spot, &c., Counsellor to King Charles, and most intimately in favour with him, because formerly he had been most dear to Henry, Prince of Wales, and Master of his Horse. But he being dead, and Charles his brother now reigning, he was made Chamberlain to the King's household, and entertained with a singular degree of favour, and advanced to great honours and wealth. In his youth he enjoyed the sweet society of Nicolas Murray, daughter to the Baron of Abercairney, his only wife, who lived with him not above eighteen months, and died in childbed with her child. When grievous old age came upon him (as weary of bad times and customs), withdrawing himself from the noise of the court, he returned to his country. He nominated Sir Archibald and Sir Robert Douglasses, baronets, sons to his elder brother, to be his heirs, dividing equally amongst them all his lands and goods, except some legacies; and they erected this monument to his memory, as a token of their gratitude.

"Nature supplied in him by sagacity what his mind wanted of education. He was inferior to none in a good capacity and candour. He would soon be angry, but was as soon calmed. This is one thing he had in his life which scarcely could be alike acceptable to all; for loyalty towards his Prince, love to his country, kindness to his relations, and charity to the poor, he was singular. In prosperity he was meek and moderate; in adversity his constancy and magnanimity prevailed to his very end. He died at Edinburgh, on the 14th day of January, and from the incarnation of the Messiah 1639, and of his age 66, being the third year above his great climacteric."

At the north-east corner of the church a noble monument to Alexander Milne, undated, is thus inscribed:—

"Tam arte, quam marte. In clarissimum virum, *Alexandrum Milnum*, Lapicidam egregium, hic sepultum, Anno Dom. 1643, Febr. 20.

Siste Hospes; clarus jacet hoc sub Marmore *Milnus;*
Dignus cui Pharius conderet ossa labor :

> Quod vel in ære Myron fudit, vel pinxit Appelles,
> Artifice hoc potuit hic lapicida manu.
> Sex lustris tantum vixit, (sine labe,) senectam
> Prodidit, et mediam clauserat ille diem."

Monteith translates thus:—

"Here is buried a worthy man and an ingenious mason, *Alexander Milne*, 20th Feb., A.D. 1643.

> Stay, Passenger, here famous Milne doth rest,
> Worthy in Ægypt's marble to be drest;
> What Myron or Appelles could have done
> In brass or paintry—that he could in stone;
> But thretty yeares hee (blameless) lived; old Age
> He did betray, and in's prime left this stage."

An elegant mural monument commemorates George Wishart, Bishop of Edinburgh. This learned prelate was born in Haddingtonshire, in 1609. He studied at Edinburgh University, and became minister at Leith. For refusing to subscribe the Covenant, he was deposed in 1638; he afterwards suffered imprisonment for his zeal in the royal cause. Rescued from Edinburgh Tolbooth by the Marquis of Montrose, he became his lordship's chaplain, and accompanied him to the Continent. He composed an account of Montrose's military exploits in Latin. For some time after Montrose's death he held the rectory of Newcastle-on-Tyne; he was consecrated Bishop of Edinburgh in June, 1662; he died in 1671. His epitaph is as follows:—

> "Hic recubat celebris Doctor Sophocardius alter,
> Entheus ille Σοφοσ καρδιαν Agricola.
> Orator fervore pio, facundior olim
> Doctiloquis rapiens pectora dura modis.
> Ternus ut Antistes Wiseheart, ita ternus Edinen.
> Candoris columen nobile, semper idem.
> Plus octogensis hinc gens Sophocardia lustris,
> Summis hic mitris claruit, atque tholis;
> Dum cancellarius regni Sophocardius, idem
> Præsul erat Fani, Regulæ Sanctæ, tui.
> Atque ubi pro regno, ad Norham, contendit avito
> Brussius, indomita mente manuque potens;

Glasguus Robertus erat Sophocardius alter,
Pro patria, qui se fortiter opposuit.
Nec pacis studiis Gulielmo, animisve Roberto,
Agricola inferior, cætera forte prior;
Excelsus sine fastu animus, sine fraude benignus,
Largus opis miseris, intemerata fides.
Attica rara fides; constantia raraque, nullis
Expugnata, licet mille petita, malis.
In regem, obsequii exemplar, civisque fidelis
Antiquam venerans, cum probitate, fidem.
Omnibus exutum ter, quem proscriptio, carcer,
Exilium, lustris non domuere tribus.
Ast reduci Carolo plaudunt ubi regna secundo,
Doctori Wiseheart insula plaudit ovans.
Olim ubi captivus, squalenteque carcere læsus,
Annos ter ternos, præsul honorus obit.
Vixit Olympiadas terquinas; Nestoris annos
Vovit Edina: obitum Scotia moesta dolet.
Gestaque Montrosei, Latio celebrata cothurno:
Quantula (proh) tanti sunt monumenta viri!"

Monteith has produced the following translation :—

"Another famous Doctor Wiseheart, here
Divine George Wiseheart lies, as may appear;
Great orator, with eloquence and zeal,
Whereby on hardest hearts he did prevail.
Three Wisehearts, Bishops, so the third was he
When Bishop of fair Ed'nburgh's diocie.
Candour in him was noble; free of stain;
In cases all, the same he did remain—
Above four hundred years great *Wiseheart's* name,
For honours, has pure and untainted fame;
While one thereof both purse and mitre bore,
Chancellor and Bishop near St. Andrew's choir;
And when brave *Bruce* did for his nation plead
At Norham, with undaunted hand and head,
Then Robert Wiseheart sat in Glasgow's chair,
With courage for his country singular.
To those great *George* was not inferior
In peace, and war elsewhere superior.
High, without pride; his bounty had no guile,
His charity to th' poor nought could defile;
His loyalty untainted—faith most rare,
Athenian faith, was constant everywhere,
And though a thousand evils did control,

None could o'ercome his high and lofty soul—
To King and Country he was faithful still;
Was good and just, e'en from a constant will.
Thrice spoil'd and banish'd, for full fifteen years,
His mind unshaken,—cheerful still he bears.
Deadly proscription, nor the nasty gaol
Could not disturb his great seraphic soul.
But when the nation's King, Charles the Second, blest
On his return from sad exile to rest;
They then received great *Doctor Wiseheart*—he
Was welcome made, by church and laity;
And where he had been long in prison sore,
He nine years Bishop did them good therefore.
At length he dy'd in honour: where his head
To much hard usage was accustomèd.
He liv'd 'bove seventy years—and Edinburgh town
Wish'd him old *Nestor's* age in great renown;
Yea, Scotland, sad with grief, condoled his fall,
And to his merits gave just funeral.
Montrose's acts, in Latin forth he drew;
Of *one* so great, ah! monuments so few."

George, fourteenth Earl of Sutherland, is commemorated by a monument thus inscribed:—

"Memoriæ illustrissimi Domini Georgii Sutherlandiæ comitis, Strathnaverniæ, &c. Dynastæ, Sutherlandiæ et Strathnaverniæ, jure hæreditario, vicecomitis, ac regalitatis domini; ex sigilli magni custodibus unius; regi Gulielmo a secretioribus conciliis; decimi noni comitis recta linea oriundi ab Allano Sutherlandiæ thano; quem, Milcolumbo tertio, haeredi legitimo regnum restituere conantem, e medio sustulit M'Bethus; cum tyrannidem occupasset, circa annum æræ Christianæ 1057. Hoc famæ perennis monumentum deflens posuit vidua, Jeanna Vemia, filiarum Davidis comitis Vemia natu maxima; quæ huic comiti peperit Joannem nunc Sutherlandiæ comitem, & Annam Arbuthnoti vicecomitissam; priori vero marito, Archibaldo Angusiæ comiti filio marchionis Duglassiorum natu maximo, Archibaldum Forfaræ comitem, & Margaretam, vicecomiti de Kingstoun, in matrimonium datam. Quinq. alii hujus dominæ liberi impuberes decesserunt.

"Natus in arce sua de Dornach, 2do Novembris, 1633. Denatus Edinburgi 4to, Martii, 1703."

Monteith supplies the following translation:—

"To the memory of the most illustrious Lord George, Earl of

Sutherland, Lord Strathnaver, &c., heritable Sheriff of said lands, and lord of the regality thereof; one of the Keepers of the Great Seal under the most renowned Prince King William, one of the Lords of Privy Council, and the nineteenth Earl descended in a right line from Allan, Thane of Sutherland, whom Macbeth, in the rage of his usurping tyranny, about the year of Christ 1057, slew for endeavouring to restore the kingdom to Malcolm III., lawful heir to the Crown. His mournful widow, Jean Wemyss, eldest daughter to David, Earl of Wemyss, erected this monument of lasting fame.

"To the defunct Earl she brought forth John, now Earl of Sutherland, and Anne, Viscountess of Arbuthnot. And to her former husband Archibald, Earl of Angus, eldest son to the Marquis of Douglas, she brought forth Archibald, Earl of Forfar, and Margaret, given in marriage to the Viscount of Kingstown. Five other children of the said Lady Dowager died in their nonage. The Earl himself was born in his own Castle of Dornoch, 2nd November, 1633, and died at Edinburgh, 4th March, 1703."

Here are also deposited the remains of William, seventeenth Earl of Sutherland, and his amiable Countess, Mary, daughter of William Maxwell, of Preston, Kirkcudbright. His lordship died at Bath, June 16th, 1766, just after he had completed his thirty-first year; and the Countess, June 1st, 1766, in her twenty-sixth year, sixteen days before the Earl. The bodies of this illustrious and affectionate pair were brought to Scotland and interred in one grave in the Abbey Church, on the 9th August, 1766.

"Beauty and birth a transient being have,
Virtue alone can triumph o'er the grave."

A flat tombstone, adorned with the family escutcheon, commemorates Isabel, Viscountess Drumlanrig, wife of William Douglas, first Viscount Drumlanrig, afterwards Earl of Queensberry, who died in 1628. She was fourth daughter of Mark Ker, first Earl of Lothian. Her elder sister, Lady Margaret, married James, seventh Lord Yester, who in 1747 founded the church in Edinburgh which bears her name.

In a monumental recess on the south wall is interred Lady Mary Ker, Marchioness of Douglas, daughter of Robert, first Marquis of

Lothian, who died on the 22nd January, 1736, aged fifty-eight. Also her daughter, Lady Jane Douglas, born 17th March, 1698, died 22nd November, 1753, aged fifty-six. The latter married secretly, in 1746, Sir John Stewart, Bart., of Grandtully, and (as was alleged) gave birth to twin sons on the 10th July, 1748. Of these the younger, Sholto Thomas Stewart, who died at Edinburgh on the 14th May, 1758, is interred with the remains of Lady Jane. From her connection with the famous Douglas cause, her ladyship is entitled to more than a passing notice. The twin children were born when she was in her fifty-first year, and it was maintained by the guardians of the infant Duke of Hamilton, heir of the Douglas estates, that the children were obtained surreptitiously. The Court of Session decided in favour of the Duke, but its decision was reversed by the House of Lords in 1769, when the surviving son of Lady Jane Douglas took possession of the estates.

A plain altar-tomb commemorates George, fifth Baron Reay, and Elizabeth, Baroness Reay, his second wife :—

"Under this stone
Are laid the remains of
The late Right Honourable George, Lord Reay,
And Elizabeth Fairley, his wife.
In the grave thus undivided,
As in life they were united in that divine bond
Of Christian Faith and Love,
Which ennobled their earthly affection,
By elevating each view and desire
In one undeviating course,
Towards another and a better world.

"George Lord Reay died 27th February, 1768, aged thirty-four; Elizabeth Lady Reay died 10th November, 1800, aged sixty-one. This stone is inscribed, January, 1810, in token of grateful respect and affection, by their daughters, the Honourable Mrs. H. Fullarton and the Honourable Georgina M'Kay."

An inscription on the tombstone of Thomas Lowes, of Ridley Hall, proceeds thus :—

"Here lies the body of Thomas Lowes, Esq., late of Ridley Hall, in the county of Northumberland; one instance among thousands of the uncertainty of human life and the instability of earthly possessions and enjoyments. Born to ample property, he for several years experienced a distressing reverse of fortune; and no sooner was he restored to his former affluence, than it pleased Divine Providence to withdraw this, together with his life. Reader, be thou taught by this to seek those riches which never can fail, and those pleasures which are at God's right hand for evermore—the gracious gift of God, and to be enjoyed through faith in Jesus Christ our Saviour. An only daughter, over whom the deceased had long watched with the tenderest care, and many friends who admired his liberal and generous mind, unite in deploring his loss. He departed this life on the eighteenth day of September, in the year of our Lord 1812, and in the sixty-first year of his age."

In the centre of the southern aisle a plain altar-tomb denotes the resting-place of Isabella, Countess Dowager of Errol. It is thus inscribed :—

"In memory of Isabella, Countess Dowager of Errol, daughter of Sir William Carr, of Etall, Bart., and widow of James, fourteenth Earl of Errol, whose life was passed in the discharge of all the duties which religion prescribes, and closed in all the hopes which it inspires. This stone is inscribed by her grateful and affectionate daughter, Augusta Carr, Countess of Glasgow. She was born March 31, 1742, and died November 3, 1808."

At the east end of the chapel a monumental tablet celebrates the deceased in Latin and English, thus :—

"Gulielmo Gramo de Hilton et Margaretæ Stuartæ consorti suæ, suisque terrena animæ indumenta cum fata vocaverint, hic deponi concessum fuit 6to cal. Sept., 1646. Hoc in cœmetereo conditur hactenus progenies tota; Alexander, Margareta, Maria una, atque alteri liberi quidem non posteri sed parentum suorum ut in morte, ita in vita et hæreditate illa æterna antecessores. O quam fluxa res humana, spes lubrica et mortalitas sæpe præpostera. O vitæ fugacis curriculum breve in quo viator hæc legens sistis nec sistis!

    Mind, passenger, thy going hence,
    From Captain Graham, his providence,
    Nor envy thou this little stone,
    Here is no proud mausoleon :
    But rather emulate his hopes,
    In which he earth far overtops
    Nilus' vast pyramids : lo! here
    A wardrobe for his soul's attire

He doth provide; he trusts at last
This coat incarnate not to cast,
But lay it off; the world may burn,
Yet shall his ashes from his urn
Muster his outside, and present
Christ's all-monarchick parliament.

ANAGRAM.

" Ah me, I gravel am and dust,
And to the grave descend I must;
O painted piece of living clay,
Man, be not proud of thy short day."

Nicol Paterson, Secretary to John, Earl of Rothes, has these epitaphs:—

"Hic habentur reliquiæ Nicolai Patersoni Nobilissimo Joanni, inclyto Rothusiæ Comiti, Clarissimo Scotorum proregi, a Secretioribus ministris. Obiit postridié Iduum Decembr. MDCLXV.

" To weep for him that's gone is surely folly :
To rest in hope is best, in spirits holy.
You see that neither youth, nor strength, nor beauty,
Can privilege one man from Nature's duty.
Howe'er, let none pass by without resent
To Death itself for his death doth repent."

John Paterson, Bailie in the Canongate, who died in 1663, is by his widow thus celebrated :—

Memoriæ dilectissimi conjugis Joannis Patersoni; qui cum suavissimo matrimonii vinculo XXXV. plus minus annos transegisset et aliquoties Balivi munere in vico (Canongate) functus esset. Obiit anno Christi MDCLXIII. Apr. XXIII., ætatis LXIII. Amoris et officii ergo. Monumentum hoc dicavit Agneta Lyall quae haec ipsa obiit A.D. MDCLXIV. Ap. XXIII. ætatis LXI.

Ecce Patersoni mortis sicura secundae,
Mens peregrinantes quæ peragenda monet,

Stay, passenger, consider well
That thou ere long with me must dwell;
Endeavouring, while thou hast breath,
How to avoid the second death ;
For on this moment do depend
Torments and pleasures without end.

> See then to sin thou daily die,
> So shalt thou live eternallie;
> And serve the Lord with all thy might,
> The day's far spent, fast comes the night.
> Mark well, my son, what here you read ;
> The best advice is from the dead."

Mary Moss, " daughter of Edward Moss," who died in 1671, aged eighteen, is commemorated in these lines :—

> " Here lies interred chaste beauty's maid,
> In whom death virtue had betrayed ;
> Meek, modest, mild, sweet Mary Moss,
> Perfection's flow'r in primely bloss,
> Transformèd now is into dust,
> Had the respect of all in trust ;
> From wedlock's hope divorcèd here,
> Stop, reader, and her worth admire."

A small tablet on the east exterior wall thus describes the worth of Mrs. Anne Fowler, who died 9th May, 1645 :—

> " Two vert'ous hands, one truth-expressing tongue,
>   A furnisht heart with piety, faith, and love ;
> A fruitful womb, whence hopeful males are sprung,
>   Two lust-free eyes, thoughts tending far above,
> The reach of nature, motionless become,
> Rest peaceably into this earthly tomb.

Till 1804, when it was removed, a tombstone in the Abbey Churchyard thus celebrated Richard Henderson, who died 30th November, 1677, aged thirty-three, and his brother Robert, who died on the 21st June, 1680, aged twenty-three :—

> " Two brethren, Hendersons, here lye below,
>   Sons to Alexander Henderson gardener,
> Struck in the prime of youth by death's sad blow,
>   Richard could write and read, Robert could cure.
>   Their arts, strength, stature, seem'd them to secure
> Longer from this attack ; but we may see
> Nothing impedes the course of destinie.

Near the southern wall are deposited the remains of the following notable persons whose monuments have perished :—

Fergus, Prince of Galloway, leader of his countrymen at the battle of the Standard in 1138, and husband of an illegitimate daughter of Henry I. of England,—he died at Holyrood in 1161; John, Bishop of Whithorn, afterwards a monk in this abbey, died 1209; Archibald Crawford, Abbot of Holyrood and Treasurer to James III., a restorer of the church; Andrew Fairfowl, Bishop of Glasgow, died November, 1663; John Paterson, successively Bishop of Galloway and Edinburgh, and afterwards Archbishop of Glasgow, died 8th December, 1708; George Douglas, Bishop of Moray, natural son of Archibald, Earl of Angus, died 1780; Henry David, tenth Earl of Buchan, died 1st December, 1767, and his wife Agnes, daughter of Sir James Stewart of Goodtrees; John, Lord Drummond (who assumed the title of Duke of Perth), died 27th October, 1757; and Sir William Hamilton of Whitelaw, one of the senators of the College of Justice and Lord Justice Clerk, died 1750.

In the abbey a magnificent monument (destroyed by Cromwell's soldiers) commemorated David Fleming, Lord Biggar and Cumbernald. On his return from accompanying Prince James to the Bass on his voyage to France in February, 1405, he was assailed and slain at Longherdmanstoun near Edinburgh by James Douglas of Balveny, afterwards seventh Earl of Douglas. He is thus celebrated by Wyntoun:—

> "Sence Davy Fleming of Cumbernald,
> Lord, a Knycht baith stout and bald,
> Trowit and livit wel with the Kyng,
> This ilke gude and gentil Knychte
> That was baith manfu' leid and wychte,
> Wes cruely mangled in hys blude,
> And now is layde in Halyrude."

In 1857 several stone coffins were discovered at the east end of the chapel, supposed to belong to the thirteenth or fourteenth century.

The following noble and distinguished persons were interred in the chapel:—

John, Lord Bellenden, died 2nd November, 1706; John, Lord Lindores, died 17th January, 1706; James Carnegie, Earl of Finhaven, died 24th March, 1707; Charles Murray, first Earl of Dunmore, died 12th May, 1710; Lord Anstruther, died 3rd February, 1711; Elizabeth, Countess of Crawford, died 26th February, 1711; Anne York, Lady Newark, died 28th February, 1713; James Douglas, twelfth Earl of Morton, one of the Commissioners for the Union, died 14th December, 1715; Robert Douglas, thirteenth Earl of Morton, died 14th December, 1730; Henry Maule, Earl of Panmure, died 25th June, 1734; James Lyon Bowes, seventh Earl of Strathmore, died 18th January, 1735; Francis, tenth Lord Semple, died 1760; the Hon. John Maule, one of the Barons of Exchequer, died 3rd July, 1781; Dunbar Hamilton Douglas, fourth Earl of Selkirk, died 24th May, 1799, and his eldest daughter, Lady Isabella Margaret, died 6th September, 1830; Euphemia, widow of William Stewart, of Castle Stewart, and daughter of Kennet, Lord Fortrose, died 14th February, 1817; Eleanor, Dowager Lady Saltoun, widow of George, fourteenth Baron Saltoun, died 13th September, 1800; Lord Webb John Seymour, died 19th April, 1819; Dame Matilda Cochrane Wishart, wife of Captain Sir Thomas John Cochrane, R.N., died 4th September, 1819; Lady Alvanley, died 17th January, 1825; Lady Caroline Anne Edgcumbe, wife of Ranald George Macdonald, Chief of Clan Ranald, and daughter of Richard, Earl of Mount Edgcumbe, died 10th April, 1824; Mary, widow of Francis, Lord Seaforth, died 27th February, 1829; Thomas Lyon-Bowes, eleventh Earl of Strathmore, died 22nd August, 1846; Charlotte, daughter of John Francis Erskine, fifteenth Earl of Mar, died 27th February, 1852; Alexander Campbell Sinclair, thirteenth Earl of Caithness, died 24th December, 1855; and Louisa Georgiana, Countess of Caithness and daughter of Sir George Richard Philips, Bart., of Weston, Warwickshire, died the 31st July, 1870.

In 1833 the Abbey Churchyard received the remains of the Right Honourable Sir John Sinclair, Bart., of Ulbster. This eminent person was born in Thurso Castle on the 10th May, 1754. Having studied at the Universities of Edinburgh, Glasgow, and Oxford, he passed Advocate; he was afterwards called to the English Bar. In 1780 he entered Parliament as M.P. for Caithness; he sat in the House of Commons for thirty years. In 1790 he devised the "Statistical Account of Scotland," which was completed in 1798 in twenty octavo volumes. Through his exertions the Board of Agriculture was established in 1793. In 1810 he was sworn of the Privy Council; in 1811 he was appointed Cashier of Excise. He died at Edinburgh on the 21st December, 1835. The author of numerous political, statistical, and agricultural works, he enjoyed the reputation of being the busiest man of his time. Near his remains rest those of his second wife, Diana, daughter of Alexander, first Lord Macdonald; she died on the 22nd May, 1845.

RESTALRIG CHURCHYARD.

One mile south-eastward from the city is the ruin of Restalrig Church, which was founded by James III. It was, as a monument of idolatry, demolished by order of the General Assembly in December, 1560, but it has latterly been restored, and is now used for public worship. In the chapterhouse is the burial vault of the House of Logan of Restalrig. This family was one of the most ancient in Scotland. "Dominus Robertus de Logan" is mentioned in a charter in the twelfth year of the reign of Alexander II. The family had possessions in different parts of Scotland, but their principal estate was the Barony of Restalrig, lying between Edinburgh and the sea, and on which the greater part of South Leith is now built. Sir Robert Logan of Restalrig married a daughter of Robert II. Several representatives of the family were chief magistrates of Edinburgh. The last owner of the barony was a turbulent and worthless person; his name is associated with the history of the Gowrie Conspiracy. The Barony of Restalrig subsequently became the property of the noble family of Balmerino. John, second Lord Balmerino, President of the Scottish Parliament, and an extraordinary Lord of Session, died on the 28th February, 1649, and was interred in the Logan family vault. According to Scott of Scotstarvet, his body was exhumed in 1650 by Cromwell's soldiers, who searched the leaden coffins in the vault for the purpose of making bullets. Arthur, sixth and last Lord Balmerino, was decapitated on Tower Hill on the 18th August, 1746, for taking up arms on behalf of Prince Charles Edward. His widow, Margaret, daughter of Captain Chalmers, died at Restalrig on the 24th August, 1765, and was interred in the Logan vault.

A plain monument in Restalrig Churchyard denotes the burial-place of Henry Brougham, of Brougham Hall, Westmoreland. This gentleman, representative of the old Saxon family of Brougham, is entitled to remembrance as father of the distinguished Henry, Lord Brougham and Vaux. He was born on the 18th June, 1742; married, 22nd May, 1777, Eleanora, only child of the Rev. James Syme, minister of Alloa, by Mary, sister of Principal Robertson, and died at Edinburgh on the 19th February, 1810, at the age of sixty-seven.

In the interior of the church is commemorated by a mural monument Alexander Wood, surgeon, Edinburgh, who died on the 12th May, 1807. Also his wife, Veronica Chalmers, daughter of George Chalmers, Writer to the Signet; she died 9th December, 1807.

A monument commemorates John Barclay, M.D., the distinguished anatomist, nephew of John Barclay, the Berean. He was born at Cairn, Perthshire, in 1760. Obtaining licence as a preacher, he accepted a tutorship in a private family, and afterwards devoted himself to the study of medicine. In 1797 he began a course of anatomical lectures at Edinburgh, which brought him reputation and emolument. He died at Edinburgh on the 21st August, 1826. He contributed the article "Physiology" to the third edition of the "Encyclopædia Britannica." His valuable anatomical collection is preserved in the Royal College of Surgeons, Edinburgh.

In the church rest the remains of Alexander Rose, successively

Bishop of Moray and Edinburgh. To the see of Edinburgh he was translated in 1687. He was in the following year, at the Revolution, deprived of his status; he survived till the 20th March, 1720. Bishop Rose was much respected for his consistent adherence to his ecclesiastical opinions.*

A handsome monument celebrates the worth and learning of the Right Rev. Michael Russell, Bishop of Glasgow and Galloway. This respectable historical writer was born at Edinburgh in 1781, studied at the University of Glasgow, and was in 1808 appointed minister of the Episcopal Church, Alloa. During the following year he was preferred to St. James's Church, Leith. In 1831 he was appointed Dean of Edinburgh, and in 1837 was elected to his bishopric. Bishop Russell was author of "History of the Church in Scotland," and of many other historical and theological works. He died at Edinburgh on the 11th April, 1848.

Restalrig Churchyard is the burial-place of the family of Campbell of Aberuchill. A tombstone is inscribed to the memory of Dame Mary Anne Brown, widow of the late Sir James Campbell, Bart., of Aberuchill, who died July 13th, 1819. Another tombstone commemorates William Campbell, Writer to the Signet, son of Sir James Campbell, Bart., of Aberuchill, who died 28th April, 1849.

There are tombstones in memory of Alexander Telfer, of Luscar, who died 28th March, 1803; Lieut.-General John Gordon, who died 26th December, 1832; and Thomas Galbraith Logan, M.D., who died 6th March, 1836.

SOUTH LEITH CHURCHYARD.

This churchyard environs the parish church of South Leith. That church was substituted for the collegiate church of Restalrig,

* For an interesting narrative of the proceedings of Bishop Rose in connection with the event of the Revolution, see Keith's "Scottish Bishops," edited by Dr. Russell, pp. 64—72. Edinb., 1824. 8vo.

and declared to be "the parish kirk" by Act of Parliament on the 24th June, 1609. Within the vestibule a mural tablet commemorates Lieut.-Colonel Adam White, Political Agent in Upper Assam, who fell during a night attack of the Kampti tribes, in Upper Assam, on the 28th January, 1839.

In the interior of the church a tablet commemorates the Rev. James Robertson, minister of the parish, who died on the 25th August, 1832, in the seventy-fifth year of his age, and fiftieth of his ministry.

These are commemorated by mural tablets. James Jameson, surgeon to the 88th Regiment, died 16th October, 1760; Lieutenant John Spence, killed at the Battle of Moodkee, 18th December, 1845; James Reoch, formerly Provost of the Burgh, and an active improver of the town, died 1848; James Miller, merchant, died 15th December, 1855.

In one of the external walls a mural monument commemorates the Rev. John Home, author of the tragedy of "Douglas," who is buried at the spot. Son of Alexander Home, town clerk of Leith, this ingenious dramatist was born at Ancrum, Roxburghshire, on the 22nd September, 1722. When a licentiate of the Church he joined a volunteer corps in support to the Government, and was present at the battle of Falkirk in 1745. In the following year he was ordained minister of Athelstaneford. His tragedy of "Douglas" was produced in 1755; it was performed at Edinburgh in the following year, when he and several of his brethren were present. The encouragement of theatricals being deemed an unclerical offence, Home escaped deposition by resigning his charge. He soon after obtained a Civil List pension of £300 a year, with the sinecure office of Conservator of Scots Privileges at Campvere. In 1802 he published a history of the Rebellion of 1845; it was unequal to his former productions. He died on the 4th September, 1808, in his eighty-sixth year.

In the churchyard is interred Hugo Arnot, the historical and antiquarian writer. Son of a merchant at Leith, he was there born on the 8th December, 1749. His family name was Pollock, but he changed it on succeeding through his mother to the estate of Balcormo, Fifeshire. In 1772 he passed Advocate. His "History of Edinburgh" appeared in 1779, and in 1785 he published his "Collection of Criminal Trials." He died on the 20th November, 1786, aged thirty-seven.

This churchyard contains the earthly remains of the Rev. Andrew Grant, D.D., Minister of St. Andrew's Church, Edinburgh. Dr. Grant was successively Minister of Kilmarnock, the Canongate and Trinity College Church; he was translated to St. Andrew's Church in December, 1812. He was one of his Majesty's Chaplains, Dean of the Chapel Royal, and Collector of the Ministers' Widows Fund. He died on the 2nd July, 1836, in the eightieth year of his age, and fifty-second of his ministry.

A monument commemorates Robert Gilfillan, the ingenious poet. Born at Dunfermline, on the 7th July, 1798, he was in his thirteenth year apprenticed to a cooper at Leith; he subsequently became clerk to a wine merchant. In 1837 he was preferred to the office of collector of poor rates in Leith. He died on the 4th December, 1850, at the age of fifty-two.

Tombstones in South Leith Churchyard commemorate the following:—Robert Ramsay, died 9th December, 1806; James Balfour, of Pilrig, died 6th March, 1795; Rev. John Colquhoun, Minister of the New North Church, Leith, died 27th November, 1827; Rev. Dr. Robert Dickson, minister of South Leith, died 25th January, 1824; Rev. Alexander Nisbet, minister of the United Associate Congregation, Portsburgh, died 12th September, 1832; John Watt, founder of the hospital at Leith, which bears his name, died 30th September, 1829; John Macfie, died 28th December, 1852; Lieut.-Colonel Archibald Kerr, died 10th February, 1850; Thomas Hutchison, of Carlowrie, Provost of Leith, died 8th May, 1852; Duncan Mathieson, Advocate and Sheriff-Substitute, of Leith, died 24th May, 1838; Adam White, of Feus, first Provost of Leith, died 31st December, 1843.

On the tombstone of Margaret White, who died in 1810, aged twenty-four, are inscribed these lines:—

> "Adieu, dear Margaret, till we meet above,
> In those pure, peaceful realms of light and love;
> Grain sown on earth is still its owner's care,
> And evening suns but set to rise no more."

In the north-east corner of the church a tablet formerly commemorated "David Gillies, skipper, who died 2nd January, 1685." The inscription was as follows:—

> "Here are consigned his ashes, understood
> No other thing but to be just and good;
> Who did endeavour God and man to please
> In all his actions, both by land and seas;
> Who all his life practised his counsel deep,
> Your mind unto yourself I bid you keep:
> Devout to God, and loyal to the king,
> In heaven now doth hallelujahs sing."

NORTH LEITH CHURCHYARDS.

There are two churchyards at North Leith, the *Old* and the *New*. The *Old Churchyard* is in a most neglected condition, reflecting the utmost discredit on the parochial authorities. Here rest the remains of the immediate progenitor of a distinguished benefactor of North Leith, and ancestor of the present Prime Minister of the Crown. A tabular tombstone denotes the spot; it is thus inscribed:—

"Beneath this stone are the remains of Ellen Neilson, spouse of Thomas Gladstones, merchant in Leith, who died July the 17th, 1806, aged sixty-six years; also the remains of the said Thomas Gladstones, who died the 11th May, 1809, aged seventy-six years; also the remains of Margaret Gladstones, eldest daughter of the above, and spouse of Peter Crowden, shipmaster, Leith, died 3rd May, 1814, aged fifty-one years."

Thomas Gladstones, who is thus commemorated, was a prosperous trader in Leith. By his marriage with Ellen, daughter of Walter Neilson, of Springfield, he became father of Sir John Gladstone, Baronet of Fasque, who was born at Leith on the 11th December,

1764. Sir John's fourth son, the Right Honourable William Ewart Gladstone, after a distinguished career as a statesman, obtained the Premiership in 1868. Sir John Gladstone, as a tribute of respect to his native town, erected and endowed at Leith a church and school in connection with the Established Church.

The following Latin inscription celebrates the personal virtues and ministerial fidelity of the Rev. James Lundie, minister of the parish, who died on the 31st March, 1696:—

"Siste gradum, viator. Hic jacet Dominus Jacobus Lundinus, theologus admodum reverendus, & verbi divini minister eximius; præclarum exemplar spectatæ morum probitatis, veræ pietatis, Christianæ humilitatis, modestæ gravitatis, certæ amicitiæ, & humanæ urbanitatis, perpetuæ fidei, curæ & vigilantiæ, in munere pastorali; quo, cum annos octodecim, in ecclesia Edinburgena, unum in Dalkethensi, summa cum laude & bonorum favore functus esset, conscientiæ suæ fide commotus ab anno MDCLXXXI. ad annum MDCLXXXVII. a publico ejusdem exercitio cessavit. Postea vero, mutato rerum statu, unanimi ecclesiæ Lethensis Septentrionalis suffragio, ad animarum curam ibidem admotus eam tenuti annos VIII. menses V. Obijt prid cal. April, anno Dom. MDCXCVI ætatis 56.

"Charissimo patri posuit filius natu maximus, Dominus Archibaldus Lundinus, verbi divini minister, apud Saltoun. Volat irrevocabile tempus."

Monteith supplies the following translation:—

"Stay, passenger. Here lieth Mr. James Lundie, a very reverend divine, and a notable minister of God's word; a most famous pattern of a good life, true piety, Christian humility, modest gravity, firm friendship, and courteous civility; of constant faithfulness, care, and vigilance, in his ministerial function; which when he had discharged for the space of eighteen years in the Church at Edinburgh, one year at Dalkeith, with great commendation, and the favour of good people, he all moved by a principle of conscience, ceased from the public exercise of his ministry, from the year 1681 to the year 1687. But afterwards the state of affairs being altered, by the unanimous call of the Church at North Leith, he was advanced to the cure there, in which he officiated for the space of eight years and five months. He died the last day of March, in the year of our Lord 1696. His age fifty-six.

"His eldest son, Mr. Archibald Lundie, minister of God's word at

Saltoun, erected this monument to his dearest father's memory. Irrecoverable time flies away."

A tombstone commemorates the Rev. David Johnston, D.D., minister of North Leith. Second son of the Rev. John Johnston, Minister of Arngask. Dr. Johnston was born on the 24th April, 1734. Licensed by the Presbytery of Selkirk in 1757, he was in the following year ordained to the ministry at Langton, Berwickshire. He was translated to North Leith parish in 1765. He died on the 5th July, 1824, in the ninety-first year of his age, and sixty-seventh of his ministry.

A tombstone commemorates the Rev. Walter Foggo Ireland, who succeeded Dr. Johnston in the ministerial charge of the parish. Having studied at the High School and University of Edinburgh, he was licensed in 1798, and in the following year was ordained assistant and successor to Dr. Johnston. He died on the 18th February, 1828, in the fifty-third year of his age, and thirtieth of his ministry.

A plain tombstone denotes the resting-place of the poet, Robert Nicoll. This short-lived son of genius was born at Auchtergaven, Perthshire, on the 7th January, 1814. For some time he kept a circulating library at Dundee. In 1836 he became editor of the *Leeds Times*. The labour of conducting a public journal undermined a constitution which was never robust. He died at Edinburgh, on the 7th December, 1837, in his twenty-third year. Several of Robert Nicoll's songs have obtained a wide popularity.

Tombstones in the Old Churchyard commemorate Samuel Lindsay, Teacher in the High School of Edinburgh, who died 18th January, 1854, and Captain John Thomson, R.N., who died 12th November, 1803.

The *New Churchyard* of North Leith is of recent construction. There is a tombstone in memory of William Gooch, brother of Sir Thomas Gooch, Bart., of Benacre Hall, Suffolk. He died on the 15th October, 1833.

EDINBURGH AND LEITH CEMETERY, ROSEBANK.

Rosebank Cemetery is situated on the east of the Water of Leith, in the vicinity of Bonnington. Among the more noted persons commemorated within its enclosure are the following:— William Child, of Glencorse, died 10th August, 1847; George Cunnynghame, of Cronan, died 9th January, 1847; Matthew Buchan, M.D., died 4th February, 1848; Lieutenant-Colonel Philip Warren Walker, died 5th November, 1850; Alexander Spence, banker, Leith, died 4th May, 1852; Robert Cook, shipowner, Leith, died 11th November, 1856; David Young, teacher, Edinburgh, died 23rd October, 1849; William Finlayson, M.D., died 26th April, 1852; John Davidson, teacher in the High School, Leith, died 23rd November, 1858; Lieutenant Edward W. Pitt, R.M., died 18th January, 1858; William Belfrage, died 22nd March, 1860; Captain John Hall, died 30th January, 1861; Robert Tulloh Easton, Surgeon, R.N., died 14th August, 1861; James Pope, died 8th November, 1866; and John Mitchell, of Mayville, Knight of the Order of Leopold, and Belgian Consul at Leith, died 24th April, 1865.

A monument commemorates Peter Macleod, of Polbeth, author of several popular Scottish melodies. He was born on the 8th May, 1797, and died on the 10th February, 1859.

A tombstone, of Aberdeen granite, is thus inscribed:—

"Sacred to the memory of Miss Ida Bonanomi, the faithful and highly esteemed dresser of Queen Victoria, who departed this life October 15th, 1854, in the thirty-seventh year of her age, beloved and respected by all who knew her. This stone has been erected by Queen Victoria as a mark of her regard."

Miss Bonanomi died at Holyrood Palace while in attendance on the Queen.

WARRISTON CEMETERY.

Warriston Cemetery is situated in the vicinity of the Botanical Gardens west of the Water of Leith, and in the immediate vicinity of Warriston Crescent. In this cemetery a handsome monument commemorates Patrick Neill, LL.D., the eminent horticultural writer. Dr. Neill was born in 1776. He engaged in business as a printer, but devoted his spare hours to the cultivation of flowers. He published several valuable works on gardening, and contributed papers to the Transactions of the Wernerian Society and the *Edinburgh Philosophical Journal.* He died at Edinburgh on the 5th September, 1851. On his monument he is described as "distinguished for literature, science, patriotism, benevolence, and piety."

A tombstone denotes the resting-place of George Outram, advocate, editor of the *Glasgow Herald.* This skilful prose-writer and ingenious poet was born in the vicinity of Glasgow, in 1805. He was called to the Scottish Bar in 1827, and for some years practised as an advocate. In 1837 he accepted his appointment in connection with the *Glasgow Herald.* He died at Rosemore, on the shores of the Holy Loch, on the 16th September, 1856, in his fifty-first year. Mr. Outram composed a MS. volume of humorous songs, which he styled "Legal Lyrics;" a few only of these compositions have been published.

An obelisk of Aberdeen granite commemorates Professor Robert Jameson, the distinguished naturalist. He was third son of Thomas Jameson, soap manufacturer, and was born at Leith on the 11th July, 1774. He studied medicine, and became keeper of the Natural History Museum in Edinburgh College. He visited the Shetland and Western Isles, and in two important works published the results of his explorations, chiefly mineralogical. Proceeding to Germany, he studied geology under the celebrated Werner. On his return to Edinburgh he was appointed to the vacant chair of Natural History in the University. He founded the Edinburgh Wernerian Society, and originated the *Edinburgh Philosophical Journal*. His indefatigable labours in connection with the Natural History Museum, of which he was keeper, led to its conversion into a National Museum. A bust of Professor Jameson, by Mr. Steell, is placed in the Museum. He died at Edinburgh on the 19th April, 1854, in his eightieth year. His works on Natural History are held in high estimation.

In Warriston Cemetery rest the remains of Robert Fleming Gourlay, an eccentric political writer. Descended from an ancient Norman family, which accompanied William the Lion to Scotland in 1174, Mr. Gourlay was born in the parish of Ceres, Fifeshire, in 1778. His father, Oliver Gourlay, proprietor of Craigrothie, was a zealous agriculturist; he expended his fortune in useless enterprises. Robert Gourlay was educated at the University of St. Andrews. Becoming a zealous politician, his extreme views necessitated his leaving his native county for England. He subsequently removed to Canada, and on his return enthusiastically advocated the cause of emigration to that colony. His next movement was to illustrate the importance of political economy, when, to indicate the sincerity of his convictions, he became a stone breaker. He accused Mr. Henry Brougham of plagiarizing his views on reform, and chastised the illustrious statesman with his whip. This escapade made him acquainted with the House of Correction. His subsequent career was occupied in political or other agitations. He died on the 1st August, 1863, in his eighty-fifth year. Though entirely lacking in discretion, Mr. Gourlay possessed considerable intellectual calibre, and was a kind and intelligent companion.

In Warriston Cemetery an elegant monument commemorates Alexander Smith, author of the "Life Drama." This ingenious poet was born at Kilmarnock on the 31st December, 1829. He began life as a pattern-drawer, but disliking the avocation employed his leisure hours in the composition of verses. In 1851 he submitted his poems to the Rev. George Gilfillan, and by that judicious critic was advised to contribute his "Life Drama" to the *Critic*, a London serial. The appearance of the poem in this well-circulated journal laid the foundation of the poet's fame. The "Life Drama" was subsequently published by Bogue. In 1854 Mr. Smith was appointed Secretary of Edinburgh University. He now contributed prose articles and tales to various periodicals. After a short career of literary activity he fell into feeble health, and died on the 5th January, 1867. His monument was reared by public subscription. Designed by Mr. James Drummond, R.S.A., it consists of an Iona cross of Binny stone, twelve feet in height, the centre of the shaft displaying a bronze medallion of the poet, executed by Brodie. In the centre of the cross is a large boss, and the four arms are covered with Scottish thistles. There are other appropriate ornaments.

In this cemetery rest the remains of Horatio M'Culloch, R.A., the celebrated landscape painter. He was born at Glasgow in 1806. Though in humble circumstances his father contrived to afford him a respectable education, both in his native city and at Edinburgh. For some time he was employed in the establishment of W. H. Lizars, the celebrated engraver. Returning to Glasgow he began out-of-door sketching in the interesting scenery of the west of Scotland. He carried his colours to the fields, and worked his pictures into life and fidelity on the spot. In 1826 he exhibited at Edinburgh a view on the Clyde which attracted considerable notice. He now became a regular exhibitor in the Scottish Academy, of which in 1836 he was elected an associate. In 1838 he exhibited his celebrated picture of *Cadzow Forest*, and in the same year was elected a Royal Academician. He had now attained a first rank as a painter of Scottish landscapes, and his pictures were in great demand, and brought high prices. Through exposure to damp in the prosecution of his art his health became shattered; he died on the 24th June, 1867, aged sixty-one.

A handsome monolith of grey Sicilian marble commemorates Robert Scott Lander, R.S.A., the great historical painter. He was born on the 25th June, 1803. After a steady progress as an artist, he was in 1826 elected an Associate of the Scottish Academy. In 1833 he visited the Art galleries in Italy and at Munich. For the next ten years he resided in London, exhibiting at the Academy many pictures illustrative of scenes in Scottish history and romance. He died at Edinburgh on the 21st April, 1869. His monument, designed and executed by Mr. John Hutchison, R.S.A., contains a medallion head of the artist in white marble.

On the 13th May, 1870, were consigned to their last resting-place the remains of Sir James Young Simpson, Bart., Professor of Midwifery at Edinburgh. This celebrated physician was born at Bathgate in 1811. His father, David Simpson, was a baker, and he was originally intended for the same trade. A love of learning marked him out for a higher position, and he was sent to the University of Edinburgh. He became M.D. in 1832. His eminence as a lecturer in obstetric science at Edinburgh justified his being appointed in 1840 to the Professorship of Midwifery in the University. He introduced chloroform into the practice of his profession in 1847, and soon afterwards was elected President of the Edinburgh College of Physicians. He was a leading member of the Scottish Society of Antiquaries, and in the Transactions of that body published useful and interesting papers. In 1866 he was created a Baronet, and appointed Physician-Accoucheur to the Queen for Scotland. He died on the 6th May, 1870, at the age of fifty-nine. His premature death was deeply lamented by the citizens of Edinburgh and the members of the medical profession. His remains were honoured with a public funeral, and a public monument is about to be erected to his memory.

In Warriston Cemetery are interred the remains of Samuel Halkett, Keeper of the Advocates Library. He was born in the Canongate, Edinburgh, in 1814. Educated at Smith's classical academy, George Street, he was apprenticed to a trade. He afterwards, in partnership with another, became a woollendraper on the North Bridge. From youth devoted to linguistic studies, he could read all and speak most of the languages of Europe. In 1853 he was elected Keeper of the Advocates Library, and in discharging the duties of this important office he proved himself efficient and laborious. For fifteen years preceding his decease he was engaged in the compilation of a dictionary of anonymous and pseudonymous British literature. After an illness of some months, Mr. Halkett died on the 19th April, 1871.

The following are also commemorated in this Cemetery:— —John Orr, of Brackraw, died February 10th, 1837; Captain John Watson, died 13th February, 1847; Major Neil Campbell, died January 14th, 1842; Robert Kendall Fair, M.D., died 19th April, 1844; James Johnston, M.D., died 6th April, 1846; Captain the Honourable William Keith, youngest son of William, 6th Earl of Kintore, died 5th January, 1846; William Fergusson, Governor of the Colony of Sierra Leone, died 19th January, 1846; Major-General Pitman, C.B., died 26th December, 1846; Lieut.-Colonel David Crichton, died 7th August, 1845; Lieut.-Colonel Martin, died 8th October, 1846; Captain John Hamilton Montgomerie, of Broomfield, died 20th May, 1846; Major-General John Ogilvie, died 20th September, 1847; Rev. John Birrell, A.M., second minister of the Collegiate Church, Cupar-Fife, died 1st February, 1842; Major-General Thomas Murray, died 30th January, 1846; William Balfour, M.D., died June, 1846; George Ogilvie, of Kirkbuddo, died 17th March, 1848; Colonel Dugald Campbell, died 4th July, 1849; Lieut.-Colonel Charles Hamilton Bell, died 20th April, 1848; Archibald Mackellar, M.D., died 31st March, 1848; George Wauchope, died 28th February, 1848; William Beilby, M.D., died 30th May, 1849; Admiral Pringle Stoddart, died 29th January, 1848; David Hatton, M.D., died May 13th, 1854; Colonel Robert Low, died 25th September, 1853; Eliza Margaret Carstairs, wife of George Harvey, R.S.A. (now Sir George Harvey, President of the Royal Scottish Academy), died 18th December, 1844, and Margaret Muir, his second wife, died 15th August, 1854; the Rev. William B. Smith, died 24th September, 1852; Peter Ramsay, banker, died August 31st, 1855; the Rev. John Willison Ferguson, minister of St. James's Episcopal Church, Edinburgh, died 27th March, 1854; Major Alexander

K

Robertson, died September 17th, 1857; George Robertson, Deputy Keeper of the Records, died 5th March, 1857; William Archibald Cadell, of Banton, died 19th February, 1855; Alexander Blackie, banker, Aberdeen (father of Professor Blackie), died 10th May, 1856; Captain John Stuart, died 14th September, 1854; David Low, Professor of Agriculture, died 7th January, 1859; Walter Nichol, LL.D., died 4th March, 1858; Charles W. Campbell, late of the 39th Regiment, son of John Campbell, of Boreland, died 18th January, 1861; John Raimes, of Cowden, died June 24th, 1858; William Simson, Secretary of the Bank of Scotland, died 31st October, 1858; Major David Munro, died 10th November, 1863; George Simson, R.S.A., died 11th March, 1862; George Walker, M.D., died 28th September, 1866; Walter Marshall, goldsmith, died 6th April, 1866; and Peter Edward, sculptor, died 2nd January, 1867.

In Warriston Cemetery are mortuary enclosures belonging to Lord Deas, one of the senators of the College of Justice, and to Charles Lees, R.S.A.

THE DEAN CEMETERY.

The Dean or Western Cemetery was opened for interments in 1846. Owing to the picturesqueness of its situation, and the remarkable taste with which it has been laid out, it is a favourite place of sepulture. It is adorned with a profusion of monumental obelisks and memorial crosses, in granite and marble.

One of the most elegant monumental erections in the Dean Cemetery is a pyramid of red granite, reared by the Right Honourable Andrew Rutherfurd, in memory of his wife, and likewise to commemorate himself. It is inscribed—

"Uxori desideratissimæ contra votum superestes moerens posuit Andreas Rutherfurd, et sibi, MDCCCLII."

The remains of Lord Rutherfurd, who died on the 13th December, 1854, have been placed in a vault under the pyramid. Andrew Rutherfurd was born at Edinburgh in 1791. Through his mother, Mrs. Janet Bervie, he was descended from the old Scottish house of Rutherfurd, and he and the other members of his family assumed this patronymic. He passed Advocate in 1812, and soon became known for his forensic talents. In 1837 he was appointed Solicitor-General, and two years afterwards Lord Advocate. He was elected M.P. for Leith. In 1851 he was raised to the bench by the title of Lord Rutherfurd, and was sworn a member of the Privy Council. He died at Edinburgh on the 13th December, 1854, in his sixty-third year. When Lord Advocate he effected by legislative enactment several valuable reforms in connection with the law of Scotland. His wife, Sophia Stewart, was daughter of Sir James Stewart, of Fort Stewart, county Donegal, Ireland. She died in 1852.

Adjoining the burial-place of Lord Rutherfurd a handsome tombstone, with a well-executed medallion head, is inscribed thus:—

"Francis Jeffrey, erected by his friends."

An acute lawyer and the greatest of British critics, Francis Jeffrey was born at Edinburgh on the 27th October, 1773. He was educated at the University of Glasgow, and Queen's College, Oxford. In 1794 he passed Advocate, but not early obtaining a remunerative practice at the Scottish Bar, he removed to London, with a view to adopting a literary profession. Returning to Edinburgh, he joined Sydney Smith, Henry Brougham, and others in establishing the *Edinburgh Review*, of which the first number appeared in October, 1802. During the first year the periodical was conducted by Sydney Smith, but thereafter Jeffrey became editor. He retained the office for twenty-five years. Under his management the *Review* not only sustained its original reputation, but obtained a position in the critical world altogether unrivalled. His success as a lawyer kept pace with his celebrity as a critic.

In 1820 he was elected Rector of the University of Glasgow, and in 1829 was chosen Dean of the Faculty of Advocates. In December, 1830, when the Liberal party came into power, he was appointed Lord Advocate, and entered Parliament. He was nominated a Lord of Session in 1834. After a period of feeble health, he died at Edinburgh on the 26th January, 1850, at the age of seventy-seven. His contributions to the *Edinburgh Review* have been collected and published in four octavo volumes.

A few feet from the grave of Jeffrey, a monument commemorates Sir James Wellwood Moncreiff, Bart., a Lord of Session under the title of Lord Moncreiff. This eminent lawyer was born on the 13th September, 1776. Completing his education at Oxford, he passed Advocate at the Scottish Bar in 1779. Early distinguished in his profession, he was in 1807 appointed Sheriff of Clackmannan and Kinross. In 1826 he was chosen Dean of Faculty. He was raised to the bench in 1829, and was also appointed a Lord of Justiciary. He died on the 30th April, 1851, at the age of seventy-five. An enlightened judge, Lord Moncreiff maintained a liberal policy in Church and State. He was distinguished for his benevolence.

Lord Cockburn, another distinguished lawyer, is entombed in the same division of the cemetery. Born on the 26th October, 1779, Henry Cockburn was educated at the High School and University of Edinburgh. In 1800 he passed Advocate. In 1806 he was appointed Advocate-Depute, and in 1830, when the Liberal party obtained power, he became Solicitor-General. Raised to the bench in 1834, he devoted his leisure to literary pursuits. In 1852 appeared his "Life of Lord Jeffrey," in two octavo volumes. His "Memorials of his Time" were published posthumously. He died at Bonaly, near Edinburgh, on the 26th April, 1854, at the age of seventy-five. Of Lord Cockburn it has been said that his homely style and unaffected utterance gave him a weight in the Jury Court such as no other Scottish pleader ever attained.

An obelisk of Aberdeen granite denotes the last resting-place of Sir William Allan, the distinguished painter. He was born at

Edinburgh in 1782, and was originally apprenticed to a coach painter. Having studied at the Trustees' Academy, he removed to London, and subsequently to St. Petersburg. After an absence of ten years he returned to Edinburgh in 1814, when he attracted the attention of Sir Walter Scott, who, with other eminent literary persons, afforded him encouragement. His professional employment became ample, and in 1838 he was chosen President of the Academy. In 1841 he was appointed limner to the Queen for Scotland, and was knighted in the following year. He died on the 23rd February, 1850, in his sixty-ninth year. Among his more celebrated paintings are "Flora Macdonald's Parting with Prince Charles Edward," "The Death of the Regent Murray," "The Murder of Archbishop Sharpe," "The Ettrick Shepherd's House-heating," and "The Author of Waverley in his Study."

David Scott, another distinguished painter, has found a resting-place in the Dean Cemetery. This ingenious artist was born at Edinburgh on the 10th October, 1806. The son of an eminent engraver, he was devoted to this branch of art, but he afterwards qualified himself in drawing, and in the use of the brush. Having visited several art galleries in France and Italy, he returned to Edinburgh, and there assiduously applied himself to the practice of his profession. His pictures evince much grandeur of conception, combined with a certain quaintness of execution, especially in the treatment of the supernatural. His death took place at Edinburgh on the 5th March, 1849, at the age of forty-two.

A handsome obelisk of polished granite marks the resting-place of Professor John Wilson. Son of a manufacturer in affluent circumstances, this celebrated person was born at Paisley on the 18th May, 1785. Having studied at the University of Glasgow, he proceeded to Magdalen College, Oxford, where he gained the Newdegate prize for the best English poem of fifty lines. On attaining his majority he succeeded to his father's estate, becoming master of £30,000. Purchasing the property of Elleray, in Westmoreland, he indulged in eccentric adventures and humorous escapades. He married in 1811, and four years afterwards passed

Advocate, and established his residence at Edinburgh. "The Isle of Palms," a poem in four cantos, appeared from his pen in 1812; he published in 1816 "The City of the Plague," a dramatic poem, which was followed by tales and sketches. On the establishment of *Blackwood's Magazine* in 1817 he became one of the principal contributors; his celebrated *Noctes Ambrosianæ*, a series of dialogues on the literature and manners of the times, appeared in that periodical from 1822 till 1835. In 1820 he was elected to the chair of Moral Philosophy in the University of Edinburgh, an office which he subsequently adorned. In 1850 he was chosen first President of the Edinburgh Philosophical Institution; in the year following he obtained a Civil List pension. He died at Edinburgh, on the 3rd of April, 1854; his remains were honoured with a public funeral. As a poet, Professor Wilson is chiefly to be remarked for serenity and pathos; as a periodical writer he will find admirers while the English language is understood. By public subscription his statue in bronze has been erected in Princes Street Gardens. It has been described (see *ante*).

A brother and a son-in-law of Professor Wilson, both men of eminence, have been interred in the Dean Cemetery. His brother, James Wilson, styled of Woodville, was born at Paisley, in November, 1795. At the age of eighteen he began to study law at the University of Edinburgh, which, however, he speedily relinquished. From 1816 to 1821 he travelled on the Continent, employing a portion of his time in the study of Natural History. In 1824 he settled at Woodville, near Edinburgh, and there resided till his death, which took place on the 18th May, 1856. His works on Ornithology and Entomology are much valued; his style is clear, precise, and elegant. On subjects of Natural History he contributed to the *Quarterly Review*, the *North British Review*, and *Blackwood's Magazine*. To the seventh edition of the *Encyclopædia Britannica* he furnished numerous articles on Natural History, and revised others in this department. His Memoir was published in 1859 by the late Dr. James Hamilton, of London.

Professor Wilson's son-in-law, whose remains rest in this cemetery, divides celebrity with himself, both as a poet and essayist. Professor William Edmonstone Aytoun, to whom has been reared a handsome monument, was descended from an old Norman family, which obtained an early settlement in Scotland. He was born at Edinburgh on the 21st June, 1813; he studied at the university of the city, and afterwards in Germany. In 1835 he was admitted a Writer to the Signet; he passed Advocate in 1840. With strong literary tastes, he became a contributor to *Blackwood's Magazine*, and in 1841 rose into fame by his share in the "Bon Gaultier Ballads." In 1843 he added to his poetical laurels by his "Lays of the Scottish Cavaliers." In 1845 he was elected to the chair of Rhetoric in the University of Edinburgh, and in 1852 was nominated to the Sheriffdom of Orkney. He died at Blackhills, near Elgin, on the 4th August, 1865. Of a humorous and kindly nature, he was much lamented by his friends. His Memoirs have been published by Mr. Theodore Martin.

A Greek cross of polished granite rests on the grave of Thomas Thomson, M.D., the distinguished chemist. Born at Crieff, on the 12th April, 1773, he was educated at Stirling under Dr. Doig, and afterwards at the Universities of St. Andrews and Edinburgh. In 1799 he commenced a course of chemical lectures in Edinburgh, which was numerously attended. He had already contributed scientific articles to the *Encyclopædia Britannica*. Many new compounds and minerals which he discovered were brought under public notice in his "System of Chemistry," of which the third edition appeared in 1807. In 1817 he was appointed Lecturer on Chemistry in the University of Glasgow, an appointment which in the following year was converted into a professorship. In 1830 he published his "History of Chemistry," and in 1836 his "Outlines of Mineralogy and Geology." After a period of failing health he died at Kilmun, Argyleshire, on the 2nd August, 1852, in his eightieth year. One of the foremost of British chemists, Dr. Thomson rendered valuable service to science by his numerous publications.

Other eminent naturalists rest in this place of tombs. One of these is the amiable and short-lived Professor Edward Forbes. He was born at Douglas, Isle of Man, on the 12th February, 1815. His father, Edward Forbes, of Oakhill, was descended from a branch of the old Scottish House of that name. The future professor was intended for an artist, but he renounced painting after a short trial, and entering the University of Edinburgh, speedily obtained distinction as a naturalist. He frequently visited the Continent to improve himself in his peculiar studies. In 1841 he published his "History of British Star-fishes," and in the same year was attached as naturalist to H.M. surveying ship *Beacon*, in which he explored some of the least known parts of Asia Minor. During his absence he was appointed to the chair of Botany in King's College, London. Subsequently he became Secretary to the Geological Society; he was a leading member of the British Association. In 1853 he was appointed Professor of Natural History and Keeper of the Museum in the University of Edinburgh. This appointment, so entirely suitable to his tastes and the object of his ambition, he was not long privileged to enjoy. After a short illness he died on the 18th November, 1854. An interesting memoir of his career has been published under the editorial care of the late Dr. George Wilson and Mr. Geikie.

An obelisk denotes the grave of Professor John Fleming. This eminent naturalist was born in 1784. Having obtained licence as a probationer, he was ordained to the ministerial charge of Bressay, Orkney: he was, in 1811, translated to the parish of Flisk, Fifeshire. In 1832 he obtained the church living of Clackmannan, which he resigned after two years, on being appointed Professor of Natural Philosophy in King's College, Aberdeen. He demitted his office in 1845, when he accepted the Professorship of Natural History in the New College, Edinburgh. He died on the 18th November, 1857. His principal works are his "History of British Animals" and his "Philosophy of Zoology." He was a contributor to the *Enclyclopædia Britannica* and the *Edinburgh Philosophical Journal*.

Henry Darwin Rogers, the eminent geologist, and latterly Professor of Natural History in the University of Glasgow, has here found his last resting-place. He was born in Philadelphia, in 1809, and in his twenty-first year became Professor of Chemistry and Natural Philosophy in Dickenson College. He subsequently undertook the geological survey of the States of New Jersey and Pennsylvania, in which he was engaged for twenty-two years. In 1857 he was elected Professor of Natural History in Glasgow College. He died at Glasgow on the 29th May, 1866. Professor Rogers's Survey has been pronounced a most valuable contribution to geological science. Professor Rogers was of Scottish extraction.

A handsome monument commemorates Robert Kaye Greville, LL.D., author of the "Scottish Cryptogamic Flora." This estimable gentleman died on the 4th June, 1866. With a first rank as a botanist, Dr. Greville obtained deserved reputation for his earnest endeavours to promote the moral and religious well-being of the community.

George Combe, the distinguished phrenologist, brother of Dr. Andrew Combe, formerly mentioned, is celebrated by an elegant monument. Born at Edinburgh in 1788, he was bred to the law, and in 1812 became a Writer to the Signet. When Spurzheim, the eminent physiologist, visited Edinburgh in 1816, Mr. Combe attended his phrenological lectures, and at length embraced his opinions. His "Essays on Phrenology" were collectedly published in 1819, and in 1825 were included in his larger work entitled "A System of Phrenology." For many years he edited the *Phrenological Journal*. His "Constitution of Man" appeared in 1828, and at once commanded an extraordinary sale, both in Britain and America. From 1837 to 1840 he travelled in the United States, delivering lectures in the principal towns; on his return he published his "Notes on the United States," in three volumes. After a period of feeble health he died at Moor Park, Surrey, on the 14th August, 1858. Mr. Combe married in 1833, Cecilia, daughter of Mrs. Siddons, the celebrated actress; she became the companion of his journeys, and contributed important materials to his work on the United States. A lady of high culture, she delighted to associate with persons of literary taste. She ably seconded her husband's efforts in rendering pleasant the literary and scientific reunions which for many years they held at Edinburgh. Mrs. Combe died at Nice on the 19th February, 1868, and, according to her express wish, her body was brought to Edinburgh and interred beside her husband's grave.

In the Dean Cemetery a handsome obelisk commemorates John Wilson, the celebrated vocalist. This ingenious illustrator of Scottish song was born at Edinburgh in 1800. For many years he was employed as a compositor and reader in the printing establishment of Ballantyne and Co. In 1827 he retired from the printing business and began to improve himself in the theory and practice of music. For a period he engaged in theatrical performances. In 1838 he commenced his public entertainments in Scottish song. These he conducted in the principal towns of the United Kingdom and in the United States. He died at Quebec, of cholera, after a few hours' illness, on the 8th July, 1849. Wilson composed several melodies. In singing the patriotic and pathetic songs of Scotland he was unrivalled.

Finlay Dun, another eminent musician, author of "The Analysis of Scottish Music," rests in this cemetery; he died at Edinburgh on the 28th November, 1853.

Captain Charles Gray, an agreeable song-writer, is commemorated by a tombstone. He was born at Anstruther on the 10th March, 1782. In his twenty-third year he procured a commission in the Royal Marines. In 1811 he produced a volume of poems, which passed into a second edition. After thirty-six years' service he retired in 1841, and established his residence in Edinburgh. At the request of his friends he published a collected edition of his verses with the title "Lays and Lyrics." He died on the 13th April, 1851. His "Cursory Remarks on Scottish Song," which originally appeared in the *Glasgow Citizen* newspaper, are copiously quoted by Mr. Farquhar Graham in his edition of the "Songs of Scotland."

By subscription an obelisk has been reared to the memory of—

"Colonel the Hon. Lauderdale Maule, Colonel James Ferguson, Captain Adam Maitland, Lieutenant F. A. Grant, Lieutenant F. J. Harrison, and Dr. R. J. Mackenzie; also 369 non-commissioned officers and men of the 79th Highlanders, who died in Bulgaria and the Crimea, or fell in action during the campaign of 1854-5."

Colonel Maule was second son of William, Baron Panmure; he was born 27th March, 1807, and died at Varna, on the 1st August, 1854. Colonel Ferguson was a member of the house of Ferguson of Raith. Captain Maitland was connected with the family of Maitland of Dundrennan.

A Greek cross commemorates William Ambrose Morehead, member of the Supreme Council of India, who died on the 1st December, 1863, aged fifty-eight. His relative, the Rev. Robert Morehead, D.D., Incumbent of St. Paul's Church, Edinburgh, and subsequently Rector of Easington, Yorkshire, was one of the early contributors to the *Edinburgh Review*.

A monument, in the form of a Greek temple, reared by his widow, celebrates the munificent liberality and Christian devotedness of James Buchanan, founder of the Institution at Glasgow which bears his name. He died on the 21st December, 1857.

In 1857 were reared handsome memorial stones in memory of Hannah Leonora, widow of Sir William Maxwell, Bart., of Calderwood, and daughter of Robert Pasley, Esq., of Mount Annan, who died on the 19th July, 1857; William H. Playfair, architect of Donaldson's Hospital, the New College, and other public buildings at Edinburgh, who died on the 19th March, 1857, and Dr. Thomas Clark, minister of St. Andrew's Church, who died on the 11th January, 1857. Dr. Clark was born in Galloway, in September, 1790. Licensed by the Presbytery of Kirkcudbright in 1819, he was, in 1824, ordained to the pastoral charge of Methven, Perthshire. In 1843 he was admitted to the collegiate charge of St. Andrew's Church, Edinburgh. In the public business of the Church

Dr. Clark took considerable interest; he was much devoted to the pastoral duties.

An obelisk of polished granite, with a bronze medallion, has been erected by the congregation of St. Stephen's Church, in memory of the Rev. Dr. William Muir, their late pastor. This esteemed clergyman was licensed in 1810, and was in 1812 ordained to St. George's Church, Glasgow. In 1822 he was translated to New Greyfriars Church, Edinburgh, from which he was transferred to St. Stephen's Church in 1828, when it was erected into a parish. In 1838 he was elected Moderator of the General Assembly. He died at Ormelie, Murrayfield, on the 23rd June, 1869. Dr. Muir was, after the Disruption in 1843, consulted by Government in the filling up of the parochial cures in the gift of the Crown. He was a laborious and faithful minister. He published several volumes of Discourses and other works.

A monument commemorates the Hon. John Lord Cunningham, of Duloch, senator of the College of Justice, who died on the 26th October, 1854. Lord Cunningham derived considerable notoriety during the period which preceded the Disruption, on account of his decisions as Lord Ordinary adverse to the views of the General Assembly.

A monument of Aberdeen granite denotes the grave of Robert Handyside, a judge of the Court of Session, by the title of Lord Handyside. Son of a Writer to the Signet, he was born at Edinburgh in 1793. In 1822 he passed Advocate, and in 1840 was appointed Sheriff of Stirlingshire. He became Solicitor-General in 1852, and in the following year was raised to the bench. He died on the 18th April, 1858.

John Riddell, Advocate, the most profound of Scottish genealolists, is interred in this cemetery. He was born in 1785, and was called to the Scottish Bar in 1807. For many years he devoted himself to the study of Scottish family history, many of the principal charter chests passing under his review. His familiarity with the law—feudal, consistorial, genealogical, and heraldic—was unrivalled. His principal work, "Inquiry into the Law and Practice in Scottish Peerages," is held as an authority. Mr. Riddell died at Edinburgh on the 8th February, 1862. A tombstone erected to his memory is thus inscribed:—

"Johannes Riddell, armiger, jurisconsultus, vir cujusque Ætatis imbutus literis; qui in antiquitate et ea præcipue quæ ad origines gentilicias pertinet, ad veritatem rerum revocanda. Prodigus laboris atque etiam felix fuit eandemque scriptis illustravit auctor animum consensu gravissimus; hoc in agro, qui proavorum ipsius olim fuit sepultus est. Natus IV° die Octobris, MDCCLXXXV. Decessit VIII° die Februarii, MDCCCLXII.; vixit annos LXXVI."

A handsome monumental cross, designed by Mr. James Drummond, R.S.A., has just been erected to the memory of Dr. Joseph Robertson, the distinguished antiquary. He was born at Aberdeen in 1811, and was educated at Marischal College. At an early age he began to write on local antiquities in the provincial journals; he subsequently became newspaper editor, first in Aberdeen, afterwards at Edinburgh. In 1839 he joined the "Spalding Club," for which he edited many ancient charters and some historical memoirs. The Maitland and Bannatyne Clubs subsequently profited by his labours. An article which he contributed to the *Quarterly Review*, on the "Ecclesiastical and Domestic Architecture of Scotland," was much commended by Mr. Lockhart, and attracted general attention. In 1853 he was appointed Curator of the Historical Department in the General Register House, Edinburgh, an office which he filled with distinguished ability. Of his various publications, the "Councils and Canons of the Scottish Church," and "Inventory of the Jewels, &c., of Queen Mary," are the most widely known. As an accurate inquirer into every department of Scottish antiquarian lore he was held to be unrivalled. Dr. Robertson died on the 13th December, 1866, aged fifty-five. He was LL.D. of the University of Edinburgh.

Sir Archibald Alison, Bart., the historian of Europe, is interred in this cemetery. Son of the Rev. Archibald Alison, author of "Essays on Taste," and scion of the family of Alison of Newhall, Forfarshire, he was born at Kenley, Shropshire, on the 29th December, 1792. Educated at the University of Edinburgh, he was admitted Advocate in 1814. For eight years he travelled on the Continent. In 1822 he was appointed Advocate-Depute, an office which he held for ten years. In 1832 he published his "Principles of the Criminal Law of Scotland," to which in the following year he added "The Practice of the Criminal Law." He was appointed Sheriff of Lanarkshire in 1834. The first volume of his great work, the "History of Europe," appeared in 1833; it extended to nineteen octavo volumes. In 1845 Sheriff Alison was elected Lord Rector of Marischal College, Aberdeen; and in 1851 he was chosen Rector of Glasgow University. In June, 1852, he was created a baronet. He was D.C.L. of Oxford, a member of many of the learned societies, a constant contributor to *Blackwood's Magazine*, and an ingenious writer on political economy. He died at his residence, Possil House, Lanarkshire, on the 31st May, 1867. Sir Archibald Alison was a zealous promoter of patriotic and benevolent enterprises.

In the Dean Cemetery monuments or tombstones commemorate the following:—Major Thomas Fairweather, died 29th September, 1846; John Aitken of Mount Aitken, Victoria, Australia, died 21st October, 1853; John Bell, W.S., died 15th November, 1852; Archibald Bell, Sheriff of Ayr, died 6th October, 1854; George Swinton, son of the Honourable George Swinton of Swinton, died 17th June, 1854; John Scott, M.D., died 3rd May, 1853; Sir John Peter Grant of Rothiemurchus, died 17th May, 1848; Lieut.-Colonel James Oliphant Clunie, C.B., died 27th July, 1851; James Greig of West Cambus, W.S., died 25th December, 1850. William Richardson Dickson of Alton, died 2nd May, 1850; Rachel Jane Aytoun, daughter of Major-General Roger Aytoun of Inchdairnie, and Mrs. Jean Sinclair Aytoun of Balgreggie, died 3rd April, 1852, and Mary their second daughter, died 24th September, 1854; James Keir, M.D., died December 16th, 1852; David Erskine of Cardross, died 28th November, 1847; Matthew Wingrave of Kirkbank, died 23rd November, 1848; James Alexander Cruikshank of Langley Park, died 25th April, 1849; Henry Marshall, M.D., died 5th May, 1851; Robert Hepburn Swinton of Swinton, died 3rd June,

1852; Thomas Robertson Chaplain of Colliston, died 7th December, 1857; John Tod, W.S., died 24th December, 1856; Rev. John Stevenson, D.D., minister of Ladykirk, died 11th August, 1858; Annabella Macartney, wife of the Honourable Lord Cowan, died 31st October, 1858; Allan Menzies, Professor of Conveyancing in the University of Edinburgh, died 13th February, 1856; Robert Ainslie, W.S., died 11th December, 1858; Mrs. Marian Anstruther, daughter of the Right Honourable Sir John Anstruther, Bart., and wife of James Anstruther, W.S., died 19th June, 1859; James Murray, of Wick, Caithness, died 24th October, 1859; Robert Reid, Crown Architect, died 20th March, 1856; John Goodall, of Rennyhill, Advocate, died 23rd October, 1854; Captain Alexander Drysdale, died 27th August, 1854; Major William Blackwood, died 8th April, 1861; Rev. Henry Wright of Largnean, died 28th June, 1861; John Taylor, M.D., died July 14th, 1856; John Knapp, M.D., died November 8th, 1857; Robert Thomson, Advocate, Sheriff of Caithness, died 26th May, 1857; Rev. Robert Stirrat, minister of Free St. Cuthbert's, died 16th January, 1852; Alexander Black, Architect, died 19th February, 1858; Monsieur Gabriel Surenne, died 12th September, 1858; Major-General John Pringle, died 29th December, 1861; Lieut.-Colonel Humphrey Hay, died 30th August, 1860; James Russell, M.D., died 21st November, 1862; James George Hunter, eldest son of John Hunter, Auditor of the Court of Session, died 7th July, 1862; Patrick S. K. Newbigging, M.D., died 10th January, 1864; Lieut.-General Thomas Robert Swinburne, died 29th February, 1864; Lieut.-Colonel John Macdougall, died 3rd June, 1865; Lieut.-Colonel Æneas John Mackay, died 9th February, 1865; John Balfour Atkinson, died 2nd May, 1866; Major James Hunter Rutherfurd, died 1st February, 1866; Mrs. Campbell Hamilton of Dalserf, died 22nd February, 1867; Robert Allan, F.R.S.E., died 6th June, 1862; John Macneill of Ardnacross, died 10th November, 1867; Major-General Carnegy, C.B., died 1st August, 1862; Honora, youngest daughter of the late Sir Henry Havelock, Bart., died 15th August, 1861; Rev. Francis Gillies, minister of Free St. Stephen's, died 10th January,

1862; Robert Bell, Procurator of the Church of Scotland, and Sheriff of Haddingtonshire, died 27th April, 1861; Major-General William John Gairdner, C.B., died 3rd February, 1861; James Carlile, D.D., LL.D., died 2nd February, 1866; and the Rev. John Le Poer, French Rector of Temple Michael, Longford, Ireland, died 29th September, 1866. Monumental erections or mortuary enclosures denote the family burial-places of Sir John Graham Macdonald, Bart.; Major-General Wardlaw; Major-General Peter Dudgeon; William Blackwood, merchant; R. C. Williamson; Douglas Maclagan, M.D.; and Haig of Bonnington.

DALRY CEMETERY.

This cemetery is situated in the south-western suburb, about two and a half miles from the General Register House; it was laid out in 1845. Within its enclosure a handsome monument celebrates Lieut.-General Sir Neil Douglas, K.C.B., Colonel of the 78th Highlanders and Commander of the Forces in North Britain. He died on the 21st September, 1853, in his seventy-ninth year.

By an elegant monument is commemorated James Burnes, of Montrose, father of Sir Alexander Burnes, C.B., the distinguished traveller. His grandfather, James Burnes, was brother of William Burnes, father of the poet Burns. He was born in 1780 at Montrose, where for many years he practised as a solicitor and served as chief magistrate. He died at Edinburgh on the 15th February, 1852. His wife Elizabeth, daughter of Adam Glegg, of Montrose, died on the 25th February, 1851: she is commemorated on the same tombstone. Two of their sons, Sir Alexander and Charles Burnes, were massacred at Cabool, India, on the 2nd November, 1841.

A monument is reared to the memory of Captain George Eddington, who died on the 10th December, 1851, and of his sons Captain

George Eddington and Lieutenant Edward W. Eddington, who were both killed at the battle of the Alma on the 20th September, 1854.

A handsome monument celebrates the ministerial devotedness of the Rev. Alexander Lockhart Simpson, D.D., minister of Kirknewton. This estimable divine was educated for the Secession Church: he subsequently joined the Establishment, and was licensed by the Presbytery of Kirkcaldy in 1810. In October, 1812, he was ordained to the ministry at Kirknewton. In 1828 he was elected joint sub-clerk of the General Assembly; in 1859 he was on a vacancy promoted to the principal clerkship. He was elected Moderator of the General Assembly in 1849. He died on the 15th December, 1861, in the seventy-eighth year of his age and fiftieth of his ministry. Dr. Simpson was one of the earliest advocates of Church extension, and was for many years Convener of the Assembly's Committee on Home Missions. He was an earnest preacher, an eloquent debater, and a friendly man.

A marble obelisk commemorates Charles McIntosh, F.R.H.S., author of "The Book of the Garden," and other works.

There are tombstones in memory of

John M'Nab, of Inglisgreen, died 25th December, 1850: Captain James Galloway, R.N., died 12th August, 1846; Alexander Stephen, M.D., died 10th August, 1848; Alexander Cruikshank, of Keithock, died 18th January, 1855; Major Archibald Macneil, died 6th November, 1855; Archibald Mackenzie, of the Orphan Hospital, died 28th April, 1866; Lieutenant Evan Macpherson, died 5th December, 1859; and William Carmichael, Assistant Clerk of Session, died 15th November, 1860.

These quaint lines commemorate John Robertson, a native of the United States, who died 29th September, 1860, aged 22 :—

> "Oh, stranger! pause, and give one sigh
> For the sake of him who here doth lie
> Beneath this little mound of earth,
> Two thousand miles from land of birth."

THE GRANGE CEMETERY.

The Grange or Southern Cemetery is situated to the south of the meadows. In the front wall a mural tablet denotes the resting-place of Dr. Thomas Chalmers. This distinguished divine was born on the 17th March, 1780, at Anstruther, Fifeshire. He studied at the University of St. Andrews, and in his nineteenth year obtained licence as a probationer. In 1803 he was appointed assistant to Professor Vilant, of the Mathematical chair at St. Andrews, and in the same year was presented to the church living of Kilmany. He was translated to the Tron Church, Glasgow, in 1814. Hitherto he had devoted his chief attention to the exact sciences and to philosophical speculation; he was henceforth to concentrate his energies on theological study and parochial work. As a preacher he attained a national celebrity. In 1819 he was translated to St. John's parish, Glasgow, and here he began to develop his system of parochial economy, which he conceived would dispense with the necessity of a poor law. He accepted in 1823 the Professorship of Moral Philosophy at St. Andrews, where his popularity as a teacher restored to that university a portion of its earlier celebrity. In 1828 he was elected Professor of Divinity in the University of Edinburgh, an office which he held till the Disruption in 1843, when he was chosen Principal of the New College. In May, 1843, he was elected first Moderator of the Free Church; he was the principal framer of its Sustentation Fund. He died on the 31st May, 1847. A man of vigorous intellect and massive eloquence, Dr. Chalmers attracted persons of all ranks by the force and splendour of his declamation. His Astronomical Discourses are the most splendid specimens of pulpit eloquence which have been published. To Dr. Chalmers a public monument is in progress of construction (see *ante*).

A monument of Peterhead granite commemorates Sir Andrew Agnew, Bart., of Lochnaw, and his wife, Lady Agnew. Sir Andrew was born at Kingsdale, Ireland, on the 21st March, 1793. He

THE GRANGE CEMETERY.   147

was only child of Lieutenant Andrew Agnew, eldest son of Sir Stair Agnew, sixth Bart. of Lochnaw, representative of a family who were long hereditary Sheriffs of Wigtonshire. In his sixteenth year he succeeded his grandfather in his title and estates. He studied at the University of Edinburgh, and at Oxford. Entering Parliament as M.P. for Wigtonshire, in August, 1830, he began to take an interest in public affairs. His movement so zealously prosecuted for the legislative protection of the Sabbath took origin in 1832, and was continued till the period of his death. After a short illness he died at Edinburgh, on the 12th April, 1850. His wife, Madeline Lady Agnew, tenth daughter of Sir David Carnegie, Bart., of Southesk, was born on the 8th January, 1796, and died on the 21st January, 1858. A memoir of Sir Andrew Agnew has been published by Dr. Thomas McCrie, of London.

Sir Thomas Dick Lauder, Bart., of Fountainhall, a learned and ingenious writer, rests in this cemetery. He was born in 1784, and was for a short time an officer in the 79th Regiment. He was one of the original contributors to *Blackwood's Magazine.* Two romances from his pen, "Lochandhu," and "The Wolf of Badenoch," were formerly popular, and have been translated into several continental languages. His interesting account of "The Moray Floods in 1829" added to his reputation. In 1839 he was appointed Secretary to the Board of Scottish Manufactures, an office with which was afterwards conjoined the Secretaryship of the British Fisheries. He died on the 29th May, 1848. Besides the works enumerated, Sir Thomas composed several others, chiefly connected with subjects of natural history.

Sir John Dick Lauder, Bart., son of the preceding, is also commemorated. He was born at Relugas, Morayshire, in 1813, and was some time in the military service of the East India Company. He died on the 23rd March, 1867.

A monument of Peterhead granite commemorates Hugh Miller, the distinguished geologist. This remarkable individual was born at Cromarty, on the 10th October, 1802. Having lost his father when he was only five years old, he was brought up under the care of two of his mother's brothers, who severally imbued him with a taste for natural history and old Scottish traditions. With a substantial training at the grammar school of his native place, he commenced in his seventeenth year to work as a stonemason. In 1829 he published a small volume of poems, which a few years afterwards was followed by "Scenes and Legends of the North of Scotland." Having renounced his handicraft occupation, he obtained employment as a bank clerk. In 1840 he accepted an invitation to become editor of the *Witness* newspaper, then started at Edinburgh. He advocated with remarkable power the claims of the Non-intrusion party, and proved of essential service in the constitution of the Free Church. In 1840 he published his work on the "Old Red Sandstone," which at once led to his recognition as an accomplished geologist. Of his subsequent publications the more prominent are his "Footprints of the Creator" and "The Testimony of the Rocks." A course of persistent study at length preyed upon his health, his brain gave way, and in a frenzy he shot himself. He died at Portobello on the 23rd December, 1856.

An elegant obelisk commemorates the literary merits and private worth of John and Mrs. Christian Johnstone, a married pair whose names are intimately associated with Scottish literature during the last half-century. John Johnstone began life as a schoolmaster at Dunfermline: he subsequently became proprietor and editor of the *Inverness Courier*. Latterly he entered into business as a printer in Edinburgh. He projected the *Schoolmaster*, a weekly serial, which he some time conducted in connection with his wife. He died on the 3rd November, 1857, in his seventy-eighth year. Mrs. Johnstone is best known as author of the "Edinburgh Tales." She was a principal contributor to *Tait's Magazine*. She died on the 26th August, 1857, at the age of seventy-six.

A marble obelisk denotes the grave of Professor John Pringle Nichol, LL.D., the astronomical writer. He was born at Brechin on the 13th January, 1804. Having studied at King's College, Aberdeen, he was, in his seventeenth year, appointed parish schoolmaster of Dun, in the neighbourhood of his birthplace. He

THE GRANGE CEMETERY.

subsequently taught at Hawick and Cupar-Fife, and was afterwards elected rector of Montrose Academy. He now took licence as a probationer, intending for the ministry of the Established Church. In 1836 he was appointed to the Professorship of Practical Astronomy in the University of Glasgow, an office which he held till his death, which took place at Rothesay, on the 19th September, 1859. Among his principal works are "View of the Architecture of the Heavens," "The Solar System," "The Stellar Universe," and the "Cyclopædia of the Physical Sciences."

The poet David Vedder rests here. Son of a small landowner in the parish of Burness, Orkney, he was born in 1790. After some experience as a seaman, he entered the Revenue service in 1815 as first officer of an armed cruiser. A writer of verses from his boyhood, he published, in 1826, "The Covenanters' Communion, and other Poems," which was followed by a second volume of prose and poetry, under the title of "Orcadian Sketches." He contributed to the leading journals. He latterly resided in Edinburgh, where he died on the 11th February, 1854.

A tombstone commemorates William Lennie, the celebrated grammarian. Mr. Lennie was originally a teacher in the city; he latterly devoted himself to the publication of his "Principles of Grammar," a work of which he issued upwards of fifty editions. From the profits he was enabled to purchase a landed estate. He died on the 20th July, 1852.

A mural tablet commemorates Dr. David Irving, one of the most erudite of modern Scotsmen. He was born at Langholm on the 5th December, 1778. At the University of Edinburgh he studied with a view to the ministry, but he afterwards chose the literary profession. His "Elements of English Composition," which has passed through many editions, was issued in 1801. In 1804 he published his "Lives of the Scottish Poets," in two octavo volumes, which was followed by his most elaborate work, "Memoirs of the Life and Writings of George Buchanan." In 1820 he was appointed Keeper of the Advocates Library, an office which he held for thirty years. Dr. Irving died at Edinburgh on the 10th May, 1860. His "History of Scottish Poetry," a work of great research, was published posthumously.

The Rev. William Steven, D.D., minister of Trinity College Church, Edinburgh, is interred in this cemetery. Dr. Steven published "History of the Scottish Church, Rotterdam," "Memoir of George Heriot," and "History of the High School of Edinburgh." He was successively minister of the National Scottish Church, Rotterdam, Governor of Heriot's Hospital, and minister of Trinity College Church. He died on the 2nd April, 1857.

A monument of Peterhead granite commemorates the Rev. William King Tweedie, D.D., minister of Free Tolbooth Church, Edinburgh, who died on the 24th March, 1863. Mr. Tweedie, who had successively ministered in the Scots Church, London Wall, and as pastor of the South Church, Aberdeen, was in 1842 appointed to the Tolbooth Church, Edinburgh. This charge he resigned at the Disruption, in 1843. He was author of many religious publications, of which the more esteemed are "Lights and Shadows in the Life of Faith," "Seedtime and Harvest," "Rivers and Lakes of Scripture," and "Ruined Cities of the East."

A handsome Gothic cross celebrates the Rev. William Maxwell Hetherington, D.D., LL.D., Professor of Divinity in the Free Church College, Glasgow. This able divine and industrious historical writer was born in the Vale of Nith, Dumfriesshire, on the 4th June, 1803. Bred a gardener, he afterwards studied at the University of Edinburgh, and obtained licence as a preacher in 1830. In 1836 he was ordained to the ministry at Torphichen. Resigning his charge at the Disruption in 1843, he in the following year became Free Church minister at St. Andrews. In 1848 he was translated to Free St. Paul's, Edinburgh; he was appointed to his Professorship in 1857. He died on the 23rd May, 1865. Among other works Dr. Hetherington published "History of the Church of Scotland," "History of the Westminster Confession," "The Fulness of Time," and "The Minister's Family."

A monument of Aberdeen granite has been reared to the memory of James Miller, M.D., Professor of Surgery in the University of

Edinburgh. Professor Miller was son of the Rev. James Miller, minister of Eassie, and was born in 1812. He studied at the Universities of St. Andrews and Edinburgh, and, devoting his attention to medicine, became a Licentiate of the Edinburgh College of Surgeons. In 1842 he was elected Professor of Surgery in the University of Edinburgh, and at once took a high rank in his profession. His "Principles of Surgery," which appeared in 1844, has passed into a fourth edition. Dr. Miller was a zealous promoter of various schemes of social and religious improvement. He died on the 17th June, 1864.

A handsome Gothic cross commemorates Charles Maclaren, F.R.S.E., an eminent geologist, and founder of the *Scotsman* newspaper. This enterprising and ingenious person was born at Ormiston, Haddingtonshire, on the 7th October, 1782. Son of a small farmer, he was intended for a handicraft occupation, but owing to a delicate constitution, he became a mercantile clerk, and afterwards entered the Customs. In August, 1816, he resolved to establish a newspaper on liberal and independent principles, and on the 25th January of the following year the first number of the *Scotsman* was issued under his superintendence. During the first two years this journal was edited by Mr. John Ramsay McCulloch, afterwards of London; but in 1820 Mr. Maclaren, resigning his post in the Customs, undertook the editorial duties. He retained office till 1847, when he was succeeded by Mr. Alexander Russel, the present editor. He was a zealous geologist and a constant contributor to the scientific journals. His principal works are a "Dissertation on the Topography of the Plain of Troy," and "The Geology of Fife and the Lothians." He died on the 10th September, 1866. Mr. Maclaren married, on the 27th January, 1842, Jean Veitch, daughter of Richard Somner, of Somnerfield. This gentlewoman died on the 6th May, 1871, and was interred near the grave of her husband. She bequeathed £2,500 to establish a scholarship in the University of Edinburgh, to be designated the "Charles Maclaren Scholarship."

A tombstone commemorates the Rev. James Bryce, D.D., who

died on the 11th March, 1866. Dr. Bryce was in 1814 promoted from the ministerial charge of Strachan, Kincardineshire, to St. Andrew's Presbyterian Church, Calcutta. In 1836 he returned to Britain. He subsequently resided at Edinburgh, devoting a large portion of his time to ecclesiastical affairs. In the General Assembly he advocated the principles of the moderate party. His principal publications are "Sketch of the State of British India," and "Ten Years of the Church of Scotland."

A monument denotes the resting-place of the Rev. John Hunter, D.D., Minister of the Tron Church. This estimable clergyman was son of the Rev. Dr. Hunter, one of the ministers of Edinburgh. Licensed to preach in 1812, he was ordained to the ministry at Swinton, Berwickshire, in 1814. From this parish he was translated to the Tron Church in 1832. Devoted to his parochial duties, Dr. Hunter avoided public display. He declined nomination as Moderator of the General Assembly. He died on the 21st June, 1866.

A tombstone, erected by public subscription, marks the grave of Robert Lee, D.D., Professor of Biblical Criticism in the University of Edinburgh, and Minister of Old Greyfriars Church. Dr. Lee was born at Tweedmouth, North Durham, in November, 1804. For some time he wrought as a carpenter. Having entered on classical studies, he proceeded to the University of St. Andrews in 1824. In 1833 he was elected minister of Inverbrothock Chapel, Forfarshire. In 1836 he was translated to the parish of Campsie, from which he was promoted to Greyfriars Church in 1843. He was appointed Professor in 1846. Dr. Lee was a contributor to the periodicals, and author of several esteemed theological works, but he will be chiefly remembered for his enlightened views as a Churchman. Through his efforts instrumental music and more reverent postures in devotion have been introduced into the worship of the Established Church. After a period of feeble health he died at Torquay on the 14th March, 1868, in the sixty-fourth year of his age and thirty-fifth of his ministry. Dr. Lee was one of the Deans of the Chapel Royal.

Other notable persons whose remains have been consigned to the

THE GRANGE CEMETERY.   153

Grange Cemetery must be simply enumerated:—Graham Speirs, Sheriff of Mid-Lothian, died 24th December, 1847; Archibald Speirs, of the Hon. East India Company's service, died 8th March, 1806; James Wyse, surgeon, died October 7th, 1828; Rev. Thomas Lockerby, minister of Cadder, died 17th December, 1851; the Rev. Robert Watt, died 23rd January, 1853; the Rev. William Galbraith, an eminent mathematician, died 27th October, 1850; Rev. David Fraser, died 10th August, 1854; Rev. David Moir, superintendent of the Edinburgh City Mission, died 11th March, 1856; Rev. John Malcolm Smith, Professor of Oriental Languages, Queen's College, Kingston, Canada, died 3rd August, 1856; Samuel Brown, M.D., died 20th September, 1856; Rev. William Brown, M.D., died May 15th, 1863, and his sons Alexander Brown, M.D., died 15th November, 1839, and Robert Ebenezer Brown, M.D., died 10th April, 1849; Augustus Maitland, W.S., fifth son of Sir Alexander Charles Maitland Gibson, Bart., of Cliftonhall, died 26th January, 1855; John Maitland, Auditor of the Court of Session, sixth son of Sir Alexander Charles Maitland Gibson, Bart., of Cliftonhall, died 6th September, 1865; Rev. Thomas Pitcairn, minister of the Free Church, Cockpen, died 28th April, 1862; Rev. Walter Fairlie, minister of the Free Church at Liberton, died 25th November, 1856; Rev. John Jeffrey, Secretary to the Missionary Board of the Free Church, died 20th October, 1858; James Colquhoun, M.D., died 27th January, 1862; Peter Redford Scott, of Redford Hill, died 23rd May, 1865; George Monro, S.S.C., died 7th April, 1866; Rev. Alexander Renton, Theological Tutor of the Presbyterian Church, died 25th October, 1863; James Brewster Balfour, M.D., died 8th November, 1861; Alexander Cowan, of Valleyfield, died 19th February, 1859, "leaving sixty-one descendants to bless his memory;" Rev. James McEwen, minister of the United Presbyterian Church, Strathaven, died 13th November, 1859; Thomas Knox Beveridge, W.S., died 11th April, 1858; Wemyss Orrok, of Orrok, died 9th August, 1856; Rev. John Sime, died 28th April, 1864; Charles Chalmers (of Merchiston), brother of the Rev. Dr. Thomas Chalmers, died 12th November, 1864; Rev. John Calvin

McNair, died 19th January, 1859; James Crawfurd, W.S., died November, 1863; General Suetonius Henry Tod, died 1st September, 1861; George Ross, Professor of Law in the University of Edinburgh, died November 21st, 1863; James Nichol, publisher, died 26th April, 1866; Benjamin Hall Blyth, civil engineer, died 21st August, 1866; William Wemyss, Deputy Commissary-General, died 8th April, 1862; James Wyld, of Gilston, died 8th May, 1860; Captain Benjamin Wyld, died 30th August, 1860; Robert Edward Scoresby-Jackson, died 1st February, 1867.

NEWINGTON BURIAL-GROUND.

Newington Cemetery is situated in the S.S.E. suburb of Edinburgh; it was opened in 1820. Here rest the remains of Dr. James Brown, Professor of Natural Philosophy in Glasgow College. This ingenious individual was born in 1764, at Auchterderran, Fifeshire. At the University of St. Andrews he distinguished himself in literature and mathematics, and in his twenty-first year was appointed assistant to Professor Vilant, of the Mathematical chair. In 1790 he was appointed to the church living of Dunino, Fifeshire. He was elected Professor of Natural Philosophy in the University of Glasgow in 1796, but after a short trial was compelled, owing to feeble health, to retire on an allowance. He afterwards resided, first at St. Andrews and afterwards at Edinburgh, where he died on the 3rd November, 1838. Dr. Brown was an interesting conversationalist and an eminent scholar. Dr. Chalmers and other eminent persons were wont to attribute their first literary aspirations to the privilege of having associated with him.

Richard Huie, M.D., the ingenious hymn-writer, rests in this burying-ground. He was born at Aberdeen in 1795. Having studied at the High School and University of Edinburgh, he

NEWINGTON BURIAL-GROUND.

became a licentiate of the Edinburgh College of Surgeons in 1815. After practising about six years at Dundee he settled at Edinburgh in 1822. In 1840 he was elected President of the College of Surgeons. In 1843 he published "Sacred Lyrics," 32mo. He died on the 10th July, 1867. Dr. Huie was an active promoter of various philanthropic enterprises.

Other prominent persons who have found a resting-place in this burying-ground are as follow:—Alexander Allan, philosophical instrument maker, died 5th April, 1839; George Carfin, commissary clerk, died 21st December, 1849; Major Thomas Laing, died 19th December, 1826; Captain Alexander Wishart, died 30th October, 1810; Captain John Macdiarmid, died October 29th, 1844; James Sibbald, M.D., died 8th September, 1824; William Calder, formerly Lord Provost of Edinburgh, died 19th August, 1824; Rev. William Limont, minister of the Relief Church, South College Street, died 3rd January, 1833; William Farquhar, M.D., died 28th July, 1832; Robert Thomson of Kaimflat, died 25th February, 1843; Captain James Clapham, R.N., died 28th January, 1851; William Moffat, S.S.C., died 6th July, 1847; Francis Graham of Morphie, died 1847; Rev. Thomas Turnbull, minister of Anworth, died 6th July, 1838; Captain Alexander Knox, died 23rd February, 1855; Alexander Knox, M.D., died 5th March 1859; John Dinning, of Mavisbush, died 18th August, 1859; Robert Wilson, of the National Bank, died 12th February, 1862; Captain Thomas Brown, died 7th July, 1863; David Craigie, M.D., an eminent medical writer, died 17th May, 1866; Rev. Alexander Philip, Minister of the Free Church, Portobello, died 18th March, 1861; Rev. John Edmonstoun, Minister of the Free Church, Ashkirk, died 8th December, 1865.

In Echo Cemetery, Newington, a tombstone commemorates Colonel Robert Sinclair Sutherland of Brabster, who died on the 4th January, 1863.

Opposite to Auchindinny Gate, near Milton Bridge, about seven miles south from Edinburgh, a triangular stone fourteen feet in height bears the following inscription :—

"Sophia Inglis, 1775."

" Muse, at that name thy sacred sorrows shed,
Those tears eternal that embalm the dead;
Call round her tomb each object of desire,
Each purer frame informed with purer fire :
Bid her be all that cheers or softens life;
The tender sister, daughter, friend, and wife;
Bid her be all that makes mankind adore,
Recall her memory, and be vain no more.

PARISH OF BORTHWICK.

In the aisle of the old church are recumbent monumental statues of William, first Lord Borthwick, and his spouse. His lordship is in full armour, Lady Borthwick in the female attire of her period. Lord Borthwick was raised to the peerage by James I. before the year 1430; he obtained a charter under the Great Seal, authorizing him to build a castle upon the lands of Lochwarret, which, under the name of Borthwick Castle, afterwards became the chief seat of the family. As Sir William Borthwick he was employed in many important concerns; he was one of the commissioners for prolonging the truce in 1404; and he sat on the assize of the Duke of Lennox and the two sons of Murdoch, Duke of Albany, in 1424. His death took place before 1448. Lady Borthwick belonged to the noble House of Douglas.

PARISH OF COLINTON.

An upright block of trap rock in the vicinity of two cairns on the lands of Comiston is variously called the Kel Stane and Camus Stane; it is supposed to denote the burial-place of a Danish prince slain in battle.

In the floor of the parish church a stone coffin was found some years ago bearing this inscription:—"Here lyis ane honorabi voman. A. Hiriot spovs to I. Fovlis of Collingtovn qvha died 8 Avgvst 1593."

The family of Foulis came to Scotland in the reign of Malcolm Canmore, and acquired lands at Colinton in 1519. James Foulis of Colinton was appointed King's Advocate in 1528, and Clerk Register in 1531.

PARISH OF CORSTORPHINE.

The parish church of Corstorphine contains several monuments, and numerous armorial escutcheons connected with the ancient House of Forrester. On the north side of the chancel a figure in a recess represents Sir John Forrester, founder of the Collegiate Church, along with one of his three wives. Sir John was one of the commissioners for negotiating the release of James I. from his English captivity, and one of the hostages for his liberation. He was on the jury at the trial of Murdoch, Duke of Albany, in 1424. In 1425 he became Lord High Chamberlain. He died in 1440. Another figure in the chancel represents Sir John Forrester, son of the preceding, who was a distinguished soldier. His effigies represents him as a man of herculean mould.

At the east end of the church, Nicol Bannatyne, Provost of the Collegiate Church, is thus commemorated:—

"Istud collegium incepit anno Domini MCCCCXXIX. Et eodem anno Magister Nicholayus Bannachtyne prepositus, subtus jacens, qui obiit anno Dom. MCCCCLXX. Cujus anniversarius sibi simulque posteris magistris celebrabitur XIIII. die mensis Junii, pro quo annuus redditus 10 librarum in villa de novo Kyrkcramond. Orati pro papa et pro eo."

Translation:—

"This collegiate church was begun in the year of our Lord 1429; and in the same year Mr. Nicol Bannatyne was provost; who, lying here below, died in the year 1470. Whose anniversary, or yearly commemoration, for him and all the succeeding masters, will be celebrated upon the 14th day of June annually, for which a yearly rent of £10 is set apart out of the lands of New Kirk Cramond. Pray for the Pope and for him."

In the south aisle a Latin inscription, now obliterated, formerly commemorated a gift bequeathed to the poor by Patrick March, of the annual rent of forty pence.

The tombstone of a person named Clarkson formerly bore these lines :—

> "Here lies a piece of earth, which God one day
> Will send the best of heaven to fetch away;
> Resting in hope that, when our Lord shall call,
> Earth shall give up her share, and heaven have all."

At Corstorphine Hill a monumental stone, sculptured with a sword and the insignia of a knight in holy orders, is supposed to commemorate Bernard Steuart, Lord D'Aubigny; it was excavated from the ancient burial-vault of the Forresters. Lord D'Aubigny was knight of the order of St. Michael. He died in the house of Archibald Forrester of Corstorphine, June, 1508, and was buried in the aisle of the Collegiate Church. According to Monteith, his place of sepulture was adorned with a cross of gold, "which," he adds, "gave origin to the name of Corstorfine; for cross in French signifies *croce*, and *d'ore* gold; and 'fine' retains its own sound and significance."

In the old churchyard of Gogar rest the remains of Sir Robert Liston, the distinguished diplomatist. He was born in the parish of Kirkliston in 1742. For nearly half a century he acted as an ambassador at foreign courts. In 1821 he retired from his public duties, and established his residence on the estate of Milburn, in the parish of Ratho. He died in 1836, at the age of ninety-four. Sir Robert spoke ten different languages; he latterly obtained distinction as an agriculturist.

PARISH OF CRICHTON.

In the parish churchyard these quaint lines are cut on a tombstone:—

"In memory of a brother,
And if ye dinna ken the name,
Ye'll just look at the muckle stane,
But see ye dinna pu' the thyme,
I planted it in 'forty-nine."

PARISH OF DALKEITH.

Attached to the parish church of Dalkeith is a burial-aisle of the ducal House of Buccleuch. Here are interred the Countess Mary, who died in 1661, in her thirtieth year. Her sister, Anne, Duchess of Buccleuch and Monmouth, likewise rests in the aisle. She was wife of the reckless and unfortunate Duke of Monmouth, natural son of Charles II., who was executed in 1685, for an attempt to usurp the throne. The Duchess died on the 6th February, 1732, in her eighty-first year. Francis, Earl of Dalkeith, who died in 1750, at the age of thirty, was buried in the aisle. His son, Henry, third Duke of Buccleuch, was likewise sepulchred in the vault; he died on the 11th January, 1812, aged sixty-six.

Within the parish church a monument commemorates the Rev. William Calderwood, minister of the parish from 1659 to 1680. Son of Thomas Calderwood, Dean of Guild, Edinburgh, he was born in 1636, studied at the University of Edinburgh, and was ordained to the ministry at Dalkeith in September, 1659. Further particulars of his career are supplied by his epitaph, which proceeds thus:—

"In memoriam Gulielmi Calderwood, pastoris Dalkethensis, patris sui; qui obiit anno Dom. MDCLXXX. mensis vero Martii die 4to. Ac etiam memoriæ Margaretæ Craig, filiæ de Riccartoun, suæ matris, quæ decessit anno Dom. MDCLXXXII. mensis Septemb.

die 3tio. Necnon memoriæ M. Ludovici Calderwood sui fratris, cæterorumque puerorum qui hic cum patre et matre requiescunt.
"Hoc quicquid est monumenti poni curavit Thomas Calderwood, filius primogenitus.
"In obitum D. Gulielmi Calderwood, pastoris Dalkethensis, annos supra vicenos.

> "Non te deflemus cœlo, vir magne, receptum;
> Ploramus nostram, nec sine jure, vicem:
> Dotibus eximiis patris, pastoris, amici,
> Vix magis ornatum protulit ulla dies.
> Dum fluit esca duplex, sylvamque amplectitur ulnis,
> Caldervode, tibi fama perennis erit."

In the churchyard a monument (now removed) commemorated the Rev. John Vetche, minister of Westruther. He was son of John Vetche, minister of Roberton; he studied at the University of Glasgow, and was ordained to the ministry at Westruther in 1648. Refusing to conform to Episcopacy, he was in 1662 removed from his charge; he returned on an indulgence, but was summoned before the Privy Council in 1680, and, not appearing, was put to the horn. He was afterwards imprisoned at Edinburgh, and deprived for not accepting the Test. On the deprivation of his successor by the Act restoring Presbyterianism, he resumed his office in 1690. He died at Dalkeith on the 16th December, 1702, aged eighty-four. The following lines of Latin verse adorned his tombstone:—

> "Hic recubant Vetchi senis et venerabilis ossa,
> Spiritus est, Christi sanguine lotus, ovans;
> Hospes erat, mastixque mali, verique patronus,
> Alterius parcus, prodigus usque sui:
> En prope tres annos, post lustra bis octo, labores
> Finivit febris vis violenta tuos.
> Undecies quinos docuisti pastor in annos
> Eloquio, vita, carcere, morte, gregem."

Mr. Vetche composed "Ane Description of Berwickshire in the Merse," which is preserved in the Advocates Library.

On the north wall of the churchyard a tombstone, nearly illegible, commemorates the Rev. Dr. William Mein, minister of the parish. He studied at the University of Edinburgh, and was ordained minister at Tweedmouth in February, 1659. In 1661 he was translated to Lochrutton. He was deprived in 1662. Refusing the Indulgence, he was denounced by the Privy Council in 1673. In 1691 he was admitted to the ministerial charge of Dalkeith. He died 11th January, 1699, aged sixty-five.

The Rev. Dr. Henry Greive, minister of Dalkeith from 1765 to 1789, is celebrated by a gravestone. He was licensed to preach in 1759, and was in 1762 ordained minister of Twynholm, Kirkcudbrightshire. During the same year he was translated to Eaglesham. In 1765 he became minister of Dalkeith. He was preferred to New Greyfriars Church, Edinburgh, in 1789. He died on the 10th February, 1810. Dr. Greive was Moderator of the General Assembly in May, 1783; he was Chaplain in Ordinary to the King.

The oldest tombstone in the churchyard is thus inscribed:—

"Here lies ane worthie man called Robert Portus, and his wyfe Euphan Wauchope, quha departed in anno 1609. Here lies his son Robert Portus, and his spouse Jene, and his son, quha departed in ——."

In the new churchyard a tombstone commemorates Alexander Barrie, teacher in Edinburgh, and author of the popular school books. He died at Dalkeith on the 9th May, 1831.

In the old churchyard a female is thus celebrated:—

"Faith, Hope, and Love, with works of Faith, were still
  The dear companions of her life and heart;
  Her soul, where Love and she shall never part.
But least the stingless king of terrors boast
Of what he's won, and what he thinks she's lost,
The trump of God shall sound, the dust be raised,
Full victory given through Christ, God's name be praised."

PARISH OF DUDDINGSTON.

In the churchyard of this parish rest the remains of James Browne, LL.D., author of "History of the Highlands," and other works. This ingenious writer was born in the parish of Cargill,

Perthshire, in 1793. Having at St. Andrews University studied for the ministry, he obtained licence as a probationer. For some time he was ministerial assistant in the parish of Kinnoull. Disappointed in obtaining a settlement, he applied himself to legal studies, and in 1826 passed Advocate. His success at the Bar did not justify his ambition; he became editor of *Constable's Magazine*, and subsequently conducted the *Caledonian Mercury*; he sub-edited the seventh edition of the "Encyclopædia Britannica." Beside his "History of the Highlands" he published "History of the Inquisition" and "Critical Examination of Dr. M'Culloch's Work on the Highlands." He died in 1841. Some years before his death he married a relative of General Stewart of Garth, by whom he was perverted to the Romish faith. Dr. Browne's "History of the Highlands" is a work of considerable value.

William Duncan, Bailie of Duddingston, who died on the 5th June, 1708, aged 71, is celebrated in these lines:—

> "Nor Dedalus, nor Tully's skill can show
> His matchless worth, that's bury'd here below;
> True to his word, just, charitable, kind,
> Of an obliging and a constant mind,
> In publick and in private matters too,
> As bailie, elder, husband, father, true
> He to his wife and children left behind
> The last tokens of a virtuous mind;
> They unto him their gratitude to prove,
> Have caus'd erect this badge of mutual love.
> But reader stay, since no enjoyments can
> Redeem thee from the common lot of man;
> Look on this fabrick with a serious eye:
> By living well prepare thyself to die.
>
>   Agricola, et Prætor, senior, colo, protego, condo,
>   Rus, jus, templa, manu, consilioque prece."

PARISH OF GLENCROSS.

On the rising ground south of Turnhouse Hill stands the "Martyrs' Tomb." This erection commemorates those Covenanters who fell at the battle of the Pentlands, or Rullion Green, fought on the 28th November, 1666, between 900 Covenanters, under Colonel Wallace, and 8,000 horse and foot, under General Dalziel. The Covenanters were at first successful in beating back their opponents, but were at length overpowered by superior numbers. Nearly fifty of them fell and about one hundred were taken prisoners. The engagement took place in a valley which skirts the base of the Pentlands. The "Martyrs' Tomb" is inscribed thus:—

"Here, and near to this place, lie the Rev. John Cruickshanks and Mr. Andrew M'Cormack, ministers of the gospel, and about fifty other true covenanted Presbyterians who were killed in this place, in their own innocent self-defence, and in defence of the covenanted work of reformation, by Thomas Dalziel of Binns, upon the 28th of November, 1866. Rev. xii. 11.: 'And they overcame by the blood of the Lamb, and by the word of their testimony, and they loved not their lives unto the death.' Erected September 28th, 1738.

> A cloud of witnesses lye here,
> Who for Christ's interest did appear,
> For to restore true liberty,
> O'erturnèd there by tyranny;
> And by proud prelates who did rage
> Against the Lord's own heritage;
> They sacrificed were for the laws
> Of Christ their King, His noble cause.
> These heroes fought with great renown,
> But falling got the martyr's crown."*

---

* The battle of the Pentlands is thus celebrated by the Baroness Nairne, who, though a member of the Church of England, was an enthusiastic admirer of those Scottish Presbyterians who, during the persecutions of the seventeenth century, consented to die rather than abjure their faith :—

John Cruickshanks or Crookshanke was son of the Rev. John Crookshanke, minister of Redgorton, Perthshire. He was sometime Regent of Humanity in the University of Edinburgh, and was ordained minister at Raphoe, Ireland, before 1661. Andrew M'Cormack or M'Cormick was bred a tailor, but subsequently qualifying himself for the ministry, he obtained a living in the Irish Presbyterian Church. Along with Crookshanke he had been banished to Scotland on account of uncompromising adherance to Nonconformity and resistance of the episcopal yoke. "Not expecting or seeking for pardon in Ireland," writes Mr. Patrick Adair,* "they joined with that party in Scotland which was broken at Pentland, and were there both killed. They were zealous men, but walked too much in a separate way from their brethren, and meddled in matters too high for them."

"The Pilgrim's feet here oft will tread
  O'er this sequestered scene,
To mark where Scotland's martyrs lie
  In lonely Rullion Green:
To muse o'er those who fought and fell,
  All Presbyterians true,
Who held the League and Covenant,
  Who waved the banner blue!

"Like partridge to the mountain driven,
  Oh! lang and sairly tried!
Their cause they deemed the cause o' Heaven,
  For that they lived and died!
Together here they met and prayed,
  Ah! ne'er to meet again!
Their windin'-sheet the bluidy plaid,
  Their grave lone Rullion Green.

"Ah! here they sang the holy strain,
  Sweet martyrs' melodie;
When every heart and every voice
  Arose in harmonie.
The list'ning echoes all round
  Gave back their soft reply,
While angels heard the hallow'd sound,
  And bore it to the sky.

"Oh, faithless King! hast thou forgot
  Who gave to thee thy crown?
Hast thou forgot thy solemn oath,
  At Holyrood and Scone?
Oh, fierce Dalziel! thy ruthless rage
  Wrought langsome misery.
What Scottish heart could ever gi'e
  A benison to thee?

"I love to wander *there* my lane,
  Wi' sad and sacred feeling,
While hallowed mem'ries wake the tear
  In waefu' eye soft stealing.
I love thy wild sequester'd glen,
  Thy bonny, wimplin' burn;
For Scotland's brave and martyr'd men
  Still does it seem to mourn."

---

* "A True Narrative of the Rise and Progress of the Presbyterian Church in Ireland," by the Rev. Patrick Adair. Belfast, 1866, 8vo., pp. 283-4.

PARISH OF INVERESK.

A square pillar at the eastern extremity of the grounds of Eskgrove commemorates the encampment at this spot of the army of the Duke of Somerset. It is thus inscribed:—

> "The Protector, Duke of Somerset,
> Encamped here, 9th September,
> 1547."

The Duke of Somerset entered Scotland on the 2nd September, 1547. After routing the forces of Lord Hume at Faside he marched to the church of Inveresk, and encamped on the spot denoted by the monument. He broke up his camp on the morning of the 10th, and proceeded to meet the Earl of Angus and the army which had been mustered to resist him. The armies met on the field of Pinkie, when the Scots were completely defeated.

An artificial eminence in the churchyard is known as "Oliver's Mound;" it is popularly described as the work of Cromwell's army, but is more likely to have been of Roman origin.*

In the churchyard the following inscription is engraved on the tombstone of the Rev. Oliver Colt, minister of the parish:—

"Memoriæ sacrum magistri Oliverii Colt, hujus ecclesiæ pastoris vigilantissimi, pientissimi, evangelistæ suavissimi, facundissimi, viri integerrimi, saluberrimi, post sedecem et amplius lustra, quorum 8, plus minus sincere, pie, candide, gregi, cujus cura illi a creatore suo demandata, delegata, invigilando exacta, tandem magis senio quam segnitie, sponte magis quam morbo in nunc tumulum delapsi. Obiit penultimo Decembris, anno Dom. MDCLXXIX. Ætatis suæ 82. Mœrens posuit magister Robertus Colt, juriscon. & filius & hæres.

> Quisquis es, amissos solitus lugere parentes,
> Huc ades, hos cineres collachrymare juvet.
> Hic pietas, hic vera fides, hic pristina virtus,
> Religionis honos & probitatis apex.

* "New Statistical Account," vol. i., pp. 275—277.

> Huic epulæ servasse animas ; huic lanta supellex,
>   Intemerata Dei gloria, cura gregis ;
> Cujus non paucos, variis erroribus actos,
>   Restituit ; teneros soverat ipse sinu.
> Octoginta annos animo vultuque serenus,
>   Pacis amans vixit, pacis amator obiit.
> Felicem O nimium vitam, mortemque beatam !
>   Contigit heu paucis, sic potuisse mori."

Mr. Colt studied at the University of Edinburgh, and was licensed to preach in 1627. He was ordained assistant minister of Inveresk in December, 1632 ; and died on the 30th December, 1679,, at the age of eighty-two.

In the churchyard a tombstone celebrates Dr. Alexander Carlyle, minister of the parish, and a distinguished leader of the Church. It is inscribed as follows :—

"Alexander Carlyle, D.D. Fifty-seven years minister of this parish. Born on the 26th January, 1722. Deceased on the 25th August, 1805. Having thus lived in a period of great lustre to the country in arts and arms, in literature and science ; in freedom, religious and civil, he too was worthy of the times. Learned and eloquent, liberal and exemplary in his manners, faithful to his pastoral charge, not ambitious of popular applause, but to the people a willing guide in the ways of righteousness and truth ; in his private connections a kind relation, an assiduous friend, and an agreeable companion ; not immersed in speculation, but earnest in action to promote the merit he esteemed or the public cause he espoused ; and when full of years calmly prepared to die in peace."

Dr. Carlyle was a native of Prestonpans, of which parish his father was minister. Having studied at the Universities of Glasgow, Edinburgh, and Leyden, he obtained licence in 1746. He was ordained minister of Inveresk in 1748. He was censured by the General Assembly for being present at the first performance of the tragedy of "Douglas," in December, 1756. In 1762 he was appointed Almoner to the King, and some time after a Dean of the Chapel Royal. He was elected Moderator of the Assembly in May, 1770.

In his advanced age Dr. Carlyle prepared an autobiography, which was published in 1860 under the editorial care of Dr. John Hill Burton, Historiographer Royal. It presents an interesting picture of the times.

A small tombstone denotes the grave of David Macbeth Moir, the ingenious poet. Born at Musselburgh on the 5th January, 1798, he studied for the medical profession, and became surgeon in 1816. He early composed verses, and in his nineteenth year, under the signature of *Delta*, became a poetical contributor to *Blackwood's Magazine*. In 1824 he published "The Legend of Genevieve, with other Tales and Poems," which was followed in 1828 by "The Autobiography of Mansie Waugh." He practised medicine at Musselburgh, and by his professional services rendered gratuitously to the poor, obtained deserved favour. His "Outlines of the Ancient History of Medicine" appeared in 1831. He died at Dumfries on the 6th July, 1851. His poetical works, edited by Mr. Thomas Aird, were published at Edinburgh in 1852. On the bank of the Esk, near Musselburgh Dr. Moir is commemorated by a statue executed by Ritchie.

Inveresk Churchyard contains the following monumental rhymes:—

"Rest while affection oft will drop the tear,
Till Fate shall summon us to join you here."

"Ah, what is life with ills compassed round!
Amidst our hopes death strikes the sudden wound."

"His boast is
Not that he derived his birth
From loins enthroned and monarchs of the earth,
But higher far his scriptural hopes arise,
The son of parents passed into the skies.
'The seed of the righteous is blessed.'"

"Rest yet awhile within this narrow room,
Ye high-prized relics of the best of men,
Till at the trumpet's sound the faithful tomb
Shall render up its trust to earth again.

>Then shall exalting choirs of angels cry,
>'Happy the man whose talent is improv'd,
>Come, heir of glory, to your master's joy,
>Come taste the applause of the God you lov'd'

>"Through life's perplexing seas
>His course he steer'd,
>With steady hand,
>He all those dangers clear'd
>Till anchor'd here.
>When all the storms are o'er,
>Has driven we hope
>Safe on Emmanuel's shore,
>Where dangers cease,
>And storms assail no more."

PARISH OF KIRKLISTON.

Two erect stones at Lochend, near Newbridge, commemorate an engagement which took place in 995 between Kenneth, illegitimate brother of Malcolm II., and commander of his forces, and Constantine, who had usurped the Government. A monumental stone by the banks of the river Almond is believed to denote the spot where Constantine was slain.

At Linsmill, on the banks of the Almond, a flat stone, supported by six uprights, is associated with a curious tradition. It is believed to commemorate the last person in Scotland who died of "the plague." Though a person of property, the fear of infection was such that none would attend the funeral, nor would any joiner make a coffin. The wife of the deceased was, in consequence, necessitated to drag the body to this place, and prepare a grave with her own hands. The stone is inscribed—

"Here lye the dust of William Lin, Right Heritor of Linsmill, who died in the year of our Lord 1645."

Lord Stair, of Newliston, who died in 1629, is thus commemorated:—

"If ye wold live and die in peace,
Then love mercy and justice;
And keep frae guile your conscience clear,
As strave the man who lyeth here."

PARISH OF KIRKNEWTON.

In the churchyard of this parish a monument denotes the resting-place of the celebrated Dr. William Cullen. This distinguished physician was born at Hamilton, on the 11th December, 1710. For some time he practised in the parish of Shotts. He then removed to Hamilton. There he secured the patronage of the Dukes of Hamilton and Argyle, on whose united recommendation he was in 1746 appointed Lecturer on Chemistry at Glasgow. In 1751 he was elected Regius Professor of Medicine in Glasgow University. He was promoted in 1756 to the chair of Chemistry in the College of Edinburgh; he subsequently became Professor of the Practice of Medicine. He died on the 5th February, 1790. He published many medical works, some of which retain professional favour. A statue of Dr. Cullen, at the cost of his students, was placed in one of the halls of Edinburgh College.

Near the grave of Dr. Cullen are entombed the remains of his eldest son, Robert, a judge, by the title of Lord Cullen. This distinguished lawyer and miscellaneous writer was admitted Advocate on the 15th December, 1764. After a brilliant career at the Bar he was appointed a Lord of Session in November, 1796. He contributed essays to the *Mirror* and *Lounger*. As a mimic he is celebrated in "Kay's Edinburgh Portraits." He died on the 28th November, 1810. His tombstone bears that he was "an eminent judge, an elegant scholar, and an accomplished gentleman."

Within the church a small tablet commemorates the Rev. Alexander Bryce, the eminent geometrician. It is inscribed—

"Here lie the remains of the Reverend Alexander Bryce, who

was minister of this parish for forty years, and one of the chaplains in ordinary to His Majesty. He was a man of true piety, of great benevolence, and of general science. He died in 1786, aged seventy-three, universally regretted."

Mr. Bryce was born at Kincardine-in-Menteith, in 1713. Having studied at Edinburgh University, he was licensed to preach in 1744. In the following year he was ordained minister of Kirknewton. As a mathematical scholar he was widely celebrated. In 1752 he discovered, among some old lumber at Stirling, the standard jug, or pint measure, which had been committed by an Act of Parliament to the keeping of the magistrates of that burgh. He contributed many scientific papers to the Transactions of the Royal Society of London, and to *Ruddiman's Weekly Magazine*. He assisted in revising the calculations of the Ministers' Widows Fund. He was a considerable poet, and composed the three last stanzas of the popular song "The Birks of Invermay."

Another monumental slab within the church celebrates Major-General Sir Alexander Bryce, K.C.B., Inspector-General of Fortifications, son of the preceding. He died at London in 1832, and was buried in St. John's Wood Chapel.

In the churchyard rest the remains of the Rev. William Cameron, minister of the parish, a poet, and one of the authors of the Church Paraphrases. He studied at Marischal College, Aberdeen, where he secured the friendship of Dr. Beattie. He was ordained minister of Kirknewton in 1786. He published "Poems on Various Subjects," and other works. A second volume of poems from his pen appeared posthumously. He composed the fourteenth, seventeenth, and sixty-sixth Paraphrases, and revised thirty-nine others. He died at Kirknewton on the 17th November, 1811.

In a private burying-ground on the estate of Meadowbank a monument denotes the grave of Allan Maconochie, Lord Meadowbank. This distinguished judge was born in 1748. When a student at Edinburgh College he founded the Speculative Society, in which so many who have afterwards adorned the walks of literature, have afforded the first evidence of their powers. He was admitted to the Scottish bar in 1770, and was raised to the bench in 1796; he was some time previously Sheriff of Renfrew, and Professor of Public Law in the University of Edinburgh. He died in 1816.

PARISH OF LASSWADE.

In an aisle of the old church rest the remains of William Drummond, of Hawthornden, the poet. Son of Sir John Drummond of Hawthornden, he was there born on the 13th December, 1585. He studied at the University of Edinburgh, and at Bourges, in France. In 1610 he succeeded his father; and retiring to his romantic seat, devoted himself to the composition of poetry. He published in 1616 "The Cypress Grove," and "Flowers of Zion, or Spiritual Poems." The death of a young lady to whom he was to be married oppressed him with melancholy: he sought relief by foreign travel. On his return he composed his "History of the Five Jameses," which, however, was not published till after his decease. He died on the 4th December, 1649. An edition of his "Poems" was printed in 1656; and his whole works were issued in 1711 under the superintendence of Ruddiman. Drummond was a strong supporter of monarchy; and the untimely fate of Charles I. is said to have hastened his own death.

A monumental stone chair at the south front of Hawthornden House bears the following inscription:—

" To the memory of Sir Lawrence Abernethy, of Hawthornden, second son to Sir William Abernethy, of Saltoun, a brave and gallant soldier, who at the head of a party in the year 1338, conquered Lord Dowglas five times in one day—yet was taken prisoner before sunset; (Ford. lib., xiii., cap. 44.) and to the memory of William Drummond, Esq., of Hawthornden, Poet and Historian, an honour to his family, and an ornament to his country, this seat is dedicated by the Reverend Dr. William Abernethy Drummond, spouse to Mrs. Drummond, of Hawthornden, and sixth son to Alex. Abernethy, of Corskie, Banffshire, heir male of the Abernethies of Saltoun, in the year 1784.

> "O sacred solitude! divine retreat!
> Choice of the prudent, envy of the great!
> By thy pure stream, or in thy waving shade,
> I court fair wisdom, that celestial maid.
> There from the ways of men laid safe ashore,
> I smile to hear the distant tempest roar;
> There happy, and with business unperplext,
> This life I relish and secure the next."

In the parish churchyard rest the remains of Henry Dundas, first Viscount Melville. This eminent statesman was son of Robert Dundas, of Arniston, Lord President of the Court of Session. He was born at Edinburgh on the 28th April, 1742. Having studied at the University of Edinburgh, he passed Advocate in 1763. He was appointed Solicitor-General in 1773, and in the following year was returned to Parliament as member for Edinburghshire. In 1775 he became Lord Advocate, and in 1782 was appointed Treasurer of the Navy, and sworn a Privy Councillor. Subsequently he became President of the Board of Control. In 1791 he was appointed Secretary of State for the Home Department. In 1802 he was raised to the Peerage as Viscount Melville. In 1804 he succeeded Lord St. Vincent as first Lord of the Admiralty. Impeached by the House of Commons for mal-appropriating the funds of the Navy, he was, on his trial before the House of Lords in April, 1806, honourably acquitted. He died at Edinburgh, on the 27th May, 1811. Lord Melville is commemorated by a monument in St. Andrew's Square, and a marble statue in the Parliament House, Edinburgh; and also by an obelisk on Dunmore Hill, Perthshire. He possessed great political sagacity, with prudence and tact as an administrator.

The following inscriptions are from tombstones in Lasswade Churchyard:—

> "God keeps his own within the grave,
>   In safe repose to lie
> Till shade of sin is past and gone,
>   And glory decks the sky."

"Farewell, all joy, since hope gives nothing new,
But like a sieve lets every pleasure through;
Farewell, ye rural plains, for she is gone,
To whose lov'd memory I erect this stone."

"Before this youth to manhood grew,
Of which there none need boast,
With length of days before his view,
He yielded up the ghost."

At Dryden a monument of curious workmanship commemorates James Lockhart Wishart, of Lee and Carnwath. The tomb, which is enclosed with a parapet and iron railing, is eight feet in height and 200 feet in circumference. There is an octagonal column twelve feet high and nine broad; it supports a cradle about eight feet long and four broad. On the top is a lantern surmounted by a groined arch, supported by four pillars, twenty feet in height and five feet square. The key-stone of the arch terminates in a globe suspended over the cradle. On the south side of the column are the armorial bearings of the Lee family, in which is an emblem of the casket which contained the heart of King Robert the Bruce, borne by Sir James Douglas, founder of the family, to the Holy Land. Under the casket are the words "Corda serata pando."

On the east side of the column a marble slab bears the following inscription :—

"James Lockhart Wishart, of Lee and Carnwath, Lord of the Bedchamber to his Imperial Majesty Joseph the Second, Emperor of Germany, Knight of the Order of Maria Teresa, Count of the Holy Roman Empire, and General of the Imperial, Royal, and Apostolical Armies, died at Pisa, in Italy, VIth February, MDCCXC, in the LXIVth year of his age."

Between the column and the railing on the east side, beneath a large stone, rest the remains of James, Count Lockhart, of Lee and Carnwath, son of General Count Lockhart; he died in 1802.

On the west side of the column a marble slab is inscribed thus :—

"Jacobus Lockhart Wishart, de Lee et Carnwath, Josephi secundi Romanorum imperatoris dominus cubicularius ordinis militaris Mariæ Teresiæ eques, sacri Romani imperii comes, et imperialium regionum, et apostolicorum exercituum prefectus generalis; decessit Pisis in Italia, anno ætatis suæ sexagesimo quarto, mensis Februarii die sexto, 1790."

Between the column and the railing on the west side, rest beneath a large stone, the remains of Marianne Matilda Lockhart, and on the adjoining pillar is a richly decorated marble tablet with this inscription:—

"Sacred to the Memory of Marianne Matilda Lockhart, relict of the late Anthony Aufrere, Esq., of Hoveton, in Norfolk, and daughter of General Count Lockhart, of Lee and Carnwath, Lanarkshire. Born 15th October, 1774. Died 14th September, 1850."

Roslin Chapel is the burial-place of the ancient house of St. Clair.* A large flagstone at the foot of the third and fourth pillars covers a vault in which were interred ten Barons of Roslin prior to the year 1690. According to the custom of the house all the barons were interred in armour and uncoffined. A coarse flat stone sculptured with the representation of a man in armour, with his hands joined as in the act of devotion, and a greyhound at his feet, is supposed to denote the tomb of Sir William St. Clair, of Rosslyn, a puissant knight and attached follower of Robert the Bruce. On the demise of that monarch Sir William accompanied Sir James Douglas in his expedition to the Holy Land with the King's heart. He fell with Sir James in contending with the Moors in Spain, on the 25th August, 1330.

On the west wall of the north aisle is the monument of George, Earl of Caithness, thus inscribed:—

> * "There are twenty of Roslin's barons bold
> Lie buried in that proud chapelle;
> *   *   *   *   *   *
> And each St. Clair was buried there
> With candle, with book, and with knell."
> *Ballad of Rosabelle* in "The Lay of the Last Minstrel."

"Hic jacet nobilis ac potens domenvs Georgivs qvondam comes Cathanensis, dominvs Sinclar jvsticiarivs hereditarivs diocesis Cathanensis; qvi obiit Edinbvrgi 9 die mensis Septembris, anno Domini 1582."

Roslin Chapel is now the burial-place of the noble family of St. Clair-Erskine, Earls of Rosslyn. Within the ancient vault are deposited the mortal remains of General Sir James St. Clair-Erskine, Bart., second Earl of Rosslyn, who died 18th January, 1837; and of his Countess, who died August, 1810. The vault also contains the remains of James Alexander St. Clair Erskine, third Earl of Rosslyn, who died 16th June, 1866, and of his Countess, Frances, daughter of Lieutenant-General Wemyss, of Wemyss, who died 30th September, 1858.

PARISH OF LIBERTON.

Two ancient burying-grounds in this parish, St. Catherine's and St. Mary's Chapel, Niddry, have with their monuments disappeared. In the parish churchyard a monument commemorates the Rev. Archibald Newtoune; it is thus inscribed:—

"Reverendus dominus Archibaldus Newtonus, honestis parentibus & liberali institutione domi felix; postea imbelli corpusculo, carceris squalore ac malis, apud purioris religionis hostes foris, attrito in patriam redux, ingenio & eloquentia sic claruit, ut primum Duddingstoniæ anno 4, & deinde 18 Libertoniæ pastor, utrobique in mutuo gregis amore, religionis & regii dignitatis constans assertor: anima tandem 2 Junii, 1657, in cœlos migravit & corporis exuvias in piorum resurrectionem hic recondi voluit."

Mr. Newtoune died on the 2nd June, 1657, aged fifty-two. He made a bequest to the kirk session of the parish. In the church tower a monument, recently renovated, commemorates the Rev. Samuel Semple, minister of the parish, who died on the 24th January, 1742, aged seventy-six. He proposed to compose a history of the Church of Scotland, an undertaking in which he was encouraged by the General Assembly, and by the Lords of the Treasury. He made important transcripts in the Bodleian and Cottonian Libraries, but afterwards abandoned his design. Of a benevolent disposition, nearly £2,000 were after his decease found due to him by those whom he had obliged with loans.

A mortuary enclosure acquired by Gavin Nisbet for his family use was thus inscribed:—

"Magister Gavinus Nisbetus, sibi & suis posteris, per actum sessionis hujus ecclesiæ, sepulchrum hic posuit. Sexto Novembris, 1631, vixit annos 70. Obiit 22, die mensis Junii, 1637.

> Adam primus homo damnavit secula pomo;
>   Abstulit at damnum filius ipse Dei:
> Mors tua, Christe; mihi vita est, victoria, regnum;
>   Labe mea morior, sanguine viva tuo.
> Unde superbit homo, cujus conceptio culpa,
>   Nasci pœna, labor vita, necesse mori?
> Nudus ut in mundum veni, sic nudus abibo;
>   Peccatis Christus sit medicina meis.
> Vivus adhuc spero, moriturus forte sub horam;
>   Mors eterni certa est; funeris hora latet.
> Pulvis et umbra sumus, vivit post funera virtus.
>
> Qui dat pauperibus, thesauros colligit astris;
>   In quos nil fures juris habere queunt."

Monteith has thus translated the Latin verse:—

> "Adam, first man, the world condemn'd by sin
> The Son of God repairs what lost therein.
> O Christ, thy death's my life, reign, victorie;
> My sin brought death, thy blood brings life to me.
> Whence is man proud? O prithee, tell me why
> Man, whose conception's in iniquity,
> Birth pain, life labour, death necessity?
> As to the world I came, so hence
> I shall depart; Christ, pardon my offence,
> On life, I hope, so shall at final hour:
> For death is certain, but its time obscure.
> All men are dust and shade; virtue survives
> The grave, and endless life to th' virt'ous gives.
>
> Who give to th' poor, in heav'ns treasures have,
> The which no thieves can either claim or crave."

PARISH OF NEWBATTLE.

The Abbey of Newbattle, now in ruins, was founded by David I. in 1140; it was planted with monks from Melrose Abbey. Within the precincts was interred John Scot, Bishop of Dunkeld. Some time before his death he resigned his episcopal office, and became a monk in this monastery. He died in 1203. His Life was composed by William Binnine, Prior of Newbattle, and afterwards Abbot of Coupar.

PARISH OF PENICUIK.

In the grounds of Penicuik House an obelisk in honour of Allan Ramsay attests the taste and good feeling of the poet's friend and patron, the celebrated Sir John Clerk, second Baronet of Penicuik. During the conflict with Napoleon, the Valleyfield paper mills were fitted up for 6,000 prisoners of war. At the termination of the war the proprietor raised a monument over the remains of 300 prisoners who were interred within the enclosure. The monument is thus inscribed:—

"Grata quies patriæ, sed, et omnis terra sepulchrum."

The parish churchyard contains these metrical inscriptions:—

"Like crowded forest trees we stand,
 And some are marked to fall;
 The axe will smite at God's command,
 And soon shall smite us all."

"If children are God's heritage,
 Why should the lonely parents grieve
When He doth call them under age,
 And a more noble life doth give?
Dear infants sing loud songs of praise,
 From sin and toil so soon set free;
In heavenly notes to Him who says,
 Forbid not babes to come to Me."

"The Lord did heal the parents' hearts
  Of those two little brothers;
When Death cut down these little flowers,
  God did their anguish smother.

"Dear parents, weep no more for us,
  Nor breathe another sigh;
For God required our souls above,
  In our home beyond the sky."

"Our parents' grief no tongue can speak,
  Nor yet no one can tell;
But rest yourselves content on earth,
  While we in heaven do dwell.

"And comfort your poor drooping hearts,
  And mind your steps full well;
For we in heaven may meet again,
  And there with Christ will dwell."

"Three loving sisters lyeth here,
  Betsey, Mary, and Ann;
But death severe soon
  Our parents' grief began.

"Our parents nursed us tenderly
  While on the earth we stayed;
But God was pleased to call us here,
  So in the grave we're laid.

"Dear father, weep no more for us;
  Dear mother, grief forbear;
For while on earth you've leave,
  We're only sleeping here."

LINLITHGOWSHIRE.

PARISH OF ABERCORN.

Attached to the parish church is the family vault of Dalyell, of Binns, erected in 1623. The family of Dalyell, of Binns, are a younger branch of the house of Dalzell of Dalzell now Earls of Carnwath. Thomas Dalyell of Binns (born 1571, died 1643) was father of Thomas Dalyell, of Binns, better known as General Dalyell. This notorious adherent of the Stuart dynasty was born at Binns, about the year 1599. He entered the army, and on the outbreak of the civil war vigorously upheld the royal cause. He commanded the garrison at Carrickfergus, and was taken prisoner by the rebels. After the execution of Charles I. he did not shave nor crop his beard. Captured at the battle of Worcester in 1651, he was committed to the Tower, and his estates were forfeited. Having effected his escape, he proceeded abroad, and for a time entered the military service of the Czar, who gave him rank as General. In 1665 he returned to Scotland, when he was by Charles II. appointed Commander-in-Chief. In 1666 he suppressed the rising at Pentland, and continued to oppress and destroy the adherents of Presbyterianism. In 1681 he raised the regiment since known as the Scots Greys. On his accession, James VII. enlarged his military commission; but he now retired to his ancestral estate, which he took pleasure in adorning. His portrait is preserved in Binns House. His remains, it is believed, were interred within the family vault.

A handsome mausoleum in Saxon architecture protects the remains of John, fourth Earl of Hopetoun. Three other monuments have been erected to his memory. (See ante.)

PARISH OF BATHGATE.

The parish churchyard surrounds the ruin of the old church. A new cemetery was laid out in 1860. In the churchyard a covenanter, who was shot by a dragoon on the dispersion of a conventicle held in the parish, is commemorated by a tombstone inscribed thus :—

"Here lies the body of James Davie, who was shot at Blackdub, April, 1673, by Heron, for his adhering to the word of God and Scotland's convenated work of reformation in opposition to Popery, prelacy, perjury, and tyranny. Repaired by a few men in this parish."

Tombstones commemorate the incumbents of the parish undernamed :—The Rev. George Blackwell, who died 7th April, 1749, in his thirty-sixth year and fourteenth of his ministry ; the Rev. Thomas Wardrobe, who died on the 7th May, 1756, aged forty-one; the Rev. Walter Jardine, who died 30th November, 1811, in the seventy-second year of his age and thirty-first of his ministry ; the Rev. Samuel Martin, minister of the parish from 1825 to 1843, and afterwards minister of the Free Church, Bathgate, who died 15th May, aged forty-eight; and the Rev. John Byers, minister of the parish, who died 26th June, 1861, aged seventy-two.

A tombstone celebrates the Rev. John Fleming, of Craigs, minister of Colinton, who died on the 23rd January, 1823, aged seventy-three. One of his ancestors having suffered persecution from the Stuart dynasty, Mr. Fleming held views on civil politics bordering on republicanism. He bequeathed £240 for the education of a number of free scholars at Colinton Parish School. The bulk of his estate he conveyed to trustees for behoof of his relatives, but provisionally for establishing Professorships of Political Economy in the Universities of Edinburgh and Glasgow.

Monuments commemorate John Tennant, of Mosside, who died September 10th, 1740, aged seventy-nine; George Norvell, of Boghall, who died June, 1725 ; Robert Geddes, of Torbanehill, born 12th April, 1744, died January, 1792 : Thomas Durham, of Boghead, died 24th July, 1750; John Ranken, of Inchcross, died January 1st, 1819; and Alexander Fleming, tenant at Kirkroads, father of the late Professor Fleming of the New College, Edinburgh. Monumental enclosures belong to the families of Calder of Drumcross; Dennistoun, of Barbaughlaw; Sandilands, of Couston; and Majoribanks, of Majoribanks and Balbardie.

A monumental statue is being reared in honour of the late Professor Sir James Young Simpson, Bart., a native of the parish.

PARISH OF CARRIDEN.

In the new churchyard a tombstone commemorates Dr. John Roebuck, projector of the Carron Iron Works. Dr. Roebuck was born at Sheffield in 1718. In 1760 he established the Carron Iron Works by means of a company of which he was the founder; he obtained a charter in 1773 for the consolidation of the company. He afterwards joined the celebrated James Watt in perfecting improvements upon the steam-engine. Engaging in several projects which required more capital than he could command, he reduced himself to indigence. He died in 1794.

PARISH OF DALMENY.

In Dalmeny Churchyard is the family vault of the Earls of Rosebery. Here is interred Sir Archibald Primrose, founder of the House; he died on the 27th September, 1679. Having remained firmly attached to the House of Stuart, he was, at the Restoration, appointed Lord Clerk Register, and a Lord of Session, by the title of Lord Carrington. He afterwards became Lord Justice-General. In 1662 he purchased the important barony of Barnbougle and

Dalmeny, from John fourth Earl of Haddington. A plate on the catacomb in which his remains are deposited is thus inscribed:—

"Hac in capsula in spe resurrectionis consignatur corpus Domini Archibaldi Primrose de Carrington, militis baronetti sub augustissimo monarchâ Carlo 1mo Secrete Concilii clerici, a resturato Carlo 2do Regni ab archivis, deinceps Justitiani Generalis facto functi viij kalend Decembris ætatis 63 anno Domini 1679."

PARISH OF ECCLESMACHAN.

This churchyard contains the remains of the Rev. Henry Liston, who died 24th February, 1836, aged sixty-five. His father, Mr. Robert Liston, was minister of Aberdour, Fifeshire. He was ordained to the ministry at Ecclesmachan in 1793. Possessed of superior attainments, he was unambitious of personal celebrity. He published an "Essay on Intonation," and contributed several articles to the *Edinburgh Encyclopædia*. His son Robert was the celebrated surgeon.

PARISH OF LINLITHGOW.

The palace of Linlithgow possesses a monumental interest as the birthplace of Queen Mary; the apartment in which she was born is exhibited to strangers. An aisle of the church is the scene in which James IV. was, through a device of his Queen, made to witness an apparition, who sought to dissuade him from going to war with England—a stratagem which was unhappily fruitless. The site of the house from which Hamilton of Bothwellhaugh shot the Regent Murray in the street of Linlithgow is pointed out. Several houses in the burgh are called "Templar Tenements," having belonged to the Preceptory of the Knights of St. John at Torphichen.

Near Linlithgow Bridge took place, in 1526, the engagement between the faction of the Earl of Angus, who had possession of the young king James V., and the party which sought to rescue him from the influence of the Douglases. The Earl of Lennox, who led the party opposed to Angus, was, after being offered quarter, slain by Sir James Hamilton. The spot of his interment is known as *Lennox Cairn*.

A stone tablet, elegantly sculptured, was found in a grave within the church. Of two compartments, one exhibits the Saviour in the act of prayer, with His three chosen disciples asleep. The other represents Him saluted by Judas and seized by the guard.

PARISH OF QUEENSFERRY.

A gravestone commemorates the Rev. James Kid, one of the twelve brethren styled "the twelve apostles," who presented a petition to the General Assembly of 1721, against an Act of the preceding Assembly condemning the "Marrow of Modern Divinity." The Assembly of 1722 administered a rebuke to the petitioners, on which Mr. Kid tendered a protest. He received and welcomed the seceding brethren at the Communion in his parish after their suspension in 1733. Mr. Kid enjoyed much celebrity as a preacher. He died on the 9th February, 1744, in his seventy-eighth year and the thirty-fourth of his ministry.

PARISH OF TORPHICHEN.

The Preceptory or chief seat of the Knights of St. John stood at Torphichen. It was founded in 1153. A portion of the transept, in elegant Gothic architecture, still remains. At the south

end an arch in the form of a canopy, about six feet in breadth, received the bodies of the knights during the performance of certain rites, previous to interment. An antiquely carved stone, built in the west side of the inner wall, contains the following inscription:—
"Gualterus Lindesay, Justiciarius Generalis de Scotland, et Principalis Preceptor Torphicensis, 1538." Sir Walter Lindsay, thus commemorated, was preceptor of the Knights of St. John. He was Lord Justice-General in the reign of James V. In Sir David Lindsay's "Testament of Squyer Meldrum" he is thus referred to:—

> "The wise Sir Walter Lindsay they him call,
> Lord of St. John and Knight of Torphichen,
> By sea and land a valiant capitane."

A stone pillar in the churchyard, with the outline of a Maltese cross carved upon it, constituted the sanctuary of Torphichen, to which persons accused of crimes less than capital might resort for protection.

PARISH OF UPHALL.

This parish contains the burial-place of the noble family of Buchan. Within that enclosure were deposited the remains of the Lord Chancellor Erskine. Thomas Erskine was youngest son of Henry David, tenth Earl of Buchan; he was born on the 10th January, 1750, and studied at the High School of Edinburgh and the University of St. Andrews. His father, who possessed an income of only £200 a year, was unable to educate him for a profession; he therefore became midshipman, and afterwards entered the army. Becoming tired of military service, he was admitted a student of Lincoln's Inn in 1775, and in the following year entered Trinity College, Cambridge. Having been called to the Bar, he at once attracted attention as a pleader. In 1783 he was returned to Parliament for Portsmouth, but he did not succeed in the House of Commons; his professional career, however, went on with increasing brilliancy. In 1786 he became Attorney-General to the Prince of Wales; he was dismissed from this office in 1792 for professionally defending Thomas Paine, when proceeded against for the publication of the second part of his "Rights of Man." In 1802 the Attorney-Generalship was restored to him, and he was likewise appointed Chancellor of the Duchy of Cornwall. In 1806 he was raised to the dignity of Lord High Chancellor, and created a peer by the title of Lord Erskine. On the dissolution of the Grenville Administration, in 1810, he retired on the usual pension of £4,000 a year. The remainder of his life was spent in comparative retirement. He latterly indulged in certain eccentricities of conduct, which, with his intellectual qualities, he seems to have inherited. He died at Amondell House, Linlithgowshire, on the 17th November, 1823, in his seventy-third year. Lord Erskine has been described as the most powerful advocate who ever pleaded at the English bar, but his decisions as a judge are pronounced apocryphal or valueless.

In the parish churchyard a handsome monument commemorates Lieut.-Colonel John Drysdale, of the 42nd Regiment, who died in 1866. The monument, which is seven feet in height, is adorned with castings in bronze, designed and executed by Mr. John Steell, of Edinburgh. It was reared at the expense of the officers, non-commissioned officers, and men of the 42nd Regiment, as a tribute of respect to one who, through his own personal merits, rose from the position of a private soldier to the command of his regiment.

HADDINGTONSHIRE.

PARISH OF HADDINGTON.

The public burial-ground of Haddington surrounds the ancient church of the Franciscans, popularly known as "the Lamp of the Lothians." In this edifice, now adapted as the parish church, an aisle formed the place of sepulture of the family of Lauderdale. A monument commemorates the Chancellor Maitland, Lord Thirlestane. It is twenty-four feet long eighteen feet wide, and eighteen feet in height; and is divided into two compartments supported by three black marble pillars with Corinthian capitals of white alabaster. Under these compartments are marble statues of Lord Thirlestane and his wife. An inscription proceeds thus:—

"Joanni Matellano, Baroni de Thyrlestane magno Scotiæ cancellario, qui a nobili Metellanæ stirpe, oriundus, vetustissimæ familiæ decus celebriore titulo auxit; cujus sincera pietas, heroica mens, eruditio singularis, gnava fortitudo, posteris æmulanda, invidenda antiquis parum vix habuerunt; liberalitas exprompta, lætus lepiduique ingenii vigor devinxit sibi publicæ omnes, privatim singulos; quem, post varia in republica præclare gesta munia Jacobus, ejus nominia sextus, Scotorum rex (omnium, quos Europa unquam vidit, regum sapientissimus) ad summum cancellariatus fastigium, acclamantibus tribus regni ordinibus, in comitiis publicis; evexit. Sed manum illud annos vix novem sustinuit; cum ea tamen prudentia, integritate ac laude, ut merito affirmari possit, brevis dignitatis ingentem fuisse gloriam. Tandem, annos natus quinquaginta, in medio fere honorum & virtutum curriculo, ereptus, acerbum sui desiderium reliquit omnibus, præcipue regi optimo, qui, versibus vernaculis supremo huic marmori incisis, demortuo parentavit. Obiit anno 1595, 5 nonas Octobris, in arce sua de Thyrlestane, a se recens extructa.

"Joannes Metellanus Lauderiæ comes, filius unigena, parentibus optimo, majore pietate quam impensa poni curavit."

Chancellor Maitland was second son of Sir Richard Maitland of Lethington, the poet, and was born in 1537. Attached to the Government of Queen Mary, he obtained the Abbacy of Kelso *in commendam* in 1566, and in April of the following year was appointed Lord Privy Seal. Owing to his adherence to the Queen in her adverse fortunes he was in 1570 deprived of his offices and emoluments, and subjected to various hardships. He retired to Edinburgh Castle, then held by Kirkaldy of Grange, and there remained till its surrender in May, 1573. By the Regent Morton he was sent as a prisoner to Tantallan Castle; after nine months he was allowed, on his parole, to reside at Lowthally. the residence of Lord Somerville. On the fall of Morton he, in 1578, obtained his liberty and proceeded to court, where he was well received by the young king, who in 1581 constituted him a senator of the College of Justice. He was afterwards knighted, and was in 1584 appointed permanent Secretary of State. In 1586 he became Chancellor. In 1589 he accompanied the King to Denmark on the occasion of the royal marriage; on his return to Scotland he was created Lord Maitland of Thirlestane. His subsequent career was considerably chequered. At his advice, James VI., in June, 1592, gave his royal sanction to the establishment of Presbyterianism. Lord Thirlestane died on the 3rd October, 1595. He composed some Latin epigrams which are inserted in the second volume of the "Delitiæ Poetarum Scotorum." His monument was erected at the cost of his son John, Earl of Lauderdale.

On the Chancellor's monument a Latin epitaph celebrates his wife Jane, only child and heiress of James, fourth Lord Fleming, Lord High Chamberlain, and of Lady Barbara Hamilton, daughter of James, Duke of Chatelherault; and who, though subsequently Countess of Cassilis, desired to be here interred beside the remains of her first husband. On the same tombstone are portrayed the virtues of their daughter Jane, who was betrothed to Robert, Earl of Winton, but died unmarried on the 6th July, 1609, in her nineteenth year. The inscriptions are as follow:—

"Janæ Flaminiæ, Jacobi Baronis Flemying, ex Barbara Hamiltona, Jacobi Ducis Castri Eraldi filia, proli unicæ, serenissimæ heroinæ cujus virilis animus, secundis juxta ac dubiis rebus, constans permansit; quæ, summæ erga Deum religionis, erga maritum fideli, amoris erga liberos (duos enim peperit, Joannem & Annam Mætellanos) nobilitatis, denique atque humanitatis erga omnes, vivens moriensque singulari præluxit exemplo: quæ quamvis secundis nuptiis Joanni Cassilissæ comiti juncta, hic tamen cum priore marito, eodem simul conditori, reponi voluit, infelici calculo extincta, Edinburgi 9 cal. Quintil. 1609, currente anno, ætatis 55. Joannes Mætellanus, Lauderiæ comes, filius unigena parentibus optimis, majore pietate quam impensa poni curavit.

" Janæ Metellanæ, Baronis de Thyrlestane, Scotiæ cancellarii & Janæ Flaminiæ filiæ, puellæ nobilissimæ, quæ, pietate, ingenio, castitate & morum elegantia insignis, Roberto Wintoniæ comiti desponsata, virgo mortua est, anno 1609, pridie non. Quintil. exacto ætatis anno 16 eodem cum matre funere elata. Joannes Matellanus L. C. unicœ sorori frater unicus mœrens posuit."

On the top of the monument a marble tablet formerly bore the following inscription, composed by James VI. to evince his attachment for the deceased Chancellor:—

"Hæc Jacobus Rex Sextus.

"Thou passenger, who spiest with gazing eyes
   This sad trophy of death's triumphant dart;
Consider, when this outward tomb thou sees,
   How rare a man leaves here his earthly part;
His wisdom and his uprightness of heart,
   His piety, his practice in our state,
His pregnant wit, well vers'd in every part,
   As equally not all were in debate.
Then justly hath his death brought forth of late,
   A heavy grief to prince and subjects all,
Who virtue love, and vice do truly hate,
   Tho' vicious men be joyful at his fall:
But for himself, most happy doth he die,
   Tho' for his prince it most unhappy be."

On another portion of the Lauderdale monument are the following inscriptions:—

"Janæ Metellanæ, virgini lectissimæ, cujus divino ingenio atque industriæ nihil difficile unquam est visum quod nobilem pudicamque puellam doceret: cujus vera pietas, formæ venustas, eximia castitas, morum suavitas, & indolis, præter sexum, præter ætatem, miraculum, invidiam parcarum excitarunt; Joannes Metellanus, Lauderiæ comes, & Isabella Setonia parentes, præpostero naturæ ordine superstites relicti, insperatum hoc memoriæ sacrum statuerunt. Vixit annos 19 m. 2 d. 8 vitam mortalem exuit. 6 idus Decembris, 1631.

"Isabella Setonia, Lauderiæ comitissa, Alexandri Fermeloduni comitis, Scotiæ cancellarii & dominæ Liliæ Drummondæ filia, viva gaudium, mortua mariti gemitus, hic sita est; quæ matronarum splendor, conjugum honos, pudicitiæ jubar, sanctimonii templum, virtutum & formæ cumulus virum (cum quo mirabili concordia annos 28 mens, 4 transegit) quindecim liberorum numero auxit, marium 7. Fœmell. 8 superstitibus tantum quatuor, Joanne, Roberto, Sophia, Carolo; quæ sic semper vixit, ut seculum ipsa haud dignum videretur; ida diem extremum clausit, ut mors omni vitæ suæ curriculo responderet: ac post incredibilem in longissimo morbo constantiam, patientiam, pietatem fessi corporis ergastulo soluta, in terris, ut cœlo frueretur, esse desiit, 2 Novembris, 1638. Annos nata 44 m. 3 d. 2. Joannes Metellanus, Lauderiæ comes, conjux desolatissimus, tantæ jacturæ propemodum intolerans, uxori in comparabili, cujus merita nullus amor æquare possit, desiderii sui perpetuum monumentum, indefesso mœrore posuit.

"Joannes Metellanus, Lauderiæ comes, locum delegit sepulturæ, ad parentum pedes, sibi & uxori Isabella Setoniæ; ne, quos singularis amor & unanimis vitæ consuetudo conjunxit, vel mors ipsa sejungeret tumulo."

These inscriptions commemorate Jane Maitland, daughter of John, first Earl of Lauderdale, who died 8th December, 1631, aged nineteen; and Isabel Seaton, Countess of Lauderdale, and second daughter of Alexander, Earl of Dunfermline, Chancellor of Scotland, who died 2nd November, 1638, aged forty-nine years. She was married in her sixteenth year, and became mother of fifteen children. She is celebrated by Arthur Johnston in one of his poems. The Earl of Lauderdale, who reared this monument for himself and his spouse, was son of the Chancellor Maitland. He was sworn à Privy Councillor in July, 1615, and in the following year was created Viscount Lauderdale. He was subsequently President of the Council and an ordinary Lord of Session. In 1624 he was created Earl of Lauderdale. He was appointed one of the Lords of the Articles in 1639; taking the side of the Parliament he was elected President in June, 1644. He died on the 20th January, 1645. Drummond of Hawthornden celebrated him in a Latin elegy.

The famous Duke of Lauderdale also rests in the Maitland family vault. His remains were deposited in a leaden coffin, which on a brass plate contained the following inscription:—

"In spem beatæ resurrectionis, hic conditur illustrissimus & nobilissimus princeps ac Dominus, D. Joannes Dux de Lauderdale, Marchio de March, Comes de Lauderdale & Guilford, vicecomes Maitland, Dominus de Thirlestane, Musselburgh, Bolton, & Petersham; sæpius ad Parliamenta & ordinum hujus regni conventus tenenda prorex; a restauratione regiæ Majestatis, per 20, annos, solus, pro regno Scotiæ, regum optimo, Carolo secundo, a secretis; præces secreti concilii, prædicto potentissimo regi, in regno Angliæ, a secretioribus conciliis & ex cubiculariis primariis unus; in Scotia, ex quatuor senatoribus collegii juridici extraordinariis unus; castelli regii Edinburgen constabularius & gubernator: nobilissimi ordinis garterii eques.

"Natus 21 Maii, MDCXVI. Leidintoniæ. Obiit 24 die Augusti, prope fontis de Tunbridge, anno humanæ salutis MDCLXXXII., Ætatis 68."

John, Duke of Lauderdale, one of the most conspicuous persons in Scottish history, was born at Lethington, parish of Hamilton, on the 21st May, 1616. A zealous Presbyterian, he was, in 1643, appointed one of the Commissioners from the Scottish Church to the Assembly of Divines at Westminster. In 1644 he was sent from the Estates of Parliament, along with some others, to treat with Charles I. at Uxbridge. He was frequently employed as a Commissioner in subsequent negotiations with the King. He succeeded his father, the first Earl of Lauderdale, in 1645. In 1648 he became a promoter of "the Engagement," and waiting upon the Prince of Wales, began an intimacy with him; he now withdrew from the Presbyterian cause. He joined the court of Charles II. at the Hague; he was taken prisoner at the battle of Worcester in 1651, and was confined in the Tower, and afterwards in

Windsor Castle till the Restoration. He was now appointed Secretary of State for Scotland. At first he was opposed to the sudden establishment of episcopacy, but he subsequently acceded to the royal wishes. In 1664 he sanctioned the erection of the Court of High Commission, a tribunal intended for the entire subversion of Presbyterianism. In 1672 he was created Duke of Lauderdale and installed a Knight of the Garter. His administration in Scotland was oppressive, and he proved so obnoxious in England, that the House of Commons, in 1674, petitioned the King to remove him from State employment. For some time he continued to retain his ascendancy, but at length his influence declined, and he was deprived of his offices. He died at Tunbridge Wells, on the 24th August, 1682, in his sixty-seventh year.

Within the church Alexander Seton, schoolmaster of Haddington, is commemorated thus :—

"In obitum magistri Alexandri Setonii, scholæ Hadinensis moderatoris.

> "Qui jacet hic, juvenum mentes mansuevit agrestes
> Excoluit dociles, erudiitque rudes;
> Ex adytis aditum reserans, mysteria pandens,
> Pieridum antistes dicier ille potest.
> "Obiit anno 1645, Maii 12, Ætatis 46."

Monteith translates :—

> "Here lies a man, who tamèd wayward youth,
> Instructing them with letters and with truth,
> The easy minds he greatly did improve,
> Inform'd the ignorant, by special love :
> He did disclose all myst'ries, and reveal
> What most abstruse, as hidden under seal.
> Consider him aright, for truly he
> Priest of the Muses well may namèd be."

Seton's wife is celebrated in English verse. She died 29th December, 1655, aged sixty.

> "If modesty commend a wife
> And providence a mother,

> Grave chastity a widow's life,
> We'll not find such another
> In Haddington as Marion Gray
> Who here doth lie till the Doomsday."

A more ambitious monument commemorates William Seton, son of the two preceding, and Provost of the burgh. He is described in a lengthened Latin panegyric as descended from the House of Seton, of Northrig, and more remotely from the noble family of the name. His epitaph is as follows:—

"Memoriæ sacrum Gulielmi Seton, natalibus hujus urbis Hadinæ cives ingenui & honesti; prosapia autem e vetustissima & nobilissima gente Setona oriundi; recta quippe serie, ex familia Setona de Northrig, jure connubii cum illius prædii hærede unica, cognomine Sinclara, per atavum suum Gulielmum Seton, familiæ Setonæ principis nepotem, olim acquisiti, originem suam ducentis; præfectura hujus civitatis, per decennium continuum, fideliter, prudenter & moderate functi, ejusdemque, ad suprema regni comitia, delegatione sæpius honorati; officio tabellarii equestris in hac urbe, per 37 annos, diplomate regio præpositi; ingenii & morum humanitate, virtute & industria, omnibus, injuria autem & dolo nemini, noti; ab avaritia, vindicta, injustitia & in concives odio prorsus alieni; pie tandem, & qua Christianum decet, animi tranquillitate, anno ætatis suæ 57. Vita functi; monumentum hoc, mœroris & conjugalis sui desiderii signum & indicium, Agneta Black, ipsius conjugio nunc viduata, extruendum curavit; locumque simul hunc, cansellis munitum in quo reconduntur ossa & cineres Alexandri Seton, scholæ publiæ hujus urbis quondam moderatoris ejus patris, Mariotæ Gray matris, Alexandri, Gulielmi, & Mariotæ, trium ipsius liberorum, dicto connubio, cum Agneta conjuge sua, procreatorum ut sibi pariter & mariti sui agnatis cognatisque cum fatis cesserint, sepulturam commodam præbeat, auctoritate parochiali, religiosum fecit. Anno 1682."

Within the church a monument with a Latin inscription commemorates John Sleich, Provost of Haddington, who died 26th January, 1686, aged ninety; also his son John, Provost of Haddington, who died 12th December, 1689, aged fifty-eight. Also John Sleich, Master of Arts, son of the preceding, a magistrate of the burgh, who died in his thirty-fifth year.

PARISH OF HADDINGTON.

In the churchyard Alexander Cockburn, of the ancient family of Cockburn of Langton, is thus commemorated:—

"Alexander Cockburnus, illustri Cockburnorum de Langtoun familia oriundus, nec splendori natalium impar, eximis magni tum animi, tum corporis dotibus, constanti in Deum & regem fide; probitate & industria existimationem & rem peperit, sine injuria, sine invidia; nec amicis & necessariis tantum, sed civibus, vicinis & accolis, prudentia, consilio & opera, utilis in primis, imo necessarius & omnibus charissimus fuit. Demum, cum diu sibi & aliis vixisset, placide obiit, anno salutis 1668, ætatis LXXI. & exuviis hic positis quiescit; verum, anima in cœlis, in terris sobole, in bonorum animis desiderio, est & vivit superstes, magnum virtutis, & quæ virtuti comes, felicitatis exemplum, viator, tibi haud lugendum, sed legendum & imitandum."

The Cockburns of Langton were descended from Sir Alexander de Cockburn, who obtained the barony of Carriden, Linlithgowshire, from David II. in 1358. Through his first wife a daughter of Sir William de Vipont he got the barony of Langton. Sir William Cockburn, of Langton, obtained in 1595 the office of Principal Usher; his son, William Cockburn, was created a baronet of Nova Scotia in 1627. The latter was in 1641 Commissioner for Berwickshire in the Scottish Parliament; having insisted on maintaining his right to the Ushership against the Earl of Wigton, who had assumed the office, he inadvertently gave offence to Charles I., when the king entered the House on the 17th August of that year. Charles ordered his apprehension; but when he ascertained that Cockburn was a member of the Estates, he caused his release, and promised not to commit any of the members during session. The family of Cockburn of Langton were distinguished for their piety, and were sufferers in the cause of civil and religious liberty.

George Hepburn of Monkrig is on his tombstone celebrated thus:—

"D. Georgii Hepburnii, a Monachagrio, ingenio, doctrina & morum elegantia eximii viri, medici vero imprimis celeberrimi, tam in vita quam in morte, omnibus bonis charissimi desideratissimique tumulus.

> Hospes, sparge rosas; jacit hac Hepburnus in urna,
> Pæonia nemo quo prior arte fuit.
> Atropos invidit partis de morte trophæis,
> Rupit & atroci pendula pensa manu.
> Ingenium excellens, virtutem candidam & artes
> Egregias heu! heu! quam brevis hora rapit!"

David Wilson, dyer in Haddington, has the following epitaph:—

"Monodia in obitum Davidis Wilsoni, tinctoris burgi de Hadingtoun, qui obiit 3 nonas Maii, anno æræ Christianæ MDCLXVIII. Ætatis LXIII.

> Qui bibulam Tyrio tingebat murice lanam,
> Wilsonum nobis mors inimica tutit;
> Largus erat miseris, frugi in se, fidus in omnes:
> Virtutis speculum conditur hoc tumulo."

Monteith thus translates:—

"A funeral song on the death of David Wilson, dyer in Haddington, who died 5th May, 1668. His age sixty-three.

> Who thirsty wool in Tyrian purple dy'd,
> Wilson from us unkind fates have convey'd;
> Who frugal was and liberal to the poor,
> Faithful to all unto his final hour,
> Mirror of virtues here lies buried sure."

John Lessels, Provost of Haddington, is on his tombstone described as "vir pius et probus, prudens, antiquæ fidei et justitiæ cultor egregius & rigidus satelles; quam plurimis beneficus, nulli injurius, omnibus æquus." He died 26th March, 1691, aged sixty-one.

A monument celebrates the Rev. James Forman, minister of the parish, who died 3rd December, 1702, in the fifty-ninth year of his age and thirty-seventh of his ministry.

The Rev. John Brown, author of the "Self-Interpreting Bible" and other works, rests in this churchyard. His tombstone bears these words:—

"To the memory of Mr. John Brown, thirty-six years minister of the gospel at Haddington, and twenty years Professor of

Divinity under the Associate Synod. After maintaining an eminent character for piety, charity, learning, and diligence, he died rejoicing in hope of the glory of God, and admiring the riches of divine grace to him as a sinner, the 19th of June, A.D. 1787, aged sixty-five years."

Mr. Brown was born at Carpow, Perthshire, in 1722. His father, a hand-loom weaver, died during his childhood. Only a short time at school, he contrived, by self-application, to become acquainted before his twentieth year with Latin, Greek, and Hebrew, and also with some of the modern languages. After some years spent in teaching he studied theology under the direction of the Associate Synod, and in 1751 was licensed to preach. Soon after he received calls from the Secession congregations at Stow and Haddington. He chose the latter, and was ordained in June, 1751. In 1768 he was elected Professor of Divinity under the Associate Synod. He published his "Self-Interpreting Bible" in 1778, which was followed by his "Dictionary of the Bible." He also composed a "History of the Church." His lectures were published under the title of "A Body of Divinity." Several of his descendants have been conspicuous for their abilities and learning.

Jean Smith, wife of "Patrick Hepburn of Abbey-mill," is commemorated in these lines :—

> "Stay, passenger, and shed a tear
> For her who lies enshrinèd here;
> If virtues could keep from the grave,
> Or features from corruption save;
> If prudence and a pious life
> And what adorns a modest wife;
> If husband's sighs and children's tears,
> Friends' warm desires and secret fears
> Could have kept her from the grave,
> Still this treasure we should have.
> But Heaven's wiser providence
> Hath ta'en from us what came from thence,
> And there where lasting joyes abound,
> Have her with bliss and glory crown'd."

George Cunningham, Sheriff-depute of Haddingtonshire and a

magistrate of the burgh, who died in February, 1755, aged sixty-two, has these lines on his gravestone :—

> "O death, how absolute thy sway!
> At thy command we must obey;
> In hardy strength 'tis vain to trust,
> Even stone thou crumblest into dust."

Monteith supplies the following; it has now disappeared :—

> "Hout, Atropos, hard-hearted Hag,
> To cut the sheugh of Jamie Craig;
> For had he lived a wheen mae years,
> He had been owre teugh for your sheirs;
> Now Jamie's deid, sua man we a',
> And for his sake I'll say this sa
> In Hei'en, Jamie, be thy saul!"

The following rhymes are from tombstones in Haddington Churchyard :—

> "Oft have I till'd the fertile soil,
> Which was my destined lot;
> But here beneath this towering elm
> I lie to be forgot."

> "Silent tomb, to thee I trust
> This sacred hoard of precious dust;
> Guard it safe, O silent tomb,
> Until a son shall ask for room."

> "He died in faith of the glorious Gospel's heavenly light,
> Whereby he lived with comfort and with comfort died;
> He viewed beyond that gloomy scene the tomb
> A life of endless happiness to come."

> "If they are happy why should we mourn
> For them whose joys are now begun?
> And if begun we may depend
> That they will never have an end."

A faithful domestic is thus celebrated :—

> "Here, within this tomb confined,
> Virtue and probity combined;
> An honest cook, who many a year
> To her employers found good cheer."

"Hannah Gilliam, who died May 8th, 1803. In justice to fidelity, honesty, and exemplary conduct in a most trusty servant, Lord Elcho has caused this memorial to be placed on her tombstone."

According to Monteith the following inscriptions were engraved on tombstones at Nungate Chapel, Haddington. John Zeaman was celebrated thus :—

"Hoc in exiguo tumulo, conduntur ossa dignissimi, Joannis Zeaman; qui, ex honesta majorum serie natus, vixit, dum mori didicerat; quique, quum Dei gratia suaque industria rem sibi congesserat, aliisque haud ullo tempore deficiens fuerat, anima ad superos profecta, exuviis hic positis, quiescit.

> Expertus mundi varios vanosque labores,
> Hic tandem jaceo, pulvis & umbra, nihil;
> Sed qui de nihilo coelum terramque creavit,
> Me cum carne mea non sinet esse nihil.

"Natus mense Martii, anno MDCXXX. Obiit mense Maio, anno MDCLXXVI."

Patrick Hepburn had the following :—

> "Cujus abundanti vivax in pectore virtus,
> Consilium prudens, intemerata fides;
> Patricius situs est Hepburnus: caetera dicent
> Candor & integritas, ingeniumque viri."

Monteith translates :—

> "To whose full breast did lively virtue fly,
> Wise counsel and untainted honesty;
> Here Patrick Hepburn lies; all what remains
> Is candour, wit, uprightness, free of stains."

A monument thus celebrates the virtues of the Rev. Robert Ker, minister of the parish, who died on the 4th February, 1677, in his sixty-eighth year, and thirty-ninth of his ministry :—

"Reverendo beataeque memoriae viro, D. Roberto Caro, generis splendore illustri; utpote nobilissina Carorum Roxburgi comitum familia oriundo; ecclesiæ Prestosalinensis primum per octo, deinde Hadinensis per 31 annos, pastori eximio, fideli, pio; ingenii acumine, animi candore, vitæ integritate, consilii prudentia, morum suavitate, constantiæ inter paucos firmitate, ministerii efficacia, in sanandis conscientiæ morbis dexteritate singulari; omnibus denique naturæ & gratiæ dotibus non leviter tincto, sed penitus imbuto: quo factum est, ut omnibus bonis vere carus, & inimicis (quos ob rem privatam nullos habuit) non admodum exosus esset. Inter preces & lachrymas suorum, in Christo placidissime sopito, Jana Ramisæa, dilecto conjugi unice dilecta mœrens posuit. Obiit, die Dominico, pridie nonas Februarii, anno Dom. MDCLXXVII., Ætatis 68, Ministerii 39, cum liberis una infantulis 7, hic sepultus.

> Quo nuper gavisa suo est Hadina ministro,
>   Sed quoque natatis Presto-salina prius;
> Hic magno proceres numero, civesque patresque,
>   Mœsti omnes sanctum composuere virum,
> Dum stetit haud varianda suis ecclesia mystis,
>   Non fuit in paucis nomen inane tuum,
> De tristi semente prius, quam fecit, opimam
>   Messem nunc hilari corde reportat ovans."

Robert Ker was second son of John Ker, minister of Prestonpans. He was born in 1609, studied at the University of Edinburgh, and was admitted assistant and successor to his father at Prestonpans in 1638. He was translated to Haddington in 1647. He refused to conform to Episcopacy, but through the influence of the Duke of Lauderdale was permitted to retain his living till the period of his death. He was grandson of Andrew Ker of Fadounside, a cadet of the noble House of Roxburgh, who married the widow of John Knox the Reformer. His father was a zealous upholder of Presbyterianism; he would have been elected Moderator of the famous General Assembly of 1638, but that his feeble health was considered to unfit him for the duties.

A long inscription commemorates the Rev. Walter Paterson, minister of Bolton, who died on the 22nd March, 1692, aged fifty-one. He was ordained to the ministry at Bolton in 1665, but quitted the cure on account of the Test in December, 1681. His merits are thus depicted in Latin verse :—

> "Tumulo hoc reliquiæ sunt sacræ reconditæ
> Viri integerrimi Patersoni, optimi
> Pastoris, omi laude fulgentissimi;
> Pro veritate proque conscientia,
> Pro pace moribusque sanctis, plurima
> Qui fecit intrepide, tulitque fortiter.
> At nunc laboribus exsoluto ergastuli,
> Datum fruisci non corona marcida."

In Nungate Chapel-yard George Wilson has the following elegy :—

> "Good people, know here lies a youth (whose name
> Engraven here) was one of a good fame;
> Opposing vice, of quick engine was he,
> Retaining virtue, wisdom, constancy;
> Grave, humble, pleasant, sober, meek, and chaste,
> Extolling mercy, pious to the last.
> And now until the trumpet last shall sound,
> In quiet grave, his bones here may be found;
> Likewise his soul, up in the heaven's high
> Solemnly joins with saints sweet melody:
> O therefore study all his steps to trace,
> Now when he's gone, the standard of his race.

He died August 6, 1702. His age fourteen years."

PARISH OF ABERLADY.

Two aisles adjoining the parish church are used for interment by the Earl of Wemyss and Lord Elibank. In the Elibank or Ballencrieff aisle an elegant marble monument celebrates the virtues of Maria Margaretta, wife of Patrick, fifth Lord Elibank, who died in June, 1762. A long inscription in elegant Latin was composed by her husband, who was celebrated for his learning. Lord Elibank was a friend and associate of Dr. Samuel Johnson.

The following quaint inscription was formerly to be found in this churchyard :—

> "Here lies John Smith,
> Whom Death slew for all his pith;
> The starkest man in Aberlady—
> God prepare and make us ready."

PARISH OF ATHELSTANEFORD.

In the churchyard of this parish a plain tombstone denotes the resting-place of the Rev. Robert Blair, author of "The Grave." This ingenious divine was born at Edinburgh, in 1699. Licensed to preach in 1729, he was in the following year presented to Athelstaneford. His celebrated poem, "The Grave," was highly approved by Dr. Isaac Watts and Dr. Doddridge, but two London publishers to whom it was submitted declined to risk money in the publication. Mr. Blair died of fever on the 4th February, 1746. In the following year his poem was published at Edinburgh, and at once obtained favour. Mr. Blair was grandson of the celebrated Robert Blair, minister of St. Andrews, and was father of Robert Blair of Avontoun, the distinguished President of the Court of Session. In 1857 a monumental obelisk was reared at Athelstaneford in honour of his memory.

A tombstone thus celebrates three members of the family of Skirving :—

"Archibald Skirving, farmer, Muirton, one of the most athletic and best tempered of men, lived only fifty-six years. His oldest son, Adam, farmer, Garleton, born 1719. Died 1803."

> "In feature, in figure, agility, mind,
> And happy wit, rarely surpassed,

With lofty or low could be plain or refined,
Content beaming bright to the last."

"His first son, and finest semblance, Archibald, born October, 1749, by peculiar excellence attained eminence as a portrait painter."

"And might have lived in affluence,
Had he not aimed at private independence
By simplifying the comforts of common life,
To beauty, virtue, talent, he would bow,
But claims from birth or rank would not allow;
Kept friends and foes at nearly equal distance;
Knew how to give, but not to take assistance.
At threescore-ten, when scarce began to fail,
He dropt at once, without apparent ail."

Adam Skirving, farmer at Garleton, composed some amusing Scottish songs. His son Archibald attained celebrity as an artist.

PARISH OF DUNBAR.

In the interior of the parish church a magnificent marble monument commemorates George Home of Manderston, Earl of Dunbar, and Lord High Treasurer. The monument, which is of most elegant workmanship, is twenty-six feet high, and twelve feet broad. The Earl, in a life-size statue, clad in mail, and wearing the cloak of the Garter, is in the act of kneeling on a cushion with his prayer-book open before him; immediately below is a handsome sarcophagus. Under an ornamental arch is the following inscription:—

"Here lyeth the Body of the Right Honble. George, Earl of Dvnbar, Baron Howme of Barwick, Lord Heich Treasr. of Scotland, Knight of the most noble order of the Garter and one of His Mat[es.] most Ho[ble] Privie Covncil, who dept[ed] this Life the XXIX day of Janvary, MDCXI."

The Earl's statue is supported by two knights in plate armour, with barbed visors shut and their helmet plumes partially concealed by the superstructure. Above these mailed figures, there is on each side, a female figure; that on the right representing Justice, with the sword and scales, the left, with an owl perched on her arm, representing Wisdom. Above the arch are two female figures in high relief, one of Fame, with a key and a trumpet, and the other of Peace, with a laurel wreath and olive branch. Above these is the Earl's armorial escutcheon, with two lions for supporters, and the motto "Rex Ditat Devs Beat." The monument was executed in Italy. When the church was restored in 1819, under the superintendence of Mr. Gillespie Graham, the utmost care was exercised to preserve intact this most interesting Memorial.

Lord Dunbar was one of those clever and courtly Scotsmen whom James VI. delighted to honour. He was third son of the Laird of Manderston, in Berwickshire, and was in early life introduced at the Scottish Court. He rose, step by step, like the king's other favourites. When James succeeded to the English throne Home followed him to London. He became Chancellor of the English Exchequer, and was created Baron Home. He was subsequently raised to the Earldom of Dunbar, in the peerage of Scotland. He zealously aided the king in his endeavours to overthrow Presbyterianism, and was chiefly instrumental in procuring parliamentary sanction for the restoration of episcopacy in 1606. His dispositions were conciliatory, and he endeavoured, though unsuccessfully, to reconcile the leading Presbyterian clergy to the new system. As an administrator he evinced considerable power, and was frequently employed on special services. The Earldom of Dunbar is at present represented by George Stirling Home Drummond, Esq., of Blair Drummond.

In the church a memorial window commemorates Rear-Admiral James Hay of Belton, who died 3rd February, 1857, aged seventy-one. Also his sons, Lieutenant David Hay, of the 22nd Oude Regular Cavalry and one of the defenders of Lucknow, who died 6th June,

1868, aged twenty-five, and Commander Edward Hay, R.N., who was killed in New Zealand, 30th April, 1864, aged twenty-nine.

In the churchyard a monument commemorates the Rev. Andrew Stevenson, minister of the parish. This reverend divine was born on the 29th October, 1588. For thirty years he held office as Regent or Professor of Philosophy in the University of Edinburgh. In 1639 he was admitted to the ministry at Dunbar. He died on the 13th December, 1664, in the seventy-seventh year of his age, and twenty-fifth of his ministry. His tombstone is thus inscribed :—

"'Εγειρεται Πνευματικόν.

"Sacris hic reconditis exuviis clarissimi & charissimi patris sui magistri Andreæ Stephanidæ, primum per annos 30, in academia Edinensi philologiæ & philosophiæ professoris celeberrimi; annos dein 25, ecclesiæ Barodunensis pastoris fidelissimi (cui micare incepit diluculum nostrum breve Octob. 29, 1588. Lux vero meridiana æterna affulgere Decemb. 13, 1664). Archibaldus Stephanides medicinæ doctor liberorum octo, (quorum M. Thomas Jacobus, Joneta, a pedibus patris requiescunt) solus cum sorore Agnesia superstes, cippum hunc qualencunque L.L.M.D.C. Q.

"Ecce satus Στεφανω situs hic ; qui lustra peregit
  Undena, officiis verna corona suis :
Spineta hic tetrici perruperat aspra Lycæi
  Junior : ast vegetum suada suprema senem
Extulit. Æternam adspiras quicunque coronam,
  Vita hujus vitæ norma sit apta tuæ."

In the churchyard a tombstone is thus inscribed :—

"Thomas Reid, 1827."

"In memory of his grandfather, Magnus Reid, who died May, 1786, aged one hundred and fourteen years. Also his sister, Janet Reid, who died August 9th, 1800, aged nineteen years. Also his father, Thomas Reid, who died January 8th, 1809, aged eighty-six years. Also his uncle, Cumberland Reid, who died July 6th, 1818, aged one hundred and five years. Also two of his children who died in their infancy."

According to tradition, Magnus Reid began business as a travelling chapman about the age of eighty, and followed this calling till within two months of his decease.

Another centenarian is celebrated thus :—

" Here lies interred the body of Lieut.-Col. William Stiell, of Belhaven, who died the 7th of February, 1810, at the advanced age of one hundred and four years. He served his king and country as an officer, with reputation and success for sixty years, in the 60th Regiment of foot. He then retired from the service, and after living many years among his friends universally beloved and respected, he died regretted by all, full of days and full of honour."

Several persons who perished in an attempt to rescue a wrecked fisherman are commemorated by a tombstone with the following inscription :—

"Sacred to the memory of Lieut. Sydenham Wylde, R.N.; William Lucas, chief boatman of the Coast guard service; Peter Darg, William Miller, and William Clements, seamen, who lost their lives on the 20th of August, 1845, in bravely and devotedly, but, alas! unsuccessfully, endeavouring to rescue a wrecked fisherman from a rock at the entrance of the harbour.
"This tablet was erected by the community of Dunbar and vicinity."

A monument commemorates Charles Middlemas of Underidge, late Provost of Dunbar and Deputy-Lieutenant of Haddingtonshire, who died 24th Oct., 1850, aged eighty-nine. And his eldest son, Robert H. Middlemas of St. Andrew's Place, Regent's Park, London, who died 2nd Jan., 1857, aged 54.

A tombstone has been reared to the memory of the Rev. John Jaffray, minister of Dunbar, who died on the 13th February, 1862, in the seventieth year of his age and forty-first of his ministry. Mr. Jaffray was a native of Stirlingshire; he was distinguished as a preacher. A zealous agriculturist, he invented several agricultural implements and improved others.

Other notable persons interred in this churchyard are as follow:— Richard Anderson, of Windygoul; Colonel Robert Anderson, of Winterfield, K.H., died 30th April, 1864, aged fifty-six; Major David Dalrymple Anderson, of Winterfield, and of the Indian Army; Major-General William Cochrane Anderson, R.A., of Winterfield, died August 30th, 1865, aged seventy-four; Lieutenant John Lorimer

Sawers, Bengal Army, died 1st October, 1860, aged thirty; David France, of Seafield, died 5th December, 1859, aged seventy; Lieutenant-General George Hardyman, Bengal Cavalry, died 28th September, 1836, aged eighty-seven; Adam Watson, of Press, died 3rd August, 1802, aged fifty-seven; Thomas Wightman, Bailie of the Lordship of Dunbar, died 1st June, 1707, aged fifty-six; Rev. Thomas Burnet, died 22nd April, 1862; Lieutenant-Colonel Robert Stiell, of the 24th Regiment, died 17th May, 1801.

James Stewart, who died 8th July, 1823, aged sixty-five, is thus commemorated by his niece :—

"Come, passenger, who e'er thou art,
And shed one mournful tear,
On his grave who by sudden death
Cut off lies buried here.
No fell disease nor racking pain,
A warning to him gave;
But hurried from life's busied scene
To moulder in the grave."

John Angus, mason, who died in September, 1821, aged twenty-one, thus exhorts :—

"In dust I lie as you must all,
O be prepared when God will call;
If not prepared what shall we say,
When we meet Christ on judgment day?"

On the tombstone of John Goodall, mariner, are these lines :—

"Afflictions sore long time I bore,
Physicians were in vain,
Till God at length did call me hence,
And eased me of my pain."

The deceased William Sang apostrophises his survivors :—

"O friends, dry up these tender tears,
Affection's sigh strive to subdue;
Yet but a few revolving years,
The tomb shall be your chamber too."

These quaint metrical epitaphs are to be found in Dunbar churchyard:—

"Here is interred within this silent grave,
An honest man unquestionably brave,
Born in Hibernia, the soldier of his day,
Who by an order that was call'd away."

"Ended was her short-lived hour,
Lodg'd within the silent tomb,
But the sweet engaging flower
Was to perpetual bloom."

"Praise to my wife is justly due,
She proved this maxim to be true,
The richest portion with a wife,
Is prudence and a virtuous life."

"Forget her, no, nor ever will,
We loved her here, we love her still;
Nor love her less although she's gone
From us to her eternal home.
For her to live was Christ, and to die is gain."

"Here lyes interred ye corps of Harriet Deans
— Loving to husband, obliging to her friends,
— Alace short while on earth she did remain,
— Her godly life lies freed from all pain.
Spouse, children, friends doe not her death deplore,
Her soul enjoys heaven's eternal glore."

PARISH OF GLADSMUIR.

We are indebted to Monteith for the two following:—

"Mungo Watson.
"Fata volunt, amen. Alias, quis dixerit amen?
Hanc urnam merito ecclesia mœsta dolet.
Conjux chara gemit, nati natæ quoque lugent,
Cuncti & collachrymant invida fata boni:

> Quippe, pius doctusque fuit, fidusque minister,
> Rerum sacrarum lampas eratque micans,
> Sed, quid lugendum ? palmam fert, morte sepulta,
> Gaudet apud superos ; molliter ossa cuberit."

Monteith thus translates :—

> " Fates cannot be controlled ; the church doth mourn,
> Deservedly his death, lies in this urn ;
> Wife, children, persons all lament and cry,
> By envious fate, this good man snatch'd away.
> He pious, learned, faithful pastor was,
> A shining lamp to divine mysteries.
> But wherefore grief ? the crown he doth obtain,
> And, maugre death, with Christ doth live and reign."

These lines of Latin verse commemorated the Rev. John Bell, minister of the parish :—

> " Publica mens, cursusque micans, facundia linguæ
> Gratia, grateolens vultu, cœlestia dona
> Lugendam Belli nostri pastoris adornant
> Urnam (proh tremimus) mens fruiturque polo."

Mr. Bell was born at Glasgow on the 2nd February, 1676. He studied at Glasgow College, was licensed in 1697, and was in the same year ordained minister of Broughton. He was translated to Gladsmuir in 1701. He died on the 30th October, 1707. He published a " Discourse on Witchcraft " and "An Abridgment of the Acts of Assembly."

PARISH OF NORTH BERWICK.

In the parish churchyard a handsome altar tomb, supported by ornamental pillars, commemorates the Rev. John Blackadder, an eminent sufferer in the cause of Presbyterianism. He was born in 1623, and was the lineal descendant and representative of the ancient family of Blackadder of Tulliallan. Having studied at the university of Glasgow, he was ordained minister of Troqueer in April, 1653. He was deprived of his living in 1662, when he retired to the parish of Glencairn. He preached frequently in the fields; and having attracted the notice of the Privy Council, he, in 1666, withdrew under hiding to Edinburgh. In 1674 his apprehension was ordered; he escaped to Rotterdam. Returning to Scotland in 1679 he resumed preaching. In April, 1681, he was apprehended at Edinburgh and sentenced to imprisonment on the Bass Rock. There he was confined upwards of four years. As his health became seriously affected the Privy Council ordered his liberation. He was unable to avail himself of the privilege, and died on the Bass in January, 1686, aged sixty-three. He succeeded to the family baronetcy, but never assumed the title. He was a most zealous preacher, and pursued his itinerating labours over a large portion of the lowlands. One of his sons, Colonel John Blackadder, deputy-governor of Stirling Castle, was distinguished for his piety. The following inscription on Mr. Blackadder's tomb was renewed some years ago by the Rev. Dr. Andrew Crichton, author of his memoirs:—

"Here lies the body of Mr. John Blackadder, minister of the gospel at Troqueer in Galloway, who died on the Bass after five years' imprisonment, anno Dom. 1685, and of his age sixty-three years.

> Blest John for Jesus' sake in Patmos bound,
> His prison Bethel, Patmos Pisgah found.
> So the blest John on yonder rock confin'd,
> His body suffered, but no chains could bind
> His heaven-aspiring soul; while day by day,
> As from Mount Pisgah's top, he did survey
> The promised land, and viewed the crown, by faith
> Laid up for those who faithful are till death.
> Grace form'd him in the Christian hero's mould,
> Meek in his own concerns, in's Master's bold,
> Passions to reason chain'd, prudence did lead,
> Zeal warm'd his breast, and reason cool'd his head.
> Five years on the bare rock, yet sweet abode,
> He, Enoch like, enjoyed and walk'd with God,
> Till by long living on this heavenly food

His soul by love grew up, too great, too good
To be confin'd in jail, or flesh and blood;
Death broke his fetters off, then swift he fled
From sin and sorrow, and by angels led
Enter'd the mansions of eternal joy.
Blest soul thy warfare's o'er; praise, love, enjoy;
His dust here rests till Jesus come again.
Even so bless'd Jesus! come, come, Lord.   Amen."

In the churchyard are the following inscriptions:—

"Death is a debt to nature due,
  Which he has paid and so must you."

"Oft have I tilled the fertile soil,
  Which was my destined lot;
But here beneath this towering elm
  I lie to be forgot."

"Oh silent grave! the wicked there
  No more the just molest,
The afflicted are at ease,
  And there the weary are at rest."

"Adieu, my body for a while,
  With me thou canst not go;
But mingle with thy native soil
  Till the last trumpet blow."

"Oh friends dry up these tender tears,
  Affection's sigh strive to subdue;
Yet but a few revolving years,
  The tomb shall be your chamber too."

"For many years afflicted sore,
Yet patiently she trouble bore,
Till God was pleased to call her home,
And lodged her in the silent tomb."

PARISH OF ORMISTON.

In an aisle attached to the old church of Ormiston, now in ruins, a monument commemorates Alexander Cockburn, younger, of Ormiston, a zealous promoter of the Reformation. Born in

1535, he improved himself by foreign travel. He was a pupil of John Knox in 1547, when that Reformer obtained shelter in the castle of St. Andrews. In his "History" Knox celebrates his accomplishments. He died in August, 1564, at the early age of twenty-eight. His monument is in the form of a square mural slab with a raised border, over a Gothic arched recess. On a brass plate is the following Latin inscription, which was composed by Buchanan :—

> " Hic conditvr M[r]. Alexander Cockbvrn,
>   Primogenitus Joannis domini Ormiston
> Et Alisonæ Sandilands, ex preclara
>   Familia Calder, qvi natvs 13 Janvarii 1535
> Port insignem lingvarvm professionem ;
>   Obiit anno ætatis suæ 28 calen. Sep[t.]

> " Omnia qvæ longa indvlget mortalibvs ætas,
>   Hæc tibi Alexander prima jvventa dedit,
> Cvm genere et forma generoso sangvine digna ;
>   Ingenivm velox ingenvvmqve animvm.
> Excolvit virtvs animvm ingenivmqve camenæ,
>   Svccessv stvdio consilioqve pari ;
> His dvcibus primvm peragrata Britannia deinde ;
>   Gallia ad armiferos qva patet Helvetios ;
> Doctvs, ibi lingvas qvas Roma, Sion, et Athenæ,
>   Qvas cvm Germano Gallia docta sonat,
> Te licet imprima rapvervnt fata jvventa :
>   Non immatvro fvnere raptvs obis,
> Omnibvs officiis vitæ qvi fvnctvs obivit,
>   Non fas hvnc vitæ est de brevitate qveri."

John Cockburn of Ormiston, father of Alexander Cockburn, was also a warm upholder of the reformed doctrines. About the close of the year 1545, George Wishart, the celebrated Reformer, after preaching at Haddington, walked with Cockburn and two of his friends to Ormiston House. During night the mansion was attacked by the Earl of Bothwell, who demanded that the Reformer should be delivered up. Cockburn refused to comply until the Earl made promise that he would preserve the Reformer from the vengeance of his enemies. The Earl promised; but he soon after placed Wishart in the hands of the governor, the Earl of Arran.

At the solicitation of Mary of Lorraine, Arran transferred the Reformer to the charge of Cardinal Beaton, who, after subjecting him to a mock trial, caused him to be burned. The execution took place at St. Andrews on the 1st March, 1546. The fire which consumed the Reformer kindled a conflagration of popular hatred to ecclesiastical tyranny, which was only extinguished in the destruction of the Romish Church. In 1547 John Cockburn was by the Regent Arran and his brother, Archbishop Hamilton, of St. Andrews, banished from the kingdom, and his estates forfeited. In 1548 he found caution of underlie the law. The House of Ormiston has produced several distinguished lawyers, statesmen, and patriots. Adam Cockburn, Lord Justice Clerk, was one of the most active politicians under William III. and Queen Anne. His son John was celebrated as an agriculturist.

In Ormiston Churchyard a husband thus laments his departed wife :—

> "Let no man boast of beauty bright,
> She that lies here was my delight;
> Till cruel death did on her call
> And left me to lament her fall."

PARISH OF PRESTONKIRK.

In the parish churchyard a tombstone commemorates Andrew Meikle, inventor of the thrashing machine. Meikle was a native of Alloa.

William Dudgeon, author of the song "The Maid that tends the Goats" and some other lyrics, is buried in this churchyard. He was born at Tynningham, about the year 1753. Bred to agricultural pursuits he rented an extensive farm at Preston, Berwickshire. During his Border Tour in May, 1787, Robert Burns met him at Berrywell, the residence of the father of his friend, Robert

Ainslie; in his journal he describes him as a "poet, a worthy, remarkable character, with a great deal of information, some genius, and extreme modesty." Dudgeon died on the 28th October, 1813. He was a zealous agriculturalist, and excelled as a painter and musician.

PARISH OF PRESTONPANS.

In Prestonpans are two churchyards. One of these surrounded a monastic chapel which was destroyed during the Earl of Hertford's invasion; it is situated in the west end of the town and contains few monuments of interest. The other surrounds the parish church. In this churchyard the earliest date is 1540: it is on a stone inserted in the south wall of the church, and bearing to have reference to a John Henderson, relative of "Sir Alexander," whose armorial bearings are pretty entire, with the legend, "Sola virtus nobilitat." Probably the oldest tombstone, though without date, is one which has in relief the representation of a high-backed chair, and a writing-table, with pen, inkstand, and portfolio, together with the following inscription :—

<blockquote>
Disce mori ut sic in æternum vivas.
Viro Probo
Jacobo Pincartono,
scribæ hujus urbis,
hic nato, hic educato, honestis
parentibus prognato, ætatis
robore cum magno popularium
Suorum luctu et mœrore
rapto.
Agnes Halla conjux parentavit."
</blockquote>

On a marble pillared tombstone erected against Prestongrange aisle on the south side of the church, and repeated on a tablet within the aisle, with additions referring to members of his family, there is the following to the memory of Lord Prestongrange, who as Lord Advocate conducted the prosecutions on the part of the Crown against those involved in the Rebellion of 1745:—

"Gulielmo Grant de Prestongrange, marito, parento, civi, fideli, pio, egregio; Advocato Regio, diserto humano; Utriusque Curiæ supremæ Judici, probo integro. In variis vitæ muneribus fama æquabili et inviola; Vidua filiæque orbatæ hoc Marmor, mœrentes, extruendum curarunt. Vixit annos 63. Obiit A. H. S. 1764.

"Juncta cum sita est Vidua ejus, supra posita, fœmina in primis spectabilis, Grishelda Millar, quæ, anno 1792, fato concessit, annos 83 nata.

"Hic quoque conditæ sunt reliquiæ Christianæ Grant, filiæ corundem natu minimæ, quæ anno 1761 diem supremum obiit 16 annos habens; Et itidem suæ neptis, Joanettæ Suttie, quæ, anno 1767, vita excessit quinquennis."

On a tombstone placed against the south-east wall of the church is the following:—

"Sacred to the memory of
"Thomas Sewell, Esq., late of Haselmere, Surrey, Captain in the Royal Westmoreland Militia, in which regiment he had served as an officer nearly twenty-four years. He died October 10th, 1805, aged fifty."

Eastward of the preceding, and on the same wall of the church, is an incased marble tablet, which it appears from the famous jury trial, "Lady Ramsay against Nairne, W. S., for defamation," cost £100; and in connection with which damages to the extent of £200 were awarded by an "intelligent jury" in 1833. The brief inscription is—

"In memory of two esteemed parents, David Ramsay of Abbotshall, deceased 1775; and Helen Kid, of Craigie, his spouse, deceased in 1789.
"This tribute of affectionate remembrance was erected by their surviving son, Sir Thomas Ramsay, Bart., of Balmain, 1827."

A marble tablet at the north-west corner of the churchyard is thus inscribed:—

"Sacred to the memory of Emma, the beloved wife of It.-

Colonel Glegg, commanding the 91st Rgt. of Foot, who departed this life, 30th Sept., 1809, aged twenty-nine years."

An elegantly sculptured sandstone slab, set in the east wall of the churchyard, contains busts of two members of the old family of Hepburn of Nunraw, with the following inscription:—

"George Hepburn, his age ninety-six; he died Feb. 25, 1671. John Hepburn, his age eighty-eight; he died Jan. 24, 1670.
If thou listeth passing by,
You'l know who in this tomb doth ly.
Memento mori."

To the south of the preceding a tombstone is thus inscribed:—

" Here lyeth the Remains
of John Steuart of Phis-
-gul, a Galloway Gentlem-
-an and Cap. in Lassel's Regt.
A man of true bravery
who died honourably in
defence of his King and coun-
-try and of sacred and civil liber-
-ty, being barbarously mur-
-der'd by four Highland-
-ers near the end of the Bat-
-tle fought in the field of
Preston, on the 21st Sept.
1745."

A tombstone commemorates the Rev. James Roy, minister of the parish and brother of the celebrated Major-General William Roy, the eminent antiquary and geometrician. He was son of John Roy, gardener, Milton, Carluke, and was born on the 6th April, 1730. Licensed in 1754, he became minister of St. Cuthbert's Chapel of Ease, Edinburgh, in 1758. In 1765 he was promoted to the living of Prestonpans. He died on the 3rd September, 1767, in the thirty-seventh year of his age and tenth of his ministry. His tombstone, reared at the expense of his brother, the Major-General, is thus inscribed:—

" Quis desiderio sit pudor aut modus
Tam cari capitis ? Optimo viro
Jacobo Roy, Ecclesiæ hujus Pastori,

PARISH OF PRESTONPANS.

Post Brevi Biennii Ministerium
Immatura morte sublato.
Vixit annos XXXVII. Obiit III. Sept.
A. H. S. MDCCLXVII.
Hunc lapidem posuit frater ejus unicus
Gul. Roy, Trib. Mil."

A tombstone commemorates the Rev. John Oswalde, minister of the parish from 1648 to 1653; he died in April, 1653, aged fifty-three. An altar-tomb covers the grave of the Rev. William Carlyle, father of the eminent Dr. Alexander Carlyle, minister of Inveresk. It is thus inscribed:—

"Here lyes
The Rev. Mr. William Carlyle, who during his ministry in this place for above forty years, possessed the affection, confidence, and esteem of his parishioners. For in him were happily joined piety, benevolence, probity of manners, and fervent zeal. He dyed 8th March, 1765, in the forty-fifth year of his ministry and the seventy-fifth of his age."

The ministerial qualities of another parochial incumbent are thus set forth—

"Sacred to the Memory of
The Rev. Peter Primrose, D.D., who died on the 29th January, 1833, in the seventy-sixth year of his age and forty-sixth of his ministry; ten of which he spent in the parish of Dalgety and thirty-six as minister of Prestonpans. This stone is erected by his parishioners, who valued him as an able Minister and loved him as a sincere friend. He was an upright man, who feared God and eschewed evil."

The father and mother of Sir William Ferguson, Bart., the eminent surgeon, rest in the west churchyard, without memorial stone.

Henry Abernethy, who died 28th July, 1804, aged eighty-eight, has his last resting-place thus inscribed:—

"Blest are the Dead, yea, saith the Word,
Who die in Christ, the living Lord;
For on the other side of death
They joyful spend their living breath."

The following inscriptions, now obliterated, were in the west churchyard:—

"Anonymi, saltem quoad me.
Læta domus patriæ tunc spes, nunc incola cœli;
Oderat hic quicquid virtus amare negat."

"William Mattheson here lies,
  Whose age was forty-one;
February seventeenth he flies,
  His Is'bel Mitchell from,
Who was his marri'd wife,
  The fourth part of his life.
The soul it cannot die,
  Tho' th' body be turn'd to clay;
Yet meet again must they,
  At the last day:
Trumpets shall sound, archangels cry,
Come forth Is'bel Mitchell, and meet Will Mattheson in the sky."

In a small enclosure to the N.W. of the parish churchyard a pillared statue in honour of Thomas Alexander, C.B., Director-General of the Medical Department of the Army has the following inscription:—

"In memory of Thomas Alexander, C.B., Director-General of the Medical Department of the British Army, born at Prestonpans, 6th May, 1812, died 1st February, 1860. Throughout a long military career he laboured incessantly to elevate the condition of the soldier, and during the Crimean war his indefatigable efforts as principal medical officer of the Light Division to alleviate the sufferings of the troops were of inestimable value in stimulating others to follow his example. The improved sanitary condition of the British army, as well as the elevation in rank and consideration of its medical officers are mainly due to his exertions. His high professional attainments and his great administrative powers were wholly devoted to the service of his country and to the cause of humanity."

Adjoining the enclosure containing Mr. Alexander's monument a marble obelisk has lately been erected in memory of his parents. It bears the following inscription:—

"In memory of William Alexander, salt manufacturer, Prestonpans, died 26th Feb., 1865, aged seventy-nine; his wife Helen Kemp, died 21st May, 1865, aged eighty; and their infant children.

Their son Thomas Alexander, Director-General of the Medical Department of the British Army, died 1st February, 1860, aged forty-seven."

PARISH OF SALTON.

A vault under the north aisle of the parish church is the burial-place of the family of Fletcher of Salton. Here are interred the remains of Andrew Fletcher, of Salton, the patriot, and his nephew Andrew Fletcher, Lord Milton. The former was born in 1653. He was educated under Dr. Burnet, afterwards Bishop of Salisbury, and spent some years in foreign travel. In 1681 he entered the Scottish Parliament as commissioner for Haddingtonshire. Opposing the arbitrary measures of the Crown, he was outlawed and his estates confiscated. In 1685 he joined the ill-advised enterprise of the Duke of Monmouth, on the failure of which he escaped to Spain, where he suffered imprisonment. At the Revolution he returned to Scotland. He again entered Parliament, strongly supporting the popular rights against what he conceived to be the undue exercise of the royal prerogative. He bitterly opposed the Union, and proposed various limitations to the royal prerogative, some of which were introduced into the Act of Security. He died at London in 1716. He was an accomplished scholar, an impressive orator, and an elegant writer. In accomplishing his purposes he was firm and energetic. But he lacked tact, judgment, and temper. He was quarrelsome, even to a proverb. He nearly throttled Lord Stair in the Parliament House for his using an expression which he conceived to reflect upon him, and he shot dead the Mayor of Lyne, when that magistrate reproved him for appropriating his horse without his leave.

Andrew Fletcher, Lord Milton, was son of Henry Fletcher, of Salton, younger brother of the patriot. He was born in 1692, admitted Advocate in 1717, and promoted as a Lord of Session in 1724; he was subsequently appointed Lord Justice Clerk and Commissioner for improving the fisheries and manufactures in Scotland. His humanity in administering the law, after the Rebellion of 1745, gained him the esteem of those who had suffered defeat. He took an active part in effecting the abolition of heritable jurisdictions, and was a zealous promoter of learning, agriculture, and commerce. He died on the 13th December, 1776, aged seventy-four.

A tombstone in the churchyard is thus inscribed:—

> "Reader! here lyes good Robert Henderson,
> Phisician, Gardner, Svrgeon all in one;
> In all which three svch svccess God did give
> And now when gone His vertues do Reqvire
> A Monvment more Ample then is Here."

PARISH OF SPOTT.

An aisle attached to the church was the burial-place of the old family of Hay, of Spott; it now belongs to the family of Sprot.

In the churchyard a Latin inscription commemorates the Rev. William Orr, minister of the parish, who died on the 5th May, 1769, in the seventy-fifth year of his age and forty-third of his ministry. Tombstones commemorate the Rev. Patrick Carfrae, minister of Dunbar, who died on the 4th March, 1822, aged eighty-one; the Rev. John Martin, minister of Spot, died 29th September, 1798; General John Carfrae, died 29th August, 1863, aged seventy-nine; the Rev. Robert Cunningham, of Balgowrie, died 24th January, 1801; and the Rev. John Copeland, died 15th September, 1866, aged sixty-eight.

From tombstones in this churchyard we have the following:—

> "Oft have our tears bedewed the urn,
> Deep where her tender ashes lie;

> But hope persuades we cease to mourn,
> Faith saw her soul exulting fly."

> "Thus ends the life
> Of feeble man below; nor pow'r, nor
> Honour, fame, nor youthful bloom
> Can gain a respite from
> The dreadful blow."

> "The grave dissolves each social tie
> And tells us too, that we must die,
> And then corruption see.
> Happy are they whose hopes arise,
> High as the pleasure of the skies,
> And then immortal be."

PARISH OF TRANENT.

In the parish church of Tranent are interred the remains of the gallant and pious Colonel James Gardiner. This distinguished officer was born at Carriden, Linlithgowshire, on the 10th January, 1688. He entered the army at an early age, and though fearless of danger and an active officer, was chiefly noted for his profligacy. In July, 1719, when perusing a book entitled "The Christian Soldier," which he had taken up to occupy an idle hour, he was suddenly awakened to a sense of his criminality and danger. He conceived that he saw a vision of the Saviour extended on the cross, and remonstrating with him on his ingratitude. For a period he experienced a feeling of distress and agony; subsequently he found peace in believing. He became a zealous and most exemplary Christian. On the outbreak of the Rebellion in 1745, he marched with his Regiment from Stirling, to join Sir John Cope at Dunbar, to give battle to the rebels. The hostile armies came in view of each other on the 20th September, in the neighbourhood of Colonel Gardiner's own house of Bankton, near Prestonpans. He remained all night under arms wrapped up in his cloak. At three in the morning he summoned his four domestic servants, to whom he addressed earnest counsel; he then engaged for about an hour in solitary meditation. Before sunrise the rebel army made an attack. Colonel Gardiner was struck by a bullet in his left breast, and soon after received a shot in his right thigh. His Regiment was seized with a panic, and he made an attempt to rally them. A Highlander attacked him with a scythe and wounded and disarmed him. He was now surrounded, dragged from his horse, and struck on the head with a Lochaber axe. He expired on the following day. An elegant obelisk, with four lions on projecting buttresses, has been reared to his memory in front of the house of Bankton, not far from the spot, where he was mortally wounded. It is inscribed thus:—

"To Colonel Gardiner, who fell in the Battle of Prestonpans, 21st September, 1745. 'A man who feared God above many.'"— Neh : vii. 2.

A tablet in the church commemorates Andrew Brown, D.D., successively minister of Falkland and Tranent. He died on the 26th April, 1805, in the sixty-first year of his age and twenty-ninth of his ministry. He is described as respected for his highly cultivated understanding, sound judgment, and liberal mind. In "him," it is added, "rational piety, true patriotism, exemplary fortitude, disinterested benevolence, and inflexible integrity, were eminently conspicuous."

In the churchyard the tombstone of Thomas Bell is thus inscribed :—

"Miles, caupo, faber, stravi, fulsi, fabricavi,
Hostes, cor, ferrum, vulnere, vite, manu."

A tablet near the S.W. corner bears to be erected by a sorrowing husband to the memory of his wife, as a tribute of *filial* (sic) regard.

In the churchyard a defaced altar-tomb covers the grave of the Rev. Robert Balcanqual, who died, minister of the parish in 1664. He was nephew of Walter Balcanqual, Dean of Durham, one of the executors of the celebrated George Heriot.

BERWICKSHIRE.

PARISH OF AYTON.

In the churchyard a tombstone denotes the grave of the Rev. George Tough, minister of the parish, an ingenious mechanician. He constructed an Orrery upon an improved plan which he presented to George IV. on his visit to Edinburgh in 1822. Mr. Tough was a native of Edinburgh, was licensed in 1798, and ordained to the ministry at Berwick-on-Tweed in 1802. He was translated to Beath, Fifeshire, in 1812, and to Ayton in 1814. He died on the 29th July, 1842, aged sixty-eight.

A tombstone contains these rhymes:—

> "Though distant climes divide us here below;
> Though far apart we moulder into dust;
> Hope says, and gently dries the tears of woe,
> You all shall meet to mingle with the dust."

PARISH OF BUNKLE.

In Preston churchyard, in this parish, a tombstone presents the following inscription:—

"To the memory of William Carlisle, who died at Blanerne, on the 16th of September, 1831, aged 108 years; and Catherine Mitchell, his wife, who died on the 10th April, 1818, aged eighty-two years."

Carlisle was coachman to Mr. Lumsden, of Blanerne. In Blanerne House is preserved his portrait, painted by Thomson of Duddingston, when he was one hundred years old.

PARISH OF CHIRNSIDE.

The remains of the Rev. Henry Areskine, father of the celebrated Ebenezer and Ralph Areskine, rest in the parish churchyard. Youngest of thirty-three children born to Ralph Areskine of Shielfield, a descendant of the noble family of Mar, he was born in 1624. He graduated at Edinburgh University, and was in 1649 settled minister of Cornhill, Northumberland. From this charge he was ejected by the Act of Uniformity in 1662. He now resided on his paternal estate, occasionally preaching, till April, 1682, when he was seized by a party of soldiers, and committed to prison. By the Privy Council he was liberated on giving his bond that he would leave the kingdom. He retired to the English border, and after a time established his abode at Monilaws, near the scene of his former labours. In 1685 he was seized by the Militia, and again subjected to imprisonment, but was soon liberated under the Act of Indemnity. In 1687 he received a call to the meeting-house at Rivelaw, parish of Whitsome. After the Revolution he became minister of Chirnside, where he died on the 10th August, 1696, in his seventy-second year and forty-seventh of his ministry. A plain tombstone marks his grave; while in honour of his struggles in the cause of religious liberty, a square pillar has been reared in the churchyard by the subscriptions of 600 individuals.

PARISH OF COLDINGHAM.

The Priory of Coldingham, founded about the year 1098 by Edgar, King of Scotland, was repeatedly dilapidated during the Border wars; it has been partially restored as the parish church. Most of the older monuments have perished. In the surrounding churchyard tombstones commemorate three incumbents. The Rev. John Dysart was translated from Langton in 1694. The majority of the parishioners being attached to Episcopacy, he was inducted under the protection of a military force. For some time he carried to the pulpit a brace of pistols, which he placed on each side of him. He died in 1732, and was interred near the north wall of the church. He made a bequest to the poor. His successor, the Rev. Robert Brydone, married his daughter Elizabeth. This reverend gentleman died 17th March, 1761, aged seventy-five; he was father of Patrick Brydone, author of a "Tour through Sicily and Malta," and father of Mary, Countess of Minto. The Rev. John Jolly, who succeeded to the cure in 1761, died on the 9th November, 1792, aged sixty-one.

The following epitaph is inscribed on a modern tombstone :—

"All ye who read my epitaph,
Seek ye the Lord and put not off;
Remember when my grave you see,
I once did live like unto thee;
But soon by death was snatched away
In bloom of youth and no decay;
Oh, for eternity prepare,
And make a future life thy care."

PARISH OF COLDSTREAM.

The parish churchyard is situated in a lonely spot by the banks of the Tweed; it is deemed safe from interference by the following announcement posted up at the gateway :—

"Take notice. An armed watch is placed here every night for the protection of this burial-ground. And has orders to fire upon any person who may enter at improper hours without permission."

On a tombstone a son thus commemorates his mother:—

"I owe thee much, thou hast deserved from me,
Far, far beyond what I can ever pay;
Oft have I proved the labours of thy love,
And the warm efforts of thy gentle heart."

By these lines David Innes celebrates his departed wife :—

> "Clos'd, ever clos'd those speaking eyes,
>   Where sweetness beam'd, where candour shone,
> And silent that heart-thrilling voice
>   Which music lov'd and call'd her own.
> Alas! before the violet bloom'd,
>   Before the snows of winter fled,
> Too certain fate my hopes consum'd,
>   For she was numbered with the dead."

William Beloe laments his wife thus :—

> "Oft to this spot
> Will memory fondly turn,
> And love's pure flame
> Still unextinguished burn
> Within their breasts, who
> Here doth mourn their loss;
> But nails their sorrows
> To a Saviour's cross.
> Oh, precious hope!
> By faith to mortals given,
> That loving hearts, which
> Hath on earth been riven,
> May through the same
> Dear Saviour's pleading love
> Again unite in realms
> Of bliss above."

PARISH OF DUNSE.

These epitaphs are from the parochial burial-ground :—

> "Here lies the only comfort of my life,
> The best of husbands to a wife.
> Great was my loss for his eternal gain,
> And hope in Christ that we shall meet again."

"Beneath this stone three infants lie,
    Say are they lost or saved?
If death's by sin, they sinned, for they are here;
If heaven's by works, in heaven they can't appear.
Revere the sacred page, the knot's untied,—
They died, for Adam sinned; they live, for Jesus died."

PARISH OF EARLSTON.

A stone built in the front wall of the parish church bears these words:—

"Auld Rhymer's race
Lies in this place."

The inscription refers to Thomas Learmont of Ercildoune (Earlston), better known as the Rhymer. In the parish the ruin of an ancient tower is pointed out as his castle. He flourished about the end of the thirteenth century, and being a person of uncommon ability and learning he has been celebrated as a prophet and poet. By the vulgar he was believed to have been snatched by the Fairy Queen to her viewless abode, from which, after seven years, he was permitted to revisit the earth to astonish his countrymen by his auguries. It is said that he still "drees his weird" in fairy-land, and will reappear in his favourite haunts. In "The Minstrelsy of the Scottish Border," Sir Walter Scott has preserved some of the prophecies ascribed to him, together with a ballad descriptive of his intercourse with the Fairy Queen.

At Mellerstain is the burial-vault of the House of Baillie of Jerviswood. A tombstone with an elegant inscription commemorates the celebrated Lady Grizel Baillie. This accomplished gentlewoman was daughter of Sir Patrick Hume, afterwards Earl of Marchmont; she was born at Redbraes Castle, Berwickshire, on the 25th December, 1665. When only twelve years old she evinced remarkable courage on two trying occasions. To Robert Baillie of Jerviswood, then imprisoned at Edinburgh, she delivered a letter from her father under circumstances of peculiar danger; and when her father concealed himself in a vault of Polwarth Church she by night brought him victuals, which she secretly provided for his use. During the exile of her father in Holland she managed the family affairs with singular prudence. At the Revolution she had the privilege of declining the situation of Maid of Honour to the Princess of Orange. She composed several ballads; one of these, "Were na' my heart light I wad dee," is well known. She married George Baillie of Jerviswood, son of the celebrated Robert Baillie. She died on the 6th December, 1746, in the eighty-first year of her age.

PARISH OF ECCLES.

At Crosshall stands a sandstone column ten feet in height, supported by a massive pedestal of the same material. On the north face it is sculptured with a Calvary cross, the upper part surrounded by a kind of shield. The west side, which becomes narrower towards the top, has at the summit a circular expansion eighteen inches in diameter, with a chevron in the dexter and sinister chiefs, and precise middle base respectively, and a St. John's cross. On the south side is an escutcheon similar to that on the west side, and beneath is an ancient double-handed sword. On the east side is a circular expansion at the top, with a cross; below is the nude figure of a man and a greyhound. Among several conjectures as to the purpose of the monument the most probable is that it was constructed after the second crusade, in 1114, in honour of the father of Sir John de Soulis, lieutenant to John Baliol. Till lately the locality of the monument was called Deadriggs. According to tradition a battle was fought in the neighbourhood.

In the parish churchyard gravestones commemorate two ministers of the parish, the Rev. Matthew Dysart and the Rev. Dr. James Thomson. The former studied at Glasgow College, and was licensed in 1728, and ordained in 1731. He assumed the name of Sandilands on succeeding to the estate of Couston in right of his mother. Having been present in the Edinburgh Theatre at the first performance of "Douglas" in 1756, he was reproved by the General Assembly. He died on the 13th June, 1773, in his sixty-ninth year, and the forty-third of his ministry. Dr. Thomson was a native of Crieff; he was ordained at Eccles in 1805. He published expositions of the Gospel according to St. Luke, and of the Acts of the Apostles, with other works; he also contributed to the *Encyclopædia Britannica*. He died on the 28th November, 1855, in the eighty-eighth year of his age, and fifty-first of his ministry.

PARISH OF EDROM.

On a portion of ground called De la Beauté's field, on the estate of Broomhouse, a cairn denotes the grave of Sir Anthony Darcy, surnamed Le Sieur de la Beauté. Sir Anthony was a native of France; he was in June, 1517, appointed by the Regent Duke of Albany, warden of the Marches and captain of Dunbar Castle in place of Lord Home. Home was treacherously slain at Edinburgh at the instigation of Darcy, who consequently became odious. A dispute arose between him and David Home, proprietor of Wedderburn, and a conflict between them and their followers took place at Langton on the 12th October, 1517. Darcy's party were worsted and put to flight. His horse stuck fast in a bog in Dunse Moor, and as he was escaping on foot he was overtaken by Wedderburn and slain. His head was fixed on the battlements of Home Castle, and a cairn reared upon his body.

Attached to Edrom Church is the burying-vault of the old family of Kelloe. Another aisle of the church formed the burial-place of the family of Blackadder. It bears the following inscription :— " Founded by Robert Blackadder, Archbishop of Glasgow, in the year 1499." On the south-east corner are these words :—" Repaired by S. John Home, of Blackadder, in the year 1696."

PARISH OF FOULDEN.

In the parish churchyard a flat tombstone is thus inscribed :—
"Heir . Lieth . Ane . Honorabil . Man . Georg . Ramsay . in . Fvlden . Bastel . vho . departed . 4 . Jan. 1592 . and of . his age . 74.
Fife . fostring . Peace . me . bred
From . thence . the . Merce . me . cald .
The . Merce . to . Marsis . lavis . led .
To . Byde . his . Battellis . bald.
Veried . Vith . Vares . and . sore . opprest .
Death . gave . to . Mars . the . foyl .
And . nov . I have . more . Qvyet . Rest .
Than . in . my . native soyl.
Fife . Merce . Mars . Mort . these fatal Fovr,
Al . hail . my . days . hes . driven . ovr."

George Ramsay was last in the male line of the Ramsays of Foulden, a branch of the family of Dalhousie. The Foulden Family flourished on the eastern border for three centuries. Their stronghold of Foulden Bastel stood on the precipitous bank of a small stream, a tributary of the Whitadder, which flows about half a mile to the southward.

PARISH OF HUTTON.

A tombstone denotes the grave of Mr. Bookles, a late schoolmaster of the parish, remarkable for his stature. He was seven feet four inches in height.

Tombstones commemorate four parochial incumbents, viz.:—James Orr, died 1694; Gilbert Laurie, A.M., died September, 1727, aged seventy-five; Robert Waugh, died 23rd February, 1756, aged seventy-two; and Philip Redpath, translator of Boethius's "Consolations of Philosophy," and editor of the "Border History" composed by his brother Philip, who died 18th May, 1788, aged sixty-eight.

PARISH OF LAUDER.

A monument in the parish church commemorates Alexander Lauder, Bishop of Dunkeld, son of Sir Alan Lauder of Haltoun, who died on the 11th October, 1440. In the churchyard tombstones celebrate the ministerial gifts and faithfulness of the Rev. James Ford, who died on the 24th September, 1810, aged eighty-seven; also the Rev. Peter Cosens, who died 20th August, 1845, aged sixty-four,—both incumbents of the cure.

The following inscription formerly celebrated Alexander Thomson, whose remains were the first which were deposited in this place of sepulture:—

"Here lyes interred an honest man,
Who did this churchyard first lie in;
This monument shall make it known
That he was the first laid in this ground.
Of mason and of masonrie,
He cutted stones right curiously.
To heaven we hope that he is gone,
Where Christ is the chief corner-stone."

PARISH OF LONGFORMACUS.

A tombstone commemorates the Rev. Robert Monteith, minister of the parish, who distinguished himself as a volunteer during the insurrection of 1745. His heroism is thus sarcastically described in the ballad of "Tranent-Muir:"—

> "Monteith the great, when hersell shot,
>   Un'wares did ding him o'er, man,
>   Yet wadna stand to bear a hand,
>   But aff fou fast did scour, man."

Mr. Monteith was ordained to the cure in 1735; he died 11th December, 1776, in his sixty-eighth year, and forty-second of his ministry.

PARISH OF MERTON.

In this parish is the interesting ruin of Dryburgh Abbey, celebrated as the burial-place of Sir Walter Scott. The abbey was reared by Hugh de Morville, Lord of Lauderdale, about the year 1150. In 1233 it was burned by the army of Edward II. Restored by King Robert the Bruce, it was again demolished by the Earl of Hertford in 1545. It has since remained a ruin. The situation is beautiful and impressive; it stands on a peninsula enclosed by a bend of the Tweed, and is environed with orchards.

Early in his career Sir Walter Scott determined that his bones should rest in this abbey. His ancestors, the Haliburtons of Newmains, had been owners of the abbey, and were interred within its precincts. On the 22nd of May, 1826, the remains of Lady Scott, wife of the illustrious minstrel, were deposited in St. Mary's aisle, near the high altar. On the 26th September, 1832, the minstrel's own remains were placed by her side. Huge blocks of granite inscribed with the names of Sir Walter and Lady Scott rest upon the graves. The scene is visited by thousands who seek to contemplate the poet's sepulchre. One who made a pilgrimage to the spot has thus recorded his impressions:—

> "I stood within the ruin'd fane,
>   Beside St. Mary's grated aisle;

No sound was in that lonely spot,
　　No voice was on the gale,
Save when at intervals there came
　　A mournful music, sweet and slow—
The murmur of his own loved Tweed
　　That calmly rolled below.

"I linger'd till the harvest moon
　　Peer'd through the ivy'd loopholes there,
And still delay'd to quit a scene
　　So gloomy, yet so fair.
And was it here—life's fever o'er—
　　In this sequester'd, holy spot,
Lay mingling with its kindred clay,
　　The dust of Walter Scott?
　　　*　　*　　*　　*　　*　　*
"Where'er the winds of Heaven have blown
　　We hear his numbers borne along,
In martial strain—or tender plaint,
　　The magic of his song.
　　　*　　*　　*　　*　　*　　*
"The grass is trodden by the feet
　　Of thousands from a thousand lands;
The prince,—the peasant,—tottering age,
　　And rosy school boy bands.
　　　*　　*　　*　　*　　*　　*
"Thou wondrous being, fare-thee-well;
　　Thou noblest, best of human kind,
Who join'd to a Nathanael's heart
　　A Shakspeare's master mind."

Descended from an old Saxon family, long potent on the Border, Walter Scott was son of a Writer to the Signet, and was born at Edinburgh, on the 15th August, 1771. He studied at the High School and University of Edinburgh, but, partly owing to delicate health, he did not distinguish himself as a scholar. Engaging in legal studies, he passed Advocate in 1792. At the Bar he attained only a moderate success, but he was fortunate in securing an independence by his marriage, which took place in 1797. In 1800 he was appointed Sheriff of Selkirk, with a salary of £300. He began to compose verses at the age of twelve; and he made his *début* as an author by publishing in 1796 some poetical translations from the German. He was more successful in editing the ballads of his own country in "The Minstrelsy of the Scottish Border," of which the first two volumes appeared in 1802. His "Lay of the Last Minstrel" was issued in 1805, and proved the pioneer of his celebrity. In 1808 he produced "Marmion," and in 1810 "The Lady of the Lake," the latter poem raising his reputation to a degree which his subsequent fame as a novelist justified, but did not exceed. "Waverley" appeared in 1814 without his name; after a short interval it was rapturously received and read everywhere. "Guy Mannering" followed; then "The Antiquary;" then the series of novels under the title of "Tales of my Landlord." Fortune was now abundantly propitious. In 1806 Scott became a principal clerk in the Court of Session, with a salary of £1,200 per annum. Each of his publications, whether in verse or prose, availed him hundreds, some, thousands of pounds. In 1811 he purchased on the south bank of the Tweed, near Melrose, a piece of ground, which he drained, planted, and built upon, and dignified by the name of Abbotsford. George IV., on his accession in 1820, created him a baronet. The mansion of Abbotsford was from time to time enlarged to meet the requirements of his family and visitors. He became the most celebrated, and apparently the most prosperous *littérateur* of his time. But he, unhappily, speculated as a partner in the printing concern of the Messrs. Ballantyne, his early friends, and the printers of his works. In the bankruptcy of Archibald Constable, his publisher, which took place in 1826, the Ballantynes were involved, and Sir Walter found himself individually responsible for a debt of no less than £120,000. He was in his fifty-fifth year, and his energies were considerably impaired, and his health shattered, but he declined to settle with his creditors by a composition, and proceeded by increased literary diligence to the work of liquidating his liabilities. In the great effort he was overcome, yet he lived to extinguish more than half his obligations, and his survivors were privileged to find at his death that, by means of a policy on his life, and the sale of his copyrights, his debts were discharged. Abbotsford too was saved for his children and heirs. He died at Abbotsford on the 21st September, 1832. His remains were accompanied to the grave by a large assemblage of friends and neighbours. In recording the event of his death, many of the public journals used mourning borders. Sir Walter has depicted Scottish life and manners with the pen of an enchanter, and has, by the impress of his genius, rendered celebrated many scenes and localities hitherto unknown. The remains of so great a magician, so renowned a minstrel, rest appropriately by the banks of the silver Tweed, within his own loved Dryburgh.

In St. Mary's aisle rest the remains of Sir Walter's eldest son, the second Sir Walter Scott, who was here entombed on the 4th May, 1847. John Gibson Lockhart, his son-in-law and literary executor, has here also found a sepulchre. This ingenious writer and expert critic was born in the manse of Cambusnethan, on the 14th June, 1794. He studied at the University of Glasgow, and proceeded on the Snell Exhibition to Baliol College, Oxford. In 1816 he was called to the Scottish Bar. He was one of the originators of *Blackwood's Magazine.* In 1820 he married Sir Walter Scott's eldest daughter, Sophia. In 1825 he was appointed editor of the *Quarterly Review,* and established his residence in London. He published four novels, "Valerius," "Reginald Dalton," "Matthew Wald," and "Adam Blair." His poetical abilities are indicated in his translations of "Spanish Ballads." He died at Abbotsford, on the 25th November, 1854, in his sixty-first year. His "Life of Sir Walter Scott" is one of the most interesting works in the language.

Amidst the ruins of Dryburgh, which formed a portion of his own estate, rest the remains of David Stewart Erskine, eleventh Earl of Buchan. This patriotic and enterprising but eccentric nobleman was born on the 1st of June, 1742. He studied at Glasgow College, and afterwards joined the army. In 1767, on his father's death, he succeeded to the earldom. He devoted himself to literary and antiquarian pursuits. In November, 1780, he established the Scottish Society of Antiquaries. He edited Henry the Minstrel's "Wallace," and contributed essays and memoirs to different periodicals. He latterly resided in Dryburgh House, and took considerable interest in the improvement of the abbey estate, which he had purchased. He died on the 20th April, 1829. Amidst some oddities and extreme personal vanity Lord Buchan possessed no inconsiderable talent. He delighted to afford countenance to persons of merit, and especially rejoiced to celebrate those who had distinguished themselves by their genius or their patriotism. He was the first to erect a monument to the Preserver of the national independence; he commissioned Mr. Smith, architect, Darnick, to construct a monumental statue of the illustrious Wallace. Mr. Smith reared a figure twenty-one feet in height, which, on the 22nd September, 1814, was placed on its pedestal, a rocky eminence overlooking the Tweed. This statue is seen at a considerable distance in the landscape.

James Thomson, author of the "Seasons," was celebrated by Lord Buchan. Besides instituting a yearly festival in his honour, he reared a Greek temple on the banks of the Tweed, which he consecrated to his memory; a bust of the poet is placed upon the dome.

In Dryburgh Churchyard these lines are inscribed upon a tombstone:—

> "Here lies the dust of James Barrie,
> Who's Bible loved to read;
> But now in silent grave lies he,
> Nor further can proceed."

PARISH OF MORDINGTON.

The following epitaphs are from the parish churchyard:—

> "Though in the grave my body ly,
> And worms do it consume,
> Still waiting for the glorious day
> When Christ shall call me home;

Though for a time my dust be loathed,
    Most beautiful I'll be,
My mortal body shall be clothed
    With immortality."

"His life was healthful,
    And his conscience clear;
His heart was honest,
    To his friends sincere.
Death ne'er did awe him,
    For he wished to die;
In silent peace,
    Here let his ashes lie."

PARISH OF POLWARTH.

In the burial-vault of the House of Hume, Sir Patrick Hume, afterwards Earl of Marchmont, sought concealment in the autumn of 1684, during the persecutions of the period. The circumstances have been noticed in connection with the name of Lady Grizel Baillie (p. 225).

A schoolmaster of the parish has these lines upon his gravestone:—

"Beneath this stone the hands of death fast bind
A form once learned, generous, and kind,
Whose liberal hand to all men did extend;
A friend to all, all men to him a friend."

PARISH OF SWINTON.

Within the parish church a monument commemorates Sir Alan de Swinton, a baron of the reign of William the Lion, and founder of the Houses of Swinton of Swinton, and of Kimmerghame, Berwickshire. Under the figure of a boar and three boars' heads, the monument presents the following inscription:—

HIC · IACET · ALANVS · SVINTONVS · MILES · DE · EODEM ·

Below is a full length figure of the baron, with his arms bent upward from the elbows and clasping a book. He obtained a charter of the barony of Swinton from Bertram, prior of Coldingham; he died about 1200. His name is assumed by Sir Walter Scott for the hero of Halidon Hill, though the knight who actually fought there was Sir John Swinton. An arched vault in front of the monument and under the floor of the church was opened a number of years ago. It was found to contain one coffin and three skulls. Of the largest skull, supposed to be that of Sir Alan, who is traditionally said to have been of gigantic proportions, a cast was taken, and presented to Sir Walter Scott, who placed it in the armory at Abbotsford, beside a similar cast of the skull of King Robert the Bruce.

PARISH OF WESTRUTHER.

Bassendean Chapel has long been used as the burying-place of the family of Home of Bassendean. George Home, a member of the family who attached himself to the Presbyterian cause during the religious persecutions of the reigns of Charles II. and James VII., is interred in the chapel. He suffered proscription, but effected his escape to Holland. After the Revolution he was restored to his estate.

A native of the parish, now in Canada, lately caused these lines to be inscribed on his family tombstone:—

> "My Father, Mother, my two sons
> Lie underneath this sod,
> Who far from me believe to see
> All one in Christ with God."

PARISH OF WHITSOME.

In Hilton Churchyard a tombstone is thus inscribed :—

"Heire lyes *Christian Forret* daughter to *James Forret* of that Ilk in Fyffe, her mother being daughter to the laird of Lethiday in Angus, married William Somervil of Moshat Girfilman in Clidisdail, with whom she lived a year and being delivered of one daughter, christianly and comfortably past from her pilgrimage to her home and husband Christ. Junii 18. 1645.

> What graces, gifts, parts, perfections rare,
> Among all other women scattered are,
> Unitly, fully, cleirly shined in that Star."

The estate of Forret is situated in the parish of Logie, Fifeshire; it belonged to a family of the same name from the reign of William the Lion till the seventeenth century. In 1466 John Forret of Forret was one of an assize for clearing the marches of the Abbot of Dunfermline. One of the family was master stabler to James IV.; his son Thomas was educated by a lady of opulence, and admitted a canon regular in the monastery of St. Colm's Inch; he was subsequently admitted to the vicarage of Dollar. He embraced the reformed doctrines, and being subjected to an assize consisting of Archbishop James Beaton and a convocation of bishops, he was sentenced to death. He was burned with four others on the castle-hill of Edinburgh, on the 28th February, 1538.

ROXBURGHSHIRE.

PARISH OF ANCRUM.

At Ancrum Moor a monument commemorates " Maiden Lilliard," a young Scottish woman who at the battle of Ancrum distinguished herself by her extraordinary valour. According to tradition she continued to fight against the national enemies after both her limbs had been struck off. The original epitaph, lately renewed, proceeds thus :—

" Fair Maiden Lilliard lies under this stane,
  Little was her stature but great was her fame ;
  Upon the English loons she laid mony thumps,
  And when her legs were cuttit aff she fought upon her stumps."

The battle of Ancrum was fought in 1545. It arose out of an inroad made into Scotland by Sir Ralph Eure and Sir Brian Layton, in an attempt to obtain possession of territory in Teviotdale and the Merse, conferred upon them by Henry VIII. Led by these barons the English troops destroyed Melrose Abbey, and ransacked and defaced the burial-place of the Earls of Douglas. The Earl of Angus being determined on revenge, joined the Earl of Arran, Norman Leslie, Master of Rothes, and Walter Scott of Buccleuch, in giving battle to the invaders, who were completely routed, 800 of them being slain, and 1,000 made prisoners.

PARISH OF BOWDEN.

Attached to the parish church is the burial-vault of the Ducal House of Roxburgh. It contains twenty-one coffins, including those of five dukes. John, third duke of Roxburgh, the celebrated book collector, has here found a resting-place. He was born in London on the 23rd April, 1740, and succeeded his father, the second Duke, in 1755. With a remarkable taste for old books he formed a large and valuable collection. He died on the 19th March, 1804. His library, consisting of ten thousand volumes, was exposed to auction in 1812, many of the books fetching fabulous prices. The Roxburgh Club, for the printing of rare and curious MSS., was established in his honour.

In the churchyard a small tombstone denotes the grave of Andrew Scott, author of "Simon and Janet," and other popular ballads. A native of the parish, he was born on the 19th April 1757. For some time he served in the army; on his discharge he, became parish sexton. He printed a volume of poems in 1805, and two volumes subsequently. He died on the 22nd May, 1839, aged eighty-two.

PARISH OF CASTLETON.

In the parish churchyard rest the remains of James Telfer, an ingenious poet and miscellaneous writer. Telfer was born in the parish of Southdean, on the 3rd December, 1800. He was originally employed as a shepherd, but afterwards qualified himself as a teacher. He conducted an adventure school at Saughtree, Liddesdale, where he died on the 18th January, 1862. In 1824 he published "Ballads and Miscellaneous Poems." A volume of "Tales and Sketches" from his pen appeared in 1852.

PARISH OF CAVERS.

John Armstrong of Gilnockie, the famous border freebooter, who was put to death by James V. in June, 1529, is interred in the burying-ground at Caerlanrig Chapel. By the peasantry Armstrong's memory is held in affectionate remembrance. The circumstances of his death form the subject of a ballad published by Allan Ramsay in "The Evergreen."

On "The Green," at Denholm, a handsome monument has lately been erected to the memory of Dr. John Leyden, the celebrated poet and orientalist. Dr. Leyden was born at Denholm, in September, 1775. He studied at the University of Edinburgh, and was licensed to preach in 1798. With an eminent reputation as a scholar he became editor of the *Scots Magazine;* he also edited the "Complaynt of Scotland," a curious political treatise of the sixteenth century, and contributed several ballads to the "Minstrelsy of the Scottish Border." Disappointed in obtaining ecclesiastical preferment, he qualified himself as a physician, and accepted the appointment of assistant-surgeon in the Hospital at Madras. He sailed for India in 1803, and at once made himself familiar with the native tongues. He was successively appointed surgeon to the Commissioners for surveying the provinces in Mysore, Professor of Hindostan in the College of Calcutta, and Judge of the Twenty-four Pargunnas of Calcutta. He accompanied the army in the expedition against Java. On the capture of Batavia, having gone to examine the library of the place, he caught a malignant fever from the tainted air of the apartment. He died on the 28th August, 1811, aged thirty-six. His poem "Scenes of Infancy" has been frequently reprinted. His lyrics are pervaded with simplicity and tenderness. As a philologist his power in mastering the peculiarities of languages was nearly unrivalled.

In the parish churchyard the following quaint epitaph commemorates some of Dr. Leyden's progenitors :—

"Here lies the body of James Leydon,
   In this churchyard beneath this stone;
  And Margaret Scott, his spouse alone,
   Lyeth also here beneath this stone;
  And their posterity that's gone,
   Lies also here beneath this stone.
  William, Adam Leydon, and John,
   Lie also here beneath this stone.
  In Earlside they lived some years agone,
   Now here they ly beneath this stone.
  But this I will keep on record,
   They were all such as fear'd the Lord,
  For the deceased, James Leydon,
   On his death-bed this he made known,
  That here no more he must remain,
   But to the dust return again;
  And that his soul at God's decree
   For ever should a dweller be
  In that most holy place above
   Where nothing is but peace and love.
  He was but fifty years of age
   When he removèd from this stage;
  The year sixteen hundred and eighty-eight,
   The twelfth of March was his last night."

PARISH OF ECKFORD.

On the south bank of the Kale near Eckford Mill a mount 218 feet in circumference, and composed of artificial layers of stones and earth, commemorates Robert or Hobbie Hall, a man remarkable for his piety and his bodily strength. On the summit of the mount a rude stone records a victory achieved by Hall over Ker of Cessford, who sought illegally to appropriate his estate. The inscription is as follows :—

  "Here Hoby Hall boldly maintained his right,
   'Gainst Reif plain force armed with lawless might,
  For twenty pleughs harnes'd in all their gear,
   Could not his valiant, noble heart make fear,

> But with his sword he cut the foremost soam
> In two : hence drove both pleughs and
> Pleughmen home. 1620."

In an aisle adjoining the parish church a monument celebrates Sir William Bennet of Grubbet, a friend of the poets Thomson and Ramsay, and the supposed prototype of Sir William Worthy in "The Gentle Shepherd." Over the entrance to the aisle is the following inscription :—

"Hoc monumentum tibi et suis bene Merentibus ponendam curavit Dominus Gulielmus Bennet, Eques auratus, anno salutis 1724."

PARISH OF EDNAM.

On a portion of rising ground at Henderside an obelisk fifty-two feet in height commemorates James Thomson, author of "The Seasons." This celebrated poet was son of the Rev. Thomas Thomson, minister of the parish, and was born on the 11th September, 1700. He studied at the University of Edinburgh with a view to the ministry; he afterwards abandoned his ecclesiastical views, and resolving to devote himself to literature proceeded to London. In 1726 he produced his poem of "Winter;" that on "Summer" appearing in the following year. His "Spring" and "Autumn" followed in 1728 and 1730. Recommended to the Lord Chancellor Talbot, he visited with his lordship's son the principal courts of Europe. He subsequently obtained a civil list pension and the sinecure office of Surveyor-General of the Leeward Islands, with a salary of £300 a year. He died of fever on the 22nd August, 1748. In 1762 a monument to his memory was erected in Westminster Abbey.

PARISH OF HAWICK.

During some recent repairs on the old parish church the workmen discovered a tombstone commemorating Sir Walter Scott of Buccleuch, who was surprised and slain in the streets of Edinburgh by Sir John Ker of Fernihurst, and his kinsman, William Ker of Cessford. An illegitimate son of Sir Walter is also celebrated on the tombstone. The inscription is as follows:—

"VALTER . SCOT . HIS . GENEALOGIE.

"Heir . lyis . in . this . sepvltvre . Valter . Scot . of . Govdilandis . Sone . Natvral . to . Sir . Valter . Scot . the . valiant . Laird . of . Bvckleych . yat . vas . slain . crevelie . be . ye . Kerris . in Edinburgh . vithin . ye . nicht . being . vnnaccvmpaneit . vith . his . friendis . or . servandis . onlie . except . tva . of . his . dependeris . attending on him . not . respecting . nor . svspecting . thair . intentiovne: This . happinit . in . September . the . 53 zeir of his . age . ye . zeir . of . God . 155(2)

"This . foresaid . Valter . Scot depairtit . th(is life) in Govdilandis in . November . ye . zeir . of . God (1)596 . and . vas . (of age at his deth.) 64 .

"THE DISCRIPTOVNE OF VALTER
SCOT OF GOVDILANDIS
HIS QVALITEIS.

"Heir lyis bvrit visdome & virthines
Heir lyis bvreit trevth & honestie
Heir lyis bvreit fridome & gentres
Heir lyis bvreit manheid & cheritie
Heir lyis bvreit lairgeness & lavtie *
Heir lyis bvreit hap and exprience
Heir lyis bvreit pietie & diligence
Glorie be to God for al things."

In consequence of the slaughter of the Laird of Cessford in an encounter with the Laird of Buccleuch at Melrose in 1526, a feud raged for many years between the Kers and Scotts. In 1529 an effort was made to terminate the feud by an engagement between the Kers and Sir Walter Scott, of Branxholm, with sundry gentlemen of his clan. In this engagement the latter party became bound to perform pilgrimages to the churches of Melrose,

* Loyalty.

Dundee, Scone, and Paisley, as a reparation for the slaughter. Bad blood was, however, kept up, and the result was the slaughter of Sir Walter Scott as above described. After a long delay Sir Walter Ker, of Cessford, yielded to the wishes of his friends by consenting in St. Giles's Church, Edinburgh, on the 23rd March, 1564, to acknowledge his guilt and ask forgiveness from Almighty God and the relatives of the slain knight. A matrimonial alliance between the families was also arranged.

A mural tablet in the old church celebrates the Rev. Alexander Orrock, minister of the parish. It is thus inscribed :—

"Siste viator. Hic jacet corpus Domini Alexandri Orrock, verbi divini in ecclesia Havico fidelissimus. Vir erat vere eximius. In vitiosis reclamandis summe audax. Ob multifariam eruditionem et vitæ innocentiam doctis piisq. viris admodum probatus. In disciplina ecclesiastica æqualium nemini secundus. Qui annos XXII. officio pastorali hac in ecclesia functus, in usum scholæ publicæ novem mille, et pauperum indigentium mille et sexcentas marcas Testamento designavit. Tandem ob dormivit in Domino annum agens sexagesimum Æræ Christianæ MDCCXI Kal Maii. Ps. cxii. 9.

    Dispersit largiens pauperibus :
    Semper ejus liberalitas stabit."

Orrock studied at the University of St. Andrews, and was licensed in 1687. Having in a sermon named the King as an idolater and denounced episcopacy, he was seized at St. Andrews by command of the archbishop and removed to Edinburgh. He was called to the second charge at St. Andrews in 1690, but the Synod refused to proceed with his settlement. He was ordained at Hawick in 1691. During the meeting of the General Assembly in 1705 he insisted on speaking, though he was not a member of the House, and was forcibly ejected. Though addicted to controversy he was faithful and exemplary as a clergyman. He bequeathed 9,000 merks Scots for the endowment of a grammar school, and 1,600 merks towards the support of the poor.

A tombstone in the old churchyard presents the following inscription :—

> "Weary of life my suffering shroud o'ercast,
> She died resigned and breathed in peace her last.
> This stone erected o'er her narrow bed,
> Tells that her clay is here, her spirit fled
> To distant realms beyond life's fleeting day,
> Unknown to death, to sadness, or decay."

In St. Mary's Churchyard a tombstone is thus inscribed:—

"Heir lyes Johnny Deans ane honest man, qua was tenant Kindlie of Hawick Mill, and slain in debit of his neigbours geer. The zeir of God, 1546."

Deans was killed in a raid of border moss-troopers. The spot of his death is known as Dean's Brae.

PARISH OF JEDBURGH.

The parish churchyard of Jedburgh surrounds the ruins of the ancient abbey. This fine old structure, the most interesting sample of Saxon and early Gothic architecture in North Britain, was founded or greatly enlarged by David I., and planted with canons regular. It was often dilapidated by the English in the course of the Border wars, and was in 1523 finally demolished by the Earl of Surrey. The western portion of the nave has been fitted up as the parish church. The north transept of the abbey is the burying-place of the noble family of Lothian. It contains a number of monuments commemorating members of this illustrious House.

In the Lady Chapel a monument denotes the grave of the Rev. Dr. Thomas Somerville, the eminent historian. Dr. Somerville studied at the University of Edinburgh, and was licensed to preach in 1762. He was ordained to the parish of Minto in 1767, and in 1772 was translated to Jedburgh. His "History of Political Transactions from the Restoration of Charles II. to the Death of King William III." appeared in 1792. In the following year he was nominated one of the Chaplains in Ordinary to the King. In 1798 he published his "History of the Reign of Queen Anne," which he was privileged to dedicate and present personally to George III. He died at Jedburgh, on the 16th May, 1830, in the ninetieth year of his age, and sixty-fourth of his ministry. His "Memoirs of His Own Life and Times" appeared in 1861.

In the eastern nave of the abbey are interred the remains of John Baron Campbell, Lord High Chancellor. This eminent lawyer and statesman was second son of the Rev. Dr. George Campbell, minister of Cupar-Fife: he was born in 1781. Having studied at St. Andrews University, he proceeded to London, where he became a newspaper reporter. In 1806 he was called to the Bar; he became King's Counsel in 1827. In 1830 he entered the House of Commons. He was nominated Solicitor-General in 1832, and attained the office of Attorney-General in 1834. He was afterwards appointed Lord Chancellor of Ireland, while his wife was created a peeress by the title of Baroness Stratheden. In 1846 he became Chancellor of the Duchy of Lancaster, and a member of the Cabinet of Lord John Russell. He was appointed Lord Chief Justice in 1850; and in 1859 was elevated to the high office of Lord Chancellor. Lord Campbell died on the 23rd June, 1861. He published "Lives of the Lord Chancellors and Keepers of the Great Seal," and "Lives of the Chief Justices." Some years before his death he purchased the estate of Hartrigge in this parish.

In the churchyard a small tombstone commemorates James Brewster, schoolmaster of the parish, and father of Sir David Brewster, the distinguished philosopher. He died in 1815.

The Rev. Thomas Boston, one of the founders of the Relief Church, and son of the celebrated Thomas Boston of Ettrick, is interred in the churchyard. He was born on the 3rd April, 1713. He succeeded his father as minister of Ettrick in 1733, and was translated to Oxnam in 1749. On a vacancy occurring at Jedburgh, the majority of the parishioners applied to the Crown for his appointment to the charge, but another was presented. Thereafter his supporters erected a meeting-house and gave him a call, which he accepted. He accordingly demitted his charge and left the Established Church. In 1761 he and several of his brethren formed themselves into a Presbytery, and constituted the Relief Church. This was in 1847 included in the United Presbyterian Synod. Mr. Boston died on the 13th February, 1767, in the fifty-fourth year of his age and thirty-fourth of his ministry. On his tombstone are these lines :—

> "The sweet remembrance of the just
> Shall flourish while he sleeps in dust,
> With heavenly weapons Boston fought
> The battle of the Lord.
> Finished his course and kept the faith,
> And waits the sure reward."

On her tombstone, Mrs. Martha Hadden, wife of a provost of the burgh, is thus commemorated :—

> "In faith she dy'd, in dust she lies,
> But faith foresees that dust shall rise,
> When Jesus calls, which hope assumes,
> And boasts his joy among the tombs."

By her bereaved husband Isabel Riddel is celebrated thus :—

> "She was a virtuous and a loving wife,
> Strong advocate for peace through life;
> Beloved in life, tho' dead I love her still,
> And to my latest breath I ever will."

On the tombstone of Thomas Winter, Bailie of Jedburgh, are these words :—

"Whoever removes this stone or causes it to be removed, may he die the last of his race."

The following elegy is engraved upon a tombstone :—

> "Here lies a Christian, bold and true,
> An antipode to Babel's crew;
> A friend to truth, to vice a terror,
> A Lamp of zeal, opposing error;
> Who fought the battles of the Lamb,
> Of victory now bears the palm."

PARISH OF KELSO.

The abbey of Kelso was founded in 1124 by David I., who planted it with Tironensian monks from an abbey at Selkirk, which he reared in 1113. It was destroyed by the English under the Earl of Hertford, in 1545, and all that now remains is a portion of the Abbey Church. On account of the brittle nature of the stone the figures and inscriptions on the older monuments are obliterated. In the churchyard rest the remains of the Rev. James Ramsay, an eminent minister of the parish. He studied at the University of St. Andrews, and obtained licence in 1692. In the following year he was ordained to the ministry at Eyemouth. In 1707 he was translated to Kelso. He was appointed one of the Deans of the Chapel Royal, and was elected Moderator of the General Assembly in 1738 and 1741. He died on the 3rd July, 1749. Mr. Ramsay was a zealous upholder of Presbyterianism, but gave his support to the moderate party in the Church. As a leader in the General Assembly he commanded respect and weight.

PARISH OF LILLIESLEAF.

In this churchyard a tombstone commemorates the Rev. William Hunter, minister of the parish. It is inscribed thus:—

"Gulielmus Hunter, A.M., Christi Crucifixi Concionator. In hac Ecclesia, fidelis et Assiduus ab. an: 1695 ad. an: 1736.
"Coeli Avidus et Coelo Maturus. Cum Deo Omnipotenti agit Ævum Obiit Nov. 13. Ætatis 79."

Mr. Hunter studied at the University of Edinburgh, was licensed to preach in 1694, and was ordained minister of Lilliesleaf in 1695. He was one of twelve ministers who submitted to the General Assembly of 1721 a petition or representation against an Act of the preceding Assembly, condemning the "Marrow of Modern Divinity."

James Hunter Wright, who was killed by falling from the steeple of Jedburgh, on the 17th October, 1765, has his tombstone inscribed thus :—

> "Stop, traveller, as you go by,
> I once had life and breath;
> But falling from a steeple high
> I swiftly passed through death.
>
> "Take you example by my fate,
> And be by me advised;
> Repent before it be too late,
> Lest you be thus surprised."

PARISH OF LINTON.

The choir of the old parish church formed the burial-place of the ancient family of Somerville. Roger de Somerville, Baron of Whichnour, in England, and one of the barons who procured *Magna Charta* from King John, having been compelled to flee from England, found refuge at Linton Tower; on his death, he was buried in the choir. There too was interred his son William, who received from William the Lion the lands of Linton, for destroying a wild animal which had committed serious ravages in the district. Above the principal door of the church was set a stone, sculptured with the representation of a man on horseback in full armour, with a falcon on his arm, in the act of thrusting his lance down the throat of a large animal; it was removed in 1858. There is a tradition that the stone was originally inscribed thus :—

> "The wode Laird of Lariestone,
> Slew the wode worm of Wormieston,
> And won all Linton parochin."

Walter de Somerville, third Baron of Linton, joined the standard of Sir William Wallace, and under that hero commanded the third brigade of cavalry at the battle of Biggar. He afterwards became a firm supporter of King Robert the Bruce. His remains are interred in Linton Church.

PARISH OF MELROSE.

Here are the remains of an abbey, which "from the symmetry of its parts, the purity of its architecture, and the beauty of its materials, appears to have been one of the most superb structures ever reared in this country." It was founded by David I. in 1136, and planted with monks of the Cistercian order. The structure was often subjected to disfigurement and pillage. Under Edward II. the English army despoiled it in 1322; it was four years after restored by Robert the Bruce. In 1384, Richard II. caused it to be burned. It was defaced at the Reformation in 1560, and was ruthlessly bombarded by Cromwell.

The ruined precincts of the abbey form the parochial burying-ground. In the chancel, near the east window, where the high altar formerly stood, Alexander II. was entombed in 1249, with the following inscription on his monument:—

> "Ecclesiæ clypeus, pax plebis, dux miserorum,
> Rex rectus, rigidus, sapiens, consultus, honestus;
> Rex pius, rex fortis, rex optimus, rex opulentus,
> Nominus istius ipse secundus erat.
> Annis ter denis et quintis rex fuit ipse,
> Insula quæ Carneri dicitur hunc rapuit,
> Spiritus alta petit, cœlestibus associatus,
> Sed Melrossensis ossa sepulta tenet."

Every vestige of this royal monument has disappeared.

Near the high altar was deposited, in a silver casket, the heart of Robert the Bruce, brought back from Spain by Sir William Keith, after the ineffectual attempt made by Sir James Douglas to carry it to Palestine and bury it at Jerusalem. Sir James fell while fighting under the banner of King Alphonso, against the Saracens; his body was recovered, brought home, and also buried in the abbey.

The tombs of the great family of Douglas formerly studded the north side of the chancel. Here was buried William Douglas, the dark knight of Liddesdale, celebrated as "the flower of chivalry." He was slain while hunting in Ettrick Forest in 1356. William, first Earl of Douglas, who died in 1384, was interred here; also James, second Earl, who fell at the battle of Otterburn, in 1388. In reference to these entombments, Sir Walter Scott has in "The Lay of the Last Minstrel" thus written:—

> " There the noblest of their race
> Sleep, lock'd in death's serene embrace,
> No sound of dangling sword or spear,
> Nor foray wakes the warrior's ear;
> No breasted fight, nor parleyed truce,
> Beats to the throbless heart of Bruce:—
> Encompass'd in its narrow urn,
> The flow'r, the soul of Bannockburn;
> Beneath that ugly, shapeless stone,
> Unhonour'd, nameless, lies alone."

Sir Michael Scott of Balwearie, the celebrated wizard, is said by some to have been buried on the south side of the chancel, but others maintain that he was consigned to the dust at Holme Cultram, in Cumberland. This remarkable individual studied at Oxford, and at several universities abroad; he outstripped his Scottish contemporaries in every department of learning. After the manner of the times he studied astrology, alchemy, and other occult sciences. He was one of the commissioners who were appointed to convey the Maiden of Norway to Scotland on the death of Alexander III. Sir Walter Scott has prominently introduced the wizard in connection with the abbey, proceeding on the tradition that his magical books were deposited in his tomb.

On the west wall of the south transept, two inscriptions commemorate John Morvo, "Master Mason," a native of France, who had superintended the erection of this and other religious houses. The inscriptions proceed thus :—

> "Sa gayes the compass ev'n about,
> So Truth and Laute do, but doubt
> Be halde to ye hende q John Morvo.

The following inscription, also referring to this Master Mason, occupies a place above one of the doors :—

> "John Morvo sum tym callit was I,
> And born in Parysse certainly;
> And had in kepying al Mason Werk,
> Of Santandroys the hye Kyrk,
> Of Glasgw, Melros and Paslay,
> Of Nyddysdayl and of Galway,
> Pray to God, and Mari baith,
> And sweet St. John keep this haly kirk frae skaith." *

At the end of the north transept a circular arched doorway leads with two steps downward to an apartment traditionally known as the wax cellar, where it is supposed the tapers used in religious worship were kept. On a stone, partly concealed by the lowest step, there is the following inscription :—

> "✠ Hic jacet Johanna : d : Ross."

On another is carved a cross and a shield, the latter being that of a knight crusader.

On the north wall of the nave, at the beautifully carved gateway, called the Valley-gate, is the burial-place of the Kers of Yair, now of Sutherland Hall. Their arms, a stag's head raised on a chevron—are engraved on the wall—with this inscription :—

> "Here lies the Race of the House of Zair."

Opposite to this burial-place are the graves of the ancient family of Ker of Kippelaw.

---

* For a full and interesting account of the inscriptions commemorative of John Morow, see a paper by John Alexander Smith, Esq., M.D., in the "Proceedings of the Society of Antiquaries of Scotland" (vol. ii., p. 166).

PARISH OF MELROSE.

An inscription upon one of the tombs reads thus :—

"Here lyes lieutenant collnel Andrew Ker of Kippelaw, who was born at Melros the 23 febbuary 1620 years and died at Kippelaw, upon the 3 febbuary 1697, in the seventy-seventh year of his age."

In the cloisters are the remains of seven seats or stalls, under the base of which are inscriptions, and the appearance of tombs partially concealed by the masonwork. On a stone is inscribed, in Saxon characters :—

"Beatrix spouse Rob : : : Fraser."

On entering the church from the west, the first division or chapel on the right hand of the nave is occupied as a burial-ground by the old family of Boston, who still possess lands in the parish, which were held of the abbey by their progenitors. On the west wall is the following inscription :—

"The dust of many generations of the Bostons of Gattonside is deposited in this place.
"We give our bodies to this holy abbey to keep."

In the third chapel a tombstone, uncovered in 1815, presents a monastic figure in the attitude of prayer, with this inscription :—

"Hic jacet, honorabilis vir George Halliburton * * * * 1 October, Anno, D.M., MDXXXVI."

In the north division is the burial-place of Pringle of Woodhouse and Whytebank. Two of the inscriptions are as follow :—

"Here lies of guid memorie Dame Margaret Ker, first wyfe . to . James . Pringil . of Woodhous, and . after . his . deceis . mareit . Sir . David . Home, of Wedderburne, Knycht . Quha . deceissit . the . 24 . of . Februare . Anno . D . 1589."

"Here lyes ane honourable voman Cristin Lundi spous to James * * * * quytbank, scho deceissit 19. July 1602. Lament for syn and styl thou murn, for to the clay * * * * ye man turn."

The fifth chapel is the burial-place of the family of Hope Pringle of Galashiels. The effigies of a member of the House, known as the Baron of Smailholm, represents him in his shroud.

An inscription runs thus:—

"Heir lies ane honourabil man Andro Pringil, feuar of Galloshiels quha decessit ye 28 of February, An. Dom. 1585."

A marble slab, eight feet by four, covers the family tomb of the Scotts of Gala. The slab seems to have been an ancient altarpiece.

In the sixth chapel from the west is the following inscription:—

"Niniani: Ratine
Thome: Pauli: Cuthbt.
te: s: Petre: Retigin."

In the chapel an elegant monument denotes the grave of the Rev. David Fletcher, minister of the parish and Bishop of Argyll, Son of Andrew Fletcher, merchant, Dundee, he was educated at St. Andrews University. In 1635 he was elected minister of St. Giles' Church, Edinburgh; he was deposed by the Commission of Assembly in 1639, for declining the Glasgow Assembly of the preceding year, and defending the Service Book. Reinstated as a minister, he was, in 1641, translated to Melrose. He was promoted to the Bishopric of Argyll in 1662, but continued to discharge his parochial duties. He died in March, 1665. He bequeathed funds to build a school-house. His monument was erected by his son William, an eminent lawyer.

In the portion of the abbey known as the Ministers' burying-place are interred the Rev. John Knox, minister of the parish, and grand-nephew of the Reformer, who died in 1623, aged sixty-eight; and the Rev. Adam Milne, minister of Melrose, and author of "A Description of the Parish," who died 8th June, 1747, in his sixty-seventh year and the thirty-seventh of his ministry.

In the parish churchyard which surrounds the abbey, the tombstones are chiefly of modern date. Of these the oldest is thus inscribed:—

"Heir lyes James Edgar, who died anno 1623."

Near the door of the south transept a tombstone is engraved

with these lines, composed in his youth by the celebrated Dr. John Leyden :—

> "Near to this stone we lifeless lie,
> No more the things of earth to spy;
> But we shall leave this dusty bed
> When Christ shall come to judge the dead.
> For He shall come in glory great,
> And in the air shall have his seat,
> And call all men before his throne,
> Rewarding them as they have done."

A tombstone belonging to James Ramsay, with the date 1761, has the following :—

> "The earth goeth on the earth glist'ring like gold,
> The earth goeth to the earth sooner than it wold;
> The earth builds on the earth castles and towers,
> The earth says to the earth, all shall be ours."

A portioner at Darnick, named Fisher, who died in 1765 is thus commemorated :—

> "Thrice sacred grave, be loyal to thy trust,
> And guard till Christ revives the hallowed dust;
> Then as a faithful steward safe restore
> The precious treasure thou canst keep no more.
> Reflect each reader on thy latter end,
> For thou must lie as now thou seest thy friend."

On the tombstone of James Simson, who died in 1810, are these lines :—

> "Lean not on earth; 'twill pierce thee to the heart,
> A broken reed at best; but oft a spear,
> On its sharp point peace bleeds and hope expires."

On a tombstone erected in 1824, by Mr. Thomas Tod of Drygrange, in memory of several members of his family, are these lines :—

> "Go blessed spirits,
> Mount where cherubs sing
> Sublime hosannas
> To the Saviour King,

> Go soar triumphant
> From earth's drear domain,
> The seat of sin, of misery and pain.
> The stars of heaven
> Will light you on the way,
> To realms of glory
> And eternal day.
> Then lift your eyes,
> Behold the bright abode
> Prepared for you
> By an indulgent God."

In the centre of the churchyard a monumental pillar within a stone enclosure commemorates several generations of the family of Smith, "portioners in Darnick." An obelisk celebrates James Smith, Master Mason for Scotland; who was born 21st September, 1779, and died 9th July, 1862.

On the south side of the abbey a small tombstone denotes the grave of Sir David Brewster, the eminent philosopher. It is thus inscribed :—

> "Sacred to the Memory of
> Sir David Brewster, K.H.   Born 11th Dec., 1781.
> Died at Allerly, 10th Feb., 1868.
> 'The Lord is my Light.'"

Sir David Brewster was born at Jedburgh on the 11th December, 1781. With a view to the ministry he studied at the University of Edinburgh. In 1808 he undertook the editorship of the *Edinburgh Encyclopædia*, to which he contributed many scientific articles. He invented the kaleidoscope in 1816. Along with Professor Jameson he in 1819 established the *Edinburgh Philosophical Journal*. In 1831 he originated the *British Association for the Advancement of Science*. He obtained in 1815 the Copley medal of the Royal Society for one of his optical discoveries. In 1819 the Royal Society awarded him the Rumford gold and silver medals for his discoveries on the polarization of light. In 1825 he became corresponding Member of the Institute of France. He was knighted in 1832, and obtained a State pension. In 1838 he was elected Principal of the United College, St. Andrews; in 1859 he was preferred to the principalship of Edinburgh University. He died at Allerly, near Melrose, on the 11th February, 1869, aged eighty-eight. Sir David was an extensive contributor to periodical literature, and author of many scientific publications.

A tombstone, erected by Sir Walter Scott, commemorates Tom Purdie, forester at Abbotsford. By Sir Walter it was thus inscribed:—

"In grateful remembrance of the faithful and attached services of twenty-two years, and in sorrow for the loss of an humble but sincere friend, this stone was erected by Sir Walter Scott, Bart., of Abbotsford."

A former keeper of the abbey is thus celebrated:—

"The precious dust beneath this stone
Once showed that ancient pile,
And formed an Israelite indeed
In whom there was no guile."

On the tombstone of his deceased wife the Rev. Edward Young has inscribed these lines:—

"And where is that spirit? Washed white in the Fountain,
Presented unblameably, pure at the throne,
The love and the favour of Jesus recounting
To souls that are stirring on joy like her own.
She came to the cross while her young cheek was blooming,
And raised to the Lord the bright glance of her eye,
And when o'er her features death's darkness was glooming,
The cross did uphold her, the Saviour was nigh.
As I saw the black pall o'er her extended,
I wept, but they were not the teardrops of woe,
And the prayer of my soul that in fervour ascended
Was, Lord, when Thou callest, like her I may go."

These lines are inscribed on a modern tombstone:—

"Why all this toil for triumphs of an hour?
What though we wade in wealth, or fortune frown,

Earth's highest station ends in ' Here he lies,'
And dust to dust concludes her noblest song.
This truth how certain when this life is o'er,
Man dies to live and lives to die no more!"

The following families possess interment ground in Melrose Churchyard:—Major Brown, of Park; Admiral Russell Elliot; Captain William Clarke, of Langhaugh; Captain James Stedman, Abbey Park; Henry Ker Cranston, Esq.; George Cole Bainbrige, of Gattonside; Thomas Tod, of Drygrange; George Leverre Legge, of Old Melrose; Nicol Milne, of Faldonside; and James Curle, of Melrose.

PARISH OF ROXBURGH.

The family of Scott Kerr of Sunlaws inter in a porch of the old church. A stone resting against the church wall bears that it was erected in 1788, to commemorate a person named Hogg, whose ancestors had resided in the locality for six hundred years. A tombstone records that the ashes of Randolph Kerr, son of Thomas Kerr, Altonburn, repose in the neighbourhood of the church. Near the west end of the church a tombstone denotes the grave of the Rev. William Wemyss, a minister of the parish. He died 17th March, 1658, aged fifty-two.

West of the church a tombstone commemorates Andrew Gemmells, the prototype of Edie Ochiltree in "The Antiquary." On one side is a full-length figure of a Blue-gown, with a staff in one hand and a bag in the other, and the inscription "Behold the end o't," representing the scene between the Bluegrown and the recruiting sergeant at St. Boswell's Fair. On the other side is the following inscription :—

"The body of the Gentleman Beggar, Andrew Gemmells, *alias* Edie Ochiltree, was interred here, who died at Roxburgh Newtown, in 1793, aged one hundred and six years. Erected by William Thomson, farmer, Over Roxburgh, 1849."

Gemmells is thus described by Sir Walter Scott in the Introduction to the Abbotsford edition of "The Antiquary." "He was a remarkably fine old figure, very tall, and maintaining a soldierlike or military manner and address. His features were intelligent, with a powerful expression of sarcasm. His motions were always so graceful, that he might almost have been suspected of having studied them; for he might, on any occasion, have served as a model for an artist, so remarkably striking were his ordinary attitudes. Andrew Gemmells had little of the cant of his calling; his wants were food and shelter, or a trifle of money, which he always claimed, and seemed to receive as his due. He sang a good song, told a good story, and could crack a severe jest with all the acumen of Shakspeare's jesters, though without using, like them, the cloak of insanity. It was some fear of Andrew's satire, as much as a feeling of kindness or charity, which secured him the general good reception which he enjoyed everywhere. In fact, a jest of Andrew Gemmells, especially at the expense of a person of consequence, flew round the circle which he frequented as surely as the bon-mot of a man of established character of wit glides through the fashionable world.

* * * * * * *

"This singular mendicant had generally, or was supposed to have, as much money about his person as would have been thought the value of his life among modern footpads. On one occasion, a country gentleman, generally esteemed a very narrow man, happening to meet Andrew, expressed great regret that he had no silver in his pocket, or he would have given him sixpence. 'I can give you change for a note, laird,' said Andrew. Like most who have risen to the head of their profession, the modern degradation which mendicity has undergone was often the subject of Andrew's lamentations. As a trade he said it was forty pounds a year worse since he first practised it. On another occasion he observed, begging was in modern times scarcely the profession of a gentleman; and that if he had twenty sons, he would not easily be induced to breed one of them up in his own line. When or where this

laudator temporis acti closed his wanderings the author never heard with certainty; but most probably, as Burns says—
> 'He died a cadger-powny's death,
> At some dike side.'"

On a tombstone in Roxburgh Churchyard was this couplet, now defaced:—
> "Here lies Peter Cairns,
> Who had three wives and nine bairns."

PARISH OF SMAILHOLME.

The remains of the paternal ancestors of Sir Walter Scott rest in Smailholme Churchyard. The farm of Sandyknowe, rented by Robert Scott, the poet's grandfather, is on the borders of the parish.

A schoolmaster has thus celebrated his wife and children on his family gravestone:—

> "Conjugis ac geminæ prolis, ah! hospita servas
> Terra, sub hoc triplici, corpora trina, tapho.
> Margaretæ, polum dum spiras, margine Twedæ,
> Exspiras, rigido bis peregrina solo;
> Mariæ natum, Mariola, psallis Iesum,
> Tuque Iacobæum parve Iacobi, Deum."

PARISH OF ST. BOSWELLS.

In the parish churchyard rest the remains of John Younger, poet, and author of a prize essay on the Sabbath, who died on the 19th July, 1860, aged seventy-five. A man of vigorous intellect and literary culture, Younger, while practising his vocation of village shoemaker, conducted correspondence with many literary persons; he composed vigorously and excelled in conversation.

PARISH OF WILTON.

In the aisle of the old church a marble tablet commemorates Dr. Samuel Charters, an eminent incumbent of the cure. Son of Thomas Charters, minister of Inverkeithing, he was licensed in 1764, and after a short residence in Amsterdam was ordained minister of Kincardine in Menteith. In January, 1772, he was translated to Wilton. He was in 1784 presented to St. Andrew's Church, Glasgow, but declined acceptance of the charge. He was much esteemed as a preacher. He was the first minister of the Church of Scotland who taught a Sunday school. He entertained a deep aversion to slavery, and in consequence did not use sugar. He was opposed to the war with the French Republic, recognising the principle of non-intervention, now the policy of this country. He distinguished himself by his exertions for the repeal of the Test and Corporation Acts. He died on the 18th June, 1825, in his eighty-fourth year, and fifty-seventh of his ministry. He published several volumes of sermons and some essays.

An ingenious local poet, Elliot Aitchison, is commemorated by a tombstone. A stocking-weaver by trade, he passed through life in circumstances of indigence. He died at Hawick on the 7th October, 1858. Specimens of his compositions are included in "The Modern Scottish Minstrel," Edinburgh, 1870, 8vo.

These inscriptions are from tombstones in Wilton Churchyard:—

"Blessed are the dead whose lives, though short, have been innocent and useful. The venerable age is not that which standeth in length of time, nor that which is measured by numbers of years. But wisdom is the grey hair unto man, and unspotted life is old age."

"Grieve not for me, my glass is run,
It is the Lord's, His will be done,
When Christ doth come, I hope to rise
Unto that life that never dies."

PEEBLESSHIRE.

PARISH OF BROUGHTON.

In this churchyard rest the remains of the Rev. Hamilton Paul, minister of the parish and an ingenious poet. Born at Dailly, Ayrshire, on the 10th April, 1773, he studied at the University of Glasgow, where he was the friend and companion of Thomas Campbell, the future poet. Obtaining licence to preach in 1800, he became ministerial assistant to several clergymen in his native county. For three years he edited the *Ayr Advertiser*. In 1813 he was ordained to the ministry at Broughton. He possessed a deep sense of humour and abounded in anecdote. He died on the 28th February, 1854, in the eighty-first year of his age, and forty-first of his ministry. Of his several publications the most popular is an edition of the poetical works of Burns, which appeared in 1819.

PARISH OF EDDLESTON.

William Purdie, farmer, Kingside, who died 10th September, 1786, has on his tombstone the following epitaph:—

> "Consider, ye that eagerly explore
> The silent grave, here lies the son threescore
> Of days. Yea, and the father sixty-three
> Full years on earth did nearly see.
> Trust not in man, for parents cannot save
> Their youngest infants from the gloomy grave;

> Nor can the sons in youth though they attend
> Their fathers dear from dreadful death defend.
> Trust in God, and let His Word divine
> Dwell in your hearts and on your conduct shine.
> He soon shall lead thee far above all strife,
> Where in His favour is unfading life."

PARISH OF KIRKURD.

On a tombstone in the churchyard William Sibbald is thus celebrated:—

> " Old William Sibbald's conversation
> Was a bright pattern in his station,
> For moral virtuous pietie,
> He did excel in his degree;
> He never any did distress,
> Nor any him by law process.
> All his affairs he managed so
> That few could say they did them know;
> For temperance there was few such,
> None e'er could say he drank too much.
> He helpèd many in their need,
> He ready was the poor to feed.
> And now he reaps the fruits in store
> Of heaven's joys for evermore."

PARISH OF WEST LINTON.

James Gifford, a stone carver of local celebrity, usually known as "Laird Gifford," has afforded a specimen of his skill in a figure of his wife placed on the top of the village well. Lately renovated, the well bears this inscription :—

"The Lady Gifford's Well, erected 1666. Renewed 1861."

A marble tombstone in the parish churchyard formerly commemorated James Oswald, of Spittals, a landowner celebrated for his social practices and eccentric habits. Possessing a table of marble at which he conducted his festivities, Oswald desired that it might be placed upon his grave as his monument. With this view he caused an inscription in Latin to be engraved on it as his epitaph. It came to be used sooner than he anticipated; he was accidently shot by his servant when they were together shooting wild ducks at Slipperfield Loch. The inscription was as follows:—

"Jacobo Oswaldo de Spittal, marito bene merenti, Grizzella Russellia, conjux mœstissima, P.C.
"Marmor hoc, quoi assidens sæpe curavi genium, mihi imponi volui. Siste viator, quisquis es, discumbas licet, et, si copia est, marmore hoc uti ego olim fruiscaris. Hoc si rite feceris, monumentum non violabis, nec manes meos habebis iratos. Vale et vive!
"Vixi an. xxx. Ob. xxviii Nov., MD. CCXXVI.',

The epitaph has been translated thus:—

"To James Oswald, of Spittal, her deserving husband, this monument was erected by Grizzel Russell, his sorrowing wife.
"This marble table, sitting at which I have often cultivated good living (propitiated my tutelar genius), I have desired to be placed over me when dead. Stop, traveller, whoever thou art; here thou mayest recline, and if the means are at hand mayest enjoy this table as I formerly did. If thou doest so in the right and proper way, thou wilt neither desecrate the monument nor offend my manes. Farewell.
"Lived thirty years, and died Nov. 28, 1726."*

* Oswald's monument became dilapidated about forty years ago, and the fragments have been carried off. ("History of Peeblesshire," by William Chambers, of Glenormiston, Edinburgh, 1864, p. 460).

PARISH OF LYNE.

A tombstone commemorates the Rev. Alexander Johnston, minister of the parish, who died 8th March, 1788, in his hundred and second year, and the sixtieth of his ministry. He had an abhorrence of medicine, and used a simple diet. He preached the Sabbath previous to his death.

A tombstone to the memory of Janet Veitch, who died in 1712, is inscribed:—

> "Life is the road to death,
>   And death heaven's care must be;
> Heaven is the throne of Christ,
>   And Christ is life to me."

PARISH OF MANOR.

The churchyard contains the remains of David Ritchie, whose remarkable deformity is portrayed by Sir Walter Scott in "The Black Dwarf." Ritchie was born in the district: as a brushmaker he obtained employment at Edinburgh, Dublin, and other places. But his extraordinary malformation had excited such derision, that he resolved to renounce his trade and live in seclusion. He rented a small hut in the vale of Manor, where Scott, who had heard of his extraordinary aspects, paid him a visit. He was scarcely three feet and a half in height, and was so distorted in face and figure that it was impossible to look upon him unmoved. He had conceived an aversion to the world which had ridiculed his defects; but he found pleasure in raising flowers in a little garden near his dwelling. He read some of the English poets, and could repeat long passages of their writings. At one period he had determined that he should not be buried where the ashes of other men were. At length he changed his mind, and was content to find a grave in Manor Churchyard.

Some trees have been planted at the spot, and the elder shepherds of the district point to the grassy mound not without expressions of awe.

On the tombstone of William Ritchie, tenant in Woodhouse, who died in 1737, are these lines :—

> "Oh that the dead might speak, and in a strain
> To charm each death-formed doubt and heartfelt pain!
> Might tell the timid sons of vital breath
> How soft and easy is the bed of death!
> Might from this moral truth rich comfort give,
> That man but lives to die, and dies to live!"

The tombstone of Robert Johnston, smith, who died in 1732, is thus inscribed :—

> "Death is a debt to nature due,
> Which we have paid, and so must you.
> Life, how short! eternity, how long!
> Then haste, oh, haste! make no delay,
> Make peace with God for the great day."

PARISH OF NEWLANDS.

In the churchyard rest the remains of Alexander Pennecuick, M.D., physician and poet. His father, who bore the same name, served as a surgeon in the Swedish army during the Thirty Years' War. Dr. Pennecuick was proprietor of the estates of Newhall and Romano. He composed a "Description of Tweeddale," which was published in 1715. His poetical compositions are descriptive of rural manners. He died in 1722. It is supposed that he furnished Allan Ramsay with the plot of the "Gentle Shepherd."

A brother and sister who had long kept house together in another part of the country, but whose burial-place was in this parish, are thus commemorated:—

"They lived respected and died regretted, and the friends they loved, Jacob-like, carried back their bones into their native Canaan, and raised this monument over them."

PARISH OF PEEBLES.

In the churchyard of Peebles a plain tombstone denotes the grave of Thomas Smibert, a native of the place, who amidst unpropitious circumstances attained considerable distinction as a writer of prose and verse. He was born on the 8th February, 1810. Obtaining licence as a surgeon, he some time practised at Innerleithen, and afterwards at Peebles. He now turned his attention to literature, and procured congenial employment as sub-editor of *Chambers's Journal*, and afterwards of the *Scotsman* newspaper. He produced an illustrated volume descriptive of the Highland clans, collated a Rhyming Dictionary, and prepared a work on "Greek History." His poetical compositions appeared in 1851. He died at Edinburgh on the 16th January, 1854. Mr. Smibert's songs indicate a fine fancy and deep pathos.

Provost Tweedie, who died in 1699, is with his wife and children thus commemorated:—

> "A silent, scattered flock about they lie,
> Free from all toil, care, grief, fear, envy;
> But yet again shall gathered be
> When the last awful trumpet soundeth hie."

Provost Tweedie's tombstone presents well-executed figures emblematic of the four seasons:—a husbandman with a sheet round his shoulders in the act of sowing; a woman with a garland of flowers in her hand; a youth with a reaping-hook over his arm; and a boy with his hands to his mouth representing winter.

Helen Muir, daughter of John Muir, chief magistrate of the burgh, who died about the commencement of the seventeenth century, had the following epitaph:—

> "In Peebles town there dwells a man,
>   His name it is John Muir,
> And Lilias Ker, his loving wife,
>   Of this I am right sure.
> A proper girl these two they had
>   Of age fifteen did die,
> And by the providence of God
>   Beneath this stone doth lie.
> She was her parents' only child,
>   In her they pleasure had;
> But since by death she is removed
>   Their hearts are very sad.
> Her name was callèd Helen Muir,
>   Both modest, mild, and meek;
> She comely in her person was,
>   And every way complete.
> But here her dust it must remain
>   Until the judgment day,
> And then it shall be raised again,
>   This is the truth I say.
> Then soul and body shall unite,
>   And never parted be,
> To sing the praises of her God
>   Through all eternity."

On the side of the stone were inscribed these lines:—

> "Beneath this stone in ground ye seed is sown,
> Of such a flower, tho' fallen ere fully grown,
> As will, when dawns the saints' first spring on high,
> Be sweet and pure as the celestial sky.
>
> "Whose looks persuaded more y^n others' speech,
> And more by deeds than words, she lived to teach.
> Hence young she from the sinful living fled,
> For safety here among the sinless dead."

On the gravestone of John Jenkinson and his wife (1693) are these lines :—

> "Full fourtie years they liv'd
> As man and wife;
> In good repute, ane honest
> Vertuous life."

Bailie John Gibson, who died in 1705, is celebrated thus :—

> "This man was always tender of God's glory,
> And even studied to be just and holy;
> His body lies entombed beneath this stone,
> His soul, no doubt, to the third heavens is gone."

On the tombstone of Thomas Hope, burgh treasurer, are the following inscriptions :—

> "Here lies three Hopes enclos'd within
> Death's prisoners, by Adam's sin;
> To rest in hope that they shall be
> Set by the Second Adam free,"

"This is the burial-place appointed for Thomas Hope, late treasurer in Peebles, his wife and children. James Hope died in the twenty-third year of his age, March, 1704. Marion Hope died in the twenty-sixth year of her age, June, 1704."

On a stone in memory of Andrew Brown, who died in 1743, are these lines :—

> "Farewell, dear wife and children all!
> Where you may still remain,
> The Lord of hosts be your defence,
> Till we shall meet again."

Anne Hay, wife of James Veitch, merchant, who died in 1804, is commemorated thus :—

> "No costly marble
> Need on her be spent;
> Her deathless worth
> Is her best monument.

"Isabel Hope died the 14th of May, 1704, of her age the twenty-eighth year.

> "Here lies a girl who died into her prime,
> Shined full bright, though now she's not in time;
> But yet shall shine more bright, in glorious ray,
> When comes the morning of eternal day."

The following lines commemorate James Hall, tenant in Eshels, who died on the 7th July, 1754, aged eighty-one; and his wife Isabel Laidlaw, who died in July, 1820, aged thirty-nine:—

> "Forbear, fond man, and weep no more, 'tis vain,
> When heaven decrees 'tis folly to complain;
> This worldly mass is subject to decay,
> And death and nature all things must obey.
> The blushing rose smiles with the morning sun,
> Just then looks gay, now withers and is gone.
> Then why, poor mortal, dost thou weep and cry?
> Think what thou art, and be content to die.
> Pardon my sin, Almighty God, I pray,
> Forgive me all, then take me hence away;
> Then my triumphant soul shall upwards fly,
> And leave with joy this worldly vanity.

A cowherd is celebrated thus:—

> "Thomas Stoddart,
> Lyes here interr'd,
> Who liv'd and dy'd
> An honest herd."

On a tombstone beneath the representation of an hour-glass are these lines:—

> "In sign of this stone John Johnston gave
> To stand at Helen Hall his dear wife's grave."

The following rhymes are also to be found in Peebles Churchyard:—

> "Just as a flower full blown at noon
> Lies dead before the setting sun,
> Just in the bloom of life cut down,
> Was she that lies beneath this stone.
> Reader, prepare to follow me."

"An affectionate and faithful wife,
  Whose tender feelings to her children dear
  Caused this erection her name to bear;
  Whose feet the sacred path of virtue trod,
  And now in hope her soul doth rest in God."

"Though born to hardship, much fatigue and toil,
Yet on his labours Providence did smile,
And gave him what is more than wealth or fame,
The dear possession of an honoured name.
Wisdom and prudence daily to discharge
His moral duties in life's latest verge;
God's word he set before him as a guide,
And not the selfish rules of human pride.
Truth every feeling of his soul refined,
And sacred honour dignified his mind."

PARISH OF SKIRLING.

In the parochial burial-ground rest the remains of James Howe, the distinguished animal painter. Son of the Rev. William Howe, minister of the parish, he was born at Skirling on the 30th August, 1780. For some time he was employed in Edinburgh as a house-painter; he subsequently obtained celebrity as a painter of animals, both at Edinburgh and in London. His large panoramic view of the battle of Waterloo was exhibited in different towns, and attracted a wide interest. From Mr. Maule, afterwards Lord Panmure, he obtained encouragement and patronage. He illustrated for Lizars, the eminent engraver, a work on the domestic animals. He died at Edinburgh on the 11th July, 1836. His habits were latterly unworthy of his genius.

PARISH OF TRAQUAIR.

In the churchyard a tombstone denotes the grave of the Rev. James Nicol, minister of the parish and an accomplished poet. Mr. Nicol was born at Innerleithen on the 28th September, 1769. Bred a shoemaker, he repaired to the University of Edinburgh, where he acquired distinction. He was licensed in 1801, and in the following year was ordained to the ministry at Traquair. In 1805 he published "Poems, chiefly in the Scottish Dialect," two vols. 8vo. He died on the 5th November, 1819. Several of his songs have obtained celebrity.

On the tombstone of the Rev. Alexander Adams, minister of the parish, who died on the 10th January, 1789, are these words:—

"To his affectionate parish, grace, mercy, and peace be multiplied."

Thomas Ballantine, who died in 1704, is celebrated thus:—

"This man when living was discreet and kind,
Religious and virtuously inclined;
But now he's dead, alas! these are;
All who survive let him deplore."

PARISH OF TWEEDSMUIR.

In the churchyard John Hunter, a Covenanter, who was shot at Corehead by General Douglas in 1685, is commemorated thus:—

"When Zion's King was robbèd of His right,
His witnesses in Scotland join'd to fight;
When Papist Prelates and Indulgency,
Combin'd 'gainst Christ to ruin Presbytery,
All who should not unto the Prelate bow,
They sought them out, and whom they found they slew.
For owning of Christ's cause I here do lie;
My blood for vengeance on His enemies doth cry."

Edward Aitchison, an itinerant minstrel, who died about fifteen years ago, is on his gravestone thus described:*—

---

* These verses are believed to have been composed by the late Mr. John Wilson, farmer, Bilholm, son of the celebrated Professor John Wilson of Edinburgh.

"Here in a lonely spot the bones repose
Of one who murder'd rhyme and slaughter'd prose;
Sense he defied, and grammar set at nought;
Yet some have read his books, and even bought.

For want of art his virtues made amends;
Foes he had none, but counted many friends;
Long was he known by Teviot and by Tweed,
An aged horseman on an aged steed.

Where'er he went he found an open door,
The folks all liked him, and the bard was poor;
A ream of paper, and a pound of snuff,
Pens and his 'specks,' and Edward had enough.
Along life's road he jogg'd at easy pace,
Dismounted here, and found a resting-place."

SELKIRKSHIRE.

PARISH OF SELKIRK.

In the market-place, Selkirk, a statue in freestone, by the late Mr. Handyside Ritchie, commemorates Sir Walter Scott as Sheriff of Ettrick Forest. The following inscription adorns the pedestal :—

> "Erected in August, 1839,
> In proud and affectionate remembrance
> of
> Sir Walter Scott, Baronet,
> Sheriff of this county
> From 1800 to 1832.
>
> By Yarrow's stream still let me stray,
> Though none shall guide my feeble way;
> Still feel the breeze down Ettrick's break,
> Although it chill my withered cheek."

In an open triangular space in the centre of the burgh, an elegant memorial statue celebrates Mungo Park, the distinguished African explorer. It was executed by Mr. Andrew Currie, an ingenious self-taught sculptor and a native of the "Forest," and was reared in March, 1839. The monument, twenty-eight feet in height, consists of a colossal statue resting on a pedestal which surmounts a massive plinth. In the statue Park is represented standing in an easy attitude, with a sextant in his right hand, and in his left a scroll, on which is inscribed the last sentence of his latest communication to Lord Camden —:" All the Europeans but myself are dead, but I will still persevere in the object of my mission, and though I succeed not, I shall at least die on the Niger." He is habited in a loose travelling cloak, with under-belt. The head, which is uncovered, presents an open massive brow, the features being in perfect repose. The likeness is admirable.

Park was on the 10th September, 1771, born at Fowlshiels, on the banks of the Yarrow, near Selkirk. Having studied medicine at the University of Edinburgh and passed surgeon, he procured, on the recommendation of Sir Joseph Banks, a professional appointment on board the *Worcester*, an East Indiaman. In 1792 he visited the island of Sumatra, and contributed a paper on its natural history to the Transactions of the Linnæan Society. Under the auspices of the African Association he undertook an expedition to the interior of Africa, for the purpose of exploring the source of the Niger. He sailed from Portsmouth on the 22nd May, 1795. After many perils he returned to England in December, 1797. His travels were published in the following year. He now sought practice as a surgeon at Peebles, but a proposal having been made to him by Government to undertake a second expedition to Africa, he left Britain for Central Africa on the 30th January, 1805. From Pisania he started with a company of forty-five, of whom thirty-six were Europeans; but when he reached the Niger in August his attendants were reduced to seven. With four companions he reached the kingdom of Houssa, where, in attempting to escape from a murderous attack of the natives, he and his attendants perished in the river. From Sansanding on the Niger in the kingdom of Bambarra he had sent his journals to Gambia in November, 1805. These, with a narrative of his second journey, were published at London in 1815. The precise date of his death is unknown.

PARISH OF YARROW.

On the hill-side north-east of St. Mary's Loch a graveyard occupies the site of the old chapel of St. Mary, or the Forest Kirk. Within this structure Sir William Wallace was in 1297 elected by the estates of Parliament governor or guardian of the kingdom.

St. Mary's Chapel is associated with the legend depicted in the ballad of "The Douglas Tragedy." Here Lord William and the fair Margaret were interred.

> "Lord William was dead lang ere midnight,
>   Lady Marg'ret lang ere day;
> And all true lovers that gang thegither
>   May they have mair luck than they!
>
> "Lord William was buried in St. Marie's Kirk,
>   Lady Margaret in Marie's quire;
> Out o' the lady's grave grew a bonny red rose,
>   And out o' the knight's a brier.
>
> "And they twa met, and they twa plat,
>   And fain they wad be near;
> And a' the warld might ken right weel
>   They were twa lovers dear.
>
> "But bye and rade the Black Douglas,
>   And wow but he was rough;
> For he pull'd up the bonnie brier,
>   And flang'd in St. Mary's Loch."

St. Mary's Churchyard was a burying-place of the Covenanters. It is the subject of a poem by the Ettrick Shepherd, commencing thus:—

> "O lone St. Mary of the waves,
>   In ruin lies thine ancient aisle,
> While o'er thy green and lowly graves
>   The moorcocks bay, and plovers wail;
> But mountain-spirits on the gale,
>   Oft o'er thee sound the requiem dread,
> And warrior shades and spectres pale,
>   Still linger by the quiet dead.
>
> "Yes, many a chief of ancient days
>   Sleeps in thy cold and hallow'd soil;
> Hearts that would tread the forest maze,
>   Alike for spousal or for spoil,
> That wist not, ween'd not, to recoil
>   Before the might of mortal foe,
> But thirsted for the Border broil—
>   The shout, the clang, the overthrow.

> "Here lie those who, o'er flood and field,
>   Were hunted as the osprey's brood;
> Who braved the power of man, and sealed
>   Their testimonies with their blood.
> But long as was that wilder'd flood
>   Their sacred memory shall be dear;
> And all the righteous and the good
>   O'er their low graves shall drop the tear."

An elegant monument in St. Mary's Churchyard commemorates John Grieve, a respectable poet and generous patron of men of letters. Mr. Grieve was born at Dunfermline in 1781. For a time he engaged in business at Alloa, but afterwards became a hat manufacturer in Edinburgh. He realized a fortune and retired to a comfortable residence at Newington, where he cultivated literary society. Suffering from impaired health, he found solace in philological pursuits, and in the composition of verses. He is celebrated in "The Queen's Wake" by the Ettrick Shepherd, who also dedicated to him his poem, "Mador of the Moor." He died on the 4th April, 1836, aged fifty-five.

Beyond St. Mary's Churchyard a small mound denotes the burial-place of the wicked priest who forms the subject of Hogg's ballad of "Mess John." The spot is named Binram's Cross. On digging here in 1806 some human remains were discovered.

From the north-west shore of St. Mary's Loch extends the wild and romantic vale of Meggat. In the centre of this defile flows the Meggat Water, which deposits its waters into the loch. About a mile from the loch, and on the left side of the Meggat Water, is Henderland Castle, the ruinous stronghold of Piers Cockburn, a famous freebooter in the reign of James V. After long resisting the royal authority, he was surprised by the King, who rode from Tushielaw, and suddenly invested his castle: he was captured and hanged. His wife took refuge in a neighbouring cave, but subsequently returned, and with her own hands interred his body. In a ballad contained in the "Border Minstelsy" she is made to say,—

> "I sewed his sheet, making my mane;
> I watched the corpse mysel alane;

> I digged a grave and laid him in,
> And happed him in the sod sae green.
>
> "Nae living man I'll love again
> Since now my lovely knight is slain;
> Wi' ae lock o' his yellow hair
> I'll chain my heart for evermair."

The spot of Cockburn's interment, called the Chapel Knowe, where his faithful wife was also subsequently laid beside him, has been enclosed, and it is denoted by a slab, on which is carved the figure of a sword and other emblems, with the inscription,—

"Here · lyis · Perys · of · Cokburne · and · hys · wyfe · Marjory."

In the centre of a triangular space, intermediate between St. Mary's Loch and the Loch of the Lowes, stands the monumental statue of James Hogg, the Ettrick Shepherd. The design of rearing a monument to the Shepherd occurred to the writer of these pages in 1858. In the spring of that year he issued circular letters inviting attention to the proposal. It was cordially entertained, and four hundred pounds were subscribed. On the 28th June, 1860, the monument was inaugurated in presence of a concourse of spectators. A great banquet on the occasion was provided by the proprietor of the site, the late Mr. John Scott, of Rodono, The writer was fortunate in securing as sculptor, Mr. Andrew Currie. who being personally acquainted with the Shepherd, entered heartily into the undertaking. Resting on a massive pedestal, the poet is seated on an oak root enveloped by an ivy stem, and with some leaves of bracken falling upon it. His head droops slightly, as he seems to be surveying the scenery of the lake. His muscular form is partially enveloped in his plaid, which crosses one shoulder and falls gracefully on his limbs. His coat is close buttoned, as if he was ready for action; he is planting his staff firmly on the ground with his right hand, while in his left he holds a scroll inscribed with the last line of "The Queen's Wake :"—

> "Hath taught the wandering winds to sing."

"Hector," his favorite dog, rests at his feet, with head erect, surveying the hills behind, as if conscious that he should tend the flocks during the poetic reverie of his master. The pedestal accords with the style and proportions of the figure; ten feet in height, it is of square form and appropriate breadth. A wreath of oak leaves and acorns surrounds the entablature, while a finely sculptured ram's head projects from each of the corners. Each side contains a square panel. The front panel represents the poetic harp surmounted by the head of Queen Mary, and a wreath of flowers, including "the briar rose and heather bell." Beneath is the inscription—

"James Hogg, the Ettrick Shepherd. Born 1770. Died 1835."

The other panels are adorned with these inscriptions from "The Queen's Wake:"—

> "Instead of arms or golden crest,
> His harp with mimic flowers was drest;
> Around, in graceful streamers, fell
> The briar rose and the heather bell."

> "At even-fall, in lonesome dale,
> He kept strange converse with the gale,
> Held worldly pomp in high derision,
> And wandered in a world of vision."

> "Oft had he viewed, as morning rose,
> The bosom of the lonely Lowes;
> Oft thrilled his heart at close of even
> To see the dappled vales of heaven,
> With many a mountain, moor, and tree,
> Asleep upon the Saint Mary."

James Hogg was born at Ettrick; he was baptized on the 9th December, 1770. Of humble parentage, he was born to the sheepfold. He taught himself to read and write on the hill-side. He attempted farming and failed. In 1810 he left the forest to attempt a literary career at Edinburgh. His "Queen's Wake" appeared in 1813, and at once established his reputation. He became the associate and correspondent of many of his more distinguished contemporaries. Sir Walter Scott, his first patron, continued his attached friend. With a true conception of his genius Professor Wilson delighted to lionize and celebrate him. Lord Byron corresponded with him. The good Duke Charles of Buccleuch invited him to his table, and at the request of the duchess bestowed on him a free life lease of the farm of Altrive in Yarrow. The Shepherd returned to Yarrow in 1817, and stocked his farm with the profits of a guinea edition of his poems. He married in 1820, and leased a second farm. In 1822 he produced two works of prose fiction, which were followed by others. He was one of the originators of *Blackwood's Magazine;* he suggested the famous Chaldee Manuscript, and composed part of it. At Altrive he exercised a generous hospitality; he was visited by admirers from all parts of Britain and America. During a visit to London in 1831 he was fêted at the tables of the nobility. On his return to Scotland he was entertained at a public banquet at Peebles under the presidency of Professor Wilson. After a period of feeble health he died on the 21st November, 1835, in his sixty-fifth year. He was unquestionably the most remarkable man who ever wore the plaid of a shepherd.

PARISH OF ETTRICK.

Ettrick Churchyard contains the mortal remains of the celebrated Thomas Boston. A handsome monument denotes his grave; on a tablet of white marble is the following inscription:—

"As a testimony of esteem for the Rev. Thomas Boston, senior, whose private character was highly respectable, whose public labours were blessed to many, and whose valuable writings have contributed much to promote the advancement of vital Christianity, this monument (by the permission of relatives) is erected by a religious and grateful public, A.D. 1806. He was born at Dunse,

March 17, 1676; ordained to the pastoral charge of Simprim, Sept. 21, 1699; removed from thence to Ettrick, May 1, 1707; and died May 20, 1732, leaving a widow and four children."

Mr. Boston was one of the twelve ministers who protested against the deliverance of the General Assembly of 1720, condemning the work entitled " The Marrow of Modern Divinity." He was much celebrated as a preacher, and was most faithful in the discharge of all the parochial duties. The tradition of his worth still lingers in the forest. Of his numerous theological works his " Human Nature in its Fourfold Estate" is the most celebrated. His works were published at London in 1854, in twelve octavo volumes.

Near Mr. Boston's grave is that of the Ettrick Shepherd; it is denoted by a plain tombstone thus inscribed:—

"Here lie the mortal remains of James Hogg, the Ettrick Shepherd, who was born at Ettrickhall in the year 1770, and died at Altrive Lake the 21st day of November, 1835. This stone is erected as a tribute of affection by his widow, Margaret Hogg."

"When the dark clouds of winter," writes Mr. Scott Riddell, "pass away from the crest of Ettrickpen, and the summits of the nearer lying mountains which surround the scene of his repose, and the yellow gowan opens its bosom by the banks of the mountain stream, to welcome the lights and shadows of the spring returning over the land, many are the wild daisies which adorn the turf that covers the remains of the Ettrick Shepherd. And a verse of one of the songs of his early days is strikingly verified when he says—

> ' Flow, my Ettrick! it was thee
> Into my life that first did drop me;
> Thee I'll sing, and when I dee,
> Thou wilt lend a sod to hap me.
> Pausing swains will say, and weep,
> Here our Shepherd lies asleep.'"

The Shepherd sleeps with his kindred. A tombstone adjoining his own, erected by himself, is thus inscribed:—

"Here lieth William Laidlaw, the far-famed Will o' Phaup, who for feats of frolic, agility, and strength, had no equal in his day. He was born at Craik, A.D. 1691, and died in the eighty-fourth year of his age. Also Margaret, his eldest daughter, spouse to Robert Hogg, and mother of the Ettrick Shepherd, born at Old Over Phaup, 1730, and died in the eighty-third year of her age; also Robert Hogg, her husband, late tenant of Ettrick-hall, born at Bowhill, 1720, and died in the ninety-third year of his age; and three of their sons."

DUMFRIESSHIRE.

PARISH OF DUMFRIES.

In Queensberry Square, an open space near the centre of the burgh, a handsome Doric column commemorates Charles, third Duke of Queensberry. It is inscribed—

"Sacred to the memory of Charles, Duke of Queensberry and Dover. Erected by the county of Dumfries, as a monument of their veneration for the character of that illustrious nobleman, whose exalted virtues rendered him the ornament of society, and whose numerous acts of public beneficence and private charity endeared him to his country. Ob. 22nd Oct., 1778; ætat. 80."

In the front wall of the Burgh Savings Bank a monumental statue commemorates the Rev. Dr. Henry Duncan, minister of Ruthwell, founder of Scottish savings banks. This eminent clergyman was born in the manse of Lochrutton on the 8th October, 1774. Having some years studied at the University of St. Andrews, he thought of adopting a mercantile profession, and entered on business at Liverpool. After a trial of merchandise and banking, he returned to his studies. At the Universities of Edinburgh and Glasgow he completed his education, and in 1798 became a licentiate of the Church. In 1799 he was ordained minister of Ruthwell. Here he sedulously devoted himself to the parochial duties, establishing friendly societies and a local savings bank; the last was begun in 1810, and its success led him to advocate the adoption of savings banks throughout the country. Owing to his exertions, an Act of Parliament establishing savings banks in Scotland was passed in 1819. He now exerted himself to establish a system of popular lectures on science, and so became founder of mechanics' institutes. In 1809 he originated the *Dumfries and Galloway Courier*, a weekly newspaper, which he conducted during the first seven years of its existence. He was the first to discover footprints of four-footed animals in the new red sandstone. In 1839 he was chosen Moderator of the General Assembly. In Church politics he entertained liberal opinions. At the disruption in 1843 he resigned his charge, and joined the Free Church. He died at Ruthwell on the 12th February, 1846, in the seventy-second year of his age, and the forty-seventh of his ministry. Of his numerous publications the most esteemed is his " Sacred Philosophy of the Seasons," in four volumes 12mo. He was a contributor to the *Edinburgh Encyclopædia*, the *Edinburgh Christian Instructor*, and the " Transactions of the Royal Society of Edinburgh."

St. Michael's Churchyard is celebrated for the number and character of its monuments. It includes three acres, and contains about 3,000 tombstones, erected at a cost of upwards of £30,000. Among the forest of tombs the most conspicuous is the mausoleum to the poet Burns in the south-east corner. It is a Grecian temple with a handsome dome, and is elegantly proportioned. It was reared by public subscription at a cost of £1,500, from a design by Mr. Thomas F. Hunt, of London, architect. The foundation stone was laid on the 5th June, 1815, and operations were completed on the 19th of September. The poet's sarcophagus was removed from its original resting-place in the north-east corner of the ground, and placed in the vault prepared for its reception. To the mausoleum were at the same time transferred the remains of two of his sons, Maxwell, a posthumous child, who died in 1799; and Francis Wallace, who died in 1803, aged fourteen. In the interior of the mausoleum a handsome piece of marble sculpture, by Turnerelli, represents the bard at the plough, while his country's genius casts upon him the mantle of inspiration. The monument also contains the original gravestone, thus inscribed :—

" In memory of Robert Burns, who died the 21st July, 1796, in the 37th year of his age; and Maxwell Burns, who died 25th April, 1799, aged two years and nine months; also of Francis Wallace

Burns, who died 9th July, 1803, aged 14 years; also of Jean Armour, relict of the poet, born February, 1765, died 26th March, 1834."*

Burns was born in a clay-built cottage at Alloway, Ayrshire, on the 25th January, 1759. His father, a nursery gardener, gave him such education as he could afford, and at an early age he began to engage in field operations. A small farm which he rented with his brother Gilbert proved a loss, and was abandoned. From his sixteenth year he had composed verses, and he now resolved to print a volume of poems by subscription, that he might by the profits possess the means of emigrating to Jamaica. This volume, published at Kilmarnock in 1786, was received with an amount of favour entirely exceeding the author's expectations. He was invited to Edinburgh, and was there introduced to persons eminent in rank and in literature. Encouraged to publish a new and enlarged edition of his poems, the profits enabled him to lease the farm of Ellisland, near Dumfries, where he settled in 1788. He married Jean Armour, whom he had celebrated by his muse. With his farm he held office in the excise. After a period he abandoned farming, and established his residence at Dumfries. His salary as an officer of excise did not exceed seventy pounds, but with his frugal habits it was sufficient for his wants. He died on the 21st July, 1796. Ten thousand persons assembled at his funeral. His songs are the best which have been written; they have been translated into every European language.

* The following Latin inscription was prepared for the mausoleum, but it has not been engraved upon it:—

"In æternum honorem Roberti Burns, poetarum Caledoniæ sui ævi longe principis cujus carmina eximia, patrio sermone scripta, animi magis ardentis, ingeniique vi, quam arte vel cultu conspicua, facetiis, jucunditate, lepore, affluentia, omnibus literarum cultoribus satis nota; cives sui, nec non plerique omnes musarum amantissimi, memoriamque viri arte poetica tam præclari, foventes hoc mausoleum, super reliquias poetæ mortales, extruendum curavere. Primum hujus ædificii lapidem Gulielmus Miller, armiger, reipublicæ architectonicæ apud Scotos, in regione australi, curio maximus provincialis, Georgio Tertio regnante, Georgio, Walliarum principe, summam imperii pro patre tenente, Josepho Gass, armigero, Dumfrisiæ, præfecto, Thoma F. Hunt, Londinensi, architecto, posuit, nonis Juniis, anno lucis VMDCCCXV, salutis humanæ MDCCCXV."

On the 26th March, 1834, Jean Armour, the poet's widow, died at Dumfries; her coffin was deposited in the vault which contained the remains of her husband and two children. Two other sons of the poet, Robert and Colonel James Glencairn, have since been entombed in the mausoleum. Robert Burns, the eldest son, died in 1857, in his seventieth year. With a view to a learned profession he attended classes in the Universities of Edinburgh and Glasgow. In 1804 he accepted a situation in the Stamp Office, London. A small income he augmented by practising tuition. In 1833 he obtained a superannuation allowance and retired to Dumfries. A considerable linguist, he was fond of philological speculation, and he was familiar with the poetical literature of his country. He composed songs, but these did not surpass mediocrity.

Along with his brother, William Nicol, who also attained a colonelcy, Colonel James Glencairn Burns obtained a commission in the East India Company's service through the interest of the Marchioness of Hastings. During their residence in India the brothers found their father's name a passport to the friendship of all with whom they associated. They contributed liberally towards the support of their widowed mother. On their return to Britain they were welcomed at a public banquet, conducted under the direction and presidency of the late patriotic Earl of Eglinton. The brothers thereafter established their residence at Cheltenham There James Glencairn Burns died in 1865.

An honoured friend of the Burns family, John McDiarmid, rests in St. Michael's Churchyard. This ingenious and benevolent gentleman was born at Glasgow in 1790. For some time he was employed in business concerns. He was associated with Charles Maclaren in originating the *Scotsman* newspaper in 1816. In the following year he accepted the editorship of the *Dumfries Courier*, which he retained till the period of his death. He died at Dumfries on the 18th November, 1852, aged sixty-three. He edited the "Scrap-book," a work of selections and original contributions in prose and verse, and published editions of several of the British

PARISH OF DUMFRIES.

poets. The newspaper which he conducted, acquired under his management a celebrity rarely attained by a provincial journal. Mr. McDiarmid is commemorated by a handsome tombstone.

The Rev. Walter Dunlop, minister of the Secession Church, Dumfries, and the most humorous of Scottish pastors, has found a grave and a tombstone in this interment-ground. He was a native of Haddingtonshire, and for some time ministered to a small congregation in Liddesdale. In 1809, one hundred members of the Secession Church at Dumfries objecting to their pastor making use of a pulpit gown, resolved to establish a new congregation of which the minister should wear "no rag of prelacy." By this body Mr. Dunlop was invited to Dumfries. He proved an acceptable preacher, and became celebrated for his conversational humour. He died at Dumfries on the 4th November, 1846, in the seventy-second year of his age, and forty-second of his ministry.

A conspicuous monument denotes the grave and celebrates the worth of Sir Andrew Halliday, the eminent physician. This distinguished individual was born at Copewood, parish of Dryfesdale, Dumfriesshire, on the 17th March, 1782. Owing to pecuniary reverses sustained by his father, he was compelled when nine years old to seek the means of living by tending cattle. He qualified himself to become teacher of a wayside school. At length he entered the University of Edinburgh; he intended to study for the ministry, but afterwards turned his attention to medicine. In 1804 he became surgeon, and in 1806 graduated as a physician. He was in 1807 appointed surgeon to the 13th Light Dragoons. In 1809 he joined the forces in Portugal, with which he remained till 1812, sharing the achievements of the Duke of Wellington. He now accepted a medical appointment in Portugal, and published a work on the military resources and social condition of that country. Returning to British military service, he was present at the assault of Bergen-op-Zoom, and at the battle of Waterloo. Of the latter he composed a narrative by order of the Duke of Clarence. On the overthrow of Napoleon he returned home and took up his abode in Edinburgh. In 1818 he became domestic physician to the Duke and Duchess of Clarence, whom he accompanied in their Continental travels. On his return to Britain he engaged in various patriotic and benevolent enterprises. In 1829 he aided in establishing King's College, London, and improved the condition of lunatic asylums. Receiving the honour of knighthood he was in 1832 sent to the West Indies as Deputy Inspector-General of military hospitals. In 1836 he permanently settled at Dumfries. He died on the 7th December, 1840. He composed a number of professional and other works. Of these the best known are his "History of the House of Guelph," and "Annals of the House of Hanover." Sir Andrew was descended from Tom Halliday, sister's son of the renowned Sir William Wallace.

Dr. James Crichton, of Friar's Carse, the munificent founder of the Royal Crichton Lunatic Asylum, Dumfries, rests in this churchyard. Long in the service of the East India Company, he settled at Dumfries in 1808. He left £100,000 to be applied for beneficent purposes "in any way that his dear wife thought proper." Acting on the advice of Sir Andrew Halliday, Mrs. Crichton resolved to erect an asylum for the insane, for which a design was furnished by Mr. Burn of Edinburgh. The Crichton Institution is one of the best conducted in the kingdom. Dr. Crichton died in 1823.

Of the older monuments one of the most interesting is that which commemorates Francis Irving, Provost of Dumfries, who died on the 8th November, 1633, aged sixty-eight. He was second son of Irving of Bonshaw, representative of the ancient House of Irving, in the parish of Annan. Educated in France, he married the daughter of Provost Herbert Raining, with whom he obtained an ample fortune. He became wine merchant, importing wines from Bordeaux. On the arrival of James VI. at Dumfries he presided at an entertainment in his Majesty's honour, at which his wife assisted. He so commended himself to the monarch as to receive in guerdon of royal approbation the office of bailie of the crownlands in Annandale. In speaking of him the King usually styled him "his own bailie." Provost Irving's monument is embellished with pillars of the Corinthian order, with gilt capitals and other ornaments. It was much defaced by Cromwell's soldiers, but was restored about thirty years ago. There is a Latin inscription—also these lines of English verse :—

> "King James at first me bailie named,
> Dumfries oft since me provost claimed;
> God hath for me a crown reserved,
> For king and country have I served."

A pyramidical monument commemorates three martyrs for the Covenant. On the three slabs placed over their remains are these inscriptions :—

> " Under this stone lo here doth ly
> Dust sacrificed to tyranny;
> Yet precious in Immanuel's sight,
> Since martyr'd for his kinglie right.
> When he condemns these hellish drudges,
> By suffrage saints shall be their judges."

"Here lies William Grierson, Pentland, martyred for his adherence to the word of God, and appearing for Christ's government in his house, and covenanted work of Reformation against Perjury and Prelacy. Executed August 2, 1667. Rev. xii. 11."

" Here lyes William Welch, Pentland, martyred for his adherence to the word of God, and appearing for Christ's kingly government in his House, and the covenanted work of Reformation against Perjury and Prelacy. Executed January 2, 1667. Rev. xii. 11."

> " Stay, passenger, read, here interr'd doth lie
> A witness 'gainst poor Scotland's Perjury,
> Whose head once fixed upon the Bridge-Port, stood
> Proclaiming vengeance for his guiltless blood."

" Here lyes James Kirk, martyr, shot dead upon the sands of Dumfries, for adhering to the work of God, and the covenanted work of Reformation against Perjury and Prelacy, 1685. Rev. xii. 11."

> "By bloody Bruce and wretched Wright,
> I lost my life in great despite;
> Shot dead without due time to try
> And fit me for Eternity;
> A witness of prelatic rage
> As ever was in any age."

A monument commemorates the Rev. John Scott, minister of Dumfries. The inscription is as follows:—

"In memory of the Rev. Mr. John Scott; he was born A.D. 1697; advanced to the ministry of the Gospel at Holywood, February 4, 1725; translated to the new church of Dumfries, November 30, 1732; and died April 17, 1770, universally esteemed and regretted. The virtues of his character in private and public life will be long remembered (and most justly) with veneration by his family, congregation, and acquaintance. He was an affectionate husband and parent, a warm and steady friend, a learned and able divine, a faithful reprover of vice, and a bright pattern of the duties he taught. He was a sensible and cheerful companion; possessed of extensive knowledge; remarkable for his accuracy in the discipline and government of this Church, and most zealous for the public weal.—2. Tim. iv. 7, 8."

The Rev. Dr. William Burnside, minister of the parish, is, on a handsome tombstone, celebrated thus:—

"Sacred to the memory of the Rev. Dr. William Burnside, admitted minister of the new church of Dumfries June 22, 1780; translated to St. Michael's June 19, 1794; he died January 6, 1806, aged fifty-five years. His fidelity in the discharge of every domestic duty, and the kindness of his heart endeared him to his family. His extensive knowledge and learning, the vivacity of his imagination, and the benevolence and liberality of his mind, rendered his conversation delightful in the circle of his friends. The eloquence and usefulness of his pastoral instructions, his rational piety, affability of manners and integrity of life, commanded the esteem and won the affections of his flock; thus endowed, and thus beloved in death, his death was generally and deeply regretted."

The Rev. Patrick Linn, minister of the second charge, has the following epitaph:—

"Here lies the body of the Rev. Mr. Patrick Linn, ordained

minister of Dumfries, May 12, 1715. Who was adorned with bright natural parts, solid learning, and unaffected piety; he, with unwearied diligence and unusual success, studied the knowledge of the several parts of divine revelation, especially the perfection of God, the depravity of human nature, man's recovery and salvation by Christ, and all the parts of practical religion, all which he delivered in public with uncommon eloquence, undaunted courage, and impartial freedom, to the edification of many : he was faithful in every relation of a truly Christian spirit, hating dissimulation and craft in every shape; candid, just, benevolent, bountiful, &c. He died August 1, 1731, in the forty-fourth year of his age."

James Corrie, of Spedock, a prosperous merchant and enterprising magistrate, is thus commemorated :—

"Here lyes James Corrie, of Spedock, merchant, who often enjoyed and faithfully discharged the office of chief magistrate within this burgh. During a long and deserved trust he acted with prudence and moderation, and a steady zeal for the public interest, active, assiduous, enterprising. He happily devised, and successfully pursued, the most commendable methods in business, revived declining trade, and excited by his example an industrious emulation in others. In every respect (for it was his ambition) he truly promoted the general weal, having joined to an unblemished integrity those rare abilities which rendered him amiable and useful in life. In death justly regretted as a good man, a sincere friend, and a worthy citizen. He died November 8, 1742 ; age fifty-nine years."

The monument of Alexander Herries Maxwell, of Munches, bears the following epitaph :—

"Sacred to the memory of Alexander Herries Maxwell, of Munches, Esq., who died on the 28th of June, 1815, in the seventy-first year of his age. Benevolent, frank, social, and warm-hearted, he was a steady and sincere friend, and always ready to advance the interests of those who had any claim to his good offices. After a residence of thirty-six years in London, ·he relinquished the medical profession, in which he had been indefatigable; and retiring to the vicinity of his native town, he devoted the remainder of his days to the exercise of his accustomed hospitality, the pursuit of agriculture, and the promotion of every plan for the improvement of the country; thus his life was extensively useful, and his death most deeply lamented."

At the south-western corner is the family monument of Sharpe of Hoddam, richly carved, and adorned with two sculptured figures.

Philadelphia, daughter of James Douglas, of Dornock, who died 6th February, 1754, aged thirty-one, has these lines upon her tombstone :—

"Nor herb, fruit, flower
"Glistening with dew, nor fragrance after showers,
Nor grateful evening mild, nor walk by moon,
Or glittering starlight, without thee is sweet."

John Paterson, who died in November, 1711, aged sixteen, has these lines inscribed on his gravestone :—

"When parents, friends, and neighbours hop'd to see
These early buds of learning, piety,
And temper good, produce some fruit,
Behold, death plucks the plant up by the root."

By the following lines John Mitchell, collector of excise, has commemorated his wife; she died 7th November, 1792, aged fifty :—

"Death wounds to cure, we fall, we rise, we reign,—
Spring from our fetters, fasten in the skies;
Where blooming Eden withers in our sight,
This king of terrors is the prince of peace."

Thomas Mouat, wigmaker, who died 18th November, 1735, is with his wife celebrated thus :—

"Two lovers true for ten years' space absented,
By stormy seas and wars, yet liv'd contented ;—
We met for eighteen years and married were,
God smil'd on us, our wind blew always fair ;
We're anchor'd here waiting our Master's call,
Expecting with Him joys perpetual."

In 1789 Captain George Williams testifies in this manner to the amiable qualities of his deceased helpmate :—

"A most affectionate and loving wife
Who while in life

> Great care of me did take,
> Which makes me to lament my dear departed mate;
> But since it was His will, which is divine,
> His blessed will ought always to be mine."

John Mitchell, who died in 1708, is celebrated thus :—

> "If grace, good manners, nor gifts of mind,
> Yea, where all moral virtues have combined
> Compleat a man, behold beneath this stone
> He lyes interr'd, whom rich and poor bemoan.
> He run his race, and an entrance got,
> His name is savoury and shall not rot."

On the tombstone of a daughter of Sir Thomas Hay, of Park, are these lines :—

> "If sense mature, even in the dawn of years,
> If beauty, youth, or innocence endears,
> Affections soft with manly spirit joined
> With gentle manners, sentiments refined,
> If heaven-born piety, serene yet bright,
> If filial tenderness the soul delight;
> If these united claim the cordial tear,
> Let feeling Nature pay the tribute here."

Sybella McMath, who died in 1838, has her tombstone inscribed as follows :—

> "A soul prepared needs no delays,
> The summons comes, the saint obeys;
> Swift was her flight, and short the road,
> She clos'd her eyes and saw her God.
> The flesh rests here till Jesus come,
> And claims the treasure from the tomb."

These verses are on a tombstone erected in 1837 :—

> "Farewell, fond husband and my darling boys,
> In whom was centred all my earthly joys;
> The triple union's broke—yet one short space
> Will reunite us in the realms of peace.
>
> Kind angels watch the sleeping dust,
> Till Jesus come to wake the just;
> Then may we wake with sweet surprise
> And in our Saviour's image rise."

The tomb of Colonel Schuyler, who died in 1832, is inscribed with the following epitaph, composed by himself:—

> " Raise no vain structure o'er my grave,
> One simple stone is all I crave,
> To say, beneath a sinner lies,
> Who died in hopes again to rise;
> Through Christ alone to be forgiven,
> And fitted for the joys of heaven."

Thomas Hogg is by his son thus celebrated:—

> " In this blest grave, amid whose frowning gloom
> Mem'ry still loves to guard her votary's tomb,
> Shall I withhold what all his virtues claim,
> The sacred tribute to a father's name?
> Whose manners gentle, his affections mild,
> In wit a man, in simplicity a child;
> Above temptation in an humble state,
> And uncorrupted even among the great."

A husband thus laments his early departed wife:—

> " Few were the nuptial years that gladdened life
> With its supremest bliss, a virtuous wife;
> When, as if sent but as an angel guest,
> For her own heaven she left my widow'd breast."

The Christian virtues of Mrs. Nicholas McDowall are portrayed thus:—

> " No smarting pain, no faithless terrors come
> To break thy slumbers in the peaceful tomb;
> Nor mournful eye, nor plaintive voice bemoan,—
> O child of God, thy Saviour's presence gone.
>
> " Thy Lord appear'd to hush thine every sigh,
> To yield thee Faith's triumphant victory;
> At ev'ning tide, ere to the realms of day
> Thy long afflicted spirit hied away."

On the gravestone of Robert Anderson, painter, who died 24th May, 1792, are these lines:—

> " They may write epitaphs who can,
> I say here lies an honest man!"

On the west side of the churchyard is the burial-place of those who died at Dumfries during the terrible visitation of Asiatic cholera in 1832. A monument at the spot is thus inscribed:—

"In this Cemetery,
and chiefly within this enclosure,
lie the mortal remains
of more than 420 inhabitants of Dumfries,
who were suddenly swept away
by the memorable invasion of
Asiatic cholera,
A.D. MDCCCXXXII.
That terrific Pestilence
entered the town on 15th September,
and remained till 27th November;
during which period it seized
at least 900 individuals,
of whom 44 died in one day,
and no more than 415 were reported
as recovered.
That the benefit of this
solemn warning
might not be lost to posterity,
this Monument
was erected, from collections made in
several churches in this town.

Psa. xc.—Thou turnest man to destruction; and sayest, Return, ye children of men. Thou carriest them away as with a flood.

Matt. xxv. 13.—Watch therefore, for ye know neither the day nor the hour."

PARISH OF ANNAN.

Annan Castle stood on an eminence on the east bank of the river west of the town; the ruin disappeared sixty years ago. A stone from the castle is built into the wall of a garden; it bears the following inscription:—

"Robert De Brus Counte De Carrick et Semour De Val De Annand. 1300."

In the parish churchyard an epitaph in Latin, intended to test the ingenuity of the reader, proceeds thus:—

"Qu   A   D   T   D   P
 os   nguis   irus   risti   ulcedine   avit
 H   Sa   M   Ch   M   L."

By a little attention these three lines may be converted into two of intelligible Latinity.

John Irwin, of Gulielands, "Justice of the Peace and Bailie of Annan," who died 19th July, 1822, is thus celebrated:—

> "He thought it honour with all his might,
> To preserve the ancient burgh's right;
> No man with bribes could for his blood
> Tempt him to hurt the common good;
> Let every one that him succeeds
> Think on his faithful words and deeds."

On her tombstone Mrs. Barbara Stewart, wife of John Room, in Stewart-town, who died at Tordoch, 16th March, 1730, leaving six children, is thus commended:—

> "Beneath this stone in silent slumber sleeps
> Her sacred dust, whose soul sweet Jesus keeps;
> Which wing'd its way thro' ether's regions high
> To be united with saints above the sky.
> In piety with virtue bright she shone,
> A tender mother, wife, and friend in one;
> Lamented death, those children dear did cost,
> Husband grief for what they had and lost."

A parochial incumbent has celebrated his deceased children in these lines:—

> "Dear children, ye were most sprightly and fair,
> Of grace, love, and smartness, instances rare;
> But in health those deaths thou, Peggie, foretold,
> And heaven much longed for, who then could withhold."

A tombstone bears the following:—

> "No darkness, no dismal neglect,
> No vapour intercepts the light.
> We see for ever face to face
> The highest Prince in highest place."

In the new churchyard the parents of a youth of nineteen lament him thus:—

> "Dearest boy, thou hast left us,
> Left us deeply drown'd in woe;
> He who gave thee takes thee from us,
> And we dare not answer no."

PARISH OF CAERLAVEROCK.

In the parish churchyard a mortuary enclosure forms the burial-place of the old family of Kirkpatrick of Conheath, ancestors of Eugénie, ex-Empress of the French. On a monument are the following inscriptions:—

"In memory of William Kirkpatrick, late of Conheath; Mary Wilson, his spouse; Isabella, Alexander, and Elizabeth Kirkpatrick, their children."

"Rosina Kirkpatrick, died at Nithbank the 5th day of April, 1833."

"Jane Forbes Kirkpatrick, the last surviving daughter of the above William and Mary Kirkpatrick, born the 18th of September, 1767; died the 21st December, 1854.

Erected by John Kirkpatrick, merchant in Ostend, eldest son of the deceased William Kirkpatrick, April, 1788."

William Kirkpatrick of Conheath was cousin-german of Sir James Kirkpatrick, Bart., of Closeburn. His daughter, Jane Forbes Kirkpatrick, also commemorated on the monument, attained her eighty-seventh year; she was aunt of the Countess de Montijo, mother of the ex-Empress.

Robert Paterson, better known as "Old Mortality," rests in this churchyard; his grave adjoins the burying-place of the Kirkpatricks. He was born in 1715. Youngest son of Walter Paterson and Margaret Scott, who rented the farm of Haggisha, parish of Hawick, he some time served an elder brother, who had a farm in Comcockle-muir, near Lochmaben. He married Elizabeth Gray, who having been cook in the family of Sir Thomas Kirkpatrick of Closeburn, procured for him an advantageous lease of a freestone quarry at Morton. Here he resided many years, labouring with exemplary diligence. From his youth attached to the sect of the Cameronians he evinced a deep interest in the memory of those who had suffered in the cause of Presbytery. Occasionally he restored their tombstones. At length his zeal in the restoration of these stony memorials acquired the force of a passion. In 1758 he began to travel from parish to parish, ever working with hammer and chisel in renewing the epitaphs of the martyrs. His self-imposed task no entreaties of wife or children could induce him to abandon. Though reduced to the verge of poverty he persisted in his labours till the last day of his existence. He died at Bankend village, near Lockerby, on the 29th January, 1801, aged eighty-six. At his death he was found possessed of twenty-seven shillings and sixpence, which were applied to the expenses of his funeral. Sir Walter Scott, who has made "Old Mortality" the subject of a novel, intended to rear a tombstone to his memory, but was unable to discover his place of sepulture. Since the discovery has been made, Messrs. Black, of Edinburgh, who possess the copyright of the Waverley novels, have reared at the grave of the old enthusiast a suitable memorial stone. It is thus inscribed:—

"Erected to the memory of Robert Paterson, the Old Mortality of Sir Walter Scott, who was buried here February, 1801.

"Why seeks he with unwearied toil
   Through death's dim walk to urge his way,
  Reclaim his long-asserted spoil,
   And lead oblivion into day?"

PARISH OF CANONBIE.

In this churchyard rest the remains of the Rev. Robert Petrie, a respected minister of the parish, and father of four sons who rose to distinction and opulence. Mr. Petrie was elected schoolmaster of Jedburgh in 1719, and was afterwards preferred to the mastership of the grammar school of Selkirk. In 1734 he was ordained minister of Canonbie. He died on the 15th July, 1764, aged sixty-four. His eldest son, Dr. Robert Petrie, was an eminent physician in Lincoln; William, his youngest son, rose to be second in command at Madras, and was distinguished for his administrative abilities.

Caroline Eliza Scott, afterwards Mrs. Richardson, an elegant poetess, is interred in the churchyard. She was born at Canonbie on the 24th November, 1777. She married her cousin, Gilbert Geddes Richardson, on the 29th April, 1799. For some years she resided with her husband at Madras. On being early left a widow she returned to Britain, and established her residence at London. In 1821 she removed to Dumfries; she subsequently rented a house at Canonbie. She died on the 9th October, 1853, aged seventy-six. Mrs. Richardson published several volumes of poems, and "Adonia," a romance.

PARISH OF CLOSEBURN.

In Dalgarno Churchyard a tombstone commemorates James Harkness, who escaped from prison when under sentence of death for maintaining the right of private judgment. His epitaph is as follows:—

"Here lyes the body of James Harkness in Lockerben, who died 6 Dec., 1723, aged seventy-two years.

Below this stone his dust doth lie,
Who endured 28 years persecution by tyranny;
Did him pursue with hue and cry,
Through many a lonesome place.
At last by Clavers he was ta'en, sentenced for to die,
But God, who for his soul took care,
Did him from prison bring.
Because no other cause they had,
But that he would not give up
With Christ his glorious king,
And swear allegiance to that beast,
The Duke of York I mean.
In spite of all their hellish rage,
A natural death he died,
In full assurance of his rest
With Christ eternally."

In Closeburn Churchyard a tombstone commemorates the Rev. Peter Yorkstoun, minister of the parish. This eminent divine was licensed in 1735; he was ordained minister of Kells in 1741. In 1763 he was translated to Closeburn; he died on the 8th December, 1776, in his seventieth year, and thirty-sixth of his ministry. An accurate scholar and an accomplished conversationalist, he was highly distinguished for his ministerial gifts.

PARISH OF DORNOCK.

The Rev. James Moffat, minister of the parish from 1694 to 1714, has thus celebrated his departed wife :—

"Scarce will an age afford such one,
So prudent, wise, and rare,
Pious, humble, modest, meek, and wise,
Loadstone-like, attractive, swete."

On the tombstone of John Graham, of Rosetrees, and his wife and son, are inscribed these lines :—

> "Praises on tombs are trifles vainly spent,
> Let each good name be its own monument,
> What's here said, ye living it doth respect,
> That thou, O man, may'st seriously reflect,
> On this memento, which in mind still have,
> That each moment on the former shuts the grave,
> Thy warrant is gone out, though dormant yet,
> Perhaps behind one moment lurks thy fate;
> Which opes the scene to eternal future things,
> Which closes all, and final sentence brings."

The following rhymes commemorate the wife of David Stewart, shoemaker, who died 11th April, 1803, aged sixty-three.

> "For twenty years and eight I liv'd a maiden's life,
> And five-and-thirty years I was a married wife;
> And in that space of time eight children I did bear,
> Four sons, four daughters, who ever lov'd most dear.
> Three of that number, as the Scriptures run,
> Preach up the way to heaven, and hell to shun."

PARISH OF DRYFESDALE.

The churchyard of this parish is situated at the hamlet of Lockerbie. A former churchyard on the bank of the Dryfe stream had been more than once rifled of its contents by sudden inundations of the river. Lockerbie Churchyard contains these inscriptions:—

> "Praises on Tombs are trifles vainly spent,
> A man's good name is his best Monument."

> "Our life's a flying shadow, God's the pole,
> The index pointing to Him is the soul;
> Death's the horizon when our sun is set,
> Who will in Christ a resurrection get."

PARISH OF DUNSCORE.

In the dilapidated sepulchre of his family in the old churchyard were deposited the remains of Sir Robert Grierson, Bart., of Lag, the noted persecutor. Representative of an ancient House, which long possessed the lands of Lag, Robert Grierson succeeded to his paternal estate in 1669. In March, 1685, he was created a Baronet of Nova Scotia; he also obtained from James VII. a pension of £200 sterling. He took an active part in hunting down the adherents of the Covenant, and in repressing freedom of worship. In 1685 he attacked John Bell, of Whiteside, and some others, in Kirkconnel-muir, parish of Tongland, and ordered them to be put to death without allowing them time for prayer; he would not permit their bodies to be buried. After the Revolution he lived quietly on his estate. He died at Dumfries, 17th April, 1736. His gravestone is inscribed thus:—

   S.   17 36.   D.
   W. G.   N. M.

In Dunscore Churchyard are interred the remains of Robert Riddell, of Glenriddell, the eminent antiquary and musician, an early patron of Burns. "With Mr. Riddell and his wife," writes Burns, "I have enjoyed more pleasant evenings than at all the houses of fashionable people in this country put together; and to their kindness and hospitality I am indebted for many of the happiest hours of my life." Burns's poem of "The Whistle" commemorates a festive event which took place at Mr. Riddell's residence, Friar's Carse Hermitage, on the 16th October, 1790. Mr. Riddell died on the 21st April, 1794. He contributed a number of papers to the Scottish Society of Antiquaries.

PARISH OF DURISDEER.

In the parish church a magnificent mausoleum commemorates James, second Duke of Queensberry, and his Duchess. This eminent statesman was born at Sanquhar Castle on the 18th December,

1662. He was educated at the University of Glasgow, and afterwards travelled on the Continent. In 1684 he was sworn a Privy Councillor and appointed Lieutenant-Colonel of Lord Dundee's regiment of horse. He cordially supported the Revolution, and William III. appointed him a gentleman of his bedchamber. In 1693 he became Lord High Treasurer. In 1700 he represented the King as High Commissioner in the Scottish Parliament. By Queen Anne in 1703 he was appointed Secretary of State; he was subsequently constituted High Commissioner on the part of Scotland to carry out the treaty of Union. In recompence of his services he received a pension of £3,000 per annum, and was created a British peer by the title of Duke of Dover. In February, 1709, he was appointed third Secretary of State for the United Kingdom. He died on the 6th July, 1711, in his forty-ninth year. He married Mary, fourth daughter of Charles Boyle, Lord Clifford. She died in 1709.

The monument of the Duke and Duchess contains their figures in marble, and is thus inscribed:—

"Mariæ, Ducissæ Queensberiæ et Doverni, quæ, paterna stirpe e Burlingtonii et Cumbriæ, materna vero, Somerseti et Essexiæ familiis prælustribus, oriunda, generis splendorem morum suavitate temperavit animi magnitudine auxit; et severiorem virtutem, honestis ingenii et formæ illecebris, jucundam reddidit et benignam marito amantissimo; dum varia rerum vice exerceretur, in secundis decus, in dubiis stabilimen, in asperis solamen; curarum thalami et consiliorum sanctissimum depositum; conjugi incomparabili, Jacobus, Dux Queensberiæ et Doverni (ea spe et hoc unico consilio, quod, sub eodem marmore, ubi hos caros deposuit cineres, suas depositurus sit) hoc monumentum extrui jussit. Obiit Londini, Octob. 2, 1709.

"Hic, in eodem tumulo, cum charissimæ conjugis cineribus, misceri voluit suos Jacobus Dux Queensberiæ et Doverni; qui, ad tot et tanta, quæ subditus attigit, evectus, Londini fato cessit, sexto die Julii, anno Christi redemptoris 1711. Ætatis 49."

The Queensberry vault contains, in addition to the remains of the Duke and Duchess, those of their daughter Elizabeth; of Isabella Douglas, wife of William, first Duke of Queensberry;

Lord George Douglas, son of the preceding; of Charles, the third Duke of Queensberry, and his wife, Catherine Hyde, daughter of Henry, Earl of Clarendon, the patroness of Gay, who said of her,—

> " Yonder I see the cheerful Duchess stand,
> For friendship, zeal, and blithesome humours known; "

of Charles, Earl of Drumlanrig, younger son of the third Duke; of Elizabeth Hope, Dowager Countess of Drumlanrig, and of Henry, Lord Drumlanrig.

In the churchyard a tombstone commemorates Daniel McMichael, a Covenanter, shot by General Dalziel, in January, 1685; the epitaph follows:—

> " As Daniel cast was into lions' den,
> For praying unto God, and not to men;
> Thus lions cruelly devoured me,
> For bearing unto truth my testimony.
> I rest in peace till Jesus rend the cloud,
> And judge 'twixt me and those who shed my blood."

PARISH OF ESKDALEMUIR.

The following epitaph celebrates the Rev. John Lawrie, successively minister of Wauchope and of this parish; he died 7th December, 1723, in his sixty-ninth year, and the thirty-third of his ministry:—

> " Here lies John Lawrie,
> Neither rich nor poor,
> Last minister of Wauchope,
> And first of Eskdalemoor."

By a tombstone is commemorated William Brown, D.D., author of the " Antiquities of the Jews." Dr. Brown was ordained to the parochial cure in 1792. He died 21st September, 1835, in his sixty-ninth year and forty-fourth of his ministry.

PARISH OF GLENCAIRN.

In the churchyard three tombstones commemorate four covenanters who were in 1685 shot by order of Colonel Douglas and Lieutenant Livingston. The inscriptions are as follow:—

On John Gibson.
" My soul's in heaven, here's my dust,
By wicked sentence, and unjust,
Shot dead, convicted of no crime
But non-compliance with the time,
When Babel's bastards had command,
And monstrous tyrants ruled the land."

On James Bennoch.
" Here lies a monument of Popish wrath;
Because I'm not perjur'd, I'm shot to death
By cruel hands; men, godless and unjust,
Did sacrifice my blood to Babel's lust."

On Robert Edgar and Robert Mitchell.
" Halt, passenger, tell if thou ever saw
Men shot to death without process of law;
We two, of four who in this churchyard ly,
Thus felt the rage of Popish tyranny."

On a portion of rising ground near the village of Minnyhive a monument was reared in 1828 in commemoration of James Renwick, the last of Scottish martyrs. This celebrated field-preacher was born on the 15th February, 1662. Having prosecuted his studies at the University of Edinburgh, he obtained in 1682 licence in Holland as a preacher of the Presbyterian Church. In January, 1683, he proclaimed the famous "Lanark Declaration," and commenced a course of itinerant preaching. By the Privy Council he was denounced a traitor, and his adherents pronounced rebels. He was hotly pursued by the Government troops, and had many signal escapes. On the accession of James VII., in 1685, he publicly protested against the event in a document known as the "Sanquhar Declaration." In October, 1687, a reward of £100 was offered for his apprehension; he was discovered in January, 1688, and was committed to the Tolbooth of Edinburgh. Tried before the Court of Justiciary for disowning the royal authority, he was declared guilty; he was executed at Edinburgh on the 17th February. He was in his twenty-sixth year. A memoir of his life and a collection of his discourses were published at Glasgow in 1777. His monument stands within a hundred yards of the spot on which he is supposed to have been born; it is twenty-five feet in height, and cost £100. It is thus inscribed:—

"In Memory of the late Rev. James Renwick, the last who suffered to death for attachment to the Covenanted Cause of Christ in Scotland: born, near this spot, 15th February, 1662, and executed at the Grass-Market, Edinburgh, 17th February, 1688. 'The righteous shall be in everlasting remembrance.' Erected by subscription, A.D. MDCCCXXVIII."

PARISH OF GRETNA.

In the old churchyard at Redkirk a monumental stone was formerly inscribed thus:—

"Here lyeth IO.N BELL, who died in ye yhere
MDX and of hys age CXXX yheres,
Here bluidy Bell baith skin and bane,
Lyis quietly styll aneath thys stane.
He was a stark moss-trooper bent,
As ever drew a nout* o'er bent,
He brynt ye Lockwood tower and hall,
And flung ye lady o'er ye wall,

* Black cattle.

> For whilk ye Johnstone, stout and wyte
> Set Blacketh a' in low by nyght;
> While cry'd a voice, as if from hell,
> Haste, open ye gates for bluidy Bell."

In the parish churchyard a tombstone commemorates the Rev. James Gatt, minister of the parish, an ingenious and learned theologian. Mr. Gatt was a native of Cullen; he studied at the University of Edinburgh, and received licence in 1727. In 1730 he was ordained assistant and successor at Gretna; he died on the 31st October, 1787, in his eighty-eighth year, and the fifty-eighth of his ministry. He translated into Latin verse the Book of Job and the Book of Proverbs, and composed many Latin poems and birthday odes. Fond of alliteration, he frequently, in his discourses, indulged in this vein. Preaching on Salvation, he spoke of " the path, the purchaser, the price, the promise, the properties, the preparation, and the preaching; the privileges and pledges, the partakers and the progress; its perfection, practical use, and proper improvement. As the blessings of salvation he enumerated regeneration, reconciliation, remission, renovation, restoration, redemption from evil, rejoicing in hope, reinforcement of grace, and reception into glory."

The old church of Gretna was formerly a burial-place of the Johnstones of Annandale.

In the parish churchyard Dr. John Wallace, physician, descended from the family of Wallace of Craigie, has on his tombstone these lines celebrating Sir William Wallace, the hero of his house:—

> " The hero of his age, and martyr for liberty,
> Upon whose body nature did display
> A manly gesture, features pleasing, gay;
> But virtue nobly did adorn his mind,
> And made him ripe for company 'bove mankind."

Mrs. Jean Mackay is on her tombstone thus commemorated :—

> " Let no man boast of beauty bright,
> She that lies here was my delight;
> Till cruel death did on her call,
> And left me to lament her fall."

PARISH OF HODDAM.

In the parish churchyard is commemorated the Rev. Matthew Reid, minister of the parish. Son of the Rev. Matthew Reid, minister of Kirkinner, he studied at the University of Edinburgh, and was licensed in 1664. During the same year he was admitted to the pastoral charge of Langholm. He was translated to Hoddam in 1666. He died 11th April, 1681, in his forty-second year, and the nineteenth of his ministry. On his tombstone his qualities are thus quaintly portrayed :—

> " His name he from St. Matthew tooke,
> His skill in physicke from St. Luke,
> A reed of John the Baptist kind,
> Not wavering with every wind ;
> Ever a true Nathanael,
> He preachèd, lived, and dyed weill."

John Irving, who died of consumption in 1805, aged twenty, is celebrated thus :—

> " Hail ! pensive wanderer, 'mid the twilight gloom,
> Approach and moralize beside this sod—
> A purer heart than that within this tomb,
> Ne'er breath'd the vow of penitence to God.
> Free from those stains that darken error's clime,
> He ask'd of mercy, ask'd to be forgiven,
> Then bow'd his head before the stroke of time,
> And, borne by angels, found repose in heaven."

A couplet on a monument resting on the church wall thus commemorates Mrs. Mary Clow :—

> " A virtuous wife, a loving mother,
> And one esteemed by all that knew her."

These lines on an altar stone commemorate a clockmaker :—

> " Here lyes a man, who all his mortal life
> Past mending clocks, but cou'dna mend his wyfe.
> The larum o' hys bell was ne'er sae shrill
> As was her tongue, aye clacking like a mill.
> But now he's gane—oh whither ? nane can tell,
> I hope beyond the soun' o' Matty's bell."

In Ecclefechan Churchyard Mr. William Nicol, of the Edinburgh High School, an associate of Burns, has erected an altar tomb over the graves of his parents.

PARISH OF HOLYWOOD.

Holywood Abbey stood in the south-east corner of the burying-ground. It was founded by Devorgilla, wife of John Baliol, Lord of Barnard Castle, and mother of John Baliol, who was in 1292 declared King of Scotland by Edward I. The abbey was taken down in 1778, and the materials used in constructing the parish church. The old monuments have disappeared. The following inscriptions are from modern gravestones :—

> "The figure fair of Agnes see,
> A loving spouse five years to me;
> Death suddenly did call her hence,
> I calm resigned to Providence.

> "Stop, passenger, in passing by,
> And view the place where you must shortly be.
> As you are now, so once was I;
> As I am now so you must be,
> Therefore prepare to follow me."

> "Adieu my wife and children all,
> I yield to the Almighty's call;
> Children dear, pray love each other,
> And cherish your affectionate mother.
> Support her in declining years,
> Oh sooth and catch each falling tear,
> And may the grace of God be given,
> To sanctify your souls for heaven."

PARISH OF JOHNSTONE.

Attached to the parish church is the family vault of the noble House of Johnstone of Annandale, now extinct; it contains the remains of many notable persons connected with the family.

PARISH OF KEIR

Near the parish church stood an upright stone six feet in height; it was known as the "grey-stone," but was uninscribed. On the ridge of Keir Hill a stone bears the initials of James Renwick; the future martyr preached at the spot.

PARISH OF KIRKCONNEL.

In the churchyard a flat tombstone displaying a cross and a sword, with the legend "Hic jacet Adamus Fleeming," is associated with a melancholy narrative on which is founded the old ballad of "Fair Helen of Kirkconnel." Helen Irving, a young lady of great personal attractions, and member of an old Annandale family, had been courted by two gentlemen; viz., Bell of Blackwood House, Middlebie, and Adam Fleming of Fleming Hall, near Mossknow. Fleming was the favoured lover, and Bell determined on vengeance. He told the young lady that if he at any time found his rival in her company he would kill him. Not long after she was walking with Fleming on the romantic banks of the Kirtle, when she discovered Bell hiding among the bushes. Perceiving that he levelled his musket, she suddenly rushed between him and his intended victim. She received the ball intended for her lover, fell back, and immediately expired. Fleming rushed towards the murderer, and slew him with his sword. A cairn was reared to denote the death-spot of the fair heroine, and her remains were interred in Kirkconnel Churchyard. Overwhelmed with grief, Fleming proceeded to Spain, where he engaged in military service. Returning home he visited Helen Irving's grave, stretched himself upon it, and died. The legend is associated with the reign of Queen Mary. The ballad to which it gave origin is presented by Mr. Charles Kirkpatrick Sharpe in the *Scots Musical Museum*, vol. iv., p. 210.

In Kirkconnel Churchyard a tombstone commemorates William Laing, a short-lived poet. A native of the parish, he supported himself by tuition. He died in June, 1858, in his twenty-ninth year. His "Poems and Songs" were published posthumously.

PARISH OF KIRKMAHOE.

In the churchyard a gravestone commemorates the Rev. Francis Irving, minister of the parish, a sufferer in the cause of Presbytery. Having studied at the University of Edinburgh, he was elected schoolmaster of Dumfries. Receiving licence, he was in 1642 ordained to the ministry at Trailflat. In 1645 he was translated to Kirkmahoe. Deprived of his charge on the restoration of Episcopacy, he refused to accept the Indulgence; being afterwards denounced by the Privy Council, he was several years imprisoned in the Tolbooths of Dumfries and Edinburgh and on the Bass. He afterwards went to Holland, but returned in 1687. After the Revolution he was restored to the living of Kirkmahoe. He died on the 8th December, 1695, in the eighty-fifth year of his age and fifty-third of his ministry.

A kind old spinster is on her tombstone thus gratefully commemorated:—

"Stranger, one fleeting moment stay,
For this is Mary Lindsay's grave,
Who practised in her low estate
Virtue, that well became the great;
Whose self-denial, chaste and kind,
An honour was to human kind.
Near yon rude cot she first drew breath,
And there she closed her eyes in death;
Pattern to all who wish to thrive
At the ripe age of eighty-five.
No husband Mary ever had,
No offspring—age's ill to glad;

But all the children round and round
In her a foster-parent found;
Their eggs she boiled, their cloaks she dried,
And soothed and coaxed them when they cried;
And when the burn ran wide and wild,
She ferried over every child.
Proficient in her loving heart,
The fremit had a mother's heart.
A gentleness and love that's higher,
And blessed was Mary's fire.
Disturb not, but respect this stone,
Raised to her memory by one
Who even in death would Mary shield,
Hannah of Bayhall, Huddersfield."

PARISH OF KIRKMICHAEL.

A large stone, named "sax corses" (six corpses), denotes the burial-place of Sir Hugh de Morland and five of his followers, who were slain by Sir William Wallace and his followers, who sallied forth to attack them from the Tor-Linn, a glen of natural oak in the vicinity.

In Garrel Churchyard is the ancient burying-ground of the Kirkpatricks, Barons of Kirkmichael. A plain tombstone commemorates the great-grandmother and great-grandfather of Eugénie, ex-Empress of the French. There is the following inscription:—

"Robert Kirkpatrick of
Glenkiln, died 12th Octr., 1746, aged 68 years.
His Superior abilities, possessed
And aided by honest Industry,
Exalted his Station in Life:
His Amiable Disposition
Endeared him to Mankind.

Mrs. Kirkpatrick, of Glenkiln,
Died 2nd June, 1771, 68th year.
Her Virtue, Piety, and
Benevolence of Heart

Procured her Universal Esteem;
Her Family feel the Loss of a
Most Affectionate Parent,
And The Poor
Their Benefactress."

PARISH OF KIRKPATRICK-JUXTA.

A parochial incumbent, who had been invited to the ministerial charge of Mousewald, but died before his translation, is thus quaintly commemorated on his tombstone:—

"The Rev. Dr. Stewart's call to Mousewald
Was turned into a call to another land."

PARISH OF LANGHOLM.

At Langholm a monumental statue commemorates Admiral Sir Pulteney Malcolm, son of George Malcolm, farmer, Burnfoot, in this parish. He was born on the 20th February, 1768. In 1778 he entered the navy as a midshipman. On board the *Penelope* he aided in the capture of the *Inconstante* frigate, which he conducted to Port Royal. In 1794 he became commander, and had direction of the seamen and marines landed to garrison on Cape Nichola Mole. After many other distinguished services, he was appointed to the command of the *Donegal*, in which he accompanied Lord Nelson in his pursuit of the squadrons of France and Spain. He greatly distinguished himself at the battle of St. Domingo in February, 1806. On his return to Britain he received the thanks of both Houses of Parliament. In 1808 he escorted the army under General Wellesley into Portugal. In 1809 he commanded the blockade of Cherbourg. In command of the *Royal Oak* he proceeded to North America in 1814, and took part in the siege of Fort Boyer, the surrender of which terminated the war. In 1815 he was nominated Knight Commander of the Bath. In 1816 he held office as Commander-in-chief at St. Helena; by his agreeable manners he won the favour of Napoleon. Sir Pulteney attained the rank of Admiral in January, 1837. He died on the 20th July, 1838.

PARISH OF LOCHMABEN.

In Lochmaben Churchyard an obelisk, without inscription, is believed to commemorate Dr. James Mounsey, physician to the Empress of Russia. Son of Thomas Mounsey, farmer, at Skipmyre, parish of Tinwald, Dumfriesshire, he settled at St. Petersburg some time before 1750, and was employed by the Emperor and Empress, to whom he subsequently became first physician. Returning to Britain before 1770, he purchased the estate of Rammerscales, in Annandale. He died soon afterwards.

A tombstone celebrates the Rev. Dr. Andrew Jaffray, minister of the parish, a friend of the poet Burns. He was licensed in 1749, and ordained to the ministry at Tundergath in 1755. Translated to Ruthwell in 1760, he was in 1783 preferred to the living of Lochmaben. Burns, who much enjoyed his society, has characterized him as "a worthy old veteran in religion and good fellowship." His daughter Jean was the heroine of Burns' song, "I gaed a waefu' gate yestreen." Dr. Jaffray died on the 3rd January, 1795, in his seventy-third year, and the fortieth of his ministry.

A handsome granite obelisk denotes the grave of William Jardine, of Lanrick Castle, M.P., a native of the parish, who died on the 27th February, 1843.

PARISH OF MIDDLEBIE.

A tombstone commemorates the Rev. James Currie, minister of the parish, and father of Dr. James Currie, the editor of Burns.

Mr. Currie was son of the Rev. James Currie, minister of Hoddam. He was ordained minister of Kirkpatrick-Fleming in 1746, and was translated to Middlebie in 1763. He died on the 24th October, 1773, aged fifty-eight.

PARISH OF MOFFAT.

In the parish churchyard rest the remains of John Finlay, an ingenious and short-lived poet. He died suddenly at Moffat on the 8th December, 1810, in his twenty-eighth year. At the age of nineteen he composed his poem of "Wallace, or the Vale of Ellerslie," which, published in 1802, attracted much attention. His "Scottish Historical and Romantic Ballads" appeared in 1808.

A monument commemorates John Loudon Macadam, the celebrated improver of roads. He was born at Ayr on the 21st September, 1756. His youth was spent in America. In 1798 he was appointed Government Agent for victualling the navy in the Western ports. On his method of improving roads he had experimented in Scotland; he now made trial of his system in the west of England. In 1815 he was appointed Surveyor-General of British roads. His method being generally adopted, he received from Government the sum of £10,000 in reimbursement of funds expended in experiments. He was also offered knighthood, which he declined. He retired to Moffat and there died on the 26th November, 1836, aged eighty.

John Williamson, who discovered the Moffat mineral spa, is celebrated by a memorial stone. He died in 1769.

A tombstone has been reared in memory of the Rev. Robert Johnstone, missionary at Madras, who died in 1853.

William Muir, in Clarefoot, and his wife, who both died in 1759, are thus quaintly commemorated:—

> "Here lies the man, the woman here,
> Their mutual love surpassing dear,
> When down she in the grave did ly,
> Here he reclined of sympathy."

Another quaint epitaph is as follows :—

> "Within this cold clay bed
> The dusty parts here lie
> The affectionate father,
> The indulgent mother,
> And their children five."

PARISH OF PENPONT.

On the estate of Bailford, an obelisk, ten feet in height, is understood to possess a memorial character, but the inscription has long been defaced.

PARISH OF RUTHWELL.

In the manse garden is an ancient cross sculptured with Christian emblems and other figures, and bearing inscriptions both in Latin and in Anglo-Saxon Runes. It was partially restored and placed in its present position by the late Dr. Henry Duncan, minister of the parish. There are four faces, two of which present Anglo-Saxon Runes, and the two others Roman characters. On the latter are Christian emblems. Dr. Duncan believed that the pillar had, since its original erection, undergone a change, and that the sculpture on the Runic sides considerably preceded that on the other two. A portion of the Runes, deciphered by Mr. Repp, the learned Danish scholar, would indicate that the structure had been reared by the authority of the Therfusian Fathers to expiate an injury. The Roman sides present Latin inscriptions, from the Vulgate version of the New Testament, and illustrate leading scenes in the Saviour's life. At the Reformation the cross stood in the parish church. In 1642 it was removed by the General Assembly, as a monument of idolatry. It was afterwards restored to the church, but was taken back to the churchyard, from which the portions were collected by Dr. Duncan in 1802. In the manse garden are two other sculptured stones about the size and shape of common gravestones, but without inscriptions, each containing the figure of an ornamented cross rising in the centre on a pedestal, and on the right side a sword of ancient form; while on the left side of the one is the coulter and sock of a plough, and on that of the other a bugle-horn. These stones were found in the churchyard, but are believed to have been connected with a small chapel, or preceptory, belonging to the knights of St. John.

In the churchyard a plain monumental slab commemorates the Rev. Gavin Young, minister of the parish, who died in 1671, in his eighty-fifth year, and fifty-fourth of his ministry. Mr. Young is remembered as the Scottish Vicar of Bray, having repeatedly changed his principles to preserve his living. "John," said he to one of his elders, "what do the folk i' the Priestside say aboot me?" "'Deed, Sir," said John, "they say ye're a turncoat." "Aye, aye, John, it's vera true they say, but ye ken we manna quarrel wi' our brose for a mote i' them." On Mr. Young's tombstone is the following inscription:—

"Here lyes the Rev. Mr. Gavin Younge, Minister of Ruthwell. He died 1671, aged eighty-five. He was minister fifty-four yhears. Also his wyfe, Jane Stewart, aged forty-three."

"Far frae our own,
Amidst our own we lye,
Of our dear bairnes,
Thirty and one us bye.

Gavinus Junius—Unius agni usui.

Jean Stewart, a true saint,
A true saint I liveit, sa I deit,
Though man saw no, my God did see it,
Blessed are they that die in ye Lord."

One of Mr. Young's daughters, Mrs. Wilson, is thus commemorated on her gravestone —

> " My dear mother near I lye,
> Ten before me, the eleventh am I ;
> Dear spous, when yhou behold this shryne,
> Think on your bonny babes and myne."

Another daughter of Mr. Young, married to one of the Carlyles of Bridekirk, is celebrated thus :—

> " Of virtue, wit, grace, truth, love, pietie,
> This woman in hyr tyme had store ;
> On small meanes she aye held grit honestie,
> And in reward has endless glore."

The Rev. Dr. Henry Duncan, minister of the parish, and afterwards minister of the Free Church, Ruthwell, is commemorated by a tombstone. He died 19th February, 1846. (See *ante.*)

Stuart Lewis, the mendicant bard, rests in Ruthwell Churchyard. He is entitled to commemoration as the author of " O'er the muir amang the heather," a song which long retained popularity. Lewis died at Ruthwell, in September, 1818, at the age of sixty-two.

PARISH OF SANQUHAR.

In the parish churchyard the Rev. Thomas Ballantine, minister of the associate congregation of Sanquhar, is celebrated thus :—

> " This sacred herald whose sweet mouth
> Spread gospel truth abroad,
> Like Timothy, was but a youth,
> And yet a man of God.

> " Soon did the young yet ready scribe
> A friend of Christ appear,
> And was among the associate tribe
> A covenanted seer.

> "He for y$_e$ Reformation cause
>   Contending for renown
> Among that noted number was
>   The first that gained the crown.
>
> "His zealous soul with hasty pace
>   Did mortal life despise
> To feed the lambs around y^e place
>   Where now his body lies."

Mr. Ballantine was the first of the Associate ministers who died after the event of the Secession. He died in 1741.

William Halliday, teacher, who died in 1836, aged nineteen, is celebrated thus:—

> "Whate'er might be his faults, the youth here laid
> Ungrudgingly the debt of nature paid,
> Without a sigh resign'd what God him gave,
> Convinc'd of brighter worlds beyond the grave."

A shepherd who died in 1830 has the following epitaph:—

> Pastoral brethren, shed the tribute tear
> On him you lov'd, to social virtue dear;
> Hope views him still to brighter regions gone,
> 'Mong Christ's redeemèd folk around the throne."

PARISH OF TINWALD.

In Trailflat Churchyard four altar-stones commemorate members of the families of Paterson, Rogerson, and Mounsey, related by intermarriage, and which severally produced William Paterson, founder of the Bank of England, and Dr. James Mounsey, and Dr. John Rogerson, physicians at the Russian Court. The inscriptions follow:—

"In memory of Margaret Wilkin, spouse to James Paterson in Skipmyre, who died February, 1694; also James Paterson in Skipmyre, who died May 29, 1722, aged 101 years; also Adam Paterson, his son, who died May 29, 1737, aged seventy-one years."

"Here lyes James Paterson, son to John Paterson, in Skipmire, who deceased the 5th of April, 1694; and John and William Paterson."

"Here lyes the corpse of John Mounsey, in Shieldhill, son to William Mounsey, in Skipmyre, who departed this life the 2nd of Aprill, 1751, aged twenty-three years. *Memento mori.*"

"In memory of John Paterson, in Skipmyre, who died February 7th, 1694.

"Also William Mounsey, in Skipmire, who died April 23, 1751, aged sixty-three years; also Margaret Rogerson, his spouse, who died Nov. 19, 1760, aged sixty-five years.

"Also Alexr. Mounsey, their son, who died July 31, 1785, aged fifty-six years; also Jean Rogerson, his spouse, who died May 3, 1820, aged eighty-one years; also Samuel Mounsey, their son, who died June 9, 1797, aged twenty-six years.

"Also William, son to the said William Mounsey, who died Jan. 23, 1793, aged sixty years.

"Also William, son to the said Alexr. Mounsey, who died 22nd Decr., 1829, aged sixty-seven."

"Here lyes Jannet Paterson, lait spouse to Thomas Munsie, merchand, Skipmyre, who died the 26th day of Novr., 1698; and here lyes T. M. and A. M., their children."

"Here lyeth the body of Thomas Monsie, in Skipmyre, who departed this life August the 6th, 1711, aged fifty-five years; also here lyeth the body of Mary Steell, spouse to Thomas Mounsie, who departed this life the 23rd of May, 1747, aged sixty-three years."

"In memory of Jean White, spouse to James Mounsey, in Skipmyre, who died June 21, 1820, aged forty-three years; also James, their son, who died Augt. 6, 1812, aged two years; also William, their son, who died 31 March, 1825, aged fourteen years; also James, their son, who died 2 June, 1825, aged twelve years; also the said James Mounsey, who died 10th March, 1635, aged fifty-five years. Also interred here, John Mounsey, M.D., his son, who died in Manchester, 26 October, 1837, aged twenty-nine years."

William Paterson, founder of the Bank of England, and projector of the Darien expedition, was born at Skipmyre, in March or April, 1655, but his father's Christian name has not been absolutely ascertained.

In an interesting publication the late Mr. William Pagan of Clayton, author of "Road Reform," has collected some important data to establish that John Paterson, in Skipmyre, and his wife, Bethia Paterson, were the banker's parents. These are not mentioned on the tombstones.*

PARISH OF TORTHORWALD.

In this churchyard rest the remains of the Rev. John Macmurdo, minister of the parish, locally celebrated for his piety and his patriotism. During the Rebellion of 1715 he led out the men of his parish as volunteers in support of the Government. According to tradition his bearing was eminently soldier-like; in giving the word of command he expressed himself with military precision. He was eminently pious, spending whole nights in devotion. The epitaph on his tomb, lately repaired by his descendants, proceeds thus :—

"Hic requiescat D: Joa: M'Murdo, V. D. M. grande quondam ecclesiæ ornamentum, ac hujus parochiæ, per XVIII. annos, fidelissimus pastor. Vir solidæ eruditionis, sinceræ pietatis, illibati candoris; vitæ innocentiâ, morumque suavitate, omnibus charus; in verbo divino prædicando præpotens ac mellifluus, Boanerges alter, alter Barnabas. Obiit XIX. Nov., A.D. MDCCXX., Ætatis XXXIX. Monumentum hoc mœrens ejus conjux, Alisa Chartres, curavit."

Mr. Macmurdo studied at Edinburgh College, and was ordained at Torthorwald in 1702. He died 19th November, 1720, in the thirty-ninth year of his age, and twelfth of his ministry. The Rev. Dr. Henry Duncan, of Ruthwell, was his great-grandson.

A farmer and his wife are on their gravestone thus described :—

> "They aimed at no titles,
> But honest and unstained characters;
> None of them were rich,
> Neither were they poor.

---

* "The Birthplace and Parentage of William Paterson," by William Pagan, F.S.A. Scot. Edinburgh, 1865, 12mo.

"But their own industry, by the divine blessing, supplied them abundantly with the necessaries of life, and with something also to relieve the distressed."

PARISH OF TUNDERGARTH.

Seven erect stones on the farm of Whiteholm are popularly known as the "seven brethren." Bones are frequently dug up in the vicinity.

In the churchyard a tombstone denotes the resting-place of the Rev. William Thomson, an eccentric minister of the parish, ordained 1691; demitted April, 1716. In the pulpit, on a Communion Sunday, he began a discourse by relating that he had dreamed that he had seen the prince of darkness, and had asked him where he was going; he replied, to Tundergarth Kirk, where he expected to find some prey. "I told him," proceeded Mr. Thomson, "that he suldna get ane except John o' Kepel-foot, and if he would lead my peats he suldna hae him either."

PARISH OF TYNRON.

On Appin Hill in this parish a cairn now invisible was believed to cover the remains of a Pictish king.

In the churchyard a tombstone commemorates William Smith, a youth of eighteen, "who was shot at the bridge end of Moniaive by command of Sir Robert Lawrie, Laird of Maxwelton, and John Douglas of Stenhouse, May, 1685." His epitaph follows:—

> "I, William Smith, now here do ly,
> Once martyred for Christ's verity.
> Douglas of Stenhouse, Lawrie of Maxwelton,
> Caused cornet Baillie give me martyrdom;
> What cruelty they to my corpse then used,
> Living may judge; me burial they refused."

PARISH OF WAMPHRAY.

In Wamphray Churchyard a tombstone celebrates Dr. John Rogerson, who was for many years first physician to the Empress Catharine of Russia and her successors. Dr. Rogerson was son of Samuel Rogerson, tenant at Lochbrow, in the parish of Johnstone. Having qualified himself as a medical practitioner, he proceeded to St. Petersburg, where he became physician to the Court. After a residence in Russia of forty years he returned to Dumfriesshire, where he purchased large estates, and established his residence at Dumcrieff, in Annandale. He died in 1823 at the age of seventy-four. His estates passed to Lord Rollo, who married his daughter and heiress.

On tombstones in Wamphray Churchyard are the following inscriptions:—

"O mortal man look here and see,
As we are now
Thou must soon be,
Thy body in the ground
Till the last day
The trumpet sound."

"Securely laid
In this thy last retreat,
Unheeded o'er thy silent dust
The storms of life shall beat."

"Weep not for me, dear children, when my grave you see,
In moderation let your sorrows be;
And say with Job, the Lord who is my stay
In mercy gives, in mercy takes away."

"Underneath this stone
His earthly part doth ly;
His soul it's hop'd
Ascended is on high.

> He resigned this world
> In peace and love,
> To meet sweet Jesus Christ
> In heaven above."

PARISH OF WESTERKIRK.

On Langholm Hill an elegant obelisk commemorates Sir John Malcolm, the eminent diplomatist. This distinguished individual was born on the 2nd May, 1769, on the farm of Burnfoot, near Langholm. In 1782 he went to India as a cadet. Applying himself to the study of languages, he attracted the notice of Lord Cornwallis, who appointed him Persian interpreter to a body of British troops in the service of a native prince. In 1795 he distinguished himself at the taking of the Cape of Good Hope; he obtained a captain's commission in 1797. On the surrender of Seringapatam he was appointed joint secretary to the commissioners for settling the government of Mysore. In 1801 he became private secretary to the Governor-General. In 1803 he was appointed resident with the Rajah of Mysore, and in 1805 chief agent of the Governor-General. Having carried out two important embassies in Persia he returned to England in 1812, when he received the honour of knighthood. In 1815 he published his "History of Persia" in two quarto volumes. Returning to India in 1817 he commanded the third division of the army with the rank of Brigadier-General; he greatly distinguished himself in the decisive battle of Mehidpoor. In 1822 he returned to Britain with the rank of Major-General, when, in appreciation of his services, the Directors of the East India Company granted him a pension of £1,000 a year. In 1827 he was appointed Governor of Bombay. In 1831 he returned to Britain and was elected M.P. for Launceston. He died on the 31st May, 1833. Shortly before his death he published a work on the Government of India. His "Life of Robert Lord Clive," in three octavo volumes, appeared posthumously. Sir John Malcolm has a monument in Westminster Abbey, and a statue by Chantrey at Bombay. On the day preceding his death he attended a meeting in London on behalf of the movement to secure the mansion of Abbotsford to the family of Sir Walter Scott.

In the churchyard a plain gravestone commemorates the father of Thomas Telford, the eminent civil engineer, a native of the parish. This stone was fashioned and engraved by the great engineer when he was apprenticed to a stone-mason in the district.

KIRKCUDBRIGHTSHIRE.

PARISH OF ANWORTH.

A granite obelisk fifty-six feet in height, reared in 1839, celebrates Samuel Rutherford, the distinguished Presbyterian divine. Son of a farmer, Rutherford was born at Nisbet, Roxburghshire, about 1600. He was educated at the University of Edinburgh, and was, in 1623, elected Regent of Humanity in Edinburgh College. In 1627 he was ordained minister of Anworth. He was summoned before the Court of High Commission in 1630, but the diet was deserted. In 1636 he was deprived by the Bishop of Galloway for nonconformity, and sentenced to confine himself to the city of Aberdeen. At Aberdeen he remained eighteen months; he there wrote the greater number of his celebrated letters. In 1638 he returned to Anworth; he was a member of the General Assembly of that year. Soon after he was appointed Professor of Divinity in the University of St. Andrews, and colleague of Mr. Robert Blair, minister of that city. In 1643 he was chosen one of the commissioners from the Church of Scotland to the Assembly of Divines at Westminster; he remained in London four years. He repeatedly preached before Parliament. In 1649 he was appointed Principal of the New College, St. Andrews. At the Restoration he was selected as an object of persecution. His "Lex Rex," a work published in reply to a defence of absolute monarchy, by the Bishop of Ross, was ordered to be burnt by the common executioner, both at Edinburgh and St. Andrews. He was deprived of his offices, and summoned to appear before Parliament on a charge of high treason, a summons he did not live to obey. After a period of feeble health, he died at St. Andrews on the 19th March, 1661. His remains were interred in the churchyard of the cathedral. Rutherford's works are chiefly controversial, and are especially suited to the times in which he lived. His volume of letters, published posthumously, has been frequently reprinted, and is held in esteem.

In Anworth Churchyard a tombstone commemorates John Bell, heir of Whiteside, who for his adherence to Presbyterianism was with four others shot, by command of Sir Robert Grierson, on Kirkconnel-muir in 1685. On his tombstone are these lines:—

> "This monument shall tell posterity
> That blessed Bell of Whitesyde here doth lye,
> Who at command of bloody Lag was shot,
> A murder strange, which should not be forgot.
> Douglas of Morton did him quarters give,
> Yet cruel Lag would not let him survive.
> This martyr sought some time to recommend
> His soul to God before his days should end.
> The tyrant said, What, dev'l you've pray'd enough
> This long seven years on mountain and in cleuch;
> And instantly caused him with other four
> Be shot to death upon Kirkconnel Moor:
> So thus did end the lives of these dear saints,
> For their adherence to the covenants."

According to Wodrow, Bell was only son of a gentlewoman, heiress of Whiteside, who after his father's death married the Viscount Kenmure. He had been forfeited in 1680, in consequence of his having fought at Bothwell Bridge. Having been surprised by Grierson on Kirkconnel-muir, he and his companions were shot without being allowed time for prayer.

PARISH OF BALMACLELLAN.

In the parish churchyard a tombstone commemorates Robert Grierson, who was slain by command of Colonel James Douglas, at Inglistoun, parish of Glencairn, in 1685. His epitaph is as follows:—

> "This monument to passengers shall cry,
> That godly Grierson under it doth ly,
> Betray'd by knavish Watson to his foes,
> Which made this martyr's days by murder close.
> If ye would know the nature of his crime,
> Then read the story of that killing time,
> When Babel's brats, with hellish plot conceal'd,
> Design'd to make our earth their hunting-field.
> Here one of five at once were laid in dust,
> To gratify Rome's execrable lust.
> If carabines, with molten bullets could
> Have reach'd their souls, these mighty Nimrods would
> Them have cut off; for here could no request
> Three minutes get to pray for future rest."

A tombstone in the churchyard thus commemorates Robert Paterson, the celebrated "Old Mortality:"—

"To the memory of Robert Paterson, stone engraver, well known as ' Old Mortality,' who died at Bankend, of Caerlaverock, 14th Feb., 1801, aged eighty-eight. Also of Elizabeth Gray, his spouse, who died at Balmaclellan village, 5th May, 1785, aged fifty-nine. Also of Robert, their son, who died 30th April, 1846, aged ninety. Also of Agnes M'Knight, his spouse, who died 5th August, 1818. Also of John, their son, who died 29 Jan., 1810, aged thirteen. Also of Alexander, who died at Wakefield, 26th Oct., 1837, aged forty-two. Also of Robert, their son, who died at Liverpool, 3rd Feb., 1865, aged sixty-five. Erected by Thomas Paterson, 1855."

Thomas Paterson, who reared this memorial stone, married Jane Murray, grand-niece of the Rev. Dr. Alexander Murray, the celebrated linguist.

PARISH OF BALMAGHIE.

In the churchyard two martyrs are commemorated. Their gravestone is thus inscribed:—

PARISH OF CARSPHAIRN.

"Here lyes David Halliday, portioner of Mayfield, who was shot upon the 21st of Feb., 1685; and David Halliday, once in Glenap, who was likewise shot upon the 11th July, 1685, for their adherence to the principles of Scotland's Covenanted Reformation.

> Beneath this stone two David Hallidays
> Doe lie, whose souls now sing their Master's praise.
> To know, if curious passengers desire,
> For what, by whom, and how they did expire,
> They did oppose this nation's perjury;
> Nor could they join with lordly prelacy.
> Indulging favours from Christ's enemies
> Quenched not their zeal. This monument then cries,
> Those were the causes, not to be forgot,
> Why they by Lag so wickedly were shot.
> One name, one cause, one grave, one heaven do tie
> Their souls to that one God eternally."

PARISH OF BORGUE.

A tombstone in the churchyard denotes the grave of Robert Macquae, shot by Colonel Douglas in 1685 for attending conventicles.

William Nicholson, author of the "Brownie of Blednoch," and other popular ballads, is interred at Borgue: he died on the 16th May, 1849.

PARISH OF CARSPHAIRN.

A monument on the moor of Crossgellioch commemorates three Covenanters, Joseph Wilson, John Jamieson, and John Humphrey, shot by Claverhouse in 1685. The monument was reared in 1827; in digging for its foundation the workmen discovered the bodies of the sufferers preserved in the moss, clad in their hosen, coats, and bonnets, just as they had fallen.

PARISH OF CROSSMICHAEL.

A tombstone in the churchyard commemorates the Rev. Nathaniel M'Kie, minister of the parish. Son of William M'Kie, minister of Balmaghie, he was licensed in 1737, and ordained at Crossmichael in 1739; he died 26th January, 1781, in his sixty-sixth year, and forty-second of his ministry. Mr. M'Kie was noted for his pulpit eccentricities. Beginning one Sunday morning an exposition in Exodus, he proceeded thus :—" 'And the Lord said unto Moses,' —sneck that door; I'm thinking if ye had to sit beside the door yoursel' ye wadna be sae ready leaving it open. It was just beside that door that Yedam Tamson the bellman gat his death o' cauld; and I'm sure, honest man, he didna let it stay muckle open. 'And the Lord said unto Moses,'—I see a man aneath that laft wi' his hat on. I'm sure ye're clear o' the soogh o' the door. Keep aff yer bannat, Tammas, and if yer bare pow be cauld, ye maun just get a grey worstit wig like mysel'; they are no sae dear—plenty o' them at Rob Gillespie's for tenpence."

PARISH OF DALRY.

A monument celebrates the Rev. William Boyd, a distinguished minister of the parish. Mr. Boyd studied at the University of Glasgow about 1685, and obtained licence abroad. Joining the Cameronians he proceeded to Holland, where he secured the friendship of William, Prince of Orange, whom he accompanied to Britain, and whose accession to the throne he proclaimed at the

Cross of Glasgow. In 1690 he was ordained minister of Dalry. He died in April, 1741, in his eighty-third year, and fifty-first of his ministry. On his tombstone is the following inscription :—

" Rev. Dom. Gul. Boyd, ecclesiam hanc periclitantem, pene dejectam, zelo fervititi propugnavit. Pro viribus sustinuit, eandem vere victricem atque stabilitam. Piatatæ, probitatæ ornavit. Doctrina, diligentia nutrivit. Huic operi, quinquaginta per annos, apud Dalry pastor, summa solertia incubuit. Laus vivum, luctus mortuum sequebantur. Anno 1741, a Christo nato : ætatis suæ 83 obiit."

PARISH OF GIRTHON.

A vault under the old church constitutes the burying-place of Mr. Murray, of Broughton, proprietor of the whole parish. In this vault is interred Robert Lennox, of Drumnick, who suffered for his adherence to the Covenant; he is commemorated thus :—

" Within this tomb lyes the corps of Robert Lenox, some time in Irelandtown, who was shot to death by Grier of Lagg, in the parish of Toungland, for his adherence to Scotland's Reformation Covenants, National Covenants, National and Solemn League, 1685."

" On the 18th December, 1684," writes Mr. M'Dowall, in his History of Dumfries, " Claverhouse surprised six Covenanters wandering destitute on the banks of the Dee at Auchencloy. Four of them, Robert Fergusson, John M'Michan, Robert Stewart, son to Major Stewart, of Ardoch, and John Grierson, were, after brief warning, left lifeless on the sward. Three of the bodies were carried away by their friends and buried at Dalry, which so irritated Claverhouse that the remains were disinterred, and were publicly exposed, after which they were recommitted to the grave. The two other captives, William Hunter and Robert Smith, were carried to Kirkcudbright, and after the semblance of a trial were hanged, and then beheaded." Three of the sufferers are commemorated by tombstones near the scene of their death. The tombstone of Robert Fergusson is inscribed as follows :—

"Memento Mori. Here lies Robert Fergusson, who was surprised and instantly shot to death in this place, by Graham of Claverhouse, for his adherence to Scotland's Reformation Covenants, National and Solemn League, 1684."

On the gravestone of Robert Stewart and John Grierson are these lines :—

"Behold! behold! a stone here's forced to cry,
Come, see two martyrs under me that ly;
At water of Dee, who slain were by the hand
Of cruel Claverhouse and's bloody band :
No sooner had he done this horrid thing,
But's forc'd to say, *Stewart's soul in heaven doth sing.*
Yet strange his rage pursu'd ev'n such when dead,
And in the tombs of their ancestors laid ;
Causing their corpses be rais'd out of the same
Discharging in churchyard to bury them.
All this they did, because they would not abjure
Our covenants and reformation pure;
Because like faithful martyrs for to die
They rather chose than treacherously comply
With cursed Prelacy, the nation's bane,
And with indulgency, our church's stain.
Perjur'd intelligencers were so rife,
Show'd their curs'd loyalty, to take their life."

PARISH OF KELLS.

Three victims of the Stuart persecutions are commemorated in the parish churchyard. These inscriptions are on their tombstones :—

"Here lyes the corps of Roger Gordon of Largmore, who dyed March, 1662, aged seventy-two years, and of John Gordon, his grandchild, who dyed January, 1667, of his wounds got at Pentland, in defence of the covenanted Reformation."

"Here lyes Adam M'Qwhan, who being sick of a fever was taken

PARISH OF KELLS.

out of his bed and carried to Newton of Galloway, and the next day most cruelly and unjustly shot to death by the command of Lieutenant-General James Douglas, brother to the Duke of Queensberry, for his adherence to Scotland's Reformation Covenants, and National Solemn League, 1685."

M'Qwhan's monument was restored in 1832, chiefly through the efforts of the Rev. Dr. Maitland, minister of the parish.

Metrical epitaphs commemorate two ministers of the parish, father and son. The Rev. John Gillespie was tutor at Lundin, Fifeshire. He was ordained minister of Kells, 29th March, 1764, and died 29th April, 1806, in his seventy-sixth year, and forty-third of his ministry, His tombstone presents the following elegy :—

"Beneath that sod where sad remembrance weeps,
The best of fathers, friends, and husbands sleeps;
Warm, friendly, generous, upright, and sincere,
In manners simple, as in judgment clear;
A minister of Christ, who faithful taught
The good in practice, the sublime in thought,
Kind as his heart, his melting accents flowed,
And led in tears the sinner to his God;
And while religion's lovely charms he drew,
His own good life proved all the picture true.
Mild was his death, as mild his life had been,
And his best lesson was his dying scene."

The Rev. William Gillespie, eldest son of the preceding, was licensed in 1798, and ordained assistant and successor to his father in 1800. He died 15th October, 1825, in his fiftieth year, and twenty-sixth of his ministry. An elegant poet, he published "The Progress of Refinement: an Allegorical Poem," 1805, 8vo, and "Consolation, with other Poems," 1815, 12mo. These lines are on his tombstone :—

"A sudden call from life's unclouded scene!
But when the Christian dies, 'tis endless gain.
A duteous son, a brother kind and dear,
A loving husband, and a friend sincere,
Rests by his parent's dust; gentle and good,
He dwelt amid his native solitude.
A faithful pastor, eloquent in truth,
Pointing the gospel path to age and youth;

His chief delight to calm affliction's sigh,
And soothe the bed of pain and poverty.
O genius, wit, and science, mourn his doom,
And deck with cypress leaves the poet's tomb;
And memory weeps! But Hope, with heavenly voice,
Points the perfections of immortal joys."

John Murray, gamekeeper to Viscount Kenmure, a provincial humorist, is celebrated by the following epitaph:—

"Ah, John, what changes since I saw you last!
Thy fishing and thy shooting days are past.
Bagpipes and hautboy thou canst sound no more;
Thy nods, grimaces, winks, and pranks are o'er;
Thy harmless, queerish, incoherent talk,
Thy wild vivacity, and trudging walk
Will soon be quite forgotten. Thy joys on earth—
A snuff, a glass, riddles, and noisy mirth—
Are vanished all, yet blest I hope thou art,
For in thy station weel thou played thy part.
                                    "A.D. 1777."

John was a noted angler. He caught with the fly a pike weighing forty-two pounds, the skeleton of which is preserved in Kenmure Castle. Elated by his achievement, John walked into the dining-room holding the pike's head over his shoulder, while the tail dragged on the floor. Stepping up to his master, he threw down the fish before him, saying, "You may catch the next yoursel', my lord." No such pike has before or since been caught in any part of Britain.

A married woman who died young in 1771 is commemorated thus:—

"Her youthful bloom fair as the morning rose,
Sleeps in the silent dust of soft repose.
Great was her soul. Integrity of life
Adorned the maid and dignified the wife.
And now beyond where stars and planets shine,
She dwells in light and love and joys divine.
Suns may decay, and stars may lose their light,
And falling worlds sink in eternal night,
Whilst through eternity she wafts her way,
And basks in beams of everlasting day."

The following inscriptions are from Kells Churchyard :—

> " Death's steps are swift,
> And yet no noise maks
> His hand unseen, and yet
> Most surely taks."

> " Here lyes the corps of Agnes Herries,
> Spouse of Robert Corion, also Mary,
> Agnes, Marion, Margaret, at one birth,
> Robert, Andrew, James, at one birth."

PARISH OF KELTON.

In the parish churchyard a tombstone celebrates Joseph Train, an ingenious antiquary, and the well-known correspondent of Sir Walter Scott. He was born at Sorn, of humble parents. Having been balloted for the Ayrshire Militia, he served in the ranks of that corps from 1799 to 1802. Through the influence of Sir David Blair, colonel of the regiment, who perceived his literary tastes, he obtained an appointment in the excise. He ultimately attained the rank of supervisor. A strong turn for antiquarian research brought him under the notice of Sir Walter Scott, who encouraged his communications; no caterer of antiquities or traditional stories proved half so useful to the illustrious novelist. On materials supplied by Train, Scott founded his novels of " Guy Mannering," " Redgauntlet," " Old Mortality," " The Surgeon's Daughter," and " Peveril of the Peak." He was also greatly indebted to Train for the traditionary matter which has been embodied in " The Lord of the Isles." Train published " Strains of the Mountain Muse," a volume of respectable poetry, a " History of the Isle of Man," and other works. He died at Lochvale, Castle Douglas, on the 7th December, 1852.

The Rev. John McClellan, minister of Kelton, who died on the 6th June, 1840, and his brother, Captain Thomas McClellan,

Deputy Judge Advocate-General in India, who died in 1845, are believed to have been the last representatives of the Earls of Kirkcudbright.

These rhymes are from tombstones in Kelton Churchyard:—

> "Our tender father we regret,
> Our loving brother dear,
> We hope they're gone to endless bliss,
> And left their sorrows here."

> "Rest, pilgrim, rest,
> Thy warfare here is o'er,
> The breast too long by conflicts torn
> Is hushed to throb no more."

At Kirkmirren, a retired churchyard on the banks of the Dee, was the burial-place of the Maclellans of Auchlane, a branch of the noble House of Kirkcudbright.

PARISH OF KIRKCUDBRIGHT.

In an aisle of the church a monument commemorates Sir Thomas MacLellan, of Bombie, who died 1607, an ancestor of the Earls of Kirkcudbright; also his wife, Grissel Maxwell, daughter of John, Lord Herries. The tomb is inscribed thus:—

> "Hic situs est Dominus T. Mc Clellanus, et uxor
> D. Grissel Maxwell; marmor utrumque tenet.
> His genitus R. D. Kirkcudbrius ecce sepulchrum
> Posuit hoc, chari patris amore sui."

In the churchyard is thus commemorated Mrs. Marion MacNaught, wife of Provost Fullerton, a woman of eminent piety, to whom Mr. Samuel Rutherford addressed several of his "Letters:"—

> "Mareon McNaught, sister to John McNaught, of Kilquhanatie, an ancient and honourable baron, and spouse to William Fullerton, Provest of Kirkcudbright, died April, 1643; age fifty-eight.

> "Sexum animis, pietate genus, generosa locumque
> Virtute exsuperans, conditur hoc tumulo."

William Hunter and Robert Smith, two of the six Covenanters captured by Graham of Claverhouse, at Auchencloy, were executed at Kirkcudbright, and interred in this churchyard. A tombstone placed on their graves was thus inscribed:—

> "This monument shall show posterity
> Two headless martyrs under it do ly,
> By bloody Graham were taken and surpris'd
> Brought to this town, and afterwards were seiz'd;
> By unjust law were sentenced to die,
> Them first they hang'd, then headed cruelly.
> Captain Douglas, Bruce, Graham of Claverhouse,
> Were those that caused them to be handled thus:
> And when they were unto the gibbet come,
> To stop their speech, they did beat up the drum,
> And all because they would not comply
> With Indulgence, and bloody Prelacy.
> In face of cruel Bruce, Douglas, and Graham,
> They did maintain, *that Christ was Lord supreme;*
> And boldly owned both the covenants,
> At Kirkcudbright thus ended these two saints."

John Halkin, another Covenanter, who was also tried and executed in Kirkcudbright, is interred in the churchyard. The inscription on his tombstone reads thus:—

"Here lyes John Halkine, who was wounded in his taking and by unjust law sentenced to be hanged. All this was done by Captain Douglas for his adherence to Scotland's Reformation Covenants national and solemn league 1685."

A tombstone in memory of Andrew Ewart bears these lines:—

> "Welcome soft bed, my sweet repose,
> And so for Christ from Heaven arose;
> Welcome sweet sleep from to awake
> Of endless joys for to partake;
> Welcome fair night, thy fairest morrow
> Drives from mine eyes eternal sorrow;

z

> Welcome soft bed, sweet sleep, fair night to me,
> Thrice welcome Christ who has sanctified you three.
>
> Repent in time, your lives amend,
> That in Christ Jesus ye a' may end."

A stone with the date 1626 is thus inscribed :—

> " By faith in Christ I lived and died,
> In hope have laid my body down;
> My soul is ascended to adore
> The Saviour in celestial glore,
> With whom she sal cum and recal
> Those corps agane out of her grave,
> And there in joy triumphantlie
> Derive delight perpetual."

A plain tombstone marks the grave of William Marshall, tinker, who died in 1792, at the remarkable age of one hundred and twenty.

In Galtway Churchyard a monument commemorates Thomas Lidderdale, of St. Mary's Isle, who died on the 10th February, 1687. St. Mary's Isle is now a seat of the Earl of Selkirk.

PARISH OF KIRKMABRECK.

A handsome granite pillar denotes the grave of Dr. Thomas Brown, the celebrated metaphysician. Dr. Brown was born in Kirkmabreck manse, on the 9th January, 1778; his father and grandfather were ministers of the parish. His father dying when he was eighteen months old, his upbringing devolved upon his mother, a woman of great worth and varied accomplishments. In 1792 he entered the University of Edinburgh, where he proved an expert student in ethical and medical science. In 1803 he passed as M.D., when he was honoured with high encomiums from Dr. Gregory. Continuing his philosophical pursuits, he was in session 1808-9 appointed to conduct the Moral Philosophy class of Professor Dugald Stewart. In the year following he was constituted joint professor. In 1814 he published his poem "The Paradise of Coquettes," which was followed by other volumes of poetry. Suffering weak health, he took up his residence at Brompton in 1819, but he was not benefited by the change; he died on the 2nd April, 1820. His remains were, according to his wish, interred beside those of his father and mother in Kirkmabreck Churchyard. Dr. Brown's verses are disfigured by morbid sentiment and occasional obscurities. As a philosopher he was one of the most original thinkers which his country has produced.

Tombstones commemorate the Rev. Samuel Brown, who died 25th July, 1779, aged fifty-five; and the Rev. Samuel Brown, who died 17th May, 1751, aged seventy-four, both ministers of the parish,—father and grandfather of the metaphysician.

In Kirkdale Churchyard is the burial-place of the ancient family of M'Culloch, of Barholm. Here also is the family vault of the Hannays of Kirkdale and Mochrum.

PARISH OF KIRKPATRICK-IRONGRAY.

On a wooded eminence about 100 yards from the parish church-yard are the graves of two martyrs for the covenant. Their tombstone is inscribed thus :—

"Here lyes Edward Gordon and Alexander McCubin, Martyrs. Hanged without law by Lagg and Cap. Bruce for adhering to the Word of God, Christ's kingly government in his house, and the covenanted work of Reformation against tyranny, perjury and prelacy. Rev. 12. 11. March 3, 1685.

> "At Lagg and bloody Bruce command,
> We were hung up by hellish hand;
> And thus, their furious rage to stay,
> We died at Kirk of Irongray;
> Here now, in peace, sweet rest we take,
> Once murder'd for religion's sake."

Gordon and McCubin were executed on the spot where they are buried, with a view no doubt to strike terror among the inhabitants of a parish especially devoted to Presbyterianism.

In the churchyard a monumental pillar, reared by Sir Walter Scott, commemorates Helen Walker, the prototype of Jeanie Deans, whose integrity and tenderness are in his "Heart of Mid-Lothian" so admirably portrayed by that great novelist. The inscription is as follows:—

"This stone was erected by the author of 'Waverley' to the memory of Helen Walker, who died in the year of God 1791. This humble individual practised in real life the virtues with which fiction invested the imaginary character of Jeanie Deans. Refusing the slightest departure from veracity, even to save the life of a sister, she nevertheless showed her kindness and fortitude in rescuing her from the severity of the law, at the expense of personal exertions which the time rendered as difficult as the motive was laudable. Respect the grave of poverty when combined with the love of truth and dear affection."

PARISH OF MINNIGAFF.

A granite column at Dunkitterick commemorates the Rev. Dr. Alexander Murray, the celebrated Oriental scholar. Dr. Murray was son a shepherd in the district. He was born on the 22nd October, 1775. The indigent circumstances of his parents prevented his being early sent to school, yet in his eighth year his love of reading and wonderful memory were celebrated in his native glen. When in his fourteenth year he became a pupil in the parish school, his extraordinary power of acquiring languages excited the admiration of his teacher. Through the good offices of the parish minister he was enabled to attend the University of Edinburgh. In 1806 he was ordained assistant and successor in the parish of Urr, and six years afterwards was appointed to the chair of Oriental Languages in Edinburgh College. He had scarcely completed the duties of one session when he was cut off after a short illness. He died 15th April, 1813, aged thirty-seven. His remains were consigned to the Greyfriars Churchyard. He published "Outlines of Oriental Philology," and left in MS. a "History of European Languages," which was published posthumously.

In the Glen of Trool a stone fence encloses the burial-place of James and Robert Dun, Alexander McAulay, John M'Lude, and Thomas and John Stevenson, who were killed by a party of dragoons in 1685 while engaged in worship on the hill-side.

In the parish churchyard an elegant monument celebrates Lieut.-General Sir William Stewart, K.C.B. This distinguished officer was second son of John, Earl of Galloway. He served in seventeen campaigns in the West Indies, Egypt, and various parts of Europe. In the expedition to Copenhagen he commanded the troops embarked with Lord Nelson; he afterwards commanded the second division of the Peninsular army. In impaired health he retired to Cumloden Cottage in this parish, where he died on the 7th January, 1827.

Tombstones in the churchyard exhibit these quaint rhymes,—

> "This grave is but a fining pot
> Unto belivers' aise,*
> For when the soul hath lost its dross
> It like the sun shall rise."

> "To serve her Saviour was her only care,
> And for His home her young heart to prepare,
> And now that Saviour in a voice of love
> Hath called her spirit to that home above."

> "Death like an overflowing stream
> Sweeps us away. Our life's a dream,
> An empty tale, a morning flower,
> Cut down and withered in an hour."

---

* Ashes.

PARISH OF NEW ABBEY.

In this parish is situated Sweetheart Abbey, founded in 1275, and planted with Cistercian monks. The foundress was Devorgilla, daughter of Alan, Lord of Galloway, wife of John Baliol, and mother of John Baliol, King of Scotland. Her husband died in 1268, and was laid beside the dust of his ancestors in Teesdale; but Devorgilla, in token of her affection, caused his heart to be embalmed, and in a silver-bound ivory casket to be preserved beside her till the erection of this Abbey constituted a shrine for its reception. The casket was built into the wall over the high altar, where it remained till Devorgilla's own death. She died in 1289, and was buried in the Abbey. The casket was now placed upon her bosom; hence the name of *Dulce Cor*, or "Sweetheart" which was given to the structure. On Devorgilla's tomb was engraved the following epitaph, composed by Hugh de Burgh, prior of Lanercost:—

"In Dervorvilla moritur sensata Sibilla;
Cum Marthaque pia, comptemplativa Maria;
Da Dervorvillam requie, Rex summe, potiri,
Quam tegit iste lapis, cor pariterque viri."

The ground under the central tower has long been used as a place of sepulture. On the oldest tombstone is the inscription "Joani Broun de Landensis," with the date "IMDCXIII." Built into a comparatively modern wall are two tablets, one with the initials "R. B.;" the other with the words "Heir lyes Gauvine Broune of Bishoptone, 1683." Gilbert Brown, the prototype of Scott's abbot of St. Marie's, was the last who bore rule over the monks of this abbey; the family exercised great influence in the district. In the churchyard a stone, rudely carved, celebrates (according to popular belief) William Gladstanes, an ecclesiastic. The inscription is as follows:—

"M
W   G
Q   Quare lapis levis sub
     Opaci, Tegmine Saxi?
     In viscere telluris,
R   Aurea Gemma latet.
          1660."

On Glen Hill, 400 feet above the level of the sea, a granite column, fifty feet in height, commemorates the battle of Waterloo; it was reared soon after the event.

PARISH OF RERRICK.

In this parish is situated near the bank of the Solway, the interesting ruin of Dundrennan Abbey, a religious house founded by Fergus, Lord of Galloway, in 1142, and planted with Cistercian monks.* Among the ancient monuments the most remarkable is the tomb of Alan, Lord of Galloway, and Constable of Scotland, who was here buried in 1233. His figure is represented in *alto relievo* cross-legged, and in chain-armour, with a buff coat, and belts across the shoulders and waist. Within the chapter-house an abbot is represented in his canonicals.

The late Honourable Thomas Maitland, a judge, by the title of Lord Dundrennan, who died in 1851, is interred in the Abbey Churchyard.

On tombstones in Dundrennan Churchyard are these inscriptions:—

"Farewell, frail world, I've seen enough of thee,
Nor do I care what thou canst say of me.
Thy smiles I court not, nor thy frowns I dread,
My heart lies easy, and at rest my head.
Grieve not for me, my wife and children dear,
For 'tis the will of God that I lie here."

* Dundrennan Abbey afforded shelter to the unfortunate Queen Mary Stuart during the last hours she spent in Scotland.

"This silent dust that sleeps beneath this sod
Whispers to youth, Prepare to meet thy God,
My sun went down ere life had reached its noon,
And what mine did, remember thine may soon.
Seek Christ, delay not, lest thy time be near,
And thou be laid my next companion here."

"He was a manly pretty boy,
His father's hope, his mother's joy:
But death did call, and he must go,
Whether his parents would or no.
Weep not for me, my parents dear,
'Tis by God's will that I lie here;
But fix your hearts on truth and love,
And then I hope we'll meet above
And still our Saviour adore,
And be far happier than before."

PARISH OF TERREGLES.

On the banks of the Nith is the ruin of Lincluden Abbey, familiar to every reader of the poetry of Burns. It was founded in 1150 by Uchtred, Lord of Galloway, as a convent for Benedictine nuns. As such it continued till the close of the fourteenth century, when it was suppressed by Archibald, Earl of Douglas, and the fabric converted by him into a collegiate church. It was now much enlarged, and a church in florid Gothic added to the pile. A quadrangular court was on the east side partly formed by a high octagon tower; this fell on the 16th February, 1851.

Among the mouldering monuments of the collegiate church, a mural tomb at the north end of the chancel commemorates Margaret, daughter of Robert III., and wife of Archibald Douglas, son of the Earl who transformed the abbey into a college. Over the tomb is sculptured a heart, the leading symbol of the House of Douglas, also three chalices placed transversely, each accompanied with a star. In the recess is the following inscription:—" Hic jacet

Dna Margarita regis Scotiæ filia quodam comtissa de Douglas Dno Gallovidiæ et vallis Annandiæ." In front of the tomb are nine heraldic shields. A figure of the countess formerly occupied the recess; it was destroyed about the beginning of the century.

Within a portion of the choir is the burying-place of the family of Maxwell of Terregles, represented by Lord Herries.

PARISH OF TONGLAND.

In the muir of Tongland a monumental pillar marks the grave of James McClymont, who along with Bell of Whiteside, Halliday of Mayfield, Lennox of Irelandtown, and another, were surprised by Sir Robert Grierson, and put to death without being allowed an interval for prayer. Bell is interred in the churchyard of Anworth.

In the parish churchyard a tombstone commemorates the Rev. Alexander Robb, incumbent of the cure, who died 26th June, 1806, in his fifty-fourth year, and ninth of his ministry. Mr. Robb was inventor of some ingenious contrivances connected with the loom. He was celebrated as a mathematician.

Of the abbey of Tongland, built in the twelfth century by Fergus, Lord of Galloway, only a small arch remains. The old tombstones have disappeared.

PARISH OF URR.

In the churchyard a tombstone celebrates the Rev. John Hepburn, a distinguished minister of the parish. Son of James Hepburn, a Morayshire farmer, he studied at King's College, Aberdeen, and was ordained at London in 1678. In 1689 he accepted the ministerial charge of this parish. Not confining himself to his parochial district, he preached in other parishes without permission of the incumbents, and was consequently suspended by the General Assembly. In 1696 he was tried before the Privy Council for declining the oaths to Government, and was sentenced to confine himself to Brechin. He was subsequently imprisoned in the Tolbooth of Edinburgh and Stirling Castle, for "seditious and delusive doctrines," and for not having dispensed the Communion for sixteen years he was deposed by the Commission of the General Assembly in 1705. He was reponed in August, 1707. He attempted to form a presbytery with another disaffected brother in 1713, but failed. During the rebellion of 1715 he raised a volunteer corps; marching at their head he displayed a large white flag inscribed, "For the Lord of hosts." He died on the 20th March, 1723. Amidst many eccentricities, Mr. Robb was an earnest preacher, a true patriot, and an excellent citizen.

WIGTONSHIRE.

PARISH OF GLASSERTON.

Within the old church at Kirkmaiden is the burial-place of the family of Sir William Maxwell, Bart., of Monreith. Several members of the family who have attained distinction are interred in the vault.

PARISH OF LESWALT.

In 1851 the inhabitants of the district erected a monument to Sir Andrew Agnew, Bart., of Lochnaw, who died in 1850. (See *ante*.) It is placed on "the Tower of Craigoch," a beautiful green hill in the form of a cone, commanding an extensive view of the Irish coast.

PARISH OF OLD LUCE.

The Abbey of Glenluce was founded in 1190, and planted with Cistercian monks. At the Reformation, Thomas Hay was appointed commendator. He subsequently acquired a portion of the abbey lands, which are still possessed by his descendants. His representative, Sir John Charles Dalrymple Hay, Bart., of Park Place, has a burying-place in the abbey churchyard.

PARISH OF PENNINGHAM.

In the new churchyard a tombstone commemorates the Rev. Robert Rowan, minister of the parish, a friend and correspondent of the historian Wodrow. Having studied at Glasgow College, he obtained licence to preach in July, 1695, and in the following year was ordained minister of Penningham. Taking deep concern in the affairs of the Church, he communicated to Wodrow minute accounts of the persecutions inflicted on his parishioners and others during the latter Stuart persecutions. He died on the 9th August, 1714, in his fifty-fifth year, and the eighteenth of his ministry.

In the old churchyard a married couple are celebrated thus :—

> "These pious saints did strive for heavenly gain,
> And now they know their labour's not in vain,
> Where they abound in everlasting glore,
> And reign with Christ their King for evermore."

PARISH OF STRANRAER.

A tablet in the parish church commemorates the Rev. Walter Laurey, minister of the parish, who died 4th May, 1742, in the forty-eighth year of his ministry. Among other boons for the benefit of his successors, he bequeathed a tomb for their use under the condition of its being kept in repair.

PARISH OF WHITHORN.

The celebrated St. Ninian, a native of Whithorn, was about the year 370 ordained at Rome Bishop of the Britons. On his return to his native place he founded a church, which he dedicated to his uncle, St. Martin of Tours. Within it he was afterwards buried. According to Bede, the church of St. Ninian was the first place of worship in the kingdom built of stone, hence its name, *Candida Casa*, or the White House. A few arches of the church remain, but there is no vestige of the founder's tomb.

By Fergus, Lord of Galloway, a priory of the Premonstratensian order was founded in the reign of David I. It contained numerous relics of St. Ninian, and was consequently the resort of pilgrims. To the priory of Whithorn Margaret, queen of James III., made a pilgrimage in 1473. James IV. also made journeys to the sepulchre of St. Ninian.

In the churchyard a gravestone, erected in 1861, is inscribed thus :—

"Cease, cease, my friends, weep not for me, but for yourselves, for there is a land of pleasure where streams of joy for ever roll, 'tis there I have my treasure and rest unto my precious soul. Tho' now my earthly course is run, my weeping relatives and friends, yet still I hope to meet each one in realms of bliss where glory reigns."

On his wife's gravestone a husband has engraved the following :—

"If you think I'm forgot, you're mistaken."

A family tombstone contains these lines :—

"The dust of friends lies mingled here we find
Sincere thro' life with honest heart and mind,
But when new moulded free from worldly toil,
Shall be transplanted to a nobler soil."

PARISH OF WIGTON.

At Windyhill, an eminence adjoining the burgh, a handsome obelisk, reared by public subscription, commemorates Margaret McLachlan, aged sixty-three, and Margaret Wilson, aged eighteen, who were on the 11th May, 1685, tied to a stake within flood mark at the mouth of the Blednoch stream, near Wigton, and there drowned for refusing to conform to episcopacy. These martyrs are also commemorated by tombstones in the churchyard. On a plain upright stone is the following legend:—

"Here lyes Margret Lachlane, who was by unjust laws sentenced to die by Lagg, surnamed Grier, Strachan, Winrame and Graham, and tyed to a stake within the flood for her adherence to Scotland's Reformation Covenants, National and Solemn League, aged sixty-three, 1685."

Margaret Wilson is on her tombstone thus commemorated:—

"Here lyes Margaret Wilson, daughter to Gilbert Wilson, in Glenvernock, who was drowned anno 1685, aged eighteen."

> "Let earth and stone still witness beare,
> Thir lys a virgine martyre here,
> Marter'd for owning Christ supreame,
> Head of His church and no more crime,
> But not abjuring Presbytery,
> And her not owning Prelacy.
> They have condemn'd by unjust law
> Of heaven or hell they stood no awe;
> Within the sea ty'd to a stake,
> She suffered for Christ Jesus' sake.
> The actors of this cruel crime,
> Was Lagg, Strachan, Winram and Graham.
> Neither young yeares, nor yet old age,
> Could stop t' fury of their rage."

Margaret McLachlan and Margaret Wilson were with Agnes Wilson, a younger sister of the latter, aged thirteen, tried at Wigton, before Sir Thomas Grierson of Lag, Colonel David Graham, brother to Claverhouse, Major Winram, Captain Strachan, and Provost Coltron, of Wigton, Commissioners appointed by James VII. for the trial of Nonconformists. The younger girl was liberated, her father having given a bond of £100 Scots that he would produce her when called on. The two others were condemned to perish by drowning.

In his "Memorials of Viscount Dundee," and a subsequent publication,* Mr. Mark Napier, an ingenious writer, has endeavoured to vindicate the upholders of the policy of James VII. from having actually carried out the sentence of death against those condemned persons. He produces a reprieve contained in the following minute of the Privy Council, bearing date, April 30, 1685 :—" The Lords of His Majesty's Privy Council doe hereby reprieve the execution of the sentence of death pronounced by the Justices against Margaret Wilson and Margaret Lauchlison untill the   day of   ; and discharges the Magistrats of Edinburgh for putting of the said sentence to execution against them, untill the aforesaid day; and recommends the said Margaret Wilson and Margaret Lauchlison to the Lords Secretaries of State to interpose with His Most Sacred Majesty for his royal remission of them." This reprieve, we would remark, is addressed to the Magistrates of Edinburgh, while a petition to the Council from Margaret McLachlan, or Lauchlison, bears that she was then " a prisoner in the Tolbooth of Wigton ;" it is a respite until a date not named ; and in respect of its finality, it is suspended on the pleasure of the king. After the amplest search in the Public Record Office, London, and in the Edinburgh Register House, no document has been found intimating the royal pardon.

On the other hand, the evidence as to the two women being, consequent on the sentence of " the Justices," actually drowned at Wigton, cannot be overcome. In the " Hind let Loose," published at London in 1687, Mr. Alexander Shields presents an engraving of the martyrdom, and uses these words: " They were tyed to stakes within floodmark till the sea came up and drowned them." In the " Short Memorial of the Society People," issued in 1690, it is stated : " Colonel or Lieut.-General James Douglas, together

---

* The titles of Mr. Napier's two works in reference to the Wigton martyrs are as follow : " Memorials and Letters illustrative of the Life and Times of John Graham, of Claverhouse, Viscount Dundee," 3 vols., Edinburgh, 1859—1862, 8vo. ; and " Case for the Crown, *in re* the Wigtown Martyrs, proved to be Myths *versus* Wodrow and Lord Macaulay, Patrick the Pedlar, and Principal Tulloch," Edinburgh, 1863. In maintaining his peculiar views Mr. Napier makes use of abusive epithets to an extent altogether unparalleled in works of a historical character.

with the Laird of Lag, and Captain Winram, most illegally condemned and most inhumanly drowned at stakes within the seamark, two women at Wigtown, viz., Margaret Lachlan, upwards of sixty years, and Margaret Wilson, about twenty years of age, the foresaid fatal year 1685."

In 1703 various pamphlets were printed in relation to the question, as to whether toleration should be granted to Episcopalians to observe their own form of worship. In a pamphlet of this year entitled "Toleration's Fence Removed," composed by James Ramsay, minister at Kelso,* these words occur : " It's well enough known that poor women were executed in the Grass mercat; sure it was not for rising in arms against the King; others of them were tyed to stakes within floodmark till the sea came up and drowned them, and this without any form or process of law." Mr. Ramsay was answered in a pamphlet of twenty pages, entitled "A Short Character of the Presbyterian Spirit." Herein the writer expresses himself vituperatively concerning the adherents of Presbytery, but while denying many things (alleged in connection with the Stuart persecutions), he admits the fact of the martyrdom at Wigton. "They generally talk," he writes, "of two women in Galloway. Drown'd they were indeed, but not *tyed to stakes within floodmark till the sea came up,* as this malicious vindicator represents. . . . And what, he adds, without any *form or process of law,* is so manifest a lye that hundreds in Galloway can testify the contrary." The author of this defence of the old policy has been accurately ascertained. He was Matthias Symson, then with his father, Andrew Symson, a printer in Edinburgh, subsequently in succession Rector of Moorby in Lincolnshire, and of Wennington, Essex, and Canon of Lincoln. He was in his thirteenth year when the women suffered, and was residing in their neighbourhood,—his father, Andrew Symson, being then minister of Kirkinner, to which parish the elder martyr belonged. On the 15th October, 1684, the minister of Kirkinner attested a list of all the inhabitants of his parish

---

* "Fasti Ecclesiæ Scoticanæ," by Hew Scott, D.D., Edinburgh, 1867, 4to., vol. i., p. 457.

PARISH OF WIGTON.

above the age of twelve, noting as "disorderly" those who did not attend his ministrations. Among those so noted was Margaret McLachlan or Lauchlison. Matthias Symson's pamphlet was issued from his father's printing press. Testimony less liable to suspicion, from Mr. Napier's point of view, it is impossible to conceive.*

In 1707 the General Assembly issued an order to the inferior courts to collect accounts of the sufferings that had been endured by Presbyterians during the period from 1662 to 1688. In obedience to this order the Synod of Galloway and the Presbytery of Wigton resolved that the several parishes within their bounds should transmit returns of the sufferings endured in their respective localities to the Presbytery. Conformably with this resolution, the Kirksessions of Kirkinner and Penningham proceeded in 1711 to prepare and put on record the occurrences connected with their respective parishes. The Kirksession of Kirkinner to which Margaret McLachlan belonged, in a minute dated 15th April, 1711, certifies that she was "about the year of God 1685, in her own house taken off her knees in prayer and carried immediately to prison, and from one prison to another without the benefit of light to read the Scriptures; was barbarously treated by dragoons, who were sent to carry her from Machirmore to Wigtoun; and being sentenced by Sir Robert Grier of Lagg, to be drowned at a stake within the floodmark, just below the town of Wigtoun, for keeping conventicles and alleged rebellion, was, according to the said sentence, fixed to the stake till the tide made, and held down within the water by one of the town officers by his halbert at her throat till she died."

Margaret Wilson belonged to Penningham. In a long minute of the Kirksession of that parish, dated 15th February, 1711, it is recorded "that upon the eleventh day of May, 1685, these two

---

* The Rev. Andrew Symson was minister of Kirkinner from 1663 to 1686, when he was translated to Douglas. There he continued till 1691, when he was "outed" by the people. In 1698 he styled himself "merchant burgess of Edinburgh;" he carried on business as a printer in that city, being employed by his Nonjuring friends. He died on the 20th January, 1712, aged seventy-three.—*Dr. Hew Scott's "Fasti."*

women, Margaret McLachland and Margaret Wilson, were brought forth to execution. They did put the old woman just into the water, and when the water was overflowing her, they asked Margaret Wilson what she thought of her in that case. She answered, What do I see but Christ wrestling there? Think ye that we are sufferers? No, it is Christ in us, for He sends none a warfare on their own charges. Margaret Wilson sang Psa. xxv. from the 7th verse, read the eighth chapter of the epistle to the Romans, and did pray, and then the water covered her. But before her breath was quite gone, they pulled her up and held her till she could speak, and then asked her again if she would pray for the King. She answered that she wished the salvation of all men, but the damnation of none. Some of her relations being on the place, cried out, 'She is willing to conform,' being desirous to save her life at any rate. Upon which Major Winram offered the oath of abjuration to her either to swear it or return to the water. She refused, saying, 'I will not. I am one of Christ's children; let me go.' And then they returned her into the water, where she finished her warfare, being a virgin martyr of eighteen years of age, suffering death for her refusing to swear the oath of abjuration and hear the curates."

The minute and circumstantial relation preserved in the Kirksession record of Penningham was drawn up by the Rev. Robert Rowan, minister of the parish, a native of the district, and who was, as appears from the inscription on his tombstone, in his sixteenth year in 1685, when the martyrdom took place. His information was not derived from rumour, the chief facts being communicated to him by Thomas Wilson, farmer at Glenvernoch, one of his parishioners, brother of the martyr Wilson, and who was himself sixteen years old when his sister suffered. Thomas Wilson was still living. He became an elder of the parish in 1719. The information thus obtained by Mr. Rowan was authenticated by the members of his Kirksession, a majority of whom were adults in 1685, when the martyrdom took place. All the elders of Kirkinner also certified the report from that parish. The reports of the two Kirksessions were transmitted to the Presbytery of Wigton, and were by that body received and confirmed. Of that court, the minister of Wigton was a member. From his parish we have strong testimony some years previously. On the 7th July, 1704, Bailie McKeand, senior, one of the magistrates of Wigton, who had been debarred from the Communion on account of taking part in the condemnation of the women, made application to the Kirksession "for the privilege of the sacrament, declaring the grief of his heart that he should have sitten on the seize of these women who were sentenced to die in this place in the year 1685."

In the churchyard of Wigton the tombstones in memorial of the two martyrs, and which narrate the circumstances of their death, were reared during the lifetime of one or more of their persecutors. Sir Robert Grierson survived till 1736. According to "The Cloud of Witnesses," Margaret Wilson's memorial-stone was to be found in the churchyard prior to 1714; that of Margaret McLachlan before 1730, when the third edition of that work was published. One circumstance in relation to the tombstone of the younger martyr has not been related heretofore. It was originally placed against the north wall of the church; when this, in the course of repairs, was removed about twenty years ago, a skull was found in a cavity immediately behind the site of the gravestone. It proved on anatomical examination to be the cranium of a young woman, and bore the mark of a blow inflicted during life.* May not the skull have been raised from the martyr's grave by some one who had had the unjustifiable curiosity to open and inspect it.

The family of Margaret Wilson have resided on the farm of Glenvernoch, in Penningham parish, ever since the period of the martyrdom, and they have preserved an unbroken tradition in reference to the event. Nor has the tradition passed through many generations. John Wilson, tenant of Glenvernoch, who died in

* I owe this information to Mr. William Macgowan, watchmaker, Wigton, who examined the skull along with Dr. Macmillan, an anatomist. I have been informed by Mr. Murray, the present chief magistrate of Wigton, that he had been assured by an aged person who died many years ago that his father remembered of having as a small boy run down the banks of the Blednoch stream to witness the drowning of the two women.

1841, aged eighty-three, was born in 1758, twenty-four years after the death of Thomas Wilson, the martyr's brother, who survived till 1734.

In a recent work,* Sir Andrew Agnew, Bart., of Lochnaw, presents the contents of a letter which in 1862 was addressed to him on the subject of the martyrdom by Mr. Broadfoot, tenant of the West Mains of Baldoon. Mr. Broadfoot states that he had been informed by Miss McKie, an old person in Wigton, that Miss Susan Heron told her that her grandfather was on Wigton Sands on the day when the women were drowned, and that his words were, "The hale sands were covered wi' cluds o' folk a' gathered into clusters here and there offering up prayers for the two women while they were being put down." Mr. Broadfoot examined the tombstones of the Herons in the old churchyard of Penningham, and there found that Miss Susan Heron died on the 19th February, 1834, aged eighty-seven, and that her grandfather, James Heron, died 31st October, 1758, aged ninety-four, showing that he was twenty years old when the women were drowned.†

In Wigton Churchyard a plain upright stone, lately renewed, commemorates three other sufferers in the cause of Presbytery. It is thus inscribed :—

"Here lyes William Johnston, John Milroy, George Walker, who were without sentence of law hanged by Major Winram, for their adherence to Scotland's Reformation Covenants national and solemn league, 1685."

These epitaphs are from tombstones in the churchyard :—

* "History of the Sheriffs of Galloway," by Sir Andrew Agnew, Bart. Edinburgh, 1864. 8vo.

† The two publications of Mr. Mark Napier denying the reality of the martyrdom remain on the shelves of the British Museum uncut—almost unopened. In Scotland the works have been read, and have drawn forth several answers, of which the most exhaustive is that by the Rev. Archibald Stewart, minister of Glasserton. An elegant marble monument to Margaret Wilson and her sister Agnes was in 1859 reared at Stirling by the late Mr. William Drummond of that place. The same benevolent gentleman made an ample provision for Margaret Wilson, daughter of the present tenant of Glenvernoch, to denote his admiration of the Christian fortitude of her great-great-grand-aunt.

> "And his son John of honest fame,
> Of stature small and a leg lame;
> Content he was with portion small,
> Kept shop in Wigtoun and that's all."

> "Frazers McCrachan near this stone here lyes,
> Twelve generations many familys;
> Those ancient clans each age to dust did come,
> May teach that here is not our fixèd home."

> "Farewell, vain world, I've had enough of thee,
> And now I'm careless what thou say'st of me;
> Thy smiles I court not, nor thy frowns I fear,
> My days are past, my head lys quiet here,
> Vain worldly pomp and grandeur shun,
> My glass is done and your's far run."

At Torhouse, three miles west of Wigton, a monument consisting of three large blocks of trap rock is known as King Galdus's Tomb. Galdus was a King of the Scots; he is supposed to have conquered this province from the Romans.

AYRSHIRE.

PARISH OF AUCHINLECK.

Near the head of Aird's Moss a stone pillar reared about thirty years ago commemorates the celebrated field preacher, Richard Cameron, who was here slain by dragoons on the 20th July, 1680. Richard Cameron was son of a small shopkeeper at Falkland, Fifeshire, and was sometime schoolmaster of his native parish. Having obtained licence to preach, he excited the hostility of those Presbyterian ministers who had accepted the indulgence for the boldness with which he asserted the independence of the Church. He afterwards went to Holland, where he was held in much esteem by the clergy living there in exile. Returning to Scotland in 1780, he began a course of field-preaching, and thereby aroused the indignation of the executive. Impelled by persecution, he renounced, at the Cross of Sanquhar, his allegiance to Charles II., on account of his having abused the Government, and proclaimed war against him and his brother the Duke of York. For his head was offered a reward of 5,000 marks, and parties of soldiers were sent out for his arrest. After many narrow escapes he was surprised at Aird's Moss, by Bruce of Earlshall, and a party of horse. In a short skirmish, he fell mortally wounded. The victors cut off his head and hands, and carried them to Edinburgh, where they were laid before his father, then imprisoned for nonconformity. They were next fixed upon the Netherbow. The followers of Richard Cameron were styled Cameronians; after the Revolution many of them entered the army of William and Mary, in which they formed the 26th or Cameronian Regiment.

At Aird's Moss the body of Richard Cameron was interred; a flat stone denotes the spot. It is inscribed with his name, and the names of Michael Cameron, John Gammel, John Hamilton, James Gray, Robert Dick, Captain John Fowler, Thomas Watson, and Robert Paterson, who were slain along with him. Then follow these lines of verse:—

> "Hail, curious passenger, come here and read
> Our souls' triumph with Christ, our glorious Head;
> In self-defence we murdered here do ly,
> To witness 'gainst the nation's perjury."

Beneath the old church of Auchinleck is the burial-vault of the old family of Boswell of Auchinleck. A tombstone commemorates Sir Alexander Boswell, Bart., elder of the two sons of James Boswell, the biographer of Johnson; he was born on the 9th October, 1775. In his twentieth year he succeeded on his father's death to the estate of Auchinleck. Devoting a portion of his time to public business, he was appointed Lieut.-Colonel of the Ayrshire Yeomanry, and was returned Member of Parliament for the county. In 1821 he was created a baronet. From his youth Sir Alexander occupied himself in literary concerns. He established a printing-press at Auchinleck, and issued reprints of curious works. An ingenious poet, he published several volumes of poetry, which attracted attention. Some of his songs became popular. He took a deep interest in the erection of the Ayrshire monument to Robert Burns. Prone to indulge a vein of sarcasm, he published in a Glasgow newspaper a severe poetical pasquinade against James Stuart, younger, of Dunearn. The discovery of the authorship was followed by a challenge from Mr. Stuart, and the parties met at Auchtertool, Fifeshire. Sir Alexander fell, mortally wounded. He was carried to Balmuto, a seat of his ancestors in the vicinity, where he expired the following day. The duel was fought on the 26th March, 1822.

PARISH OF AYR.

On the site of an old building in the High Street of the burgh stands the Wallace Tower, erected about thirty years ago in commemoration of the Scottish hero. Built from a design by the late Mr. Hamilton, of Edinburgh, it is 115 feet in height, and is in elegant Gothic architecture. A statue of Wallace occupies a niche in the front wall.

At Wellington Place a bronze statue commemorates Brigadier-General James Neill, C.B., who fell at the Relief of Lucknow on the 25th September, 1857, aged forty-seven. " General Neill," writes the author of "British India," "was hardly second, whether for deeds done, or promise given of a yet brighter future, to any which the Indian Rebellion brought out before the gaze of wondering nations. In all Havelock's army no other man, certainly not Havelock, probably not even Outram, inspired his comrades with so deep a trust in the military leader, with so loyal a liking for the man. The great struggle produced no leader more trustworthy, no soldier more forward, than James Neill. The news of his death came like a dreadful shock on his countrymen in all parts of the world. To the men of his own brigade, to his own Madras fusileers, to his particular friends and intimates, it seemed as if all their brightest hopes lay buried in the presidency graveyard with the corpse of their own especial hero." *

A monument in the form of a drinking fountain has, in Sandgate Street, been reared to the memory of Primrose William Kennedy, sometime provost of the burgh, who died in 1863, aged sixty-four years.

Seven martyrs for the Covenant, viz.,—James Smith, Alexander Mac Millan, James Mac Millan, George Mac Cartney, John Short, John Graham, and John Muirhead, were executed at Ayr on the 27th December, 1666; their tombstone is thus inscribed:—

* "History of the British Empire in India," by Lionel James Trotter. London, 1866; 8vo., vol. ii., p. 178.

> "Here lye seven martyrs for our covenants,
> A sacred number of triumphant saints,
> Pontius Mac Adam th' unjust sentence past;
> What is his own the world shall know at last.
> And Herod Drummond caused their heads affix;
> Heav'n keeps a record of the sixty-six.
> Boots, thumbkins, gibbets, were in fashion then;
> Lord, let us never see such days again."

On a tombstone at the place of execution Andrew MacGill, who there suffered in 1684, is commemorated in these lines:—

> "Near this abhorrèd tree a sufferer lies
> Who chus'd to fall, that falling truth might rise.
> His station could advance no costly deed,
> Save giving of a life the Lord did need.
> When Christ shall vindicate his way, he'll cast
> The doom which was pronounced in such a haste,
> And incorruption shall forget disgrace,
> Design'd by the interment in this place."

In the parish churchyard Charles Abercrombie, civil engineer, who died in 1817, has the following epitaph:—

> "A noble Abercrombie's dust lyes here,
> A name to Britons dear;
>   But O to you,
> Ye poor of Ayr, St. Cyrus, and Maybole,
> And you in Glasgow Infirmary district,
> With gratitude his mercy record,
> Who on you thought, in your sad state forlorn,
>   Like him of Uz;
> And made your widowed hearts to sing.
> Can you this first and best of men forget?
>   That were strange.
>   Ah, I want words!
> And language fails to sing
>   Of such matchless worth;
> Worth which now ripens in a happier clime,
> And brighter sun beyond the bounds of time."

By her husband and children a woman is thus commemorated:—

> "Our tears and sighs did flow amain,
> In such distress accumulated woe,

> This trifling tribute to her shrine is due,
> From us, her widower and children dear.
> A victim sure to our distress she fell.
> Fate, drop the curtain, we can weep no more:
> 'Religion then, O lend thy heavenly aid,'
> As Young in his 'Night Thoughts' immortal sung."

By his family a father is commemorated in these lines:—

> "Faith and philosophy possessed,
> The parent's honour warm'd his breast,
> Greatly resign'd with ills opprest,
> He linger'd long, sure now is bless'd."

These quaint lines are from a tombstone in the old churchyard:—

> "Life is a voyage on a sea,
> Where tempests, rocks, and shipwrecks be;
> Religion pilots, as sure guide,
> To the far distant other side;
> The harbour's death, and heaven the land
> Where we for ever hope to stand.
> What though we're dash'd upon the shore?
> The cargo's safe and ventur'd o'er,
> As he when this the moral shows,
> Safe now beneath each wind y^t blows,
> Who left his house, his memorie,
> Example and weel won' supply."

The churchyard of Alloway, on the banks of the Doon, is associated with the "auld haunted kirk," celebrated by Burns in "Tam o' Shanter." Alloway Kirk is the burial-place of Crawford of Doonside, and of Cathcart of Auchendrane. The Hon. David Cathcart, a senator of the College of Justice, by the title of Lord Alloway, has an elegant mausoleum. Son of Elias Cathcart, a Virginian trader, and sometime chief magistrate of Ayr, he studied at Edinburgh University, and passed Advocate in July, 1785. He became a judge in 1813, and was appointed Lord of Justiciary in 1826. By his marriage he acquired the estate of Auchendrane. He died on the 27th April, 1829, aged sixty-five.

A plain tombstone commemorates William Burnes, father of Robert Burns the poet. Though in the condition of a market gardener he was member of a family of respectable rank in Kincardineshire. Discovering the genius of his son, the future poet, he endeavoured to secure him a proper education. On his tombstone the poet has thus portrayed his generous qualities :—

> "O ye whose cheek the tear of beauty stains,
>   Draw near with pious reverence and attend;
> Here lie the loving husband's dear remains,
>   The tender father and the generous friend,
> The pitying heart that felt for human woe,
>   The dauntless heart that feared no human pride,
> The friend of man—to vice alone a foe,
>   For e'en his failings leant to virtue's side."

The poet's own monument, an elegant Greek temple, occupies a commanding position on the east bank of the Doon. A triangular base, sixteen feet in height, and built of large undressed stones, represents the three divisions of the county—Kyle, Carrick, and Cunningham. From the base rise nine circular columns, with Corinthian capitals, topped by a projecting cupola, surmounted by a tripod with three inverted dolphins sacred to Apollo. The height of the monument is sixty feet. A circular apartment contains a portrait of the poet, the Bible in two volumes which he presented to "Highland Mary," and other memorials. Within the grounds, which are enclosed with shrubbery intersected by promenades, a suitable erection contains Thom's figures of Tam o' Shanter and Souter Johnnie. These after being exhibited in the principal towns were here appropriately deposited. The proposal of rearing a monument to Burns on the banks of the Doon was originated by Sir Alexander Boswell, of Auchinleck. Resolving to commence the undertaking with the wonted formalities, he convened by advertisement in the newspapers a public meeting in the Court House of Ayr. The day and hour came, but none appeared in the place of meeting save Sir Alexander and his steward. Sir Alexander took the chair, and the steward acted as clerk. Resolutions were proposed, seconded, and recorded, thanks were voted to the chairman, and a report of the meeting was printed and circulated. Within two years the sum of £3,300 for the erection of the monument was subscribed. Sir Alexander laid the foundation-stone on the 25th January, 1820.

PARISH OF BEITH.

On a tombstone in the churchyard is the following inscription:—

"This stone was erected by John Vicar, in gratitude to the memory of his parents, Margaret Smith, who died January 29th, 1808, aged sixty years; William Vicar, who died May 7th, 1814, aged seventy-two years.

> " Meek and gentle were their spirits,
> Prudence did their lives adorn;
> Modest, they disclaimed all merit,
> Tell me—am I not forlorn?
> But I must and will resign them
> They're in better hands than mine,
> But I hope again to join them,
> In the realms of love divine."

From other tombstones we have the following:—

> " These children died when young indeed,
> Which made their parents' hearts to bleed."

> " Distress'd with grief, oppress'd with woe,
> Bereaved of children ten,
> Our only comfort here below,
> We're near our journey's end."

> " Since the last end
> Of the good man is peace,
> Night-dews fall not more gently to the ground,
> Nor weary, worn-out words expire so soft."

PARISH OF COLMONELL.

In the churchyard Matthew Meiklewrath, a Covenanter slain by Claverhouse, is commemorated thus :—

> " I, Mathew M'Ilraith, in parish of Colmonell,
> By bloody Claverhouse I fell,
> Who did command that I should die
> For our Covenanted Presbytery,
> My blood a witness still doth stand
> 'Gainst all defections in this land."

Near the cross-water of Dusk, John Murchie and Daniel Meiklewrath, Covenanters, are on their gravestone celebrated in these lines :—

> " Here in this place two martyrs lye,
> Whose blood to heaven hath a loud cry;
> Murder'd contrary to divine laws,
> For owning of King Jesus' cause;
> By bloody Drummond they were shot,
> Without any trial, near this spot."

PARISH OF CUMNOCK.

In the churchyard of Cumnock a time-worn tombstone and two aged thorns denote the grave of the celebrated Alexander Peden. This uncompromising and eloquent upholder of Covenanting principles was born in the parish of Sorn in 1626. He was originally parish schoolmaster of Tarbolton. In 1659 he was ordained pastor of New Luce, in Galloway, but after three years was ejected for refusing to acquiesce in the establishment of Episcopacy. In 1666 he was by the Privy Council pronounced a rebel for continuing to exercise his ministerial functions. Captured in 1673, he was confined to the Bass till 1678. He was now with sixty others put on board a vessel for transportation to Virginia. The captain, having refused to be the instrument of carrying out a sentence of banishment against so many earnest persons, Peden obtained his liberty. After preaching in the north of England, he returned to Scotland in 1679. He ministered under hiding in different parts of Scotland and Ireland till, worn out with suffering, he returned to Sorn, where he lived in a cave prepared for his reception. There he died in January, 1686, at the age of sixty. His remains were committed to the churchyard of Auchinleck, but forty days afterwards his body was disinterred by a troop of dragoons, who dragged it to Cumnock, proposing there to suspend it on a gibbet. At the intercession of his countess, the Earl of Dumfries prevented the indignity. The body was therefore interred at the gallows-foot. So many persons in dying desired to rest beside the dust of Peden, that the scene of his second interment at length became the parochial burying-ground.

A tombstone in the churchyard commemorates Thomas Richards, Simon Patison, and David Dunn, Covenanters, slain by order of Colonel Douglas. A gravestone at Stonepark denotes the burial-place of John McGeahan, a Covenanter.

PARISH OF CRAIGIE.

On Barnweill Hill a memorial tower was reared in 1855 by the late Mr. William Patrick, of Roughwood, in commemoration of Sir William Wallace, the Scottish patriot. From Barnweill Hill Wallace is supposed to have witnessed the result of his stratagem in destroying by fire the *barns* or barracks of Ayr, in revenge for the wanton treachery of the English governor in entrapping and slaying Sir Ranald Crawfurd, his maternal uncle. As the hero observed the flames and smoke ascending from the dwellings of his country's foes, he exclaimed, " The barns burn weel ;" hence the name of this hill. Barnweill monument is about eighty feet in height; the top, reached by a spiral staircase, commands a wide and interesting prospect. On the external walls are the following inscriptions:—

"Erected MDCCCLV,

"In honour of Scotland's great national Hero, the renowned Sir William Wallace—born MCCLXX—who after performing numerous exploits of the most consummate bravery in defence of the independence of his country, was basely betrayed into the hands of his enemies, by whom, to their everlasting disgrace, he was most unjustifiably put to death on the XXIII of August, MCCCV.

"Centuries have not dimmed the lustre of his heroic achievements; and the memory of this most disinterested of patriots shall through all ages be honoured and revered by his countrymen.

> A soul supreme, in each hard conflict tried,
> Above all pain, all passion, and all pride;
> The frown of power, the blast of public breath,
> The love of lucre, and the dread of death.

Sir William Wallace;
Regent of Scotland MCCXCVII.

"In resistance to treacherous invasion, and in defence of the laws and liberties of his country, he fought against fearful odds, the desperate battles of Biggar, Stirling, Black Earnside, and Falkirk; between these actions in little more than a year he stormed and took from the invaders every fortress, castle, and town which they had seized in the kingdom. Though worsted at Falkirk by overwhelming numbers, aided by fatal dissensions in his own army, his undaunted spirit was not subdued, but ever animated by the noblest patriotism, he continued warring with the oppressors of his native land until his foul betrayal, seven years after that disastrous battle, by the execrable Monteith.

> At Wallace' name what Scottish blood
> But boils up in a spring-tide flood!

"Ever honoured be the memory of the matchless Sir William Wallace, the first of his countrymen who in age of despair, arose and—

> Dar'd to nobly stem tyrannic pride.

throw off the yoke of foreign oppression and maintain the independence and nationality of Scotland; and who, by deeds of surpassing valour and stainless patriotism, has glorified this, his native land,

and imperishably associated his name with the defence of national rights and the liberties and immunities of freeborn men.

"From Greece arose Leonidas; from Scotland Wallace; and from America Washington,—names which shall remain through all time the watchwords and beacons of liberty."

PARISH OF DAILLY.

In the parish churchyard two Covenanters are thus celebrated:—

"Here lyes the corps of John Semple, who was shot by Kirkiron at command of Cornet James Douglas. Also here lyes Thomas McLagan, who was shot uncertain by whom, for their adherence to the word of God and the covenanted work of Reformation."

PARISH OF DUNDONALD.

In the churchyard a gravestone is inscribed—

"Heir lye ye corpis of ane honovrable man, callit David Hameltovne, of Bothelhavche, spovs to Elesovne Sanclar in his tyme, qvha desisit the 14 of Merche, 1619."

Janet MacFadzon, a pedlar's wife, who died in 1761, has on her tombstone these lines:—

> " Now, reader, wonder think it none,
> Tho' I do speak that am a stone
> For in this place here lyes her dust,
> And I do *keep it* but in trust;
> Twenty-four years I lived a maiden life,
> And three years I was a married wife.
> In time I lived a happie life,
> I travelled with him from town to town,
> Until by death I was cut down;
> I in my sister's house did die,
> And here at Crosbie kirk I ly;
> Where I my rest and sleep will take,
> Until at last I be awaked;

> It will not be with tuck of drum,
> But it will be with the trumpet's sound,
> And when I'll my Redeemer see,
> Who shed his precious blood for me."

William Guthrie thus laments his son, a youth of twelve years:—

> "O much lamented youth, in early bloom,
> Relentless death consigned thee to the tomb;
> Mild were thy manners, and thy soul was kind,
> And gen'rous friendship form'd thy opening mind;
> Thy breast a son's, a mother's kindness felt;
> Love warmed thy bosom, in thy accents dwelt.
> Long shall we weep the sad, the mournful day.
> Reader! the life of man, how frail! how vain!
> O seek by Christ immortal joy to gain."

In 1803 William Guthrie celebrates his wife thus:—

> "A second prey the tyrant death hath won,
> A mother's laid beside her much lov'd son,
> In her whate'er the feeling heart can boast,
> The tender friend, the virtuous wife, we lost."

George Bryan, in 1830, thus commemorates a departed relative:—

> "Beneath this chilling earth, the worms' defence,
> Rests one whose virtues never were pretence,
> Whose heart was kind, benevolent, and just,
> Free from deceit, and true to every trust.
> In quiet but secure repose
>   Beneath this solemn stone:
> While living was best loved by those
>   To whom he best was known."

These rhymes are from tombstones in Dundonald Churchyard:—

> "Here lies James Bredine, closed within,
> Death's prisoner through Adam's sin;
> But still our hope is he shall be
> Set by the second Adam free."

> "About the grave's devouring mouth
> Our bones are scattered round,
> As wood which men do cut and cleave
> Lies scattered on the ground."

PARISH OF DUNLOP.

An aisle attached to the parish church is the family burial-place of the old House of Dunlop of Dunlop. Alexander Dunlop of Dunlop was a zealous supporter of the covenant. On the suspicion of his having been at Bothwell Bridge in 1679 he was arrested in 1682, and compelled to surrender a portion of his estate. Afterwards emigrating to America, he was, in 1685, appointed sheriff of South Carolina. John Dunlop of Dunlop, grandson of the preceding, was husband of Frances Anne, daughter of Sir Thomas Wallace, of Craigie. This gentlewoman is celebrated as the early friend and correspondent of Burns.

A small vaulted chamber, known as the picture-house, is the burial place of the parochial incumbents; it was assigned for this purpose by Hanis Hamilton, vicar of the parish, who was here interred. His monument consists of a sarcophagus upholding two marble figures in the attitude of devotion, these representing himself and his wife. Over the tomb is the following inscription:—

"Heir lyes the bodies of Hanis Hamilton, sonne of Archibald Hamilton, of Raploch, servant to King James the fift., and of Janet Denham, his wife, davchter of James Denham, Laird of West Shilde. They lived maryed together forty-five yeeres, dvring which tyme the said Hanis served the cvre at this church. They were much beloved of all that knew him, and especially of the parishioners. They had six sonnes, James, Archibald, Gavin, John, William, and Patrick, and one davchter Jeane, maryed to William Mvre, of Glanderstovne.

> "The dvst of two lyes in this artefvll frame,
> Whose birth them honor'd from an honored name,

A painefvll pastor and his spotless wife,
Whose devout statves emblems heere their life.
Blest with the height of favors from above,
Blood, grace a blest memoriall all men's love,
A frvitfvl ofspringe on whom the Lord hath fixt
Fortvnes with virtve and with honor mixt.
Then live the dead above in endless joyes,
Heere in their seid ane noble Clandeboyes;
In whom (grant soe, O heavens) their honoured name
May never die but in the death of fame.

"Heir lyes Hanis Hamilton, vicar of Dunlope, quha deceisit ye 30th Maii, 1608, [at] ye aige of seventy-two ziers, and of Janet Denham, his spovse."

Hanis Hamilton was promoted to the vicarage of Dunlop in 1563. By his marriage with Janet, daughter of James Denham of West Shield, he had six sons and one daughter. James, the eldest son, was sent to Ireland by James VI., in 1587, to ascertain the views of the Irish in the event of Queen Elizabeth's death. To conceal his design he opened a school at Dublin for the education of Protestant youth. He was appointed to a Fellowship in Trinity College, then newly founded. On the accession of James to the English throne he received in reward of service grants of forfeited lands in Ulster. In 1622 he was created Baron Hamilton and Viscount Clandeboye. By Charles I., in 1647, he was created Earl of Clanbrassil. His five brothers followed him to Ireland and shared his good fortune. From Archibald, the second son, descended Archibald Hamilton Rowan, notorious in the Irish Rebellion of 1798. From the Vicar of Dunlop have also descended the noble families of Roden, Massarene, and Dufferin. Two of his great-grandsons were Principal Carstares, of Edinburgh, and Principal Dunlop, of Glasgow.

Barbara Gilmour, who first made the far-famed Dunlop cheese, was interred in Dunlop Churchyard in 1731.

PARISH OF FENWICK.

In Fenwick Churchyard a monument commemorates Captain John Paton, the celebrated Covenanter. Son of a farmer in the parish, he was employed in agriculture till the age of manhood, when he went abroad and engaged as a volunteer in the German wars; he was promoted as captain for heroic conduct during a siege. On his return to Scotland he took an active part in the military affairs of the Covenanters. He was present at the battle of Kilsyth in 1645, and proved his valour amidst the untoward circumstances of defeat. He fought at the battle of Worcester, where his heroism so impressed his opponent, General Dalziel, that he afterwards endeavoured to save his life. At Bothwell Bridge he held rank as colonel; after the defeat he was declared a rebel, and a price set upon his head. His escapes were numerous and remarkable. At last he was apprehended by five soldiers, who surrounded the house in which he sought shelter. He was taken to Kilmarnock, then to Glasgow, and afterwards to Edinburgh. There he was met by Captain Dalziel, who promised to exert himself on his behalf. He was indicted on a charge of rebellion before the Justiciary Court. On his own statement he was held guilty, and was condemned. He was executed in the Grass Market, Edinburgh, on the 9th May, 1684. His Bible, which he handed to his wife on the scaffold, is, along with his sword, preserved by his descendants. Captain Paton's monument is thus inscribed:—

"Sacred to the memory of Captain John Paton, late in Meadowhead, of this parish, who suffered martyrdom in the Grass Market, Edinburgh, May 9th, 1684. He was an honour to his country, on the Continent, at Pentland, Drumclog, and Bothwell. His heroic conduct truly evinced the gallant officer, brave soldier, and true patriot. In social and domestic life he was an ornament, a pious Christian and a faithful witness for truth, in opposition to the encroachments of tyrannical and despotic power in Church and State.

> Who Antichrist do thus oppose,
> And for truth's cause their lives lay down,
> Will get the victory o'er their foes,
> And gain life's everlasting crown.

"The mortal remains of Captain Paton sleep amid the dust of kindred martyrs, in the Greyfriars Churchyard, Edinburgh.

"Near this is the burying-place of his family and descendants."

Two tombstones in Fenwick Churchyard commemorate four martyrs. The inscriptions follow:—

"Here lies the dust of John Fergushill and George Woodburn, who were shot at Midland by Nisbet and his party, 1685.

> When bloody prelates, once these nations' pest,
> Contrived that cursed self-contradicting test,
> These men for Christ did suffer martyrdom,
> And here their dust lies waiting till he come."

"Here lies the body of James White, who was shot to death at Little Blackwood by Peter Inglis and his party, 1685.

> This martyr was by Peter Inglis shot,
> By birth a tyger rather than a Scot,
> Who that his monstrous extract might be seen,
> Cut off his head and kick't it o'er the green.
> Thus was that head which was to wear a crown
> A football made by a profane dragoon."

A tombstone, now obliterated, formerly bore the following legend:—

"Here lies the corpse of Peter Gemmel, who was shot to death by Nisbet and his party, 1685, for bearing his faithful testimony to the cause of Christ, aged twenty-one years.

> "This man, like holy anchorist of old,
> For conscience' sake was thrust from house and hold
> Bloodthirsty red-coats cut his prayers short,
> And even his dying groans were made their sport.
> Ah, Scotland! breach of solemn vows repent,
> For blood, thy crime will be thy punishment."

Fenwick Churchyard contains the family tombstone of the Howies of Lochgoin, who sprung from a family of the Waldenses, and were intimately associated with Covenanting struggles. During the persecuting period, John Howie, farmer at Lochgoin, gave shelter to the wanderers and supplied them with provisions. Being surrounded with a morass, and thus inaccessible to cavalry, his residence was particularly adapted as a place of shelter. It did not, however, escape the vigilance of the persecutors, since it was on twelve occasions assailed and plundered. Howie always contrived to escape. He died peacefully three years after the Revolution. The most noted member of the family was John Howie, great-grandson of the preceding, and author of the " Scots Worthies." He was born at Lochgoin on the 14th November, 1735. With a taste for literary pursuits, he experienced delight in recording the lives of Scottish confessors and martyrs. The first edition of the "Worthies" was published in 1775. It has been frequently reprinted. John Howie died at Lochgoin on the 5th January, 1793, aged fifty-seven. The descendants of the family occupy the same farm. They preserve a flag and drum and other interesting relics of Covenanting struggles.

The tombstone of the Howie family is thus inscribed:—

> " The dust here lies under this stone
> Of James Howie and his son John.
> These two both lived in Lochgoin,
> And by death's power was call'd to join
> This place, the first November twenty-one,
> Year sixteen hundred and ninety-one;
> The second, aged ninety years,
> The first of July was brought here,
> Years seventeen hundred and fifty-five.
> For owning truth made fugitive
> Their house twelve times, and cattel all
> Once rob'd, and family brought to thrall.
> All these before the Revolution
> Outlived Zion's friends, 'gainst opposition.

"'And he said unto me, These are they which came out of great tribulation.'—Rev. vii. 14.

"Memoriæ sacrum. Here lies the dusty parts of John Howie, who lived in Lochgoin, A man who witnessed for truth and religion in his life, and died April 9th, 1754, aged fifty-four years; also his wife and eight children. This is likewise the burial-place of his son, John Howie, where is interred his first wife and two children, his uncle and others; also of his son John, who lived in Lochgoin, author of the "Scots Worthies," and other publications, who died January 5th, A.D. 1793, aged fifty-seven years, and his spouse, Janet Howie, who died 1st April, A.D. 1815, aged seventy-six years; also his son John, who died September, A.D. 1792, aged thirty-one years; likewise his two children who died in infancy, all of whose remains are interred here.

> "In silent throng and earth's cold womb,
> Here in repose we ly,
> But mind this state ere here we come,
> All you who do pass by.
> "Rev. xiv. 13."

These metrical epitaphs are from Fenwick Churchyard:—

> "In calm repose my mental part doth rest,
> The wreck of Nature's overwhelming tide,
> No waves of trouble now disturb my breast,
> Still as my daughter mouldering by my side."

> "On parents' knees a naked new-born child,
> Weeping thou satest, while all around thee smiled,
> So like that sinking in thy final sleep,
> Calm thou may'st smile while all around thee weep."

PARISH OF GALSTON.

By public subscription a monument has been reared to those who in this parish suffered during the Stuart persecutions. It is inscribed as follows:—

"This stone is erected by public contribution in the parish of Galston, in honour of those belonging to it who suffered at the glorious era of Scotland's covenanted Reformation. May it stand for ages as a monument of abhorrence at tyranny in Church and State, as a grateful and well-merited tribute to those illustrious men who successfully struggled to resist it! May it excite in the breasts of posterity an attachment to the noble cause of religious and civil liberty, and, if ever circumstances should require it, an ardour to imitate the noble deeds of their ancestors."

In the churchyard a tombstone presents the following :—

"In memory of John Richmond, younger, of Know, who was executed at the Cross of Glasgow, March 19, 1684, and interred in the High Churchyard there, and James Smith, East Threepwood, who was shot near Bank-on-Burn, ann. 1684, by Captain Inglis and his dragoons in a tumult there; also James Young and George Campbell, who were banished in 1679, and the Rev. Alexander Blair, who suffered imprisonment, 1673."

"Here lies Andrew Richmond, who was killed by bloody Graham of Claverhouse, June, 1679, for his adherence to the word of God and Scotland's Covenanted work of Reformation.

> When bloody tyrants here did rage
> Over the Lord's own heritage,
> To persecute His noble cause
> By mischief framed into laws,
> 'Cause I the gospel did defend,
> By martyrdom my life did end."

In the interior of the church a handsome marble monument commemorates Lieut.-Colonel Hutchison, of the 98th Regiment, a native of the parish, who died in 1782.

On her tombstone Mary Watson, who died in 1808, aged fourteen, is commemorated thus :—

> "What though no boasted honours graced her name,
> Nor highly polished song her fame proclaim;
> Yet shall her grave with rising flowers be drest,
> And the green turf lie lightly on her breast,
> While angels with their silver wings o'ershade
> The ground now sacred by her reliques made."

By these lines John Kerr, who died in 1823, is thus celebrated:—

> "Pause, serious reader, learn who moulders here,
> Whose care, and pain, and labour's at an end;
> A friend to worth, whose friendship was sincere,
> The tender husband, and the orphans' friend."

PARISH OF IRVINE.

In the parish churchyard a tombstone thus commemorates James Blackwood and John M'Caul, martyrs for the covenant, who suffered 31st December, 1666:—

"Stop, passenger, thou treadest near two martyrs, James Blackwood and John M'Caul, who suffered at Irvine on the 31st of December, 1666.

> These honest countrymen whose bones here ly,
> Both victims fell to prelates' cruelty;
> Condemned by bloody and unrighteous laws,
> They died martyrs for the good old cause,
> Which Balaam's wicked race in vain assail;
> For no enchantments 'gainst Israel prevail.
> Life and this evil world they did contemn,
> And dy'd for Christ, who died first for them.
> They liv'd unknown
> Till persecution dragg'd them into fame,
> And chas'd them up to heav'n.

"Erected by friends to religious liberty, 31st December, 1823."

A handsome monument denotes the grave of John Fergusson of Cairnbrock, an opulent gentleman who died in January, 1856. Besides providing for his relatives Mr. Fergusson bequeathed £500,000 for religious and educational purposes.

David Niven, ship-carpenter, and his wife thus commemorate their son James, an officer in the Royal Navy, who perished on the African coast 5th December, 1812:—

> "Stand still, all passengers that pass by,
> With mourning parents drop a tear;

> Behold our sorrow for a son
>   We loved so tenderly and dear.
> But callèd from his native home,
>   And on a strange and foreign shore,
> To pay the tribute due to death,
>   But hopes to meet to part no more."

William Crooks, captain of the ship *Abyss*, who perished at sea 26th November, 1791, aged twenty-two, is lamented thus:—

> "Pray, gentle reader, drop a tear
>   At his untimely fate;
> You like to him may dread no fear,
>   And dangers you await.
> He that did give can take away
>   That life which was his own,
> Either on the briny sea
>   Or lands in frozen zone.
> He here lies anchored with his fleet,
>   Companions not at strife,
> In hopes his Saviour, Christ, to meet.
>   So reader, lead a sound life."

By these lines John Docherty celebrates his wife, Sarah Kerr, who died 25th December, 1818, aged thirty-eight years:—

> "My love here in the dust doth lie,
> Deprived of life, and so must I;
> Four orphans dear for her may mourn,
> But, alas! to them she cannot return.
> You readers all, as you pass by,
> On your sister's memory cast an eye;
> Her glass is run, and yours is running,
> Refrain from sin, for judgment's coming."

The following epitaphs are from Irvine Churchyard:—

> "Art thou a parent? reverence this bier,
> The parent's fondest hopes lie buried here.
> Art thou a youth, prepared on life to start,
> With opening talents and a genuine heart,
> Fair hopes and flattering prospects all thine own?
> Lo! here their end—a monumental stone."

"Four brothers by fierce tempestuous waves
At diverse times have all lost their lives;
One of their bodies here in dust doth sleep,
The other three lie in the watery deep."

"What can preserve my life, or what destroy?
An angel's arm can't snatch me from the grave,
Legions of angels can't confine me there."

PARISH OF KILBIRNIE.

In the churchyard a monument, bearing date 1594, appears to have been erected for himself and spouse by Captain Thomas Craufurd of Jordanhill. Of an oblong form, measuring nine feet and a half in length, six feet in width, and six feet six inches in height, it is built of chiselled freestone, and covered with the same material. At the angles the walls are finished with columns separated by hollow curves. Through an aperture in the east end, aided by a faint light admitted through a slit in the south wall, are seen two recumbent statues,—one of the founder in military garb, the other of his wife in the costume of her period. On the exterior of the north wall, in relieved letters, is the following inscription:—

" God · Schaw.
The · Richt.

Heir · lyis · Thomas.   And · Janet · Ker · His.
Cravfvrd · of · Jor-   Spous · Eldest · Doc-
Danhil · Sext · Son.   Hter · to · Robert · Ker.
To · Lavrence · Crav-   Of · Kerrisland.
Fvrd · of · Kilbirny.   1 · 5 · 9 · 4."

In the centre of the inscription is a shield bearing quarterly the arms of Craufurd and Ker, and having for crest a rock, representing Dumbarton Castle. Captain Craufurd was sixth son of Laurence Craufurd of Kilbirnie, and Helen, daughter of Sir

Hugh Campbell, of Loudoun. A brave and enterprising officer, he in 1571 performed the extraordinary feat of storming the nearly impregnable Castle of Dumbarton. For this and other services he received a grant of lands in the neighbourhood of Glasgow; hence his title of Jordanhill. He spent the last twenty years of his life in retirement. His wife was heiress of Kersland. A vault in the church was the burying-place of the ancient house of the Craufurds of Kilbirnie.

In the churchyard several flat stones, each bearing the figure of a sword, are believed to commemorate certain Knight Templars supposed to have been buried at the spot.

An altar tombstone commemorates Lucres Scrimgeour, wife of the Rev. William Russell, minister of the parish, who died 3rd September, 1637. Mr. Russell was minister of Kilbirnie from 1619 till 1661. As a preacher he was not very acceptable; he caused one of his parishioners to be rebuked by the Presbytery for characterizing his doctrine as "dust and grey meal."

The Rev. James Smith, who died minister of the parish, 11th February, 1733, is on a tombstone, erected by his widow, celebrated in these lines:—

> "Buried here lys a worthy man,
> Whose life, alas! was but a span;
> He pleasure took by God's command,
> To lead us to Emmanuel's land.
> He was a blessing to our place,
> Where he did preach by power of grace,
> Bidding us Jesus' footsteps trace,
> And from all sinning strive to cease.
> To us, alas! he is no more,
> His soul triumphs in endless glore;
> Why should we then his loss deplore,
> Who joinèd has the heavenly choir?
> To make his character complete,
> Nature blest him with temper sweet.
> Kind to his own, to all discreet,
> All who do love his memory
> Must like him live, and like him dy,
> Then ye'l enjoy eternity,
> In ever praising the Most High."

These lines are from the tombstone of William Miller, of Dykes, who died 12th October, 1753:—

"Though tombs prove faithless to their trust,
And bodies moulder into dust;
A good man's name shall ever last,
In spite of every nipping blast."

James Orr, weaver thus celebrates his wife and children:—

"Affliction sore with meekness long I bore,
Physicians were in vain;
Till God did please that death should seize
And eas'd me of that pain.
Here also lies 2 girls and 2 boys,
They were part of my earthly joys;
But life's a jest, and all things show it,
I once thought so, but now I know it."

James Allan, who died in 1786, aged thirty-four, has these lines on his gravestone:—

"An opening flower, at brightest hour,
In spite of every physic power,
Was suddenly cut down;
This blossom rare, which promised fair,
Beyond all temporal repair,
Fell by the deadliest frown."

On the tombstone commemorating James Steel, weaver, his wife, son, and grandson, is the following:—

"Pause, reader, pause, whoe'er thou be,
Thus age, thus youth, admonish thee;
Think on the tomb, prepare for home,
To death, to judgment, thou must come."

A tombstone is inscribed thus:—

"Awake, thou sluggard of the dust,
The Eternal Son doth cry,
Forth into judgment come thou must,
Thy actions for to try."

> "O all ye saints who's full of wants,
> Love God and sin abhor;
> From sin I rest and every blast,
> In this my silent bower."

PARISH OF WEST KILBRIDE.

In the churchyard Thomas Ritchie, seaman, who died in 1786, has on his tombstone these lines:—

> "Though winds and waves and raging seas
> Have tost me to and fro,
> Yet by the hand of Providence
> I harbour here below,
> Safe from the dangers of them all,
> And rest as in a sleep,
> Till He who calleth me do call
> To join the vocal fleet."

Allan Spier, farmer, Kilrusken, who died in 1789, aged seventy-three, and his child, are thus commemorated:—

> "You that pass by, pray lend an eye,
> Think on this and behold,
> You see the grave all sorts it craves,
> The young as well as old.
> Submit to death, no health or strength
> Will save that fatal hour,
> For you like I must yield and die
> By unconquerable power."

These lines are from a tombstone reared by Alexander Wylie, farmer, Overtoun, in memory of his wife and son:—

> "Feeble mortal, why so vain
> To lengthen out thy destined line?
> The world affords but grief and pain,
> Strive in virtue's deeds to shine.
> To heaven at death thy soul shall fly,
> Whilst low in earth thy flesh doth lye."

Robert Miller, farmer, Sandeland, thus celebrates his departed wife:—

> "Remember, thou that passes by,
> *Thou* must return to dust as I;
> Though in youth's bloom and vigour brave,
> Thou must descend into the grave.
> Let precious time be now well spent,
> For it will give thy mind content
> When thy last moments do appear,
> For there is no repentance here."

A humble parishioner is commemorated thus:—

> "Here lye the banes of Thomas Tyre,
> Wha lang had trudged thro' dirt and mire,
> In carrying bundles and sik like,
> His task performing wi' sma fyke,
> To deal his snuff Tam aye was free,
> In's life obscure was naething new.
> Yet we must own his faults were few,
> Although at Yule he sip'd a drap,
> And in the Kirk whiles took a nap.
> True to his word in every case,
> Tam scorned to cheat for lucre base.
> Now he is gane to taste the fare
> Which none but honest men will share."

In the romantic burial-place of the island of Little Cumbray a tomb covers the remains of a son and granddaughter of the Rev. Robert Wodrow, the celebrated historian. Robert Wodrow, second son of the historian, was born on the 21st December, 1711. Licensed in 1733, he was ordained successor to his father at Eastwood in 1735. He demitted his charge in 1757, and died in Little Cumbray, 13th May, 1784. His daughter, who predeceased him, selected this romantic churchyard as her place of sepulture, and his remains were consigned to the same tomb.

PARISH OF KILMARNOCK.

At the head of Soulis Street a stone pillar, nine feet in height, commemorated Lord Soulis, an English nobleman, killed on the spot by one of the Boyds in 1444. The monument was renewed in 1825, when a fluted pillar, surmounted by a vase, was placed near the site of the older erection, in a niche of the wall enclosing the burial-ground. On the pediment is the following inscription :—

> "To the memory of Lord Soulis, A.D. 1444.
> Erected by subscription, A.D. 1825.
>
> 'The days of old to mind I call.'"

In the parish church a monument celebrates Sir Thomas Boyd, of Kilmarnock, who died in 1432. It is thus inscribed :—

> "Hic jacet Thomas Boyde, dominus de Kilmarnock, qui obiit septimo die mensis Julii, 1432; et Johanna Montgomery eius spousa. Orate pro iis."

Sir Thomas Boyd was a prominent statesman in the reign of James I.; he was one of the hostages for the ransom of that monarch in 1424.

A tablet in the church commemorates Robert, fourth Lord Boyd, a zealous promoter of the Reformation. With the Earls of Moray and Argyll he took up arms on the occasion of Queen Mary's marriage with Lord Darnley; he was consequently denounced rebel. He escaped to England, but returned after the death of Rizzio, when he received a full pardon. He was a member of the assize which acquitted Bothwell for the assassination of Darnley. After Bothwell's marriage with the Queen he joined the association for the protection of the Prince. He subsequently returned to the Queen's party; he fought on her behalf at Langside. He afterwards joined the party of the Regent Lennox, by whom he was appointed an extraordinary lord of session. He became a member of the Privy Council, and held several other offices. In 1582 he engaged in the Raid of Ruthven, but was pardoned on condition that he would retire to France. He was subsequently permitted to resume his office of lord of session. He died on the 3rd January, 1590, in his seventy-second year. His monumental tablet is inscribed as follows :—

> "Heir lyis yt godlie, noble, wyis lord Boyd,
> Quha kirk and king and commin weill decoird
> Quhilke war (quhill they yis jowell all injoyd),
> Defendit, counsaild, governd be that lord.
> His ancient hous, (oft parreld) he restoird :
> Twyis sax and saxtie zeirs he leivd, and syne,
> By death, (ye thrid of Januare) devoird ;
> In anno thryis fyve hundreth auchtye nyne."

In the Low Church burying-ground two martyrs for the Covenant are on a tombstone thus celebrated :—

"Here lie the heads of John Ross and John Shields, who suffered at Edinburgh, December 27th, 1666, and had their heads set up at Kilmarnock.

> "Our persecutors mad with wrath and ire ;
> In Edinburgh members some do lye, some here ;
> Yet instantly united they shall be,
> And witness 'gainst this nation's perjury."

John Nisbet, a native of Loudoun, who was tried and hanged at Kilmarnock for having fought at Bothwell Bridge, rests in the Low Churchyard. The spot occupied by the gibbet is marked by the initials of his name, formed in white stones. His tombstone bears the following inscription :—

"Here lies John Nisbet, who was taken by Major Balfour's party, and suffered at Kilmarnock, 14th April, 1683, for adhering to the word of God and our Covenants.—Rev. xii. 11.

> " Come, reader, see here pleasant Nisbet lies,
> His blood doth pierce the high and lofty skies ;
> Kilmarnock did his latter hour perceive,
> And Christ his soul to heaven did receive.

> Yet bloody Torrence did his body raise,
> And buried it in another place;
> Saying, 'Shall rebels lye in graves with me?
> We'll bury him where evil-doers be.'"

In 1823 a monument was reared to six martyrs connected with the district. Under the representation of an open Bible it presents the following inscription:—

"Sacred to the memory of Thomas Finlay, John Cuthbertson, William Brown, Robert and James Anderson (natives of this parish), who were taken prisoners at Bothwell, June 22nd, 1679, sentenced to transportation for life, and drowned on their passage near the Orkney Isles. Also of John Finlay, who suffered martyrdom, Dec. 15th, 1682, in the Grass Market, Edinburgh.

> Peace to the Church, her peace no friend invade;
> Peace to each noble martyr's honoured shade;
> They with undaunted courage, truth, and zeal,
> Contended for the Church and country's weal;
> We share the fruits, we drop the grateful tear,
> And peaceful altars on their ashes rear."

At the Cross an elegant monumental statue celebrates the late Sir James Shaw, Bart. This estimable individual was son of the farmer at Mosshead, parish of Riccarton, near Kilmarnock. He was born on the 26th August, 1764. In his seventeenth year he procured a commercial appointment at New York. Returning to Britain, he became junior clerk in a mercantile house at London, in which he rose to be a partner. In 1798 he was chosen alderman, and in 1805 he attained the office of Lord Mayor. In the following year he was elected a member for the city. In 1809 he was created a baronet. He was elected Chamberlain of London in 1831. He died on the 22nd October, 1843, aged seventy-nine. Retaining a deep interest in the place of his nativity, he was a liberal and constant benefactor of its institutions. On the death of the poet Burns he zealously promoted a subscription on behalf of his widow. When Lord Mayor he revived the claim for the precedency of the chief magistrate. At the funeral of Lord Nelson in 1806 he took precedency of the Prince of Wales, but waived the privilege when the procession entered St. Paul's. Sir James Shaw's monument was inaugurated on the 4th August, 1848. The statue is of Carrara marble, and was sculptured by Fillans.

In the parish churchyard is interred Thomas Samson, an early friend of the poet Burns, and on whom he composed "Tam Samson's Elegy." Samson was a prosperous seedsman, and an estimable, kind-hearted man. On his tombstone—a plain slab, set in the west end of the church—is the following:—

"Thomas Samson, died the 12th December, 1795, aged seventy-two years.

> Tam Samson's weel-worn clay here lies,
> Ye canting zealots, spare him;
> If honest worth in heaven arise,
> Ye'll mend, or ye win near him.—BURNS."

James Wilson, merchant, who died in August, 1825, while in the act of praise at family worship, has his tombstone thus inscribed:—

> "The strain which mortal tongue began
> Was finished on an angel's lyre;
> The body dropped a lifeless corpse,
> The spirit sought the heavenly choir."

On the tombstone of his son, a boy of eight years, who was killed by a cart passing over him in January, 1809, Robert Webster has presented the representation of a wheel, with these rhymes:—

> "Ye little children that survey
> The emblem'd wheel that crush'd me down,
> Be cautious as you careless play,
> For shafts of death fly thick around.
> Still rapid drives the car of time,
> Whose wheel one day shall crush you all;
> The cold, low bed that now is mine
> Will soon be that of great and small."

PARISH OF KILMAURS.

In the parish churchyard a richly sculptured mausoleum, partly in ruins, formed the burying-place of the noble family of Glencairn. The last two Peers of the House, including James, the fourteenth earl, celebrated as the patron of Burns, were interred elsewhere. The following lines are from a tombstone in this churchyard:—

> " Here precious dust lies hid beneath this clod,
>   Laid here, in firmest hope and union bound
> To pure transcendent love—the incarnate God,
>   Whose high accented praise eternally he'll sound.
> The constant flux of seasons, days, and years,
>   That's rolling down the rapid stream of time,
> If we consider with the numerous straws
>   That do surround us in this wretched clime,
> All loudly call for us to ready make
>   For this long home, where vast eternity
> Widely expanded is. O drowsy souls, awake,
>   To change your state for heaven's felicity."

PARISH OF KILWINNING.

The ancient monuments connected with Kilwinning Abbey have disappeared. The abbey was founded by Hugh de Morville, Constable of Scotland, in 1140. At the Reformation it was partially demolished by the Earl of Glencairn, but was afterwards fitted up for Presbyterian worship.

In the churchyard is the burial-aisle of the noble House of Eglinton. Here are deposited the remains of Archibald William, thirteenth Earl of Eglinton and fifth Earl of Winton. This excellent nobleman was born on the 29th September, 1812; he succeeded his grandfather, Hugh, twelfth Earl of Eglinton, in

December, 1819. He was Lord Lieutenant of Ayrshire, a Privy Councillor, and on two occasions Lord Lieutenant of Ireland. Strongly imbued with the love of chivalry, Lord Eglinton held a tournament at Eglinton Castle in 1839. When the sons of Burns finally returned from India he arranged a grand banquet for their reception, at which he appropriately presided. He died on the 4th October, 1861.

These quaint lines commemorate John Cunningham, who died on the 15th January, 1712, aged nineteen :—

> "Stop, pilgrims, as you go by,
> Behold my early destiny;
> Before I was twentie years old
> Death upon me did take hold;
> This stone stands witness at my head,
> Which makes my parents' heart to bleed."

PARISH OF KIRKMICHAEL.

In the parish churchyard a tombstone commemorates Gilbert M'Adam, a martyr for the Covenant. In 1685 he was taken prisoner and carried to Dumfries on a charge of Nonconformity, but was liberated on a heavy caution. Not long after he was again apprehended, and on refusing the oath of supremacy was banished to the Plantations. He effected his escape, but was found by a body of militia while conducting a prayer meeting in this parish. On attempting to escape by a window he was shot dead. M'Adam's tombstone was renewed in 1829.

PARISH OF LARGS.

A small eminence, known as the Castle Hill, bears traces of an encampment connected with the battle of Largs, fought in 1263.

At the back of the mansion-house of Haylie, a tumulus called St. Mary's Law is another vestige of the battle. A rude stone pillar commemorates the spot where Haco, the Norwegian commander, was slain. In a garden wall adjoining is the following inscription:—

> "Substit. Hic Gothi Furor.
> Conditur hic Haco Steniensis, et undique, circum
> Norvegios fidos terra tegit Socias:
> Huc regnum venere petentes; Scotia victor
> Hostibus hic tumulos, præmia justa dedit.
> Quarto ante nonas Octobris, A.D. 1263."

The Skelmorly aisle of the old church was reared in 1639 by Sir Robert Montgomery of Skelmorly, to contain the ashes of his wife, Lady Margaret Douglas. In his youth Sir Robert was a man of blood; in old age his devotion bordered on austerity. To this tomb he was in the habit of retiring, and by the embalmed body of his wife pondering on the errors of his youth. His remains are deposited by her side. The aisle exhibits an arched ceiling of carved oak, adorned with emblems and mottoes appropriate to the place.

Near Brisbane House a flat stone denotes the grave of the Rev. William Smyth, minister of the parish, who died of the plague in 1647. He was celebrated for his piety, and the short inscription on his tombstone has been repeatedly renewed.

A family mausoleum contains the remains of General Sir Thomas Makdougal Brisbane, the distinguished soldier and astronomer. Born at Brisbane, in this parish, on the 23rd July, 1773, he entered the army in his sixteenth year. In the Flanders campaign he took part in all the engagements, and in the West Indies, to which he was sent in 1796, he acquired considerable distinction. In 1812 he commanded a brigade under the Duke of Wellington in Spain. For his bravery on the field of Orthes he received the thanks of Parliament. In 1821 he was appointed Governor of New South Wales. While in Australia he catalogued 7,385 stars, for which he received the Copley Medal from the

Royal Society. In 1825 he was appointed to the colonelcy of the 34th Regiment. For his services in founding an observatory in New South Wales he was, in 1828, awarded a Gold Medal by the Astronomical Society. In 1832 he was elected President of the Royal Society of Edinburgh, and in 1833 he became President of the British Association. In 1836 he was created a baronet. He erected an observatory at Makerstoun in 1841; the observations which he made there have been published in three large volumes. He founded two gold medals for scientific merit, one to be awarded by the Royal Society, and the other by the Society of Arts. He died on the 27th January, 1860, at the advanced age of eighty-seven.

These lines are from the tombstone of John Paton, who died in 1802, aged eighty-eight, and of his son, who died in 1795, aged eighteen years:—

> "Reader, I do it of thee crave
> When thou does me go by;
> All you, my scholars that were,
> Remember you must die,
> And in the days of youth prepare
> For long eternity."

Archibald Hendry, who died in 1801, is commemorated thus:—

> "How loved or valued once avails not me,
> For now I lodge in this dark destiny;
> Remember, man in youthful prime,
> That thou must lie and lodge with me.
> Time was like thee, I life possest,
> And time shall be when thou must rest."

By these quaint lines is celebrated John Ewing, merchant, who died in 1763:—

> "O passenger, as thou goest by,
> Upon this stone think, listen, aye,
> And think on death while life is lent thee,
> For God himself commands it so to be."

Under the representation of a hammer crowned, are these lines commemorating Theophilus Rankin, who died in 1724:—

> "Of all mechanicks we have renown,
> Above the hammer we wear the crown."

Hugh Morris thus commemorates his daughter Elizabeth; she died in September, 1805:—

> "She ne'er knew joy
> But friendship might divide,
> Or gave her father grief
> But when she died."

Mary M'Naught, who died young, has her tombstone thus inscribed:—

> "Here in this grave a woman lys,
> Who was cut off in youth,
> A warning given to all mankind
> To live in faith and truth.
> For death may come in various shapes
> When we may least expect;
> O that all youth in time may be
> Prepar'd for such a step!"

These epitaphs are on tombstones in this churchyard:—

> "Mother Earth, to thee I trust
> These bonnie heaps o' precious dust,
> Keep them safely, sacred tomb,
> Till a parent asks for room."

> "Many die in fears,
> Both great and small;
> All ye that's young in years,
> Embrace the gospel call.
> And when you walk alone,
> Distant from companie,
> Think often then upon
> Death and long eternity."

PARISH OF LOUDOUN.

A vault in the parish church constitutes the burial-place of the noble family of Loudoun. Here were deposited the remains of Sir John Campbell, Earl of Loudoun. Descended from the noble family of Argyle, John Campbell was eldest son of Sir James Campbell of Lawers. He married in 1620 Margaret Campbell, Baroness of Loudoun, and consequently obtained the style and dignity of Baron Loudoun. In 1633 he was created Earl of Loudoun, but owing to his opposition to Court measures his patent was suspended for eight years. He resisted the unconstitutional attempt of Charles I. in 1637 to force Episcopacy on the nation; he was a member of the General Assembly of 1638; and in 1639 he garrisoned, for the Covenanters, the Castles of Strathaven, Douglas, and Tantallan. He was one of the Scottish Commissioners, who settled the pacification of Berwick. In 1640, having proceeded to London as Commissioner from the Committee of Estates, he was arrested on a charge of high treason and committed to the Tower; he soon regained his liberty and was permitted to kiss the king's hand. In August, 1640, he held command in the Scottish army at the battle of Newburn; he presided at the opening of the Estates in July following. During the royal visit in 1641 he was appointed Lord High Chancellor and first Commissioner of the Treasury. With two others he was sent to treat with the king at Carisbrooke Castle in 1647; he at first concurred in the "Engagement," but afterwards withdrew from it. On the defeat of Charles II. at Worcester in 1651, he joined the Earl of Glencairn on the king's behalf, but soon after retired into private life. By Cromwell he was excepted from the Act of Grace in 1654; at the Restoration he was deprived of his chancellorship and fined £12,000 Scots. He died at Edinburgh on the 13th March, 1663.

In the Loudoun vault rest the remains of Lady Flora Hastings. This excellent and accomplished gentlewoman was eldest daughter of Earl Moira, afterwards Marquis of Hastings. Her mother, the

Countess of Loudoun, married Earl Moira in 1804. Lady Flora was born at Edinburgh on the 11th February, 1806. In 1834 she was appointed one of the ladies of the bedchamber to the Duchess of Kent, with whom she remained till the period of her death. She died at Buckingham Palace on the 5th July, 1839. A posthumous volume of poems from her pen were published in 1841, edited by her sister, the Marchioness of Bute.

John Nisbet, a native of the parish, who suffered martyrdom at Edinburgh, on the 4th December, 1685, has been commemorated by a monument erected by public subscription. It is thus inscribed:—

"To the memory of John Nisbet, of Hardhill, who suffered martyrdom at the Grass Market, Edinburgh, 4th December, 1685.

"Animated by a spirit to which genuine religion alone could give birth, and the pure flame of civil and religious liberty alone could keep alive, he manfully struggled for a series of years to stem the tide of national degeneracy, and liberate his country from the tyrannical aggressions of the perjured House of Stuart; in an age distinguished above all others for unbounded licentiousness, and dereliction of principle, he stood the firm friend of the real interests of his country; and as a leader of the Persecuted Patriot Band, evinced a courage which no hardships could subdue. His conduct in arms at Peutland, Drumclog, and Bothwell, in opposition to prelatic encroachments, and in defence of Scotland's Covenanted Reformation, is recorded in the annals of these oppressive times. His remains lie at Edinburgh, but the inhabitants of this his native parish, grateful for the privileges his exertions tended to procure, and friends to the cause for which he fought and died, have caused this monument to be erected."

Nisbet was born in 1627; he was lineally descended from Murdoch Nisbet, of Hardhill, one of those who about the year 1500 were styled the Lollards of Kyle. During his youth he engaged in military service abroad. Returning to Scotland in 1650, he was present at the coronation of Charles II. at Scone. He married and settled at Hardhill. In 1664 he offended the Episcopal minister of his parish by having a child baptized by an ejected minister, and he was consequently exposed to various persecutions. He joined in renewing the covenant at Lanark in 1666; he was on the 28th November of that year severely wounded at Rullion Green. On his recovery he again took up arms; he fought at Drumclog and Bothwell Bridge. On the dispersion of the Covenanters he was denounced a rebel, a reward being offered for his apprehension. At Midland, in the parish of Fenwick, he was surprised by a party of dragoons in November, 1685. His companions were killed, but he was preserved for the sake of the reward. He was conveyed to Edinburgh and examined before the Privy Council, and was eventually condemned to be hanged. He met his death with resignation and fortitude.

At Loudoun another martyr for the Covenant is thus commemorated:—

> "'Cause I Christ's prisoners reliev'd,
> I of my life was soon bereav'd,
> By cruel enemies with rage,
> In that rencounter did engage;
> The martyr's honour and his crown,
> Bestow'd on me, oh, high renown!
> That I should not only believe,
> But for Christ's cause my life should give."

From Loudoun Churchyard we have the following:—

"Heir lyes ane right honest man, called Matthew Fvlton, maister meson to Lovdone, qvha decesit in the 10 Jvne, in the year of God 1632.

> I go to grave as to my bed, yet no heir to remain,
> A qvhil for to repos therin, and then to rise again."

> "Remember still the solemn tye,
> Is in this land to the most hie!
> Dead bodies in the grave do lie,
> Their souls go to eternity,
> Until the day that Christ do call,
> To raise the dead both great and small,
> For to receive eternal hire
> In heaven's joys or hell's fire."

PARISH OF MAUCHLINE.

On the green at Town-head a tombstone commemorates five martyrs for the Covenant, viz., Peter Gillies, John Bryce, Thomas Young, William Fiddison, and John Bruning, who, without trial, were hanged by the Commissioners of James VII. The tombstone bore these lines:—

> "Bloody Dumbarton, Douglas and Dundee,
> Moved by the Devil and the Laird of Lee,
> Dragged these five men to death with gun and sword,
> Not suffering them to pray nor read God's word;
> Owning the work of God was all their crime,
> The eighty-five was a saint-killing time."

A more imposing monument in honour of the five sufferers was by public subscription reared in 1830.

A tombstone denotes the grave of the Rev. William Auld, minister of the parish, who died on the 12th December, 1791, in his eighty-third year, and fiftieth of his ministry. Mr. Auld, who was a conscientious clergyman, is mentioned in the poetry of Burns.

PARISH OF MAYBOLE.

The collegiate church, now in ruins, is used as a burying-place of the noble family of Cassilis, represented by the Marquis of Ailsa.

The following inscriptions are from tombstones in the old church-yard:—

> "How vain are all things here below!
> How false, and yet how fair!
> Each pleasure has its poison too,
> And every sweet a snare."

"Under these neighbouring monuments lys the golden dust of Man and Wife,
Of pious line both soon shall rise to long-expected glorious life,
They for their constancy and zeal, still to the back did prove good steel,
For our Lord's royal truths and laws, the ancient covenanted cause
Of Scotland's famous Reformation, declining laws of usurpation."

"The man's name was John McLymont, who lived in Achaltown, and dyed the 1st of November, age sixty-nine, 1714."

PARISH OF MONKTON.

In the churchyard at Prestwick rest the remains of James Macrae Governor of Madras. Son of an agricultural labourer, he was born in the parish of Ochiltree, about 1684. During his childhood his father died, and his mother, with her two children, a boy and girl, proceeded to Ayr, where she obtained employment as a washerwoman. Young Macrae became a cowherd; he afterwards joined the navy as a seaman. In the navy he attained the rank of captain. Obtaining the confidence of the Board of Directors he was sent on a special mission to the English settlement on the west coast of Sumatra. Having acquitted himself to the satisfaction of his employers, he was appointed Deputy-Governor of Fort St. David. In 1724 he became second member of Council at Fort St. George. In the following year he was appointed Governor of Madras. He sailed for England in January, 1731, bearing to his native land a fortune of one hundred thousand pounds. On his arrival in Britain he proceeded to Ayr, where he found that his sister was married to a carpenter. The couple had four daughters, and to their training as gentlewomen the Governor devoted the efforts of his remaining years. The eldest daughter married William, thirteenth Earl of Glencairn, and on the occasion received from her uncle the barony of Ochiltree, with diamonds to the value of

£45,000; James, fourteenth Earl of Glencairn, the patron of Burns, was her second son. The Governor's second niece married James Erskine, a Lord of Session by the title of Lord Alva; the third married a person of his own family name. Macrae's youngest niece wedded Charles Dalrymple, and received the estate of Orangefield. Governor Macrae died in 1746. He presented an equestrian statue of William III. to the city of Glasgow, and lent to the City corporation £5,000 to meet the sum levied from them by Prince Charles Edward in 1745.

PARISH OF MUIRKIRK.

On the farm of Priesthill a handsome monument has been reared to the memory of John Brown "the Christian carrier," who at his own door was shot by Graham of Claverhouse on the 1st of May, 1685. One of Graham's party pointed out Brown's lifeless body to his wife, and asked what she thought of her husband. She answered, "Mair than ever I did, but the Lord will avenge this another day." On the original tombstone were recorded these lines, which form an acrostic:—

> "I n death's cold bed the dusty part here lies
> O f one who did the earth, as dust, despise.
> H ere, in this place, from earth he took departure,
> N ow he has got the garland of the martyr.
>
> B utcher'd by Clavers and his bloody band,
> R aging most rav'nously o'er all the land.
> O nly for owning Christ's supremacy,
> W ickedly wrong'd by encroaching tyranny.
> N othing, how near soever, he too good
> E steem'd, nor dear, for precious truth, his blood."

In Muirkirk Churchyard the tombstone of James Smith, a martyred Covenanter, is thus inscribed:—

> "When proud apostates did abjure
> Scotland's Reformation pure,
> And fill'd this land with perjury,
> And all sorts of iniquity;
> Such as would not with them comply,
> They persecute with hue and cry.
> I in the chase was o'erta'en,
> And for the truth by them was slain."

PARISH OF STEVENSTON.

A tombstone commemorates the Rev. John Bell, minister of the parish. Son of Mr. John Bell, minister of Stevenston, he studied at the University of Glasgow, and was in 1640 settled in the parish of Glasford, Lanarkshire. In 1642 he succeeded his father as minister of Stevenston. He died in September, 1652. His tombstone is thus inscribed :—

> "The childless mother's resolution.
> "Strength to my tryal hath my Lord made even,
> Oh to bedew his feet that tears were given;
> His weel's my weel, in him my sole content,
> Nor grieves to go, nor give what he hath lent."

On the tombstone of Alexander Crawford, his wife, and two sons, are these lines :—

> "How vain are all our earthly joys!
>   Stop, passenger, and shed a tear;
> A father, mother, and two boys,
>   Within six months interr'd lie here.
> Presume not then that wealth nor strength
>   Will save thee from the fatal hour,
> For thou, like these, must yield at length
>   To death's unconquerable power."

PARISH OF STEWARTON.

James Wilson and his wife, who both died in February, 1721, have the following epitaph :—

"O foolish people, and unwise,
   That love to live in sin,
Amend your ways now speedily,
   For danger is therein.
Sin is the cause of all the woes
   That ever did befall
To any in this present life,
   Or that hereafter shall ;
Therefore I do you all advise
   In time now to repent,
Least that the fatal stroke of death
   Do all your work prevent.
Let holiness towards your God
   Be all which you intend,
Be just and righteous to all men,
   E'en to the very end.
So finish all your work and come,
   Lie down with us and sleep,
Here all your bones shall be at rest,
   The Lord your dust shall keep,
And when he calls we shall awake,
   And rise again shall we.
O let that time be hastenèd !
   Amen— so let it be."

Ann Gray, who died September, 1820, aged twenty-two, is by her husband thus commemorated :—

"To all who read, I sleep in death,
O live to die by Christ in faith,
While youth and vigour gild your brow ;
Remember still thy days are few.
To God's blest house I long to be,
When last I viewed these tombs you see,
I did the silent graves review,
And look'd as fair for life as you ;

But ere next Sabbath did return,
They laid me in this lonely urn.
A blessed rest for them that be
From suffering, sin, and death set free.
Then kindred dear, aloud I call,
Prepare, for death will meet you all.
Should you like me next Sabbath lie,
I ask, are you prepared to die?"

PARISH OF STRAITON.

Thomas M'Haffie, a Covenanter, who in 1685 was taken out of his sick bed and shot, is on his tombstone in the churchyard celebrated thus :—

"Though I was sick, and like to die,
Yet bloody Bruce did murder me;
Because I adhered in my station
To our covenanted reformation;
My blood for vengeance yet doth call
Upon Zion's haters all."

PARISH OF TARBOLTON.

In the vicinity of Coilsfield House an enclosed mound with two upright stones is described as the burial-place of Coil, King of the Britons, who here fell in battle. In 1837 the mound was opened, and under the depth of four feet a circular flagstone was found overlying several urns full of calcined bones. The principal urn was seven inches in height and of similar diameter; it was supposed to contain the ashes of the pre-historic king. According to Boece the Scots and Picts surprised the Britons by night and put nearly the whole of them to the sword. The central district of Ayrshire, in which this parish is situated, is known as Kyle, after the name of the British king.

In the churchyard the tombstone of William Shillilaw, a martyred Covenanter, is thus inscribed :—

"Here lys William Shillilaw, who was shot at Woodhead by Lieut. Lauder for his adherence to the word of God and Scotland's covenanted work of Reformation, 1685."

A tombstone celebrates the theological learning and pastoral devotedness of Dr. William Ritchie, one of the ministers of Edinburgh, and Professor of Divinity in the university of that city. He was born at Foulis-Wester, Perthshire, in December, 1747. In his sixteenth year he was elected parish schoolmaster of Newtyle, Forfarshire. Having studied at the University of St. Andrews, he was licensed to preach in 1774. For some years he travelled abroad. He was ordained minister of Tarbolton in 1793, and in 1798 was translated to Kilwinning. In 1801 he was elected Moderator of the General Assembly. In 1802 he was translated to St. Andrew's Church, Glasgow. He introduced instrumental music into St. Andrew's church, an act which proved obnoxious to the Lord Provost, and was condemned by the Presbytery. Dr. Ritchie was preferred to the High Church, Edinburgh, in 1808. He was in the following year elected Professor of Divinity. He died at Tarbolton on the 29th January, 1830, in his eighty-third year, and the thirty-sixth of his ministry.

RENFREWSHIRE.

PARISH OF CATHCART.

In the parish churchyard three Covenanters are commemorated thus:—

"This is the stone tomb of Robert Thome, Thomas Cooke, And John Urie, martyrs, for owning the Covenanted work of Reformation, the 11th of May, 1685.

> The bloody murderers of these men
> Were Major Balfour and Captain Metlaun,
> And with them others were not free
> Caused them to search in Polmadie.
> As soon as they had them outfound,
> They murthered them with shot of guns;
> Scarce time did they to them allow
> Before their Maker their knees to bow.
> Many like in this land have been,
> Whose blood for vengeance crys to heav'n;
> This cruel wickedness you see
> Was done in loan of Polmadie.
> This may a standing witness be
> 'Twixt Presbytrie and Prelacie."

A tombstone, reared in 1689, in memory of John Hall and his wife, presents these lines:—

> "Time's rapid stream, we think, does stand,
>   While on it we are blown down
> To a vast sea that knows no land,
>   Nor e'er a shore would own;

> In which we shall for ever swim,
>   The blest through eternity;
>   Or sink beneath wrath's dreadful stream
>   In deepest misery."

On the gravestone of James Hall, of Cathcart Mill, we have the following :—

> "A foe death is not to the wise and good,
>   Though he appears a porter rude,
>   But faithful messenger and friendly hand
>   To waft us to Immanuel's land:
>   Here with pure untold pleasures to behold
>   The joys of heaven, and brightness of our Lord;
>   To which none entered these fields of bliss
>   But by the gate alone of righteousness;
>   Not of our own indeed, but of another,
>   Th' anointed Christ, our Friend and elder Brother."

A tombstone commemorates the Rev. George Adam, who died minister of the parish on the 6th February, 1759. On an event in his history Mr. J. G. Lockhart has founded his tale entitled "Some Passages in the Life of Mr. Adam Blair." Mr. Adam became minister of Cathcart in 1738. He took part in the revivals at Cambuslang in 1742, and was greatly esteemed for his ministerial gifts and amiable qualities. In April, 1746, he acknowledged himself guilty of improper behaviour with a female, to the astonishment of his friends, among whom he maintained a high character. He underwent a course of ecclesiastical discipline, and was deposed from his office. Sympathy on his behalf was everywhere awakened. His patron, heritors, elders, and parishioners petitioned the General Assembly for his restoration. He was re-admitted to his charge in August, 1748, and thereafter applied himself with increased diligence and fidelity to his sacred duties.

PARISH OF EAGLESHAM.

In the churchyard the grave of two Covenanters is protected by a tombstone, which is thus inscribed :—

"Here lies Gabriel Thomson and Robert Lockhart, which were killed for owning the Covenanted, . . . by a party of highlandmen and dragoons, under the command of Ardencaple, May 1st, 1683.

> These men did search through moor and moss
> To find out all who had no pass;
> These faithful witnesses were found,
> And slaughterèd upon the ground;
> Their bodies in this grave do ly,
> Their blood for vengeance yet doth cry.
> This may a standing witness be
> For Presbytery 'gainst Prelacy."

The following elegy celebrates the Rev. William Findlay, minister of the parish :—

> "Sublime of genius and with science blest,
> Of every brilliant excellency possess'd :
> Beyond the common standard learn'd and wise,
> Of conduct artless and above disguise.
> In whom but equals few, superiors none,
> The friend, the husband, and the father shone :
> A tutor form'd t'implant in yielding youth
> And into fruit mature the seeds of truth.
> A writer elegant in manly charms,
> Who like the sun enlightens while it warms;
> A pastor blending, with divinest skill,
> A seraph's knowledge with a seraph's zeal;
> Not only taught religion's path but trod,
> And like illustrious Enoch walked with God.
> Findlay, these rich embellishments combin'd
> Were thine! but who can paint an angel's mind?
> Heaven saw thee ripe for glory, and in love
> Remov'd thee hence to grace the realms above."

Mr. Findlay was admitted to the parochial charge in 1797. He died 19th September, 1816, in his sixty-fourth year, and twentieth of his ministry.

William Baird, farmer at Brakinridge, has thus celebrated his departed spouse, who died in 1811, aged seventy-five:—

> "Adieu, blest woman, partner of my life,
> A tender mother and a faithful wife;
> From scandal free, most ready to command,
> Most loath to hurt, most proud to be a friend;
> Her partner's comfort and his life's relief,
> Once his chief joy, and now his greatest grief.
> Her God has called her where she's sure to have
> Blessings more solid than herself once gave."

The following lines are inscribed on the tombstone of Michael Young, who died 17th March, 1818, aged eighty-three:—

> "How awful is the scene while here I tread
> These venerable mansions of the dead!
> Time was these ashes liv'd, and time shall be
> When others thus shall stand and gaze on me.
> Awake, then, O my soul, true wisdom learn,
> Nor till to-morrow the great work adjourn."

Alexander Young and his wife are commemorated thus:—

> "Here lies interr'd in silent throng
> The corps of Alexander Young;
> In Floors of Eaglesham he dwelt,
> But now the power of death has felt;
> From mortal stage he took his way
> On June the one and twentyth day,
> Seventeen hundred and seventy years,
> As by old history appears.
> Renownèd age his head did crown
> Ere to the grave he did go down;
> Threescore and two years was full spent
> Ere through death's gloomy path he went.
> But he alone doth not reside
> In gloomy mansions of the dead,
> For her who was his wife most dear
> Doth also sleep entombèd here;
> And those that now his children are,
> This shall your future rest prepare."

PARISH OF EASTWOOD.

In Eastwood Churchyard two Covenanters, James Algie and John Park, who suffered at the Cross of Paisley in 1685, are on their tombstone commemorated thus:—

> "Stay, passenger, as thou goes by,
> And take a look where these do ly,
> Who, for the love they bare to truth,
> Were deprived of their life and youth.
> Tho' laws made then caused many die,
> Judges and 'sizers were not free;
> He that to them did these delate,
> The greater count he hath to make;
> Yet no excuse to them can be:
> At ten condemned, at two to die.
> So cruel did their rage become,
> To stop their speech caus'd beat the drum.
> This may a standing witness be
> 'Twixt Presbytery and Prelacy." *

An aisle of the parish church is the burial-place of the Baroneted House of Maxwell of Pollok, now represented by Sir William Stirling Maxwell, Bart., of Keir. Walter Steuart, of Pardovan, author of the celebrated "Collections" in connection with the Scottish Church, died while on a visit at Pollok House, and was interred in the family aisle. A marble monument erected to his memory is thus inscribed:—

"Within this aisle lyes Walter Steuart, of Pardovan, son of Walter Steuart, of Pardovan, and grandson to Archibald Steuart, of Blackhall, a gent well skilled in most parts of useful learning, and in the constitution of his country, and eminent for his unbiass'd zeal for its ancient and real interests; which he shewed by his early appearance for the Protestant religion, in accompanying King William from Holland at the glorious Revolution, 1688, and afterwards by his faithful services in our Scots Parliament, where he for many years represented the borough of Linlithgow. Of such distinguished piety and zeal for our holy religion that he mortified 20,000 merks to the society in Scotland

---

* This inscription is repeated on a monument to these martyrs in Paisley Cemetery (see *postea*).

for propagating Christian knowledge. He dyed March 8th, 1719, aged fifty-two years, at the seat of his affectionate kinsman, Sir John Maxwell, of Pollok, one of the senators of the Colledg of Justice; and is interred in the burial-place of that honorable family, which, by permission of the honorable proprietor, is likewise design'd for the burial-place of his dear spouse, Katherin Cornwall, daughter of James Cornwall, of Bonhead, who has erected this monument to the memory of her dearly beloved husband."

A tombstone denotes the resting-place of the Rev. Robert Wodrow, the celebrated historian. Youngest son of Mr. James Wodrow, Professor of Divinity in the University of Glasgow, he was born in that city in 1679. Having studied at Glasgow College, he became librarian to the institution. Licensed in 1703, he was in the same year ordained minister of Eastwood. His acceptance as a preacher led to his receiving calls from Glasgow and Stirling, both of which he declined. At the Union in 1707, he was member of a committee for supporting the interests of the Church. On the accession of George I. he was with some others deputed by the General Assembly to plead with Government for the abolition of Church patronage. His great work "The History of the Sufferings of the Church of Scotland from the Restoration to the Revolution," was published in 1721-2, in two folio volumes. It was approved by the General Assembly, and dedicated to George I., who presented the author with 100 guineas in token of his royal approval. Mr. Wodrow designed to publish a series of biographical memoirs of eminent ministers of the Church of Scotland; many of these are preserved in MS. in the Library of Glasgow University. The materials on which he founded his "History," including twenty-four volumes of his correspondence, are preserved in the Advocates Library, and in the archives of the Church. Selections from his memoirs entitled "Collections upon the Lives of the Reformers," in two quarto volumes, were published at Glasgow in 1834 and 1845. Three octavo volumes of his "Correspondence" and his "Analecta," or Diary, in four volumes, have also been printed. Mr. Wodrow died 21st March, 1734, in his fifty-fifth year, and the thirty-first of his ministry.

PARISH OF GREENOCK.

A monumental statue of the celebrated James Watt, by Chantrey, occupies a conspicuous position in the Watt Institution. The statue, which is of white marble, represents the great engineer holding in his right hand a diagram, while with the other he is applying to it a pair of compasses. The pedestal presents the following inscription, composed by Lord Jeffrey :—

" The inhabitants of Greenock have erected this statue of James Watt, not to extend a fame already identified with the miracles of steam, but to testify the pride and reverence with which he is remembered in the place of his nativity, and their deep sense of the great benefits his genius has conferred upon mankind. Born 19th January, 1736. Died at Heathfield, in Staffordshire, August 25, 1819."

Son of a small trader who bore the same Christian name, James Watt, received an ordinary education at the Grammar School of Greenock; and having selected a mechanical trade, he proceeded to London, and in his eighteenth year became apprentice to a mathematical instrument maker at Cornhill. At the end of a year ill-health compelled him to return to Greenock. In 1757 he proposed to settle in Glasgow as a mathematical instrument maker, but being opposed by the corporation of hammermen, he sought and obtained employment within the walls of the university. His workshop in Glasgow College became the resort of professors and men of science. In 1767 he was employed to make surveys and prepare estimates for a canal to unite the Forth and Clyde; he afterwards prepared a survey for the canal between Fort William and Inverness. His attention had in 1759 been directed to the capabilities of steam as a motive power, and some time after he tried experiments on the force of steam by means of a Papin's digester. In 1763, when repairing a Newcomen engine used for pumping water out of mines, he discovered its defects, and forthwith proceeded to construct a machine of an improved character. He now formed a partnership with Dr. Roebuck of the Carron Ironworks, for the construction of steam engines; and a model was erected at Kinneil, near Borrowstounness. Dr. Roebuck's unexpected embarrassments led him to seek another partnership, and he was fortunate in forming such a connection with Matthew Boulton, of Soho, near Birmingham. Aided by this ingenious person, he was enabled to carry out his invention in all its details, and to secure by a series of patents the benefits of his discovery. After twenty-seven years' labour at Soho, he retired from business in 1800, conveying to his two sons his interest in the prosperous business which he and Boulton had established. Watt was admitted to membership of most of the learned societies in the United Kingdom and on the Continent. He died at Heathfield, Staffordshire, on the 25th August, 1819. In 1824 his statue, by a national subscription, was erected at Birmingham, and monuments or institutions in his honour have been reared in the principal towns.

In the west church burying-ground two altar stones, placed contiguously, denote the burial-place of James and Thomas Watt, father and grandfather of the engineer. On the tombstone of the engineer's grandfather is an inscription, executed by an illiterate stone-hewer; it is subjoined *verbatim*:—

"T. W. M. S.

"This is teburrialplace of Thomas Watprofesor of the Matematicks in Graford-dykhis wife and children 1701.

Names.	Age.			Time of death.
	Y	M	D	
Marg	0	11		6 Oct. 1683.
Catren	0	00		10 Dec. 1687.
Thomas	2	4		4 Feb. 1687.
Dorithie	18	5		20 Aug. 1706.

"Thomas Watt died Feb. 28th 1734 aged 92. Margaret Sherrer his spouse died March 21 1755 aged 79, lived in marredge 55 years."

The other tombstone was erected by the engineer, in memory of his parents and an only brother. It is inscribed thus:—

"In memory of James Watt, merchant in Greenock, a benevolent and ingenious man, and a zealous promoter of the improvements of the Town who died 17 2 aged ". Of Agnes Muirheid his spouse who died 1733 aged 50, and of John Watt their son who perished at sea 1765 aged 25. To his revered parents and to his brother, James Watt has placed this memorial."

Thomas Watt, the engineer's grandfather, was born in Aberdeenshire, where his family had previously resided. His father, the great-grandfather of the engineer, farmed a little property of his own. He was killed while fighting on the side of the Covenanters against the Marquis of Montrose.

A memorial slab in the interior of the old church commemorates Thomas Crawfurd of Cartsburn, who died 3rd February, 1743. This branch of the house of Crawfurd descends from the family of Crawfurd of Kilbirnie. George Crawfurd, author of the "Genealogical History of the Royal Family of Stewart," "A Description of the Shire of Renfrew," and other works, was a member of the family.

An elegant monument has by public subscription been erected at the grave of Mary Campbell, celebrated by Burns. It contains a sculpture representing the parting of Burns and Mary, surmounted by a figure weeping over an urn, with these lines beneath:—

"My Mary dear, departed shade,
Where is thy place of blissful rest?"

Within a railed enclosure a small tombstone is thus inscribed:—

"This burying-place belongs to Peter McPherson, ship carpenter in Greenock, and Mary Campbell his spouse, and their children, 1787."

Burns became acquainted with "Highland Mary" about the year 1785, when she was serving his friend Gavin Hamilton at Mauchline. She is described as a sprightly blue-eyed girl, possessed of true modesty and real worth. She was a native of Dunoon; her father, who was a sailor in a revenue cutter, afterwards resided at Campbelton. On Sunday, the 14th of May, 1786, Mary and Burns held a farewell meeting in a secluded spot on the banks of the Ayr. Their adieu was performed with a striking ceremonial, common to the rural courtships of the West. The lovers stood on each side of a small brook; they laved their hands in the stream, and, holding a Bible between them, vowed mutual fidelity. Mary presented the poet with a Bible in one volume; Burns handed her in return a more elegant one in two volumes. The lovers never again met. Mary returned to Campbelton, where she some months resided with her parents. Meanwhile her younger brother, Robert, was entered as an apprentice with Peter McPherson, ship carpenter at Greenock, whose wife was a cousin of Mary's mother. Mary accompanied her brother to Greenock, with the double purpose of seeing him safely transferred to the care of her relation, and of taking farewell of Burns before his intended departure for the West Indies. On the day following his arrival at Greenock Mary's brother fell ill; Mary attended him with care and tenderness, and he recovered. But Mary was seized next, and her illness proved to be fever of a most malignant type. In a few days she expired, and her remains were interred in McPherson's burial-place. She died in November, 1786.

On his tombstone a lengthened inscription celebrates the learning and personal qualities of John Wilson, Master of the Grammar School in Greenock, who died on the 2nd June, 1789, aged sixty.

On the tombstone of Robert Andrew Macfie and his wife and children are these lines:—

> "The saints, in early life remov'd,
> In sweeter accents sing,
> And bless the swiftness of the flight
> That bore them to their King."

James Shaw, butcher, who died in 1799, is by his widow celebrated thus:—

> "A tender parent, a dear friend,
> A loving husband to the end.

This truth is certain,
When this life is o'er,
Man dies to live,
And lives to die no more."

In the cemetery a handsome monument of Aberdeen granite commemorates Robert Wallace of Kelly, who died on the 1st April, 1855. It is thus inscribed:—

"Robert Wallace was the descendant and representative of the renowned champion of Scottish independence, and inherited no small portion of the patriotic spirit and indomitable energy of his ancestor. He sat in Parliament as member for Greenock from 1832 to 1845, being returned four times in succession free of expense, and by his indefatigable and successful labours in the cause of legal and post office reform, he not only justified the choice of the electors, but established a title to the lasting gratitude of his countrymen. His casting vote as chairman of the committee of the House of Commons secured to the nation the benefit of the penny postage."

Mr. Wallace was lineally descended from Sir Richard Wallace of Riccarton, uncle of the patriot. His father, John Wallace of Cessnock, Ayrshire, purchased in 1792 the estate of Kelly, having previously sold Cessnock. Robert Wallace succeeded his father in 1805. For many years he engaged in business as a West India merchant. In 1832 he was elected M.P. for Greenock, which he represented for thirteen successive years. His important services in connection with post office reform were widely appreciated. He died in his eighty-second year.

An elegant monument celebrates the personal worth and public spirit of Walter Baine, chief magistrate of the burgh, and subsequently its representative in Parliament.

In an elevated portion of the cemetery a cairn composed of stones from different parts of the world has been piled in honour of James Watt.

A handsome obelisk of Peterhead granite commemorates the Rev. Patrick M'Farlan, D.D., minister of the Free West Church. In the inscription Dr. M'Farlan is thus described:—

"A man of God, nobly gifted, and learned in the Word, he faithfully prosecuted the blessed gospel and adorned it by his life. His sterling worth, sweetened by courtesy, exalted him in public esteem and endeared him to his flock. A wise counsellor of the Church in her difficulties, he stood firm in her trials, and despising for conscience' sake her temporal gains, was called amidst devoted labours to his honoured rest. Born 4th April, 1781; died 13th November, 1849."

In the burgh a memorial fountain of polished granite commemorates John Galt, the eminent novelist. This ingenious writer was born at Irvine, on the 2nd May, 1779. With an ordinary education he engaged in mercantile concerns at Greenock, and afterwards in London. He subsequently entered at Lincoln's Inn, but eventually abandoned legal pursuits. From failing health he proceeded to the Mediterranean. At Gibraltar in 1809 he made the acquaintance of Lord Byron and his friend Mr. Hobhouse, and in their company sailed to Sicily, whence he proceeded to Malta and Greece. He devised a scheme for creating a mercantile establishment in the Levant, but his suggestions were not accepted by Government. In 1804 he published anonymously a poem entitled "The Battle of Largs," which he afterwards endeavoured to suppress. In 1811 he published his "Travels in the East." Other works followed, but he first evinced decided power as a writer in "The Ayrshire Legatees," which was published in *Blackwood's Magazine* in 1820. "The Annals of the Parish" appeared in the following year. Having now attained a high literary reputation, he continued to issue a series of romances, which became more or less popular. Along with his literary labours he much occupied himself in commercial speculations. In 1824 he became superintendent of the Canada Company for disposing to emigrants portions of the Crown lands in Upper Canada. This office yielded him £1,000 a year; but having become involved in disputes with the Government, he in 1827 tendered his resignation. After a life of extraordinary labours and unhappy vicissitudes he retired to Greenock, where he died on the 11th April, 1839. Many of his works are forgotten; others maintain a steady popularity. In portraying the peculiarities of Scottish village life he is altogether unrivalled.

PARISH OF HOUSTON.

In the aisle of the Red Friars monastery are several monuments. A magnificent tomb contains under a canopy two statues the size of life; one is supposed to represent Sir Patrick Houston of that ilk, who died in 1440, the other Sir Patrick's wife, Agnes Campbell, who died in 1456. Sir Patrick is dressed in a coat of mail, his head resting on a pillow, and his feet upon a lion with a lamb in its paws. Both figures have their hands elevated as in the act of prayer. An inscription on the tomb has become illegible.

A monument on the south wall of the aisle represents a variety of emblematical figures. On the top an old man crowned with long flowing hair and a loose robe places his foot on a large globe, on each side of which is a small image blowing a trumpet. A chain thrown across the globe hangs down on each side, and is grasped by two children, one having three faces, the other with a cloth bound over his eyes. Beneath is the following inscription:—

"Hic sita est Domina Anna Hamilton, delectissima Domini Patricii Houston, eodem, Baronetti conjux sua, quæ obiit tertio die idus Maias, anno salutis partæ, milesimo sexcentesimo et septuagesimo octavo."

PARISH OF INCHINNAN.

In the churchyard of Inchinnan several ridged stones having figures of swords engraved on their sloping sides are believed to commemorate some members of the Knights Templars, who possessed a settlement in the district.

PARISH OF INNERKIP.

In the parish churchyard is the burying-place of Sir Gabriel Wood, founder of the Mariners' Institution at Greenock which bears his name. A tombstone commemorates his father, Gabriel Wood, a highly respected merchant of Greenock, who died 23rd October, 1828, aged eighty-four.

PARISH OF KILMALCOLM.

The old family of Porterfield, of that ilk, interred in a vault connected with the old church; it bore the following inscriptions:—

> " Bvreit heir lyis,
> That deth defyis,
>   Of Porterfeild's the race;
> Qvho be the sprit,
> To Christ unite,
>   Are heirs of gloir throw grace.
>   1566."

> " This anagrame vnfold my bvilder sal,
> His name qvha vil into this sentence seik,
> Til flie the il, mak gvid report of al:
> Gvilliame sal find, Porterfeild of that ilk.
> Zeirs sevintie fyve, to live, he livit and mo,
> And nov for ay livs with the Gods but vo."

PARISH OF LOCHWINNOCH.

Within the walls of the Old Collegiate Church is the burying-place of the old family of Sempill, of Castle Semple.

In the churchyard Elizabeth, daughter of Hugh Montgomerie of Broadly, who died in 1819, aged twenty-seven, is commemorated thus :—

> "Kind to the poor, here virtue's path she trod,
> Now robed in white she stands before her God."

These lines are from the tombstone of Hugh Montgomerie, who died in 1819, aged sixty-eight :—

> "Of judgment clear, of firm decided mind,
> The lover and the friend of human kind,
> Spotless through life he steer'd his onward way,
> His death the evening of a beauteous day."

A handsome monument, reared by public subscription, commemorates Dr. Andrew Crawfurd, a local antiquary, who died at Lochwinnoch on the 27th December, 1854.

PARISH OF PAISLEY.

Malcolm IV., on attaining his majority in the summer of 1163, visited his Castle of Fotheringay, in Northamptonshire; and on the 1st of July of that year met his second cousin, Henry II. of England, at Woodstock. The King of Scots was accompanied by Engelram his chancellor, Walter his steward, Richard his chaplain, and a retinue of attendants becoming his dignity. During his residence at Fotheringay, Walter the High Steward sealed a charter establishing a house of devotion at Paisley of Cluniac monks from Wenlock, Shropshire, the county of his progenitors. The house was founded as a priory; fifty-six years afterwards, in 1219, it was constituted an abbey by Pope Honorius III.

The priory consisted of a chancel, choir, transept, and nave, and was munificently endowed by the Steward and his successors. The abbey buildings were burned and destroyed by the English in

1306, and were not fully restored till 1451. It may properly be designated the burial-place of the House of Stuart. It contains the remains of Walter, the founder of the church, his son Alan, his son Walter; his grandson James, his son Walter, and Marjory Bruce his wife, daughter of King Robert the Bruce, and of Elizabeth Mure and Euphemia Ross, the two consorts of Robert II. In a charter erecting the village of Paisley into a burgh of barony on the 19th August, 1488, James IV. refers to the monastery as the burial-place of many of his ancestors, his words being—

"Vbi plvrima progenitorvm nostrorvm,
Corpora sepelivntvr et reqviescvnt."

St. Mirin's aisle is the burying-place of the ducal house of Abercorn. Before the Reformation interments were made in the chancel and nave, and also in the yard of St. Roque's Chapel. In 1789, when Dr. Boog, one of the ministers of the church, made his renovations in the nave, the tombstones lying on the floor were put into the wall—which has fortunately preserved them. The tombstones in the chancel are of dates subsequent to the Reformation. The present burial-ground, lying to the north of the nave and transept, was opened about 1608, and shortly thereafter interments in the nave and St. Roque's Chapel were discontinued.

The old stones are of a dark hard texture, and the inscriptions are generally in bas-reliefs coiled along the margin, and in fine specimens of Saxon and Roman letters.

In the nave are six monuments: that of Abbot John Lithgow is thus inscribed:—

"iohes · a · lychtgw · abbas · huius · monastii · xx · die · mesis · January · ano · dm · M · cccc xxxiij · Elegit · fieri · sua · sepultura."

This tablet, which is inserted in the north porch of the nave, bears that John Lithgow, abbot of the monastery, on the 20th

January, MCCCCXXXIII., selected his place of sepulture. John Lithgow was Abbot of Paisley in January, 1368, as appears from an instrument in his favour defining the privileges of the monastery. Abbot Lithgow was appointed by Robert III., grandson of King Robert the Bruce. He lived to an old age, having held the pastoral staff for the long period of sixty-four years. He is the only abbot whose name appears on the monastery buildings.

A tablet commemorates James Crawfurd, of Kilwinnet, with the following inscription :—

"Hic Jacet Jacobz Crawfurd d Kilbynet q · obit xx
. . . . . . cccc° nonage° ix Orate · p · aia eius."

James Crawfurd was a cadet of the family of Crawfurd of Thirdpart, in the parish of Kilbarchan, and county of Renfrew; he and his wife, Elizabeth Calbraith, acquired the lands of Kilwinnet, an estate in the earldom of Lennox and county of Stirling. He also acquired the lands of Seedhill and Wellmeadows, in the burgh of Paisley, in May, 1490. In 1493 Abbot George Schaw appointed him one of the two bailies of Paisley. On the 15th July, 1499, he and his wife founded a chapel and constituted a chaplain to the altar of Saint Mirin and Saint Columba, giving for endowment his lands of Wellmeadow and Seidhill. The chapel was erected after his death : it is known as Saint Mirin's Aisle, or more popularly the *Sounding Aisle,* and of which Pennant said in 1771, " It had the finest echo, perhaps, in the world." James Crawfurd before his death exchanged the lands of Kilwinnet for one-half of the lands of Spango, in the parish of Innerkip. Mrs. Crawfurd died about three years after her husband.

A tablet in memory of William Pyrre is inscribed thus :—

"William. Pyrre died on ye first day of Junj ye zer of god. m° n° and ix. zers orate."

The Pyrres were for a century and a half an opulent family in Paisley. William Pyrre's tablet is inserted in the south wall of the nave. His son, who bore the same Christian name, was chosen a bailie of Paisley in 1511, and on the 20th October, 1520, mortified xiiis iiijd to the altar of St. Peter. His son John was appointed a bailie of Paisley in 1540.

In the interior of the north aisle of the nave a stone, inscribed in Roman letters, contains the Hamilton arms for an ecclesiastic, with the initials I. H. and the motto—

"MISERICORDIA ET PAX."

It commemorates Abbot John Hamilton, one of the three natural sons of James Hamilton, first Earl of Arran. Appointed in 1625, through the favour of his father, he exercised great influence over his brother James, second Earl of Arran, Governor of Scotland during the minority of Queen Mary. He was appointed Bishop of Dunkeld in 1543, and promoted to the Archbishopric of St. Andrews in 1549. A firm adherent of Queen Mary, he was condemned by the regent Lennox, and was hanged at Stirling on the 1st April, 1570.

A monument commemorates Captain Robert Crawfurd, chamberlain of Paisley; it is thus inscribed:—

"heir lyis ——— aiptane robert craufurd granter of paslay i ye sepultur of James Craufurd of Sedil qlk decessit ye fourt of Julij ye zeir of God, 1575, quha neuir racebit honors of na man and hir maid to mony sundry."

Captain Crawfurd was grand-nephew of James Crawfurd of Seidhill. At the death of the Laird of Seedhill, his brother Alexander made up titles to the lands of Spango, which had been exchanged for those of Kilwinnet. In 1517 James Crawfurd, the eldest son of Alexander, succeeded to the lands of Spango, which he disposed in 1541 to his two natural sons, James and Robert Crawfurd. Robert resigned his half to his brother James. The inscription completes Robert's history, by showing that he was both captain and chamberlain to the monastery. The mortuary biographer further gives his opinion that Robert Crawfurd was a very independent gentleman, because he never received honours from any man, and had conferred on many sundry favours. On the 1st June, 1597, the Town Council, patrons of the chaplaincy of Saints Mirin and Columba, mortified by James Crawfurd of Seedhill, and Donators of the Crown after the Reformation, feued the lands of Seedhill to Hew Crawfurd, son to the deceased Robert Crawfurd, sometime granter of Paisley.

A stone inserted in the north wall of the aisle thus celebrates James Steuart of Cardonald:—

"heir lyis ane honorabill man James Stewart of Cardonald. Somtyme capitane of ye Gard of Scotland to France quha decessit ye xb day of Januar ano dm 1584.
☧ lord I comend my saul into yi handis qlk yob hes Redemit by yi precious blud."

The House of Darnley Lennox furnished many valiant captains to the military service of France; their courage secured them preferment and fame. The Scots guard at the fatal field of Verneuil, fought on 16th August, 1424, was chiefly composed of men, actually natives of Scotland. Scotsmen continued to join the Scots guard in France, and Captain Steuart, following the spirit of his ancestors, volunteered his services to the French king. According to the Scripture quotation on his tombstone, now inserted in the north wall of the nave, he died in Christian hope. Captain Steuart was grandson of Allan Steuart, *filio carnali* of John, first Earl of Lennox. He built the mansion-house of Cardonald (lately taken down), in which there was a stone tablet, containing his armorial bearings with his initials and motto:—

"I S
TOVIOVRS
AVANT, 1562."

In 1569 Margaret Steuart, only child of the preceding, married Sir John Stewart of Mynto, Provost of Glasgow. Walter Stewart, the eldest son of that marriage, was appointed Commendator of Blantyre in 1580, and created Lord Blantyre in 1606. The present Lord Blantyre is his lineal descendant.

A tablet in the north wall of the nave commemorates certain members of the family of Inglis. This inscription, which is in bas-relief, reads thus:—

"Heir lyis Thomas Inglis Bailze of PASLAY qvha Decessit ye 1502. And David Inglis his sone 1533. Johnne Inglis sone to DAVID 1559. THOMAS INGLIS SONE to IHONEV BAILIIS of ye BVRGH for YE TYME AND ISSABELL MVIR SPOVSE TO ye SAID THOMAS."

The first Thomas Inglis must have been a bailie between 1493 and 1502; David, his son, was a bailie in 1530, 1531, and 1533; John, his son, was a bailie in 1538 and 1544; Thomas, his son, was a bailie nine times between 1592 and 1617 : he died in 1622, aged seventy-eight. All the four were lawyers in Paisley; the last, Thomas, was town-clerk and agent for Claud Hamilton, Lord Paisley, and his son, the Marquis of Abercorn.

In the chapel erected from money bequeathed by James Crawfurd of Kilwinnet and Seidhill, and dedicated to Saints Mirin and Columba, now called Saint Mirin's Aisle, is a massive altar tomb of composite construction, vulgarly called "Queen Blearie's Tomb." Queen Blearie was Marjory Bruce, daughter of King Robert the Bruce, and mother of Robert II., who had bloodshot or blear eyes. In the chancel, prior to 1789, lay a statue of a female, believed to represent Marjory Bruce. In 1789 Dr. Boog, minister of the abbey church, discovered other sculptured stones among a heap of rubbish. These were all put together, and in 1817 Dr. Boog had the whole very ingeniously erected in St. Mirin's Aisle. A stone with three coats of arms, one representing the Paisley shield, forms the end; sculptured stones from the rubbish heap constitute three sides, and a slab with the female statue and canopy surmounts the whole. On the right and left sides there are nine compartments, with half-compartments at each end. On the right side the first compartment is occupied by an abbot, holding in his hand a pastoral staff. In the fourth compartment is a bishop at prayer, with the name on a scroll, robert wyshard. On the left side an abbot is celebrating at the altar, with the name ioḣes ꝺ lẏtcḣtgw, and there is an abbot at prayer with the name ioḣes ꝺ lẏcḣtgw. Such of the other compartments as are filled represent monks in the attitude of prayer. Robert Wishard was Bishop of Glasgow; he died in 1316. From the repetition of the name of *Abbot Lychtgw*, it is obvious that this portion is supplied from a monument erected in commemoration of that abbot. The statue of the female is supposed to refer to Marjory Bruce.

Three children of Claud Hamilton, Lord Paisley, are on a tombstone commemorated thus:—

"D. O. M.

"Piæ . infantvm . Margaretæ . Henrici . et . Alexandri . Hamiltoniorvm . memoriæ . Clavdivs . Hamiltonivs . Pasleti . dominvs . et . Margareta . seton . eivs . vxor . proli charissime . cvm . lachr : poss : obiere . Margareta . an : sal : 1577 . x . Kalen : ian : nata . menses tres . dies . xxii.   Henricvs . 1585 id : Mar . natvs . menses tres . dies . dvos . Alexander . 1587 . xi . kal . Decemb . natvs . menses . Octo . dies tres.

Felices . anime . vobis . svprema . parentes
Solvvnt . vos . illis solvereqvæ . decvit." *

Claud Hamilton was third son of James, second Earl of Arran, and first Duke of Chatelherault. He was born in Blackness Castle, in September, 1543. When he had attained the age of fourteen, his illegitimate uncle, Abbot John Hamilton, conveyed to him the temporalities of the abbey. After undergoing many vicissitudes of fortune, he was by James VI. created Lord Paisley in 1587. He married Margaret Seton, daughter of George, sixth

---

* TRANSLATION.

"God, the Governor of the World.—In memory of the pious infants, Margaret, Henry and Alexander Hamilton, the beloved children of Claud Hamilton, Lord Paisley, and Margaret Seton his wife. They died much lamented: Margaret, 23rd December, 1577 ; aged 3 months and 22 days: Henry, 15th March, 1585; aged 3 months and 2 days: Alexander, 11th December, 1587; aged 8 months and 3 days.

Blessed souls, to your death this is devoted:
He that hath taken you hath done what beseemeth Him."

Lord Seton, by whom he had other five children, beside those named on the monument. He converted St. Mirin's Chapel into a burial-place for the use of his family. In the aisle a vault was constructed for the reception of his remains. His descendants, the members of the noble family of Abercorn, also interred in the vault.

When the vault was opened a few years ago, consequent on the competition between the late Duke of Hamilton and the present Duke of Abercorn to the Dukedom of Chatelherault, the plates on the coffins of the Earls of Abercorn were found to bear the French title of Duke of Chatelherault.

In the chancel of the abbey a monument thus celebrates Mrs. Marion Montgomerie, relict of Patrick Peebles, Provost of Irvine:—

"Here . lyes . a . faithfvl . sister . Marion . Montgomerie . spovs . to . vmqll . Patrik . Peblis . of . Brvmelands . Provost. of . Irvine. and mother . in . law. to. Thomas . Inglis . of . Corsflet . Bailie . of . Paislay qvha deceissit 28 Ian 1620 yeiris."

Thomas Inglis is in the chancel commemorated thus :—

"Heir lyes a faithfvl broher Thomas Inglis of Corsflat qvha decisst the 27 of May 1622 etatis sve 78."

Thomas Inglis inherited from his ancestors several properties in Paisley; and on the 31st May, 1578, he and his first wife, Isobel Muir, purchased the lands of Corsflat, adjoining the abbey garden. In 1612 he granted his property situated at the West Port of Paisley for an hospital for the maintenance of "sax puir men." The Town Council, on 30th April of that year, ordained that the Chapel of Saint Rocque, in Broomlands, of Paisley, should be taken down, and "the staines timmer and sclates" applied in the erection of the hospital or almshouse. In 1724 the hospital was rebuilt; it was again taken down in 1808. On the front wall was the following inscription :—

> "He that has pitie on the pvir
> Of grace and mercie sal be svir
> Qvha gives the pvir to God he lends
> And God agane mair grace him sends."

In the chancel a monument to Allan Lockhart, of Hindschelwood, is inscribed as follows :—

"Heir lyes ane worthie · Gentelman · Allan · Lockhart · of . Hindschelvod lait baile of Paslay · qvha . decisit · the · 10 · of · Apryl · ano · 1635 etatis · 42. I · have · fovght a good fight I have finished my covrse · I · have · kepit · the faith. 2 : Tim. 4 : 7."

Allan Lockhart was son of Allan Lockhart, of Cleghorn, parish of Lanark, and was born in 1593. In connection with a matter of family history he claims more than a passing notice. He married Marion Peibles, widow of Thomas Inglis, of Corsflat. Inglis had expressed a wish that his only daughter, Anna, should be married to Montgomerie, of Hesilhead, a kinsman by her mother's side. In direct contravention of this desire, Lockhart, on marrying Inglis's widow, caused the daughter, then under twelve years, to accept as her husband William Cunningham, younger, of Aitket. Aitket fell into dissipated habits, and maltreated his young wife. Mr. Robert Baillie, in his "Letters," under date 20th August, 1641, writes as follows :—

"Friday, 6th. A world of Bills came to be referred to the Parliament. Among the rest, Anna Inglis complaining that her husband, young Aiket Cunynhame, having received 40,000 merks tocher with her, had deserted her after frequent tormenting her with strokes and hunger, he debauching all with harlots in Paisley. We sent two with this bill to the Parliament to get present order. The justice of God was in this matter. The damsel's father had left her to be married to Mr. Hugh Montgomerie, of Hesilhead, his wife's near cousin. After, his widow fell in conceit with Allan Lockhart, and gives herself to him, and by his persuasion makes her daughter when scarce twelve years of age, without proclamation, to be married to his cousin Aiket. For her reward, her husband, Allan, leaves her to pay 10,000 merks of his debt, which made her a poor vexed widow."

In the Court of Session, Anna Inglis raised an action of Reduction of her marriage, on the plea of minority and lesion, and the Court found the action competent. Her husband died in 1645. On 8th April, 1668, her son, James Cunningham, became a burgess of Paisley.

John Hutchinson, a magistrate of Paisley, and factor for Lord Paisley, is celebrated thus :—

"Here lyeth ane faithful · brother · called Johne Hutchesone Baillie of Paislay who decessit the 22 of Februar, 1625."

An inscription in the chancel thus celebrates two members of the old family of Henderson :—

"Heir lyeth Robert Henderson and Magdalen Hovstovne, 1629; Thomas Henderson and Malie Cochrane."

David Maxwell is thus commemorated :—

"Here lyeth Ionete · Delop · spovs · to · David Maxwal · merchand · bvrges of Paisley, qvha decesed 1643."

David Maxwell was chosen treasurer of the burgh in 1635. His cousin, Jean Knox, only child of William Knox of Selvieland and his second wife Margaret Maxwell, conveyed the whole to David Maxwell and his wife Janet Dunlop, on the 12th May, 1642. William Knox of Selvieland by his first wife had a son, Alexander, who succeeded to the lands of Selvieland. David Maxwell died before 1658.

In the chancel a flat stone with the date 1648 is inscribed with the initials of Robert Alexander of Blackhouse, Ayrshire, and with the initials of his two wives, and their respective shields. Robert Alexander was born in 1604. He had a long and successful career as a solicitor in Paisley; he was also town clerk. He was elected a magistrate in 1647. He purchased Blackhouse in 1648; he afterwards acquired properties in Paisley and elsewhere. He also purchased properties for his several children for their advancement in the world. His first wife was Marion Hamilton, daughter of Claud Hamilton of Blackhole. He married secondly Janet Henderson, daughter of David Henderson of Paisley. His tombstone was placed by himself to denote his right of sepulture in the abbey church.

In the church an elegant monument commemorates William

M'Dowall of Castlesemple and Garthland, Lord Lieutenant of Renfrewshire, and representative of the county in Parliament. The monument was reared by public subscription in 1810.

A mortuary enclosure protects the remains of the noble family of Cathcart. A monument commemorates William Schaw Cathcart, first Earl of Cathcart, born 17th September, 1755, died 16th June, 1843, and his countess, who died 14th December, 1847; also Augusta Sophia Cathcart, their youngest daughter, born 25th November, 1792, died 18th November, 1846.

A mural tablet celebrates Lieutenant-General the Honourable Sir George Cathcart, *aide-de-camp* to his father, General Earl Cathcart. " He fell gloriously in command of the fourth division at the battle of Inkermann, on the 5th November, 1854."

In the Abbey Churchyard Bailie Thomas Peter is thus celebrated:—

" Heir lyis ane honest man callit Thomas Piter, bailzie of Paslay, qvha decissit ye 10 of Nov., Anno 1609, & Ionet Vrie his spovs; & Iohne Piter thair sone and Margaret Craig his spovs, qvha deceissit ye 30 of Octob., Anno 1617."

Thomas Peter was a bailie of Paisley in 1605. He was one of the first interred in the Abbey Churchyard. One of his descendants went to Glasgow and became a successful merchant in that city, of which he was elected dean of guild. He presented to the magistrates of Paisley three thousand merks Scots, the annual rent of which was to be applied to the maintenance of decayed burgesses.

John Alexander, a prosperous shoemaker, is celebrated thus:—

" Heir lyis Iohne Alexander, Cordovner, bvrges of Paslay, and Bessie Carswall his spovs, J. A."

John Alexander's eldest son Robert became town clerk of Paisley in 1636, and a very successful man of business. He was founder of the Newton, Southbar, and Ballochmyle families.

The tomb of William Algeo is thus inscribed:—

" Heir · lyis · ane · faithfwl · brother · called · William · Algeo ·

Bvrges · of · Paisley & Cirstin-Keibill · his · spovs · qvha · deseisit
. ye · zeir of God 1660."

The Algeo family came from Italy with one of the Abbots, and were connected with the monastery. John Algeo or Aldjoy, was proprietor of Bladoyard in 1490. One of the descendants, Peter Algeo, married Margaret Morton, heiress of Easter Walkingshaw, about the end of the sixteenth century.

The tombstone of William Skeoch, cordiner, and his wife Marion Kerlie, presents the following inscription :—

> " Remember · all · that · come · this · rod
> Hou · your · meeting · uill · be · uith · God
> If · it · be · sueet · you · may · be · shour
> That · Christ · is · been · the · opening · door."

Skeoch was one of the twenty founders of the Cordiners or Shoemakers' Society of Paisley, formed on 16th December, 1701. The motto of the society was—

> " GOD'S PROVIDENCE IS OUR INHERITANCE."

William Skeoch was first deacon of the craft. His grandson, Alexander Skeoch, was town clerk of Paisley and laird of Gockston. The Shoemakers' Society, after existing 158 years, was dissolved in 1859.

A tablet, now forming the door lintel of a house in Wallneuk Street, commemorates Abbot George Schawe. The inscription, in Saxon letters, is as follows :—

> " Ya callit ye abbot georg of schawe
> about yis abbay gart make yis waw
> A thousande four hundereth zheyr,
> Auchty ande fywe the date but weir,
> Pray for his soulis salvacioun,
> Yat made thus nobil fundacioun."

Son of the laird of Sauchie and Greenock, George Schaw was born in 1434. He was elected Abbot of Paisley in 1476, demitted in 1498, and died in 1506, aged seventy-two. In great favour with the government of King James IV., he held high offices in the state. The great wall named in the inscription was nearly a mile in circumference, and was built with square ashlar stones. When the abbey garden was feued by the Earl of Abercorn in 1777, the wall was nearly all taken down. A portion remains on the bank of the Cart river.

On Tuesday, the 3rd February, 1685, James Algie and John Park, joint tenants of a small piece of land at Kinnieshead, near Pollokshaws, were tried for refusing to take the test oath, and were condemned and executed at the Cross of Paisley. Their bodies were buried in the Gallowgreen, then the place of execution. Some years after the Revolution a memorial stone was erected over their graves, bearing the following inscription:—

"Here lyes James Algie and John Park, in the Parroch of Eastwood, who suffered for the oath of Abjuratione, 1685.

"Stay, passenger, as thou goest by,
And take ane look qr they doe ly,
Who for the love they bore to truth,
Depryved were of yr life and youth,
The Lawes made then caused many dye,
Yett Judges and Sysers were not free
He yt to them did these delate,
The greater count he has to make;
Yett nae excuse to them can be,
Att ten condemned and two to dye,
Soe cruel did yr rage become,
To stop yr speech by took of drum,
There's cause to murne for qt was done;
For guiltless blood doeth cry to Heaven,
This may ane standing witness be
Betwixt Presbytrie and Prelacy."

In 1779 the martyrs' tomb was renewed. In 1835, by public subscription, a handsome monument, twenty feet in height, was reared in substitution for the older erection. Along with a modern version of the original inscription, it is inscribed as follows:—

"Their blood is shed,
In confirmation of the noblest claim—
Our claim to feed upon immortal truth,
To walk with God, to be divinely free,
To soar, and to anticipate the skies.

> Yet few remember them. They lived unknown,
> Till persecution dragged them into fame,
> And chased them up to heaven.—*Cowper*.

"Erected by the contributions of Christians of different denominations in and about Paisley, to renew and perpetuate a memorial of the respect and gratitude with which posterity still cherish the memory of the Martyrs of Scotland. MDCCCXXXV."

In 1845 the Paisley Cemetery was formed in the immediate neighbourhood of the martyrs' monument; it is now included in the grounds.

In the cemetery a handsome obelisk, erected by public subscription in 1867, commemorates Andrew Hardie and John Baird, who were executed at Stirling in 1820; and of James Wilson, who was executed at Glasgow in the same year, on convictions for high treason.

An elegant monumental statue commemorates the Rev. Patrick Brewster, one of the ministers of the abbey church. Youngest son of James Brewster, Rector of the Grammar School of Jedburgh, he was born on the 20th December, 1788. Obtaining licence as a probationer in 1817, he was in the following year ordained to the second charge of the Abbey Church. Taking a deep interest in political concerns, he upheld his opinions with a vehement pertinacity which occasionally provoked recrimination. He died on the 26th March, 1859, in his seventy-first year, and forty-first of his ministry. On his tombstone he is described thus :—

"He was a sincere Christian, an elegant and powerful advocate for the political enfranchisement of the people, the abolition of negro slavery, a national system of education, the repeal of the corn laws, the cause of temperance, and the rights of our ablebodied and infirm poor."

A handsome monument with a bronze bust marks the grave of Andrew Park, the ingenious poet. Park was born at Renfrew on the 7th March, 1807. In his fifteenth year he entered a commission warehouse in Paisley, and not long after published his first poem, entitled "The Vision of Mankind." About his twentieth year he commenced business in Glasgow as a hat manufacturer; after some years he disposed of his stock and proceeded to London. He returned to Glasgow in 1841, and became a bookseller. In 1856 he visited Egypt and other Eastern countries, and in the following year published a narrative of his travels, entitled "Egypt and the East." Of his twelve volumes of poems his "Silent Love" is the most popular. Several of his songs have been set to music. Park died at Glasgow on the 27th December, 1863.

In the cemetery a handsome obelisk commemorates James Kerr, M.D. It was erected in 1853 by public subscription, "in testimony of public respect for his private and professional character, and grateful acknowledgment of his invaluable services as the originator and promoter of the plan for supplying Paisley with water."

On his grave in the churchyard of the West Relief Church, a handsome monument of grey granite was erected in 1868, in memory of the poet Tannahill. Robert Tannahill was born at Paisley on the 3rd June, 1774. With an ordinary education at the burgh school, he was apprenticed to a cotton weaver. Collecting old or obscure airs he began to compose to them suitable words, which he jotted down on a rude writing-desk attached to his loom. Several of his songs were afterwards set to music by Robert Archibald Smith, the eminent composer. In 1805 he published a volume of "Poems and Songs," which at once became popular. Of a melancholy temperament, Tannahill was cheered by congenial society, but his habits became irregular, and his mind lost its balance; he threw himself into the river Cart and perished. He died on the 17th May, 1810, at the age of thirty-six. His more popular songs are " Jessie, the Flower o' Dumblane," "Bonnie Wood o' Craigie Lea," "Loudoun's Bonnie Woods and Braes," and "The Braes of Balquhither."

The churchyards of Paisley exhibit the following monumental rhymes:—

> "Frail as the leaves which quiver on the sprays,
> Like them man flourishes, like them decays."

"A wife's a feather, and a chief's a rod,
An honest man's the noblest work of God.

"Not gone from memory, not gone from love,
But gone to our Father's home above."

"O hear me still, my children dear,
When you my tomb pass by;
Think on the dark and silent grave
Where you must shortly lie."

"He was——
But words are wanting to say what :
Think what a friend should be,
And he was that."

"Beyond the sky
Our home is fixed,
Thereon be fixed our love;
Nor seek from earth what
Earth can ne'er supply."

"Though in the stream of time thy vessel glide,
And pure as heaven the waters seem to roll,
Ere long in calm or tempest shall the tide
Cast on a land unknown thy naked soul.
Ah, then, when life and death no more shall be,
Where, reader, wilt thou spend eternity?"

"My dust shall slumber in the ground,
Till the last trumpet's joyful sound,
Then burst the chains with sweet surprise,
And in my Saviour's image rise."

PARISH OF RENFREW.

On the farm of Knock an octagonal column ten feet in height, resting on a pedestal six feet in diameter, is, on very doubtful authority, alleged to denote the death-scene of Marjory Bruce, daughter of Robert the Bruce, and wife of Walter the High Steward. It was known as "Queen Blearie's Stane."* According to tradition, the princess had been hunting, and her horse having stumbled in a marsh, she was thrown from her saddle. Being far advanced in pregnancy, premature labour supervened, and the child was separated from her by a surgical operation at the cost of her life. The absurdity of the popular notion that her child was brought into the world by the Cæsarian operation, Lord Hailes has been at pains to refute. Marjory's child became Robert II., and a peculiar delicacy of eyesight, which he inherited from his grandfather, King Robert, led to his being styled Blearie, an appellation also attached to his royal mother. Marjory Bruce was by her husband committed to his family burying-place in Paisley Abbey.

In the old parish church are two sculptured figures, believed to represent Sir John Ross of Hawkhead, and his wife Marjory Mure. Sir John attained distinction by overcoming, in single combat, an English champion, sent by his sovereign to challenge all Scotland. The Englishman was of gigantic stature, while Ross was under the middle height. To compensate for his inequality of size he clothed himself in a dress of skin, the smooth side out, which he rendered slippery with oil. The stratagem succeeded. In struggling with him the Englishman was unable to retain his grasp, while Ross at length contrived to throw both his antagonist's arms out of joint. The statues now occupy a place in the aisle; they originally stood under an arch, which was surrounded by the following inscription, still legible:—

* The monument was removed in 1781, and the materials used in constructing a farm steading in the neighbourhood.

"Hic jacet Johēs: ros miles quōdem : dominus de hawkehede et marjoria uxor sua; orate pro meis, qui obiit."

In Renfrew Churchyard a tombstone bearing date 1691 is thus inscribed :—

> "Come, courteous reader, come and see
> This tomb of great antiquity;
> Three hundred years and more this stone
> Has covered corps called Robertson.
> And still for George, one of that race,
> This tomb remains the appointed place.
> Elizabeth Ritchie, his wife,
> Who by connection formed in life,
> Does jointly claim with him this place,
> Designèd by them for their race."

LANARKSHIRE.

PARISH OF AIRDRIE.

The churchyards of Airdrie abound in metrical epitaphs. The following are from Broomknoll burying-ground:—

"Grave, the guardian of our dust,
   Grave, the treasure of the skies;
Every atom of thy trust
   Rests in hope again to rise.
Hark, the judgment trumpet calls,—
   Soul, rebuild thy house of clay,
Immortality thy walls,
   And eternity thy day."

"Soon happier days in happier climes shall smile,
   Through earth's thronged visions while we toss;
'Tis tumult all and rage and endless strife;
But these shall vanish like the dreams of morn,
When death awakes us to immortal life."

"Babes thither caught from womb and breast,
   Claim right to sing above the rest;
Because they find the happy shore
They never saw or sought before."

"Be taught, vain man, how fleeting are thy joys,
   Thy boasted grandeur and thy glittering store;
Death comes and all thy favoured bliss destroys,
   Quick as a dream it fades and is no more.
And sons of sorrow, though the threatening storm,
   Of angry fortune overhang awhile,
Let not her frowns your inward peace deform."

Wellwynd Churchyard contains the following:—

"'Tis hard to part with those we love,
E'en when they go to rest above."

"My lovely flowers were plucked too soon,
But not too soon for glory;
Whom the gods love die young."

"Short though it seemed since we were one,
On this dark distant shore;
And oh, how small the stream that runs,
When death divides no more!"

"This tribute to a mother's care,
Affection prompts me here to show;
'Twas love unmixed that I did share
From her who lies interred below."

"The young, the gay,
This scene of earth explore,
The young, the gay!
Alas, is now no more.
A sudden call, a hapless doom,
Consigned his body early to the tomb."

"Young in years but old in knowledge,
And here she rests, for all her works are o'er;
She is not dead, but only gone before,
Christina, 'midst her loving friends,
Hath breathed the bitter blast;
And oh, her beauty soon did end,
As over her it passed.
'Tis well with her in youthful bloom,
From pain and sorrow gone;
But oh, we grieve so soon the tomb,
Hath claimed her for its own!"

PARISH OF AVONDALE.

On the battle-field of Drumclog a monumental obelisk, twenty-three feet in height, commemorates the victory which was here obtained by the soldiers of the Covenant. The monument is inscribed thus:—

"In commemoration of the victory obtained in this battle-field, on Sabbath, the 11th January, 1679, by our Covenanted forefathers over Graham of Claverhouse and his dragoons."

In the parish churchyard, on two tombstones, three Presbyterian martyrs are commemorated. The tombstone of William Dingwall is inscribed thus:—

> "This hero brave, who here doth lye,
> Was persecute by tyranny;
> Yet to the truth he firmly stood,
> 'Gainst foes resisting unto blood,
> Himself and th' gospel did defend,
> Till for Christ's cause his life did end."

William Paterson and John Barrie have the following epitaph:—

"Here lies the corpses of William Paterson and John Barrie, who were shot to death for their adhering to the word of God and covenanted work of reformation, anno 1685.

> "Here lie two martyrs severally who fell
> By Captain Inglis and by bloody Bell;
> Posterity shall know, they're shot to death,
> As sacrifices unto Popish wrath."

PARISH OF BIGGAR.

In the parish churchyard Alexander Wardlaw, chamberlain to the Earl of Wigton, is on his tombstone thus celebrated:—

> "Here lyes a man whose upright heart
> With virtue was profusely stored,
> Who acted well the honest part
> Between the tenants and their lord.

> "Betwixt the sands and flinty rock
> Thus steered he in the golden mean,
> While his blithe countenance bespoke
> A mind unsullied and serene.
>
> "As to great Bruce the Flemings proved
> Faithful, so to the Flemings' heir
> Wardlaw behaved, and was beloved
> For justice, candour, faith, and care.
>
> "This merit shall preserve his fame
> To latest ages free from rust,
> Till the archangel raise his frame
> To joyn his soul amongst the just."

James Affleck and James Brown, two local poets, rest in Biggar Churchyard. The former died in 1835, the latter in 1836.

PARISH OF BLANTYRE.

A tombstone in the parish churchyard thus commemorates the Rev. John Heriot, minister of the parish:—

> "Here lies a pastor, ten years and fourscore,
> Who taught his flock 55 years and more;
> During which time, to his immortal praise,
> So blameless behaved himself always
> In holy order, doctrine sweet and sound,
> As did become his reverend gospel gown;
> His soul in heaven, his body in the clay
> Waits a reunion at the latter day."

Heriot graduated at the University of Glasgow in 1603; he was ordained at Blantyre in 1607, and died in December, 1662.

PARISH OF BOTHWELL.

In this parish, on the 22nd June, 1679, was fought the battle of Bothwell Bridge, between the Duke of Monmouth, commanding the King's forces, and the army of the Covenanters, numbering about 4,000 men. The Covenanters suffered defeat; of their number 400 were slain and 1,200 made prisoners. No trace of the battle remains.

In the aisle of the parish church an elegant monument with a long Latin inscription celebrates Lord William Douglas, afterwards Duke of Hamilton. The Duke held various offices of state. He died on the 18th April, 1694.

In the churchyard a blacksmith is thus commemorated:—

> "My sledge and hammer lies declined,
> My bellows' pipe have lost its wind,
> My forge's extinct, my fire's decayed,
> And in the dust my vice is laid;
> My coals is spent, my iron is gone,
> My nails are drove, my work is done."

By her husband a wife is celebrated in these lines:—

> "Here rests in peace one good without pretence,
> Blest with plain reason and with sober sense;
> Passion and pride were to her soul unknown,
> Convinced that virtue only is our own."

PARISH OF CAMBUSNETHAN.

In the old churchyard of Cambusnethan, situated in a sequestered hollow on the bank of the Clyde, a handsome mausoleum protects the remains of the late Lord Belhaven and Stenton. The mausoleum, which is in form of a parallelogram, is thirty-eight feet in height. On each corner of the wall which supports the roof is placed a sphinx, the spaces between which on the sides are filled with a row of lions' heads; in the pediments above the façade and the back wall are the arms of the Belhaven family. Below, wreaths of flowers surround the building, the rest of the walls being relieved by plain massive mouldings. Along with appropriate scriptural quotations is presented the following inscription:—

"Here rests Robert Montgomerie, Lord Belhaven and Stenton, Baron Hamilton of Wishaw, Lord Lieutenant of Lanarkshire, forty years Convener of the county, twenty-seven years Lord High Commissioner to the General Assembly of the Church of Scotland. Born A.D. MDCCXCIII., died A.D. MDCCCLXVIII." This tomb is erected by Lady Belhaven, his loving partner through life, now his sorrowing widow, who hopes to be laid by his side, as he desired, humbly but confidently trusting to meet him hereafter, through the merits of our Saviour."

In the old churchyard is the burial vault of the baronetted House of Coltness and Allanton. It contains the remains of Sir James Denham Steuart, Bart., of Coltness, the eminent political economist. Born at Edinburgh on the 10th October, 1713, he succeeded his father, the second baronet, in 1727. In 1734 he passed advocate. In the course of a Continental tour he was at Rome introduced to Prince Charles Edward, and when the Prince reached Edinburgh in 1745, he, after some hesitation, joined his cause. By the Prince he was despatched on a mission to the court of France; he thus happily escaped being at the battle of Culloden. Having been excepted in the Act of Indemnity, he remained on the Continent eighteen years. In 1758 he published at Frankfort a vindication of Newton's Chronology and a "Treatise on German Coins." In 1763 he returned to Scotland, and was allowed to reside on his estates, which had not been forfeited. In 1767 he published his "Principles of Political Economy." He subsequently published a treatise on "The Principles of Money as applied to the Coin of Bengal." In 1771 he obtained a full pardon from the Government. He died on the 26th November, 1780. Sir James's collected works in six volumes octavo were published in 1805, accompanied with a memoir. He married Lady Frances, eldest daughter of the Earl of Wemyss, with whom he enjoyed much domestic happiness. In an arbour near Coltness House, immediately above a seat in which he often sat with his wife, a marble tablet is thus inscribed:—

"The favourite seat of Sir James and Lady Frances Steuart, inscribed to their memory, 1815.

> Blest and united by the ties that bind
> The generous spirit and the virtuous mind;
> To their loved homes the exiles came at last,
> Courted this safe retreat, and smiled on perils past.
>
> Thus, arm in arm, enjoying and enjoyed,
> Musing on life, no moment misemployed,
> The pilgrims paused to hail the happier shore,
> Where love is ever young, and virtue weeps no more."

In the old churchyard the tombstone of a Presbyterian martyr has the following legend:—

"Here lyes Arthur Inglis in Nethertoun, who was shot at Stockelton Dyke by bloody Graham of Claverhouse, July, 1679, for his adherence to the word of God and Scotland's covenanted work of reformation. Rev. xii. 11. Erected in the year 1733.

> When I did live, such was the day,
> Forsaking sin made men a prey
> Unto the rage and tyranny
> Of that throne of iniquity
> Who robbed Christ, and killed His saints,
> And brake and burned his covenants;
> I at that time this honour got
> To die for Christ upon the spot."

Inglis was put to death with circumstances of great barbarity. On his farm he was watching his cows, when some dragoons came up. He held a book which they correctly supposed to be a Bible, in those times a sign of Nonconformity. One of the dragoons discharged his carbine at him, while another cut him down with his sword. His monument was renewed in 1836.

The following monumental rhymes are from the New Churchyard:—

"Soul of the just, companion of the dead,
Where is thy house, and whither art thou fled?
Soft be thy sleep, dear partner, may my mind
Like thine be ever to God's will resigned:
And when the mortal life I shall resign,
O may some kind friend lay my bones with thine!"

"Hark, passenger, as you go by,
And view the place where we do lie;
You'll hear for once our threefold cry
To think of death before you die."

"Religion should our thoughts engage
Amidst our youthful bloom;
'Twill fit us for declining age,
Or for an early tomb."

"A child in bud, a wife in bloom,
One dreary grave contains;
But, like the fading flower's perfume,
In memory sweet remains."

"Reader, learn, or over noon
The rose may be plucht in its bloom
In your young years seek the Most High,
For younger than you here doth lie."

"We mourn, but not for her removed from pain;
Our loss, we trust, is her eternal gain;
With her we'll strive to win the Saviour's love,
And hope to join her with the blest above."

"A mother and a friend indeed,
To all she found her want or need;
She left this world of tears and sighs
To meet with Christ above the skies.
Her friends do mourn her absent smile,
But hope to meet her in a while."

On a tombstone James Weir, a child of seventeen months, who died in 1821, is thus described:—

"This child, when only thirteen months old, measured 3 feet 4 inches in height, 39 inches round the body, 20½ inches round the thigh, and weighed 5 stone. He was pronounced by the faculties of Edinburgh and Glasgow to be the most extraordinary child of his age upon record."

PARISH OF CARLUKE.

A mound near Mauldslie Castle, surrounded with large trees, was an ancient burial-place. On its summit was interred Brigadier-General James Carmichael, second Earl of Hyndford. He died 16th August, 1737.

In the churchyard a tombstone commemorates the Rev. Peter Kid, minister of the parish. It is inscribed as follows:—

> "A faithful, holy pastor here lies hid,
> One of a thousand, Mr. Peter Kid,
> Firm as a stone, but of a heart contrite.
> A wrestling, praying, weeping Israelite;
> A powerful preacher, far from ostentation,
> A son of thunder, and of consolation.
> His face, his speech, and humble walk might tell
> That he was in the mount and Peniel.
> He was in Patmos, and did far surpass
> In fixèd steadfastness the rocky Bass.
> His love to Christ made his life to be spent
> In feeding flocks and kids beside his tent.
> His frail flesh could not equal paces keep
> With his most willing sp'rit, but fell asleep.
> His soul's in heaven, where it was much before,
> His flesh rests here in hopes of future glore.
> Passenger! ere thou go, sigh, weep, and pray,
> Help, Lord, because the godly do decay."

A native of Fifeshire, Mr. Kid was a student of St. Andrews University. Obtaining license, he was forcibly inducted into the pastoral charge of Douglas in 1654. He was deprived in 1662, but accepting the indulgence, was allowed to minister at Carluke in 1672. For not observing the anniversary of his Majesty's Restoration, he was in 1673 fined by the Privy Council in half his stipend. Having in 1677 refused to read the proclamation respecting the King's deliverance from the Rye House Plot, his indulgence was withdrawn. He was in 1685 made a prisoner in the Bass; but was released the following year. He died in 1694.

PARISH OF CARMICHAEL.

A vault in the parish churchyard contains the remains of John Carmichael, third Earl of Hyndford, son of James, second Earl. He was born on the 15th April, 1701. For some time he served as an officer in the third regiment of Foot Guards. In 1737 he succeeded his father in his title and estates. In 1739-40 he held office as Lord High Commissioner to the General Assembly. In 1741 he was sent as envoy to the court of Berlin, where he succeeded in adjusting those differences which led to the invasion of Silesia. Ambassador at the court of Russia for six years preceding 1750, he contributed to accelerate the peace concluded at Aix-la-Chapelle. On his return to England he was sworn a Privy Councillor; he afterwards undertook an important mission to the court of Vienna. In 1764 he became Vice-Admiral of Scotland. For some years he resided on his estate in Lanarkshire. He took a deep interest in agriculture and rural affairs. His lordship died on the 19th July, 1767.

PARISH OF CARNWATH.

An aisle of Gothic architecture, built in 1424, has successively been used as a burial-place by the Barons Somerville, the Earls of Carnwath, and a branch of the House of Lockhart. The church, of which the aisle formed a part, was founded in 1386 ; it was endowed by Lord Somerville in 1424.

In the churchyard a monument commemorates Robert Anderson, M.D., editor of the "British Poets." This ingenious individual was born at Carnwath on the 7th January, 1750. With a view to the Church he studied at Edinburgh University; he subsequently became a physician, and sought medical practice at Alnwick, in Northumberland. With a moderate independence obtained by his marriage, he settled at Edinburgh in 1784. He now devoted himself wholly to literature. The first volume of his "British Poets" appeared in 1792; the fourteenth and last in 1807. He was a zealous patron of youthful talent. To his patronage Thomas Campbell was especially indebted; he dedicated "The Pleasures of Hope" to his benefactor. In 1796 Dr. Anderson published "The Miscellaneous Works of Tobias Smollett" accompanied with a memoir. He composed an elaborate life of Dr. Samuel Johnson, and for some years edited the *Edinburgh Magazine.* Dr. Anderson died on the 20th February, 1830, aged eighty-one. He desired that his dust might rest with that of his kindred in Carnwath Churchyard.

PARISH OF CRAWFORDJOHN.

The Rev. William Miller, who died minister of the parish, on the 3rd February, 1801, has his tombstone thus inscribed :—

> "Enclosed within this coffin here doth lie,
> Exempt from cares and from all troubles free,
> A man whose virtues were such that
> Few can them well express, less imitate ;
> Lo ! here's a proof that death doth oft arrest,
> In this sad instance not the worst, but best.
> Much like those worms that often still
> Devour the fairest flowers, but spare the ill."

Mr. Miller died in his eighty-second year, and fifty-first of his ministry. He was much esteemed for his theological learning and ministerial faithfulness.

PARISH OF DALSERF.

Near the south-east corner of the church is the resting-place of the Rev. John M'Millan, one of the founders of the Reformed Presbyterian Church. Born at Barncachla, parish of Minnigaff, Kirkcudbrightshire, he studied at the University of Edinburgh, and became a probationer in November, 1700. In September, 1701, he was ordained to the ministry at Balmaghie. With strong sympathies for the Cameronian party, he incurred the displeasure of his brethren, who, in 1703, proceeded to depose him for "disorderly and schismatical practices." Having refused to vacate his pulpit, he was summoned before the Commission of Assembly in June, 1704; he then submitted himself, and desired restoration to the clerical office. As the Commission delayed to revoke the sentence of deposition, he afterwards renounced the Church's authority. Joined by a clerical brother and a lay elder, he, in August, 1743, constituted "The Reformed Presbytery." Mr. M'Millan died at Broomhill, parish of Bothwell, on the 1st December, 1753, in his eighty-fourth year. In 1840 a monument to his memory in Dalserf Churchyard was reared by public subscription.

PARISH OF DALZIEL.

In the east end of the old parish church is a former burial-place of the family of Dalziel, ancestors of the Earls of Carnwath. One of the family tombstones is inscribed thus :—

"Heir lyes James Dalyell, Mearchant Bvrger Edr. lawful sone to umql. Thomas Dalyell, wch. Thomas wes lawful sone to the Right Honl. umql. William Dalyell of the ilk, procreat betwix him and his Lady Gelis Hamilton, lawful daughter to the Laird Preston, wch. James depairt tys lyf, at the place of Dalyell, the 8th of March, 1608, being of the age of 78 yeiris."

PARISH OF DOUGLAS.

An aisle in the old parish church is the original burial-place of the ancient and famous House of Douglas. The monuments, though considerably defaced, are still remarkable for elegance of sculpture. One of the oldest is that of Sir James Douglas, the attached friend and follower of King Robert the Bruce. He is represented by a recumbent statue, cross-legged, to denote that he was a crusader. Sir James was eldest son of William, Lord of Douglas, a companion of Wallace. A page to Bishop Lamberton, of St. Andrews, he in his eighteenth year joined Bruce's standard, after the death of Comyn. He was present at the coronation at Scone, and constantly attended the King during the struggles which terminated at Bannockburn. In March, 1307, he surprised the English garrison which occupied his castle of Douglas, and casting the stores in a heap, flung the dead bodies upon it, and so produced what is known as "the Douglas Larder." In March, 1313, he took by stratagem the Castle of Roxburgh; he was henceforth known among the English as "the Black Douglas." At the battle of Bannockburn he commanded the centre division of the Scottish van; after the victory he pursued Edward II. to Dunbar. Appointed Warden of the Middle Marches, he distinguished himself in successful raids against the English. When King Robert was on his death-bed, he commissioned Sir James to carry his heart to the holy sepulchre at Jerusalem. With this intent he left Scotland in June, 1330. On reaching Flanders he learned that Alphonso, the young King of Castile, was engaged in warfare with Osmyn, the

Moorish King of Granada; and he hastened to join him with his retinue. On the 25th August, 1330, a battle took place near Tebason, on the frontier of Andalusia. The Moors were defeated, and Douglas joined in the pursuit. Taking from his neck the silver casket which contained his precious charge, he threw it before him, exclaiming, " Pass on before us, gallant heart, as thou wert wont; Douglas will follow thee or die." He fell, mortally wounded. His body, recovered from the field, was carried to Scotland and interred in the family aisle.

In the Douglas aisle a richly sculptured monument commemorates Archibald Douglas, Duke of Touraine, fifth Earl of Douglas, who died in 1438. He was one of the ambassadors to England, in 1424, in treaty for the ransom of James I. His monument is thus inscribed:—

" Hic jacet Archibaldus Douglas, Dux Toureniæ, Comes de Douglas et Longville, Dominus Gallovidiæ, Wigtoniæ, et Annandiæ, locum tenens Regis Scotiæ, obiit 26 die mensis Junii, 1438."

On the south side of the aisle a tomb of exquisite workmanship has the following legend :—

" Hic jacet magnus et potens princeps, Dominus Jacobus de Douglas, Dux Toureniæ et Comes de Douglas, Dominus Annandiæ, Gallovidiæ, Liddaliæ, Jedburg Forestiæ, de Balveniæ magnus Wardanus, Dominus regni Scotiæ versus Angliam, &c.; qui obiit 24 die mensis Matii, anno Domini 1443."

James Douglas was brother of Archibald, the fifth Earl, to whose estate and title he succeeded on the murder of his two sons in the Castle of Edinburgh. His tomb presents recumbent statues of himself and spouse, and figures of their ten children.

An inscription, in these words, commemorates the countess and her children :—

" Hic jacet Domina Beatrix de Sinclair (filia Domini Henrici Comitis Orcadum, Domini de Sinclair, &c.), Comitissa de Douglas, et Aveniæ, Domina Gallovidiæ."

" Hæ sunt proles inter prædictos Dominum et Dominam generatæ. 1mo, Dominus Wilhelmus, primogenitus et hæres dicti

Domini Jacobi, qui successit ad totam hæreditatem prædictam. Jacobus, 2do genitus, Magister de Douglas. Archibaldus, 3tio genitus, comes Moraviæ. Hugo, 4to genitus comes Ormundiæ. Joannes, 5to genitus, Dominus de Balvenia. Henricus, 6to genitus. Margareta, uxor Domini de Dalkeith. Beatrix uxor Domini Joannis Constabularii Scotiæ. Janeta, uxor Domini de Biggar et de Cumbernauld. Elizabeth Douglas, 4ta filia erat."

On the leaden coffins in the Douglas vault are the following inscriptions:—

"Gul. Angus. Dominus ex Jacobo Marchione Douglasiæ et Dom. Maria Kerr filia Comitis Lothianæ conjuge, primogenitus, natus 15 Oct., 1693, obiit 20 Mar., 1694. Maria Gordon filia Georgii primi Marchionis de Huntly, quam Gulielmus primus Marchio de Douglas in uxorem secundo duxit, quæque anno suæ ætatis sexagesimo quarto, salutis humanæ 1644, mortem obiit, Hic situm est corpus Gul. Marchionis Douglasiæ eo titulo primi, qui ex diversis et mutuis thalamis ab Hamiltoniorum et Gordoniorum gente suam progeniem continuatam, Hamiltoniorum vero instauratam, reliquit. Obiit 11. cal. Mart. anno 1660. ætat, vero 71. Margaret Hamiltown, Angusiæ Comitissa, obiit 38 anno ætatis suæ, 11 Septembris, 1623. Anna Stewarta duc. Lennoxiæ et Richmondiæ filia, Archibaldo Angusiæ Comiti per xviii. annos nupta, obiit xvi. die Augusti, anno MDCXLVI. ætat. xxxi. D. O. M. Hic positum est corpus Margaretæ, filiæ promogenitæ Gul. Marchionis de Douglas, relictæ ex matrimonio cum Margareta: obiit 1mo Jan. 1660. Katharina conjuga Domini de Torphichen, item Joanna Gul. Alexandri Comitis de Sterl., ætatis 49."

The coffin of the last Marquis of Douglas is thus simply inscribed:—

"J. M. D., ætatis 54; obiit 25 Februarii, 1700."

In a vault under the new parish church are deposited the remains of the Duke and Duchess of Douglas, and of other members of the House who have died within a modern period.

In the churchyard tombstones commemorate two parochial incumbents—William M'Cubbin, a noted humorist, who was ordained to the charge in 1770, and died on the 18th April, 1820, in his eighty-fourth year, and fifty-first of his ministry; and Alexander Stewart, LL.D., a native of Edinburgh, who was ordained to the cure in 1820, and died in 1862, in his eighty-first year, and forty-third of his ministry. Dr. Stewart published a "History of Scotland," "A Compendium of Modern Geography," a "Life of Principal Robertson," and other works; he was one of the contributors to the *Edinburgh Encyclopædia*.

PARISH OF GARTSHERRIE.

Gartsherrie Churchyard abounds in metrical epitaphs. A clergyman who died young has these lines on his gravestone:—

> "Young and happy while thou art,
>   Not a furrow on thy brow,
> Not a sorrow in thy heart,
>   Seek the Lord thy Maker now.
> In its freshness bring the flower,
>   While the dew upon it lies;
> In the calm and fragrant hour
>   Of the morning sacrifice."

On his wife's tombstone Andrew Gordon has inscribed the following:—

> "Farewell, farewell, till God me call,
>   Although no more in time we meet;
> My memory warmly cherish shall
>   Thy features calm and mildly sweet.
> But no, that look is not the last,
>   We yet shall meet where seraphs dwell;
> Where love no more deplores the past,
>   Nor breathes that withering word farewell."

Sorrowing parents commemorate their children thus:—

> "They, ere a cloud obscured their day,
> Have paid the debt we all must pay.
> They, ere life's sorrows had begun,
> Have run the race we all must run.
> Then weep not, parents, at the doom
> Which gave thy babes an early tomb;
> Mourn not the merciless behest
> Which sent thy innocents to rest."

On a daughter's tombstone her parents have inscribed the following lines :—

> "Then weep not for her who will weep no more,
> But follow her steps to that peaceful shore,
> Where the withering flower ne'er meets the eye,
> And that which is fairest shall never die;
> And there's no more sorrow and no more night,
> But all is happy, and blessed, and bright."

A son and daughter have thus commemorated their parents :—

> "It is a blessed thing to die,
> To know no sin, no tear, no sigh,
> To pass into a world of light,
> Where faith itself is lost in sight.
> To leave a world of pain and strife,
> To find an entrance into life,
> To see our Saviour eye to eye,—
> It is a blessed thing to die."

PARISH OF GLASFORD.

In the churchyard a monumental pillar commemorates William Gordon of Earlston, one of the Presbyterian martyrs. This devoted person was born in 1614, on his paternal estate of Earlston, Kirkcudbrightshire. He early evinced a decided attachment to Presbyterianism. In granting leases on his estate he stipulated that the tenants should observe family worship and every Sabbath attend the Presbyterian Church. In 1663 he refused an order of the Commissioners to assist in settling at Dalry an Episcopal clergyman, nominated by the bishop, while he was himself patron of the cure. For his declinature he was summoned before the Privy Council, but he ignored the citation. Charged with keeping conventicles, he was summoned before the Council a second time. He was commanded to depart the kingdom within a month, and meanwhile to live peaceably, under the penalty of £10,000. Disobeying the sentence, he was, in 1667, turned out of his house by a military force. Hastening to join the Covenanters after the battle of Bothwell Bridge, he was encountered near the field by a party of dragoons, by whom he was shot dead. He was buried in the churchyard of Glasford, his grave being denoted by an unlettered gravestone. It was thus inscribed by his great-grandson :—

"To the memory of the very worthy Pillar of the Church, Mr. William Gordon, of Earlston in Galloway, shot by a party of dragoons, on his way to Bothwell Bridge, 22nd June, 1679, aged sixty-five; inscribed by his great-grandson, Sir John Gordon, Bart., 11th June, 1772."

PARISH OF GLASGOW.

In the city, at the east end of Trongate, stands a bronze equestrian statue of William III.; two guns at its base were used at the Battle of the Boyne. This monument to the great constitutional king was erected, as an inscription bears, by "*Jacobus Macrae*, Gubernator Madrasii in 1734." The cost of erection was £3,000, which Mr. Macrae solely defrayed. A sketch of Mr. Macrae will be found at page 397 of this volume.

Near the entrance to the "Green," a beautiful pleasure ground, two and a half miles in circumference, a column in imitation of Trajan's pillar at Rome commemorates Horatio, Viscount Nelson; it is 143 feet in height, and is suitably inscribed.

In front of the Royal Exchange, the Duke of Wellington is represented in an elegant equestrian statue; the pedestal is adorned with appropriate sculptures.

George Square is adorned with several elegant monuments. In the centre a fluted Doric column eighty feet in height, surmounted by a colossal statue, is the tribute of the West of Scotland to the genius of Sir Walter Scott. At the corners are memorial statues of James Watt; General Sir John Moore; Sir Robert Peel, Bart.; and Lord Clyde.

The statue of Watt, executed by Chantrey, is constructed of

bronze. It represents the great engineer seated, and as in deep thought; it rests on a granite pedestal.

The statue of Sir John Moore is of bronze, and was executed by Flaxman. On the pedestal, which is of granite, are these words:—"To commemorate the military services of Lieut.-General Sir John Moore, K.C.B. Native of Glasgow, his fellow-citizens have erected this monument 1819." Son of John Moore, M.D., an eminent physician and man of letters, and on the mother's side grandson of the celebrated Professor Simson, Sir John Moore was born at Glasgow on the 13th November, 1761. In his fifteenth year he entered the army, and as Colonel served with distinction in Corsica. As Brigadier-General, he distinguished himself in the West Indies. He was engaged in suppressing the Irish Rebellion in 1798, and accompanied the expedition to Holland as a General of the staff. In Egypt, under Sir Ralph Abercromby, he commanded the army of the reserve. After serving in Sicily, and Sweden, he was in 1808 sent to the Peninsula, where he assumed the chief command. In the attempt to expel the French from the Peninsula his operations were retarded by the apathy of the Spaniards, and the unsatisfactory character of the commissariat. After a march of 250 miles through a mountainous country, he arrived with his troops at Corunna, where he intended to embark. In the process of embarkation he was assailed by Soult, and a battle ensued. While animating the 42nd Regiment in a brilliant charge, he was struck by a cannon ball on the left shoulder; he expired, in the moment of victory, on the 16th January, 1809. By order of Parliament a monument to his memory was reared in St. Paul's Cathedral, and his generous enemy, Marshal Soult, commemorated his prowess on the spot where he fell.

The statue of Sir Robert Peel was executed by Mossman. The great statesman appears in walking costume on a pedestal of Aberdeen granite.

The statue of Lord Clyde was reared by public subscription in 1868; it is executed by Foley in bronze. In easy military undress, the great commander stands with the left foot advanced, and with the left hand grasping a telescope, while in the right hand he holds a veiled hat or helmet. The pedestal is in raised letters thus inscribed:—

> "Field-Marshal Lord Clyde,
> G.C.B., K.S.I.
> Born in Glasgow, 20th Oct. 1792
> This Memorial
> of his Distinguished Military Services
> is Erected by
> his Fellow-Citizens.
> 1868."

Colin Campbell was son of John Macliver, a native of Mull, and for many years an operative cabinet-maker in Glasgow. His mother was daughter of a member of the clan Campbell, who owned a small estate in the island of Islay. Her brother, an officer in the army, attracted the notice of the Duke of York. On the early death of his sister, Mrs. Macliver, he undertook the education of his nephew, and sent him to the military academy at Gosport. The youth took his uncle's family name, and as Colin Campbell was gazetted ensign in the 9th Regiment of Foot on the 26th May, 1808; he was present at the battle of Vimiero, on the 21st August of the same year. He was with his regiment in the Corunna campaign and in the expedition to Walcheren. Returning to Spain in 1810, he was present at most of the great actions, till the conclusion of the war. He took part in the expedition for relieving Tarragona, and in the affair for relieving the posts in the valley of Malaga. He was present at the battles of Osma and Vittoria, and led the column of attack at the siege of San Sebastian and at the passage of Bidassoa. In 1813 he became captain, and in the following year was transferred to the 60th Rifles. In the American War he was present at the battles of Bladensburg and New Orleans. In 1823 he aided in subjugating the slave insurrection in Demerara.

Lieut.-Colonel Campbell went to China in 1842 in command of the 98th Regiment; he took an active part at the taking of Chin-kiang-foo, and the operations at Nankin. His next destination was India, where he commanded the third division under

Lord Gough in the Punjaub campaigns of 1848-9; he distinguished himself at the battle of Chillianwallah, where he was wounded, and at Goojerat, when the Sikhs were crushed. In 1849 he was created K.C.B.; for his conduct at Goojerat he received the thanks of Parliament. As Brigadier-General he commanded the Peshawur district in 1851, and in the following year distinguished himself in the expedition against the Octmankbail tribes. On the outbreak of the Russian War he, as Major-General, took command of the Highland Regiments. For his successful impetuosity at the battle of the Alma, he won much fame, which was greatly enhanced by his successful resistance of the Russian cavalry on the field of Balaclava. In 1856, he was promoted as Lieut.-General, received the Grand Cross of the Bath, was created D.C.L. of Oxford, and had conferred on him many Continental military honours. The city of London admitted him to its freedom, and the citizens of Glasgow voted him a sword value £300, and entertained him at a public Banquet. When tidings of the Indian Mutiny reached this country he was appointed to the chief command; he requested only twenty-four hours for preparation. He arrived at Calcutta on the 29th August, and reached the Alumbagh early in November. On the 3rd November he fought the battle of Cawnpore, and again defeating the insurgents at Gwalior, effected the liberation of the garrison of Lucknow, on the 17th of the same month. After defeating the rebels at Futteghur on the 2nd January, 1858, he reduced Lucknow early in the following March; and suppressed the insurrection. For these important services he received the thanks of both Houses of Parliament, and was created a Baron by the title of Lord Clyde, with a pension of £2,000. In 1860, he was appointed Colonel of the Coldstream Guards, and was raised to the military rank of Field-Marshal on the 9th November, 1862. After a short illness, he died at the Government House, Chatham, on the 14th August, 1863. His remains were placed in Westminster Abbey.

Near the centre of George Square two elegant equestrian statues celebrate Her Majesty the Queen, and H.R.H. the late Prince

Consort. The Queen's statue was erected in 1849, in memorial of Her Majesty's first visit to the city. The statue of the Prince Consort was inaugurated on the 20th October, 1866, in presence of his Royal Highness the Duke of Edinburgh. The statue, which was executed by Marochetti, represents the Prince in a Field-Marshal's uniform, reining in his charger with the left hand, while the right, holding a plumed hat, rests on his thigh in an easy posture. The horse is posed, similarly to that on which the Queen is mounted, with the exception of the head, which is thrown into a curvetting attitude, with the ears pointing backwards. As in the Queen's statue, there is a basement of grey granite, with a superstructure of red Peterhead granite, the latter having a bronze column at each of the four corners. At the north end of the pedestal is a bronze panel bearing the letter "A," encircled by a wreath. A similar panel at the south end exhibits the inscription, "Albert, Prince Consort." On the east and west sides are bas-reliefs, also in bronze, composed of symbolical figures, representing the arts, literature, commerce, manufactures, and agriculture. The monument was reared at the cost of £6,000, defrayed by public subscription.

In Sauchiehall Street, at the corner of Crescent Place, an elegant monumental statue commemorates James Oswald, M.P. Fronting Castle Street, a memorial tablet celebrates three martyrs for the covenant; it is thus inscribed:—

"Behind this stone lies James Nisbet, who suffered martyrdom at this place, June 5th, 1684; also James Lawson, and Alexander Wood, who suffered martyrdom October 24, 1684, for their adherence to the word of God, and Scotland's covenanted work of Reformation.

> "Here lye martyrs three
>   Of memory
> Who for the covenant die,
> And witness is
> 'Gainst all these nations perjury.
> Against the covenated cause
> Of Christ, their royal King;

The British rulers make such laws,
Declar'd 'twas Satan's reign.
As Britain lyes in guilt you see,
'Tis ask'd O reader! art thou free?"

The following lines of Latin verse, are engraved on the front wall of the hospital in Trongate, reared in 1642 by George and Thomas Hutchison, brothers:—

" Nobilis hospitii si forte requiris alumnos,
Orphanus hic habitat pauper, inopsque senex;
Tu ne temne domos, ignarus sortis : egestas
Forte tuum senium progeniemque premet.
Quis scit, an hinc veniant, quas publica fama celebret,
Sive armis surgat gloria, sive toga?

" Adspicis Hutchesonos fratres ; his nulla propago
Cum foret, et numero vix caperentur opes;
Hæc monumenta pii, votum immortale, dicarunt,
Dulcia quæ miseris semper asyla forent.
O bene testatos! hæredes scripsit uterque
Infantes inopes invalidosque senes."

THE CATHEDRAL.

Glasgow Cathedral was founded in 1123, by John Achaius, Bishop of the See. It is 319 feet long, 63 feet broad, and has two great towers, one of which supports a spire, making the whole height 225 feet. At the Reformation the cathedral escaped destruction, and the choir has since been used for Presbyterian worship. During a recent restoration of the structure, painted glass windows have been introduced into the nave and transept—some of a commemorative character. With these elegant accessories, the cathedral has been rendered one of the most interesting in the kingdom. In the choir a memorial copper-plate has the following inscription:—

" Heir ar bvreit Sr Waltir, Sr Thomas, Sr Jhone, Sr Robert, Sr Jhone, and Sr Mathev, by lineal descent to vtheris barons and knichis of the hovs of Mynto^i w^t thair vyffis bairnis and bretherein."

In the crypt are interred the remains of Edward Irving, the celebrated preacher. This remarkable individual was born at Annan, on the 15th August, 1792. He studied at the University of Edinburgh, where, by his mathematical attainments, he attracted the notice of Professor Leslie. For some time he taught in academies at Haddington and Kirkcaldy. Obtaining license as a preacher, he was appointed by Dr. Chalmers, his assistant in St. John's Church, Glasgow. In 1822 he accepted an invitation from a congregation of Scottish Presbyterians in London, to become their pastor. From the eloquence of his discourses, conjoined with his remarkable pulpit fervour, he attracted crowds; orators and statesmen flocked to his ministrations. A volume of discourses which he published in 1823, passed within six months into a third edition. In 1827 he issued his "Dialogues on Prophecy," in three octavo volumes. In 1829 a large and handsome church in Regent Square was reared for his use by the contributions of his numerous adherents. At length his theological opinions awakened some misgivings. By the Presbytery of London he was, in 1830, charged with maintaining the sinfulness of Christ's human nature, and with denying the doctrines of atonement and substitution. Soon afterwards he sanctioned belief in "unknown tongues," which, uttered by deluded persons of his congregation, he pronounced to be manifestations of the Holy Ghost. His deposition from the ministry was pronounced by the Presbytery of Annan which ordained him, and he was dispossessed of his charge as minister of Regent Square Church. He continued to uphold his peculiar opinions, obtaining crowded audiences wherever he conducted service. He died of consumption at Glasgow, on the 8th December, 1834, at the age of forty-two. His followers, styling themselves members of the Catholic Apostolic Church, have a cathedral in London, and places of worship elsewhere.

An aisle of the cathedral contains the remains of Robert Haldane, of Airthrey, the eminent lay preacher and theological writer. Eldest son of Captain James Haldane, of Airthrey, he was born at London on the 28th February, 1764. With his younger brother

James—who subsequently was associated with him in his public labours—he was educated at the Grammar School of Dundee and the High School of Edinburgh. He was inclined towards the ministry of the Scottish Church, but on the counsel of his guardians he joined the *Monarch* ship of war, under his uncle, Admiral Duncan. On the peace of 1783, he retired from the navy, and returning to Scotland, entered as a student the University of Edinburgh. He afterwards travelled abroad, and having married in 1785, settled on his estate of Airthrey in the autumn of that year. At first he devoted himself to the improvement of his estate, but, becoming the subject of deep religious convictions, he withdrew himself from worldly pursuits. In 1798 he sold his estate, resolving to devote the proceeds towards a mission to the Hindus. To his intention the Board of Control and the Company's directors having interposed an insuperable barrier, Mr. Haldane began to dedicate himself to the propagation of the Gospel at home. Aided by the zealous efforts of his brother James, he carried on a system of itinerant preaching, throughout Scotland and the Orkneys. In Edinburgh and other populous towns he erected large buildings for public worship; thereto appointing pastors with adequate emoluments. Personally, he took a general superintendance of the churches, distributed copies of the Scriptures, and constituted classes for aspirants to the ministry. From 1798 to 1810 he expended £70,000 in promoting the extension of Christian truth. In 1816 he proceeded to France and Switzerland, and at Montauban and Geneva sought to awaken the dormant energies of the Protestants in those places. He instructed inquiring young men in correct Christian doctrine. One whom he taught at Geneva was Merle D'Aubigné, the future historian. Robert Haldane died at Edinburgh on the 12th December, 1842. His principal works are his "Evidence and Authority of Divine Revelation," his "Exposition of the Epistle to the Romans," and his work on the "Verbal Inspiration of the Scriptures."

In the cathedral churchyard a tombstone commemorates Thomas

Hutchison, founder of the hospital which bears his name; it is inscribed thus:—

"Conditur hic D. Thomas Hutchisonus, quem semper innocentia sero opulentia beavit, cujus brevem possessionem amplis in egenos largitionibus compensavit humana cuncta ficta, falsa, fabula, et vanitatum vanitas. Obiit. kal. Septembris anno 1641. Ætatis suæ 52."

In the external wall of the Dripping aisle nine Presbyterian martyrs are on a mural tombstone thus commemorated:—

"Here lies the corps of Robert Bunton, John Hart, Robert Scot, Matthew Patoun, John Richmond, James Johnston, Archibald Stewart, James Winning, John Main, who suffered at the cross of Glasgow for their testimony to the Covenant and work of Reformation, because they durst not own the authority of the then tyrants, destroying the same betwixt 1666 and 1688.

> "Years sixty-six and eighty-four
> Did send their souls home in glore,
> Whose bodies here interred ly,
> Then sacrific'd to tyranny;
> To Covenants and Reformation
> 'Cause they adhered in their station,
> These nine with others in this yard,
> Whose heads and bodies were not spar'd,
> Their testimonies, foes, to bury,
> Caus'd beat the drums then in great fury:
> They'll know at resurrection day,
> To murder saints was no sweet play.

The original stone and inscription repaired and new lettered, 1827, at the expense of a few friends of the cause for which the martyrs suffered."

A mural monument, bearing date 1616, commemorates Bessie Adam, wife of James Hamilton, of Aikenhead; it is thus inscribed:—

> "Ye gazers on this trophie of a tombe,
> Send out one grone for want of her, whose lyf;
> Once borne of earth, and now lyes in earth's wombe,
> Lived long a virgine, then a spotless wyf.

Heir is inclosed man's grief, earth's lose, friend's paine,
Religiones lampe, vertvs light, heaven's gain.
Dvmbe senseless state of some lyveless stones,
Rear'd wp for memrie of a blessed sovle;
Thow holds bvt Adam—Adames blood bemones
Her lose, shees fled none can her ioys controvle.
O happy thow! For zeale and Christiane love,
In earth beloved, and now in heavens above."

Dr. Peter Low, a physician, who died in 1612, is on his tombstone celebrated thus:—

" Stay, passenger, and view this stone,
For under it lyes such a one
Who cuired many whill he lieved,
Soe gracious he noe man grieved,
Yea, when his physick's force oft failed,
His pleasant purpose then prevailed,
For of his God he got the grace
To live in mirth and die in peace.
Heavin hes his soul,—his corps this stone,
Sigh, passenger, and soe be gone."

An elegant monument to Archbishop James Law is inscribed as follows:—

" Sat vixi; quid non corpus sine pectore vixi:
Mi curæ Christus religione fuit,
Structa alibi, titulis stant mausolæa superbis;
Urna LAI brevis est, fama perennis erit.
Laudat, hyperboreos inter, quæ gesserat, Orcas,
Hic, qui, Glotta, tuis accola gaudet aquis.
Gymnasii reditus, domus hospita, plumbea fani
Tecta, scholæ tanti sunt monumenta viri,
Exitus in Domino placidus, sine labe peractis
Bis septem lustris, præsule dignus, erat
Obiit 3 Idus Octobres, 1632.
Omnibus hæc calcanda via est mortalibus; at qui
Calcat eam, Christo sub duce, salvus erit."

Son of John Law, portioner of Lathrisk, Fifeshire, James Law studied at St. Andrews University, and obtaining license, was ordained minister of Kirkliston in 1585. He was appointed one of the State Commissioners for the maintenance of religion in the sheriffdom of Linlithgow. In 1605 he was preferred to the bishopric of Orkney. In 1615 he became Archbishop of Glasgow. He died at Glasgow on the 13th October, 1632. He completed the leaden roof of the cathedral, and bestowed considerable largesses on schools and hospitals in the city. A "Commentary" which he composed on various passages of Scripture remains unprinted.

Dr. Robert Mayne, Professor of Medicine in the University, is on his tombstone commemorated thus:—

"Hic jacet Robertus cognomento Magnus, multis nominibus revera magnus, philosophus, orator, poeta, medicus, omnigeno, virtute ac eruditione clarus, medicinæ in Academia Glasguensi professor. Obiit nonis Februarii anno Dom. ciciccxlvi. Ætatis suæ sexies septimo climaterico."

Sir Alexander Thomson, a distinguished military officer, who died on the 18th October, 1699, aged sixty-three, has the following epitaph:—

"Memoriæ sacrum Domini Alexandri Thomsone, equitis aurati, quondam in regio præsidio centurionis spectatissimi, fortissimi, vigilantissimi; qui pie et placide in Domino obdorimivit Octob. 18, anno Dom. 1669. Ætatis 63.

"Gentis honos, virtvtis amor, fama integra, candor,
Thomsonum ornabant vivum; nunc, ære perenni
Firma magis, famæ stant monumenta ducis.
Est sacer hic tumulus, necnon venerabilis urna;
Quam tegit augustus, quem capit urna, cinis.
Vita mihi mors est, mors mihi vita nova."

A Latin epitaph also celebrates James Anderson, merchant, Glasgow, who died in 1702:—

"Memoriæ sacrum Jacobi Andersoni, mercatoris Glasguensis, patris amantissimi; liberi monumentum hoc posuerunt. Obiit anno æræ christianæ 1688. Necnon in memoriam Jacobi Andersoni filii sui primogeniti constituerunt. Natus anno 1679, denatus anno 1702."

A monument thus commemorates William Hamilton, son of

Thomas Hamilton, Professor of Anatomy in the University of Glasgow, and father of Sir William Hamilton, Bart., the distinguished metaphysician:—

"M. S.
"Gulielmi F. Thomæ Hamilton, patriæ virtutes et muneris hæredis, anat. et bot. in academia Glascuensi profesoris celeberrimi; qui, capacis et exculti vi ingenii, jucunda disciplinam tradendi facultate, felici in morbis curandis industria et succesu prisca fide et pietate et unica morum comitæ. Auditorum venerationem ægrotorum fiduciam collegarum et suorum amorem. Bonorum omnium benevolentiam sibi vivus conciliavit; tam cari capitis desiderium, cui nec modus, extinctus reliquit. Pientiss. et mœstiss. conjunx Elizabetha Stirling, P. Natus pridii cal. Aug. A.D. MDCCLVIII. obiit iii. idus Martias A.D. MDCCXC. Heu! tales terris quod monstrant fata, nec ultra esse sinunt."

In the churchyard rest the remains of Thomas Watt, M.D., compiler of the "Bibliotheca Britannica." Son of a small farmer, Dr. Watt was born at Stewarton in May, 1774. In early life he was a ploughboy, and afterwards a joiner's apprentice. At eighteen he entered as a student the University of Glasgow. He subsequently attended medical classes at Edinburgh, and obtained license as a surgeon. In 1799 he settled as a surgeon in Paisley; he subsequently sought practice in Glasgow. He published several medical works, and was a contributor to the medical and surgical journals. His great work, the "Bibliotheca," was commenced at an early period, and in 1817 he retired from medical practice in order to devote himself exclusively to its completion. After a period of severe affliction, Dr. Watt died on the 12th March, 1819. The "Bibliotheca Britannica" was published posthumously in four quarto volumes, but it is believed that the author's family derived from it no pecuniary advantage. As a monument of literary industry it is nearly unrivalled.

A plain gravestone denotes the resting-place of John Donald Carrick, an eminent miscellaneous writer. Born at Glasgow in April, 1787, he was placed in an architect's office, but not relishing his employment, he proceeded to London, making the journey on foot. He engaged himself as a porter; subsequently he was employed in a pottery warehouse. In 1811 he returned to Glasgow and opened a large stoneware establishment in Hutcheson Street. Retiring from business in 1825, he devoted himself exclusively to literary concerns. His "Life of Sir William Wallace" appeared in *Constable's Miscellany* in 1825; it is the best memoir of the patriot which has been published. He afterwards edited "The Laird of Logan," an interesting collection of Scottish anecdotes, and contributed interesting papers to the periodicals. In 1833 he edited the *Perth Advertiser*, and in the following year conducted the *Kilmarnock Journal*. After a period of illness, he died on the 17th August, 1837.

George Rodger, junior, one of the managers of the Barrowfield Works, who died on the 9th September, 1824, aged twenty-six, has on his tombstone the following elegy:—

> " He whose loved ashes moulder here below
> Was once the gentlest model of his kind,
> He lived, nor made himself a single foe,
> He died, nor left one enemy behind."

Dr. William Chrystal, Rector of the Grammar School of Glasgow, an eminent scholar, is on a handsome monument, commemorated thus:—

"M. S.
"Gulielmi Chrystal, L.L.D., schol. gram. Glasguensis rectoris; quem freto Glottiano submersum. Mors immatura abstutit. Hoc pietatis monumentum acerbe lugentes posuerunt alumni, et familiares. Natus est vi. idus Jun., MDCCLXXVI. Obiit vii. idus Jun., MDCCCXXX."

In the churchyard, monuments commemorate Provost John Anderson, representative of the city in the first Parliament after the Revolution, who died in 1710; William Cochran, portrait painter, who died 23rd October, 1785, aged forty-seven; John Bowman of Ashgrove, Lord Provost, who died 24th November, 1797; James Lumsden, Lord Provost, who died in 1856; John

Orr, of Barrowfield, advocate, principal town clerk of Glasgow, who died 16th December, 1863; Lieut.-Colonel the Hon. Henry Cadogan, of the 71st Regiment, who fell at the battle of Vittoria, 21st June, 1813; Lieutenant John Stirling, of the Bombay Army, who fell while leading the assault against the fort of Dundhootee, India, on the 3rd January, 1828, aged twenty-three; Major William Middleton, who died 13th April, 1859; Robert Burn Anderson, lieutenant in the Bombay Fusileers, "taken prisoner when in command of an escort under protection of a flag of truce and died a victim to the cruelty of a barbarous foe," 27th September, 1860; and James McConechy, M.D., editor of the *Glasgow Courier*, who died 3rd October, 1866.

Monuments commemorate the Rev. William Taylor, D.D., minister of the High Church and Principal of the University, who died 29th March, 1823, in the fifty-first year of his ministry; and the Rev. John Muir, D.D., minister of St. James's Church, Glasgow, who died 1st February, 1857, in the seventy-ninth year of his age and fifty-fourth of his ministry.

In the interior of the cathedral an elegant monument, erected by himself, celebrates George Baillie, formerly sheriff substitute of Dunblane. An inscription intimates the founder's intention of bequeathing £20,000 to unsectarian schools.

Mural monuments commemorate Major Robert Murray Bonner, Brevet-Major John Anstruther, and others who fell in action or died during the Crimean campaign of 1854-6; also those officers and men of the 71st Light Infantry who died during the campaign on the north-west frontier of India in 1863.

COLLEGE CHURCHYARDS.

A mural tablet commemorates Robert Simson, M.D., the eminent mathematician. Eldest son of John Simson, of Kirton Hall, Ayrshire, he was born on the 14th October, 1687. Intended for the

Church he entered Glasgow College. In that seat of learning he became Professor of Mathematics in his twenty-fourth year. His edition of the "Elements of Euclid," published in 1750, widely extended his reputation. Other works on the higher mathematics proceeded from his pen. He died on the 1st December, 1768, bequeathing to the university his mathematical books and MSS. His monumental tablet is inscribed as follows:—

"H. S. E.

"Robertvs Simson, matheseos in academia Glasgvensi per annos LVIII. professor prisca morvm simplicitate simvl atqve probitate insignis omniqve doctrina excvltvs vetervm græcorum geometriam per annos bis mille fere deperditam, in pristinvm splendorem restitvit vnvs. Monvmentvm qvidem perenne sibi geometricis svis operibvs ipsi exegit marmor avtem hoc cadvcvm reliqvis egregii viri mortalibvs sacrvm posveri testamenti cvratores Jac. Clow, Gvl. Rouet, Ioa, Bvchanan jvnior. Obiit ipsis kalendis Octobris anno æræ Christianæ MDCCLXVIII., ætatis LXXXI."

A monument celebrates Dr. Thomas Reid, the eminent philosopher. He was born in the manse of Strachan, Kincardineshire, on the 26th April, 1710—his father being minister of the parish. At Marischal College, Aberdeen, he highly distinguished himself, especially by his attainments as a mathematician. After ministering at New Machar, Aberdeenshire, for fifteen years, he was appointed Professor of Moral Philosophy, King's College, Aberdeen, in 1752. His "Inquiry into the Human Mind" appeared in 1764, and at once brought him high reputation as a philosopher. Soon after he received D.D. from the University of Aberdeen, and was elected Professor of Moral Philosophy in Glasgow College. In 1781 he withdrew from his public duties that he might entirely devote himself to philosophical investigation. In 1785 he published his "Essays on the Intellectual Powers." His other philosophical works appeared subsequently. He died on the 7th October, 1796, in his eighty-sixth year. His tombstone is thus inscribed:—

"Memoriæ sacrum Thomæ Reid. S. T. P., quondam in schola regia Aberdoniensi, philosophiæ professoris, nuper vero, in universitate Glasguensi, ab anno 1764, usque ad annum 1796, philosophiæ moralis professoris : qui, in scientia mentis humanæ, ut olim in philosophia naturali illustris ille Baconus verulamius, omnia instauravit, qui ingenii acumine, doctrinæque omnigenæ, summam morum gravitatem, simul atque comitatem adjunxit: qui obiit 7° Oct., 1796, annos natus 86 : cuiusque ossa cum cineribus Elisabethæ Reid, conjugis carrissmæ. Triumquæ filiarum, morte præ matura abreptarum sepulchro hic condita sunt hoc monumentum poni jussit filia piissima unica superstes, Martha Carmichael."

In the College Churchyard tombstones commemorate Robert Roger, merchant in Glasgow, who died in 1700; James Baillie, D.D., professor of divinity in the University, who died 28th April, 1778 ; Josiah Walker, professor of humanity, who died 28th August, 1831 ; Hugo Macleod, professor of ecclesiastical history, who died June, 1800; William Meikleham, LL.D., professor of natural philosophy, who died 7th May, 1846; and George Gray, D.D., professor of oriental languages, who died 23rd June, 1850.

In the churchyard, at the old university buildings, a monument commemorates William Dunlop, Principal of the University and Royal Historiographer for Scotland. Son of Alexander Dunlop, minister of Paisley, and through his mother related to the Mures of Caldwell, he studied at Glasgow College, and was licensed to preach about 1679. Owing to the troubles which oppressed the Scottish Church he emigrated to Carolina, where he remained till the Revolution. In 1690 he was presented to the parish of Ochiltree; but was immediately thereafter appointed to the Principalship of Glasgow College. Through his efforts with Government a yearly grant of £1,200 from the bishops' rents was voted to the Scottish Universities. He died in March, 1700. His epitaph is as follows :—

"Memoriæ sacrum D. Wilielmi Dunlop academiæ et collegii Glasguensis vicecancellarii et præfecti dignissimi, vigilantissimi, ecclesiæ ibidem pastoris fidelissimi ; serenissimis principibus Wilielmo et Mariæ historiographi peritissimi, qui obiit viii. Idus Martii, anno Dom. MDCC. Ætatis suæ xlvii."

Over the gateway of the college buildings stood a bust of the celebrated Zachary Boyd, surrounded with the following inscription:—

"Mr Zacharias Bodivs fidelis ecclesiæ svbvrbanæ pastor 20,000 lib. qva ad alendos qvotannis tres adolescentes theologiæ stvdiosos; qva ad extrvendas novas has ædes vna cvm vniversa svpellectili librariæ almæ matri academiæ legavit."

Descended from the old family of Boyd of Pinkhill, Ayrshire, Zachary Boyd was born about the year 1585. Having studied at the Universities of Glasgow and St. Andrews, he afterwards proceeded to France and became a student at the University of Saumur under his cousin Robert Boyd, of Trochrig. At Saumur he was appointed a regent in 1611; he subsequently declined the office of principal. In 1617 he was presented to the church of Notre Dame, but owing to the persecution of the Protestants, he relinquished it, and returned to Britain. He became minister of the Barony parish of Glasgow in 1623; he was elected Rector of the University in 1634, and on two occasions subsequently. Warmly attached to the cause of Charles I., he at first refused to subscribe the Covenant; he did so latterly, and adhered faithfully to its provisions. Preaching before Cromwell at Glasgow in September, 1650, he loaded him with reproaches, but being afterwards invited to a private interview, he became reconciled to the Protector. He died in March, 1653. Boyd is chiefly remembered as author of "Zion's Flowers" and "The Last Battell of the Soule in Death," two works in verse. His versification is homely, and has excited ridicule, but it is withal pervaded by strong devotional feeling. His MSS. are preserved in the library of Glasgow College. He bequeathed £20,000 Scots to the University funds.

Michael Wilson, another benefactor of the University, is thus commemorated in the college buildings:—

"Magister Michael Wilson, civis Glasguensis (qui literas humaniores in Anglia professus, obiit ibidem anno Dom. 1617) sex mille libras Scoticanas, in pios academiæ usus, testamento legavit; cujus voluntas egregia plane irrita fuisset, nisi accessisset serenissimi regis Jacobi benignitas, singulari studio et opera clarissimi, viri, et multifariam de hoc collegio optime meriti, secretis, impetrata: quorum nomen et merita, perenni memoria pie celebratura academia, hoc tantæ rei exile monumentum, extare voluit."

TRON CHURCH.

A gravestone discovered in the south aisle of the old Tron Church when it was taken down in 1794, thus celebrates the Rev. John M'Laurin, minister of the North-West Parish:—

" Adorn'd with learning, taste, and manly sense,
Wisdom with genius, wit without offence,
Modest, yet resolute in virtue's cause,
Ambitious, not of man's but God's applause,
Each talent that enriched his heaven-born mind,
By Jesus given to Jesus he resigned,
Swift was his race, with health and vigour blest,
Soft was his passage to the land of rest.
His work concluded, ere the day was done,
Sudden the Saviour stooped, and caught him to His throne."

Mr. M'Laurin was born at Glendaruel in 1693. Having studied at the University of Glasgow he was licensed in 1717, and was ordained minister of Luss in May, 1719. He was translated to Glasgow in 1723. He died 8th September, 1754, in the sixty-first year of his age and thirty-sixth of his ministry. His theological works were reprinted in 1860.

RAMSHORN CHURCHYARD.

In this churchyard a monument commemorates David Dale, an eminent manufacturer. Son of a small trader at Stewarton, he was born in that place on the 6th January, 1739. Originally apprenticed to a Paisley weaver, he in 1761 became clerk in the office of a silk mercer in Glasgow. In 1775 he established the first works in Scotland for dyeing cotton Turkey red, and ten years afterwards began to erect the cotton mills at New Lanark. For his workers he established schools, and made other efforts for their improvement. He was elected a magistrate of Glasgow, and in that city originated and helped forward many charitable enterprises. He died on the 17th March, 1806.

THE NECROPOLIS.

The Necropolis was opened for interments in March, 1833. It includes the sloping side of the West Craigs, which here project into a promontory 225 feet above the level of the Clyde. Extending to twenty-four acres, it embraces the ancient Fir Park, a portion of waste land, formerly the property of the Merchants' House.

On the summit of the Craigs stands a monument of John Knox, the illustrious Reformer. Of this structure the foundation-stone was laid on the 22nd September, 1825, when a discourse suitable to the occasion was preached by Dr. Thomas Chalmers in St. George's Church. The monument represents a colossal statue of the Reformer resting on a fluted Doric column fifty-eight feet in height. The base of the column is fifteen feet square; it presents the following lengthened inscription:—

"To testify gratitude for inestimable Services in the cause of Religion, Education, and Civil Liberty; to awaken admiration of that Integrity, Disinterestedness, and Courage, which stood unshaken in the midst of trials, and in the maintenance of the highest objects; finally, to cherish unceasing reverence for the Principles and Blessings of that Great Reformation, by the influence of which our Country, through the midst of Difficulties, has arisen to Honour,

THE NECROPOLIS.   471

Prosperity, and Happiness: this monument is erected, by voluntary contribution, to the memory of John Knox, the Chief Instrument, under God, of the Reformation of Scotland on the xxii. day of September, MDCCCXXV. He died, rejoicing in the faith of the Gospel, at Edinburgh, on the xxiv. of November, A.D. 1572, in the sixty-seventh year of his age.

"The Reformation produced a revolution in the sentiments of mankind, the greatest as well as the most beneficial that has happened since the publication of Christianity.

"In 1547, and in the city where his friend George Wishart had suffered, John Knox, surrounded with dangers, first preached the doctrines of the Reformation. In 1557, on the 24th of August, the Parliament of Scotland adopted the Confession of Faith presented by the Reformed Ministers, and declared Popery to be no longer the religion of this kingdom.

"John Knox became then a minister of Edinburgh, where he continued to his death, the incorruptible guardian of our best interests. 'I can take God to witness,' he declared, 'that I never preached in contempt of any man; and wise men will consider that a true friend cannot flatter, especially in a case that involves the salvation of the bodies and souls, not of a few persons but of a whole realm.' When laid in the grave the Regent said, 'There lieth he who never feared the face of man, who was often threatened with dag and dagger, yet hath ended his days in peace and honour.'

"Among the early and distinguished friends of the Reformation should be especially remembered Sir James Sandilands, of Calder; Alexander, Earl of Glencairn; Archibald, Earl of Argyle; and Lord James Stewart, afterwards known by the name of 'The Good Regent'; John Erskine of Dun, and John Row, who were distinguished among the Reformed Ministers for their cultivation of ancient and modern literature; Christopher Goodman and John Willock, who came from England to preach the gospel in Scotland; and John Winram, John Spottiswood, and John Douglas, who with John Row and John Knox, compiled the first Confession of Faith, which was presented to the Parliament of Scotland; and also the first Book of Discipline.

"Patrick Hamilton, a youth of high rank and distinguished attainments, was the first martyr in Scotland for the cause of the Reformation. He was condemned to the flames at St. Andrews in 1528, and the twenty-fourth year of his age. From 1530 to 1540 persecution raged in every quarter. Many suffered the most cruel deaths, and many fled to England and the Continent. Among those early martyrs were Jerome Russell and Alexander Kennedy, two young men of great piety and talent, who suffered at Glasgow in 1538. In 1544 George Wishart returned to Scotland, from which he had been banished, and preached the gospel in various quarters. In 1546 this heavenly-minded man, the friend and instructor of Knox, was also committed to the flames at St. Andrews."

Seven years before the erection of the Knoxian monument, a proposal was instituted by the poet Motherwell to rear on the West Craigs a national monument to Wallace. In a prospectus issued in 1818 by the enthusiastic poet, he thus wrote:—"The site considered most eligible for this monument is the Fir Park, a commanding eminence to the east of the Glasgow Cathedral, and separated from the heights on which that ancient and noble edifice stands by the Molendinar Burn. Over and above its many local advantages there are other circumstances which plead strongly in favour of this spot. In its immediate vicinity was laid the scene of one of Wallace's earliest skirmishes, ending in the complete rout of the English commanded by Percy. From it can be seen Elderslie, the place of Wallace's nativity, as well as Robroyston, where he was betrayed. . . . The monument will be a lofty circular tower of unhewn whinstone, quarried from the rock on which it is proposed to be erected. It will have a spiral staircase, so that visitors may enjoy the lovely and extensive prospect to be obtained from its summit."

Motherwell's proposal was so far entertained; 252 persons subscribed a guinea each, and a meeting was held at Glasgow in March, 1819, when, under the presidentship of the Lord Provost, the Earl of Buchan and other notable persons made suitable orations. A committee of sixty noblemen and gentlemen were appointed to raise additional funds and to procure a suitable design. The proposal fell into abeyance, and the balance of subscriptions, some £60, were deposited in the Union Bank at Glasgow, to augment the unclaimed deposits of that prosperous corporation.

William Motherwell, the poet, has in these romantic grounds long since found a grave and a tombstone. He was born in High Street, Glasgow, on the 13th October, 1797. His father was an ironmonger in the city. His parents having removed to Edinburgh early in the century, he attended the High School of that city; he afterwards studied at the Grammar School of Paisley. For one session he attended classes in Glasgow College. In 1819 he was appointed Sheriff Clerk Depute of Renfrewshire, an office which he held till 1830, when he accepted the editorship of the *Glasgow Courier*. From boyhood he evinced poetical talent of a high order; he produced the first draught of his beautiful ballad of "Jeanie Morrison" in his fourteenth year. In 1819 he edited the "Harp of Renfrewshire," to which he contributed an introductory essay and valuable notes. His "Minstrelsy Ancient and Modern" appeared in 1827, and secured him the correspondence of Sir Walter Scott. In 1832 he published his best poetical compositions in a small volume entitled "Poems, Narrative and Lyrical." He died suddenly on the 1st November, 1835, at the age of thirty-eight. In admiration of his genius the citizens of Glasgow have raised in the Necropolis a monument to his memory,—a Gothic temple twenty feet in height. It contains his bust by Fillans, while on the pedestal and four pilasters are carvings illustrating passages in his works. The inscription is as follows:—

"Erected
By admirers of the poetic genius of
William Motherwell,
Who died 1st November, 1835, aged 38 years.

" Not as a record he lacketh a stone!
'Tis a fond debt to the singer we've known—
Proof that our love for his name hath not flown,
With the frame perishing
That we are cherishing
Feelings akin to the lost poet's own."

The proposal to erect a monument to John Knox at Glasgow was suggested by William McGavin, author of "The Protestant." This excellent individual was born on the 25th August, 1773, in the parish of Auchinleck, Ayrshire. Only a short time at school, he was apprenticed to a silk-weaver in Paisley; he afterwards became assistant to a bookseller. In 1793 he conducted a seminary, but soon relinquished the drudgery of tuition. Entering the office of a cotton merchant at Glasgow, he obtained charge of the business, and in 1813 was accepted as a partner. For some years he acted as collegiate pastor in an Independent church. From 1818 to 1822 he edited *The Protestant*, a periodical publication devoted to the exposure of papal error. This work was subsequently printed in four large volumes, and commanded wide attention. In 1822 Mr. McGavin became manager of the Glasgow Branch of the British Linen Bank. He died suddenly on the 23rd August, 1832. His remains were interred in the crypt of Wellington Street Chapel, and in the following year a monument to his memory was by public subscription reared in the Necropolis. It is thirty-five feet in height; and consists of a pedestal projecting into four wings, in form of a St. Andrew's cross, surmounted by an elegant statue. The pedestal is thus inscribed:—

"To the memory of William M'Gavin, author of *The Protestant*, &c., &c., who died on the 23rd August, 1832, aged fifty-nine years. This monument has been erected by his fellow-citizens MDCCCXXXIV."

A monument designed by Fillans commemorates Dugald Moore, an ingenious and short-lived poet. He was born in Stockwell Street, Glasgow, in 1805. Bred a tobacco-boy, he was afterwards received into the copper-printing establishment of James Lumsden and Son, booksellers. Under the patronage of Mr. Lumsden, senior, he published in 1829 a volume of poems entitled, "The African; a Tale, and other Poems." Several other volumes of poems appeared from his pen. From the profits of his writings he opened a bookselling establishment in Queen Street, which became the rendezvous of men of letters. Moore died unmarried on the 2nd January, 1841, aged thirty-six. His monument was reared by public subscription; it contains his bust in marble, accompanied by these lines from his poem, "The Bard of the North":—

"School'd in adversity; he was reared
  By her in winter; and he went

> Forth in the frosty pilgrimage of life
> To face the tempests, and to fling them back
> With the strong arm of virtue and resolve."

Though slightly known to fame, Moore is entitled to a respectable place among Scottish minor poets. His themes are lofty and his language rich and copious.

Alexander Rodger, another minor poet, is in the Necropolis honourably commemorated. His monument, a handsome erection, presents a medallion of the poet's head, along with the following inscription:—

"To the memory of Alexander Rodger, a poet, gifted with feeling, humour, and fancy; a man animated by generous, cordial, and comprehensive sympathies, which adversity could not repress nor popularity enfeeble, this monument is erected in testimony of public esteem. Born at Mid-Calder, 16th July, 1784, died at Glasgow, 26th September, 1846.

> "What though with Burns thou couldst not vie,
> In diving deep or soaring high;
> What though thy genius did not blaze
> Like his, to draw the public gaze;
> Yet thy sweet numbers, free from art,
> Like his can touch, can melt the heart."

Rodger was apprenticed in his twelfth year to a silversmith in Edinburgh. He afterwards became a weaver in Glasgow, when he also acted as a music-master. Extreme in his political opinions he was led in 1819 to support a journal which promoted disaffection; he was convicted of revolutionary practices and sent to prison. He was subsequently employed in the Barrowfield Works. In 1836 he became assistant-editor of the *Reformer's Gazette*, a situation which he held till his death. Many of his poems are disfigured by coarse political allusions, but several of his songs are of a high order, and are deservedly popular.

A handsome cenotaph commemorates Thomas Atkinson, bookseller and miscellaneous writer. He was born at Glasgow in 1801. On completing the usual apprenticeship he commenced business as a bookseller in the city in partnership with David Robertson, subsequently King's publisher. Of active habits, he conducted with his partner a successful bookselling trade, yet found leisure for literary pursuits. At an early age he published the "Sextuple Alliance," a series of poems on Napoleon Buonaparte. In 1827 he produced "The Ant," a work in two volumes. "The Chameleon," a sort of annual, which he commenced in 1831, extended to three octavo volumes. Distinguished as a liberal politician, Mr. Atkinson was invited to become a candidate in the liberal interest for the parliamentary representation of the Stirling burghs at the general election subsequent to the passing of the Reform Bill. The fatigues of the canvass superinduced an illness which terminated in consumption. During a voyage he had undertaken to Barbadoes for the recovery of his health he died at sea, on the 10th October, 1833. His remains, placed in an oaken coffin which he had taken along with him, were buried in the deep. He bequeathed a sum, to be applied after accumulation in founding a hall in Glasgow for the furtherance of adult education.

These lines, of his own composition, adorn his cenotaph :—

> "While, when beneath the verge of time,
> I've sped—as soon I know 'twill be—
> I rise, but in another clime—
> Uncircling—fixed eternity."

David Robertson, the business partner of the preceding, is commemorated by an elegant monument reared by subscription. Son of a farmer in the Vale of Menteith, Perthshire, he was there born in 1795. In his 15th year he was apprenticed to a bookseller in the Trongate, Glasgow, on whose death, in 1823, he succeeded to the business. In 1832 he published "Whistle Binkie," a collection of Scottish modern songs. He afterwards issued "The Laird of Logan," a collection of anecdotes chiefly connected with the West of Scotland. He died of cholera on the 6th October, 1854, much lamented by a large circle of attached friends.

Another Glasgow bookseller of literary tastes rests in the Necropolis—Robert Stuart, author of "Caledonia Romana." This ingenious individual was born at Glasgow on the 21st January, 1812. After some desultory education in town and country, he joined his father in a bookselling establishment at Glasgow in 1826. In his 20th year he began to insert short poems to the *Literary Rambler*, a local periodical; he afterwards contributed to *Chambers's Journal* and *Tait's Magazine*, and in 1834 produced a small volume entitled "Ina and other Fragments in Verse." As the result of several years' labour he published in 1844, in an elegant quarto, his "Caledonia Romana," a descriptive account of the occupation of Scotland by the Romans. In 1848 he published a second quarto, entitled "Views and Notices of Glasgow in Former Times." He died of cholera on the 23rd December, 1848, at the age of thirty-seven, leaving a widow and several children. A second edition of "Caledonia Romana" was issued in 1852, to which is prefixed a short memoir of the author's life.

A plain monument commemorates Michael Scott, an ingenious and entertaining writer. He was born in Edinburgh on the 30th October, 1789. From 1806 to 1822 he resided in Jamaica. He subsequently engaged in mercantile pursuits at Glasgow. To *Blackwood's Magazine* he contributed anonymously his entertaining sketches "Tom Cringle's Log" and "The Cruise of the Midge," which at the time of their appearance and subsequently attracted much attention. He died at Glasgow on the 6th November, 1835.

An elegant tomb, of octagonal form, celebrates William Rae Wilson, LL.D., author of "Travels in the Holy Land." He was born in Paisley, on the 7th June, 1772; his father's name was Rae, but he assumed the family name of Wilson on succeeding to the estate of his uncle, John Wilson, one of the Town Clerks of Glasgow. Bred to legal pursuits, he occupied himself chiefly in foreign travel. He died at London in 1849, and in compliance with his request, his body was brought to Glasgow and interred in the Necropolis. On a tablet of statuary marble his monument is thus inscribed:—

"In Memory of William Rae Wilson, LL.D., late of Kelvinbank, who died 2nd June, 1849, aged seventy-six, author of 'Travels in the Holy Land,' and editor of other works written on that and other countries during many years.

> "Thy servants take pleasure in her stones,
> And favour the dust thereof.
>
> "This tablet is inscribed by his affectionate wife."

A hexagonal temple, resembling the monument of Lysicrates at Athens, celebrates the Rev. John Dick, D.D., Professor of Divinity in the United Secession Church; it is inscribed as follows:—

"To the Memory of John Dick, D.D., Professor of Theology to the United Secession Synod, and minister of Greyfriars' Church, Glasgow; who was born at Aberdeen the 10th of October, 1764, and died at Glasgow, the 25th of January, 1833.

"Erected by his congregation, 1838."

Having studied at King's College, Aberdeen, and the Divinity Hall of the Secession Church, Dr. Dick was licensed as a preacher in 1785. He was ordained at Slateford in October, 1786, where he continued till 1801, when he became collegiate pastor of Greyfriars Secession Church, Glasgow. In 1820 he was appointed Professor of Theology to the Associate Synod. He died on the 25th January, 1833, in the sixty-ninth year of his age and forty-seventh of his ministry. His theological lectures were published posthumously; these, and his "Essay on the Inspiration of the Scriptures," have obtained deserved commendation.

An obelisk of red granite commemorates the Rev. Hugh Heugh, D.D., minister of the Secession Church, Blackfriars Street. Son of the Rev. John Heugh, minister of the anti-burgher congregation at Stirling, he was born on the 12th August, 1782. Having studied at the University of Edinburgh and the University Hall of the Associate Synod, he was licensed to preach on the 22nd February, 1804. In 1806 he was ordained colleague to his father at Stirling. In 1819 he was elected Moderator of the Associate Synod, and was afterwards invited to the pastorate of a congregation in Blackfriars Street, Glasgow. To that charge he was translated in September, 1821. On the outbreak of the voluntary controversy in 1832 he took a prominent part in the discussions, and obtained celebrity as a platform orator. He died on the 10th June, 1846. For many years Dr. Heugh exercised a powerful advocacy on behalf of religious and charitable institutions.

A monument of Peterhead granite, surmounted by a bust, celebrates the Rev. Ralph Wardlaw, D.D., the eminent theological writer. Dr. Wardlaw was descended from the ancient family of Wardlaw of Pitreavie, one of the members of which was the celebrated Bishop Wardlaw, of St. Andrews, founder of the University in that city. His father was one of the magistrates of Glasgow, and his mother granddaughter of the celebrated Ebenezer Erskine. Born at Dalkeith on the 22nd September, 1779, he became a student at the theological seminary of the Secession Church, when the brothers Haldane began their lay preaching in 1797. Attracted by the new movement he attached himself to the Congregationalists, and in 1803 became pastor of the Independent Church, Albion Street, Glasgow. In 1811 he was appointed theological tutor in the Academy of the Scottish Congregational Church. Though frequently offered important preferment he continued to minister at Glasgow to his large and attached flock. He died on the 17th December, 1853, in his seventy-fourth year and fiftieth of his ministry. Dr. Wardlaw was author of numerous works in theology, homiletics, and Christian biography. His memoirs have been published by the Rev. William Lindsay Alexander, D.D.

In an elevated spot of the Necropolis an elegant monument, reared by public subscription, celebrates Duncan Macfarlan, D.D., minister of the High Church and Principal of Glasgow College; it is thus inscribed:—

"In memory of the Very Rev. Duncan Macfarlan, D.D. Born 1771. Died 1857. Succeeded his father as minister of Drymen, 1792. Became Principal of Glasgow College 1820, and minister of St. Mungo, the original parish of Glasgow, 1824. Erected 1861."

"Principal Macfarlan, as a minister of the gospel, was faithful and diligent; as a member of the Church of Scotland, his knowledge of its constitution and history, his zeal for its stability and extension, and his sound judgment and sagacious counsel in circumstances of difficulty obtained for him the confidence and respect of his brethren, and the singular honour of having twice filled the chair of the General Assembly.

" In the University he strenuously upheld its privileges, and judiciously watched over its interests; he enjoyed the confidence of his colleagues and the respect of the students.

" In the management of the public institutions of the city, his great sagacity and good sense, joined to an extensive experience, and a singular aptitude for business, made his services valuable, while his firm adherence to principle, and his dignified yet courteous demeanour, secured for him the esteem of all who had intercourse with him. To erect this memorial of his honoured and useful life all classes of the community cordially contributed."

Dr. Macfarlan was born at Auchingray, on the 27th September, 1771; his father, who bore the same Christian name, was ordained minister of Drymen in 1743, and died in 1791. Having studied at the University of Glasgow he was licensed to preach in 1791, and in the following year was ordained at Drymen as his father's successor. In 1815 he was appointed one of His Majesty's Chaplains, and in May, 1819, was elected Moderator of the General Assembly. In 1820 he became Principal of Glasgow College, and was in 1824 admitted minister of the High Church. In 1835 he originated the colonial scheme of the General Assembly, and continued its convener till 1856. On the event of the Secession in May, 1843, he was a second time elected Moderator of Assembly. He died on the 25th November, 1857, in his eighty-seventh year and the sixty-sixth of his ministry.

An obelisk of Peterhead granite, resting on a basement of black marble, commemorates Henry Monteith, of Carstairs, a prosperous and enterprising citizen. Third son of James Monteith, of Anderston, he was born in 1765. Prior to 1801 he carried on a manufacturing business as junior partner in the house of Robertson and Monteith; he subsequently became principal partner of the opulent firm of Henry Monteith, Bogle, & Co., whose manufactory of Bandana handkerchiefs became celebrated over Europe. In 1819 he purchased the estate of Carstairs, near Lanark. In 1814, and on a subsequent occasion he was elected Chief Magistrate of Glasgow, and he continued to evince a deep interest in civic affairs. For many years he was parliamentary representative of the Lanark burghs. He died on the 14th December, 1848.

A monument, representing the stage and proscenium of a theatre, celebrates John Henry Alexander, of the Theatre Royal, Glasgow. This ingenious individual was born at Dunse, Berwickshire, on the 31st July, 1796. At an early age his parents removed to Glasgow, where, in his thirteenth year, he was apprenticed to a hosier. With a remarkable taste for mimicry he practised private theatricals; and having attracted the notice of the managers of Queen Street Theatre, he obtained an opportunity of publicly exhibiting his gifts. In his sixteenth year he adopted the histrionic profession. For some seasons he was employed in a theatre at Newcastle; he subsequently performed at Carlisle, and afterwards in the Theatre Royal, Edinburgh. At Edinburgh his successful impersonations of Dandie Dinmont and other characters of the Waverley novels gained him the friendship of Sir Walter Scott. After some changes he accepted the managership of the Dunlop Street Theatre, Glasgow, of which he became proprietor in 1829. He rebuilt the structure in 1840; it was partially destroyed by fire on the 17th February, 1849, when 65 persons unhappily perished. The shock which he experienced on this occasion seriously affected his health, and in 1851 he found it expedient to retire from his profession. He died on the 15th December, 1851, aged fifty-five. On his tombstone are inscribed these lines from the pen of Mr. James Hedderwick, the editor of the *Glasgow Citizen:*—

> "Fallen is the curtain, the last scene is o'er,
> The favourite actor treads life's stage no more.
> Oft lavish plaudits from the crowd he drew,
> And laughing eyes confessed his humour true;
> Here fond affection rears this sculptured stone,
> For virtues not enacted, but his own.
> A constancy unshaken unto death,
> A truth unswerving, and a Christian's faith;
> Who knew him best have cause to mourn him most.
> Oh, weep the man, more than the actor lost!

Unnumbered parts he play'd, yet to the end
His best were those of husband, father, friend."

Robert Kettle, President of the Scottish Temperance League, is commemorated by a handsome obelisk. Born at Kintillo, near Perth, on the 18th December, 1791, he at first entertained views towards the ministry. These were abandoned, and he engaged in mercantile concerns. In 1815 he became clerk to William Kelly & Co., manufacturers, Glasgow, with whom he remained till 1829, when he began business on his own account. He joined the temperance movement in 1830. In 1838 he was elected President of the Glasgow Abstinence Society; in the following year he undertook the editorship of the *Scottish Temperance Journal*. He latterly recommended the cause of Savings Banks. He died on the 23rd March, 1852, deeply lamented by his fellow-citizens.

A monument celebrates James Reddie, LL.D., advocate and City Clerk. Born at Dysart, Fifeshire, in November, 1775, he studied at the University of Edinburgh, and passed advocate in 1797. With a high reputation as a lawyer, he was, in 1804, unanimously elected Town Clerk of Glasgow, and Presiding Judge in the Burgh Court. The onerous duties of his appointment he discharged with great ability and unceasing vigilance. In 1840 he published "Inquiries, Elementary and Historical, in the Science of Law;" and in the following year "An Historical view of the Law of Maritime Commerce." His subsequent publications, "Inquiries in International Law," and "Researches, Historical and Critical in Maritime International Law," are, with the former, held as standard authorities. Dr. Reddie died on the 5th April, 1852.

A colossal statue of white marble, executed by Park, commemorates Charles Tennant, of St. Rollox. This enterprising individual was born at Ochiltree House, Ayrshire, in 1768. Apprenticed to a silk weaver at Paisley, he subsequently became a bleacher in the neighbourhood of that town. Having in 1797 discovered the chloride of lime as a bleaching agent, he took out a patent for his invention, and two years afterwards erected the chemical works at

THE NECROPOLIS. 483

St. Rollox. As principal owner of these works Mr. Tennant exercised a powerful influence, which he employed in promoting the best interests of the community. He accelerated the construction of railways in the west of Scotland. He died on the 1st October, 1838, aged seventy-one.

A massive sarcophagus of Peterhead granite celebrates James Ewing, LL.D. Second son of Walter Ewing, West India merchant, he was born at Glasgow, on the 5th December, 1775. Educated at the High School, he entered on business at an early age; he was elected Dean of Guild, in 1815. In 1817 he published his "History of the Merchant's House." He exerted himself in procuring the abolition of the Burgess oath, which, after some opposition, he accomplished. In 1827 he took an active part in promoting the erection of the Royal Exchange; in the following year he initiated the movement for the construction of the Necropolis. He was, in 1831, elected Lord Provost, and in the following year was chosen one of the city's representatives in the Reformed Parliament. Soon after, he received the degree of LL.D. from the University. In 1836 he purchased the estate of Levenside, afterwards Strathleven, and retiring from public affairs devoted himself to rural pleasures and works of benevolence. He died on the 20th November, 1853; he bequeathed £70,000 to charitable purposes.

An elegant monumental sarcophagus commemorates the Rev. Thomas Brown, D.D., minister of Free St. John's Church. This eminent clergyman was born in the parish of Closeburn, Dumfriesshire, on the 9th August, 1776. Educated at Wallacehall, and afterwards at the Universities of Edinburgh and Glasgow, he was licensed to preach in 1804. In 1807 he was ordained minister of Tongland, Kirkcudbrightshire; he there ministered till 1826, when he accepted a call to St John's Church, Glasgow. For some years preceding the Disruption in 1843 he actively upheld the views of the dominant party, and on the event of the Disruption he adhered to the Free Church. He ministered in Free St. John's Church till within a few weeks of his decease; he died on the 23rd January,

1847, in his seventieth year and fortieth of his ministry. On his monument he is commended thus:—

"He walked with God like Enoch : preached with the fervor of Apollos: and, combining undaunted firmness with great gentleness and benevolence, presented, through grace, a bright example of Christian excellence and pastoral fidelity."

The Rev. Edward Irving, whose remains rest in the Cathedral crypt* is with his sister, Mrs. Dickson, commemorated by an elegant monument of Aberdeen granite, inscribed thus:—

"Sacred to the memory of the Rev. Edward Irving, A.M., who was born at Annan, Dumfriesshire, on the 4th August, 1792; and died at Glasgow, on the 8th December, 1834, aged forty-two years. His remains are interred in the crypt of the adjoining Cathedral.

"Janet Irving, sister of the late Rev. Edward Irving, and wife of Robert Dickson, Esquire, late of Annan, Dumfriesshire, who died at Glasgow, on the 29th August, 1849, aged fifty-five years."

An elegant monument celebrates Robert Muter, D.D. Born at Stonehouse, Lanarkshire, on the 13th August, 1771, he studied at the Divinity Hall of the Associate Synod, and obtaining license was invited in 1800 to undertake the pastorate of the Associate Church, Duke Street, Glasgow. There he ministered till his death, which took place on the 5th May, 1842, in the seventy-first year of his age, and forty-second of his ministry.

The Rev. William Brash, United Presbyterian minister, is commemorated by a monument of Elizabethan architecture. Born at Edinburgh, on the 1st March, 1794, he was educated at the High School and University of that city. After some preparatory studies at the Theological Hall of the Associate Synod, he was licensed to preach in March, 1815. In December of the same year he was ordained collegiate minister of East Campbell Street congregation, where he continued to minister till his death, which took place on the 24th November, 1851.

* See page 458.

A tall and massive monument commemorates William Dunn of Duntocher. This enterprising mechanician and successful agriculturist was born at Kirkintilloch, on the 5th October, 1770. Having been apprenticed to a machine maker, he in 1798 commenced business on his own account, and obtained a high reputation for the superiority of his machines. He subsequently carried on a large business as a cotton spinner. Through his enterprise the village of Duntocher became a centre of manufacturing industry. He realized a fortune of £500,000, a portion of which he bequeathed to charitable purposes. He died on the 13th March, 1849.

A plain monument celebrates Thomas Thomson, M.D., F.R.S., Professor of Chemistry in the University. Dr. Thomson's remains are interred in the Dean Cemetery, Edinburgh, where he is also commemorated by a monument (see *ante*, p. 135).

A granite pillar marks the grave of Colin Dunlop of Tollcross. Descended from an old family in Lanarkshire, he was born in 1775. Educated for the Scottish bar he became proprietor of the Clyde Iron Works, and engaged in business pursuits. In 1835 he became a candidate for the representation of the city in the liberal interest, and was returned. He died suddenly, on the 27th July, 1837. Mr. Dunlop was much esteemed for his public usefulness and private worth.

An elegant monument, in the form of a sarcophagus, celebrates James Sheridan Knowles, the ingenious dramatist. Son of James Knowles, an eminent teacher of elocution, he was born at Cork on the 12th May, 1784. For some time he held a commission in the army; he afterwards performed as an actor at Dublin. Subsequently he taught elocution at Belfast and Glasgow. He next devoted himself to dramatic composition, and from first to last produced fifteen plays, which, though not exhibiting high genius, have been pronounced the best acting plays produced by any modern Englishman. In 1845 he relinquished the stage, and devoted himself to serious studies. He died at Torquay, Devonshire, on the 30th November, 1862.

A handsome monument of Aberdeen granite denotes the resting-place of John Strang, LL.D., City Chamberlain. This accomplished scholar was son of a wine merchant, and was born in the city in 1795. Devoted to literary pursuits, he, in early manhood, travelled in France and Italy, and prosecuted philosophical studies in Germany. Having visited some of the chief art galleries on the Continent, he obtained celebrity as a fine art critic. In 1830 he published, under the pseudonym of Jeoffrey Crayon, jun., " A Glance at the Exhibitions of the Works of Living Artists, under the patronage of the Glasgow Dilletanti Society." His small volume, entitled " Necropolis Glasguensis," published in 1831, essentially contributed to the success of the movement for the construction of the Necropolis. In 1836 he published "Travels in Germany," in two octavo volumes. About the same time he was elected Chamberlain of the city. His most popular work, " Glasgow and its Clubs," was issued in 1855, and soon passed into a second edition. Dr. Strang died on the 8th December, 1863, aged sixty-eight. He was a laborious student, and an acute and vigorous administrator of public affairs.

Massive and elegant monuments celebrate James Mackenzie, of Craig Park, who died 13th June, 1838, aged thirty-seven; Hugh Cogan, of the firm of Cogan and Bartholomew, died 28th August, 1855, aged sixty-three; John Tait, editor of the *Glasgow Liberator*, died 19th October, 1836, aged forty-one; John Spittal, M.D., died 27th March, 1840, aged thirty-four; James Dennistoun, manager of the Glasgow Bank, died 11th October, 1835; Andrew Henderson, author of "Collection of Scottish Proverbs," died 9th April, 1835; Major Archibald Douglas Monteith, died 15th June, 1842; James Connell, LL.D., mathematical master in the High School, born 7th September, 1804, died 26th March, 1846; Lieut.-Colonel Alexander Hope Pattison, K.H., Commander of the troops in the Bahamas, died 11th January, 1843, aged forty-eight; Hugh Hamilton, a political orator, born 25th June, 1791, died 25th December, 1837.

Among the other notable persons commemorated in the Necropolis are the Rev. William Black, D.D., minister of the Barony Church, Glasgow, died 15th January, 1851, in the fiftieth year of his age and twenty-fifth of his ministry; the Rev. John Fairley, minister of the Reformed Presbyterian Church, Glasgow, died 8th August, 1837; the Rev. James Gardner, minister of Fairlie, died 17th December, 1836; John Dymock, LL.D., one of the masters of the Grammar School, died 9th November, 1838; Lieut.-Colonel James McNair, K.H., died 11th May, 1836; Patrick Playfair, of Dalmarnock, born 14th September, 1765, died 26th November, 1836; James Towers, Professor of Midwifery in the University of Glasgow, died 24th July, 1820; Peter Lawrence, sculptor, died 27th January, 1839; Alexander Hope Pattison, Lieutenant and acting Adjutant of the 2nd West India Regiment, died 28th September, 1834, aged twenty-one; the Rev. Robert Ross, minister of Free St. Mark's, died 12th October, 1847; Rev. William France, Wesleyan minister, died 11th October, 1850; the Rev. John Kirkland, Chaplain to the Forces, died 7th December, 1854; Robert Baird, of Auchmedden, Lord Dean of Guild, died 7th August, 1856; Dr. Alexander Hannay, died 22nd January, 1846; Dr. George Black, died 7th January, 1847; Dr. John Black, died 8th January, 1865; Robert Douie, master of the Grammar School, died April, 1853; James Buchanan, of Dowanhill, died 15th April, 1844; James Davidson, of Ruchill, died 1850; James Jeffrey, M.D., Professor of Anatomy in the University, born 1759, died 1848; William Johnston, of Glenorchard, died 6th December, 1864; William Campbell, of Tillichewan, born 15th January, 1794, died 11th April, 1864; Donald Cuthbertson, LL.D., died 8th December, 1864; Rev. James Robertson, D.D., minister of Shamrock Street, U. P. Church, died 14th January, 1861; Rev. Matthew Barclay, D.D., minister of the Free Church, Old Kilpatrick, died 22nd January, 1865, aged seventy-six; William Maclean, of Plantation, died 22nd February, 1867; John Graham Gilbert, R.S.A., died 4th June, 1866, aged seventy-two; Robert Stewart, of Murdostoun, Lord Provost of Glasgow from 1851 to 1854, born 16th January, 1811, died 12th September, 1866; John Panton, M.D., died 28th July,

1864; Charles S. P. Tennent, of Well Park, died 19th February, 1864, aged forty-seven; Rev. John Maclaren, minister of U. P. Church, New City Road, died 21st June, 1859; William Symington, D.D., minister of the Reformed Presbyterian Church, Glasgow, died 28th January, 1862; and James Boyd, D.D., minister of the Tron Church, Glasgow, died 27th March, 1865, in the seventy-ninth year of his age and forty-eighth of his ministry.

A monument commemorates Francois Foucart, an officer in the Imperial Guard of France, Knight of the Legion of Honour, and Professor of fencing in the Royal Academy of Paris, born at Valenciennes in 1781, died at Glasgow in 1862. On his tombstone are inscribed the following lines, composed by J. Sheridan Knowles :—

> "Talk you of scars ?—that Frenchman bears a crown!
> Body and limb his vouchers palpable;
> For many a thicket he has struggled through
> Of briery danger, wondering that he
> Came off with even life, when right and left
> His mates dropp'd thick beside him. A true man,
> His rations with his master gone—for he
> Was honor's soldier, that ne'er changes sides.
> He left his country for a foreign one
> To teach his gallant art, and earn a home.
> I knew him to be honest, generous,
> High soul'd, and modest, every way a grace
> To the fine martial nation whence he sprang."

On the tombstone of John Pattison, of Kelvingrove, merchant in Glasgow, who died 28th December, 1807, aged fifty-seven, and of his wife Hope Margaret Moncrieff, who died 3rd December, 1833, aged seventy-seven, are the following stanzas :—

> "This native stone—what few vain marbles can ?—
> May truly say, Here lies an honest man!
> A manly form, a firm yet brilliant mind,
> Open as day, his heart loved all mankind;
> A lively faith, from superstition free,
> A love of truth, and hate of tyranny.
> Such this man was, who now from earth removed,
> At length enjoys the liberty he loved.

"And thou, his best beloved, his faithful wife,
The pride and solace of his wedded life;
Our gentle mother—honored, loved, revered—
Whose sweet voice blest us, and whose bright eye cheered,
Thou too hast left us in this world of woe;
Nor dare we murmur while we mourn the blow;
'For we would ill requite thee to constrain
Thine unbound spirits into bonds again.'"

To denote the site of his father's dwelling, John Mitchell, painter in Glasgow, has in the Necropolis erected an obelisk inscribed as follows:—

"In childhood's years, when full of sportive glee,
Here have I prattled on my mother's knee,
Received her kind caress, her holy care,
As oft she breath'd for me her fervent prayer.

"Here did our parents and their children meet,
A happy circle joined in concord sweet;
While upwards rose the voice of prayer and praise,
That God would lead us in his holy ways.

"As on this spot I drew my infant breath,
Here let me rest when I repose in death;
And when the last trump's pealing notes shall sound,
Oh, may our lot among the blest be found."

From the numerous metrical epitaphs to be found in the Necropolis, we have selected the following:—

"This little flower was early crop't,
But crop't by love divine."

"What joy when she resigned her breath,
For as her eyelids closed, she smiled in death."

"Thy word, O God, was found of me,
And I did eat it, and it was to me the joy
And rejoicing of mine heart."

"Thou wert not, Solomon, in all thy glory,
Arrayed, the lilies cry, in robes like these,

How vain your grandeur, Ah, how transitory
  Are human flowers!"

"Learn then, ye living! By the mouths be taught
  Of all these sepulchres, instructors true,
That, soon or late, death also is your lot,
  And the next opening grave may yawn for you."

"The grave has eloquence; its lectures teach
In silence louder than divine can preach.
Hear what it says, ye sons of folly, hear,
It speaks to you—lend an attentive ear."

"Keep safe these treasures, chest of clay,
  Till they are called for at the judgment-day;
For while these jewels here are set,
  The grave is but their cabinet."

"Here sleeps a saint whose soul was ne'er cast down,
By earthly troubles; now a heavenly crown
His brow adorns, while angels of the light
Hail him as brother in those regions bright
Where all is glorious, Christ in all appears,
And souls live happy through eternal years."

"She is gone; she is gone to the land of light,
Where the glorious day ne'er sets in night;
Where a cloud ne'er comes across the sky,
Where the tears are wiped from every eye,
Where all is holiness, love, and bliss—
And none regret a world like this."

SOUTHERN NECROPOLIS.

In this cemetery rest the remains of Hugh Macdonald, an ingenious and short-lived poet. Born at Bridgeton, Glasgow, on the 4th April, 1817, he was, after a short attendance at school, apprenticed in the block-printing works of Monteith and Co., Barrowfield. He afterwards opened a provision shop at Bridgeton, but the venture did not succeed, and he returned to his trade. From his house at Bridgeton to the block-printing works at Colinslie, near Paisley, where he was now employed, he walked every morning, a distance of eight miles, and after twelve hours' labour again walked home. During these long journeys he improved himself by reading and reflection, and he began to send contributions, both in prose and verse, to the public journals. During a visit to Edinburgh in the summer of 1846, he met with a kind reception from Professor Wilson, who commended his verses. In 1849 he became sub-editor of the *Glasgow Citizen*. In the columns of the *Citizen* he commenced his "Rambles Round Glasgow," a series of interesting and amusing sketches, which, subsequently collected in a volume, established his reputation. In 1855 he accepted the editorship of the *Glasgow Times*; he contributed to that journal a series of papers descriptive of the scenery of the Clyde, which he afterwards published with the title of "Days at the Coast." Joining the literary staff of the *Morning Journal*, a daily newspaper started at Glasgow in June, 1858, he continued in this connection till his death, which took place on the 16th March, 1860. His poetical compositions were in 1865 published at Glasgow in a duodecimo volume. Mr. Macdonald is commemorated by a short inscription on a tombstone which he erected to the memory of his wife. She died on the 25th October, 1855, and is by her husband celebrated thus:—

> "The blighted flower shall bloom again,
> The fallen star shall rise
> Triumphant from the gloom of death
> To glory in the skies."

An obelisk, erected by his friends, commemorates the Rev. Peter Mathie, upwards of fourteen years editor of the *Christian News.* He died 11th January, 1864, aged seventy-two.

Two advocates of total abstinence are commemorated by handsome obelisks reared by the friends of temperance—Malcolm McFarlane, who died 20th February, 1862, aged fifty-two, and James Mitchell, who died 18th January, 1862, aged sixty-six.

An obelisk of Peterhead granite, erected by his congregation, celebrates the pastoral diligence of the Rev. Jonathan Anderson, minister of "Knox's Kirk of Scotland Tabernacle, Glasgow," who died 10th January, 1859, aged fifty-six.

On his family tombstone Robert Muir has thus celebrated a hopeful son:—

> " Beneath this sacred monumental stone,
> Designed for other mem'ry than his own,
> The youthful architect to earth is given.
> No, no; this tomb his first and last attempt in art,
> But marks without intent his mortal part,
> He lives, whence his design with art, in heaven."

Andrew Thomson commemorates his infant daughter thus:—

> " See gentle patience smile on pain,
> Till dying hope revives again;
> Hope wipes the tear from sorrow's eye,
> And faith points upward to the sky."

In these lines William Brown laments the loss of his infant son:—

> "These ashes few, this little dust,
> Our Father's care shall keep,
> Till the last angel rise and break
> The long and peaceful sleep."

Dr. Robert Parker, who died in 1861, is thus lamented by his widow:—

> " Sleep on, lov'd one, thy troubles o'er,
> From care and suffering free;
> The grief that rends this widowed heart
> Can ne'er be felt by thee."

Peter Delacourt has inscribed these lines on his wife's gravestone :—

> "Shed not for her the bitter tear,
> Nor give the heart to vain regret;
> 'Tis but the casket that here lies,
> The gem that filled it sparkles yet."

Edward Morris, a temperance advocate, who died 1st August, 1860, has his tombstone inscribed thus :—

> "Dust to its narrow house beneath
> Sent to the home on high!
> They that have seen thy look
> In death no more need fear to die."

William Wood and his wife thus lament their infant son :—

> "Fare thee well, our last and fairest,
> Dear wee Willie, fare thee well;
> God, who lent thee, hath recalled thee
> Back, with Him and His to dwell."

On his short-lived wife Robert Macintyre has composed these verses :—

> "How soon her marriage morn is shaded,
> But yesterday she was a bride;
> But scarce her orange flower had faded
> When she, herself a flower, hath died."

> "She lives in Christ, we dare not sorrow
> That Christ her spouse hath called her home;
> But breaking hearts from this will borrow
> Comfort for the days to come."

The children of William Cameron thus lament their departed mother :—

> "Mother, thou wast mild and lovely,
> Gentle as the summer breeze,
> Pleasant as the air of evening
> When it floats among the trees;
> Peaceful be thy silent slumber,
> Peaceful in the grave so low,

Thou no more wilt join our number,
   Thou no more our songs shalt know.
Dearest mother, thou hast left us,
   Here thy loss we deeply feel,
But 'tis God that hath bereft us,
   He can all our sorrow heal.
Yet again we hope to meet thee
   When the day of life is fled,
Then in heaven with joy to greet thee,
   Where no farewell tear is shed."

In these touching stanzas Alexander Stewart mourns an infant daughter :—

"Our wee smilin' cherub just lent to our hearth
How we miss thy bit prattle an' innocent mirth,
Your merry guffaw, an' your sweet lispin' glee,
Your mammie's whole heart an' your daddie's ae e'e.
There's a blank by our hearth an' a blank by our knee,
And ilka bit plaything reminds us o' thee;
A wee seat stan's empty, a wee dish an' spoon
Gars us think on our infant nicht, mornin', and noon."

"Ay, we saw thee in pain, what my tongue couldna tell,
And kiss'd thy fair flushed cheek an' thocht 'twould be well;
And we dreamit na that death, sae relentless an' stern,
Was sae near to thy wee heart, our ain bonnie bairn.
Then farewell our dear infant, farewell for a wee,
The time's fast approaching, we'll a' follow thee;
Our dust, mixed in thine, will be sma' late or soon,
And may we a' meet a family aboon."

On her tombstone Janet Grant, who died 19th April, 1858, is described as having reached the age of one hundred and eleven years.

SIGHTHILL CEMETERY.

Situated in the northern part of the city, Sighthill Cemetery was constructed in 1840.

SIGHTHILL CEMETERY.

A monument commemorates the Rev. James Seaton Reid, D.D., author of "History of the Presbyterian Church in Ireland." Born at Lurgan, in the province of Ulster, Dr. Reid studied at the University of Glasgow. Licensed to preach in 1818, he was in the same year ordained minister of the Presbyterian church at Donegore. In 1822 he was transferred to Carrickfergus, where he ministered for fifteen years. In 1827 he was elected Moderator of the Synod of Ulster. He was appointed Professor of Ecclesiastical History in the Academical Institution, Belfast, in 1837, and four years thereafter was preferred to the chair of Church History in the University of Glasgow. He died on the 26th March, 1851. The first volume of his work on the Irish Presbyterian Church appeared in 1834. The third and last was published posthumously in 1853.

Tombstones commemorate William Mossman, sculptor, and Samuel Edmund Glover, of the Glasgow Theatre; the former died 14th August, 1851, aged fifty-eight, the latter 24th October, 1860.

An elegant monument celebrates John Baird and Andrew Hardie, political martyrs. It is inscribed thus:—

"Erected by public subscription July, 1847, to the memory of John Baird, aged thirty-two, and Andrew Hardie, aged twenty-eight, who, for the cause of freedom, suffered death at Stirling, 8th September, 1820.

"Here lie the slain and mutilated forms
  Of those who fell like martyrs true,
Faithful to freedom through a time of storms,
  They met their fate, as patriots always do,
  Despising death, which ne'er can noble souls subdue.

"Calmly they viewed death's dread and dark array,
  Then, heaven directed, turned their prayerful eyes,
Serene in hope, they triumphed o'er dismay
  Their country's wrongs alone drew forth their sighs,
  And those to them endear'd by nature's holiest ties.

"But truth and right have better times brought round,
  Now no more traitors scared by passing breath;

> For weeping Scotland hails this spot of ground,
>   And shrines with all who fell for freedom's faith,
>   Whose sons of hers, now fam'd, made glorious by their death."

"During the erection of this monument the committee applied to Her Majesty's Government for permission to remove the mortal remains of the two martyrs from Stirling to this spot, and after a lengthened correspondence the following letter was received from the Lord Advocate:—

"Gwydyr House, Whitehall,
"London, 5th May, 1847.

"Sir,

"I have laid the memorial for the relatives of Andrew Hardie and John Baird before Secretary Sir George Grey, and I have the satisfaction of informing you that, if the Kirksession of Stirling see no objections upon other grounds, opposition will not be made on the part of Government to the removal of the remains of these unfortunate men from their present place of interment.

"But the permission is given under the express condition that the removal shall take place without any public notice or intimation, and without any procession, or concourse, or attendance of people, but in the presence of a few friends only.

"Andrew Rutherfurd.

"In accordance with these instructions the exhumation took place at an early hour on the morning of the 20th July, 1847, and the remains were reinterred in front of the monument on the same day in presence of a considerable assembly of friends.

> "Here, then, they rest, and far in future years
>   Shall freedom dew the spot with memory's tears.

"This monument was repaired at considerable expense in 1865 by a few friends, under the superintendence of the original Hardie and Baird and Martyrs' Stone Committee."

Margaret Humbie thus commemorates her departed husband:—

> "I know 'tis wrong in me to sigh,
>   Thy spirit's fled unto the sky,
>   Where thy sweet form I yet shall see,
>   As I still hope to be with thee."

William Robertson has on his wife's tombstone inscribed these lines:—

> "A little while between our souls
> The shadowy gulf must be;
> Yet have we for our communing
> Still, still, eternity."

On the gravestone of his infant son, Thomas Dunlop has engraved the following:—

> "Kind parents, why those tears,
> And why those bursting sighs?
> No weeping here bedims
> Your little lov'd one's eyes."

Robert and Amelia Brownlee thus commemorate their infant daughter:—

> "Here lies the body of a beloved child,
> With talents rare and manners mild;
> The Almighty marked her for His own,
> And she from earth to heaven has flown."

In memory of his infant daughter, James Sharpe has inscribed the following:—

> "So fades the lovely blooming flower,
> Frail, smiling offspring of an hour;
> So soon our transient comforts fly,
> Pleasures which only bloom to die."

The tombstone of William Walker, who died in 1841, presents the following:—

> "This languishing head is at rest,
> Its drooping and aching are o'er;
> This quiet, immovable breast,
> Is heav'd by affliction no more."

Peter Rodger, sailor, thus celebrates his brother John and his wife:—

> "Our anchor is cast, cast down at last,
> We hear no sound of storm or blast,
> We see no rain, we feel no wind;
> But let us to our Saviour come,
> A sailor's brother lyes here,
> Also his wife he loved so dear."

On the gravestone of his infant son David Minto has inscribed these lines :—

"Now is his cradle bed under the sod,
But the spirit enjoys the sweet presence of God;
In the morning of life he has gone to that shore
Where earth's mourners may meet and rejoice evermore.
The opening bud shall there blossom for ever,
Kind feelings shall ripen, and friends separate never."

John Hamilton, who died in 1844, is by his widow lamented thus :—

"Bear with me, O my God,
If in the bitterness of mortal woe
I've dared to murmur at Thy high decree,
Look on my babe, who now no father has
But Thee. Oh, shield his helpless infancy
From sin and danger, and give me strength
To train him to do Thy will."

On the tombstone of William Miller, who died in 1851, are these verses :—

"Pause here and think; a monitory rhyme
Demands one moment of thy fleeting time;
Consult life's silent clock, thy bounding vein,
Seems it to say, health here has long to reign.

"Hast thou the vigour of thy youth; an eye
That beams delight? a heart untaught to sigh?
Yet fear, youth ofttimes healthful and at ease
Anticipates a day it never sees."

William Bruce commemorates his daughter thus :—

"Life ne'er exulted in so rich a prize
As Jeanie lovely from her native skies;
Nor envious death so triumphed in a blow
As that which laid th' innocent Jeanie low.
Thy form and mind, sweet child, we'll ne'er forget,
In richest ore the brightest jewel set;
In the high heaven above was truest shown,
As by His noblest work the Godhead best is known."

Captain William Douglas, of Maitland, Nova Scotia, has inscribed these verses on his son's gravestone :—

> "Let me go! let me go! for the purple is dawning,
>   Is mantling the dull dark tomb of time;
> And there stealeth the ray of a blissful morning,
>   That blushes and burns in a deathless clime.
>
> "I have done with sin, I have done with sorrow,
>   I fly to the spotless realm of light;
> Where the day that is breaking shall have no morrow,
>   And the sun that is rising shall have no night."

On a tombstone commemorating their five young children, Hugh Paterson and his wife have inscribed these verses:—

> "There fell upon our house a sudden gloom,
>   A shadow on those features fair and thin,
> And softly from that hushed and darkened room,
>   Two angels issued where but one went in.
>
> "And the mother gave in tears and pain
>   The flowers she most did love;
> She knew she should find them all again,
>   In the fields of light above.
>
> "They shall all bloom in fields of light,
>   Transplanted by my care;
> And saints, upon their garments white,
>   These sacred blossoms wear."

JANEFIELD CEMETERY.

This place of tombs, otherwise styled the Eastern Necropolis, presents the following metrical epitaphs.

Sergeant William Robertson, who died October, 1847, is celebrated thus:

> "He whose kind ashes moulder here below,
>   Was once the gentlest model of his kind;
> He lived—nor made himself a single foe,
>   He died—nor left one enemy behind."

George Porter thus laments his infant daughter:—

> "Here lies a rose, a budding rose,
>   Blasted before its bloom,
> Whose innocence did sweets disclose
>   Beyond that flower's perfume
> To those who for her loss are grieved
>   This consolation's given
> She's from a world of woe relieved
>   And blooms a rose in heaven."

Mrs. Sophia Brown thus commemorates her son, who died in September, 1860, aged twenty-four:—

> "Months have rolled on, yet thou art not forgot;
> Years may roll on, yet I'll remember thee;
> No time nor change can ever, ever blot
> Thy chastened image from my memory;
> No; for thou art entwined around this heart;
> And while it beats, thou never can'st depart.

> "For the calm sweet impression of that face
> Death or the grave or time cannot efface
> Such thoughts were selfish, thou art happier far.
>   Far, far, removed from sorrow, pain and grief;
> Thou hadst thy share of ills; and I can bear
> Thy loss, assured that thou hast found relief
> From all the cankering cares which man annoy
> From sin, from suffering, everything but joy."

WOODSIDE CEMETERY, ANDERSTON.

From tombstones in this churchyard we have the following:—

> "Sleep on, sweet Babe, high heaven's all gracious King
> Hath to eternal summers chang'd thy spring
> Short tho' thy bloom the opening flower began
> The promise fair when ripened into man."

> "An aged Christian slumbers here
> Whose faith was strong, her love sincere;
> Content she passed life's little span
> In fearing God and serving man."

"As those we love decay we die in part,
String after string is sever'd from the heart;
Till loosened life at last but breathing clay
Without one pang is glad to flee away.
Unhappy she who latest feels the blow,
Whose eyes have wept o'er every friend laid low;
Dragg'd lingering on from partial death to death,
Till, dying all, she can resign her breath."

"Here lies the cold remains of one who seem'd to be
A flower to flourish in this world of woe;
And tread the path along its stormy sea,
That path thus doom'd to mortals here below;
This was my lot, sweet flower, that bloom'd to fall,
An early victim to death's fatal dart;
But in thy death thou triumphed over all
For Heaven, dear youth, holds thy immortal part."

PARISH OF GOVAN.

In the vestibule of the old parish church a marble tablet commemorates the Rev. Hugh Binning, minister of the parish and a celebrated preacher. Son of John Binning, of Dalvennan, a landowner at Straiton, in Ayrshire, he was born about 1627. Having distinguished himself as a student at Glasgow College, he was appointed Regent of Philosophy in that University in his nineteenth year. In 1650 he was invited by the parishioners of Govan to become their pastor, and accepting the call, was ordained to the charge. In 1651 he joined the Protesting party in the church; with a view to effect reconciliation between them and the Resolutioners, he composed his "Treatise on Christian Love." In the disputation which Cromwell caused to be held at Glasgow between his own Independent ministers and the Scottish Presbyterians, Binning's fervid eloquence astonished even the Protector himself. Binning died of consumption in September, 1653, in his twenty-seventh year and the fourth of his ministry. His chief publications, besides his "Treatise on Christian Love," are "The Common Principles of the Christian Religion," "The Sinner's Sanctuary," and "Fellowship with God." His tombstone is inscribed with a Latin epitaph, composed by Principal Gillespie, of Glasgow College.

PARISH OF HAMILTON.

Within the enclosures of Hamilton Palace stands the magnificent mausoleum of the Dukes of Hamilton. It was constructed at the cost and under the superintendence of Alexander, the tenth Duke. His Grace died on the 18th August, 1852, and his remains were deposited in a sarcophagus which he caused to be prepared during his life. The mausoleum also contains the remains of William Alexander Anthony Archibald, son of the preceding, the eleventh Duke of Hamilton. He died at Paris on the 15th July, 1863, aged fifty-two. To his memory a monument has been reared on a projecting cliff of the Avon, near the entrance to Cadzow Forest. This monument, which was erected by the tenantry on the Hamilton estates, is of elegant construction. An open circular temple, twenty-six feet in height and twenty-two feet in diameter, is raised upon a rusticated basement, from which spring nine pillars of Aberdeen granite, supporting an entablature. In the interior a pedestal of grey granite is surmounted by a bust of the Duke, executed by Mossman.

In the old burial-place of the Hamilton family a monument commemorates Lord William Douglas, second Duke of Hamilton; it is inscribed thus :—

"Memoriæ sacrum illustrissimi principis Gulielmi secundi, Hamiltoniorum ducis, Clidisdaliæ marchionis, Araniæ, Lanerici, &c., comitis Avaniæ, Polmontii, Macdaniæ, &c., reguli, celcissimi Duglassiorum marchionis, ex secundis nuptiis, cum Maria Gordon marchionis de Huntly filia, filii natu maximi; regii palatii Sanctæ Crucis custodis perpetui: in trium regni ordin. comitiis sæpius proregis; secretiori conciliis regni Scotiæ præsidis; tribus etiam regibus succedaneis ab intimis regni Angliæ conciliis;

sacri ibidem ærarii comitis; in supremo foro juridico senatoris extraordinarii; regni Scotiæ thalassiarchæ; nobilissimi ordinis periscelidis equitis socii; patriæ propugnatoris strenui; familiæ instauratoris tanquam divinitus missi; hoc (famæ nunquam interituræ) monumentum mœrens posuit vidua Anna (post seriem tredecim procerum familiæ principem) ipsa familias hæres; præter Jacobum hæredem, quinque alios reliquit filios, tres itidem filias, illustrissimi familiis in matrimonium collocatas. Natus 24 die Decembris, 1634, dentatus 18 Aprilis, 1694."

In the churchyard the Rev. Robert Wyllie, minister of the parish, has thus commemorated his wife, who died in childbirth, on the 15th July, 1694 :—

"P.M. lectissimæ, dilectissimaque conjugis, Rachel Murray, ex illustri ac perantiqua gente Moraviorum a Philiphaugh, prognatæ; eximiis vero tum naturæ tum gratiæ dotibus, quam stemmatis splendore, longe illustrioris : quæ nata pridie cal. Oct. CICICCLXIV. denata XVI. cal. sextil. CICICCXCIV. annorum XXIX. Biennio conjugali vixdum exacto, febri ex secundo puerperio correpta, vitam, filiolo quam dederat in terris peragendam, lubens deseruit; ad supernam, cui matura inhiabat, evecta, magno sui desiderio apud omnes probos relicto : cippum hunc, luctuosi tesseram amoris quo etiam primogenitus infans, nomine Jacobus, propter matrem, conditur, Robertus Wyllie, ecclesiæ Hamiltoniensis antistes, expectans, dum, ad suos aggregatus, in spem beatæ resurrectionis, ipse simul seminetur orbitatem interea suam mœrens, posuit. Matrem secuta est altera proles, Thomas Διμηνος infans.

Robert Wyllie was son of Thomas Wyllie, minister of Kirkcudbright. He studied at the University of Glasgow, and was some time employed as a tutor. Obtaining license as a probationer in 1687, he was ordained minister of Yarrow in 1690. He was translated to Ashkirk in 1691, and to Hamilton in 1692. By Wodrow, he is commended as " a man of shining piety, fine taste, excellent sense, and singular accomplishments in every branch of valuable knowledge and learning." He died on the 14th February, 1715, in the twenty-sixth year of his ministry. His wife, whom he has so affectionately commemorated, was descended from the family of Murray of Philiphaugh; she died in her twenty-ninth year.

In the churchyard were interred the heads of John Parker, Gavin Hamilton, James Hamilton, and Christopher Strong, four

Presbyterian martyrs, who suffered at Edinburgh on the 7th December, 1666. A tablet in the churchyard wall, opposite the spot, is thus inscribed:—

> "Stay, passenger, tak notice what thou reads
> At Edinburgh lie our bodies, here our heads;
> Our right hands stood at Lanark, these we want
> Because wi' them we swore the Covenant."

From tombstones in the churchyard we have the following inscriptions:—

> "Livest thou, Thomas? Yes, with God on high!
> Art thou not dead? Yes, and here I lie;
> I that with man on earth did live to die,
> Died for to live with Christ eternally."

> "He took the cup of life to sip,
> Too bitter it was to drain;
> He put it meekly from his lip,
> And went to sleep again."

> "Short here thy stay for souls of holiest birth,
> Dwell but a moment with the sons of earth;
> To this dim sphere by God's indulgence given,
> Their friends are angels and their home is heaven."

> "The seas he ploughed for twenty years
> Without the smallest dread or fears;
> And all that time was never known
> To strike upon a bank or stone;
> But when the Lord his time had tryed,
> He brought him home and there he died.

PARISH OF LANARK.

In front of the Town Hall a colossal statue celebrates Sir William Wallace, the Scottish chief. Wallace married Marion Braidfoot, the heiress of Lamington, and after his marriage resided in the district. In Bonnington House, several curious relics, said to have belonged to the hero, are carefully preserved. Among these are a broad oaken seat, and a small oak cup or quaigh; both are evidently of great antiquity.

In the churchyard a tombstone thus commemorates a martyr for the Covenant:—

"Heir lyes William Howie, who suffered at the Cros of Lanark, the 2 of March, 1682, aged thirty-eight, for his adherence to the word of God and Scotland's covenanted work of Reformation."

The following epitaphs are from Lanark Churchyard:—

"Here ashes meet in death's dark shade
A solemn proof that all must fade;
Here's all on earth we hold most dear,
A bosom friend, a friend sincere."

"How awful is the scene which here I tread
The venerable mansions of the dead!
Time was these ashes liv'd, and time shall be
When others thus shall stand and gaze on me.
Awake, then, O my soul, true wisdom learn,
Nor till to-morrow the great work adjourn."

PARISH OF LESMAHAGOW.

At Blackwood, a tombstone denotes the burial-place of John Brown, a Presbyterian martyr, who suffered in 1685. The inscription is as follows:—

"Murray might murder such a godly Brown,
But could not rob him of that glorious crown,
He now enjoys. His credit, not his crime,
Was non-compliance with a wicked time."

In the parish churchyard David Steel, a Presbyterian martyr, is commemorated thus:—

"David, a shepherd first, and then
Advanced to be king of men,
Had of his graces in this quarter,
This heir a wand'rer, now a martyr;

> Who, for his constancy and zeal,
> Still to the back did prove good steel;
> Who, for Christ's royal truths and laws,
> And, for the covenanted cause
> Of Scotland's famous reformation,
> Declining tyrant's usurpation;
> By cruel Crichton murder'd lies,
> Whose blood to heav'n for vengeance cries."

PARISH OF WANDELL.

In the old church of Lamington a marble monument commemorates Elizabeth Dundas, Lady Ross Baillie, who died in 1817. She was eldest daughter of the Lord President Dundas, and was heiress of the Lamington estates; she married Sir John Lockhart Ross, of Balnagowan.

In Lamington churchyard a large flat tombstone commemorates several progenitors of the late Professor Jardine, of Glasgow College.

PARISH OF WALSTON.

In a vault, which formed the burying-place of the old family of Baillie, of Walston, a member of that house, who died in 1665, has as an epitaph these lines:—

> "Thow passing that lviks
> Vpon this Tomb,
> Learn this Lesson Remenbir
> On thv Hom;
> Give Heaven thy Mynd, thy
> Bodie Dee It mvst,
> Remember Man, thow art
> Bvt mortal Dvst."

INDEX.

A

Abercairney, The Baron of, 105.
Abercorn, Duke of, 424.
Abercorn, Parish of, 179.
Abercrombie, Charles, 361.
Abercrombie, John, M.D., 64.
Abercromby, Sir Ralph, 453.
Aberlady, Parish of, 199.
Abernethy, Alexander, of Corskie, 172.
Abernethy, Henry, 215.
Abernethy, Sir Lawrence, 171.
Abernethy, Sir William, 171.
Achaius, Bishop John, 457.
Adam, Bessie, 460.
Adam, Dr. Alexander, 83.
Adam, Francis, 49.
Adam, James, 50.
Adam, John, of Blair-Adam, 47.
Adam, John, jun., Blair-Adam, 48, 49.
Adam, Mrs. Eleanora, 49.
Adam, Mrs. Jean, 49.
Adam, Mrs. Mary, 48.
Adam, Rear-Admiral Sir Charles, 49, 50.
Adam, Rev. George, 404.
Adam, Right Hon. William, 47.
Adam, Robert, 50.
Adam, William George, 48.
Adam, William Patrick, 50.
Adams, Rev. Alexander, 272.
Adamson, Principal, 19.
Advocates Library, 5, 14, 36.
Affleck, James, 438.
Agnew, Frances Georgiana Vans, 71.
Agnew, Lady, 146, 147.
Agnew, Lieutenant Andrew, 147.
Agnew, Sir Andrew, Bart., 146, 347, 356.
Agnew, Sir Stair, Bart., 147.
Aikenhead, David, 52.
Ailsa, Marquis of, 396.
Ainslie, Robert W. S., 143.
Ainslie, Robert, 212.
Airdrie, Parish of, 435.
Airds Moss, 358.
Aitchison, Edward, 272.
Aitchison, Elliot, 261.
Aitken, John, of Mount Aitken, 142.
Albany, Duke of, 100, 156, 157.
Albert, Prince, Monuments to, 18, 455.
Alexander II., 250.
Alexander, John, 427.
Alexander, John, M.D., 71.
Alexander, John Henry, of the Glasgow Theatre, 481.
Alexander, Rev. William L., 479.
Alexander, Robert, of Blackhouse, 426.
Alexander, Thomas, C.B., 216.
Alexander, William, 216.
Algeo, William, 427.
Algie, James, 429.
Alison, Professor William P., 73.
Alison, Rev. Archibald, 72, 141.
Alison, Sir Archibald, Bart., 141.
Allan, Alexander, 155.
Allan, David, the Painter, 96.
Allan, James, 381.
Allan, Robert, F.R.S.C., 143.
Allan, Sir William, 2, 132.
Alloway, Churchyard of, 362.
Alston, Professor Charles, 89.
Alva, Lord, 71, 398.
Alvanley, Lady, 115.
Ancrum, Parish of, 238.
Anderson, Colonel Robert, of Winterfield, 204.
Anderson, General William C., 204.
Anderson, James, 386, 462.

508 INDEX.

Anderson, Lieutenant Robert B., 465.
Anderson, Major David D., 204.
Anderson, Provost John, 464.
Anderson, Rev. Jonathan, 492.
Anderson, Rev. Robert, D.D., 53, 54.
Anderson, Richard, of Windygoul, 204.
Anderson, Robert, 294, 386.
Anderson, Robert, M.D., 445.
Angus, Earls of, 108, 109, 114, 165, 238.
Angus, John, 205.
Annan, Parish of, 295.
Annand, Dean William, 52.
Anstruther, James, W.S., 143.
Anstruther, Lord, 115.
Anstruther, Major John, 465.
Anstruther, Mrs. Marian, 143.
Anstruther, Sir John, Bart., 143.
Anworth, Parish of, 326.
Arbuthnot, Anne, Viscountess of, 109.
Arbuthnot, Sir William, Bart., 79.
Areskine, Ralph, of Shielfield, 222.
Areskine, Rev. Henry, 222.
Argyle, Earls of, 101, 471.
Argyle, Jane Stewart, Countess of, 101.
Argyle, Marquis of, 28, 31.
Armour, Jean, 285, 286.
Armstrong, John, of Gilnockie, 240.
Arnot, Hugo, 119.
Arran, Earls of, 103, 238, 420, 423.
Arthur, Prince, 99.
Athelstaneford, Parish of, 200.
Athole, Duke of, 8.
Atkinson, John Balfour, 143.
Atkinson, Thomas, 476.
Auchinleck, Parish of, 358.
Aufrere, Anthony, 174.
Auld, Rev. William, 396.
Avondale, Parish of, 436.
Ayr, Parish of, 360.
Ayton, Parish of, 221.
Aytoun, John Marriott, 15.
Aytoun, Major-General Roger, 142.
Aytoun, Mary, 142.
Aytoun, Mrs. Jean, of Balgregie, 142.
Aytoun, Professor W. E., 135.
Aytoun, Rachel Jane, 142.

B
Bailford, Obelisk at, 316.
Baillie, George, of Jerviswood, 226.
Baillie, Lady Grizel, 225.
Baillie, Lady Ross, 506.
Baillie, Professor James, 467.
Baillie, Robert, of Jerviswood, 225.
Baillie, Sheriff George, 465.
Baillie of Walston, Family of, 507.
Bain, Rev. James, 84.
Bainbrige, George C., of Gattonside, 258.
Baine, William, 413.
Baird, John, 430, 495.
Baird, Robert, of Auchmedden, 487.
Baird, William, 406.
Balcanquel, Dean Walter, 220.
Balcanquel, Rev. Robert, 220.
Balfour, James Brewster, M.D., 153.
Balfour, James, of Pilrig, 120.
Balfour, Major, 385.
Balfour, William, M.D., 129.
Baliol, John, 309, 342.
Ballantine, James, 5.
Ballantine, Rev. Thomas, 318.
Ballantine, Thomas, 272.
Ballantyne, John, 91.
Balmaclellan, Parish of, 327.
Balmaghie, Parish of, 328.
Balmerino, Arthur, Sixth Lord, 117.
Balmerino, John, Second Lord, 117.
Bank of Scotland, 1.
Bannatyne, Nicol, 157.
Bannatyne, Thomas, 23.
Bannerman, Sir Alexander, Bart., 77.
Bannockburn, 7.
Barclay, Rev. John, the Berean, 92, 93, 117.
Barclay, John, M.D., 117.
Barclay, Rev. Matthew, D.D., 487.
Barnard Castle, 308.
Barnett, John, 35.
Barrie, Alexander, 161.
Barrie, James, 234.
Barrie, John, 437.
Bathgate, Parish of, 180.
Beatson, Lieutenant Douglas, 75.
Beauté's, De la Field, 227.
Beilby, William, M.D., 129.

Beith, Parish of, 364.
Belfrage, William, 124.
Belhaven, Robert, Lord, 439.
Belhaven, Robert, First Lord, 104, 105.
Bell, Archibald, 142.
Bell of Blackwood House, 312.
Bell, Colonel Charles H., 129.
Bell, John, 306.
Bell, John Montgomerie, 71.
Bell, John, W.S., 142.
Bell, John, of Whiteside, 327, 345.
Bell, Rev. John, 207, 399.
Bell, Robert, Sheriff, 144.
Bellenden, John, Lord, 115.
Beloe, William, 224.
Bennet, Sir William, of Grubbet, 242.
Bennoch, James, 305.
Bervie, Mrs. Janet, 131.
Bethune, Alexander, of Longhirdmonston, 28.
Beugo, John, 50.
Beveridge, Thomas Knox, W.S., 153.
Biggar, Lord, 114.
Biggar, Parish of, 437.
Binnine, Prior William, 177.
Binning, John, of Dalvennan, 501.
Binning, Rev. Hugh, 501.
Binram's Cross, 277.
Birrell, Rev. John, 129.
Black, Alexander, Architect, 143.
Black, Dr. George, 487.
Black, Dr. John, 487.
Black, Joseph, M.D., 52.
Black, Rev. David, 71.
Black, Rev. William, D.D., 487.
Blackadder, Archbishop Robert, 228.
Blackadder, Colonel John, 208.
Blackadder, Rev. John, 207.
Blackadder of Tulliallan, 208.
Blackie, Alexander, Banker, 130.
Blacklock, Dr. Thomas, 82.
Blackwell, Rev. George, 180.
Blackwood, James, 377.
Blackwood, Major William, 143.
Blackwood, William, Publisher, 94.
Blackwood, William, Merchant, 144.
Blair, Anne Hunter, 38.
Blair, Capt. Robert, 50.

Blair, Dr. Hugh, 40.
Blair, General Thomas Hunter, 38.
Blair, Lord President, 13, 50, 200.
Blair, Rev. Alexander, 376.
Blair, Rev. Robert, of St. Andrew's, 40, 200.
Blair, Rev. Robert, Author of "The Grave," 50, 200.
Blair, Sir James Hunter, 38.
Blake, Helen, 45.
Blantyne, Parish of, 438.
Blantyre, Lord, 421.
"Blearie, Queen," 422, 433.
Blednoch, Stream of, 350.
Blyth, Benjamin H., C.E., 154.
Bonanomi, Ida, 124.
Bonner, Major Robert M., 465.
Bonnington House, Relics at, 505.
Boog, Rev. Dr., 418, 422.
Bookles, Mr., 227.
Borgue, Parish of, 329.
Borthwick, Lady, 156.
Borthwick, Parish of, 156.
Borthwick, Sir William, 156.
Borthwick, William, First Lord, 156.
Boston of Gattonside, 253.
Boston, Rev. Thomas, of Relief Church, 246.
Boston, Thomas, of Ettrick, 246, 280.
Boswell, Alexander, W.S., 53.
Boswell, Sir Alexander, Bart., 359, 363.
Boswells, Burial-place of the, 359.
Bothwell, Adam, Bishop of Orkney, 101, 102.
Bothwell Bridge, Battle of, 30, 439.
Bothwell, Earls of, 20, 101, 210.
Bothwell, Sir Francis, 57, 101.
Bothwell, Parish of, 439.
Boulton, Matthew, 410.
Bowden, Parish of, 239.
Bowman, John, of Ashgrove, 464.
Boyd, George, Publisher, 99.
Boyd, John, of Maxpoffle, 96.
Boyd, of Pinkhill, 468.
Boyd, Rev. James, D.D., 488.
Boyd, Rev. William, 330.
Boyd, Rev. Zachary, 468.
Boyd, Sir Thomas, 384.

INDEX

Boyd, The Lords, 384.
Boyle, Lord President, 14.
Braidfoot, Marion, heiress of Lamington, 505.
Brash, Rev. William, 484.
Bredine, James, 369.
Brewster, James, 246, 430.
Brewster, Rev. Patrick, 430.
Brewster, Sir David, 16, 246, 256.
Brisbane, Dame Darcy, 42.
Brisbane, General Sir Thomas Makdougal, 390.
Brisbane, Thomas, of Brisbane, 42.
Broadfoot, Mr., 356.
Brodie, Marjorie, 32.
Brodie, W., Sculptor, 7, 14, 16, 86
Broomknoll, Burying-ground at, 435.
Brougham, Henry, of Brougham Hall, 117.
Brougham, Henry, Lord, 117, 126, 131.
Broughton, Parish of, 262.
Brown, Alexander, M.D., 153.
Brown, Captain Thomas, 155.
Brown, Dame Mary Anne, 118.
Brown, Dr. John, 97.
Brown, Gavin, of Bishoptone, 342.
Brown, James, 32, 55.
Brown, James, Author, 54.
Brown, James, Poet, 438.
Brown, John, 506.
Brown, John, the "Christian Carrier," 398.
Brown, Major, of Park, 258.
Brown, Mrs. Sophia, 500.
Brown, Professor Andrew, 53.
Brown, Professor James, 154.
Brown, Professor Thomas, 338.
Brown, Rev. Dr. Andrew, 220.
Brown, Rev. John, 97, 194.
Brown, Rev. Samuel, 339.
Brown, Rev. Thomas, D.D., 483.
Brown, Rev. William, M.D., 153.
Brown, Robert Ebenezer, M.D., 153.
Brown, Samuel, M.D., 153.
Brown, William, Martyr, 386.
Brown, William, 492.
Brown, William, D.D., 304.
Brown, William, M.D., 52.

Browne, Gilbert, 342.
Browne, James, LL.D., 161.
Brownlee, Robert, 497.
Bruce, Captain Andrew, 71.
Bruce, King Robert the, 6, 173, 174, 236, 250, 296, 370, 387, 411, 418, 433, 447.
Bruce, Marjory, 422, 433.
Bruce, Mrs. Jane, 71.
Bruce, William, 498.
Bruning, John, 396.
Bryan, George, 369.
Bryce, David, R.S.A., 11.
Bryce, General Sir Alexander, 170.
Bryce, John, 396.
Bryce, Rev. Alexander, the Geometrician, 169.
Bryce, Rev. James, D.D., 151.
Brydone, Patrick, 223.
Brydone, Rev. Robert, 223.
Buccleuch, Anne, Duchess of, 159.
Buccleuch Churchyard, 81, 85.
Buccleuch, Dukes of, 1, 159.
Buccleuch, House of, 159.
Buccleuch, The Countess Mary of, 159.
Buccleuch, Walter, Earl of, 103.
Buccleuch, Walter, Lord, 103.
Buchan, Earls of, 114, 184, 233, 472.
Buchan, Matthew, M.D., 124.
Buchanan, George, 16, 17, 19, 54.
Buchanan, James, 54, 139.
Buchanan, James, of Dowanhill, 487.
Bunkle, Parish of, 221.
Bunton, Robert, 460.
Burnes, Charles, 144.
Burnes, James, 144.
Burnes, Sir Alexander, C.B., 144.
Burnes, William, 363.
Burnet, Rev. Thomas, 205.
Burns, Ayrshire Monument to, 363.
Burns, Colonel James Glencairn, 7, 286.
Burns, Colonel W. N., 7, 286.
Burns, Francis Wallace, 284.
Burns, Maxwell, 284.
Burns, Robert, 7, 41, 44, 82, 85, 93, 144, 211, 284, 314, 344, 363.
Burns, Robert, jun., 286.
Burnside, Rev. Dr. William, 290.
Burt, Captain James R., 14.

INDEX.   511

Byers, Rev. John, 180.

C

Cadell, Robert, of Ratho, 50.
Cadell, W. A., of Banton, 130.
Cadogan, Hon. Henry, 465.
Caerlaverock, Parish of, 297.
Cairns, Peter, 260.
Caithness, Countess of, 115.
Caithness, Earls of, 116, 174.
Calder, of Drumcross, 181.
Calder, William, 155.
Calderwood, Rev. William, 159.
Calderwood, Thomas, 159.
Calton Hill, Edinburgh, 5, 7.
Cambusnethan, Parish of, 439—443.
Cameron, Michael, 359.
Cameron, Richard, 358.
Cameron, William, 493.
Cameron, Rev. William, 170.
Campbell of Aberuchill, 118.
Campbell, Agnes, 415.
Campbell, Charles W., 130.
Campbell, Colonel Dugald, 129.
Campbell, Colonel James Mure, 83.
Campbell, General Sir John, Bart., 75.
Campbell, George, 376.
Campbell, George, of Boreland, 130.
Campbell, John, Baron, 246.
Campbell, Lady, 9.
Campbell, Major Archibald Argyle, 95.
Campbell, Major Neil, 129.
Campbell, Mary, 411.
Campbell, Mr., Sculptor, 10, 11.
Campbell, Professor Archibald, 93.
Campbell, Rev. John, D.D., 52.
Campbell, Sir Colin, 453.
Campbell, Sir Hugh, of Loudoun, 380.
Campbell, Sir James, Bart., of Aberuchill, 118.
Campbell, Sir John, 393.
Campbell, Thomas, the Poet, 445.
Campbell, William, of Tillichewan, 486.
Campbell, William, W.S., 118.
Candlish, Rev. Dr. Robert S., 96.
Canonbie, Parish of, 299.
Canongate Churchyard, 85, 91.
Carfin, George, 155.

Carfrae, Gen. John, 218.
Carfrae, Rev. Patrick, 218.
Carlile, James, D.D., LL.D., 144.
Carluke, Parish of, 443.
Carlyle of Bridekirk, 318.
Carlyle, Dr. Alexander, 166, 215.
Carlyle, Michael, Fourth Lord, 103.
Carlyle, William, Master of, 103.
Carlyle, William, 221.
Carlyle, Rev. William, 215.
Carmichael, General James, 443.
Carmichael, John, Lord, 101.
Carmichael, Parish of, 444.
Carmichael, William, 145.
Carnegie, Sir David, Bart., 147.
Carnegy, Major-General, C.B., 143.
Carnwath, Earls of, 179.
Carnwath, Parish of, 444.
Carr, Sir William, of Etall, Bart., 111.
Carrick, John Donald, 464.
Carriden, Parish of, 181.
Carruthers, John, of Holmains, 95.
Carson, Dr. A. R., 14, 51.
Carsphairn, Parish of, 329.
Carstairs, Eliza Margaret, 129.
Carstairs, Principal, 371.
Cassilis, Countess of, 187.
Cassilis, Noble Family of, 396.
Castle, John, 5.
Castleton, Parish of, 239.
Cathcart, Elias, 362.
Cathcart, General Sir George, 427.
Cathcart, Hon. David, 362.
Cathcart, Parish of, 403.
Cathcart, William, Earl of, 427.
Cathedral, The Glasgow, 457—465.
Chalmers, Captain, 117.
Chalmers, Charles, of Merchiston, 153.
Chalmers, Dr. Thomas, 10, 146, 458, 470.
Chalmers, George, W.S., 117.
Chalmers, Veronica, 117.
Chambers, Robert, LL.D., 83.
Chambers, William, of Glenormiston, 16, 17, 264.
Chantrey, Sir Francis, 10, 14.
Chaplain, Thomas R., of Colliston, 143.
Chatelherault, Duke of, 187, 423, 424.

Charles Edward, Prince, 61, 440.
Charles I., 104.
Charles II., Statue of, 12.
Charters, Dr. Samuel, 261.
Charters, Rev. Thomas, 261.
Cheyne, Robert, 99.
Chiesley, John, of Dalry, 29.
Child, of Glencorse, 124.
Chirnside, Parish of, 222.
Cholera, Monument to those who died of, 295.
Christison, Professor Alexander, 52.
Chrystal, Dr. William, 464.
Clandeboye, Viscount, 371.
Clarke, Captain William, of Langhaugh, 258.
Clarke, Dr. Thomas, 139.
Clarkson, person so named, 158.
Clements, William, 204.
Clephane, Captain James, 155.
Clerk, Sir James, of Penicuik, 86.
Clerk, Sir John, Bart., of Penicuik, 177.
Clockmaker, Verses on a, 308.
Closeburn, Parish of, 299.
Clow, Mrs. Mary, 308.
Clunie, Colonel James O., 142.
Clyde, Lord, 452, 453, 454, 455.
Cochran, William, Painter, 464.
Cochrane, Captain Sir Thomas John, 115.
Cochrane, Isabella Maccomb, 77.
Cochrane, Rupert John, 76.
Cockburn, Adam, Lord Justice Clerk, 211.
Cockburn, Alexander, 193.
Cockburn, Alexander, of Ormiston, 209.
Cockburn, Captain Adam, 82.
Cockburn, John, of Ormiston, 210.
Cockburn, Lord, 14, 132.
Cockburn, Mrs. Alison, 82.
Cockburn, Patrick, 82.
Cockburn, Piers, 277.
Cockburn, Sir Alexander de, 193.
Cockburn, Sir William, 193.
Cockburn, Sir William, Bart., 193.
Cogan, Hugh, 486.
Coil, King of the Britons, 401.
Coldingham, Parish of, 222.
Coldstream, Parish of, 223.

Colinton, Parish of, 156.
College Churchyards, Glasgow, 465—469.
Colmonell, Parish of, 365.
Colquhoun, James, M.D., 153.
Colquhoun, Rev. John, 120.
Colt, Rev. Oliver, 165.
Coltron, Provost, 350.
Combe, Andrew, M.D., 65, 137.
Combe, George, 137.
Combe, Mrs. George, 138.
Connell, James, LL.D., 486.
Constable, Archibald, 51, 93.
Constable, Elizabeth, 51.
Cook, Robert, 124.
Cooke, Thomas, 403.
Cope, Sir John, 210.
Copeland, Rev. John, 218.
Corion, Robert, 335.
Corrie, James, of Spedock, 291.
Corstorphine, Parish of, 157.
Cosens, Rev. Peter, 229.
Cousin, David, Architect, 516.
Covenanters, Tombs of, 30, 163, 180, 272, 289, 299, 304, 305, 306, 322, 327, 328, 329, 331, 332, 337, 339, 345, 349, 350, 351, 352, 353, 354, 355, 356, 358, 359, 361, 365, 370, 372, 373, 374, 375, 376, 377, 385, 386, 389, 394, 395, 396, 397, 398, 401, 402, 403, 405, 406, 407, 429, 430, 436, 437, 441, 451, 456, 460, 504, 505, 506.
Cowan, Alexander, of Valleyfield, 153.
Cowan, Lord, 143.
Cowper, Bishop William, 51.
Craig, Jamie, 196.
Craigie, David, M.D., 155.
Craigie, Parish of, 366.
Cranstoun, William, Fifth Lord 71.
Craufurd, Captain Thomas, of Jordanhill, 379.
Craufurd, Laurence, of Kilbirnie, 379.
Crawford, Abbot, Archibald, 114.
Crawford, Alexander, 400.
Crawford, of Doonside, 362.
Crawford, Elizabeth, Countess of, 115.
Crawfordjohn, Parish of, 445.
Crawfurd, Alexander, 420.

INDEX. 513

Crawfurd, Captain Robert, 420.
Crawfurd, Dr. Andrew, 417.
Crawfurd, George, Author of " History of the Stuarts," 411.
Crawfurd, James, of Seidhill, 420, 421, 422.
Crawfurd, James, of Spango, 420.
Crawfurd, James, of Thirdpart, 419.
Crawfurd, James, W.S., 154.
Crawfurd, of Kilbirnie, 411.
Crawfurd, Sir Ranald, 366.
Crawfurd, Thomas, of Cartsburn, 411.
Creech, Rev. William, 44.
Creech, William, 44.
Crichton, Colonel David, 129.
Crichton, Dr. James, 288.
Crichton, Mrs., of Friar's Carse, 288.
Crichton, Parish of, 159.
Crichton, Rev. Dr. Andrew, 208.
Cringletie, Lord, 45.
Cromartie, Countess of, 87.
Cromwell, Oliver, 117, 165, 289.
Crooks, Captain William, 378.
Crookshanke, Rev. John, 164.
Crossgellioch, Martyrs' Monument at, 329.
Crossmichael, Parish of, 330.
Cruickshanks, Rev. John, 163, 164.
Cruikshank, Alexander, of Keithock, 76, 145.
Cruikshank, George, 6.
Cruikshank, James A., of Langley Park, 142.
Cruikshank, Lieut. James, 76.
Cullen, Dr. William, 169.
Cullen, Lord, 169.
Cullen, William, M.D., 23.
Cumbernald, Lord, 114.
Cumnock, Parish of, 365.
Cunningham, George, 195.
Cunningham, James, 425.
Cunningham, John, 389.
Cunningham, Lord, 140.
Cunningham, Rev. Robert, 218.
Cunningham, Sir Hugh, of Bonnington, 52.
Cunningham, William, of Aitket, 425.
Cunnynghame, George, of Cronan, 124.

Curle, James, of Melrose, 258.
Currie, Andrew, Sculptor, 274, 278.
Currie, Dr. James, 314.
Currie, James, 30.
Currie, Rev. James, 314.
Curtis, Jacobina, 60.
Cuthbertson, Donald, LL.D., 487.
Cuthbertson, John, 386.

D

Dailly, Parish of, 368.
Dale, David, 469.
Dalgarno Churchyard, 299.
Dalhousie, Earl of, 10.
Dalkeith, Parish of, 159.
Dalmeny, Parish of, 181.
Dalry Cemetery, 144, 145.
Dalry, Parish of, 330.
Dalrymple, Charles, of Orangefield, 398.
Dalserf, Parish of, 446.
Dalzel, or Dalziel, Family of, 179, 446.
Dalzel, Professor Andrew, 41, 51.
Dalziel, General, 163, 179, 304, 372.
Dalziel, Parish of, 446.
Darcy, Sir Anthony, 227.
Darg, Peter, 204.
Darnley, House of, 421.
Darnley, Lord, 17, 20, 99, 100, 101.
D'Aubigné, Dr. Merle, 459.
D'Aubigné, Lord, 158.
David I., 99, 177, 250.
David II., 100.
Davidson, James, of Ruchill, 487.
Davidson, John, 124.
Davie, James, 180.
Dean Cemetery, 130, 144.
Deans, Harriet, 206.
Deans, John, 245.
Deas, Lord, 130.
Delacourt, Peter, 493.
Denham, James, of West Shield, 370, 371.
Denholm, Monument at, 249.
Denniston, of Barbaughlaw, 181.
Dennistoun, James, 486.
Devorgilla, wife of John Baliol, 309.
Dewar, Henry, of Lassodie, 71.
Dick, General Sir Robert Henry, 14.
Dick, Rev. Professor, 478.

2 L

Dick, Robert, 359.
Dickson, Rev. David, 63.
Dickson, Rev. David, D.D., 63.
Dickson, Rev. Dr. Robert, 120.
Dickson, Robert, Annan, 484.
Dickson, William R., Alton, 142.
Dingwall, William, 437.
Dinning, John, of Mavisbush, 155.
Docharty, John, 378.
Donaldson, James, 66.
Douie, Robert, 487.
Dornock, Parish of, 300.
Douglas, Archibald, 344, 448.
Douglas, Bishop George, 114.
Douglas, Captain William, of Maitland, 498.
Douglas Cause, The, 110.
Douglas, Colonel James, 305, 327, 337, 366, 368.
Douglas, Earls of, 114, 344, 448.
Douglas, General Sir Neil, 144.
Douglas, House of, 156, 447.
Douglas, Isabella, 303.
Douglas, James, of Balveny, 114.
Douglas, James, of Dornock, 292.
Douglas, John, of Stenhouse, 322.
Douglas, Lady Elizabeth, 20, 303.
Douglas, Lady Isabella Margaret, 115.
Douglas, Lady Jane, 110.
Douglas, Lord, 171.
Douglas, Lord George, 304.
Douglas, Lord James, 102.
Douglas, Malcolm, of Mains, 104.
Douglas, Marquis of, 108, 109, 449.
Douglas, Mary, Marchioness of, 109.
Douglas, Parish of, 447.
Douglas, Philadelphia, 292.
Douglas, Sir Archibald, 104.
Douglas, Sir James, 173, 174, 250, 447.
Douglas, Sir James, of Parkhead, 103.
Douglas, Sir Robert, 104.
Douglas, Sir William, 251.
"Douglas," Tragedy of, 119, 276.
Drumclog, Battle-field of, 436.
Drumlanrig, Charles, Earl of, 304.
Drumlanrig, Elizabeth, Countess of, 304.
Drumlanrig, Henry, Lord, 304.
Drumlanrig, Isabel, Viscountess of, 109.

Drumlanrig, William, First Lord, 109.
Drummond, Bailie George, 54.
Drummond, Dr. W. A., 171.
Drummond, George, of Newton, 88.
Drummond, George Stirling H., 202.
Drummond, James, R.S.A., 7, 127, 141.
Drummond, John, Lord, 114.
Drummond, Mrs., of Hawthornden, 171.
Drummond, Sir John, 171.
Drummond, William Stirling, 356.
Drummond, William, of Hawthornden, 171, 190.
Dryburgh Abbey, 230, 234.
Dryden, Monument at, 173.
Dryfesdale, Parish of, 301.
Drysdale, Captain Alexander, 143.
Drysdale, Colonel John, 185.
Drysdale, Sir William, of Pitteuchar, 71.
Duddingston, Parish of, 161.
Dudgeon, General Peter, 144.
Dudgeon, William, 211.
"Dumbarton, Bloody," 396.
Dumfries, Earl of, 366.
Dumfries, Parish of, 283—295.
Dun, Finlay, musician, 138.
Dun, James, 341.
Dun, Robert, 341.
Dunbar, Eliza, 60.
Dunbar, George, Earl of, 201.
Dunbar, Parish of, 201, 206.
Dunbar, Professor George, 51.
Dunblane, Bishop of, 100.
Duncan, Andrew, sen., M.D., 84.
Duncan, Bailie William, 162.
Duncan, Henrietta, Viscountess, 90.
Duncan, Henry Francis, 85.
Duncan, Provost George, 88, 89.
Duncan, Rev. Dr. Henry, 283, 316, 318, 321.
Duncan, Viscount, of Camperdown, 90.
Dundas, Elizabeth, 506.
Dundas, Lord Chief Baron, Statue of, 14.
Dundas, Lord President Robert, 90, 172.
Dundonald, Parish of, 368.
Dundrennan Abbey, 343.
Dundrennan, Lord, 343.
Dunfermline, Alexander, Earl of, 189.

INDEX.   515

Dunlop, Alexander, of Dunlop, 370.
Dunlop, Colin, of Tolcross, 485.
Dunlop, John, of Dunlop, 370.
Dunlop, Mrs., 370.
Dunlop, Parish of, 370.
Dunlop, Principal William, 371, 467.
Dunlop, Rev. Walter, 287.
Dunlop, Rev. William, 467.
Dunlop, Thomas, 497.
Dunmore, Charles, First Earl of, 115.
Dunn, David, 366.
Dunn, William, of Duntocher, 485.
Dunscore, Parish of, 301.
Dunse, Parish of, 224.
Durham, Thomas, of Boghead, 180.
Durisdeer, Parish of, 302.
Dymock, John, LL.D., 487.
Dysart, Rev. John, 222.
Dysart, Rev. Matthew, 227.

E
Eaglesham, Parish of, 405.
Earlston, Parish of, 225.
Easton, Robert Tulloh, Surgeon, 124.
Eastwood, Parish of, 407.
Eccles, Parish of, 226.
Ecclesmachan, Parish of, 182.
Eckford, Parish of, 241.
Edgar, James, 254.
Edgar, Robert, 305.
Edgcombe, Lady Caroline, 115.
Eddington, Captain George, 144.
Eddington, Lieut. Edward W., 145.
Eddleston, Parish of, 262.
Edinburgh, Monuments at, 1—156.
Edmonstoun, Rev. John, 155.
Ednam, Parish of, 242.
Edrom, Parish of, 227.
Edward II., 79.
Edward, Peter, Sculptor, 130.
Eglinton, Archibald, Earl of, 287, 388.
Eglinton, Jean, Countess of, 102.
Elibank, Patrick, Fifth Lord, 199.
Elizabeth, Queen, 101.
Elliot, Admiral Russell, 258.
Elphinston, Tenth Lord, 49.
Epitaphs, Quaint, 167, 172, 177, 196, 205, 206, 234, 261, 269, 341, 343, 357,

362, 364, 368, 378, 380, 382, 383, 385, 387, 391, 392, 398, 399, 400, 406, 416, 431, 432, 434, 435, 436, 438, 439, 442, 443, 445, 450, 451, 461, 492, 493, 494, 497, 498, 499, 500, 501, 504, 506, 507.
Errol, Countess Dowager of, 111.
Errol, James, Fourteenth Earl of, 111.
Erskine, David, of Cardross, 142.
Erskine, James, of Alva, 71.
Erskine, John, of Carnock, 41.
Erskine, John, of Dun, 471.
Erskine, Lady Ann, 35.
Erskine, Lord Chancellor, 184.
Erskine, Rev. Ebenezer, 222.
Erskine, Rev. John, D.D., 41.
Erskine, Rev. Ralph, 222.
Eskdalemuir, Parish of, 304.
Ettrick, Parish of, 280.
Eure, Sir Ralph, 235.
Ewart, Andrew, 339.
Ewing, James, LL.D., 483.
Ewing, John, 391.
Ewing, Walter, 483.

F
Fair, Robert Kendall, M.D., 129.
Fairfowl, Bishop Andrew, 114.
Fairley, Elizabeth, 110.
Fairley, Rev. John, 487.
Fairlie, Rev. Walter, 153.
Fairweather, Major Thomas, 142.
Falconer, Alexander, of Falcon Hall, 53.
Falconer, Sir David, 52.
Falconer, Sir James, 52.
Farquhar, William, M.D., 155.
Farquharson, Colonel John, 53.
Fenwick, Parish of, 372.
Fergus, Prince of Galloway, 114.
Ferguson, Rev. John W., 129.
Ferguson, Sir William, Bart., 215.
Fergusson, Colonel James, 139.
Fergusson, Governor, William, 129.
Fergusson, Robert, 331, 332.
Fergusson, Robert, the Poet, 85.
Ferrier, James, 70.
Ferrier, John, W.S., 70.
Ferrier, Professor James Frederick, 70.
Fettes, Sir William, Bart., 87.

Fiddison, William, 396.
Findlay, Rev. William, 405.
Finhaven, James, Earl of, 115.
Finlay, John, 315, 386.
Finlay, Thomas, 386.
Finlayson, Rev. Dr. James, 54.
Finlayson, William, M.D., 124.
Fisher, —, Darnick, 255.
Fisher, Thomas, 33.
Fleming, Adam, 310.
Fleming, Alexander, 181.
Fleming, David, 114.
Fleming, James, Fourth Lord, 187.
Fleming, Professor John, 136.
Fleming, Rev. John, 180.
Fleming, Rev. Thomas, D.D., 62.
Fletcher, Andrew, 254.
Fletcher, Andrew, of Salton, 217.
Fletcher, Andrew, Lord Milton, 217.
Fletcher, Henry, of Salton, 217.
Fletcher, Rev. David, 254.
Forbes, Edward, of Oakhill, 136.
Forbes, Lord President, 13.
Forbes, Professor Edward, 136.
Forbes, Sir John, Bart., 1.
Forbes, Sir William, 38.
Forest Kirk, The, 275.
Forrest, Sir James, Bart., 3.
Forrester, Archibald, 158.
Forrester, Sir John, 157.
Forfar, Earls of, 100, 109.
Forman, Rev. James, 194.
Forret, Christian, 237.
Forret, James, 237.
Forret, John, of Forret, 237.
Forsyth, Robert, 90.
Fortrose, Kennet, Lord, 15.
Foucart, François, 488.
Foulden, Parish of, 228.
Foulis, James, of Colinton, 157.
Foulis, I., of Colinton, 157.
Fowler, Captain John, 359.
Fowler, Mrs. Anne, 113.
France, David, of Seafield, 205.
France, Rev. William, 487.
Fraser, Admiral Alexander, 98.
Fraser, Rev. David, 153.
Fraser, Robert, 253.

Fraser, William, of Broughton Place, 98.
Fullarton, Hon. Mrs. H., 110.
Fullerton, Provost, 336.
Fulton, Matthew, 395.

G
Gairdner, General William J., 144.
Galbraith, Rev. William, 153.
Galdus, Tomb of King, 357.
Gall, Richard, 93.
Galloway, Captain James, 145.
Galloway, Lords of, 342, 343, 344, 345, 349.
Galston, Parish of, 375.
Galt, John, 414.
Gammel, John, 359.
Gardiner, Colonel James, 219.
Gardner, Rev. James, 487.
Garrell Churchyard, 312.
Gartsherrie, Parish of, 450.
Gatt, Rev. James, 307.
Ged, William, Inventor of Stereotyping, 52.
Geddes, Robert, of Torbanehill, 180.
Gemmel, Peter, 373.
Gemmell, Andrew, 258.
George IV., 6, 10.
Gerald, Joseph, 92.
Gib, Rev. Adam, 38.
Gibson, Bailie, John, 269.
Gibson, John, 305.
Gibson, Sir Alexander Charles Maitland, of Clifton Hall, Bart., 53.
Gilbert, John Graham, R.S.A., 487.
Gillespie, Rev. John, 333.
Gillespie, Rev. William, 333.
Giffard, James, 263.
Giffard's Well, 264.
Gilfillan, Rev. George, 126.
Gilfillan, Robert, the Poet, 120.
Gillian, Hannah, 197.
Gillies, Adam, Lord, 53.
Gillies, David, 121.
Gillies, Peter, 396.
Gillies, Rev. Francis, 143.
Gilmour, Barbara, 371.
Girthon, Parish of, 331.
Gladsmuir, Parish of, 206.

INDEX.

Gladstanes, Archbishop, 25.
Gladstanes, William, 342.
Gladstone,. Right Hon. W. E., 122.
Gladstone, Sir John, Bart., of Fasque, 121.
Gladstones, Margaret, 121.
Gladstones, Thomas, 121.
Glasford, Parish of, 451.
Glasgow, Parish of, 452—501.
Glasgow, Augusta, Countess of, 111.
Glasserton, Parish of, 347.
Glegg, Adam, 144.
Glegg, Colonel, 214.
Glencairn, Earls of, 61, 388, 397, 471.
Glencairn, Parish of, 505.
Glencross, Parish of, 163.
Glen Hill, Monument at, 343.
Glenlee, Lord, 96.
Glenorchy, John, Lord, 81.
Glenorchy, Viscountess, 81.
Glover, Samuel Edmund, 495.
Goldie, George, 38.
Gooch, Sir Thomas, Bart., of Benacre Hall, 123.
Gooch, William, 123.
Goodall, John, of Rennyhill, 143.
Goodall, John, 205.
Goodman, Christopher, 471.
Gordon, Andrew, 450.
Gordon of Cluny, 72.
Gordon, Edward, 339.
Gordon, General John, 118.
Gordon, Roger, of Largmore, 332.
Gordon, Sir John, Bart., of Invergordon, 87.
Gordon, William, of Earlston, 451.
Gourlay, Oliver, of Craigrothie, 126.
Gourlay, Robert Fleming, 126.
Govan, Parish of, 501.
Gowrie Conspiracy, 116.
Graham, Admiral John, of Coldoch, 98.
Graham, Captain, of Hilton, 111.
Graham, of Claverhouse, 332, 337, 398, 437, 441.
Graham, Colonel David, 350.
Graham, Colonel Thomas, 76.
Graham, Farquhar, 138.
Graham, Frances, of Morphie, 155.

Graham, James Gillespie, of Orchill, 53, 202.
Graham, John, 360.
Graham, John, of Rosetrees, 300.
Grahame, James, 32.
Grammont, Duchess de, 101.
Grange Cemetery, 146—154.
Grange, Lady, 30.
Grant, Christian, 213.
Grant, Janet, 494.
Grant, John, of Kilgraston, 59.
Grant, Mrs. Ann, 64.
Grant, Patrick, of Elchies, 52.
Grant, Peter, of Glenlochy, 59.
Grant, Rev. Andrew, D.D., 120.
Grant, Rev. James, 64.
Grant, Sir John Peter, 142.
Grant, William, of Prestongrange, 213.
Gray, Ann, 400.
Gray, Captain Charles, 138.
Gray, Elizabeth, 328.
Gray, James, 359.
Gray, Professor George, 467.
Greenock, Parish of, 409.
Greig, James, of Cambus, 142.
Gretna, Parish of, 306.
Greville, Robert Kaye, LL.D., 137.
Grey, Rev. Henry, D.D., 66.
Greyfriars Churchyard, 19—57.
Greig, John R., of Lethangie, 99.
Greyfriars Monastery, 19.
Grierson, John, 332.
Grierson, Sir Robert, Bart., of Lag, 301, 327, 355.
Grierson, William, 289.
Grieve, John, 277.
Grieve, Rev. Dr. Henry, 161.
Guthrie, William, 369.

H

Hadden, Mrs. Martha, 247.
Haddington, John, Fourth Earl of, 182.
Haddington, Parish of, 186, 199.
Haig, of Bonnington, 144.
Haig, James, of Blairhill, 98.
Haldane, Captain James, 68, 458.
Haldane, James Alexander, 68.
Haldane, Robert, of Airthrey, 67, 458.

Hall, Captain John, 124.
Hall, Helen, 270.
Hall, James, 270.
Hall, James, of Cathcart Mill, 404.
Hall, John, 403.
Hall, Rev. James, 37.
Hall, Robert, 241.
Halliburton, George, 253.
Haliburtons, of Newmains, The, 230.
Halkin, John, 337.
Halkett, Samuel, 128.
Halliday, David, 329, 345.
Halliday, Sir Andrew, 287.
Hamilton, Abbot John, 420, 423.
Hamilton, Archbishop, 211, 420.
Hamilton, Archibald, of Raploch, 370.
Hamilton, Claud, 423.
Hamilton, David, of Bothwellhaugh, 368.
Hamilton, Dr. James, 134.
Hamilton, Dukes of, 6, 110, 424, 439, 502.
Hamilton, Gavin, 504.
Hamilton, Hugh, 486.
Hamilton, James, 504.
Hamilton, James, of Aikenhead, 460.
Hamilton, James, of Bothwellhaugh, 182.
Hamilton, John, 359.
Hamilton, Lady Anne, 415.
Hamilton, Lady Barbara, 187.
Hamilton, Marian, 426.
Hamilton, Mrs. Campbell, 143.
Hamilton, Parish of, 502.
Hamilton, Patrick, the Martyr, 471.
Hamilton, Professor Thomas, 463.
Hamilton, Professor Sir William, Bart., 73.
Hamilton, Rev. Harris, 370.
Hamilton, Rev. Robert, D.D., 84.
Hamilton, Sir William, Bart., 463.
Hamilton, Sir William, of Whitelaw, 114.
Hamilton, Thomas, Architect, 95.
Hamilton, William, 462.
Handyside, Lord, 140.
Handyside, William, of St. Petersburg, 98.
Hannah, of Bayhall, 312.
Hannay, Dr. Alexander, 487.
Hannay, of Kirkdale, 339.
Hardie, Andrew, 430, 495.

Hardy, Professor Thomas, 90.
Hardy, Rev. Henry, 90.
Hardyman, General George, 205.
Harkness, James, 299.
Harrison, Lieutenant F. Y., 139.
Hart, John, 460.
Harvey, Sir George, 129.
Hastings, Lady Flora, 393.
Hastings, Marquis of, 393.
Hatton, David, M.D., 129.
Havelock, Honora, 143.
Havelock, Sir Henry, Bart., 143.
Hawick, Parish of, 243.
Hay, Alexander, of Park, 102.
Hay, Anne, 269.
Hay, Colonel Humphrey, 143.
Hay, Commander Edward, 203.
Hay, Elizabeth, 54.
Hay, General Sir James, 53.
Hay, Lieutenant David, 202.
Hay, Margaret, 80.
Hay, Rear-Admiral James, 202.
Hay, Sir John C. D., Bart., of Park Place, 347.
Hay, of Spott, 218.
Hay, Thomas, 347.
Hay, Sir Thomas, of Park, 293.
Hedderwick, Mr. James, 481.
Henderland, Lord, 60.
Henderson, Alexander, 113.
Henderson, Andrew, 486.
Henderson, David, 426.
Henderson, John, 212.
Henderson, Rev. Alexander, 24, 25.
Henderson, Richard, 113.
Henderson, Robert, 113.
Henderson, Robert, Physician, 218.
Henderson, Robert, Paisley, 426.
Henderson, Thomas, 426.
Hendry, Archibald, 391.
Henry, Prince, 104.
Henryson, Alexander, 24.
Henryson, Dr. Edward, 24.
Henryson, Sir Thomas, 24.
Hepburn, George, of Nunraw, 214.
Hepburn, George, of Monkrig, 193.
Hepburn, James, 345.
Hepburn, John, of Nunraw, 214.

INDEX. 519

Hepburn, Patrick, of Abbey Mill, 195, 197.
Hepburn, Rev. John, 345.
Herd, David, 83.
Herries, Agnes, 335.
Herries, Lord, 336, 345.
Heriot, A., 157.
Heriot, David, 19.
Heriot, George, 19.
Heriot, Rev. John, 438.
Heron, Miss Susan, 356.
Hetherington, Rev. Professor, 150.
Heugh, Rev. Hugh, D.D., 479.
Heugh, Rev. John, 479.
Hoddam, Parish of, 308.
Hogg, James, the Ettrick Shepherd, 278.
Hogg, Robert, 282.
Hogg, Thomas, 294.
Holstein, Duke of, 17.
Holyrood Abbey Churchyard, 99, 116.
Holywood, Parish of, 309.
Home, Alexander, 119.
Home, David, of Wedderburn, 227.
Home, George, of Bassendean, 236.
Home, George, of Maunderston, 201.
Home, Joseph, of Ninewells, 92.
Home, Rev. John, 119.
Home, Sir John, Bart., 52.
Honyman, Sir Richard B. J., Bart., 71.
Hope, Isabel, 269.
Hope, James, 269.
Hope, Lady Henrietta, 61.
Hope, Marion, 269.
Hope, Sir Thomas, 22.
Hope, Thomas, 269.
Hopetoun, Earls of, 9, 10, 179.
Houston, Magdalen, 426.
Houston, Parish of, 415.
Houston, Sir Patrick, 415.
Howe, James, the Painter, 271.
Howe, Rev. William, 271.
Howie, James, 374.
Howie, John, of Lochgoin, 374.
Howie, William, 505.
Huie, Richard, M.D., 154.
Hume, David, 91, 92.
Hume, House of, 235.
Hume, John, General Register House, 99.

Hume, Lord, 165.
Hume, Sir Patrick, 225, 235.
Humphrey, John, 329.
Hunt, Thomas F., Architect, 284.
Hunter, Alexander Gibson, of Blackness, 52.
Hunter, Captain William, 77.
Hunter, James George, 143.
Hunter, John, Merchant, Ayr, 38.
Hunter, John, LL.D., Edinburgh, 143.
Hunter, John, Covenanter, 272.
Hunter, Rev. John, D.D., 152.
Hunter, Rev. William, 248.
Hunter, William, 337.
Hutchison, George, 457.
Hutchinson, Bailie John, 426.
Hutchison, Colonel George, 71.
Hutchison, John, Sculptor, 54, 128.
Hutchison, Lieut.-Colonel, 376.
Hutchison, Thomas, 457, 460.
Hutchison, Thomas, of Carlowrie, 120.
Hutton, Parish of, 228.
Hyndford, Earls of, 443, 444.

I

Inchinnan, Parish of, 415.
Inglis, Anna, 425.
Inglis, Arthur, 441.
Inglis, Bailie Thomas, 422.
Inglis, Captain, 376.
Inglis, Rev. Dr. John, 54, 96.
Inglis, Rev. Harry, 96.
Inglis, Sophia, 156.
Inglis, Thomas, of Corsflat, 424.
Innerkip, Parish of, 416.
Innes, David, 224.
Innes, Gilbert, of Stow, 52.
Innes, Rev. William, D.D., 67.
Inveresk, Parish of, 165.
Ireland, Rev. Walter F., 123.
Irvine, Parish of, 377.
Irving, of Bonshaw, 288.
Irving, Dr. David, 149.
Irving, John, 308.
Irving, Provost Francis, 288.
Irving, Rev. Edward, 458, 484.
Irving, Rev. Francis, 311.
Irwin, John, of Gulielands, 286.

J

Jaffray, Rev. Dr. Andrew, 314.
Jaffray, Rev. John, 204.
James I., 156, 157.
James II., 99, 101.
James III., 99, 116.
James IV., 99.
James V., 100, 101.
James VI., 17, 101, 188, 288.
Jameson, James, Surgeon, 119.
Jameson, Professor Robert, 125.
Jameson, Robert, Advocate, 63.
Jameson, Thomas, 125.
Jamesone, George, the Painter, 52.
Jamieson, John, 329.
Jamieson, Rev. John, D.D., 62.
Janefield Cemetery, Glasgow, 499.
Jardine, John, D.D., 88.
Jardine, Professor, 506.
Jardine, Rev. Robert, 88.
Jardine, Rev. Walter, 180.
Jardine, Sir Henry, 89.
Jardine, William, of Lanrick Castle, 314.
Jedburgh, Abbey of, 245.
Jedburgh, Parish of, 245.
effrey, John, 53.
Jeffrey, Lord, 3, 14, 52, 73, 131.
Jeffrey, Rev. John, 153.
Jenkinson, John, 269.
Jobson, William, of Lochore, 61.
Johnson, Dr. Samuel, 18, 200.
Johnston, James, M.D., 129.
Johnston, John, 270.
Johnston, Rev. Alexander, 265.
Johnston, Rev. David, D.D., 123.
Johnston, Rev. John, 123.
Johnston, Robert, 266.
Johnston, William, of Glenorchard, 489.
Johnstone, of Annandale, 309.
Johnstone, John, 148.
Johnstone, Mrs. Christian, 148.
Johnstone, Parish of, 309.
Johnstone, Rev. John, 62.
Johnstone, Rev. Robert, 315.
Jolly, Rev. John, 223.
Jones, Rev. Thomas Snell, 71, 81.
Julius II., Pope, 99.

K

Kay, John, the Caricaturist, 53.
Keir, James, M.D., 142.
Keir, Parish of, 310.
Keith, Hon. William, 129.
Keith, Sir William, 250.
Kelloe, Family of, 228.
Kells, Parish of, 332.
Kel Stane, The, 156.
Kelso, Parish of, 248.
Kelso, Abbey of, 248.
Kelton, Parish of, 335.
Kemp, George Meikle, 268.
Kenmure, Viscount, 327.
Kennedy, Alexander, 471.
Kennet, Lord Easter, 102.
Ker, Andrew, of Fadounside, 198.
Ker, Andrew, of Kippelaw, 253.
Ker, Dame Margaret, 253.
Ker, Lady Jane, 71.
Ker, Lady Mary, 109.
Ker, Rev. John, 198.
Ker, Rev. Robert, 197.
Ker, Sir John, of Fernihurst, 243.
Ker, William, of Cessford, 243.
Kerr, Colonel Archibald, 120.
Kerr, James, M.D., 431.
Kerr, John, 376.
Kerr, Randolph, 258.
Kerr, Scott, of Sunlaws, 258.
Kerr, Thomas, Altonburn, 258.
Kers, of Yair, 252.
Kettle, Robert, 482.
Kid, Helen, of Craigie, 213.
Kid, Rev. James, 183.
Kid, Rev. Peter, 443.
Kilbirnie, Parish of, 379.
Kilmalcolm, Parish of, 416.
Kilmarnock, Parish of, 384.
Kilmaurs, Parish of, 388.
Kilwinning, Parish of, 388.
Kingstown, Viscount, 108, 109.
Kinloch, Lord, 70.
Kinloch, Sir Francis, Bart., of Gilmerton, 58.
Kinniburgh, Robert, Edinburgh, 98.
Kintore, William, Sixth Earl of, 129.
Kirk, James, 289.

INDEX.

Kirkconnel, Parish of, 310.
Kirkcudbright, Earls of, 336.
Kirkcudbright, Parish of, 336.
Kirkdale Churchyard, 339.
Kirkinner, Parish of, 353.
Kirkland, Rev. John, 487.
Kirkliston, Parish of, 168.
Kirkmabreck, Parish of, 338.
Kirkmahoe, Parish of, 311.
Kirkmichael, Parish of, 312.
Kirkmichael, Parish of, Ayrshire, 389.
Kirkmirren Churchyard, 336.
Kirknewton, Parish of, 169.
Kirkpatrick-Irongray, Parish of, 339.
Kirkpatrick, Jane Forbes, 297.
Kirkpatrick, John, 297.
Kirkpatrick-Juxta, 313.
Kirkpatrick, Mrs., of Glenkiln, 312.
Kirkpatrick, Robert, of Glenkiln, 312.
Kirkpatrick, Rosina, 297.
Kirkpatrick, Sir James, Bart., of Closeburn, 297.
Kirkpatrick, William, of Conheath, 297.
Kirkurd, Parish of, 263.
Knapp, John, 143.
Knowles, James Sheridan, 485, 488.
Knox, Alexander, M.D., 155.
Knox, Captain Alexander, 155.
Knox, Jean, 426.
Knox, John, the Reformer, 12, 19, 46, 198, 210, 470.
Knox, Mary, 77.
Knox, Rev. John, 254.
Knox, William, of Selvieland, 426.

L

L'Amy, James, of Dunkenny, 53.
Lady Glenorchy's Chapel, 81.
Lady Yester's Churchyard, 80.
Laidlaw, William, 282.
Laing, David, LL.D., 16, 19.
Laing, Major Thomas, 155.
Laing, William, 311.
Lamp of the Lothians, 186.
Lampe, John Frederic, 91.
"Lanark Declaration," 305.
Lanark, Parish of, 505.
Langholm, Parish of, 313.

Langside, Battle of, 20.
Largs, Parish of, 389.
Lariestone, Laird of, 249.
Lasswade, Parish of, 171.
Lauder, Bishop Alexander, 229.
Lauder, Parish of, 229.
Lauder, Robert Scott, 127.
Lauder, Sir Alan, 229.
Lauder, Sir Andrew Dick, of Grange, 54.
Lauder, Sir John Dick, Bart., 147.
Lauder, Sir Thomas Dick, Bart., of Fountainhall, 147.
Lauderdale, John, Duke of, 190.
Lauderdale, John, First Earl of, 189.
Laurey, Rev. Walter, 348.
Laurie, Rev. Gilbert, 229.
Law, Archbishop James, 461.
Law, John, of Lathrisk, 461.
Lawrence, Peter, Sculptor, 487.
Lawrie, Rev. John, 304.
Lawrie, Sir Robert, 322.
Lawson, James, 456.
Layng, John, Keeper of Signet, 22.
Layton, Sir Brian, 238.
Leach, Sir John, 50.
Leach, Thomas, 50.
Learmont, Thomas, 225.
Learmouth, John, of Dean, 53.
Lee, Principal John, D.D., 69.
Lee, Rev. Dr. Robert, 54, 152.
Lees, Charles, R.S.A., 130.
Legge, George L., of Old Melrose, 258.
Leith Churchyards, 118, 123.
Lennie, William, the Grammarian, 149.
Lennox, Cairn, 183.
Lennox, Earl of, 183.
Lennox, of Irelandtown, 345.
Lenox, Robert, 331.
Le Poer, Rev. John, 144.
Leslie, Norman, 238.
Leslie, Peter, 45.
Lesmahagow, Parish of, 506.
Lessels, Provost John, 194.
Leswalt, Parish of, 347.
Lewis, Stewart, 318.
Leyden, Dr. John, 240, 255.
Leydon, Adam, 241.
Leydon, James, 241.

Leydon, John, 241.
Liberton, Parish of, 175.
Lidderdale, Thomas, 338.
Lilliard, Maiden, 238.
Lilliesleaf, Parish of, 248.
Limont, Rev. William, 155.
Lin, William, of Linsmill, 168.
Lincluden Abbey, 344.
Lindores, John, Lord, 115.
Lindsay, Mary, 311.
Lindsay, Samuel, 123.
Lindsay, Sir David, 184.
Lindsay, Sir Walter, 184.
Linlithgow, Parish of, 182.
Linn, Rev. Patrick, 290.
Linsmill, Flat Stone at, 168.
Linton, Parish of, 249.
Liston, Rev. Robert, 182.
Liston, Robert, the Surgeon, 182.
Liston, Sir Robert, 158.
Liston, Rev. Henry, 182.
Lithgow, Abbot John, 418.
Livingstone, Lieutenant, 305.
Lizars, John, 67.
Lizars, William Home, 67, 127.
Lochend, Erect Stones at, 168.
Lochmaben, Parish of, 314.
Lochwinnoch, Parish of, 416.
Lockerbie Churchyard, 301.
Lockerby, Rev. Thomas, 153.
Lockhart, Allen, of Cleghorn, 425.
Lockhart, Allen, of Hinschelwood, 425.
Lockhart, General Count, 173.
Lockhart, John Gibson, 233, 404.
Lockhart, Marianne M., 174.
Lockhart, Robert, 405.
Lockhart, Sir George, 29.
Lockhart, Sir James, of Lee, 30.
Logan, Thomas Galbraith, M.D., 118.
Logan, Sir Robert, of Restalrig, 116.
Lollards of Kyle, 394.
Lorimer, Dean of Guild, 15, 70.
Lothian, First Marquis of, 104.
Lothian, Mark, First Earl of, 109.
Lothian, Second Marquis of, 71.
Lothian, Third Earl of, 80.
Loudoun, Countess of, 83.
Loudoun, Noble Family of, 393.

Loudoun, Parish of, 393.
Louis, Robert, of Plean, 72.
Low, of Balmakelly, 83.
Low, Colonel Robert, 129.
Low, Dr. Peter, 461.
Low, Professor David, 130.
Lowes, Thomas, of Ridley Hall, 110.
Lucas, William, 204.
Lumsdaine, Archibald, 60.
Lumsden, of Blanerne, 221.
Lumsden, Lord Provost James, 464, 474.
Lundie, Christian, 253.
Lundie, Rev. Archibald, 122.
Lundie, Rev. James, 122.
Lyne, Parish of, 265.

M

MacAdam, John Loudon, 315.
Macartney, Annabella, 143.
MacCartney, George, 360.
Macdiarmid, Captain John, 155.
Macdonald, Chief of Clan Ranald, 115.
Macdonald, Hugh, Poet, 491.
Macdonald, Lord, 116.
Macdonald, Sir John Graham, Bart., 144.
Macdougall, Colonel John, 143.
MacFadzon, Janet, 368.
Macfarlan, Principal Duncan, 479.
Macfie, John, 120.
Macfie, Robert Andrew, 412.
MacGill, Andrew, 361.
Macgowan, William, 355.
Macintyre, Duncan Ban, 42.
Macintyre, Robert, 493.
Mackay, Charles, 94.
Mackay, Colonel Æneas J., 143.
Mackay, Mrs. Jean, 307.
Mackellar, Archibald, M.D., 129.
Mackenzie, Archibald, 145.
Mackenzie, Dr. R. J., 132.
Mackenzie, Henry, Author of "The Man of Feeling," 45.
Mackenzie, James, of Craig Park, 486.
Mackenzie, John, 80.
Mackenzie, Joshua, 45.
Mackenzie, Joshua Henry, 45.
Mackenzie, Sir George, of Rosehaugh, 28, 29.

INDEX. 523

MacKnight, Dr. James, 50.
MacKnight, Rev. William, 59.
Maclagan, Douglas, M.D., 144.
Maclaren, Charles, F.R.S.E., 151.
Maclaren, Rev. John, 488.
Maclaurin, Professor Colin, 35.
Maclean, William, of Plantation, 487.
Maclellan, of Auchlane, 336.
MacLellan, Sir Thomas, 336.
Macleod, Flora, 83.
Macleod, Lord, 87.
Macleod, Peter, of Polbeth, 124.
Macleod, Professor Hugo, 467.
MacLiver, John, 454.
Macmath, Janet, 33.
MacMillan, Alexander, 360.
Macmillan, Dr., 395.
MacMillan, James, 360.
Macmoran, Bailie, 17.
Macmurdo, Rev. John, 321.
Macnair, Rev. John Calvin, 154.
Macneil, Major Archibald, 145.
Macneill, John, of Ardnacross, 143.
Macpherson, James, 41.
Macpherson, Lieutenant Evan, 145.
MacPherson, Peter, 411.
Macquae, Robert, 329.
Macrae, Governor James, 397, 452.
Macvey, John, of Kirkintilloch, 73.
McAulay, Alexander, 341.
McCheyne, Adam, W.S., 63.
McCheyne, Rev. Robert Murray, 63.
McClellan, Captain Thomas, 335.
McClellan, Rev. John, 335.
McClimont, James, 345.
McConechy, James, 465.
McCrachan, Family of, 357.
McCrie, Dr. Thomas, 46.
McCubin, Alexander, 339.
McCulloch, John R., 151.
McDiarmid, John, 286.
McDowall, Mrs. Nicholas, 294.
McEwen, Rev. James, 153.
McFarlane, Malcolm, 492.
McGavin, William, Author of "The Protestant," 474.
McGeahan, John, 366.
McIntosh, Charles, F.R.A.S., 145.

McKeand, Bailie, 355.
McKie, Miss, 356.
McLachlan, Margaret, 349, 356.
McLagan, Thomas, 368.
McLean, Rev. Archibald, 71.
McLymont, John, 397.
McMath, Sybella, 293.
McMichael, Daniel, 304.
McNair, Colonel James, 487.
McNaught, John, of Kilquhanatie, 336.
McNaught, Mrs. Marion, 336.
McVicar, Rev. Neil, 61.
M'Adam, Gilbert, 389.
M'Cormack, Rev. Andrew, 163, 164.
M'Caul, John, 377.
M'Cubbin, Rev. William, 449.
M'Culloch, of Bartholm, 339.
M'Culloch, Horatio, R.A., 127.
M'Donald, Colonel David Robertson, 40, 75.
M'Dowall, Mr., 331.
M'Dowall, William, of Garthland, 427.
M'Farlan, Rev. Patrick, D.D., 413.
M'Haffie, Thomas, 401.
M'Kay, Hon. Georgina, 110.
M'Kie, Rev. Nathaniel, 330.
M'Kie, Rev. William, 330.
M'Knight, Agnes, 328.
M'Laurin, Rev. John, 469.
M'Lude, John, 341.
M'Michan, John, 331.
M'Millan, Rev. John, 446.
M'Nab, John, of Inglisgreen, 145.
M'Naught, Mary, 392.
M'Qwhan, Adam, 332.
M'Vicar, Dunan, 64.
Magdalene, Queen, 100, 101.
Maida, The Dog, 4.
Maiden, The, Instrument so called, 21.
Main, John, 460.
Maitland, Captain Adam, 139.
Maitland, Chancellor, 186.
Maitland, Hon. Thomas, 343.
Maitland, Jane, 189.
Maitland, John, Accountant of Court of Session, 153.
Maitland, Rev. Dr., 333.
Maitland, Sir Richard, of Lethington, 187.

Malcolm, Admiral Sir Pulteney, 313.
Malcolm, George, 313.
Malcolm IV., 417.
Malcolm, Mrs., 9.
Malcolm, Sir John, 324.
Manor, Parish of, 265.
Mar, John Francis, Fifteenth Earl of, 115.
March, Patrick, 158.
Marchmont, Earl of, 225, 235.
Margaret of Denmark, 99.
Margarot, Maurice, 92.
Marjoribanks, of Marjoribanks, 181.
Marshall, Henry, M.D., 142.
Marshall, Walter, 130.
Marshall, William, 338.
Martin, Lieutenant-Colonel, 129.
Martin, Rev. John, 218.
Martin, Rev. Samuel, 180.
Martin, Theodore, 135.
Martyrs' Monument, 30.
"Mary, Highland," 411.
Mary of Gueldres, Queen, 101.
Mary, Queen of Scots, 17, 19, 99, 101, 183, 343.
Mason, John, 60.
Mathie, Rev. Peter, 492.
Mathieson, Duncan, Advocate, 120.
Mattheson, William, 216.
Mauchline, Parish of, 396.
Maule, Colonel Lauderdale, 139.
Maule, Hon. John, 115.
Maxwell, Alexander H., of Munches, 291.
Maxwell, David, Treasurer of Paisley, 426.
Maxwell, Hannah Leonora, 139.
Maxwell, of Pollok, 407.
Maxwell, of Preston, 109.
Maxwell, of Terregles, 345.
Maxwell, Sir Walter, of Pollok, 42.
Maxwell, Sir William, Bart., of Calderwood, 139.
Maxwell, Sir William, Bart., of Monreith, 347.
Maxwell, Sir William Stirling, Bart., 407.
Maxwell, William, of Preston, 81.

Maybole, Parish of, 396.
Mayne, Dr. Robert, 462.
Mayne, Major-General, 77.
Meadowbank, Lord, 170.
Medina, Sir John, the Painter, 52.
Megget, Mrs. Mary, 71.
Meikle, Andrew, 211.
Meikleham, Professor William, 467.
Meiklewrath, Matthew, 365.
Meiklewrath, Daniel, 365.
Mellis, Rev. David Barclay, 53.
Melrose Abbey, 2.
Melrose, Parish of, 250.
Melville, Henry, First Viscount, 9, 14, 172.
Melville, Robert, Second Viscount, 10.
Menzies, Professor Allan, 143.
Merton, Parish of, 230.
Middlebie, Parish of, 314.
Middlemas, Provost Charles, 204.
Middlemas, Robert H., 204.
Middleton, Major William, 465.
Miller, Hugh, the Geologist, 147.
Miller, James, 119.
Miller, Patrick, of Dalswinton, 53.
Miller, Professor James, 150.
Miller, Rev. James, 151.
Miller, Rev. William, 445.
Miller, Robert, 383.
Miller, Sir William, Bart., 96.
Miller, William, 498.
Miller, William, of Dykes, 381.
Miller, William, Seaman, 204.
Milne, Alexander, 105.
Milne, John, Master Mason, 27, 28.
Milne, Nicol, of Falconside, 258.
Milne, Rev. Adam, 254.
Milroy, John, 356.
Milton, Lord, 217.
Minnigaff, Parish of, 340.
Minnyhive, Village of, 305.
Minto, David, 498.
Minto, Mary, Countess of, 223.
Mitchel, Isabel, 216.
Mitchell, Catherine, 221.
Mitchell, James, 492.
Mitchell, John, Collector, 292.
Mitchell, John, 293.

INDEX.

Mitchell, John, Painter, 489.
Mitchell, John, of Mayville, 124.
Mitchell, Robert, 305.
Moffat, Parish of, 315.
Moffat, Rev. James, 300.
Moffat, William, S.S.C., 155.
Moir, Rev. David, 153.
Moir, David Macbeth, the Poet, 167.
Moir, Professor George, 74.
Moncreiff, Hope Margaret, 488.
Moncreiff, Lord, 132.
Moncreiff, Sir James W., Bart., 132.
Monkton, Parish of, 397.
Monmouth, Duchess, 159.
Monmouth, Duke of, 159.
Monro, George, S.S.C., 155.
Monteith, Major Archibald D., 486.
Monteith, Rev. Robert, 229.
Monteith, Robert, 20.
Montgomerie, Captain John Hamilton, 129.
Montgomerie, of Hesilhead, 425.
Montgomerie, Mrs. Marion, 424.
Montgomery, Hugh, of Broadly, 417.
Montgomery, Sir Robert, of Skelmorly, 390.
Montrose, Marquis of, 106.
Monypenny, Alexander, W.S., 53.
Moore, Dugald, Poet, 474.
Moore, General Sir John, 10, 452, 453.
Moray, John, Twelfth Earl of, 16.
Mordington, Parish of, 234.
Morehead, Rev. Robert, D.D., 139.
Morehead, William Ambrose, 139.
Morland, Sir Hugh de, 312.
Morris, Edward, 493.
Morris, Hugh, 392.
Morton, George, Earl of, 79.
Morton, James, Twelfth Earl of, 115.
Morton, The Regent, 20.
Morton, Robert, Thirteenth Earl of, 115.
Morville, Hugh de, 230, 238.
"Morvo, John," 2, 251.
Moss, Edward, 113.
Moss, Mary, 113.
Mossman, William, Sculptor, 495.
Motherwell, William, the Poet, 472, 473.
Mouat, Thomas, 292.

Mounsey, Alexander, 320.
Mounsey, Dr. James, 314, 320.
Mounsey, John, 320.
Mounsey, John, M.D., 320.
Mounsey, Thomas, 314, 320.
Mounsey, William, 320.
Mount Edgecumbe, Richard, Earl of, 115.
Mousewald, Parish of, 313.
Muir, Dr. William, 149.
Muir, Helen, 268.
Muir, Isabel, 39, 424.
Muir, James, 92.
Muir, John, 268.
Muir, Margaret, 129.
Muir, Rev. John, D.D., 465.
Muir, Rev. Dr. William, 160.
Muir, Robert, 492.
Muir, William, 315.
Muirhead, Agnes, 411.
Muirhead, John, 360.
Muirkirk, Parish of, 398.
Munro, Major David, 130.
Munsie, Thomas, 320.
Murchie, John, 365.
Mure, of Caldwell, 38, 46.
Mure, Marjory, 433.
Murray, Alicia Stewart, 46.
Murray, of Broughton, 331.
Murray, Captain George, 72.
Murray, General Thomas, 129.
Murray, James, of Deuchar, 26.
Murray, James, of Wick, 143.
Murray, James Wolfe, Lord Cringletie, 45.
Murray, Jane, 328.
Murray, Lord, 8, 9.
Murray, Nicholas, 105.
Murray, Provost, 355.
Murray, Rev. Dr. Alexander, 328—340.
Murray, Sir John Archibald, 60.
Murray, Sir Patrick, of Ochtertyre, 72.
Murray, The Regent, 15, 182, 471.
Murray, William, of Henderland, 60.
Muter, Rev. Robert, D.D., 484.
Mynto, Sir Walter, 457.
Mynto, Sir Thomas, 457.

N

Nairne, Baroness, 163.

INDEX.

Napier, Fifth Lord.
Napier, John, of Merchiston, 57.
Napier, Major-General Mark, 61.
Napier, Mr. Mark, 351.
Napier, Professor Macvey, 73.
Napier, Sir Alexander, 57.
Napoleon I., 6.
Nasmyth, John, Monument of, 21.
National Monument, Edinburgh, 6.
Necropolis, The, Glasgow, 470, 490.
Neill, General James, 360.
Neill, Patrick, LL.D., 126.
Neilson, Ellen, 121.
Neilson, Walter, of Springfield.
Nelson, Lord, 5, 6, 452.
New Abbey, Parish of, 342.
New Calton Burial-ground, 96, 99.
Newark, Lady, 115.
Newbattle, Parish of, 177.
Newbigging, Patrick S. K., M.D., 143.
Newington Burial-ground, 154, 156.
Newlands, Parish of, 266.
Newton, Lord, 102.
Newton, W. W. Hay, of Newton, 79.
Newtoune, Rev. Archibald, 175.
Nichol, James, Publisher, 154.
Nichol, Professor, 148.
Nichol, Walter, LL.D., 130.
Nicholson, William, Author of "The Brownie of Blednoch," 329.
Nicol, Rev. James, 271.
Nicol, William, of the Edinburgh High School, 309.
Nicoll, Robert, the Poet, 123.
Niddry, Burial-ground at, 175.
Ninety-third Regiment, Monument to officers and men of, 15.
Nisbet, Alexander, Author of "System of Heraldry," 52.
Nisbet, Henry, of Dean, 58.
Nisbet, James, 456.
Nisbet, John, 385—394.
Nisbet, Rev. Alexander, 120.
Nisbet, Rev. Gavin, 176.
Niven, David, 377.
North Berwick, Parish of, 207.
Norvell, George, of Boghall, 180.

O

Observatory, Edinburgh, 6.
"Ochiltree Edie," 258.
Ogilvie, General John, 129.
Ogilvie, George, of Kirkbuddo, 129.
Ogilvy, Sir John, Bart., 71.
Ogilvy, Walter, Lord, 87.
Old Calton Burial-ground, 91—96.
Old Luce, Parish of, 347.
Oliphant, Sir William, 51.
Oliver's Mound, 165.
Ord, Clara Jane, 98.
Ord, Thomas, 98.
Ormiston, Parish of, 209.
Orr, James, 381.
Orr, John, of Barrowfield, 465.
Orr, John, of Brackraw, 129.
Orr, Rev. James, 229.
Orrock, Rev. Alexander, 244.
Orrok, Wemyss, of Orrok, 153.
Oswald, James, M.P., 456.
Oswalde, Rev. John, 215.
Outram, George, 125.

P

Pagan, William, of Clayton, 321.
Paisley, Parish of, 417, 432.
Palmer, Thomas Tyshe, 92.
Panmure, Earl of, 115.
Panmure, William, Baron, 139.
Panton, John, M.D., 487.
Park, Andrew, 430.
Park, John, 429.
Park, Mungo, 274.
Park, Patrick, Sculptor, 97.
Parker, Dr. Robert, 492.
Parker, John, 504.
Pasley, Robert, of Mount Annan, 139.
Paterson, Bailie John, 112.
Paterson, Bishop John, 114.
Paterson, Hugh, 499.
Paterson, James, 320.
Paterson, Janet, 320.
Paterson, John, 292.
Paterson, John, Skipmier, 320.
Paterson, Nicol, 112.
Paterson, Rev. Walter, 198.
Paterson, Robert, "Old Mortality" 298, 328.

INDEX.

Paterson, Thomas, 328.
Paterson, William, 437.
Paterson, William, Founder of Bank of England, 319, 320.
Patison, Simon, 366.
Paton, Captain John, 372.
Paton, Matthew, 460.
Patrick, William, of Roughwood, 366.
Pattison, Colonel Alexander H., 486.
Pattison, John, of Kelvingrove, 488.
Pattison, Lieutenant Alexander H., 487.
Paul, Rev. Hamilton, 262.
Paul, Rev. William, 58.
Paxton, Rev. George, D.D., 62.
Paxton, Rev. John Dunlop, 96.
Peden, Rev. Alexander, 13, 365.
Peebles, Parish of, 267.
Peel, Sir Robert, 452, 453.
Penicuik, Parish of, 177.
Pennecuick, Alexander, M.D., 266.
Penney, William, Advocate, 70.
Penningham, Parish of, 348, 353.
Penpont, Parish of, 316.
Pentlands, Battle of the, 163.
Perth, Duke of, 114.
Peter, Bailie Thomas, 427.
Peter the Great, 34.
Peters, Sir John, 52.
Petrie, Dr. Robert, 299.
Petrie, Rev. Robert, 299.
Petrie, William, 299.
Philip, Rev. Alexander, 155.
Philips, Sir George Richard, Bart., 115.
Pinkerton, James, 212.
Pinkie, Battle of, 165.
Pitcairn, Elizabeth, 34.
Pitcairn, Dr. Archibald, 34.
Pitcairn, Janet, Countess of Kellie, 35.
Pitcairn, Margaret, 35.
Pitcairn, Rev. Thomas, 153.
Pitcairnes, Rev. Thomas, 71.
Pitman, Major-General, 129.
Pitt, Lieutenant Edward W., 124.
Pitt, William, 10.
Playfair, Patrick, of Dalmarnock, 487.
Playfair, Professor John, 7, 95.
Playfair, William H., 2, 7, 66, 139.
Pollok, Sir Robert Crawford, Bart., 90.

Polwarth, Parish of, 235.
Pont, Rev. Robert, 58, 59.
Pope, James, 124.
Porteous, Captain John, 53.
Porter, George, 500.
Portus, Robert, 161.
Pratt, David, of Seggie, 98.
Preston, Sir Simon, 17.
Prestongrange, Lord, 213.
Prestonkirk, Parish of, 211.
Prestonpans, Parish of, 212.
Primrose, Peter, D.D., 215.
Primrose, Sir Archibald, 181.
Pringle, Andrew, 254.
Pringle, General John, 143.
Pringle, Hope, of Galashiels, 253.
Pringle of Whitebank, 253.
Pringle of Woodhouse, 253.
Purdie, Tom, 257.
Purdie, William, 262.
Pyrre, William, 419.

Q
Queensberry, Charles, Duke of, 283.
Queensberry, Earl of, 109.
Queensberry, James, Second Duke of,
Queensberry, Mary, Duchess of, 303.
Queensferry, Parish of, 183.
Queen Victoria, 8, 124, 453.
Quincey, Thomas de, 67.

R
Raeburn, Sir Henry, 72.
Raimes, John, of Cowden, 130.
Raining, Provost Herbert, 288.
Ramsay, Allan, 8, 17, 37, 96.
Ramsay, Bishop James, 89.
Ramsay, David, of Abbotshall, 213.
Ramsay, Dean, 10, 79.
Ramsay, Dowager Lady, 77.
Ramsay, General, 9.
Ramsay, George, of Foulden Bastel, 228.
Ranken, of Inchcross, 181.
Ramsay, James, 255.
Ramsay, Lady, 213.
Ramsay, Mrs. Allan, 9.
Ramsay, Mrs. Isabella, 79.
Ramsay, Peter, 129.

Ramsay, Principal, 89.
Ramsay, Rev. James, 248, 352.
Ramsay, Robert, 120.
Ramsay, Sir Alexander, Bart., 77.
Ramsay, Sir Thomas, Bart., 213.
Ramshorn Churchyard, Glasgow, 469.
Rankin, Theophilus, 392.
Rattray, Baron Clerk, 79.
Reay, Elizabeth, Baroness, 110.
Reay, George, Fifth Baron, 110.
Reddie, James, LL.D., 482.
Redpath, Rev. Philip, 229.
Redkirk, Churchyard at, 306.
Register House, Edinburgh, 7.
Reid, Cumberland, 203.
Reid, Janet, 203.
Reid, Magnus, 203.
Reid, Professor James Seaton, 495.
Reid, Professor Thomas, 73, 466.
Reid, Rev. Matthew, 308.
Reid, Robert, Architect, 143.
Reid, Thomas, 203.
Renfrew, Parish of, 433.
Renton, Rev. Alexander, 153.
Renwick, Rev. James, 31, 306, 310.
Reoch, Provost James, 119.
Restalrig Churchyard, 116, 118.
Reynolds, Sir Joshua, 72.
Richard II., 99.
Richards, Thomas, 366.
Richardson, Mrs. Caroline E., 299.
Richmond, Andrew, 376.
Richmond, John, 460.
Richmond, John, of Know, 376.
Riddel, Isabel, 247.
Riddell, General Henry James, 53.
Riddell, Henry Scott, 281.
Riddell, John, Advocate, 140.
Riddell, Robert, Advocate, 53.
Riddell, Robert, of Glenriddell, 302.
Riddell, Thomas, of Carrieston, 85.
Rigby, William, 60.
Ritchie, Christian, 94.
Ritchie, David, 265.
Ritchie, Dr. David, 77.
Ritchie, Dr. William, 402.
Ritchie, Thomas, 382.
Ritchie, William, 266.

Rizzio, David, 101.
Robb, Rev. Alexander, 345.
Robert II., 116.
Roberts, David, R.A., 2, 94.
Roberts, John, 94.
Robertson, Captain James, 75.
Robertson, David, Bookseller, 476.
Robertson, Dr. Joseph, 141.
Robertson, George, 130.
Robertson, Hon. William, 40.
Robertson, Jane, 145.
Robertson, Major Alexander, 130.
Robertson, Principal William, 39, 54.
Robertson, Professor James, 71.
Robertson, Rev. James, 119.
Robertson, Rev. James, D.D., 487.
Robertson, Sergeant William, 499.
Robertson, William, 497.
Robertson, Patrick, Lord, 15, 79.
Robison, Sir John, 77.
Rocheid, Sir James, 58.
Rodger, Alexander, Poet, 475.
Rodger, George, jun., 464.
Rodger, Peter, 497.
Roebuck, Dr. John, 181, 410.
Roger, Robert, 467.
Rogers, Henry Darwin, 136.
Rogerson, Dr. John, 319—323.
Rogerson, Jean, 320.
Rogerson, Margaret, 320.
Rogerson, Samuel, 323.
Room, John, 296.
Rose, Bishop Alexander, 118.
Rosebank Cemetery, 124.
Rosebery, Countess of, 72.
Rosebery, Earls of, 1, 72, 181.
Roslin, Barons of, 174.
Roslin Chapel, 174.
Ross, Admiral Sir John Lockhart, Bart., 72.
Ross, of Balnagowan, 506.
Ross, Dame Margaret, 103.
Ross, George, Advocate, 72.
Ross, Lord James, 103.
Ross, Johanna, 252.
Ross, John, 385.
Ross, Professor George, 154.
Ross, Rev. Robert, 487.

INDEX.

Ross, Sir John, of Hawkhead, 433.
Rosslyn, Earls of, 175.
Rosslyn, Frances, Countess of, 175.
Rothes, John, Earl of, 112.
Row, John, 471.
Rowan, Rev. Robert, 348, 354.
Roy, Major-General William, 214.
Roy, John, 214.
Roy, Rev. James, 213.
Royal Bank, Edinburgh, 9.
Royal Institution, Edinburgh, 9.
Roystoun, Lord, 30.
Roxburgh Club, The, 239.
Roxburgh, Dukes of, 239.
Roxburgh, Parish of, 258.
Roxburghe, Jane, Countess of, 101.
Ruddiman, Thomas, 36.
Ruddiman, William, M.D., 36.
Rullion Green, Battle of, 163.
Runciman, Alexander, 86, 96.
Runciman, John, 86.
Russel, Alexander, 151.
Russell, Bishop Michael, 118.
Russell, James, M.D., 143.
Russell, Jerome, 471.
Russell, Rev. William, 380.
Rutherfurd, Andrew, 496.
Rutherfurd, Lord, 130, 131.
Rutherfurd, Major James H., 143.
Rutherfurd, Mrs. Alison, 82.
Rutherfurd, Rev. Samuel, 326, 336.
Rutherfurd, Robert, of Fernylee, 82.
Ruthwell, Parish of, 316.

S

Salton, Parish of, 217.
Saltoun, Dowager Lady, 115.
Saltoun, George, Fourteenth Baron, 115.
Samson, Thomas, 387.
Sandford, Bishop Daniel, 73.
Sandford, Sir Daniel, 79.
Sandilands, of Couston, 181.
Sandilands, Sir James, 471.
Sang, William, 205.
"Sanquhar Declaration," 306.
Sanquhar, Parish of, 318.
Sawers, Lieutenant John L., 205.
Schaw, Abbot George, 419, 428.

Schuyler, Colonel, 294.
Scoresby, Jackson Robert E., 154.
Scot, Bishop John, 177.
Scot, Robert, 460.
Scott, Andrew, Poet, 239.
Scott, Caroline Eliza, 299.
Scott, David, the Painter, 133.
Scott, John, M.D., 142.
Scott, John, of Rodono, 278.
Scott, Lady, 62, 230.
Scott, Margaret, 298.
Scott, Michael, 477.
Scott, Mrs. Anne, 79.
Scott, Peter Redford, 143.
Scott, Rev. John, 290.
Scott, Rev. Robert, 100.
Scott, Robert, Sandyknowe, 260.
Scott, Sir Michael, of Balwearie, 251.
Scott, Sir Walter, 1, 5, 14, 18, 51, 62, 68, 79, 83, 91, 93, 94, 133, 225, 230, 251, 257, 260, 265, 274, 280, 325, 335, 340, 342, 452, 480.
Scott, Sir Walter, of Branxholm, 243.
Scott, Sir Walter, of Buccleuch, 243.
Scott, Sir Walter, Lieut-Colonel, 62, 233.
Scott, Sophia, 233.
Scott, Walter, W.S., 79, 231.
Scott, of Gala, 254.
Scrimgeour, Lucres, 380.
Scrymgour, Daniel, 53.
Seaforth, Earl of, 29.
Seaforth, Lord Francis, 115.
Seaforth, Mary, Countess of, 115.
Seaton, Isabel, 189.
Selkirk, Earls of, 115, 338.
Selkirk, Parish of, 274.
Sempill, of Castle Semple, 416.
Semple, Francis, Tenth Lord, 115.
Semple, John, 368.
Semple, Rev. Samuel, 175.
Seton, Alexander, 191.
Seton, Margaret, 423.
Seton, of Northrig, 192.
Seton, William, 192.
Seventy-second Regiment, Monument to officers and men of, 15.
Seventy-eighth Regiment, Monument to officers and men of, 11.

Sewell, Thomas, of Haselmere, 213.
Seymour, Lord Webb John, 115.
Sharpe, Charles Kirkpatrick, 310.
Sharpe, of Hoddam, 291.
Sharpe, James, 497.
Shaw, James, 412.
Shaw, Sir James, Bart., 386.
Sherrer, Margaret, 410.
Shields, Alexander, 351.
Shields, John, 385.
Shillilaw, William, 402.
Short, John, 360.
Sibbald, James, M.D., 155.
Sibbald, Sir Robert, 100.
Sibbald, William, 263.
Siddons, Cecilia, 137.
Siddons, Henry, 52.
Siddons, Mrs., 137.
Sighthill Cemetery, Glasgow, 494, 499.
Sime, Rev. John, 153.
Simpson, Colonel John, 99.
Simpson, David, 128.
Simpson, David, of Teviot Bank, 53.
Simpson, Rev. Alexander, LL.D., 145.
Simpson, Sir James Young, Bart., 128, 181.
Simson, George, R.S.A., 130.
Simson, James, 255.
Simson, John, of Kirton Hall, 465.
Simson, Professor Robert, 465.
Simson, William, 130.
Sinclair, Captain Archibald, R.N., 76.
Sinclair, Catherine, 11, 74.
Sinclair, Elesoune, 368.
Sinclair, Sir John, Bart., 11, 76, 115.
Sinclair, Lady, 116.
Skene, Andrew, 97.
Skene, Dr. George, 97.
Skene, Sir James, Bart., 52.
Skeoch, Alexander, 428.
Skeoch, William, 428.
Skirling, Parish of, 271.
Skirving, Adam, 200.
Skirving, Archibald, 200.
Skirving, Archibald, Artist, 201.
Skirving, William, 92.
Sleich, John, 192.
Smailholme, Parish of, 260.

Smellie, Alexander, F.R.S.E., 52.
Smibert, Thomas, the Poet, 267.
Smith, Alexander, the Poet, 126.
Smith, Dr. Adam, 86.
Smith, James, Martyr, 360, 398.
Smith, James, Architect, 234, 256.
Smith, Jean, 195.
Smith, John, 200.
Smith, John Alexander, M.D., 252.
Smith, Margaret, 364.
Smith, Rev. James, 380.
Smith, Rev. Professor, 153.
Smith, Rev. William B., 129.
Smith, Robert, 331, 337.
Smith, Robert Archibald, 65.
Smith, Sydney, 131.
Smith, William, 322.
Smollett, Tobias, 17.
Smyth, Mrs. Mary, 59.
Smyth, Rev. William, 390.
Somerset, the Protector, 165.
Somerville, Dr. Thomas, 245.
Somerville, Lords, 187, 444.
Somerville, Roger de, 249.
Somerville, Walter de, 249.
Somner, Richard, of Somnerfield, 151.
Soulis, Lord, 384.
Soulis, Sir John de, 226.
Southern Necropolis, Glasgow, 491, 494.
Spence, Alexander, 124.
Spence, Lieutenant John, 119.
Spier, Allan, 382.
Spiers, Archibald, 153.
Spiers, Sheriff Graham, 153.
Spittal, John, M.D., 486.
Spott, Parish of, 218.
Spottiswood, John, 471.
Spottiswood, Robert, 95.
Sprott, Family of, 218.
Sprott, Lieutenant George H., 14.
Stair, Lord, of Newliston, 168.
Standard, Battle of the, 114.
Stanley, Captain Edward, 75.
St. Boswell's, Parish of, 260.
St. Clair, Sir William, of Rosslyn, 174.
St. Cuthbert's Churchyard, 57, 72.
Stedman, Captain James, 258.
Steel, David, 506.

INDEX. 531

Steel, James, 381.
Steell, John, Sculptor, 3, 5, 8, 9, 10, 18, 185.
Steell, Mary, 320.
Stiell, Colonel Robert, 204, 205.
St. Giles's Church, Edinburgh, 12, 14, 15, 16, 19, 58, 244.
St. John's Episcopal Church, Edinburgh, 72, 79.
St. John, Knights of, 182, 183.
St. Mary's Churchyard, 276.
St. Ninian, Church of, 348.
Stephen, Alexander, M.D., 115.
Steuart, Archibald, of Blackhall, 407.
Steuart, Bernard, 158.
Steuart, John, of Phisgyl, 214.
Steuart, Lady Frances, 441.
Steuart, Lord Provost David, 71.
Steuart, Sir James D., Bart., of Coltness, 440.
Steuart, Walter, of Pardovan, 407.
Steven, Rev. William, D.D., 150.
Stevenson, Elizabeth, 34.
Stevenson, John, 341.
Stevenson, Rev. Andrew, 203.
Stevenson, Rev. John, D.D., 143.
Stevenson, Robert, C.E., 97.
Stevenson, Thomas, 341.
Stevenston, Parish of, 399.
Stewards, The High, 417, 418.
Stewart, Alexander, 494.
Stewart, Archibald, 460.
Stewart, David, 301.
Stewart, General, of Garth, 162.
Stewart, General Sir William, 341.
Stewart, James, 205.
Stewart, James, of Cardonald, 421.
Stewart, Lord James, 471.
Stewart, Major, of Ardoch, 331.
Stewart, Margaret, 421.
Stewart, Mrs. Barbara, 296.
Stewart, Professor Dugald, 7, 73, 87.
Stewart, Rev. Alexander, LL.D., 449.
Stewart, Rev. Dr., 313.
Stewart, Robert, 331.
Stewart, Robert, of Murdostoun, 487.
Stewart, Sholto Thomas, 110.
Stewart, Sir James, of Fort Stewart, 131.

Stewart, Sir James, of Goodtrees, 114.
Stewart, Sir John, Bart., of Grandtully, 110.
Stewart, Sir John, of Mynto, 421.
Stewart, Sophia, 131.
Stewart, William, 103.
Stewart, William, of Castle Stewart, 115.
Stewart, Walter, 421.
Stewarton, Parish of, 400.
Stirling, General Alexander Graham, 76.
Stirling, Lieutenant John, 465.
Stirling, Sir George, of Keir, 103.
Stirrat, Rev. Robert, 143.
Stoddart, Admiral Pringle, 129.
Stormouth, James, of Lednathy, 84.
Strachan, Captain, 350.
Straiton, Parish of, 401.
Strang, John, LL.D., 486.
Stranraer, Parish of, 348.
Strathmore, James, Seventh Earl of, 115.
Strathmore, Thomas, Eleventh Earl of, 115.
Strathnavar, Lord, 100.
Strong, Christopher, 504.
Stuart, Captain John, 130.
Stuart, Mrs. Rachel, 61.
Stuart, James, of Dunearn, 351.
Stuart, Margaret, 111.
Stuart, Robert, Author of "Caledonia Romana," 477.
Surenne, Gabriel, 143.
Sutherland, Alexander, 71.
Sutherland, Colonel Robert S., 155.
Sutherland, George, Fourteenth Earl of, 108, 109.
Sutherland, John, Earl of, 108, 109.
Sutherland, Mary, Countess of, 109.
Sutherland, William, Seventeenth Earl of, 109.
Suttie, Janet, 213.
Suttie, Sir George Grant, 90.
Sweetheart Abbey, 342.
Swinburne, General Thomas R., 143.
Swinton, Alexander, of Mersingtoun, 55.
Swinton, George, 142.
Swinton, of Kimmerghame, 235.
Swinton, Robert Hepburn, 142.
Swinton, Sir Alan de, 235.
Swinton, of Swinton, 235.

Syme, Eleanora, 117.
Syme, Professor James, 74.
Syme, Rev. James, 117.
Symington, Rev. William, D.D., 488.
Symson, Matthias, 352.
Symson, Rev. Andrew, 352.

T

Tait, John, of Glasgow, 486.
Tait, Rear-Admiral J. H., 71.
Tannahill, Robert, 65, 431.
Tarbolton, Parish of, 401.
Taylor, John, M.D., 143.
Taylor, Rev. Principal William, 465.
Telfer, Alexander, of Luscar, 118.
Telfer, James, Poet, 239.
Telford, Thomas, 325.
Tennant, Charles, of St. Rollox, 482.
Tennant, John, of Mosside, 180.
Tennent, Charles, S. P., of Well Park, 488.
Terregles, Parish of, 344.
Thirlestane, Lord, 186.
Thomas, the Rhymer, 225.
Thome, Robert, 403.
Thomson, Alexander, 229.
Thomson, Andrew, 492.
Thomson, Captain John, R.N., 123.
Thomson, Dr. Andrew, 66.
Thomson, Dr. John, 66.
Thomson, James, the Poet, 234, 242.
Thomson, Professor Thomas, 135, 485.
Thomson, Rev. Dr. James, 227.
Thomson, Rev. Thomas, Edinburgh, 95.
Thomson, Rev. Thomas, Ednam, 242.
Thomson, Rev. William, 322.
Thomson, Robert, Advocate, 143.
Thomson, Robert, of Kaimflat, 155.
Thomson, Sir Alexander, 462.
Thomson, William, 258.
Tinwald, Parish of, 319.
Tod, Alexander Bruere, 76.
Tod, Captain, 60.
Tod, General Suetonius H., 154.
Tod, John, W.S., 143.
Tod, Provost Archibald, 26.
Tod, Thomas, of Drygrange, 255, 258.
Tongland, Parish of, 345.

Torphichen, Parish of, 183.
Torphichen, Preceptory at, 183.
Torthorwald, Parish of, 321.
Tough, Rev. George, 221.
Touraine, Duke of, 448.
Towers, Professor James, 487.
Trail, Rev. Robert, 54.
Trailflat Churchyard, 319.
Train, Joseph, 335.
Traquair, Parish of, 271.
Trinity College Church, Edinburgh, 101.
Tron Church, Glasgow, 469.
Trool, Glen of, 341.
Trotter, John, of Morton Hall, 33.
Trotter, William, of Ballendean, 52.
Tundergarth, Parish of, 322.
Turnbull, Rev. Thomas, 155.
Turner, Claud, 500.
Turner, General William, C.B., 98.
Turnerelli, Sculptor, 284.
Tweedie, Captain Alexander Lawrence, 76.
Tweedie, Provost, 267.
Tweedie, Rev. William, D.D., 150.
Tweedsmuir, Parish of, 272.
Tynron, Parish of, 322.
Tyre, Thomas, 383.
Tytler, Alexander Fraser, 43.
Tytler, Patrick Fraser, 43.

U

Uphall, Parish of, 184.
Urie, John, 403.
Urr, Parish of, 345.

V

Valleyfield, Monument to French Prisoners at, 177.
Vedder, David, the Poet, 149.
Veitch, James, 269.
Veitch, Janet, 265.
Veitch, Jean, 151.
Vetche, Rev. John, 160.
Vicar, John, 364.
Vicar, Wiliam, 364.
Vilant, Professor, 146.
Vipont, Sir William de, 193.

W

Walker, Bishop James, 74.
Walker, Colonel Philip W., 124.
Walker, Dr. John, 89.
Walker, George, 356.
Walker, Helen, prototype of Jeanie Deans, 340.
Walker, Professor Josiah, 467.
Walker, William, 497.
Wallace, Colonel, 163.
Wallace, Dr. John, 307.
Wallace, Professor William, 53.
Wallace, Richard, 413.
Wallace, Robert, of Kelly, 413.
Wallace, Sir Thomas, of Craigie, 370.
Wallace, Sir William, 275, 307, 312, 360, 366, 472, 505.
Wallace Statue at Lanark, 505.
Wallace Tower at Ayr, 360.
Wallace Tower at Barnweill, 366.
Walston, Parish of, 507.
Wamphray, Parish of, 323.
Wandell, Parish of, 506.
Wardlaw, Alexander, 437.
Wardlaw, Major-General, 144.
Wardlaw, Rev. Ralph, 479.
Wardrobe, Rev. Thomas, 180.
Warriston Cemetery, 125, 130.
Watson, Adam, of Press, 205.
Watson, Captain John, 129.
Watson, James, the celebrated Printer, 52.
Watson, Mary, 376.
Watson, Mungo, 206.
Watt, James, 16, 409, 413, 452.
Watt, John, 120.
Watt, John, Greenock, 411.
Watt, Rev. Robert, 153.
Watt, Thomas, 410.
Watt, Thomas, M.D., 463.
Wauchope, Euphan, 161.
Wauchope, George, 129.
Waugh, Rev. Robert, 229.
Webster, Dr. Charles, 34.
Webster, Robert, 387.
Weir, James, an Extraordinary Child, 443.
Welch, William, 289.

Wellington, Duke of, Monuments to, 7, 452.
Wellwood, Rev. Sir Henry Moncreiff, Bart., 58.
Wellwynd Churchyard, 436.
Welsh, Rev. David, D.D., 65.
Wemyss, Commissary William, 154.
Wemyss, Earls of, 109, 199.
Wemyss, Jean, 109.
Wemyss, Rev. William, 258.
Westerkirk, Parish of, 324.
West Kilbride, Parish of, 382.
West Linton, Parish of, 243.
White, Colonel Adam, 119.
White, James, 373.
White, Jean, 320.
White, Margaret, 120.
White, Provost Adam, 120.
Whithorn, John, Bishop of, 114.
Whithorn, Parish of, 348.
Whyte, Bain, W.S., 71.
Whyte, Sir Robert, of Bennochy, 52.
Wightman, Thomas, 205.
Wigton, Earls of, 193, 437.
Wigton, Parish of, 349.
Wilkin, Margaret, 319.
William III., Statue of, 452.
William, the Lion, 235, 249.
Williams, Captain George, 292.
Williamson, John, 315.
Williamson, R. C., 144.
Willock, John, 471.
Wilson, Agnes, 350.
Wilson, David, 194.
Wilson, Dr. George, 95, 136.
Wilson, George, 199.
Wilson, James, 387, 400.
Wilson, James, of Woodville, 134.
Wilson, John, of Greenock, 412.
Wilson, John, Vocalist, 138.
Wilson, Joseph, 229.
Wilson, Margaret, 70.
Wilson, Margaret (the Martyr), 349, 356.
Wilson, Michael, 468.
Wilson, Mrs., 318.
Wilson, Mrs. Catherine, 52.
Wilson, Professor John, 8, 9, 133.
Wilson, Robert, 155.

Wilson, Thomas, of Glenvernoch, 354, 355.
Wilson, William Rae, 478.
Wilton, Parish of, 261.
Wingrave, Matthew, of Kirkbank, 142.
Winning, James, 460.
Winram, John, 471.
Winram, Major, 350, 354, 356.
Winter, Bailie Thomas, 247.
Winton, George, 71.
Winton, Robert, Earl of, 187.
Wishart, Bishop George, 106, 108.
Wishart, Captain Alexander, 155.
Wishart, Dame Matilda Cochrane, 115.
Wishart, George, the Martyr, 210, 471.
Wishart, James Lockhart, of Lee, 173.
Wodrow, Professor James, 408.
Wodrow, Rev. Robert, 383, 408.
Wood, Alexander, Martyr, 456.
Wood, Alexander, Surgeon, 117.
Wood, Sir Gabriel, 416.
Wood, William, 493.
Woodburn, Captain John, 77.
Woodburn George, 373.
Woodhouselee, Lord, 43.
Woodside Cemetery, Anderston, Glasgow, 1, 50.

Wright, James Hunter, 249.
Wright, Rev. Henry, of Largnean, 143.
Wyld, Captain Benjamin, 154.
Wyld, James, of Gilston, 154.
Wylde, Lieutenant Sydenham, 204.
Wylie, Alexander, 382.
Wyllie, Rev. Robert, 503.
Wyse, James, 153.

Y

Yarrow, Parish of, 275.
Yester, James, Seventh Lord, 109.
Yester, Lady Margaret, 80, 109.
York, Frederick, Duke of, 11, 454.
Yorkstoun, Rev. Peter, 300.
Young, Alexander, 406.
Young, David, 124.
Young, James, 376.
Young, Michael, 406.
Young, Rev. Edward, 257.
Young, Rev. Gavin, 317.
Young, Thomas, 396.
Younger, John, 260.

Z

Zeaman, John, 197.